BEE COUNTY COLLEGE LIBRARY
3800 CHARCO ROAD
BEEVILLE, TEXAS 78102
(512) 354-2740

BEE COUNTY COLLEGE
DATE DUE

DEC 6 1976		
DEC 2 1977		

26624

GV
1060.5
.B586

Bowerman
Coaching track and field

26624

GV
1060.5
.B586

Bowerman
Coaching track and field

BEE COUNTY COLLEGE

You have accepted the responsibility of either returning this book when due or paying the $1 a week penalty. NO overdue notice will be mailed to you. The college business office will notify you if money is owed the college. This book can be renewed for one week either in person or by phone (358-7032). A book returned by 10 a.m. on the third overdue day will not be charged a fine.

Coaching Track and Field

Coaching Track and Field

WILLIAM J. BOWERMAN
Professor of Physical Education, University of Oregon
Head Track Coach, United States Olympic Team, 1972

edited by WILLIAM H. FREEMAN
Assistant Professor of Physical Education
Gardner-Webb College, North Carolina

HOUGHTON MIFFLIN COMPANY BOSTON
Atlanta Dallas Geneva, Illinois
Hopewell, New Jersey Palo Alto London

Photographs on page 75: courtesy of William Freeman. All other photographs: Toni Nett, Germany.

Copyright © 1974 by Houghton Mifflin Company. All rights reserved. No part of this work may be reproduced or transmitted in any form or by any means, electronic or mechanical, including photocopying and recording, or by any information storage or retrieval system, without permission in writing from the publisher. Printed in the U.S.A.

Library of Congress Catalog Card Number: 73-22591
ISBN: 0-395-17834-7

GV 1060.5.B586

Contents

26624

Preface

It was almost forty years ago that circumstances led me, a prospective medical student, into an unforeseen teaching career. Two years after the great Los Angeles Olympiad of 1932, the lean times of the Depression encouraged me to take a fling at teaching. Teachers are always needed, I reasoned, and more importantly, teaching would allow me to save tuition money and go on to medical school. But the two years I allotted to this detour were filled with so many exciting experiences that medicine was left to those dedicated to the sick, while I continued to work with the healthy. The premed background has nonetheless been of inestimable value to me.

Teaching was and still is fun. Like any other job, it has its tribulations and boredom, but the rewards have been generous: for one, the satisfaction of contributing to the growth of several generations of Americans. I am proud to be a teacher and to be associated with a group of men and women who, on the whole, love youngsters and do not give a whoop if their critics, the vocal few, cause them to be underpaid, underestimated, and overworked.

I think that our schools are among the best in the world because of such teachers. Their efforts and the support of involved parents and students have made our schools the educational, cultural, and athletic centers of our communities. As both a teacher and a coach, I feel fortunate to be part of this great program.

Coaching Track and Field is an outgrowth of my years of coaching in schools. There are a number of ways to present a text on track and field, and in fact, many excellent books on the subject have been published. I have tried to read them all and continue to run into old ones, as well as those that are "hot off the press." Each has something good to offer, and many are so full of "meat" that rereading often turns up appetizing new morsels.

Nonetheless, I believe that *Coaching Track and Field* has something new and unique to offer. Through the years, it has been my pleasure to attend clinics on track, both as a listener and as an "expert" in presentations to athletes and coaches. My observation has been that most teacher-coaches and athletes would prefer to know *how* to train for, or to train a person for, an event, rather than *why* to train that way. This presentation will therefore be devoted to the "how," with training schedules which have been used by champion athletes as a special feature. Other materials related to training methods are included, plus bibliographies directing the reader to further materials in each area.

It is my hope that this book will have value in its entirety as a step-by-step guide for the teacher-coach in his first years. I would hope, too, that the experienced coach will find its systematic and complete analyses of form and training methods a useful addition to his own methods. Finally, it should be possible for the individual working alone to adapt the workout materials in single sections, such as "Distance training and racing," to a training program tailored to his own goals and informed by the experience of decades of champion athletes.

WJB

Coaching Track and Field

Using this book

1

Coaching Track and Field was written especially for two types of people: the teacher-coach who lacks experience in training athletes in a particular event or events, thereby needing detailed training information based on solid experience; and the athlete who has no knowledgeable coach and limited personal training experience. It is an attempt to fill a need in the field of current coaching publications for more detailed and pertinent information on "how" to train.

The book provides a number of valuable training aids, organized in a convenient way, for each of the events covered. A synopsis of the arrangement of the event chapters will demonstrate these features.

The chapters on training usually begin with a discussion of *training methods* for the event in question. The most common training techniques for the event are explained, enabling the athlete and coach to see how the fundamentals of training are actually applied. It should be noted that no specific weight training is indicated. At Oregon weight training is not assigned, but it is acknowledged as important in all events and athletes are encouraged to develop programs suited to their individual capabilities and requirements.

Next, photographic sequences of the performances of champion athletes, both male and female, are presented and discussed. The primary purpose of this section is to show the athlete how skilled athletes perform the event. In some cases, more than one athlete is presented because no two performers are exactly the same. There are unique points to each person's performance, and this book does not seek to convince any coach or athlete that there is one perfect method of training or performance. It is believed that a rigidly copied training system or form will develop only a second-rate athlete; when studied closely, the photographs will illustrate that the champion is one who takes the "basic" form of an event and molds it to accommodate his strengths and his limitations.

Both male and female athletes are shown because it is hoped that the book will be useful to women teachers, coaches, and athletes as well as to men. Basic training methods and event skills are the same for women as for men, but the author does not pretend that the book is equally appropriate for both men and women. The author's experience has been primarily with male athletes, and the book has been written from that point of view. The bulk of the supportive material, the workouts, are men's workouts, and most women will require some adaptations to use them. But the author will not suggest that they be reduced by a fraction for women's use, an approach advocated by some which undercuts the potential of many women athletes. Rather, it is hoped that women will experiment with the workouts and adapt them to their individual capabilities. Women's track and field is growing rapidly in scope and quality in the United States; and it is time for the women to control and develop their own athletic programs, rather than allow men coaches and administrators to train "little men." We firmly believe that women coaches will find this book more useful than most texts written for women in track and field, but the author has no wish to present himself as a knowledgeable coach of women.

The training schedules are the "meat" of the chapters and the most valuable portion of the book. A typical training manual will tell the athlete how to train for a week or several weeks. The workouts will usually be theoretical ones which no living athlete performing on a high level has used or is likely to use. The workouts in this book, however, are all taken from *actual* training files; they follow an athlete through his daily training for an entire training year, from the fall until June, when his most important meets are contested. The workouts were used by quality athletes, sub-4:00 milers, 60-foot shot-putters, 9.2-to-9.4-second 100-yard runners, and so on. Since these competitors have been national-class and world-class athletes, where actual times and paces are given, the coach or athlete should adapt them to the appropriate level of ability. For younger athletes, the quantity of work should also be adapted. Other than these precautions, the workouts are absolutely usable by any athlete. They solve a great problem for the inexperienced coach or athlete: *what* should the athlete do to train well? In the training schedules, he has what he needs.

Following the training schedules, the meaning of the symbols on the training schedule sheets is explained in detail. In addition, the origin of the schedule sheets and a presentation of their use and interpretation, as well as a general discussion of training, appear in Chapter 2.

The explanation of the training fundamentals is followed by a bibliography of additional sources regarding that particular event or activity. It is a selection of materials, mostly periodical articles, which have appeared in print since 1960. Although it is not intended to be exhaustive, it should provide enough further material to satisfy the most interested of readers. The author does not necessarily agree with the content of every article, but this book tries to stress that there is no "one way" to reach success.

After the events are covered, some general administrative problems are discussed in the final chapters. The importance of an all-around track program is covered, as well as methods which have been successfully applied for finding track talent in the school. Materials which can aid the coaching process are presented in a brief chapter, and finally, the techniques and problems involved in running track and field meets, both small and large, are discussed in some detail.

Throughout this book the emphasis is on one thing: "how?"

Coaching Track and Field does not attempt to explain *why* a training method works, because most coaches and athletes are primarily interested in *what* will work (the "how" of training). If it works, they are satisfied, and the materials given here have worked in the past and are working today. If coaches and athletes use these materials and find that they have been helped, the purpose of this book will have been met.

A last word on reference materials is necessary. There are many valuable publications devoted to sports, and several of them are cited frequently in this book. A brief annotated bibliography following this introduction will give details on some of the more important of these publications.

Annotated Bibliography

What Is Going On in Track and Field

Track and Field News. $9.00. This publication is absolutely essential to any person interested in what is going on around the world in track and field. P.O. Box 296, Los Altos, California 94022. Published 18 times per year (twice a month in season).

Runner's World Magazine. Monthly publication devoted primarily to distance running. $4.00 per year from P.O. Box 366, Mountain View, California 94040.

Women's Track and Field World. Claremont, California.

Articles on Training and Technique

Athletic Journal. $4.00 per year from 1719 Howard Street, Evanston, Illinois 60202.

Scholastic Coach. $4.00 per year from 50 West 44th Street, New York, New York 10036.

Track and Field Quarterly Review. Publication of the United States Track Coaches Association. Sent to all members. Contains much valuable material. Ann Arbor, Michigan.

Track Technique. Quarterly magazine which has digests of foreign articles. Extremely valuable. Available through *Track and Field News* for $4.00 per year.

Rulebooks and Officiating Materials

AAU Rule Book. Rules of competition of the United States Amateur Athletic Union, available from AAU headquarters in Indianapolis, Indiana.

Handbook of the IAAF. The official international rulebook, source of all track rulebooks, published every two years by the International Amateur Athletic Federation, 162 Upper Richmond Road, Putney; London, S.W. 15, England.

Official Collegiate Track and Field Guide. Rules of the National Collegiate Athletic Association, published annually and distributed through the Collegiate Athletics Publishing Service, 349 East Thomas Road, Phoenix, Arizona.

Scoring Table for Men's Track and Field Events. Table formed in 1962, with a revised addition in 1971. The *International Edition of the Metric Conversion Tables* should be purchased at the same time for a combined total of about $3.50 (scoring table at 50 pence, conversion table at 80 pence; women's pentathlon tables, 1971 edition, at 30 pence). Available through the IAAF address above.

Track and Field Official's Manual, 1972–1973. Very helpful details for running and officiating at meets. Published for $1 by the United States Track and Field Federation, 1225 North 10th Ave., Tucson, Arizona 85705.

National Alliance Edition of Track and Field Rules and Records. Rules for high schools, NAIA schools, junior colleges and women's competition. Published annually by the National Federation of State High School Associations, 400 Leslie Street, Elgin, Illinois 60120, for $1.

one

The Distances

The fundamentals of distance training

2

The basic philosophy of the Oregon system is to seek the greatest improvement possible in the athlete while working for *his* benefit. This means that the good of the athlete is the first consideration, rather than the maximum use which the school can get from his abilities. To help the athlete reach his potential, his training schedule is planned to improve his performances gradually over a period of time, aiming for peak performances at the time of the conference and national meets.

Fall and winter are not emphasized as competitive seasons, but are part of this training cycle of gradual improvement. Cross country is used to give the runners a solid training background. Though some cross country meets are entered, these few meets are more for the purpose of stimulating the runners and giving them something to look forward to than for actual competition. The indoor track season is also passed over, for the most part. There is one "home" meet in Portland each year, the Oregon Invitational; but except for that meet, few of the Oregon athletes have any official winter competition. Instead, they run against the clock in three-quarter effort trials every two or three weeks from midfall until just before the competitive season begins.

When spring arrives, Oregon competes almost every week against some of the best teams in the world, the Pacific Eight conference teams. A runner might not compete every week even during this season. A distance man will rarely compete in two events in a single meet. The reasons are simple: (1) the athlete needs to be "hungry," anxious to compete; and (2) a runner reaches his potential more surely (and is more likely to remain there for some time) if he does not go out every week feeling the need to "make up points" for his team. The coach may like to win as much as anyone, but the good of the runner must come first. An athlete who has to compete in two events regularly will usually be holding back in the first event and tired during the second. As a result, he will not be likely to reach his potential in either event.

The Oregon training system had its genesis in the coaching theories of William H. Hayward, Oregon track coach from 1904 to 1947. "Colonel Bill," a volunteer assistant coach and trainer for the U.S. Olympic Team at several Olympics and coach of several world record holders, always stressed a program of gradual conditioning and a reasonable limit on the number of competitive races. The Oregon system of training has its roots in his four and a half decades of service to the University and to American track and field.

Upon returning to the University as track coach in 1948, William Bowerman found a small track team and a "stable" of one distance runner, junior Pete Mundle. At this time he knew mostly the American theories of distance training, so he had Pete conduct some library research to learn what training methods seemed to offer the best possibilities for success. After some study, Mundle wrote a term paper recommending that they try interval training and fartlek, a method which was not too widely known or understood in the United States at that time.

Pete then became the "guinea pig," and those experiments laid the groundwork from which the Oregon system of distance training grew. This research led to the discovery of the great value of fartlek to the training program and to further development of the "hard-easy" principle of training. Fortunately, some fine young distance runners chose to come to Oregon, and they in turn brought more good runners. For many years this has been the primary means of recruiting runners.

Principles and Theory of Distance Training

These training theories are not new or unusual. Nothing is done which is not practiced around the world. These theories developed primarily from what was learned about Gosta Holmer's work with fartlek, observations of John Landy's training before the 1954 British Empire Games, Franz Stampfl's writings on interval training, the theories of Mihaly Igloi, and personal contacts with Arthur Lydiard, plus useful ideas from many fine American coaches.

The basic principles are simple. The first was expressed well by Lydiard: "train, don't strain." The athlete should enjoy training. He should complete his workout feeling exhilarated, not exhausted, as Holmer suggested with fartlek training. Training must be fun, or else why do we train?

It is better to undertrain the runner than to overtrain him. Overtraining can result in staleness, a loss of interest in practice and in competition. Staleness can also result from too frequent competition, which can interfere with the best performances and progress of our athletes. An ideal situation is competition every two weeks, occasionally every three weeks. It is difficult to understand how a team or a coach can accomplish much in the school or college season with two meets a week. When do they learn or teach?

To those coaches who prefer two or three meets a week and point to the summer European programs where American athletes have performed outstandingly, we emphasize that those distance runners are usually mature, twenty-five years or older. Furthermore, during that time all they have to do is compete, eat, and rest. The school or college athlete is not only competing; he is also getting his education, which should be his first concern. This requires considerable evening study.

Evolution of the System

The basic system discussed here is a combination of interval training and fartlek. It has been developing around those basic concepts for almost twenty-five years now, and it is still developing. It began with the written materials given to Pete Mundle in the late 1940s, has combined with what was learned from coaches around the world since then, and has synthesized through years of coaching practice into the present system.

We have found no better system for the athletes for whom it was developed: college students between the ages of seventeen and twenty-four. Here the work level is lower than that cited for many world-class athletes. Keep in mind, however, that those athletes are often five years or more older than the older college students and ten years older than the high school athletes.

The first major outside influence on the system was that of Gosta Holmer of Sweden, the namer, if not the developer, of fartlek. He also contributed a ten-day training pattern, which was adapted into our first pattern of training. His writings and assistance were a great contribution to the system.

Franz Stampfl provided the framework around which this version of the yearly pattern of interval training, with a gradually quickening pace, was developed. Stampfl's book, published in 1955, was perhaps the most widely circulated writing on interval training in the English language. It was an attempt to put interval training into a system in which the level of training progressed scientifically. It was probably more widely circulated among English-speaking coaches than the work of interval training's major developer, Woldemar Gerschler of Germany.

Mihaly Igloi made considerable contributions also. Bowerman's first contact with his training methods was through a letter from the late Dale Ranson, coach at the University of North Carolina. After Igloi's defection from Hungary following the 1956 Olympics, he and several of his runners spent some time in Chapel Hill, North Carolina, where they were observed by Coach Ranson. Later Oregon's Pete Mundle trained after graduation under Igloi in southern California, providing more information and insight into the methods of Igloi, who is a fine, knowledgeable, but misunderstood coach.

Finally, but by no means least, much was learned from Arthur Lydiard of New Zealand. His insights into training opened up new areas of experimentation. Though we do not agree with everything he says, as we are sure he does not agree with all our teachings, there is no better distance coach in the world. His year-round training patterns were very interesting, as were a number of his practices which were adapted and are now used in one form or another.

The "Hard-Easy" Training Approach

The athlete should not compete before he has been properly conditioned. Competing too soon causes the athlete to risk injuring himself, since his body is not properly prepared for the stresses of competition. For that same reason, the athlete should not use or be made to use meets as a means of conditioning.

The training pattern follows a "hard-easy" sequence, with each day of hard training being followed by a day of light or "easy" training, primarily jogging and light fartlek. The reason for this cycle is basic to all training: the body must have rest. Rest is always necessary for the body to recover and replenish itself. Furthermore, the light days will allow more work in the training sessions on the hard days, giving greater progress in the long run. This cycle is basic, but it is not inflexible. Some runners are strong enough to take two hard days for every easy day; others can take only one hard day and then need two easy days.

An experiment was conducted with the Oregon runners to see how long they could hold up under conditions of heavy training, with no recovery days. Most of the runners lasted no more than a week, including several who, after returning to the hard-easy cycle, later ran under 4:00 for the mile. Only one runner lasted two weeks: Bill Dellinger, then a twenty-five-year-old graduate student and veteran of two Olympics. At the end of three weeks, even he could no longer take the unrelieved hard days.

In this same vein, it is preferable to keep the runners short of their peak, not over the hill. Once an athlete has been properly conditioned and has a good background of training, it takes little extra work to bring him to a peak. However, an athlete cannot remain at peak condition for very long. For that reason, we prefer to hold the athletes short of their peak and sharpen them at the end of the season for the most important meets. Many athletes can be observed who are world beaters in the early season, but who cannot make the finals in the national meets. We want to avoid that.

The athletes work toward objectives and goals in their training. If they don't know where they are going, how will they get there? How will they know how close they are? The athletes and the coach set personal goals for the end of the year, then gradually progress toward those goals through training sessions and test efforts run at the three-quarter-effort level.

The athlete must also train to the competition. No athlete can train without taking account of his competitors. This involves training to reach the same level, or a better one, as the competitors, and also involves training in tactics and their uses.

One of the purposes of training is to improve the runner's strengths, so that his assets become greater assets, and to overcome his weaknesses, so that his handicaps will be eradicated, if possible, or at least minimized.

The athlete should continue with light exercise after hard training or competition. This is sometimes referred to as "cooling down." The reason is quite simple: during strenuous exercise the body builds up lactic acid, a by-product of muscular activity, in the muscles. If the lactic acid is not removed from the muscles, it can result in cramping and possibly muscular injury. Easy jogging after heavy exercise keeps the blood circulating rapidly, gradually drawing the excess lactic acid from the muscles. For this reason also, an easy trot on the morning after heavy exercise is beneficial to the body.

The morning run is now considered an essential of distance training. The practice is excellent, if the runner can handle it. It helps to wake him up in the morning and get his metabolic processes started for the day. It also encourages him to go to bed earlier. If the runner will not do this, however, it becomes a destructive process. If the runner has heavy studies or is involved in a romance, he should not try the morning run, nor should the coach force him to try it. The athlete is going through the biology of youth, and it must be accommodated because it cannot be changed.

Compared to other world-class athletes, Oregon athletes do not train very hard. At the moment, 100 or more miles a week is considered by many people to be necessary for success in distance running. We do not believe this, nor has experience suggested it. Oregon athletes run anywhere from 60 to 80 miles a week in training, averaging about 70 miles a week. None of them covers 100 miles a week except in rare circumstances, yet over a dozen sub-4:00 milers have been produced at Oregon. While mileage helps, it is by no means the only variable involved in training, and perhaps it is not the most important one.

It is our belief that 100 miles a week is more than is necessary for successful distance competition. Though Arthur Lydiard has been pointed to as the source for this magic mark, his training schedules call for that amount of training for only about two months, while at other times they call for only 40 to 60 miles per week of training. Every athlete's training method should be taken with a grain of salt, experimented with, and then adapted to the specific needs and abilities of the individual who wishes to use them. The coach must keep in mind that: (1) the student-athlete is supposed to be studying, and (2) there are other things in life besides running. The athlete should learn to keep his appetite up for running, not make it the most important thing in his life. If he passes up other things in life, he will be isolating himself, which is not good.

The age at which training should begin is simple to pick: the age at which the youngster *wants* to train. If a four-year-old likes to run, he is old enough to train (as distinct from *being* trained). If an eighteen-year-old must be driven out to the track and flogged around it, he is too young to train, or his appetite is gone. The key is *enjoyment:* the athlete should enjoy what he is doing; he should not have to be forced into training.

Physiology of Training

Of the physiological phenomena which are a measure of a person's ability to run a race of over 100 yards, one of the best indicators is oxygen debt and its related reactions. To explain it scientifically would take a chapter, if not a volume, but we can mention it here.

When a miler runs, he is burning internal fuels and is using oxygen for the burning, just as a camper burns wood which consumes oxygen. If the lungs can supply enough oxygen to the fuel to carry the runner for a mile at a comfortable pace, there is no distress. If there is insufficient oxygen supplied to maintain the pace, or if the pace is too fast for the amount of oxygen supplied, the runner goes into oxygen debt.

Other related biochemical factors produce the same sort of inability to maintain pace. Too much smoke in the chimney prevents good combustion in the stove. Similarly, production of carbon dioxide and related wastes in greater quantities than can be eliminated by the circulatory and respiratory systems interferes with oxygen exchange and contributes to oxygen debt.

Some coaches speak of fatigue tolerance or tolerance to oxygen debt. Is it a superior level of fitness which permits an athlete not only to turn in a world-record performance, but to do it repeatedly? We suspect that it is a combination of his fitness, his tolerance, his coach, and, of course, his superior physical equipment.

Other Distance Training Principles

We believe in weight training for runners. By weight training we do not mean the development of Olympic weight lifters, or hours of time spent weekly. A short list of exercises is used which concentrates upon the upper body, back, and arms, all of which tend to be neglected with most runners. Strengthening these areas, particularly the back and abdomen, assists in improving the posture, which in turn permits the body to take in more oxygen, permitting the athlete to run faster and farther. We experimented with a group of runners in a study testing weight training and half-mile times. With two groups of previously equal performance levels, the group which lifted weights for fifteen minutes a day, three days a week, rather than doing extra running at that time, averaged two seconds per man faster than the nonlifting group after eight weeks of training. That is an extra 15 or more yards gained.

Swimming also appears to be beneficial to runners. Though this is accepted today, twenty years ago it was considered taboo. It is good for relaxing and loosening tight muscles, and it is very helpful for a runner with knee or ankle problems, since he can exercise the muscles without antagonizing the joints. In fact, a few years ago a varsity swimmer at Oregon came out for the mile during his fifth year of school. At the end of the year he ran a 4:05.2 mile, followed by a 1500-meter race at a faster pace. He has since become an Olympic modern pentathlon performer.

The final principle might be better described as a practice. During their early season training, all the distance runners at Oregon practice the techniques of the steeplechase occasionally. Since few of them have ever encountered this event before coming to the University, this is a way of finding runners who show natural ability or interest in this event. Those athletes will continue to work on steeplechase activities. This work consists primarily of practicing clearance of the barriers, pace work over the barriers, and work on the water-jump, begun with stepping onto and then over sections of logs. A number of good steeplechasers began on Oregon's Douglas firs.

Components of Running Ability

There are three essential components to successful racing over the middle distances. The first two are of equal importance, and the third is nice to have, but not absolutely necessary. These essentials are: (1) endurance, (2) pace judgment, and (3) speed. It is entirely possible that a fourth essential has been added by Emil Zatopek and Vladimir Kuts. It might be called varied-pace or aggressive tactics.

Endurance is necessary for the body's ability to withstand the continued stress of a distance race. The runner must develop this strength to endure before he will be able to compete well. The coach and athlete should remember that endurance is not solely a physical or physiological matter; it is also a state of mind and a function of will power. The champion not only has greater physiological endurance, but he also has greater mental endurance. He can drive himself closer to his real capacity before his mind tells him to stop. Tolerance to stress requires considerable mental training in addition to physical training.

Pace judgment is extremely important. Most inexperienced runners will begin a race at a very fast pace, slow down too much during the race, and then try to make a sprint finish. Not only is such a tactic painful and thus discouraging to the young athlete, but also it is physiologically foolish. The easiest way to run a given time, from a physiological standpoint, is by following even space. The ability to run even pace, or any pace, requires training in pace judgment, not just endurance training. The world's best distance runners are all excellent judges of pace. It is the work of years of training and racing experience, and it is essential to success.

The third component is speed. While it is not the most important factor, it is still very helpful. Obviously if all other factors and abilities are the same, the runner with the best speed will win. However, all other factors and abilities are rarely equal, and many tactical variations have been used to equalize the inequities among runners. Speed can be improved in runners in most instances. Where it can be improved, it should be improved.

The tentative fourth essential is varied-pace or aggressive tactics. This is the method of shifting from one pace to another during the race, throwing in a short sprint here, a running long, quick section there, and attempting to hold a reasonably stiff pace for the rest of the race. It is a difficult type of race to run. It is physiologically much harder than an evenly paced race, and the runner has the disadvantage of having to lead the race all the way, while hoping to "kill off" his opponents without exhausting his own physiological resources. However, it is as psychologically exhausting on the opponents as it is physically exhausting, for they never know when a fast burst may be used or how long it will last, thus being less decided about how to cope with it.

Training Methods

Interval Training

The Oregon version of interval training includes ideas from Franz Stampfl, Billy Hayes, Woldemar Gerschler, and Mihaly Igloi, to name a few. We try to fit the workout to the individual. Some athletes can handle more work than others. Some show more improvement on intervals, others on fartlek. The two are combined with a little speed work until we learn what kind of fertilizer makes our flowers grow best.

We say of interval training that 1 to 2½ times the racing distance, preceded by a warm-up and followed by some fartlek or speed work, is a heavy workout. Experience has shown that one-quarter of the racing distance is the ideal distance for practicing intervals. Distances shorter and longer than quarter-distance are used, and the intensity is increased by reducing the rest or recuperative intervals.

If a runner is working toward a 4:40 mile, he would run 4 to 12 quarters at 70 seconds each. For variety he would have some 220s at a slightly faster pace or some 660s at a slightly slower pace. The total distance covered during a workout would be one to three times his racing distance, or 1 to 3 miles. His "full" rest would also be 1 to 3 miles. If he wants the workout a bit more intense, he cuts down the length of the rest interval to 220 or even 110 yards after running each fast 440.

Experience has suggested that nothing is gained by training ahead of pace (a 4:40 miler training at a 65- or 60-second pace per 440 yards), except for one-eighth of the distance (220 yards) at the slightly faster goal pace, followed by work at the date pace. The runner will reach higher goals by getting in a greater volume of work than if he tries to carry too fast a pace and "poops out" before the workout is completed. We don't know how many freshmen have said, "But I can run faster than 75s (or 70s). I can run ten times at 64."

The answer should be a question: "But can you run a mile in 4:16?" The courage of the young athlete who wants to try is admirable, but having tried and found himself wanting, we doubt his judgment if he will not turn himself over to his coach.

There are five variables involved in interval training: (1) the duration of the effort (distance run), (2) the intensity of the effort (speed of the run), (3) the number of repetitions, (4) the duration of the recovery (length of the rest intervals), and (5) the nature of the recovery interval (jogging, walking, or complete rest). Many articles are available which describe interval training and its practice, so it will not be discussed further here. Numerous sources of information are listed in the bibliography at the end of this chapter.

Repetition Running

Repetition running is a useful variant of interval training. While interval training technically includes only short runs (not over 660 yards) with only partial recovery between each run, repetition running involves longer intervals run at a slower pace, usually with complete rest between each run, allowing complete or near-complete recovery. Repetition running is done less often than interval training, but it is still very useful to the overall training pattern.

Fartlek

Gosta Holmer of Sweden is generally recognized as the man who introduced his fartlek, or "speed play," training to running. We are indebted to him for the ideas of "Holmer-type" fartlek. How does one train with Holmer fartlek? All the elements of a race are interspersed with periods of rest or partial recuperation. The length of the training session depends upon the amount of time available and the energy of the runner.

Assume that a period of thirty minutes, forty-five minutes, an hour, or even longer will be used. Begin by having the runner jog slowly at a pace of seven to eight minutes per mile for two or three miles. This fifteen or twenty minutes is for warming up, to bring the cardiovascular and respiratory systems into a condition of readiness for hard work. Then have the runner pick up to what feels like race pace and carry it for 400 yards, 600 yards, half a mile, or however far until a sense of fatigue is felt. Then, without letting him rest, have him sprint for 50 to 150 yards until it begins to "hurt." This is followed by a very slow jog or a walk to recover. Next comes a series of short sprints of perhaps 50 yards, alternating sprinting and walking that distance until it is quite an effort, then recovering with another jog or walk.

Now have him imagine that it is a race. The athlete will stride at racing pace up to the shoulder of an imaginary opponent, pass with a quick burst, then settle into racing pace for 200 to 400 yards, followed by a recuperative jog or walk. Have another imaginary race, this time with his opponent on his shoulder. The athlete should accelerate enough to hold off a challenge or series of challenges and then finish with another walking or jogging rest. Anything that can happen or be imagined in a race can be practiced in Holmer's fartlek. Fartlek is a personal, not a group, "tool."

Where should a runner practice fartlek? Soft surfaces are best. Holmer suggests the woods and fields. Runners might use the local golf courses. You should get written permission to use the courses from the president and board of each course every year. The ground rules for the runners are simple:

1. Always stay on the outside of a fairway and "run with the grain" or direction of play.
2. Do not cut across a fairway.
3. Go behind a tee and around a green.
4. If a player is addressing a ball, *stop.*

The second type of fartlek which is used is "Lydiard fartlek." Lydiard also uses variations of the "speed play." However, to differentiate between what we want our runners to do, we call the steady running "Lydiard fartlek." We agree with Lydiard that no runner is ready to start training until he can run steadily without stopping for 45 minutes to one hour. How does a runner reach that stage? He should wear a watch and start at an eight-to-ten-minute-per-mile pace (60 to 75 seconds per 220 yards), head down the street for ten minutes, and then return, all at that same pace. Add time gradually until he can go out for thirty minutes and then return, a total of one hour. Then he is ready to go on a schedule.

We continue to use Lydiard's slow, steady running fartlek and Holmer's "speed play" throughout the year, following the principles which each of them suggested. Holmer said, "You should finish the workout feeling exhilarated, not exhausted." Lydiard said, "You should train, not strain." Both men produced champions and world record holders.

Overdistance and Road Training

Overdistance training is essential to a balanced program of training for the distance races. This consists simply of long runs, usually at a steady pace. As for what constitutes a "long" run, it depends to some extent upon the normal competitive distance of the athlete. To most half-milers, a 6- or 8-mile run is a long distance, but for a 3- or 6-miler it is not long at all. Generally speaking, a long run would be any distance over 6 miles. The longest distance any of our runners uses with any regularity is 14 to 16 miles, though some marathon runners occasionally run as far as 30 miles in a long training session. We have a series of "loops" or training courses laid out around the town and surrounding countryside. These are almost entirely on roads, as a matter of simple necessity: the Willamette Valley is a bit damp for six or eight months a year. Our shortest loop is a 3-mile loop through Hendricks Park on a low ridge near campus, and our longest loop (16 miles) wanders around nearby Spencer's Butte. There is a much longer course running up the McKenzie River, but it is used only on rare occasions. We are fortunate in our location in a flat river valley which also has many convenient hills and buttes surrounding our city. This provides us with both easy and difficult terrain, depending upon what we want or need in our training.

Other Overdistance Training Theories

Arthur Lydiard suggested a period of training which he termed "marathon training." Thus his recommendation of a minimum of 100 miles a week is considered something of a sacred rite for any runner who wishes to be successful. In the first place, that training period was not over 15 percent of his suggested annual cycle. In the second place, we don't consider that much mileage to be entirely necessary. The purpose of the heavy mileage was to lay an endurance basis for the later speed work and races. We are not entirely convinced that runs of more than 10 miles at a time are necessary to successful running. We definitely do not believe that over 70 or 80 miles a week are needed for success on the international level.

A variation of overdistance training is a trend which is not yet too common among racers: "long slow distance," commonly abbreviated LSD. Some runners have discovered that they are able to progress just as well (and sometimes better) as with previously used, more difficult training techniques. It is just what the name implies: long distances run at speeds rarely under 7 minutes per mile and as slowly as 10 or more minutes per mile. Little experimentation has been done with it as yet, however. It does serve to illustrate that "there's more than one way to skin a cat" in training and still get good results.

Regardless of the type of training which is preferred, one cardinal principle should never be forgotten: Variety is the spice of life." Every runner needs variety, if for no other reason than to prevent mental staleness. The system always must recognize that individuals are different. Schedules are only guides. Just as a balanced diet makes for a healthier, happier person, so does a varied and balanced training schedule make for a more efficient, eager runner. A continuous, nonvaried schedule usually makes an automatic, unimaginative runner.

Introducing the Runners to Training

Finding Candidates

The best way to find your first candidates is by testing everyone in the physical education classes. Have every man run an 880 and record the time. An untrained person who can run under 2:30 has enough natural speed and endurance to be considered a good prospect. Experience in high school and college over a period of years has proven this to be a reliable indicator of inherent talent. (See Chapter 18 for more information.)

Most of the great middle distance champions have been of average or slightly over average height, slightly built, and with well-defined (but not bulky) muscles. They generally have had slower than average pulse rates. However, there have been notable exceptions to each of these characteristics.

Champions must be serious, with abundant energy and tenacity. They must be willing to endure grueling workout schedules regardless of weather conditions, day in and day out, year after year. They must be eager to push themselves to the limit of their capacities, as well as anxious to defeat their opponents. The two greatest characteristics of the champion have always been dedication and hard work.

Equipment

The runner's equipment is almost as meager as the swimmer's, with one exception: his shoes. Every runner should have three pairs of shoes, if possible. One is for wearing to and from the track and during road work; the second is for regular practice; and the last is for competition.

We recommend a flat, rubber-soled warm-up shoe. A shoemaker can take the soles off a pair of worn-down spiked shoes and replace them with a sole about half an inch thick and between the hardness of sponge and regular sole rubber (called Number 18 Iron). The shoes must have a heel between one-quarter -inch and one-half-inch thick, also of rubber. Our runners have preferred the rebuilt shoes better than any they have been able to buy.

For practice sessions, a sturdy but comfortable shoe is essential. A four-spike model is a frequent choice. The four-spike competition shoe must be comfortable and of the lightest possible construction. Every fraction of an ounce counts. This fact can be demonstrated by comparing a typical American-made pair of shoes which weighs sixteen ounces to another pair which weighs twelve ounces. The extra four ounces in the heavier pair of shoes will amount to the runner's having picked up literally 220 extra pounds in the course of a 1-mile race (4 ounces X 880 strides). This energy could be more profitably spent in getting ahead than in dragging an anchor.

Running trunks and jersey should also be made of the lightest possible material. Names or emblems can be silk-screened rather than sewn on, thereby avoiding useless, weighty junk. The only necessary stripe across the chest is the one at the finish line.

Practice gear may be as inexpensive as it is practicable. "Long johns" may be substituted for sweat pants, not only for economy, but also because they do not get clammy when wet and can be worn in competition during cold weather.

Stocking caps are good protection against the cold, but a sweat shirt with a hood attached is probably more practical, since the hood cannot be forgotten or lost. All the training clothing should be kept clean, either washed or dry-cleaned as frequently as possible.

Work on Mechanics and Posture

We work to improve the mechanics of our runners because the runners gain much from it. A champion is able to do a certain job with less effort than a non-champion. The reason for this is that his body has been trained to do that task more efficiently. We are trying to improve the mechanical efficiency of our runners to enable them to do the same amount of work with less effort, so they will be able to devote the energy which they have saved to running a faster race. The effort expended will be the same, but the time will be faster, because the body worked more efficiently, yielding greater output without requiring a greater effort.

Good posture comes from good muscle tone. If the muscles of the stomach, lower back, and hips are well developed, they will assist in maintaining an upright posture. Weight lifting and other exercises can help in this area of need.

The best postural position for the middle distance runner is an upright one. A line from the ear straight down to the ground should show that the back is perpendicular to the ground while running. The widely accepted belief is that the body needs to lean forward to run well. Extensive tests conducted with Dr. Donald Slocum[1] show that this belief is incorrect. The results show that champion runners have basically an upright posture while striding at racing speed. This is true even for sprinters, once they have finished accelerating.

Photograph 2.1, page 19, is a side view of a group of runners in an 880-yard run. Times on this lap varied from 51 to 53 seconds, so they are running at race pace. Notice that they are all running erectly, with little or no body lean, though there are some personal eccentricities of form shown. The upright posture is simply more efficient, because when any body part is out of alignment, some muscles have to strain to keep the body balanced, diverting part of the body's energies from the task of running a fast race.

In our work with runners, we try to point out the mechanical advantages of this upright "form." We have the runners practice these principles in their fartlek and interval training, so they will become part of the runner's natural technique. We do try to keep in mind that there are individual variations to this "perfect" form. There are very few "picture" runners, for most men have some physical characteristics which require minor compensations.

We found in our research that the pelvic position is the key to control of the runner's posture. The pelvis should be "tucked under" or brought forward in relation to the rest of the body. This assists in straightening the spine, which helps maintain an upright posture. The chest is directly in line above the hips, keeping the back in a straight line perpendicular to the ground. The head is up, the chest raised, and the arms swing slightly across the chest. This basic running form permits easier use of the leg muscles and aids in taking air into the lungs. If the horizon seems to be bounding, the runner may be overstriding.

The arm carry and swing also affect the posture. We teach an angle of sixty to ninety degrees at the elbow as optimum, though the athlete with very muscular arms, someone like Peter Snell, might need to use a more open angle. This angle contributes to running efficiency in three ways. The first contribution is the improvement of circulation. The little bit of downward flow from hand to

[1] Donald B. Slocum and William J. Bowerman, "The Biomechanics of Running," in *Proceedings of the Second National Conference on the Medical Aspects of Sports* (Chicago: American Medical Association, 1961), pp. 53–58.

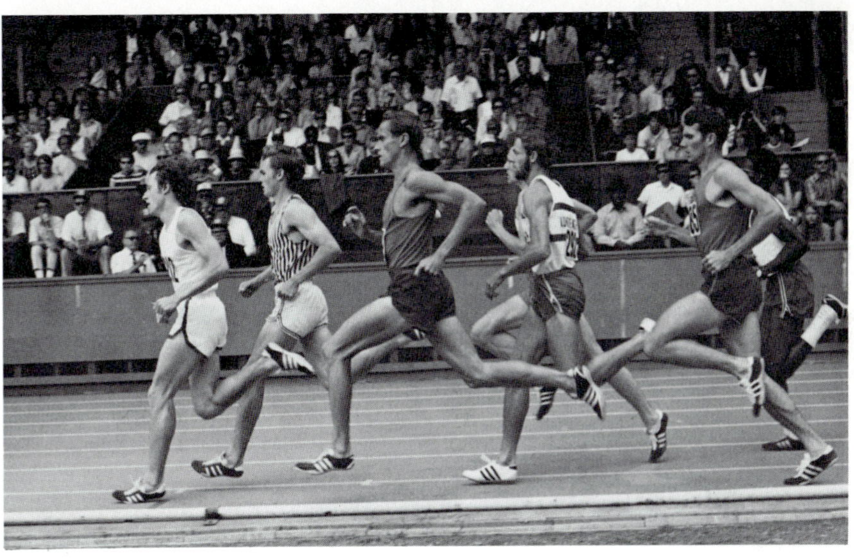

Photograph 2.1 Side view of runners moving at race pace demonstrating an erect posture.

elbow makes the heart's job that much easier. There is also centrifugal force to be considered. Like the water in the bucket swung at arm's length, centrifugal force will be acting to keep the blood from returning from the hands, if the arms are carried very low.

The second advantage of the elbow angle is mechanical. The lower the arms are carried, the longer the stride tends to be. The longer the stride, the greater is the energy output required to maintain a given pace and stride length. Since the arms and legs work in opposite pairs, we try to get the short, quick, economical stride by keeping the upper extremities moving in a shorter working radius also.

The third advantage is the contribution to balance. The swing of the arms contributes to equilibrium balance or imbalance. The wild swinging of one or both arms must be compensated for with a shift of weight on the opposite side of the center of gravity or through the expenditure of additional energy. When a runner is fresh, he can swing an arm way out of line and get away with it. When he comes down the home stretch and fatigue and tension are riding him, he may vibrate all over the track, or if too fatigued he may even fall.

It is recommended that runners use their arms in the following manner: with an elbow bend of sixty to ninety degrees, the hand is swung in an arc from about the top of the hip bone to the breast bone in the center of the body, with the arms naturally alternating this movement. The hand and arm are swung from the shoulder; the elbow does not open and close. There are times when the runner may want to rest or save the arms for the final drive by carrying them for a while. This motion is one where the hands remain about three to six inches apart and swing in rhythmical tempo back and forth across the chest.

The quick, light stride is the most economical, and it is most easily maintained when the body is running in an upright position, rather than leaning forward. The leg swing should be as effortless as possible. The knee lift is moderately high, but there is no conscious effort to reach with the knee. The leg and foot are dropped directly under the body for the stride, and the leg is not fully extended in front of the body. A relatively short stride is the most efficient. It is better to understride than to overstride. The runner should watch an object on the horizon to see if it is moving up and down. If the object is bounding, then the runner is bouncing, having to lift his body at every stride. He is probably overstriding, a very common fault, and he is certainly running inefficiently.

There are three ways to plant the foot while running: heel-to-ball, flat-footed, and ball-to-heel. The ball-to-heel is basically running on the toes, as sprinters do, and is out of place in distance running. It is less efficient for a runner, since it requires more energy and puts additional strain on the calf muscles. Most great runners use either the heel-to-ball or flat-footed stride. The runners should experiment to see which is most comfortable for them. The flat style involves landing flat-footed and rocking forward, while the heel-to-ball covers landing in the area of the heel of the foot and rolling forward to the toes to push off.

Three of the items we have discussed are worth repeating: stride length, body mechanics, and body posture. Stride length is important because it, combined with stride cadence and economy of energy, determines in part how soon the race will be finished. The "long, beautiful stride" is often a disadvantage because it acts as a brake when the foot lands ahead of the center of gravity, and it requires more energy since it lifts and drops the body with every stride. Overstriding is the most common fault of high school distance runners. A short, economical, quick stride is better and more efficient.

Body mechanics are important because when improper mechanics are used, the body is faced with a much greater energy drain. The body should be used as efficiently as possible, so the energy saved by good mechanics may be diverted to faster running.

Posture is also important from the standpoint of efficiency. If the mechanical and postural advantages are deleted, there are still two good advantages of the upright running posture: (1) it enables the body to take more air into the lungs, since the upright trunk allows the lungs more space in the body cavity, and (2) it permits the knees to be lifted higher, allowing the runner to swing the legs more freely and easily while running.

Work on Pace Judgment

Pace judgment is one of the most important abilities of the champion runner. Generally speaking, the most efficient way to run a race is with even pacing. Pace judgment is not inherent; it is learned. Once pace judgment is acquired, the athlete can plan his race more easily, and he can better utilize his strengths and negate his weaknesses.

The significant thing is that pace judgment is one of the weapons with which an athlete arms himself. He knows what his pace is and deviates from it only as a weapon, as did Vladimir Kuts in the 1956 Olympics against Gordon Pirie in the 10,000 meters. By using a mixture of sprints combined with his otherwise even pacing, Kuts forced Pirie to try what Pirie was unable to do, resulting in a run-away victory for Kuts.

The penalties of poor pacing can be described by telling of a simulated race between a good college miler of 4:10 ability and a high school 4:20 miler. On the first lap, the high school runner goes out quickly, leading the veteran by 2 seconds, 60 to 62 seconds. The veteran is running comfortably, since he is quite close to his racing pace: but as the runners enter the second lap, the high school runner is already going into oxygen debt because he ran a full 5 seconds below his pace. At the half the runners are even in 2:05. Though the veteran kept on pace with a 63 for his lap, the other runner was already feeling the effects of his fast first lap, so he slowed to a 65. On the third lap the younger runner is struggling because of oxygen debt, so he can only manage a 70-second lap, while the veteran continues with another 63 to lead at the 1320 by 50 yards, 3:08 to 3:15. On the last lap the veteran may hold his pace with a 62, or he may even be able to "kick in" in 56 seconds or so, giving him a time of 4:10 to as low as 4:04. Meanwhile, the high school runner is failing, and he struggles through in 70 to 75 seconds for a 4:25 to 4:30 mile, not only losing painfully by 100 yards or more, but also unable to reach his capability of 4:20.

The reason for this poor race was primarily that the high school runner was unable to judge his pace well. By running too fast in the early stages of the race, he built up an oxygen debt which he was unable to pay off without slowing down greatly. Had the high school runner trained more at developing his pace judgment, he would have been less likely to make that error. Practice perfects rhythm at any pace. A person can be strong of wind and heart and in good condition, but not have practiced pace work long enough to establish his rhythm.

To start teaching pace to our new runners, we put a small stake in the middle of each straight and each turn of the track, dividing the track into four 110-yard or 100-meter segments. The runners are shown a pace card with the 440-, 220-, and 110-yard splits for mile paces of 4:00, 4:16, 4:32, 5:00, and 6:00, which appears as follows:

4:00	4:16	4:32	5:00	6:00
60	64	68	75	90
30	32	34	37½	45
15	16	17	19	22½

Their practice consists of watching our large pace clock and jogging into a paced 110 when the second hand reaches any of the quarter-circle points: 0, 15, 30, or 45 seconds. They try to reach the 110 mark in 20 to 25 seconds, then walk or jog a 110, and repeat the paced run until they have run ten 110s. It is interesting how many run at a pace faster than a four-minute mile on the first 110, but reassuring to see how soon pain teaches the first lesson of 20 to 25 seconds per 110. When the runners can do this, we drop down to the five-minute mile pace and increase the distances to a 220, 330, or even a 440.

It is doubtful that any runner can be dead sure of his pace. Our runners have a margin of error of ±2 seconds per 440 in the mile and 3- mile and ±1 second in the 880. Our pace chart, which was first presented in a clinic in 1952, now looks like Figure 2.1 on page 23.

In practicing pace, we not only expect errors in judgment, but we permit the runner to be off a bit, as long as he remains within allowable limits. We expect the margin to appear in any of the segments of the race, but we do not want a big deviation, for example, in the third or fourth quarter of the race. If the runner is trying for a 1:56 half and he hits 28 and 29 for a 57 at the 440, this is acceptable. If he then rests with a 32, he is running like a schoolboy and either is not capable of running a 1:56 or has not yet found the courage to pour it on and make his own race.

It is frustrating to see a well-conditioned good judge of pace hold back and save something for the last 100 yards against a competitor who is known to have a better kick. If he is going to win, make him *earn* it. The weapons for the slower, stronger man are through his pace judgment either (1) to get a lead that the sprinter cannot overcome, or (2) to take him on a pace ride that will take all the kick out of him.

Timing Intervals

Eugene, Oregon, is a distance man's paradise, with the most knowledgeable and enthusiastic track fans in the world. We probably have more stop watches per capita than any city in the world. With all these watches available, how do we time intervals? We use a large clock! With a squad of sixty or more men in seventeen events, it is impossible to spend an hour with each man or be with every event every day. It is also expensive to turn a watch over to a runner or a group of runners, so we use our clock.

Our clock is homemade. We took a piece of sheet tin three feet square, cut a round hole which was two inches in diameter in the middle, and painted the face black. A ruler compass was used to lay out the major sixty points of a circle with a three-foot diameter. Each fifth or five-second mark was painted yellow, and the other four points were painted smaller and white. We now had a three-foot clock face.

Our original clock was "begged" from a drugstore. We made a second hand which was three feet long and painted one half black and the other half yellow. We then mounted it on the "axle" of the clock and carefully counterbalanced it so that the small motor could make it go steadily. Our clock can be used anywhere that we have an electrical outlet, and when mounted above the ground, it is visible clearly from all points around the track.

Vandals have occasionally disabled our clock, since it is left outdoors. It would be easy to say, "If they're going to act that way, we will not leave our

Photographs 2.2 and 2.3 Emil Puttemans, Belgium, and Herb Elliott, Australia, world-class long distance runners.

Figure 2.1 Theoretical races

One Mile

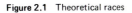

110	220	440	880	3/4	Mile
18-19-20	36-37-38	73-75-77	2:26-2:30-2:34	3:39-3:45-3:51	4:52-5:00-5:08
	34-35-36	68-70-72	2:16-2:20-2:24	3:24-3:30-3:36	4:32-4:40-4:48
	33-34-35	66-68-70	2:11-2:15-2:19	3:16-3:22-3:28	4:22-4:30-4:38
	32-33-34	63-65-67	2:06-2:10-2:14	3:09-3:15-3:21	4:12-4:20-4:28
	30-31-32	60-62-64	2:00-2:04-2:08	3:00-3:06-3:12	4:02-4:10-4:18
14-15-16	29-30-31	58-60-62	1:56-2:00-2:04	2:54-3:00-3:06	3:52-4:00-4:08
Margin of Error	+1 +1	-2 +2	-4 +4	-6 +6	-8 +8

880 Yards

	110	220	440	660	880
	16-17-18	33-34-35	66-68-70	1:40-1:42-1:44	2:11-2:15-2:19
	15-16-17	31-32-33	63-65-67	1:35-1:37-1:39	2:06-2:10-2:14
	14-15-16	30-31-32	60-62-64	1:31-1:33-1:35	2:01-2:05-2:09
	14-15-16	29-30-31	58-60-62	1:28-1:30-1:32	1:56-2:00-2:04
	13-14-15	28-29-30	56-58-60	1:25-1:27-1:29	1:52-1:56-2:00
	13-14-15	27-28-29	54-56-58	1:22-1:24-1:26	1:48-1:52-1:56
Margin of Error	-1 +1	-1 +1	-2 +2	-2 +2	-4 +4

equipment out." Because of a few troublemakers, sixty or more people who want to participate may be denied a facility. For this reason, we try to keep our clock and some of our other equipment out and available for anyone's use. As Ray Hendrickson has said, "The real test of a facility is that it is being used."

Workout Sheets

The chart form of workout sheets which we use (Figure 2.2) developed from necessity. While coaching for the State Department in Pakistan, Bowerman faced the problem of communicating with coaches and athletes who spoke several different languages. It seemed obvious that he could save time and improve general understanding if he could have an interpreter translate a single list of "fundamentals" for each event. These charts were mimeographed, together with a weekly training calendar. The coach then had to refer to each exercise only by its number. For example, if he wanted the runners to run 8 × 440 in 70 to 73 seconds, he wrote 8 × 5E1. A fartlek assignment was 2 (this was pre-Lydiard). He knew what he was assigning, since his copy was in English, and the runner knew what the coach wanted, because his own copy, with the same numbering system, was printed in Urdu or Hindustani or what-have-you. Thus the coach could communicate with the Pakistani athletes "by the numbers," and the system worked so well that it was put into use with his own squad when he returned.

The charts are updated every year, so there are slight variations from year to year. As an example of how we record the workouts, we are showing here (Figure 2.3) a copy of the February 1960 workouts of Jim Grelle, who made the U.S. Olympic Team that year, running 4:00.1 in the mile. In 1966, he ran a 3:55.4 mile and an 8:25.2 2-mile as a thirty-year-old veteran. As an example, note his workout on the tenth of that month. He warmed up, then ran 4 × 440 in 64 seconds, The workout record saves much of this space. The records are retained, some of them going back to the late 1940s. The coach is then able to compare the progress of one miler against his previous progress or that of any of his predecessors, giving a more concrete comparison of the runner's current progress. We believe that it is the quickest way to communicate with our runners.

The General Training Patterns

The Annual Cycle

At Oregon a master plan is developed for each three-month period. The early training during October, November, and December consists of conditioning, cross country, and testing. The pretrack and long distance training in January, February, and March stresses fundamentals and increasing strength. During the competitive season, April, May, and June, all the efforts are directed toward keeping the athletes in top physical and psychological condition.

The volume of work is rather modest at the start of a training period. It builds

Figure 2.2 Workout Sheet

Runner's Schedule NAME DATE

1. A. Jog 1 to 3 miles
   B. Weights & jog
2. Fartlek A. Varied (1) 30 min. (2)
   B. Steady (1) 2-4 mi. (2) 4-6 mi. (3) 7-10 mi.
   (4)
3. Weights
4. High knee and power run
5. Intervals
   A. 110 (1) 18-16-14 (2) 17-15-13
   B. 165 (1) 25 (2)
   C. 220 (1) 35 (2)
   D. 330 (1) 52 (2) 48 (3) 45 (4)
   E. 440 (1) 70-73 (2)
   F. 660 (1) 1:45 (2)
   G. 880 (1) 70 (2)
   H. 3/4 (1) 70 (2)
   I. Mile (1) 72 (2) 68-70 (3) 64-67 (4)
   J.
   K.
   L.
6. Sets A. 660-440-330-220-110
   (1) 1:45-68-49-32-15 (2)
   B. 440-660-440-220 (1) 63 (2)
   C. 550-165-165 (1) 55 pace (2)
   D.
7. Squad meeting
8. Special A. Sauna B. Swim C.
9. Drills A. Sprint-float-sprint (165)
   B. 1-step acceleration (165)
   C. 40-30 drill (1) 4 laps (2)
   D. 70-90 drill (1) 1-1 (2) 2-1
   (3) 3-1 (4)
   E. Cut-downs (1) 110 (2) 165 (3) 220
   (4) 330 (5) 440 (6) 880 (7)
   F. Simulate race drills (1) 1st 220-last 220
   (2) 2½–1½ (3) 10 miles–3/4 drill (4)
   G. 2-4 miles at (1) 80 (2) 75 (3)
10. A. Test B. Trial C. Compete
    (1) 3/4 date pace (2) Over (3) Under
11. Hill interval A. 110 B. 220 C.
12. With coach (A) Bill B. (B) Bill D. (C)
14. A. Wind sprint B. Hurdle drill
    C. Spring and bound D.
15. Finish work
16. Acrobatics or apparatus
17. 3/4 effort
18.
19.
20. Secondary event
21. A. Pictures B. Film

M
T
W
T
F
S
S

M
T
W
T
F
S
S

M
T
W
T
F
S
S

M
T
W
T
F
S
S

Figure 2.3 Oregon Runner's Schedule: Jim Grelle

DATE							
Feb. 1	1	2x 9D	2x 6C	2x 5D	12	11	F
2	1	3					
3	1	10x 7F	11				
4	1	3					
5	1	3					
6-7	2	Saturday and Sunday					
8	1	1x 10	2x 4D	11			1/2
9	1	3					
10	1	4x 7F	4x 6C	4x 5D	3		
11	1	3					
12	1	3					
13	1	1x 3/4	64s		1x 660	29s	
14	1	16	2				
15	1	2					1/4
16	1	3					
17	1	10x 7F	3				
18	1	3					
19	1	1x 9D					
20-21	2	Saturday and Sunday					1/4
22	1	4x 6C	4x 5C	12	9		
23		3					
24	1	1x 9	1x 14	4x 5C	9		
25		3					
26		3					
27	1	1x 3/4	64s		1x 660	29s	
28							

1. Warm-up weight work or arm and shoulder work on rope, rings, or apparatus.

2. Fartlek

3. Light fartlek

4. Repeats. 110, A.20; B.18; C.16; D.14; E.12; F.11

5. Repeats. 220, A.38; B.35; C.33; D.31; E29; F.28; G.27; H.26

6. Repeats. 330, A.54 B.51; C.48; D.45; E.42; F.39; G.38; H.37

7. Repeats. 440, A.75; B.72; C.70; D.68; E.66; F.64; G.62; H.60; I.58

8. Selected longer distance repeats.

9. Sets.

	660	- 440	- 220
A.	1:50	70	34
B.	1:45	68	32
C.	1:42	66	30
D.	1:39	64	29
E.	1:36	62	28
F.	1:33	60	27
G.	1:30	58	26

10. Bunches. 2 or 3 660s; 3 to 6 440s; 6 to 10 220s; Use same time as (9) A, B, Etc.

11. Run ot after each competition or workout.

12. Wind sprints.

14. Reduced interval 440s. Run 440, rest, 440, run 440, rest, 220; 440, rest 110, run 440. Use letters as (7).

15. Alternate sprint 55, shag 55.

16. Up and down hill.

NAME Grelle

up as the year progresses, reaches a peak just before the competitive season, and then is somewhat reduced as the weekly competition demands maximum strength and attention. During all the seasons, the schedules generally follow a pattern of a hard day (one to two hours of work) followed by an easy day (about thirty minutes of work).

During the early season, assignments are made to the runners as a group. During the competitive season each person has a separate workout sheet on which his workouts are blocked out for a week at a time. An example of the rough progression of training throughout the year for a miler who can run in the 4:00 range *already* is shown in Table 2.1. The pace given is for a 440 interval, the volume is the workout mileage in terms of the number of times the racing distance ("2" for a miler would be 2 miles), and the rest interval is proportionate to the interval being run (if running 440s and the interval is one-half, the rest interval will be 220 yards of walking or jogging). (See page 30 for a more detailed explanation of these terms.) This general workout pattern must, of course, be adapted to the individual runner.

Above all, the runners must have variety. There should be the pleasurable variety offered by fartlek, the discipline of interval training, some special speed work, and regular exercises to increase the runner's strength. The runner needs a bit of almost everything, including a balanced training diet, both for his overall improvement and for the prevention of the boredom which is sometimes called "staleness."

At this point, some terms which will be used frequently need to be defined. The first is *date pace.* Date pace is the actual pace at which the runner is clocked in a test effort or time trial in which he is attempting to run at three-quarter effort. This is usually expressed as the time for the 440. If the runner can already run a 4:24 mile, his date pace, or DP, is 66. After his next test effort, it will be adjusted to reflect his improvement. We try to get the runner to improve by one second per 440 during each training period (two to three weeks).

The *race pace* is the time which the runner has actually done in all-out competition. The *goal pace* is the 440 time the runner wants to be able to reach at the climax of his season, such as the national championships. If he wants to reach a 4:00 mile, his goal pace, or GP, is 60. If his goal is a 4:48 mile, his GP is 72.

The ten-day, fourteen-day, and twenty-one-day schedules are named for how long their cycle of training at a set pace requires. Each pattern is concluded with a *test effort.* The test effort, often marked simply as "test," is a time-trial run at *three-quarter* effort. It is *not* an all-out effort. There is more detail on our trials on page 31.

The Running Patterns

We have already mentioned that the individual's schedule should be tailored to fit his needs, ambitions, and goals. These schedules are a conglomerate of training methods which we have tried and found helpful in our case. The first

Table 2.1 Oregon Training Schedule Outline (for a 4:00 miler)

Month	*Week*	*Pace*	*Volume*	*Rest interval*
Oct.	1	75	2	full
	2	75	2–3	½
	3	75	2	¼
	4	75	2–3	¼
Nov.	1	70	2	full
	2	70	2–3	½
	3	70	2	¼
	4	70	2–3	¼
Dec.	1	68	2	full
	2	68	2–3	½
	3	68	2	¼
	4	68	2–3	¼
Jan.	1	66	2	full
	2	66	2–3	½
	3	66	2	¼
	4	66	2–3	¼
Feb.	1	64	2	full
	2	64	2–3	½
	3	64	2	¼
	4	64	2–3	¼
March	1	62	2	full
	2	62	2–3	½
	3	62	2	¼
	4	62	2–3	¼
April	1	61	2	full
	2	61	2–3	½
	3	61	2	¼
	4	61	2–3	¼
May	1	60	2	full
	2	60	3	½
	3	60	2	¼
	4	60	2–3	¼
June	1	59	2	full
	2	59	2–3	½
	3	59	2	¼
	4	59	2–3	¼
July	1	58	2	full
	2	58	2–3	½
	3	58	2	¼
	4	58	2–3	¼
Aug.	1	57	2	full
	2	57	2–3	½
	3	57	2	¼
	4	57	2–3	¼

pattern which was developed was a *seven-day pattern.* It developed simply as a way to plan ahead of time where to put the training emphasis for a given period. At this time our runners did not begin regular training until the first of January or February, and they did not train or compete with any regularity after mid-June. The pattern, based on the hard-easy sequence, was like this:

Monday:	heavy training
Tuesday:	light training
Wednesday:	heavy
Thursday:	light
Friday:	heavy
Saturday:	light
Sunday:	heavy

You will notice that this schedule throws two hard days, Sunday and Monday, together. In applying the principle of hard-easy, or heavy-light, training, we must recall that every person is different. Some runners will benefit from the two heavy days, while others will need to make Sunday a light or rest day also.

The idea of the ten-day pattern comes from Gosta Holmer of Sweden, and we believe that his program fits the progress of conditioning, testing, and preparation better than the one which most of us are forced into by the Gregorian and school calendar of seven days to a week, which usually puts us into a 14-day training period. The adapted Holmer ten-day schedule would appear as follows:

Monday:	heavy training
Tuesday:	light training
Wednesday:	heavy
Thursday:	light
Friday:	heavy
Saturday:	light
Sunday:	heavy
Monday:	light
Tuesday:	light
Wednesday:	test effort

This schedule points out another principle: there usually should be at least two days of light training before a hard test effort or competition.

Our school calendar being what it is, we are forced to use the two-week training cycle, or *fourteen-day pattern.* The two-week pattern also brings up our strong belief that runners will compete best if their major efforts are two weeks apart. We recognize that large meets may have trials and final races over a period of two, three, or even four days. We plan and train for such situations with the individual runner. The basic two-week pattern calls for alternating days of heavy and light training, beginning with a hard day on the first Sunday and including two light days, the second Thursday and Friday, before the competition or test effort on the second Saturday. The specific fourteen-day pattern which we follow is like this:

Sunday:	Steady fartlek: 6 to 15 miles
Monday:	Varied fartlek (light)
Tuesday:	Goal pace; date pace; light fartlek
Wednesday:	Steady fartlek (light)
Thursday:	Rhythm or quick; fartlek; cut-downs
Friday:	Light fartlek (light)
Saturday:	Overdistance; underdistance; date pace; fartlek
Sunday:	Steady fartlek: 6 to 15 miles
Monday:	Varied fartlek (light)
Tuesday:	Goal pace; steady fartlek; light running
Wednesday:	Steady fartlek (light)
Thursday:	Quick, light fartlek; cut-downs; or simulated race
Friday:	Light fartlek
Saturday:	Test effort (date pace); steady fartlek; cut-downs

Some of the above words will be clearer if we elaborate a bit. "Overdistance" work is understandable. "Goal" refers to intervals run at the goal pace. The athlete will run intervals totaling his racing distance at that pace. For example, a miler with a goal pace of 60 seconds per 440 would run 4 × 440 in 60 as his "goal" part of the workout, or he might run a set of 660-, 440-, 330-, 220-, and 110-yard intervals all at that pace, or any combination totaling one mile. "Date" refers to intervals run at the date pace. If the same miler is at a 4:20 mile in his date pace, he might next run 1 to 2 miles of intervals on a 65-second 440 pace. He would finish his workout session with some fartlek.

"Sprints" consist of a small number of fast, short intervals. They are followed by a moderate to heavy amount of fartlek. The workout is concluded with increasingly fast, short intervals, or "cut-downs." These are usually 110s run at a pace which gradually quickens. For example, 4 × 110 in 16, 15, 14, 13. The "overdistance or underdistance" in the schedule for the first Saturday refers to a test effort at either a longer or shorter distance than is usual. For example, a miler might run an 880 or he might run 2 or 3 miles.

The workout for the second Thursday consists of a small number of short, quick sprints, followed by a moderate, but not heavy, fartlek workout. The final day is a test effort conducted at the date pace.

The *twenty-one-day pattern* is a combination of two ten-day patterns, with a day of rest tossed in at a convenient spot. Most of our training before the meets begin is just this type of pattern. The schedule progresses like this:

Sunday:	Steady fartlek: 6 to 15 miles
Monday:	Varied fartlek (light)
Tuesday:	Goal pace; date pace; light fartlek; cut-downs
Wednesday:	Steady fartlek (light)
Thursday:	Rhythm; light fartlek; cut-downs

Friday:	Light fartlek
Saturday:	Overdistance trial; steady fartlek; cut-downs
Sunday:	Steady fartlek: 6 to 15 miles
Monday:	Varied fartlek (light)
Tuesday:	Heavy intervals; light fartlek; cut-downs
Wednesday:	Steady fartlek (light)
Thursday:	Quick; light fartlek; cut-downs
Friday:	Light fartlek
Saturday:	Underdistance trial; date pace; light fartlek; cut-downs
Sunday:	Steady fartlek; 6 to 15 miles
Monday:	Varied fartlek (light)
Tuesday:	Goal pace; steady fartlek; cut-downs
Wednesday:	Steady fartlek
Thursday:	Quick; light fartlek; cut-downs; *or* simulated race
Friday:	Light fartlek
Saturday:	Date pace trial; steady fartlek; cut-downs

"Rhythm" is simply the opposite of "lack of rhythm." It is not a pace. "Tempo" is similar to rhythm, but we use it as an *action* (an exercise in which the hands are held about six inches apart and swung quickly back and forth across the chest as a break in the monotony of running, a "breather" or "wake up" exercise). "Speed" is the same thing as the short sprints which are done as speed work. We might do 4 × 50-yard fast sprints, or one or two 165s, with the middle 55 extremely fast. There should not be many intervals of this type, as the risk of injury is high.

Trials and What They Mean

We use test efforts or time trials to assess the runners' progress at different points throughout the year. However, our trials are not all-out efforts. Our trials are similar to the system of trials used by Arthur Lydiard. They are three-quarter-effort trials in which we try to achieve a predetermined time (our date pace) by running an evenly paced race.

For example, if a runner ran a 4:24 mile in his trial three weeks ago, his present goal (date pace) would probably be a 4:20 mile (65 pace). Actually, to avoid trying to push the athlete too fast, we average several times to get his new goal. We add twice his previous trial time to his new tentative goal (4:20) and divide by three, yielding a more accurate goal for his new pace (4:22.5).

He would run his trial at an even pace (65.5, 2:11, 3:16.5) as nearly as possible, following the suggested limits of variance in Figure 2.2. His run will be a *controlled effort* in which he knows he could have run faster and in which he kicks or speeds up below his date pace in the last one-fourth or less of his race. The race will thus show how far toward his goal the runner has progressed, and at the same time it will give him practice in the most efficient way of running his race: even pace.

Setting Goals

Each individual should have a goal, and if he is a good runner, the goal should be high. If a young man was a 4:28 high school miler, we sit down with him and ask, "How fast do you want to run next year?" Too many freshmen say, "Four minutes." We feel it is a good goal, but we want to know what to aim for during the immediately coming year. After all, 4:28 is only 4 × 67 seconds. Let us assume that 4:16 is a reasonable goal for this eighteen- or nineteen-year-old freshman. Let us make two more assumptions: (1) if he is capable of better than 4:16, let's help him as far as his ability will carry him; and (2) if he falters somewhere in his progress toward 4:16, the schedule will be adjusted to a slower time of 4:20 or 4:24 or possibly 4:28, which may be as fast as he will ever run.

Each runner should have a goal. It should be a good goal, but it should be realistic. We want our runners to make steady progress year after year, rather than progress rapidly one year, only to stagnate or regress during the next several years. Now that we have given the rudiments of our distance training system, we will get down to the specific training for the individual middle distance and distance races in the next several chapters.

Distance Training Bibliography

Distance Running Basics

Abosi, Stefan, and Bohus, Branislav. "Training for oxygen shortage," *Track Technique,* No. 51 (March 1973), pp. 1624–26.

Adams, William S., and Bernauer, Edmund M. "The effect of selected pace variations on the oxygen requirement of running a 4:37 mile," *Research Quarterly* 39 (December 1968): pp. 837–46.

Amery, Richard. "A new view of distance training," *Track Technique,* No. 46 (December 1971), pp. 1451–59.

———. "Pacing in middle and long distance running," *Track Technique,* No. 42 (December 1970), pp. 1325–29.

Bloomfield, John. "The specificity of interval training," *Track Technique,* No. 44 (June 1971), pp. 1402–5.

Bork, John. "Mihaly Igloi: the man and the coach," *Track Technique,* No. 18 (December 1964), pp. 551–53.

———. "Principles of training middle distance runners," *Track Technique,* No. 39 (March 1970), pp. 1230–31.

Bowerman, Bill. "Some principles for distance runners," *Track and Field Quarterly Review* 73 (September 1973): 142–45.

Bowles, Charles J., and Sigerseth, Peter O. "Telemetered heart rate responses to race patterns in the one-mile run," *Research Quarterly* 39 (March 1968): pp. 36–46.

Bradshaw, James W. "Discovering potential distance runners," *Track Technique,* No. 40 (June 1970), pp. 1259–60.

Brodt, Mel. "Middle and distance running at Bowling Green," *Track and Field Quarterly Review* 72: 83–91.

Brodt, Mel. "The training of Dave Wottle," *Track and Field Quarterly Review* 73 (September 1973): 160–69.

Brown, Bobby. "Salt and water," *Track and Field Quarterly Review*, December 1964, pp. 50–51.

Brown, Stanley R. "Specific fitness for middle dis ›nce running," *Track Technique*, No. 25 (September 1966), pp. 785–86.

Buehler, Al. "Distance training — Duke University' · 'power tempo,' " *Track and Field Quarterly Review* 72: 152–56.

Bures, Milan. "Training of Czech women midd. distance runners," trans. by Glen B. Hoidale, *Track Technique*, No. 35 (March 1969), pp. 1115–18.

Butler, Guy. *The Art of Pace Judgement*. N.P.: n.d. 24 pp.

Caviness, Herm. "Running the distances at Ferris High School," *Track and Field Quarterly Review* 72: 176–82.

Cerutty, Percy W. *Middle Distance Running*. London: Pelham Books Ltd., 1964. 192 pp.

Clarke, Ron, and Clayton, Derek. "Clarke-Clayton on distance training," *Track Technique*, No. 42 (December 1970), pp. 1323–25.

Cooter, G. Rankin. "Heat control in athletics," *Scholastic Coach* 42 (October 1972): 56, 58.

Corbitt, Ted. "Strain: the Valsalva phenomenon," *Track Technique*, No. 19 (March 1965), p. 602.

Costill, David L., and Kammer, Walter F. "Distance running in the heat," *Distance Running News* 4 (March 1969): 8–9.

_______. "To drink or not to drink," *Distance Running News* 4 (September 1969): 12–13.

_______, ed. *What Research Tells the Coach about Distance Running*. Washington: AAHPER, 1968. 49 pp.

Dellinger, Bill, with Steve Prefontaine. "University of Oregon distance training," *Track and Field Quarterly Review* 73 (September 1973): 146–59.

Dodds, Deloss. "Middle distance and distance training at Kansas State University," *Track and Field Quarterly Review* 70 (May 1970): 22–25.

_______. "Physiological and practical bases for planning middle distance training at Kansas State," *Track and Field Quarterly Review* 72: 143–51.

Doherty, J. Kenneth. "Relaxation in endurance running," *Track Technique*, No. 16 (June 1964), pp. 483–88.

_______. "The role of the coach in endurance running," *Track and Field Quarterly Review*, February 1964, 56–63.

Down, Michael Geoffrey. "An appraisal of interval training," (12-part series), *Track Technique*, Nos. 18–29 (December 1964–September 1967), pp. 571–74, 593–96, 637–39, 655–57, 681–84, 732–35, 764–66, 791–94, 818–22, 860–63, 867–69, 918–22.

_______. "Speed through endurance — a reply," *Track Technique*, No. 51 (March 1973), pp. 1627–29.

Ekblom, Bjorn, Goldbarg, Alberto N., and Gullbring, Bengt. " 'Blood boosting: its effects on exercise," *Track Technique*, No. 51 (March 1973), pp. 1614–17.

Ferguson, Max B. " 'Second wind,' " *Track Technique*, No. 25 (September 1966), p. 800.

———. "Temperature changes in runners," *Track Technique,* No. 28 (June 1967), pp. 884–85.

Formichev, A., and Fruktov, A. "Effectiveness of twice-a-day training," trans. by Gar Williams, *Track Technique,* No. 4 (June 1961), pp. 98–99.

Freeman, William H. "Basic elements of all the distance training programs," *Scholastic Coach* 40 (March 1971): 62, 64, 110.

———. "Variety in distance training," *Scholastic Coach* 39 (January 1970): 78, 80, 103–4.

Gaislova, Jirina. "Load and intensity in women's training," *Track Technique,* No. 27 (March 1967), pp. 843–44.

Garfoot, B. P. "Review of warming up," *Track Technique,* No. 40 (June 1970), pp. 1284–88.

Gerschier, Woldemar. "Interval training," trans. by Leonard Almond, *Track Technique,* No. 13 (September 1963), pp. 391–96.

———. "Training for middle and long distance running," trans. by Gerry Weichert, *Track Technique,* No. 17 (September 1964), pp. 530–32.

Grodjinovsky, Amos, and Magel, John R. "Effect of warm-up on running performance," *Research Quarterly* 41 (March 1970): 116–19.

Groves, Harry. "A distance training program," *Track and Field Quarterly Review,* June 1969, pp. 25–27.

———. "Penn State distance running program," *Track and Field Quarterly Review* 73 (September 1973): 170–77.

Guilliams, Glenda. "Female cardio-respiratory responses," *Track Technique,* No. 51 (March 1973), pp. 1617–18.

Hamrick, Robert. "The 880 at Jesse H. Jones High School (Houston, Texas)," *Track and Field Quarterly Review* 71: 39–43.

Henderson, Joe. "L.S.D. — long slow distance," *Track Technique,* No. 38 (December 1969), pp. 1196–98.

Higdon, Hal. "The third sport," *Track and Field Quarterly Review*, 72: 183–85.

Hoffmann, Karel. "Stature, leg length, and stride frequency," trans. by Prue Cochran and Karen Suuring, *Track Technique,* No. 46 (December 1971), pp. 1463–69.

Holmer, Gosta. "Development in running," *Track Technique,* No. 50 (December 1972), pp. 1584–85.

Huntsman, Stan. "Distance running," *Track and Field Quarterly Review*, February 1965, pp. 62–71.

Hyman, Martin. "Mechanical analysis of running," *Track Technique*, No. 53 (September 1973), pp. 1675–77.

Ingelsrud, Don. "Biorhythms and the athlete," *Track Technique,* No. 16 (June 1964), pp. 501–3.

Jacoby, Edward G. "Physiological implications of interval training" (2 parts), *Track and Field Quarterly Review,* March 1969, pp. 43–78; June 1969, pp. 28–42.

Jensen, Clayne. "The controversy of warmup," *Track and Field Quarterly Review,* May 1968, pp. 7–11.

Kahler, Robert W. "The influence of cold applications upon running performance," *Track and Field Quarterly Review,* December 1968, pp. 56–61.

Kashlahov, Yevgeniy. "Varying work loads in middle distance training," trans. by Peter Tschiene, *Track Technique,* No. 43 (March 1971), pp. 1375–77.

Kruger, Arnd. "Observing Mihaly Igloi," *Track Technique,* No. 30 (December 1967), pp. 953–54.

Lowe, John M., Jr. "Bases for endurance training methods," *Track Technique,* No. 44 (June 1971), pp. 1387–96.

Lucas, John A. "Telescoping — the acid test of distance training," *Track Technique,* No. 25 (September 1966), pp. 787–88.

Lumian, Norman C., and Krumdick, Victor F. "Physiological and psychological aspects of marathon training for distance runners," *Athletic Journal* 45 (April 1965): 68, 70–71.

Lydiard, Arthur. "Marathon training," *Track and Field Quarterly Review* 70: 9–28.

_______, and Gilmour, Garth. *Run to the Top.* 2d rev. ed. Auckland: Minerva Ltd., 1967. 149 pp.

McDavid, Robert F. "The effects of intermittent and continuous work patterns on oxygen intake," *Track and Field Quarterly Review* 71: 178–87.

McFadden, James. "Summer distance running precautions," *Scholastic Coach* 40 (June 1971): 38.

McFadden, Karen. "Our unwanted athletes," *Scholastic Coach* 37 (March 1968): 42, 44.

McFarlane, Brent. "The chemistry for an even-paced 800-meters," *Track Technique,* No. 49 (September 1972), pp. 1550–53.

Mach, Richard. "Comparison of energy expenditures in running," *Track Technique,* No. 20 (June 1965), pp. 618–19.

Mather, D. N., and Vanketeshwaralu, K. "Influence of interval training on blood sugar level," *Track Technique,* No. 35 (March 1969), pp. 1098–1100.

Mayhew, J. L. "Current research studies in endurance training," *Track Technique,* No. 53 (September 1973), pp. 1680–90.

Miller, George J. "Coaching the young distance runners," *Scholastic Coach* 40 (April 1971): 20, 22, 85.

Mooberry, Jack, and Lindgren, Gerry. "Distance running," *Track and Field Quarterly Review,* October 1969, pp. 52–60.

Mulak, Jan. "Mihaly Igloi's training methods," trans. by Robert Z. Opiola, *Track Technique,* No. 8 (June 1962), pp. 228–32.

Nett, Toni. "Foot plant in running," *Track Technique,* No. 15 (March 1964), pp. 462–63.

Noble, Noel A. "Breath control in running," *Track Technique,* No. 11 (March 1963), pp. 349–51.

Oglesby, Burch E. "Preparing the part-time high school middle distance runner," *Scholastic Coach* 38 (May 1969): 66, 68, 91.

Osler, Tom. *The Conditioning of Distance Runners.* Woodbury, N.J.: Long Distance Log, 1963. 29 pp.

Pyke, Frank S. "Dilemma of the distance coach," *Track Technique,* No. 45 (September 1971), pp. 1424–25.

"Ralph Doubell — assured champion," *Track Technique,* No. 40 (June 1970), pp. 1281–82.

Randolph, John H. "Middle distance running at William and Mary," *Track and Field Quarterly Review* 70 (November 1970): pp. 11–15.

Rompotti, Kalevi. "The blood test as a guide to training," *Track Technique,* No. 1 (September 1960), pp. 7–8.

———. "Sauna and relaxation," *Track Technique,* No. 12 (June 1963), pp. 361–62.

Rosandich, Thomas P. "The American technique of distance training," *Athletic Journal* 49 (February 1969): 48, 52, 54, 105, 107.

———. *Olympia Cross Country Clinic Notes.* Upson, Wisc.: Olympia Sport Publications, 1967. 120 pp.

Rose, Kenneth D., and Dunn, F. Lowell. "Telemeter electrocardiography: a study of heart function in athletes," *Track and Field Quarterly Review,* February 1965, pp. 12–20.

Rynda, Eleanor C. "Physiological aspects of competition for women," *Track Technique,* No. 42 (December 1970), pp. 1346–48.

Schmidt, Paul. "Don't be afraid of a fast start," *Track Technique,* No. 35 (March 1969), pp. 1109–11.

Schorez, Pavel. "Extent and intensity of distance training," trans. by H. von Quillfeldt and Walter D. Morris, *Track Technique,* No. 45 (September 1971), pp. 1425–27.

Spindler, John. "The physiological basis of interval training" (2 parts), *Track and Field Quarterly Review,* December 1966, pp. 43–78; March 1967, pp. 28–35.

Sprecher, P. "Visit with Dr. Woldemar Gerschler," trans. by Brother G. Luke, *Track Technique,* No. 9 (September 1962), pp. 282–84.

Stampfl, Franz. *Franz Stampfl on Running.* London: Herbert Jenkins Ltd., 1955. 159 pp.

Sterner, John. "Distance running in hot weather," *Track Technique,* No. 6 (December 1961), pp. 169–70.

———. "Stroke and heat exhaustion in athletics," *Track Technique,* No. 25 (September 1966), pp. 773–75.

Travers, P. R. "Physiological principles of training," *Track Technique,* No. 9 (September 1962), pp. 268–70.

Truex, Max. "My views on distance running," *Track and Field Quarterly Review,* April 1964, pp. 13–18.

Van Aaker, Ernest. "Endurance work as protection against coronary and circulatory disorders," *Track Technique,* No. 4 (June 1961), pp. 114–15.

———. "Running and the chemistry of the blood," trans. by Phil Diamond, *Track Technique,* No. 3 (March 1961), pp. 93–95.

———. "Speed or endurance training," trans. by Nolan Fowler, *Track Technique,* No. 1 (September 1960), pp. 3–6.

Von Ruden, Tom, and Metcalf, Jim. "440, 880 and mile training at Oklahoma State University under Ralph Higgins," *Track and Field Quarterly Review,* October 1969, pp. 31–35.

Ward, A. P. "Distance running training weekend," *Track Technique,* No. 25 (September 1966), pp. 776–78.

———. *Middle Distance Running.* London: AAA, 1972. 56 pp.

———. "Modern concepts of middle distance training," *Track Technique,* No. 30 (December 1967), pp. 931–35.

Watt, Edward A., Plotnicki, B. A., and Buskirk, E. R. "The physiology of single and multiple daily training programs," *Track Technique,* No. 49 (September 1972), pp. 1554–56.

Weiland, Jerome, and O'Hara, Tom. "Remarks on distance running," *Track and Field Quarterly Review*, October 1965, pp. 29–39.

White, Bob. "Developing a distance running program at the junior high school level," *Distance Running News* 4 (January 1969): 37–39.

Wilt, Fred. "Comments on running," *Track and Field Quarterly Review,* June 1965, pp. 60–64.

_______. *How They Train, vol. 1: middle distances.* Los Altos: Tafnews Press, 1973. 128 pp.

_______. *How They Train, vol. 2: long distances.* Los Altos: Tafnews Press, 1973. 128 pp.

_______. *Run Run Run.* Los Altos: Tafnews Press, 1961. 281 pp.

Winrow, Ed. "Footwear weight and energy expenditure," *Track Technique,* No. 40 (June 1970), pp. 1270–71.

Woodell, Thomas. "Fun and games in distance and cross-country running," *Track Technique,* No. 39 (March 1970), pp. 1242–43.

Young, George. "Methods of training for distance running," *Track and Field Quarterly Review* 73 (September 1973): 180–83.

Long Distance Running

Cirulnik, Nat. "Training for the super distances" (2 parts), *Distance Running News,* No. 2 (April 1967), p. 12; No. 3 (July 1967), p. 26.

Corbitt, Ted. "Aspects of running ultramarathon races," *Distance Running News* 2 (January 1967): 20–22.

_______. "How to recover from a marathon," *Distance Running News* 4 (January 1969): 42–43.

Goodsell, Peter. "The handling of long distance road runners," *Distance Running News* 2 (January 1967): 14–16.

Dirksen, Jay. "Marathon running for beginners," *Distance Running News* 4 (November 1969): 34–35.

Henderson, Joe. "Marathoning," *Track and Field Quarterly Review* 71: 224–29.

Kaslauskas, V. "Food intake in marathon races," *Distance Running News* 3 (January 1968): 26.

Reid, Robert. "Diet and marathon training," *Track Technique,* No. 40 (June 1970), p. 1262.

Rose, John J. "Marathon training in high altitudes," *Distance Running News* 1 (July 1966): 1, 3–5.

Altitude Training

"Altitude stress research in the Peruvian mountains," *Track and Field Quarterly Review,* October 1966, pp. 9–19.

Arnesen, Arne U. "Comparison of performances at sea-level and above 5300 feet," *Track and Field Quarterly Review,* December 1965, pp. 65–67.

Balke, Bruno. "Effects of altitude on maximum performance," *Track Technique,* No. 18 (December 1964), pp. 554–58.

Bannister, E. W. "Training for altitude," *Track Technique,* No. 26 (December 1966), pp. 804–7.

Bowerman, William J.; Higgins, Ralph; Tracy, Robert; Lewis, Harley; and Cooper, Carl. "Preliminary report on 1967 Olympic development program," *Track and Field Quarterly Review,* January 1968, pp. 16–22.

———. "United States Olympic altitude training," *Track and Field Quarterly Review,* March 1969, pp. 10–18.

Edelen, Buddy. "Training and racing at high altitude — guides and considerations," *Distance Running News* 3 (April 1968): 12–14.

Hanley, Daniel F. "Report of the medical section of the United States team to the Games in Mexico City — October, 1965," *Track and Field Quarterly Review,* March 1966, pp. 29–38.

Le Masurier, John. "Project Mexico City," *Track Technique*, No. 28 (June 1967), pp. 870–74.

LeMessurier, D. H. "Physiology of altitude acclimatization," *Track Technique,* No. 27 (March 1967), pp. 845–47.

Lucas, John. "Summary of altitude research," *Track and Field Quarterly Review,* March 1967, pp. 57–65.

Mach, Richard S., and Favor, Cutting B. "Training and racing at altitude," *Track and Field Quarterly Review,* June 1967, pp. 16–24.

Olds, L. W. "Observations of the effects of high altitude on athletic performances," *Track and Field Quarterly Review,* December 1966, pp. 24–26.

Potts, Frank C. "Running at high altitude," *Track and Field Quarterly Review*, January 1968, pp. 26–27.

Robinson, Sid. "Performance at high altitude," *Track and Field Quarterly Review*, October 1966, pp. 20–24.

Shephard, R. J. "Physical performance of unacclimatized men in Mexico City," *Research Quarterly* 38 (May 1967): 291–99.

Staikov, Ivan. "Training schedules for high altitude acclimatization," *Track and Field Quarterly Review,* May 1968, pp. 12–19.

Distance training and racing

Racing Tactics

A runner who wants to run the best possible time in his race is usually better off if he runs as closely as possible to even pace for the entire distance. However, many racing situations call for tactics which consider not what will yield the fastest time but what will give the greatest chance of victory against a particular opponent. A knowledge of tactics then becomes vital to the athlete.

To use tactics well the runner must know two things. The first was inscribed at the entrance to the Delphic Oracle: "Know Thyself." What are the athlete's personal strengths and weaknesses as a racer? Can he carry a solid pace for the entire racing distance? How far can he carry a final sprint? This is something to learn in the test efforts, then put to practice in racing situations. The athlete must learn his capabilities and weaknesses well, both to know how he can use them to his advantage and to know how his opponent might use them against him.

The second thing an athlete must know is his opponent. What are his strong and weak points? These will point the way to how he can be beaten. The comparison between oneself and one's opponent will indicate which of the following tactical considerations might be of the greatest value.

If the athlete is clearly better than his opponent, then he should practice some *part* of his race during the competition. This work on strengthening one particular phase of the race will help in an obvious way, but it also serves another purpose: it conceals the athlete's strengths. The athlete should no more show all his racing weapons against a weak opponent than he should use a sledgehammer on an ant. Instead, he should concentrate on some section of the race, such as the first, middle, or last part.

This concealment of his weapons leads to another aspect of tactics: the athlete should not always run the same kind of race. He should have a plan for every race, and it should be a different one in some respect. If the athlete runs only one kind of a race, a good tactician will notice it, analyze it, and beat him. Being obvious is rarely a tactical virtue, unless it is planned to mislead an opponent.

If the athlete's strong point is the last part of the race, he should work to make it his best weapon. The athlete should *work* to improve what he is endowed with, rather than accepting it as it is and working on other areas of his ability. This does not mean that the athlete works only on his strengths; he must also train to overcome his weaknesses. A person with only one weapon in his bag may meet someone else with the same weapon, only to find that the other weapon is bigger. Again, the athlete should beware of tipping his hand. He may, in fact, use his greatest weapon only once in a year, at the time of his most important race.

One artificial tactic is varied-pace running. It is also a tactic of which the runner should beware. Some athletes can use it, but other runners will be destroyed by it. It is a *very* big weapon for the person who can use it. However, if the athlete knows he *cannot* use it, he should beware of a contest with someone who can use it. He must let the runner go, then reel him in like a fish, making sure not to let him get too far ahead. He should not at any time go with the opponent when he surges. Rather, as soon as he is close enough to the finish to hold it to the end, he should go into his sprint finish. If the athlete runs his opponent's race, he will have a very bad experience, because it is a devastating way to run a race.

An example of this tactic occurred in the 10,000-meter Olympic final in 1956, with Vladimir Kuts using this pacing tactic. Gordon Pirie attempted to stick with Kuts and was gradually destroyed, finishing far back in a race in which he should have been no worse than second. Arne Kvalheim ran a two-mile race at Oregon against Gerry Lindgren, who was using the varied-pace tactic as his weapon. Kvalheim let his opponent run away, while he ran a steady race at 10 yards and more behind. Late in the race he went into his final sprint, easily defeating Lindgren in an NCAA record of 8:33.2. In their next meeting, Kvalheim ran on Lindgren's shoulder throughout the race, while the same varied-pace tactic was employed. On this occasion Lindgren ran away with the race, his tactic being particularly successful because his opponent obligingly offered himself as a lamb for the slaughter. Never try to fight an opponent on his own choice of battleground.

Whenever an athlete is tempted to try to beat an opponent by letting the opponent use his favorite club in the contest, the athlete should remember one thing: wisdom and judgment are a great deal more important than determination. There is more pleasure in being a wise victor than a determined loser.

The runner must be cautious in the first part of the race, for it is very important. It is easily the most dangerous part of the race. Most athletes tend to start too fast, which will put them quickly into oxygen debt and make the late stages of the race very difficult. Few athletes are strong enough to lead all the way. Pace judgment is extremely important in this case, for by running too fast in the first one-eighth to one-fourth of the racing distance the runner stands the greatest chance of making a fool of himself. If the athlete has good pace judgment, he should be onto his correct pace by the end of the first one-fourth of the racing distance. If he does not have good pace judgment, he need not worry, for he has little chance in top competition anyway. When tempted to overwhelm his opponents with a fast start, the runner should remember one vital fact: all the points are awarded at the finish line.

No matter how good the runner is, he *must* know what is going on at the front of the race. If the runner dawdles in the rear of the pack, someone may break away and not be noticed until it is too late. The athlete probably has some advantage if he can run in the rear for the first half of the racing distance, but he must progress to one of the first three places by the time he reaches the halfway point in the race so that he can keep an eye on what is going on at the front. To stay in the first three places, the runner must be careful not to get "boxed in" or blocked as other runners move up in position. Each time a competitor moves up to go by, the runner should "take one" — moving out a lane or so and going with the new competition to ensure his position at the front of the race. Moving out from the curb also helps prevent being boxed in and unable to move if an opponent tries to break away from the leaders.

In the last 300 yards of the race, a good competitor should attempt to get in front, *if* he can sprint that far. Once the athlete is in front, he becomes the other runners' problem. The athlete should use up to nine-tenths of his effort to get in front. He should not use 100 percent, because he needs to have a bit of reserve to prevent his being passed in the last 50 yards of the race. The athlete should not try to win from fifth place on the last straight of the track, a very foolish tactic. If he prefers to race with that tactic, he should enter the 100-yard dash instead.

Cross Country

Cross country means many things to many people. At Oregon it is more of a preparatory season than a competitive season. Though a few meets are contested, they are relatively incidental to the primary purpose of the season: building a "base" of cardiovascular conditioning for the spring track season. Because the big meets in May and June are the most important of the year, cross country meets are not a large part of the schedule, any more than are the indoor track competitions.

This season begins after the opening of school, about the first of October. The program is begun with a "run," not a race. The distance is equal to the racing distance at the end of the season, which (for university competition) is 6 miles. The athletes run this distance at a pace of 6 to 7 minutes per mile, aiming for a time of 36 to 42 minutes for the full 6-mile distance. This is a submaximal pace, but we want it to be a comfortable, successful run for the athlete.

Before the start of the run, each athlete must declare his pace. The times are given at the 1- and 2-mile points to give the runners an idea of how close they are to their pace. If an athlete reaches a mark in a time much below his declared pace, he is made to stop until his pace time comes up on the watch. After the 2-mile point, the next time is given at 4 miles, then times are recorded at 5 miles. The athletes are allowed to run the last mile as fast as they wish. When the 6-mile times are compared to the 5-mile times, the athlete's pace for his interval training is determined. If his last mile was 4:30 or 4:40, his training pace for intervals will be 70 seconds per 440, as in the case of a Prefontaine. If his last mile was 6 minutes, his pace will be 90 seconds. The pace will be changed as he improves during his racing season. His pacing will generally be set at an average of his last three times in the cross country runs.

During the cross country season, the training will go a bit heavier on fartlek than on interval training, since the primary object is cardiovascular development. Interval training will generally be used only one day per week, usually on Tuesdays; and it will be run on the date pace, as explained in the previous chapter. The training included in this section does not follow this description exactly, as it was used in a slightly more competitive situation.

The athletes should have a minimum of three weeks of training before they compete in any meets. There should not be more than one competition per week in any instance. If the athletes race twice a week, they will have a difficult time making any real progress. With such a heavy schedule they would be better off with a bookkeeper than a coach.

The cross country pattern which has been used at Oregon is a fourteen-day cycle based upon years of training patterns. Like any other dynamic training program, it is still undergoing periodic changes and improvements. The present system was described by Bill Dellinger as following this pattern:

(1) Sunday:	Steady fartlek
(2) Monday:	Varied fartlek
(3) Tuesday:	Cut-down intervals; date pace intervals; light fartlek; cut-downs
(4) Wednesday:	Steady fartlek
(5) Thursday:	Hill intervals; light fartlek
(6) Friday:	Light fartlek
(7) Saturday:	Overdistance; simulated race; varied fartlek
(8) Sunday:	Steady fartlek
(9) Monday:	Varied fartlek over hills
(10) Tuesday:	Date pace intervals; steady fartlek; cut-downs
(11) Wednesday:	Steady fartlek
(12) Thursday:	Quick; light fartlek; cut-downs
(13) Friday:	Light fartlek
(14) Saturday:	Competition or test effort

Figure 3.1a Cross Country Training Schedule

Cross Country NAME DATE *October*

1. A. Jog 1 to 3 miles
   B. Weights & jog
2. Fartlek A. Varied (1) 30 min. (2) *Light*
   B. Steady (1) 2-4 mi. (2) 4-6 mi. (3) 7-10 mi.
   (4) *3-5 mi.* *(5) Easy run* *(6) 8-15 mi.*
3. Weights
4. High knee and power run
5. Intervals
   A. 110 (1) 18-16-14 (2) 17-15-13
   B. 165 (1) 25 (2) *24-26*
   C. 220 (1) 35 (2)
   D. 330 (1) 52 (2) 48 (3) 45 (4)
   E. 440 (1) 70-73 (2) *72-75* *(3) 62*
   F. 660 (1) 1:45 (2)
   G. 880 (1) 70 (2)
   H. 3/4 (1) 70 (2) *69* *(3) 68* *(4) 66*
   I. Mile (1) 72 (2) 68-70 (3) 64-67 (4)
   J.
   K.
   L.
6. Sets A. 660-440-330-220-110
   (1) 1:45-68-49-32-15 (2)
   B. 440-660-440-220 (1) 63 (2)
   C. 550-165-165 (1) 55 pace (2)
   D.
7. Squad meeting
8. Special A. Sauna B. Swim C.
9. Drills A. Sprint-float-sprint (165)
   B. 1-step acceleration (165)
   C. 40-30 drill (1) 4 laps (2)
   D. 70-90 drill (1) 1-1 (2) 2-1
   (3) 3-1 (4)
   E. Cut-downs (1) 110 (2) 165 (3) 220
   (4) 330 (5) 440 (6) 880 (7) *Mile*
   F. Simulate race drills (1) 1st 220-last 220
   (2) 2½-1½ (3) 10 miles-3/4 drill (4)
   G. 2-4 miles at (1) 80 (2) 75 (3)
10. A. Test B. Trial C. Compete
    (1) 3/4 date pace (2) Over (3) Under
11. Hill interval A. 110 B. 220 C.
12. With coach (A) Bill B. (B) Bill D. (C)
14. A. Wind sprint B. Hurdle drill
    C. Spring and bound D.
15. Finish work
16. Acrobatics or apparatus
17. 3/4 effort
18.
19.
20. Secondary event
21. A. Pictures B. Film

	A.M.	*P.M.*
M	*2B(4)*	*2A(1)-6x 5A (grass)*
T	*2B(4)*	*12-16-20x 5E(2) -2B(1)- 6x 9E(1)*
W	*2B(4)-8x 5A*	*2B(3)*
T	*2B(4)*	*16-24x 5B(2) -1A-7*
F	*1A*	*1A*
S		*5E(3)-2B(3)-6x 9E(4)*
S		*2B(5)*
M	*2B(4)*	*2B(2)-6x 5A (grass)*
T	*2B(4)*	*4x 5H(2 or 3)-3x 9E(7)[72-70-68 or 80-75-70]*
W	*1A*	*1A*
T	*2B(4)*	*12x 5D (grass)*
F	*1A*	*1A*
S		*5I.(3)-12x 9E(5)[72-70-68]*
S		*2B(6)*
M	*2B(5)*	*2B(5)*
T	*2B(4)*	*12x 5D(1)-2B(1)-6x 9E(1)*
W	*2B(4)*	*2B(3)*
T	*2B(4)*	*16x 9E(2) -2B(5)(grass)*
F	*1A(grass)*	*1A(grass)*
S		*10B (6 miles)*
S		*2B(6)*
M	*2B(4)*	*2B(2)-4x 9E(1)*
T	*2B(4)*	*3x 5H(1-3-4)-3x 9E(6)-9E(5)-3x 9E(3)-1A-3x 9E(4)*
W	*2B(4)-9x 9E(1)*	*2B(3)*
T	*2B(4)*	*12x 5D(grass)*
F	*1A*	*1A*
S		*9F(3)-3x 5A*
S		*1A*

Figure 3.1b Cross Country Training Schedule

Cross Country NAME DATE *November*

1. A. Jog 1 to 3 miles
   B. Weights & jog
2. Fartlek A. Varied (1) 30 min. (2) *Light*
   B. Steady (1) 2-4 mi. (2) 4-6 mi. (3) 7-10 mi.
   (4) *3-5 mi.* *(5) Easy run* *(6) 8-15 mi.*
3. Weights
4. High knee and power run
5. Intervals
   A. 110 (1) 18-16-14 (2) 17-15-13
   B. 165 (1) 25 (2) *21-22*
   C. 220 (1) 35 (2) *27* *(3) 30*
   D. 330 (1) 52 (2) 48 (3) 45 (4)
   E. 440 (1) 70-73 (2) *66-68*
   F. 660 (1) 1:45 (2) *1:42*
   G. 880 (1) 70 (2) *68*
   H. 3/4 (1) 70 (2)
   I. Mile (1) 72 (2) 68-70 (3) 64-67 (4)
   J.
   K.
   L.
6. Sets A. 660-440-330-220-110
   (1) 1:45-68-49-32-15 (2)
   B. 440-660-440-220 (1) 63 (2)
   C. 550-165-165 (1) 55 pace (2)
   D.
7. Squad meeting
8. Special A. Sauna B. Swim C.
9. Drills A. Sprint-float-sprint (165)
   B. 1-step acceleration (165)
   C. 40-30 drill (1) 4 laps (2) *6 laps*
   D. 70-90 drill (1) 1-1 (2) 2-1
   (3) 3-1 (4)
   E. Cut-downs (1) 110 (2) 165 (3) 220
   (4) 330 (5) 440 (6) 880 (7)
   F. Simulate race drills (1) 1st 220-last 220
   (2) 2½–1½ (3) 10 miles–3/4 drill (4)
   G. 2-4 miles at (1) 80 (2) 75 (3)
10. A. Test B. Trial C. Compete
    (1) 3/4 date pace (2) Over (3) Under
11. Hill interval A. 110 B. 220 C.
12. With coach (A) Bill B. (B) Bill D. (C)
14. A. Wind sprint B. Hurdle drill
    C. Spring and bound D.
15. Finish work
16. Acrobatics or apparatus
17. 3/4 effort
18.
19.
20. Secondary event
21. A. Pictures B. Film

	A.M.	P.M.
M	1A	2B(2)
T	2B(4)	5H(1)-2X 5G(2)-6X 5D(2)-2A(2)-3X 9E(1)
W	2B(4)	2A(1)
T	1A	4X 9E(2)-2A(2)-4X 9E(1)-7
F	1A	1A
S		10C-Northern Division Meet
S		2B(6)
M	2B(4)	2B(4)
T	2B(4)	9F(3)-9X 9E(4)
W	2B(4)	2B(2)-9X 9E(1)
T	12X 9E(4)	2X 5C(2)-2B(2)-6X 5C(1)
F	1A	1A
S	3X 5I(2)-12X 5D	2B(2)
S		2B(6)
M	1A	4X 9E(1)
T	2B(4)	4X 5F(2)-4X 5E(2)-4X 5D(2)-4X 5C(3)-1A
W	2B(4)	2B(3)
T	1A	2X 5B(2)-9G(1)-4X 9E(1)
F		Travel-light over course
S		10C-Pac 8 Meet
S		2B(5)
M		2B(5) (6 miles)-4X 9E(1)
T	2B(2)	2-3X 9C(2)-2B(5)-6X 9E(4)
W	2B(4)	2B(5) (45 min)
T	2B(2)	8-12X 5D(1-2)-2B(2)-6X 9E(4)
F		2B(5)
S		Travel
S	Jog course	Monday=N.C.A.A. Meet

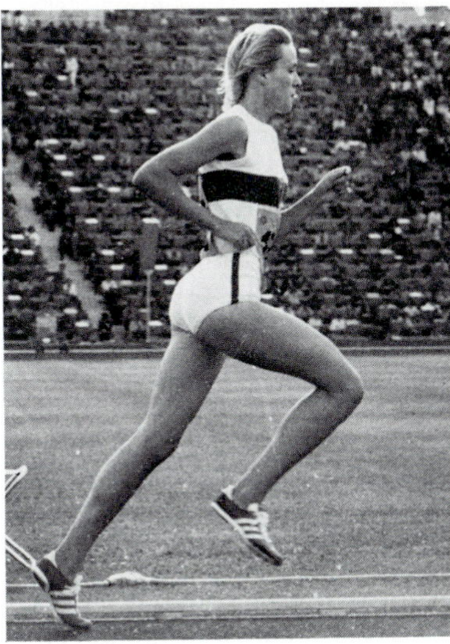

Photograph 3.1 Hildegard Falck, West Germany, in the 800 meters.

The terms used in the training schedule on page 42 have already been described. The heavy use of fartlek, as described both by Gosta Holmer (varied) and by Arthur Lydiard (steady), is evident.

The athlete needs to learn to run on hills as well as on the flat. His posture should still be relatively upright, as on the track, though the slopes will cause some leaning. The runner must try not to let the slopes cause him to lean to his disadvantage, though. When running uphill or downhill, the legs should be kept a bit bent at the knee, to allow for more "play" in a joint in case of unexpected changes in the ground. When going uphill, he should try not to lean too far forward, which can result in back strain and "stabbing" at the ground with his feet. When running downhill, the runner should try to avoid leaning back, since hitting a wet spot might cause a rough landing on the wrong part of the anatomy. Cross country is the season for developing a "base" which will help the runner throughout the year.

The Distance Man's Sprint and the Golden Mile

Training for the 880-yard run and the mile are essentially the same. The first object of the training is to get good, solid cardiovascular training which will permit the athlete to run up to 6 miles, though the athlete does not have to race up to distances that long. As the runner does the longer distance training runs, he will find that such training will take away his basic speed. The athlete should not be worried about this loss. A man can get back his speed to its maximum level in a period of three to six weeks of quality or "sharpening" work. However, he *cannot* build up his cardiovascular system in six weeks.

The training program should combine the speed-developing training activities and the conditioning training from the fall of the year right through to the end of the competitive season. While this is contrary to some training systems and theories, experience has proved it to be as successful as any other system. It has a further advantage, largely psychological, but still important: the athletes will get more pleasure out of their training if the "quality" and "quantity" training are combined, rather than attacked separately at different times in the year.

The training cycle for half-milers and milers should begin in the fall and continue throughout the year, if the best results are to be obtained. After school begins, the athletes will participate in the cross country training described earlier. The fall is a period of much work on cardiovascular development. At the conclusion of the cross country season in late November, the athletes move into training patterns aimed more specifically at their particular racing distance.

The coach must remember that all runners are individuals. Some athletes will prefer interval training, while others will prefer the long runs. Some will not thrive on the "who can get in the most miles" philosophy, and men have run the four-minute mile on as little as 30 miles a week or less in training. These "quick types" will usually do their best on 50 to 80 miles per week in training. Other athletes may be the slower "warriors" who love the long distance training and will destroy an opponent with work, trying to set a devastating pace to get out of the range of the sprinter. The teacher-coach must know his runner, just as the athlete must know himself. In training, there are many roads from A to B, and the shortest is not always the quickest or the best, any more than would be the longest.

In using the following training schedules, the athlete and coach should keep in mind that these schedules have been used by successful athletes. They should be viewed as a departure point and example of how the theories of training have been applied, rather than seen as "the" way to train.

The Middle Distances: Two Miles to Ten Kilometers

The training principles and patterns are the same for the longer distance races as those given for the shorter middle distance runs. The fall training is described in detail in the section on cross country training (page 42). At the conclusion of the cross country season in late November, the distance runners switch to training schedules more specific to their racing distances on the track. These schedules are given fully here, but several training considerations should be mentioned before the programs are given.

As in other events, the "hard-easy" principle is followed in planning the athletes' training programs. This is an area of danger, if the coach attempts to overwork the athlete. The runner must not be sent beyond his personal tolerance

Figure 3.2a 880-Yard Run Training Schedule

880-Yard Run NAME DATE September/October

1. A. Jog 1 to 3 miles
   B. Weights & jog
2. Fartlek A. Varied (1) 30 min. (2) 45 min.
   B. Steady (1) 2-4 mi. (2) 4-6 mi. (3) 7-10 mi.
   (4)
3. Weights and jog
4. High knee and power run
5. Intervals
   A. 110 (1) 18-16-14 (2) 17-15-13
   B. 165 (1) 25 (2)
   C. 220 (1) 35 (2) 28
   D. 330 (1) 52 (2) 48 (3) 45 (4)
   E. 440 (1) 70-73 (2)
   F. 660 (1) 1:45 (2)
   G. 880 (1) 70 (2)
   H. 3/4 (1) 70 (2)
   I. Mile (1) 72 (2) 68-70 (3) 64-67 (4)
   J.
   K.
   L.
6. Sets A. 660-440-330-220-110
   (1) 1:45-68-49-32-15 (2)
   B. 440-660-440-220 (1) 63 (2)
   C. 550-165-165 (1) 55 pace (2)
   D. 440-330-220
7. Squad meeting
8. Special A. Sauna B. Swim C.
9. Drills A. Sprint-float-sprint (165)
   B. 1-step acceleration (165)
   C. 40-30 drill (1) 4 laps (2)
   D. 70-90 drill (1) 1-1 (2) 2-1
   (3) 3-1 (4)
   E. Cut-downs (1) 110 (2) 165 (3) 220
   (4) 330 (5) 440 (6) 880 (7)
   F. Simulate race drills (1) 1st 220-last 220
   (2) 2½-1½ (3) 10 miles-3/4 drill (4)
   G. 2-4 miles at (1) 80 (2) 75 (3)
10. A. Test B. Trial C. Compete
    (1) 3/4 date pace (2) Over (3) Under
11. Hill interval A. 110 B. 220 C.
12. With coach (A) Bill B. (B) Bill D. (C)
14. A. Wind sprint B. Hurdle drill
    C. Spring and bound D.
15. Finish work
16. Acrobatics or apparatus
17. 3/4 effort
18. Steeplechase A. Hurdle drill B. Water jump C.
19. Park A. Around B. Hill
20. Secondary event
21. A. Pictures B. Film
22. Golf course A. Around B. Short C. Long

M	7 (organization-lockers-equipment)
T	3-2B
W	2x 2x 1A-5D-5C-2A(1)
T	3-2B
F	1A
S	10 a.m.:3 mile or 6 mile fall road run
S	

M	3
T	2x 2x 2x 3x 2x 4x 1A-18A-5G-5A-5F-5E-6D
W	Light and 3
T	19A (45 min.)-5A
F	Light
S	2A(2) (park)
S	

M	4x 10x 1A-5D-19A-5A(16-18)
T	3
W	8x 3x 1A-5C(2)-6A(1)-22A
T	16 (rope climbing)-3-2 (20 min.)
F	3x 4x 5A(1)-30 min. out-30 min. back-5A
S	6A(1) (grass)-easy jog
S	

Day	A.M.	Workout
M	A.M. Jog	6-10x 5C or D (110 rest-20 secs.)
T		16-3 (20 min. jog)
W	Jog	6x 3x 5D(2-3) (220 rest)-6A(1)-1A
T		16 (rope and parallel bars)
F	Jog	3x/5A(1)-30 out-30 back (7-10 min./mile)
S		1A
S		

Figure 3.2b 880-Yard Run Training Schedule

880-Yard Run NAME DATE October/November

1. A. Jog 1 to 3 miles
   B. Weights & jog
2. Fartlek A. Varied (1) 30 min. (2) 60 min.
   B. Steady (1) 2-4 mi. (2) 4-6 mi. (3) 7-10 mi.
   (4)
3. Weights and jog
4. High knee and power run
5. Intervals
   A. 110 (1) 18-16-14 (2) 17-15-13
   B. 165 (1) 25 (2)
   C. 220 (1) 35 (2)
   D. 330 (1) 52 (2) 48 (3) 45 (4)
   E. 440 (1) 70-73 (2)
   F. 660 (1) 1:45 (2) 1:39
   G. 880 (1) 70 (2) 68
   H. 3/4 (1) 70 (2)
   I. Mile (1) 72 (2) 68-70 (3) 64-67 (4)
   J.
   K.
   L.
6. Sets A. 660-440-330-220-110
   (1) 1:45-68-49-32-15 (2) 1:42-66-46-30-14
   B. 440-660-440-220 (1) 63 (2) 28-30/220y.
   C. 550-165-165 (1) 55 pace (2) Date pace (880)
   D. 220-440-220 (1) 29 pace
7. Squad meeting
8. Special A. Sauna B. Swim C.
9. Drills A. Sprint-float-sprint (165)
   B. 1-step acceleration (165)
   C. 40-30 drill (1) 4 laps (2)
   D. 70-90 drill (1) 1-1 (2) 2-1
   (3) 3-1 (4)
   E. Cut-downs (1) 110 (2) 165 (3) 220
   (4) 330 (5) 440 (6) 880 (7)
   F. Simulate race drills (1) 1st 220-last 220
   (2) 2½-1½ (3) 10 miles-3/4 drill (4)
   G. 2-4 miles at (1) 80 (2) 75 (3)
10. A. Test B. Trial C. Compete
    (1) 3/4 date pace (2) Over (3) Under
11. Hill interval A. 110 B. 220 C.
12. With coach (A) Bill B. (B) Bill D. (C)
14. A. Wind sprint B. Hurdle drill
    C. Spring and bound D.
15. Finish work
16. Acrobatics or apparatus
17. 3/4 effort
18.
19.
20. Secondary event
21. A. Pictures B. Film

M	4x 5H(1)-2-5A(1)
T 1A	3-8A
W	1A
T 1A	3x 6A(2)-2A(2)
F	1A-3
S	440-440-440-220-220 10A(68- 68- 68- 34-9/10)-2A(1)
S	
M 1A	2x 2x 1A-5G(2)-5F(2)-2A(2)
T	1A-3-8A
W 3-6x 5A(1)	440-440-440-220-220 Mile(80- 80- 80- 29-9/10-2A(1)
T	Jog and stretch
F 1A	9A(660 to 1320)- 2A-9A(330 to 660)
S	6A(2)-6D(1)-2A
S	
M 1A	4x 1A-5G(2)-1A
T	3-8A
W 3-6x 5A(1)	3x 1A-6D-6A(1)-2A(2)
T	9A(880 to 1320)-2A
F	1A-3
S	
S	220 6x 10A(880)(30-30-28-9/10)-2A-5A(1)
M	1A-2A-5A(1)
T 1A	4x 2x 6C(2)-5E-6A(1)-1A
W	3-8A
T 5A(1)	4x 1A-6B(2)-2A-5A(1)
F	3-8A
S	2-3x 1A-6A (60 sec. pace)-6A(1)-1A
S	

Figure 3.2c 880-Yard Run Training Schedule

880-Yard Run NAME DATE November/December

1. A. Jog 1 to 3 miles
   B. Weights & jog
2. Fartlek A. Varied (1) 30 min. (2) 60 min.
   B. Steady (1) 2-4 mi. (2) 4-6 mi. (3) 7-10 mi.
   (4) 10 miles
3. Weights
4. High knee and power run
5. Intervals
   A. 110 (1) 18-16-14 (2) 17-15-13
   B. 165 (1) 25 (2) 7/8 effort
   C. 220 (1) 35 (2)
   D. 330 (1) 52 (2) 48 (3) 45 (4) 42
   E. 440 (1) 70-73 (2) 59 (3) 58
   F. 660 (1) 1:45 (2) 1:27
   G. 880 (1) 70 (2)
   H. 3/4 (1) 70 (2)
   I. Mile (1) 72 (2) 68-70 (3) 64-67 (4)
   J. 770 (1) 58 at 440
   K.
   L.
6. Sets A. 660-440-330-220-110
   (1) 1:45-68-49-32-15 (2)
   B. 440-660-440-220 (1) 63 (2)
   C. 550-165-165 (1) 55 pace (2)
   D.
7. Squad meeting
8. Special A. Sauna B. Swim C.
9. Drills A. Sprint-float-sprint (165)
   B. 1-step acceleration (165)
   C. 40-30 drill (1) 4 laps (2)
   D. 70-90 drill (1) 1-1 (2) 2-1
   (3) 3-1 (4)
   E. Cut-downs (1) 110 (2) 165 (3) 220
   (4) 330 (5) 440 (6) 880 (7)
   F. Simulate race drills (1) 1st 220-last 220
   (2) 2½-1½ (3) 10 miles-3/4 drill (4)
   G. 2-4 miles at (1) 80 (2) 75 (3)
10. A. Test B. Trial C. Compete
    (1) 3/4 date pace (2) Over (3) Under
11. Hill interval A. 110 B. 220 C.
12. With coach (A) Bill B. (B) Bill D. (C)
14. A. Wind sprint B. Hurdle drill
    C. Spring and bound D.
15. Finish work
16. Acrobatics or apparatus
17. 3/4 effort
18.
19.
20. Secondary event
21. A. Pictures B. Film

M 1A	1A-5F(2) [2x]-5E(2)-5D(1-2) [8x]-1A-5A [4x]
T	3-8A
W 5A	2A(2)(grass)
T	Light jog
F	10A(880 date pace)-2A(45min)-5A(1)
S	2B(3)(7-9 min. pace per mile)
S	

M 1A	1A-5J(1)-5E(3)-5D(3-4) [2x]-6A(1) [3x]-1A-5A(1)
T	3-8A
W	9A(660)-2A(45min)-5B(2) [2x]
T 1A	1A-3-8A
F	10A(Mile)(440-440-440-440 / 68-68-68-9/10 effort)
S	2B(4)(8-10min pace)
S	

M	
T	
W	
T	
F	
S	
S	

M	
T	
W	
T	
F	
S	
S	

Figure 3.2d 880-Yard Run Training Schedule

880-Yard Run NAME DATE January

1. A. Jog 1 to 3 miles
   B. Weights & jog
2. Fartlek A. Varied (1) 30 min. (2) 60 min.
   B. Steady (1) 2-4 mi. (2) 4-6 mi. (3) 7-10 mi.
   (4)
3. Weights and jog
4. High knee and power run
5. Intervals
   A. 110 (1) 18-16-14 (2) 17-15-13 (3) 15
   B. 165 (1) 25 (2) 22½ (3) 19½
   C. 220 (1) 35 (2) 30
   D. 330 (1) 52 (2) 48 (3) 45 (4)
   E. 440 (1) 70-73 (2) 59-62
   F. 660 (1) 1:45 (2)
   G. 880 (1) 70 (2)
   H. 3/4 (1) 70 (2)
   I. Mile (1) 72 (2) 68-70 (3) 64-67 (4)
   J.
   K.
   L.
6. Sets A. 660-440-330-220-110
   (1) 1:45-68-49-32-15 (2)
   B. 440-660-440-220 (1) 63 (2)
   C. 550-165-165 (1) 55 pace (2)
   D.
7. Squad meeting
8. Special A. Sauna B. Swim C.
9. Drills A. Sprint-float-sprint (165)
   B. 1-step acceleration (165)
   C. 40-30 drill (1) 4 laps (2)
   D. 70-90 drill (1) 1-1 (2) 2-1
   (3) 3-1 (4)
   E. Cut-downs (1) 110 (2) 165 (3) 220
   (4) 330 (5) 440 (6) 880 (7)
   F. Simulate race drills (1) 1st 220-last 220
   (2) 2½-1½ (3) 10 miles-3/4 drill (4)
   G. 2-4 miles at (1) 80 (2) 75 (3)
10. A. Test B. Trial C. Compete
    (1) 3/4 date pace (2) Over (3) Under
11. Hill interval A. 110 B. 220 C.
12. With coach (A) Bill B. (B) Bill D. (C)
14. A. Wind sprint B. Hurdle drill
    C. Spring and bound D.
15. Finish work
16. Acrobatics or apparatus
17. 3/4 effort
18.
19.
20. Secondary event
21. A. Pictures B. Film

M	Recheck organization-1A or 3
T	2B-3-8A
W	5I or 5G (3/4 effort)-2A-8A
T	3-8A
F	1A-8A
S	Reestablish date pace 5I or 5G (1/2 effort)-2A2-8A
S	
M	1A-4X 5C-3X 5D-2X 6A(1)-2A(1)-2X 5A(1)
T	Jog and stretch-8A
W	3-6B-2B-2X 5C(1)
T	1A-3-8A
F	1A-8X 5C(2)-4X 9A-2A-5C(1)
S	10A(1)
S	
M 1A	1A-11X 5B(2)-2A(1)-2X 5C(1)
T Jog	2X 6A(1)-1A-6X 5B(3)-2X 5C(1)
W	1B-8A
T 1A	5B(3)-2A or B-5X 5A(3)
F Jog	1B-8A
S	Mile (80-80-60-9/10 effort)-2A
S	
M Jog	4X 5E(2)-3X 5B(3)-2A-8A
T Jog	9A (660)-2A(1)-8A
W 2X 5A(1)	1B
T	1A-6X 5B-2A-4X 5A(3)
F Jog	Check indoor gear-1A
S	Indoor 1,000 or 2B(1)
S	

Figure 3.2e 880-Yard Run Training Schedule

880-Yard Run NAME DATE February

1. A. Jog 1 to 3 miles
   B. Weights & jog
2. Fartlek A. Varied (1) 30 min. (2) 60 min.
   B. Steady (1) 2-4 mi. (2) 4-6 mi. (3) 7-10 mi.
   (4)
3. Weights and jog
4. High knee and power run
5. Intervals
   A. 110 (1) 18-16-14 (2) 17-15-13
   B. 165 (1) 25 (2)
   C. 220 (1) 35 (2) 28 (3) 25-26
   D. 330 (1) 52 (2) 48 (3) 45 (4)
   E. 440 (1) 70-73 (2) 60
   F. 660 (1) 1:45 (2)
   G. 880 (1) 70 (2)
   H. 3/4 (1) 70 (2)
   I. Mile (1) 72 (2) 68-70 (3) 64-67 (4)
   J.
   K.
   L.
6. Sets A. 660-440-330-220-110
   (1) 1:45-68-49-32-15 (2)
   B. 440-660-440-220 (1) 63 (2)
   C. 550-165-165 (1) 55 pace (2)
   D. 220-440-220
7. Squad meeting
8. Special A. Sauna B. Swim C.
9. Drills A. Sprint-float-sprint (165)
   B. 1-step acceleration (165)
   C. 40-30 drill (1) 4 laps (2)
   D. 70-90 drill (1) 1-1 (2) 2-1
   (3) 3-1 (4)
   E. Cut-downs (1) 110 (2) 165 (3) 220
   (4) 330 (5) 440 (6) 880 (7)
   F. Simulate race drills (1) 1st 220-last 220
   (2) 2½-1½ (3) 10 miles-3/4 drill (4)
   G. 2-4 miles at (1) 80 (2) 75 (3)
10. A. Test B. Trial C. Compete
    (1) 3/4 date pace (2) Over (3) Under
11. Hill interval A. 110 B. 220 C.
12. With coach (A) Bill B. (B) Bill D. (C)
14. A. Wind sprint B. Hurdle drill
    C. Spring and bound D.
15. Finish work
16. Acrobatics or apparatus
17. 3/4 effort
18.
19.
20. Secondary event
21. A. Pictures B. Film

M Jog	4x 2x 1A-5E(2)-5C(2)-6A(1)
T 2x 5A(1)	1A-4-3-8A
W Jog	2A
T	2x 4x 2x 2x 10A(Mile)-5B-5D-5B-2A-5A(1)
F 5x 5A(1)	2A(1)-3-8A
S	2x 10A(500 or 1,000)-2A-5A(1)
S	2B(3)
M Jog	3x 4x 1B-5C(1)-2A(1)-55y.
T 2x 5A(1)	2x 4x 1A-6D-6A(1)-2A(2)-5A (grass)
W Jog	1B-8A
T 2x 5A(1)	1A-6C-9A (880)-2A(1)
F	2x Light jog-5B(7/8 effort)
S	10A(1,000 or 500)-2A
S	2B(3)
M Jog	2x 1A-5B(9/10 effort)-2A
T 2x 5A(1)	2x 2x 1A-5C(3)-6C-6B-6A(1)-5A(1)
W Jog	3x 3x 1A-5A(1)-2B(2)-5A(1)-8A
T Jog	3x 2A-5A(1)
F 2x 5A(1)	2x 2x 1A-9A-9A(220)
S	2A(2)
S	Country jog
M Jog	3-6x 2A(2)-5A(1)
T 2x 5A(1)	2x 3x 1A-6C-2B(2)-5A(1)
W Jog	3x 1A-5B(9/10 effort)-2A(1)-5A(1)
T 2x 5A(1)	1A-3-8A
F	1A
S	10A (600y.)
S	Run-choice

Figure 3.2f 800-Yard Run Training Schedule

880-Yard Run NAME DATE *March*

1. A. Jog 1 to 3 miles
   B. Weights & jog
2. Fartlek A. Varied (1) 30 min. (2) *60 min.*
   B. Steady (1) 2-4 mi. (2) 4-6 mi. (3) 7-10 mi.
   (4) *45 min.*
3. Weights *and jog*
4. High knee and power run
5. Intervals
   A. 110 (1) 18-16-14 (2) 17-15-13 *(3) 12.5 (4) 12.0*
   B. 165 (1) 25 (2) *19*
   C. 220 (1) 35 (2) *25-27 (3) 27*
   D. 330 (1) 52 (2) 48 (3) 45 (4)
   E. 440 (1) 70-73 (2) *65-70 (3) 63*
   F. 660 (1) 1:45 (2)
   G. 880 (1) 70 (2)
   H. 3/4 (1) 70 (2)
   I. Mile (1) 72 (2) 68-70 (3) 64-67 (4)
   J.
   K.
   L.
6. Sets A. 660-440-330-220-110
   (1) 1:45-68-49-32-15 (2) *1:42-66-46-30-14*
   B. 440-660-440-220 (1) 63 (2)
   C. 550-165-165 (1) 55 pace (2)
   D. *220-440-220*
7. Squad meeting
8. Special A. Sauna B. Swim C.
9. Drills A. Sprint-float-sprint (165)
   B. 1-step acceleration (165)
   C. 40-30 drill (1) 4 laps (2)
   D. 70-90 drill (1) 1-1 (2) 2-1
   (3) 3-1 (4)
   E. Cut-downs (1) 110 (2) 165 (3) 220
   (4) 330 (5) 440 (6) 880 (7)
   F. Simulate race drills (1) 1st 220-last 220
   (2) 2½-1½ (3) 10 miles-3/4 drill (4)
   G. 2-4 miles at (1) 80 (2) 75 (3)
10. A. Test B. Trial C. Compete
    (1) 3/4 date pace (2) Over (3) Under
11. Hill interval A. 110 B. 220 C.
12. With coach (A) Bill B. (B) Bill D. (C)
14. A. Wind sprint B. Hurdle drill
    C. Spring and bound D.
15. Finish work
16. Acrobatics or apparatus
17. 3/4 effort
18.
19.
20. Secondary event
21. A. Pictures B. Film

Day	A.M.	P.M.
M	*1A*	*3X 9E(3)(33-30-27)-2A(1)-3X 5A(1)*
T	*2A(2)*	*1A-4X 5A(3)-4X 5C(2)-6A(1)-2A(2)*
W	*1A*	*2A(1)-3-2X 5A(1)*
T	*2A(1)*	*1A-5B(9/10)-2B(4)-2X 9E(4)(48-45-42)*
F		*1A-3-4X 9E(3)(36-33-30-27)*
S	*1A*	*1A-6C-2A(2)-2-3X 5C(1)*
S		*Runner's choice*
M	*2X 5A(1)*	*3*
T	*1A*	*10A(330 at pace, 220 jog, 330 at pace)-2X 6A(2)-3-5X 5A(1)*
W	*2X 5A(1)*	*1A-3-8A*
T	*1A*	*6X 5B(2)-2A(2)-2-3X 9F(4)(51-48-45)*
F	*3X 5A(1)*	*5B-2A-4X 5A(3)*
S	*2A*	*10A(880 at date pace)-2A(2)*
S		*Runner's choice*
M	*1A*	*1A-4X 5E(2)-5C(3)-2A(2)-2X 9E(4)(48-45-42)*
T	*2B*	*4X 5A(4)-2A-3X 5A(1)*
W	*1A*	*1A-5E(2)-2X 5B(9/10 effort)-2A*
T	*2A*	*2A or 2B-5A(1)*
F	*1A*	*2X 5A-3-2X 5A*
S		*10C or 10A*
S		*Travel to spring trip*
M	*2A*	*1A-2A or 2B-2X 5A(1)*
T	*2B(1)*	*1A-4X 5E(3)-6D-2A(1)-4X 5A*
W	*2A*	*2A or 2B-2X 5A(1)*
T	*2X 5A(1)*	*4X 5C(3)-2A*
F	*2X 5A(1)*	*Jog*
S		*10C*
S		*Home and re-register (spring term)*

Figure 3.2g 880-Yard Run Training Schedule

880-Yard Run NAME DATE April

1. A. Jog 1 to 3 miles
   B. Weights & jog
2. Fartlek A. Varied (1) 30 min. (2) 45 min.
   B. Steady (1) 2-4 mi. (2) 4-6 mi. (3) 7-10 mi.
   (4)
3. Weights and jog
4. High knee and power run
5. Intervals
   A. 110 (1) 18-16-14 (2) 17-15-13 (3) 11.5-12
   B. 165 (1) 25 (2)
   C. 220 (1) 35 (2)
   D. 330 (1) 52 (2) 48 (3) 45 (4)
   E. 440 (1) 70-73 (2)
   F. 660 (1) 1:45 (2)
   G. 880 (1) 70 (2)
   H. 3/4 (1) 70 (2)
   I. Mile (1) 72 (2) 68-70 (3) 64-67 (4)
   J.
   K.
   L.
6. Sets A. 660-440-330-220-110
   (1) 1:45-68-49-32-15 (2) 1:42-66-46-30-14
   B. 440-660-440-220 (1) 63 (2)
   C. 550-165-165 (1) 55 pace (2)
   D. 220-440-220 (1) 26 pace for 220
7. Squad meeting
8. Special A. Sauna B. Swim C.
9. Drills A. Sprint-float-sprint (165)
   B. 1-step acceleration (165)
   C. 40-30 drill (1) 4 laps (2)
   D. 70-90 drill (1) 1-1 (2) 2-1
   (3) 3-1 (4)
   E. Cut-downs (1) 110 (2) 165 (3) 220
   (4) 330 (5) 440 (6) 880 (7)
   F. Simulate race drills (1) 1st 220-last 220
   (2) 2½-1½ (3) 10 miles-3/4 drill (4)
   G. 2-4 miles at (1) 80 (2) 75 (3)
10. A. Test B. Trial C. Compete
    (1) 3/4 date pace (2) Over (3) Under
11. Hill interval A. 110 B. 220 C.
12. With coach (A) Bill B. (B) Bill D. (C)
14. A. Wind sprint B. Hurdle drill
    C. Spring and bound D.
15. Finish work
16. Acrobatics or apparatus
17. 3/4 effort
18.
19.
20. Secondary event
21. A. Pictures B. Film
22. Golf course A. Around B. Short C. Long

M 1A	3x 4x 3x 1A-9A-6D(1)-2A(2)-5A(1)
T	3-2A
W 3x 5A(1)	3x 3x 1A-6D-9E(4)(50-47-44)-2A-5A(1)
T	Light
F 1A	10A:880(220 in 35; go last 550:13-26-52-65)-2A
S	10C or 660 at date pace-2B
S	Runner's choice
M 2x 5A(1)	4x 2x 1A-5C-6D-6A(2)-2A(1)
T	3-1A-8A
W 1A	3x 6C-22A or 22B-5A(1)
T	2x 5B(9/10 effort)-2B
F	Gear ready-light jog
S	10C-880 and Relay
S	Runner's choice
M	4x 2x 1A-5C-5C-2A(1)-9E(4)(48-45-42)
T 1A	4x 3x 5A(3)-2A(1)-5A(1)
W	2x 1A-6B-5B(9/10 effort)-2B
T 2x 5A(1)	9A-2B
F	4-6x 5A(quick)-relay work
S	10C (mile and relay)
S	Runner's choice
M 1A	2-3x 2A-5A(1)(grass)
T	6x 2x 1A-6D-5D(2-3)-6A(1)-2A(2)-5A(1)
W 2x 5A(1)	1B-2A-8A
T	1A-5F(14-26-54-68-1:22- 6x/5C-2A-2x/5A(1)
F 1A	Jog
S	10C (Easy, perhaps relay only)
S	Runner's choice

Figure 3.2h 880-Yard Run Training Schedule

880-Yard Run NAME DATE May

1. A. Jog 1 to 3 miles
   B. Weights & jog
2. Fartlek A. Varied (1) 30 min. (2) 45 min.
   B. Steady (1) 2-4 mi. (2) 4-6 mi. (3) 7-10 mi.
   (4)
3. Weights and jog
4. High knee and power run
5. Intervals
   A. 110 (1) 18-16-14 (2) 17-15-13
   B. 165 (1) 25 (2)
   C. 220 (1) 35 (2) 27
   D. 330 (1) 52 (2) 48 (3) 45 (4) 39-42
   E. 440 (1) 70-73 (2)
   F. 660 (1) 1:45 (2)
   G. 880 (1) 70 (2)
   H. 3/4 (1) 70 (2)
   I. Mile (1) 72 (2) 68-70 (3) 64-67 (4)
   J. 770 (1) Race pace
   K.
   L.
6. Sets A. 660-440-330-220-110
   (1) 1:45-68-49-32-15 (2) 1:42-66-46-30-14
   B. 440-660-440-220 (1) 63 (2)
   C. 550-165-165 (1) 55 pace (2) 52 pace
   D. 220-440-220
7. Squad meeting
8. Special A. Sauna B. Swim C.
9. Drills A. Sprint-float-sprint (165)
   B. 1-step acceleration (165)
   C. 40-30 drill (1) 4 laps (2)
   D. 70-90 drill (1) 1-1 (2) 2-1
   (3) 3-1 (4)
   E. Cut-downs (1) 110 (2) 165 (3) 220
   (4) 330 (5) 440 (6) 880 (7)
   F. Simulate race drills (1) 1st 220-last 220
   (2) 2½-1½ (3) 10 miles-3/4 drill (4)
   G. 2-4 miles at (1) 80 (2) 75 (3)
10. A. Test B. Trial C. Compete
    (1) 3/4 date pace (2) Over (3) Under
11. Hill interval A. 110 B. 220 C.
12. With coach (A) Bill B. (B) Bill D. (C)
14. A. Wind sprint B. Hurdle drill
    C. Spring and bound D.
15. Finish work
16. Acrobatics or apparatus
17. 3/4 effort
18.
19.
20. Secondary event
21. A. Pictures B. Film
22. Golf course

M	2x 5A(1)	4x 1A-5C(2)-2A(2)
T	1A	2x 1A-5B(9/10 effort)-8A-8B
W	2x 5A(1)	1A-5J(1)-6A(1)
T	1A	4x 2x 5C-5B(9/10 effort)-2A(1)
F		Gear ready-1A
S	2x 5A(1)	10C (880 and Relay)
S		Runner's choice
M	2A	3-1A-8A-8B
T	2x 5A(1)	3x 2x 5D(4)-6A(1)-22-5A(1)
W	2A	4x 2-3x 5C(2)-2B-5A(1)
T	2x 5A(1)	2x 5B(7/8 effort)-2A
F		Gear ready-baton work
S	2A	10C (440 or mile and relay)
S		Runner's choice
M	1A	1A
T	2x 5A(1)	1A-6D-6B-6A(2)-2A
W	1A	Light-8A-8B
T	2x 5A(1)	Gear ready-5C-5B-5A-2A
F		2-4x 2A(1)-5B(quick)
S	1A	10C(880) Northern Division
S		Runner's choice
M		2-4x 6C(2)-2A(1)-5B
T	1A	5C(2)-5D(4)-5C(2) -5B(9/10 effort)-2B
W		1-2x Jog-5B-2A(1)
T		2x Jog-5A(quick)
F	1A	10C-Trials-Pac 8 Meet
S	1A	10C-Finals
S		2A or 2B

Figure 3.2i 880-Yard Run Training Schedule

880-Yard Run NAME DATE *Late May or June*

1. A. Jog 1 to 3 miles
   B. Weights & jog
2. Fartlek A. Varied (1) 30 min. (2) *60 min.*
   B. Steady (1) 2-4 mi. (2) 4-6 mi. (3) 7-10 mi.
   (4)
3. Weights
4. High knee and power run
5. Intervals
   A. 110 (1) 18-16-14 (2) 17-15-13
   B. 165 (1) 25 (2) *19½*
   C. 220 (1) 35 (2) *26-28 (3) 26*
   D. 330 (1) 52 (2) 48 (3) 45 (4)
   E. 440 (1) 70-73 (2) *59 (3) 53*
   F. 660 (1) 1:45 (2)
   G. 880 (1) 70 (2)
   H. 3/4 (1) 70 (2)
   I. Mile (1) 72 (2) 68-70 (3) 64-67 (4)
   J. *2½ laps (1) 60-65*
   K.
   L.
6. Sets A. 660-440-330-220-110
   (1) 1:45-68-49-32-15 (2) *1:42-66-46-30-14*
   B. 440-660-440-220 (1) 63 (2)
   C. 550-165-165 (1) 55 pace (2)
   D.
7. Squad meeting
8. Special A. Sauna B. Swim C.
9. Drills A. Sprint-float-sprint (165)
   B. 1-step acceleration (165)
   C. 40-30 drill (1) 4 laps (2)
   D. 70-90 drill (1) 1-1 (2) 2-1
   (3) 3-1 (4)
   E. Cut-downs (1) 110 (2) 165 (3) 220
   (4) 330 (5) 440 (6) 880 (7)
   F. Simulate race drills (1) 1st 220-last 220
   (2) 2½-1½ (3) 10 miles-3/4 drill (4)
   G. 2-4 miles at (1) 80 (2) 75 (3)
10. A. Test B. Trial C. Compete
    (1) 3/4 date pace (2) Over (3) Under
11. Hill interval A. 110 B. 220 C.
12. With coach (A) Bill B. (B) Bill D. (C)
14. A. Wind sprint B. Hurdle drill
    C. Spring and bound D.
15. Finish work
16. Acrobatics or apparatus
17. 3/4 effort
18.
19.
20. Secondary event
21. A. Pictures B. Film

M	*5B-1A*	*Jog*
T	*1A*	*Twilight meet*
W	*5A*	*2A*
T		*4X 5C(2) – 2X 6A(2) – 2A*
F	*4X 5A*	*2A – 8B*
S	*2A*	*5E(2) or 5C(2)–2A(2)–6X 5B(2)*
S		*Jog*
M	*Jog*	*5C (9/10 effort)–2A–6X 5A(1)*
T	*Jog*	*5J(1) – 2B – 4X 5C*
W	*Jog*	*4–1A–8A and B*
T	*Jog*	*6C – 2X 5B – 2A – 3X 5A(1)*
F		*5C(3)–5E(3)–5C(9/10 effort)–1A–2X 5A*
S		*6X 5B(2)– 2B – 2X 5A (7/8 effort)*
S		*Jog*
M		*6X 5B(2) – 2A – 4X 5A (7/8 effort)*
T		*Light*
W		*Light*
T		*Trials*
F		*Semi-finals*
S		*Finals*
S		*Jog*
M		
T		
W		
T		
F		
S		
S		

Figure 3.3a One-Mile Run Training Schedule

One-Mile Run NAME DATE *September/October*

1. A. Jog 1 to 3 miles
   B. Weights & jog
2. Fartlek A. Varied (1) 30 min. (2) *45 min.*
   B. Steady (1) 2-4 mi. (2) 4-6 mi. (3) 7-10 mi.
   (4)
3. Weights
4. High knee and power run
5. Intervals
   A. 110 (1) 18-16-14 (2) 17-15-13
   B. 165 (1) 25 (2)
   C. 220 (1) 35 (2) *32-35*
   D. 330 (1) 52 (2) 48 (3) 45 (4)
   E. 440 (1) 70-73 (2)
   F. 660 (1) 1:45 (2)
   G. 880 (1) 70 (2)
   H. 3/4 (1) 70 (2)
   I. Mile (1) 72 (2) 68-70 (3) 64-67 (4)
   J.
   K.
   L.
6. Sets A. 660-440-330-220-110
   (1) 1:45-68-49-32-15 (2)
   B. 440-660-440-220 (1) 63 (2)
   C. 550-165-165 (1) 55 pace (2)
   D. *220-440-220 (1) 29-58-29*
7. Squad meeting
8. Special A. Sauna B. Swim C.
9. Drills A. Sprint-float-sprint (165)
   B. 1-step acceleration (165)
   C. 40-30 drill (1) 4 laps (2)
   D. 70-90 drill (1) 1-1 (2) 2-1
   (3) 3-1 (4)
   E. Cut-downs (1) 110 (2) 165 (3) 220
   (4) 330 (5) 440 (6) 880 (7)
   F. Simulate race drills (1) 1st 220-last 220
   (2) 2½–1½ (3) 10 miles–3/4 drill (4)
   G. 2-4 miles at (1) 80 (2) 75 (3)
10. A. Test B. Trial C. Compete
    (1) 3/4 date pace (2) Over (3) Under
11. Hill interval A. 110 B. 220 C.
12. With coach (A) Bill B. (B) Bill D. (C)
14. A. Wind sprint B. Hurdle drill
    C. Spring and bound D.
15. Finish work
16. Acrobatics or apparatus
17. 3/4 effort *A. Mile*
18. *Steeplechase A. Hurdle drill B. Water jump*
19. *Park A. Around B. Short Hill*
20. Secondary event
21. A. Pictures B. Film

	A.M.	P.M.
M	*Jog in the*	*Organization-lockers-equipment-1A*
T	*mornings if*	*3-2B*
W	*time permits*	*1B-2x 5D-2x 5C-2A(1)*
T	*1A*	*3-2B*
F	*1A*	*1A-2x 6D(1)-9A(880-mile)-2B*
S		*2A(1)*
S		*2B(3)*
M	*1A*	*3*
T	*1A*	*1A-2x 18A-2x 5G-2x 5A-3x 5F-4x 5E, D, C-7*
W	*1A*	*1A*
T	*1A*	*18-17A*
F	*1A*	*2(light)*
S		*2A(2)*
S		*2(light)*
M	*1A*	*1A-4x 5C-19A-10x 5A(16-18)*
T	*1A*	*1B*
W	*1A*	*1A-4x 5D(1-2)-3-4x 6A(1)-3x 5A(1)*
T	*1A*	*1B*
F	*1A*	*1A-4x 5C(2)-2A(2)-3x 5A(1)*
S		*2(light)*
S		*2A(2)-19A*
M	*1A*	*2(light)*
T	*1A*	*10A-2-3x 6A*
W	*1A*	*2B(1)-3*
T	*1A*	*2A(2)*
F	*1A*	*2(light)*
S		*10A or cross country*
S		*2(light)*

Figure 3.3b One-Mile Run Training Schedule

One-Mile Run NAME DATE *October/November*

1. A. Jog 1 to 3 miles
   B. Weights & jog
2. Fartlek A. Varied (1) 30 min. (2) *45 min.*
   B. Steady (1) 2-4 mi. (2) 4-6 mi. (3) 7-10 mi.
   (4)
3. Weights
4. High knee and power run
5. Intervals
   A. 110 (1) 18-16-14 (2) 17-15-13
   B. 165 (1) 25 (2)
   C. 220 (1) 35 (2)
   D. 330 (1) 52 (2) 48 (3) 45 (4)
   E. 440 (1) 70-73 (2) *65-70*
   F. 660 (1) 1:45 (2)
   G. 880 (1) 70 (2)
   H. 3/4 (1) 70 (2)
   I. Mile (1) 72 (2) 68-70 (3) 64-67 (4)
   J.
   K.
   L.
6. Sets A. 660-440-330-220-110
   (1) 1:45-68-49-32-15 (2) *1:42-66-46-30-14*
   B. 440-660-440-220 (1) 63 (2)
   C. 550-165-165 (1) 55 pace (2)
   D.
7. Squad meeting
8. Special A. Sauna B. Swim C.
9. Drills A. Sprint-float-sprint (165)
   B. 1-step acceleration (165)
   C. 40-30 drill (1) 4 laps (2)
   D. 70-90 drill (1) 1-1 (2) 2-1
   (3) 3-1 (4)
   E. Cut-downs (1) 110 (2) 165 (3) 220
   (4) 330 (5) 440 (6) 880 (7)
   F. Simulate race drills (1) 1st 220-last 220
   (2) 2½–1½ (3) 10 miles–3/4 drill (4)
   G. 2-4 miles at (1) 80 (2) 75 (3)
10. A. Test B. Trial C. Compete
    (1) 3/4 date pace (2) Over (3) Under
11. Hill interval A. 110 B. 220 C.
12. With coach (A) Bill B. (B) Bill D. (C)
14. A. Wind sprint B. Hurdle drill
    C. Spring and bound D.
15. Finish work
16. Acrobatics or apparatus
17. 3/4 effort *A. Mile*
18. *Steeplechase A. Hurdle drill B. Water jump*
19. *Park run A. Around B. Short hill*
20. Secondary event
21. A. Pictures B. Film

22. Golf course run A. Around

	A.M.	P.M.
M	1A	2-19A-2B(3)(7-8 min. pace)
T	1A	2B(1)-3
W	1A	2X 4X 1-2X 2-18A-5D(2-3)-19A-19B-2A(2)
T	1A	2A(1)
F	1A	9A (1320-mile)-4
S		3
S		6A-2A(2)
M	1A	3
T	1A	10A(17A)-2A-19A
W	1A	3
T	1A	10A (17A)-22
F	1A	2 (light)
S		5-9X 22A
S		2A (light)
M	1A	2A (light)
T	1A	2X 1A-4-6A (1 or 2)-2A (2)
W	1A	3
T	1A	1A
F	1A	Light
S		10C-Cross country regional meet
S		2 (light)
M	1A	3-2A
T	1A	4X 2X 5E(2)-6A(1)-2B(2)
W	1A	3
T	1A	6-10X 22A
F	1A	2 (light)
S		4X 2X 5-6X 5E(2)-5H(1)-5A-2A
S		2 (light)

Figure 3.3c One-Mile Run Training Schedule

One-Mile Run NAME DATE November/December

1. A. Jog 1 to 3 miles
   B. Weights & jog
2. Fartlek A. Varied (1) 30 min. (2)
   B. Steady (1) 2-4 mi. (2) 4-6 mi. (3) 7-10 mi.
   (4)
3. Weights
4. High knee and power run
5. Intervals
   A. 110 (1) 18-16-14 (2) 17-15-13
   B. 165 (1) 25 (2)
   C. 220 (1) 35 (2)
   D. 330 (1) 52 (2) 48 (3) 45 (4)
   E. 440 (1) 70-73 (2) 60
   F. 660 (1) 1:45 (2)
   G. 880 (1) 70 (2)
   H. 3/4 (1) 70 (2)
   I. Mile (1) 72 (2) 68-70 (3) 64-67 (4)
   J.
   K.
   L.
6. Sets A. 660-440-330-220-110
   (1) 1:45-68-49-32-15 (2)
   B. 440-660-440-220 (1) 63 (2)
   C. 550-165-165 (1) 55 pace (2)
   D.
7. Squad meeting
8. Special A. Sauna B. Swim C.
9. Drills A. Sprint-float-sprint (165)
   B. 1-step acceleration (165)
   C. 40-30 drill (1) 4 laps (2)
   D. 70-90 drill (1) 1-1 (2) 2-1
   (3) 3-1 (4)
   E. Cut-downs (1) 110 (2) 165 (3) 220
   (4) 330 (5) 440 (6) 880 (7)
   F. Simulate race drills (1) 1st 220-last 220
   (2) 2½-1½ (3) 10 miles-3/4 drill (4)
   G. 2-4 miles at (1) 80 (2) 75 (3)
10. A. Test B. Trial C. Compete
    (1) 3/4 date pace (2) Over (3) Under
11. Hill interval A. 110 B. 220 C.
12. With coach (A) Bill B. (B) Bill D. (C)
14. A. Wind sprint B. Hurdle drill
    C. Spring and bound D.
15. Finish work
16. Acrobatics or apparatus
17. 3/4 effort
18. Steeplechase A. Hurdle drill
19. Park run A. Around
20. Secondary event
21. A. Pictures B. Film
22. Golf course A. Around

	A.M.	P.M.
M	1A	2A(1)-3
T	1A	4x 4x 3-5x 5E(2)-18A-6A
W	1A	1B
T	1A	9A(1-1½ miles)-2B
F	1A	1B
S		4x 6A-19A
S		Pleasant jog
M	1A	10C-area cross country race
T	1A	Home-1A
W	1A	4x 6-10x 18A-5G(1)
T	1A	1B
F	1A	2A or 2B
S		Light
S		10A(1½ miles)-19A
M		Vacation:
T		Fartlek runs
W		+rest
T		+recreation
F		
S		
S		
M		
T		
W		
T		
F		
S		
S		

Figure 3.3d One-Mile Run Training Schedule

One-Mile Run NAME DATE January

1. A. Jog 1 to 3 miles
   B. Weights & jog
2. Fartlek A. Varied (1) 30 min. (2) 45 min.
   B. Steady (1) 2-4 mi. (2) 4-6 mi. (3) 7-10 mi.
   (4) 45 min. out, 45 min. back
3. Weights
4. High knee and power run
5. Intervals
   A. 110 (1) 18-16-14 (2) 17-15-13
   B. 165 (1) 25 (2)
   C. 220 (1) 35 (2)
   D. 330 (1) 52 (2) 48 (3) 45 (4)
   E. 440 (1) 70-73 (2) 60
   F. 660 (1) 1:45 (2)
   G. 880 (1) 70 (2) 61
   H. 3/4 (1) 70 (2)
   I. Mile (1) 72 (2) 68-70 (3) 64-67 (4)
   J.
   K.
   L.
6. Sets A. 660-440-330-220-110
   (1) 1:45-68-49-32-15 (2)
   B. 440-660-440-220 (1) 63 (2)
   C. 550-165-165 (1) 55 pace (2)
   D.
7. Squad meeting
8. Special A. Sauna B. Swim C.
9. Drills A. Sprint-float-sprint (165)
   B. 1-step acceleration (165)
   C. 40-30 drill (1) 4 laps (2)
   D. 70-90 drill (1) 1-1 (2) 2-1
   (3) 3-1 (4)
   E. Cut-downs (1) 110 (2) 165 (3) 220
   (4) 330 (5) 440 (6) 880 (7)
   F. Simulate race drills (1) 1st 220-last 220
   (2) 2½-1½ (3) 10 miles-3/4 drill (4)
   G. 2-4 miles at (1) 80 (2) 75 (3)
10. A. Test B. Trial C. Compete
    (1) 3/4 date pace (2) Over (3) Under
11. Hill interval A. 110 B. 220 C.
12. With coach (A) Bill B. (B) Bill D. (C)
14. A. Wind sprint B. Hurdle drill
    C. Spring and bound D.
15. Finish work
16. Acrobatics or apparatus
17. 3/4 effort A. Mile
18. Steeplechase A. Hurdle drill
19. Park run A. Around B. Short hill
20. Secondary event
21. A. Pictures B. Film

Day	A.M.	P.M.
M		Class or squad organization
T		Register and 1B
W		2-3x 4x 4x 2x 1A-18A-5D(2-3)-5G-6A-1A
T		2B(1)
F		1B-2B
S		2B(4)
S		Recreation
M		1B-2B
T	1A	11x4x 4x 2x 7-5B-9A-19B-5A(1)
W		1B-2B
T		10x 3x 2x 1A-9A-6A(1)-5D-2B
F		1A-3
S		Easy 220's
S		2
M	1A	1B-1A
T	1A	10x 8x 5D(3)-5F-2B
W	1A	1B
T	1A	1A
F		Gear ready-1A
S		10C-Indoor mile or 10A
S		Pleasant jog
M	1A	1B
T	1A	10x 4x 1A-5B-5C-14A
W	1A	1B
T	1A	7
F	1A	Gear ready-1A
S		10C-2 mile indoor
S		Recreation

Figure 3.3e One-Mile Run Training Schedule

One-Mile Run NAME DATE February

1. A. Jog 1 to 3 miles
   B. Weights & jog
2. Fartlek A. Varied (1) 30 min. (2)
   B. Steady (1) 2-4 mi. (2) 4-6 mi. (3) 7-10 mi.
   (4) 12-15 min.
3. Weights
4. High knee and power run
5. Intervals
   A. 110 (1) 18-16-14 (2) 17-15-13
   B. 165 (1) 25 (2)
   C. 220 (1) 35 (2) 28 (3) 29
   D. 330 (1) 52 (2) 48 (3) 45 (4) 42
   E. 440 (1) 70-73 (2) 65-70 (3) 62
   F. 660 (1) 1:45 (2) 1:30
   G. 880 (1) 70 (2)
   H. 3/4 (1) 70 (2)
   I. Mile (1) 72 (2) 68-70 (3) 64-67 (4)
   J.
   K.
   L.
6. Sets A. 660-440-330-220-110
   (1) 1:45-68-49-32-15 (2) 1:42-66-46-30-14
   B. 440-660-440-220 (1) 63 (2)
   C. 550-165-165 (1) 55 pace (2)
   D. 220-440-220
7. Squad meeting
8. Special A. Sauna B. Swim C.
9. Drills A. Sprint-float-sprint (165)
   B. 1-step acceleration (165)
   C. 40-30 drill (1) 4 laps (2)
   D. 70-90 drill (1) 1-1 (2) 2-1
   (3) 3-1 (4)
   E. Cut-downs (1) 110 (2) 165 (3) 220
   (4) 330 (5) 440 (6) 880 (7)
   F. Simulate race drills (1) 1st 220-last 220
   (2) 2½-1½ (3) 10 miles-3/4 drill (4)
   G. 2-4 miles at (1) 80 (2) 75 (3)
10. A. Test B. Trial C. Compete
    (1) 3/4 date pace (2) Over (3) Under
11. Hill interval A. 110 B. 220 C.
12. With coach (A) Bill B. (B) Bill D. (C)
14. A. Wind sprint B. Hurdle drill
    C. Spring and bound D.
15. Finish work
16. Acrobatics or apparatus
17. 3/4 effort A. Mile
18. Steeplechase A. Hurdle drill B. Water jump
19. Park run A. Around B. Short hill C. Long hill
20. Secondary event
21. A. Pictures B. Film
22. Golf course A. Around

Day	A.M.	P.M.
M	1A	4X 19A - 2X 5A(1)
T	1A	4X 5E(2) - 6X 5D(3) - 5A(9/10 effort) - 4X 5C(2) - 2B(1)
W	1A	1B
T	1A	2-4X 19A - 2X 19B - 2-3X 5A(1)
F		2
S		10C
S		2B(3)
M	1A	1A
T	1A	4-6X 22A - 3X 5A(1)
W	1A	1B-1A
T	1A	3X 5F(2) - 2X 5A(9/10 effort) - 4X 5E(3) - 2X 5A(9/10 effort) - 2X 6A(2)
F		1A
S		2
S		1A
M	1A	3X 5A(1) - 2B(1)
T	1A	2A(1) - 6B - 4X 5D(2-3) - 4X 5C(3) - 9A(880)
W	1A	3X 5A(1) - 2B(1)
T	1A	1A - 6D - 22A - 5C(1)
F		Light
S		10A(17A) - 19A - 19C - 19B
S		2
M	1A	2B - 4X 18A - 4X 18B - 4X 5E - 2X 5A - 4X 5D(4) - 3X 5A(1)
T	1A	2A - 6X 19A
W	1A	2A
T	1A	2B(4)
F		4X 18A - 4X 18B - 12X 5D(3)(9/10 effort every 3d) - 2B
S		2A(1) - 3
S		2

Figure 3.3f One-Mile Run Training Schedule

One-Mile Run NAME DATE *March*

1. A. Jog 1 to 3 miles
   B. Weights & jog
2. Fartlek A. Varied (1) 30 min. (2)
   B. Steady (1) 2-4 mi. (2) 4-6 mi. (3) 7-10 mi.
   (4)
3. Weights
4. High knee and power run
5. Intervals
   A. 110 (1) 18-16-14 (2) 17-15-13
   B. 165 (1) 25 (2)
   C. 220 (1) 35 (2)
   D. 330 (1) 52 (2) 48 (3) 45 (4) *42*
   E. 440 (1) 70-73 (2) *66* *(3) 60*
   F. 660 (1) 1:45 (2)
   G. 880 (1) 70 (2) *63*
   H. 3/4 (1) 70 (2)
   I. Mile (1) 72 (2) 68-70 (3) 64-67 (4)
   J.
   K.
   L.
6. Sets A. 660-440-330-220-110
   (1) 1:45-68-49-32-15 (2) *1:42-66-46-30-14*
   B. 440-660-440-220 (1) 63 (2)
   C. 550-165-165 (1) 55 pace (2)
   D.
7. Squad meeting
8. Special A. Sauna B. Swim C.
9. Drills A. Sprint-float-sprint (165)
   B. 1-step acceleration (165)
   C. 40-30 drill (1) 4 laps (2)
   D. 70-90 drill (1) 1-1 (2) 2-1
   (3) 3-1 (4)
   E. Cut-downs (1) 110 (2) 165 (3) 220
   (4) 330 (5) 440 (6) 880 (7)
   F. Simulate race drills (1) 1st 220-last 220
   (2) 2½-1½ (3) 10 miles–3/4 drill (4)
   G. 2-4 miles at (1) 80 (2) 75 (3)
10. A. Test B. Trial C. Compete
    (1) 3/4 date pace (2) Over (3) Under
11. Hill interval A. 110 B. 220 C.
12. With coach (A) Bill B. (B) Bill D. (C)
14. A. Wind sprint B. Hurdle drill
    C. Spring and bound D.
15. Finish work
16. Acrobatics or apparatus
17. 3/4 effort *A. Mile*
18. *Steeplechase A. Hurdle drill B. Water jump*
19. *Park run A. Around B. Short hill*
20. Secondary event
21. A. Pictures B. Film

	A.M.	P.M.
M	*1A*	*1A-4-2B(1)*
T	*1A*	*2-6X 4-6X 2X* *1B–19B–19A–5A(1)*
W	*1A*	*1A-1B*
T	*1A*	*4X 4X* *18A-18B-9A(1320)-2B(1)*
F		*Light*
S		*10B(17A)-2*
S		*2*
M	*1A*	*1B-4*
T	*1A*	*2*
W	*1A*	*1B-4*
T	*1A*	*2-4X* *6B-18AB-6A(2)-2A*
F		*1B-4-2B*
S		*Light*
S		*2*
M		*Exam week-2A(1)*
T		*2X 2X 3-4X 2X 4-6X 6X* *5G(3)-5A-5F(1)-5A-5E(2)-5D-2A*
W		*1B-2B(1)*
T		*2B*
F		*Gear ready-14A*
S	*Travel*	*10C-Dual meet*
S		*Travel-Spring trip*
M	*1A-14A*	*4X 3X* *5E(3)-2A(1)-6A(1)-2A(1)*
T	*1B-14B*	*3X 2X* *5D(4)-5A(9/10 effort)-2*
W	*1A*	*Light*
T	*1A-14A*	*2 (Hills)*
F		*1B*
S		*10C-Triangular meet*
S		*Travel home-registration*

Figure 3.3g One-Mile Run Training Schedule

One-Mile Run NAME DATE April

1. A. Jog 1 to 3 miles
   B. Weights & jog
2. Fartlek A. Varied (1) 30 min. (2)
   B. Steady (1) 2-4 mi. (2) 4-6 mi. (3) 7-10 mi.
   (4)
3. Weights
4. High knee and power run
5. Intervals
   A. 110 (1) 18-16-14 (2) 17-15-13
   B. 165 (1) 25 (2)
   C. 220 (1) 35 (2)
   D. 330 (1) 52 (2) 48 (3) 45 (4)
   E. 440 (1) 70-73 (2)
   F. 660 (1) 1:45 (2)
   G. 880 (1) 70 (2)
   H. 3/4 (1) 70 (2)
   I. Mile (1) 72 (2) 68-70 (3) 64-67 (4)
   J. 1100y (1) 60
   K.
   L.
6. Sets A. 660-440-330-220-110
   (1) 1:45-68-49-32-15 (2) 1:42-66-46-30-14
   B. 440-660-440-220 (1) 63 (2)
   C. 550-165-165 (1) 55 pace (2)
   D.
7. Squad meeting
8. Special A. Sauna B. Swim C.
9. Drills A. Sprint-float-sprint (165)
   B. 1-step acceleration (165)
   C. 40-30 drill (1) 4 laps (2)
   D. 70-90 drill (1) 1-1 (2) 2-1
   (3) 3-1 (4)
   E. Cut-downs (1) 110 (2) 165 (3) 220
   (4) 330 (5) 440 (6) 880 (7)
   F. Simulate race drills (1) 1st 220-last 220
   (2) 2½-1½ (3) 10 miles-3/4 drill (4)
   G. 2-4 miles at (1) 80 (2) 75 (3)
10. A. Test B. Trial C. Compete
    (1) 3/4 date pace (2) Over (3) Under
11. Hill interval A. 110 B. 220 C.
12. With coach (A) Bill B. (B) Bill D. (C)
14. A. Wind sprint B. Hurdle drill
    C. Spring and bound D.
15. Finish work
16. Acrobatics or apparatus
17. 3/4 effort
18.
19. Park run
20. Secondary event
21. A. Pictures B. Film
22. Golf course run

Day	A.M.	P.M.
M	2A	1A-1B
T	2B	4-6x 1A-6A-9G(1)-2A
W	2A	1A-1B
T	2B	1A-19
F		Gear ready-1A
S		Relay Meet-10C(2 mile)
S		2
M	2A	4x 4x 4-5x 7-1A-5F(2)-5F(3)-6A(2)-2B(1)
T	2B	1B-9F(2)(60's)-22
W	2A	Light
T	2B	14A
F		Gear ready-1A
S		10C-dual meet-mile
S		2
M	2B	1A-2(easy)-1B
T	2A	2-3x 5A(1)-5J(1)-5F(2)-2B
W	2B	1A-1B
T	2A	2 (easy)
F		Gear ready
S		10C-Dual Meet
S		2(easy)
M	2A	7-2B(grass)
T	2B	4x 3x 1A-5E(3)-6A(1:39-64-45-29-13½)-2A(1)
W	2A	2-1B
T	2B	2 (easy)
F		Travel-1A
S		Dual meet-10C (2 miles)
S		Home-loosen up

Figure 3.3h One-Mile Run Training Schedule

One-Mile Run NAME DATE May

1. A. Jog 1 to 3 miles
   B. Weights & jog
2. Fartlek A. Varied (1) 30 min. (2)
   B. Steady (1) 2-4 mi. (2) 4-6 mi. (3) 7-10 mi.
   (4)
3. Weights
4. High knee and power run
5. Intervals
   A. 110 (1) 18-16-14 (2) 17-15-13
   B. 165 (1) 25 (2)
   C. 220 (1) 35 (2)
   D. 330 (1) 52 (2) 48 (3) 45 (4)
   E. 440 (1) 70-73 (2) 60
   F. 660 (1) 1:45 (2)
   G. 880 (1) 70 (2) 61
   H. 3/4 (1) 70 (2)
   I. Mile (1) 72 (2) 68-70 (3) 64-67 (4)
   J.
   K.
   L.
6. Sets A. 660-440-330-220-110
   (1) 1:45-68-49-32-15 (2) 1:42-66-46-30-14
   B. 440-660-440-220 (1) 63 (2) 59
   C. 550-165-165 (1) 55 pace (2)
   D. 880-660-220 E. 330-660-330
7. Squad meeting
8. Special A. Sauna B. Swim C.
9. Drills A. Sprint-float-sprint (165)
   B. 1-step acceleration (165)
   C. 40-30 drill (1) 4 laps (2)
   D. 70-90 drill (1) 1-1 (2) 2-1
   (3) 3-1 (4)
   E. Cut-downs (1) 110 (2) 165 (3) 220
   (4) 330 (5) 440 (6) 880 (7)
   F. Simulate race drills (1) 1st 220-last 220
   (2) 2½-1½ (3) 10 miles-3/4 drill (4)
   G. 2-4 miles at (1) 80 (2) 75 (3)
10. A. Test B. Trial C. Compete
    (1) 3/4 date pace (2) Over (3) Under
11. Hill interval A. 110 B. 220 C.
12. With coach (A) Bill B. (B) Bill D. (C)
14. A. Wind sprint B. Hurdle drill
    C. Spring and bound D.
15. Finish work
16. Acrobatics or apparatus
17. 3/4 effort
18. Steeplechase A. Hurdle drill B. Water jump
19.
20. Secondary event
21. A. Pictures B. Film

	A.M.	P.M.
M	1A	4x 4x 7-18A-5E(2)-2A
T	2A	2x 1A-6B-6D(2:14-1:37½-63-30)-2A(1)
W	2x 1A-5A(1)	Light
T	2A	14A-2 (easy)
F		Gear ready-1A
S		10C-Dual meet-mile
S		2
M	7	3x 2x 1A-5D(3)-5A(9/10 effort)-2A(1)
T	1A	2x 2A(1)-5E(2)-5G(2)-5E(2)-6A(2)-2B
W	2A	Light
T	1A	2B (easy)
F	2A	Gear ready
S		10C-Traditional dual meet
S		2
M	2A	4x 4x 2x 1A-5E(2)-5E(2)-9B-2A(1)
T	1A	2x 1A-6E-6A
W	2A	1A-1B-2A(1)
T	1A	2
F		Travel
S		10C-Relay (4 x 1 mile)
S		Home-2
M	1A	2x 7-18AB-2A(2)
T	2A	2-4x 18A(330's)-6B(2)-2A(1)
W		1A
T		2B (easy)-14A
F		Gear ready
S		10C-Division championship
S		2

Figure 3.3i One-Mile Run Training Schedule

One-Mile Run NAME DATE June

1. A. Jog 1 to 3 miles
   B. Weights & jog
2. Fartlek A. Varied (1) 30 min. (2)
   B. Steady (1) 2-4 mi. (2) 4-6 mi. (3) 7-10 mi.
   (4)
3. Weights
4. High knee and power run
5. Intervals
   A. 110 (1) 18-16-14 (2) 17-15-13
   B. 165 (1) 25 (2)
   C. 220 (1) 35 (2) 27
   D. 330 (1) 52 (2) 48 (3) 45 (4) 42
   E. 440 (1) 70-73 (2) 60 (3) 58
   F. 660 (1) 1:45 (2) 1:30 (3) 1:27
   G. 880 (1) 70 (2) 59 (3) 60
   H. 3/4 (1) 70 (2)
   I. Mile (1) 72 (2) 68-70 (3) 64-67 (4)
   J.
   K.
   L.
6. Sets A. 660-440-330-220-110
   (1) 1:45-68-49-32-15 (2)
   B. 440-660-440-220 (1) 63 (2)
   C. 550-165-165 (1) 55 pace (2)
   D.
7. Squad meeting
8. Special A. Sauna B. Swim C.
9. Drills A. Sprint-float-sprint (165)
   B. 1-step acceleration (165)
   C. 40-30 drill (1) 4 laps (2)
   D. 70-90 drill (1) 1-1 (2) 2-1
   (3) 3-1 (4)
   E. Cut-downs (1) 110 (2) 165 (3) 220
   (4) 330 (5) 440 (6) 880 (7)
   F. Simulate race drills (1) 1st 220-last 220
   (2) 2½–1½ (3) 10 miles–3/4 drill (4)
   G. 2-4 miles at (1) 80 (2) 75 (3)
10. A. Test B. Trial C. Compete
    (1) 3/4 date pace (2) Over (3) Under
11. Hill interval A. 110 B. 220 C.
12. With coach (A) Bill B. (B) Bill D. (C)
14. A. Wind sprint B. Hurdle drill
    C. Spring and bound D.
15. Finish work
16. Acrobatics or apparatus
17. 3/4 effort A. Mile
18.
19. Park run A. Around B. Short hill
20. Secondary event
21. A. Pictures B. Film
22. Golf course A. Around B. Short C. Long

	A.M.	P.M.
M	1A	1A-3
T	2A	5G(2)-5F(2)-5E(2)-5C(2)-2A(1)
W	1A	1A
T	2A	22 (easy)
F		Travel
S		10C-Mile
S	Home	2x 19A – 2x 19B – 3x 5A(1)
M	2A	2A
T	1A	1A
W		10C-Twilight Meet (2 mile)
T		3
F		17A – 2A
S		2x 6C – 2B
S		2
M	2x 5A(1)	5G(3)-5F(3)-5E(3)-5D(4)-5C(2)-2A(1)
T	1A	2B – 14A
W	2x 5A(1)	1A
T		Trials – NCAA Meet
F		Semifinals
S		Finals (Mile)
S		
M		
T		
W		
T		
F		
S		
S		

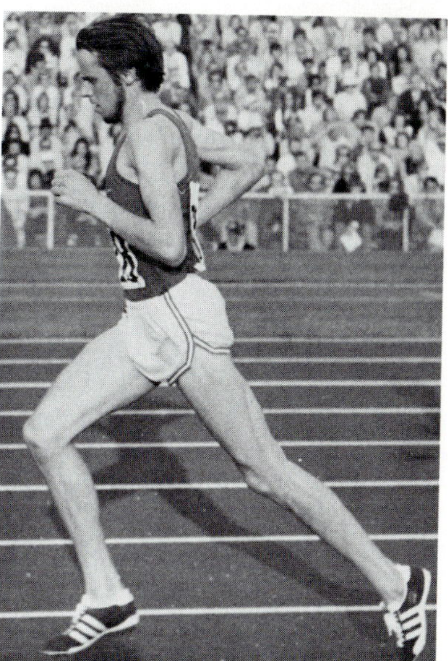

Photograph 3.2 Lasse Viren, Finland, champion in the middle distances.

level in training. The basic cycle used is one day of hard or heavy training, followed by a day of light or easy training. However, this pattern is not universal. Some athletes need two light days after each heavy day of training. An example of this was Ken Moore, who developed into an Olympic marathoner after graduating from college. Many athletes are not really physically mature until they have reached their early twenties, so the teacher and coach should be careful of the workload assigned to young athletes.

Other athletes are extremely strong and can go two hard days for every easy day. Examples in this case are Dyrol Burleson, who ran under 4 minutes in the mile a number of times as an undergraduate and was three-time NCAA mile champion, and Steve Prefontaine, who set an American record in the 5 kilometers as a college sophomore. These athletes might even be able to progress on a program of three hard days for each easy day, but the coach must be very cautious in following up such possibilities. Each individual has his own tolerance level for work. If he is pushed beyond that level, his performance will go into a nose dive. Once this happens, it is very difficult to reverse the process and get the athlete's performances moving in the right direction.

The training patterns for the longer distances are the same as for the shorter distances, but the mileage covered is greater. This does not mean 100 miles a week, which for most athletes is foolish. It means that where a miler or half-miler might run 6 to 10 miles for his long run of the week on Sunday, the three-miler may go as many as 15 miles or more. Interval work is essentially proportionate to the racing distance, varying from 1½ to 3 times the racing distance. Where an 880 runner will cover no more than 1¼ to 1½ miles in a long interval session,

Figure 3.4a Middle Distances Training Schedule

Middle Distances NAME DATE *November*

1. A. Jog 1 to 3 miles
   B. Weights & jog
2. Fartlek A. Varied (1) 30 min. (2) *45 min.*
   B. Steady (1) 2-4 mi. (2) 4-6 mi. (3) 7-10 mi.
   (4) *8-12 mi.*
3. Weights
4. High knee and power run
5. Intervals
   A. 110 (1) 18-16-14 (2) 17-*16-15-14*
   B. 165 (1) 25 (2)
   C. 220 (1) 35 (2) *28 (3) 27*
   D. 330 (1) 52 (2) 48 (3) 45 (4) *42*
   E. 440 (1) 70-73 (2)
   F. 660 (1) 1:45 (2) *1:39*
   G. 880 (1) 70 (2)
   H. 3/4 (1) 70 (2)
   I. Mile (1) 72 (2) 68-70 (3) 64-67 (4)
   J.
   K.
   L.
6. Sets A. 660-440-330-220-110
   (1) 1:45-68-49-32-15 (2)
   B. 440-660-440-220 (1) 63 (2)
   C. 550-165-165 (1) 55 pace (2)
   D.
7. Squad meeting
8. Special A. Sauna B. Swim C.
9. Drills A. Sprint-float-sprint (165)
   B. 1-step acceleration (165)
   C. 40-30 drill (1) 4 laps (2)
   D. 70-90 drill (1) 1-1 (2) 2-1
   (3) 3-1 (4)
   E. Cut-downs (1) 110 (2) 165 (3) 220
   (4) 330 (5) 440 (6) 880 (7) *3/4 effort* *(8) Mile*
   F. Simulate race drills (1) 1st 220-last 220
   (2) 2½–1½ (3) 10 miles–3/4 drill (4)
   G. 2-4 miles at (1) 80 (2) 75 (3)
10. A. Test B. Trial C. Compete
    (1) 3/4 date pace (2) Over (3) Under
11. Hill interval A. 110 B. 220 C.
12. With coach (A) Bill B. (B) Bill D. (C)
14. A. Wind sprint B. Hurdle drill
    C. Spring and bound D.
15. Finish work
16. Acrobatics or apparatus
17. 3/4 effort *A. 3 miles on date pace*
18.
19.
20. Secondary event
21. A. Pictures B. Film

	A.M.	*P.M.*
M	*1A*	*2B(2)-5A(2)*
T	*2B(2)*	*8-12x 5D(on hill)-2B(1)*
W	*2B(1)*	*2A(2)*
T	*1A*	*3x 9E(7)(67-66-64)-3x 9E(8)(75-70-68 or 69)-6x 9E(4)-7*
F	*1A*	*1A (grass)*
S		*6x 5D(on hill)-2B(2)-6x 5D (track)*
S		*Easy run*
M		*Light-5A(2)*
T	*2B(1)*	*2x 5F(1)-2x 5F(2)-2x 5F(1)-2x 5D(1-2)-2x 5D(3-4)-2x 5D(2)-2B(1)*
W	*2B(2)*	*2B(3)*
T	*Easy*	*2x 5C(2)-9G(1) (sawdust)-5A(2)*
F	*Light*	*Light*
S		*10B(17A)-2B(2)-6x 9E(4)*
S		*Easy run*
M		*2A(1)-5A(2)*
T	*2B(1)*	*9C(1)-880 rest-9C(1)-880 rest-9C(1)-1A-6x 9E(4)*
W	*2B(1)*	*2B(3)*
T	*2B(2)*	*2x 5C(3)-2B(2)-5A(2)*
F	*Light*	*Light*
S		*16-24x 5D(1-2) (sawdust)*
S		*Easy-long*
M		*2A(1)-5A(2)*
T		*2B(3)*
W		*2A(2)*
T		*Light run-Thanksgiving*
F		*2B(4)*
S		*12-24x 5D(50-52)*
S		*Easy running*

Figure 3.4b Middle Distances Training Schedule

Middle Distances NAME DATE December

1. A. Jog 1 to 3 miles
   B. Weights & jog
2. Fartlek A. Varied (1) 30 min. (2) 45 min.
   B. Steady (1) 2-4 mi. (2) 4-6 mi. (3) 7-10 mi.
   (4) 12-15 mi. (5) 8-12 mi.
3. Weights
4. High knee and power run
5. Intervals
   A. 110 (1) 18-16-14 (2) 16-15-14
   B. 165 (1) 25 (2)
   C. 220 (1) 35 (2) 27-28
   D. 330 (1) 52 (2) 48 (3) 45 (4)
   E. 440 (1) 70-73 (2)
   F. 660 (1) 1:45 (2)
   G. 880 (1) 70 (2)
   H. 3/4 (1) 70 (2)
   I. Mile (1) 72 (2) 68-70 (3) 64-67 (4)
   J. 4 miles (1) 6:30-7:00
   K.
   L.
6. Sets A. 660-440-330-220-110
   (1) 1:45-68-49-32-15 (2)
   B. 440-660-440-220 (1) 63 (2)
   C. 550-165-165 (1) 55 pace (2)
   D.
7. Squad meeting
8. Special A. Sauna B. Swim C.
9. Drills A. Sprint-float-sprint (165)
   B. 1-step acceleration (165)
   C. 40-30 drill (1) 4 laps (2) 6-12 laps
   D. 70-90 drill (1) 1-1 (2) 2-1
   (3) 3-1 (4)
   E. Cut-downs (1) 110 (2) 165 (3) 220
   (4) 330 (5) 440 (6) 880 (7)
   F. Simulate race drills (1) 1st 220-last 220
   (2) 2½-1½ (3) 10 miles-3/4 drill (4)
   G. 2-4 miles at (1) 80 (2) 75 (3)
10. A. Test B. Trial C. Compete
    (1) 3/4 date pace (2) Over (3) Under
11. Hill interval A. 110 B. 220 C.
12. With coach (A) Bill B. (B) Bill D. (C)
14. A. Wind sprint B. Hurdle drill
    C. Spring and bound D.
15. Finish work
16. Acrobatics or apparatus
17. 3/4 effort A. 3 miles at 70 ± 1 sec.
18.
19.
20. Secondary event
21. A. Pictures B. Film

	A.M.	P.M.
M	2B(2)	2A(2)
T	2B(2)	3x 9D-5J(1)-9E(4)(52-49-46)
W	2B(2)	2B(3)(6:30-7:00 pace)
T	2B(2)	6x 6x 6x 2A(2)(include 5G-5E-5B)
F	2B(2)	2B(2)
S		3x 4x 9F(3)(5H)-9E(4)-2B(2)
S		2B(4)
M	2B(2)	2A(2)
T	2B(1)	6x 6x 5D(2)-2B(3)-9E(4)
W	2B(2)	2B(3)(easy)
T	2B(1)	2x 5C(2)-2A(1)-5A(2)
F	Light	Light grass
S		6x 10B(17A)-2B(2)-9E(4)
S		2B(4)
M	2B(1)	2A(2)
T	2B(2)	12-24x 5D(1-2)
W	2B(1)	2B(3)
T	2B(2)	4x 4x 4x 4x 2A(2)(include 5G-5E-5C-5A)
F	2B(1)	Light run
S		2B(5)
S		2B(5)(Light)
M	2B(1)	2A(2)
T	2B(2)	3x 3x 3x 6x 5H-5G-5E-5C
W	2B(1)	2B(5)-5A(2)
T	2B(2)	4x 5C(1)-2A(1)-5A(2)
F	2B(2)	Light run (30-40 min.)
S		2B(5)
S		6x 9C(2)-2B(1)-9E(4)

Figure 3.4c Middle Distances Training Schedule

Middle Distances NAME DATE January

1. A. Jog 1 to 3 miles
   B. Weights & jog
2. Fartlek A. Varied (1) 30 min. (2) 45 min.
   B. Steady (1) 2-4 mi. (2) 4-6 mi. (3) 7-10 mi.
   (4) 12-15 mi.
3. Weights
4. High knee and power run
5. Intervals
   A. 110 (1) 18-16-14 (2) 17-16-15-14
   B. 165 (1) 25 (2) 24
   C. 220 (1) 35 (2) 29
   D. 330 (1) 52 (2) 48 (3) 45 (4) 54 (5) 50
   E. 440 (1) 70-73 (2) 68
   F. 660 (1) 1:45 (2)
   G. 880 (1) 70 (2)
   H. 3/4 (1) 70 (2)
   I. Mile (1) 72 (2) 68-70 (3) 64-67 (4)
   J.
   K.
   L.
6. Sets A. 660-440-330-220-110
   (1) 1:45-68-49-32-15 (2)
   B. 440-660-440-220 (1) 63 (2)
   C. 550-165-165 (1) 55 pace (2)
   D.
7. Squad meeting
8. Special A. Sauna B. Swim C.
9. Drills A. Sprint-float-sprint (165)
   B. 1-step acceleration (165)
   C. 40-30 drill (1) 4 laps (2)
   D. 70-90 drill (1) 1-1 (2) 2-1
   (3) 3-1 (4)
   E. Cut-downs (1) 110 (2) 165 (3) 220
   (4) 330 (5) 440 (6) 880 (7) Mile (8) 1320
   F. Simulate race drills (1) 1st 220-last 220
   (2) 2½-1½ (3) 10 miles-3/4 drill (4)
   G. 2-4 miles at (1) 80 (2) 75 (3)
10. A. Test B. Trial C. Compete
    (1) 3/4 date pace (2) Over (3) Under
11. Hill interval A. 110 B. 220 C.
12. With coach (A) Bill B. (B) Bill D. (C)
14. A. Wind sprint B. Hurdle drill
    C. Spring and bound D.
15. Finish work
16. Acrobatics or apparatus
17. 3/4 effort
18.
19.
20. Secondary event
21. A. Pictures B. Film

	A.M.	P.M.
M		2A(2)
T	2B(2)	15x 5E(2)-2B(2)-6x 9E(4)
W	2B(2)-5A(2)	2B(2)
T	2B(2)	4x 5D(3)-2A(1)-7
F	2B(2)	2B(1)
S		9D(4)-2 (light)
S		2B(4)
M	2B(2)	2A(2)
T	2B(2)	1A-8F(1)-5A(1)
W	2B(1)	7-2B(2)
T	2B(2)	5I(3)-9G(1)-1x 9E(7) (80-75-70-65)
F	1A	1A
S		12x 5D(1-2)-2B(2)-5A(2)
S		2B(4)
M		2A(2)
T	2B(2)	8x 5D(1-2)-2B(2)-5A(2)
W	2B(2)	2A(2)
T	2B(2)	4x 9E(8)(72-70-68-66)-3x 9E(7)(75-72-68)-1A
F	1A	1A
S		22x 5B(2)-9G(1)-5A(2)
S		2B(4)
M		2A(2)
T	2B(2)	6x 5D(4)-6x 5D(5-1)-6x 5D(2-5)-1A-5A(2)
W	2B(1)	2 (easy - 1 hour)
T	2B(1)	2x 5C(2)-9G(1)-6x 9E(4)(2x 52-2x 50-48-46)
F	1A	1A
S		10C - Portland Indoor
S		

Figure 3.4d Middle Distances Training Schedule

Middle Distances NAME DATE February

1. A. Jog 1 to 3 miles
   B. Weights & jog
2. Fartlek A. Varied (1) 30 min. (2) 45 min.
   B. Steady (1) 2-4 mi. (2) 4-6 mi. (3) 7-10 mi.
   (4) 12-15 mi. easy
3. Weights
4. High knee and power run
5. Intervals
   A. 110 (1) 18-16-14 (2) 17-16-15-14
   B. 165 (1) 25 (2)
   C. 220 (1) 35 (2) 30 (3) 32-34 (4) 27-28
   D. 330 (1) 52 (2) 48 (3) 45 (4)
   E. 440 (1) 70-73 (2) 68 (3) 62
   F. 660 (1) 1:45 (2)
   G. 880 (1) 70 (2) 62-64
   H. 3/4 (1) 70 (2)
   I. Mile (1) 72 (2) 68-70 (3) 64-67 (4) 63
   J. 6 miles (1) 6 min./mile
   K.
   L.
6. Sets A. 660-440-330-220-110
   (1) 1:45-68-49-32-15 (2)
   B. 440-660-440-220 (1) 63 (2)
   C. 550-165-165 (1) 55 pace (2)
   D.
7. Squad meeting
8. Special A. Sauna B. Swim C.
9. Drills A. Sprint-float-sprint (165)
   B. 1-step acceleration (165)
   C. 40-30 drill (1) 4 laps (2)
   D. 70-90 drill (1) 1-1 (2) 2-1
   (3) 3-1 (4)
   E. Cut-downs (1) 110 (2) 165 (3) 220
   (4) 330 (5) 440 (6) 880 (7)
   F. Simulate race drills (1) 1st 220-last 220
   (2) 2½–1½ (3) 10 miles–3/4 drill (4)
   G. 2-4 miles at (1) 80 (2) 75 (3)
10. A. Test B. Trial C. Compete
    (1) 3/4 date pace (2) Over (3) Under
11. Hill interval A. 110 B. 220 C.
12. With coach (A) Bill B. (B) Bill D. (C)
14. A. Wind sprint B. Hurdle drill
    C. Spring and bound D.
15. Finish work
16. Acrobatics or apparatus
17. 3/4 effort
18.
19.
20. Secondary event
21. A. Pictures B. Film

M	2A(1-2) (light)
T 2B(2)	6x 6x 5D(4)-2B(2)-9E(1)
W 2B(2)	2B(3)
T 2B(1)	4x 8x 5G(2)-1A(light)-9E(4)(50-48-46-44)
F 1A	1A
S	8x 6x 5C(2)-2B(2)-9E(1)
S	2B(4)
M	2A(2)
T 2B(2)	6x 5E(2)-5J(1)-5A(2)
W 1A	2B(2)
T 2B(2)	3-4x 5H(1)-2B(1)
F 2B(1)	2B(1)
S	12-20x 5C(3)-1A
S	2B(4)
M 2B(1)	2A(2)
T 2B(2)	4x 8x 5E(3)-5E(2)-2B(1)
W 2B(2)	2B(3)
T 2B(2)	2x 6x 5C(4)-2B(2)-9E(1)
F 2B(2)	1A
S	6x 5I(4)-9G(1)-9E(4) 2B(4)
S	2B(4)
M	2A(2)
T 2B(2)	6x 6x 5D(4)-2B(2)-9E(1)
W 2B(2)	2B(3)
T 2B(2)	3-4x 5H(1)-2B(1)
F 2B(2)	2B(1)
S	16x 5D-1A
S	2B(4)

Figure 3.4e Middle Distances Training Schedule

Middle Distances NAME DATE *March*

1. A. Jog 1 to 3 miles
   B. Weights & jog
2. Fartlek A. Varied (1) 30 min. (2) *45 min.*
   B. Steady (1) 2-4 mi. (2) 4-6 mi. (3) 7-10 mi.
   (4) *12-15mi. easy (5) 8-12 mi.*
3. Weights
4. High knee and power run
5. Intervals
   A. 110 (1) 18-16-14 (2) 17-*16-15-14*
   B. 165 (1) 25 (2)
   C. 220 (1) 35 (2) *32-34 (3) 27*
   D. 330 (1) 52 (2) 48 (3) 45 (4) *46-47*
   E. 440 (1) 70-73 (2) *68*
   F. 660 (1) 1:45 (2)
   G. 880 (1) 70 (2)
   H. 3/4 (1) 70 (2)
   I. Mile (1) 72 (2) 68-70 (3) 64-67 (4)
   J.
   K.
   L.
6. Sets A. 660-440-330-220-110
   (1) 1:45-68-49-32-15 (2)
   B. 440-660-440-220 (1) 63
   C. 550-165-165 (1) 55 pace (2)
   D.
7. Squad meeting
8. Special A. Sauna B. Swim C.
9. Drills A. Sprint-float-sprint (165)
   B. 1-step acceleration (165)
   C. 40-30 drill (1) 4 laps (2)
   D. 70-90 drill (1) 1-1 (2) 2-1
   (3) 3-1 (4) *2-2*
   E. Cut-downs (1) 110 (2) 165 (3) 220
   (4) 330 (5) 440 (6) 880 (7)
   F. Simulate race drills (1) 1st 220-last 220
   (2) 2½-1½ (3) 10 miles-3/4 drill (4)
   G. 2-4 miles at (1) 80 (2) 75 (3)
10. A. Test B. Trial C. Compete
    (1) 3/4 date pace (2) Over (3) Under
11. Hill interval A. 110 B. 220 C.
12. With coach (A) Bill B. (B) Bill D. (C)
14. A. Wind sprint B. Hurdle drill
    C. Spring and bound D.
15. Finish work
16. Acrobatics or apparatus
17. 3/4 effort
18.
19.
20. Secondary event
21. A. Pictures B. Film

Day	A.M.	P.M.
M	*1A*	*2A(2)*
T	*2B(2)*	*6x 5E(2)-9G(1)-5A(2)*
W	*2B(2)*	*2B(2)*
T	*2B(2)*	*3-4x 5H(1)-2B(1)*
F	*1A*	*2B(1)*
S		*12-20x 5C(2)*
S		*2B(4)*
M	*2B(1)*	*2A(2)*
T	*2B(2)*	*6x 5D(4)-2B(2)-6x 9E(4)*
W	*2B(2)*	*2B(3)*
T	*2B(2)*	*9D(4)*
F	*1A*	*1A*
S		*10A (880)-2B(3)-6x 9E(4)*
S		*2B(4)*
M	*2B(1)*	*2A (1-2)-5A(2)*
T	*2B(1)*	*6x 9E(4)-2B(1)-6x 9E(3)(32-30-28)*
W	*2B(1)*	*2B(2)-5A(2)*
T	*1A*	*2x 5C(3)-9G(1)(2mi.)-5A(2)*
F	*1A*	*1A*
S		*10C-Fresno meet*
S		*2B(5)*
M	*2B(1)*	*2A(2)-5A(2)*
T	*2B(1)*	*6x 5D(4)-2B(1)-6x 9E(4)*
W	*2B(1)*	*2B(2)*
T	*2B(1)*	*2x 5C(3)-9G(1)-5A(2)*
F	*1A*	*1A*
S		*10C*
S		*2B(4)*

Figure 3.4f Middle Distances Training Schedule

Middle Distances NAME DATE April

1. A. Jog 1 to 3 miles
   B. Weights & jog
2. Fartlek A. Varied (1) 30 min. (2) 45 min.
   B. Steady (1) 2-4 mi. (2) 4-6 mi. (3) 7-10 mi.
   (4) 8-12 mi. easy (5) 8-15 mi. easy
3. Weights
4. High knee and power run
5. Intervals
   A. 110 (1) 18-16-14 (2) 17-16-15-14
   B. 165 (1) 25 (2)
   C. 220 (1) 35 (2)
   D. 330 (1) 52 (2) 48 (3) 45 (4) 47
   E. 440 (1) 70-73 (2) 66
   F. 660 (1) 1:45 (2)
   G. 880 (1) 70 (2) 90
   H. 3/4 (1) 70 (2) 67-68
   I. Mile (1) 72 (2) 68-70 (3) 64-67 (4)
   J.
   K.
   L.
6. Sets A. 660-440-330-220-110
   (1) 1:45-68-49-32-15 (2)
   B. 440-660-440-220 (1) 63 (2) 62
   C. 550-165-165 (1) 55 pace (2)
   D. 330-220-110 (1) 48-31-14
7. Squad meeting
8. Special A. Sauna B. Swim C.
9. Drills A. Sprint-float-sprint (165)
   B. 1-step acceleration (165)
   C. 40-30 drill (1) 4 laps (2)
   D. 70-90 drill (1) 1-1 (2) 2-1
   (3) 3-1 (4)
   E. Cut-downs (1) 110 (2) 165 (3) 220
   (4) 330 (5) 440 (6) 880 (7) 1320
   F. Simulate race drills (1) 1st 220-last 220
   (2) 2½-1½ (3) 10 miles-3/4 drill (4)
   G. 2-4 miles at (1) 80 (2) 75 (3)
10. A. Test B. Trial C. Compete
    (1) 3/4 date pace (2) Over (3) Under
11. Hill interval A. 110 B. 220 C.
12. With coach (A) Bill B. (B) Bill D. (C)
14. A. Wind sprint B. Hurdle drill
    C. Spring and bound D.
15. Finish work
16. Acrobatics or apparatus
17. 3/4 effort
18.
19.
20. Secondary event
21. A. Pictures B. Film

	A.M.	P.M.
M		2B(2)
T	2B(2)	4x/5E(2)-Rest/5G(2)-4x/5E(2)- 2B(1)-4x/9E(4)(51-49-47-45)
W	2B(2)	2B(2)
T	2B(1)	5F(1)-5D(4)-5A(14)-1A-5A(2)
F	1A	1A
S		10C (2 mile)
S		2B(4)
M	2B(2)	2A(2)
T	2B(2)	6x 6B(2)-2B(2)-9E(4)
W	2B(2)	2B(2)
T	2B(2)	4x 9G(1)-9E(4)(52-50-48-46)
F	2B(2)	2B(1)
S		3x 2x 4x 5H(2)-5I(1, 2)-1A-9E(4)
S		2B(5)
M	2B(1)	2A(1)
T	2B(1)	8x 6x 7-5D(2)-1A-9E(3)(34-32-30)
W	1A	7-2B(2)
T	1A	2x 6D(1)-1A-5A(2)
F	1A	1A
S		10C (2 or 3 mile)
S		2B(4)
M	2B(2)	2A(2)
T	2B(2)	4x 3x 5D(4)-9E(7)(70-68-66)
W	2B(1)	2x 2B(2)-9A
T	2B(1)	2x Light grass-5A(14)
F	1A	9G(1)
S	1A	1A
S		10C-Twilight meet

Figure 3.4g Middle Distances Training Schedule

Middle Distances NAME DATE *May*

1. A. Jog 1 to 3 miles
   B. Weights & jog
2. Fartlek A. Varied (1) 30 min. (2) *45 min.*
   B. Steady (1) 2-4 mi. (2) 4-6 mi. (3) 7-10 mi.
   (4) *8-12 mi. easy*
3. Weights
4. High knee and power run
5. Intervals
   A. 110 (1) 18-16-14 (2) 17-*16-15-14*
   B. 165 (1) 25 (2) *8-6-8*
   C. 220 (1) 35 (2) *33* *(3) 31*
   D. 330 (1) 52 (2) 48 (3) 45 (4) *46*
   E. 440 (1) 70-73 (2) *62*
   F. 660 (1) 1:45 (2)
   G. 880 (1) 70 (2) *64*
   H. 3/4 (1) 70 (2) *66*
   I. Mile (1) 72 (2) 68-70 (3) 64-67 (4)
   J.
   K.
   L.
6. Sets A. 660-440-330-220-110
   (1) 1:45-68-49-32-15 (2)
   B. 440-660-440-220 (1) 63 (2)
   C. 550-165-165 (1) 55 pace (2)
   D.
7. Squad meeting
8. Special A. Sauna B. Swim C.
9. Drills A. Sprint-float-sprint (165)
   B. 1-step acceleration (165)
   C. 40-30 drill (1) 4 laps (2)
   D. 70-90 drill (1) 1-1 (2) 2-1
   (3) 3-1 (4)
   E. Cut-downs (1) 110 (2) 165 (3) 220
   (4) 330 (5) 440 (6) 880 (7)
   F. Simulate race drills (1) 1st 220-last 220
   (2) 2½–1½ (3) 10 miles–3/4 drill (4)
   G. 2-4 miles at (1) 80 (2) 75 (3)
10. A. Test B. Trial C. Compete
    (1) 3/4 date pace (2) Over (3) Under
11. Hill interval A. 110 B. 220 C.
12. With coach (A) Bill B. (B) Bill D. (C)
14. A. Wind sprint B. Hurdle drill
    C. Spring and bound D.
15. Finish work
16. Acrobatics or apparatus
17. 3/4 effort
18.
19.
20. Secondary event
21. A. Pictures B. Film

	A.M.	*P.M.*
M		*2A(2)*
T	*2B(1)*	*8x 5D(2)-2B(2)-5F(1)-5D(4)-5A(13)*
W	*2B(2)*	*2B(2)*
T	*2B(1)*	*2x 5B(2)-9G(1)(2 miles)-5A(2)*
F	*/A*	*/A*
S		*10C - Dual meet*
S		*2B(4)*
M		*2 (light)*
T	*2B(1)*	*9x 9E(4)(50-48-46)-2B(2)-3x 9E(4)(48-46-44)*
W	*2B(1)*	*2B(2)*
T	*/A*	*4x 9E(4)(52-50-48-46)-/A-5A(2)*
F	*/A*	*/A*
S		*10C - 3 mile*
S		*2B(4)*
M	*2B(1)*	*2A(2)*
T	*2B(1)*	*5H(2)-5G(2)-5E(2)-/A-6x 9E(4)(50-48-46)*
W	*2B(1)*	*2B(2)*
T	*2B(1)*	*6x 5C(2)-2B(1)-5A(2)*
F	*/A*	*/A*
S		*10C -Northern Division meet*
S		*2B(4)*
M	*2B(1)*	*2A(2)(easy)*
T	*2B(1)*	*6x 5D(2)-2B(1)-3x 9E(4)(48-46-43)*
W	*2B(2)*	*2B(2)*
T	*2B(1)*	*4x 5C(3)-Light grass-3x 9E(3)(31-29-27)*
F		*Light grass*
S		*10C - Pac 8 meet*
S		*2B(4)*

Figure 3.4h Middle Distances Training Schedule

Middle Distances NAME DATE June

1. A. Jog 1 to 3 miles
   B. Weights & jog
2. Fartlek A. Varied (1) 30 min. (2) 45 min.
   B. Steady (1) 2-4 mi. (2) 4-6 mi. (3) 7-10 mi.
   (4) 8-12 mi.
3. Weights
4. High knee and power run
5. Intervals
   A. 110 (1) 18-16-14 (2) 17-15-13 (3) 15-14-13
   B. 165 (1) 25 (2)
   C. 220 (1) 35 (2) 27-28
   D. 330 (1) 52 (2) 48 (3) 45 (4)
   E. 440 (1) 70-73 (2) 60-64
   F. 660 (1) 1:45 (2)
   G. 880 (1) 70 (2)
   H. 3/4 (1) 70 (2) 62-68
   I. Mile (1) 72 (2) 68-70 (3) 64-67 (4)
   J. 7 miles (1) 6 min. pace
   K.
   L.
6. Sets A. 660-440-330-220-110
   (1) 1:45-68-49-32-15 (2)
   B. 440-660-440-220 (1) 63 (2)
   C. 550-165-165 (1) 55 pace (2)
   D.
7. Squad meeting
8. Special A. Sauna B. Swim C.
9. Drills A. Sprint-float-sprint (165)
   B. 1-step acceleration (165)
   C. 40-30 drill (1) 4 laps (2)
   D. 70-90 drill (1) 1-1 (2) 2-1
   (3) 3-1 (4)
   E. Cut-downs (1) 110 (2) 165 (3) 220
   (4) 330 (5) 440 (6) 880 (7)
   F. Simulate race drills (1) 1st 220-last 220
   (2) 2½-1½ (3) 10 miles-3/4 drill (4)
   G. 2-4 miles at (1) 80 (2) 75 (3)
10. A. Test B. Trial C. Compete
    (1) 3/4 date pace (2) Over (3) Under
11. Hill interval A. 110 B. 220 C.
12. With coach (A) Bill B. (B) Bill D. (C)
14. A. Wind sprint B. Hurdle drill
    C. Spring and bound D.
15. Finish work
16. Acrobatics or apparatus
17. 3/4 effort
18.
19.
20. Secondary event
21. A. Pictures B. Film

	A.M.	P.M.
M	2B(1)	2A(2)
T	2B(2)	6x 5E(2) – 2A(1) – 6x 9E(4)
W	2B(2)	2B(2)
T	2B(2)	4x 5H(2) – 12x 5D(1-2) – 1A
F	2B(2)	Light run
S		3x 9E(4)(48-45-43) – 5J(1) – 3x 9E(4)(48-45-43)
S		2B(4)
M	2B(1)	Light grass – 5A(3)
T	2B(1)	1-2x 5C(2) – 9G(1) – 5A(2)
W		Light grass
T		10C-5km. Trials or light grass (NCAA)
F		Light grass or 10C-Finals-10km (NCAA)
S		10C-Finals-5km (NCAA)
S		
M		
T		
W		
T		
F		
S		
S		
M		
T		
W		
T		
F		
S		
S		

the three-miler may cover from 3 to 6 miles of intervals. Even so, most athletes at Oregon would rarely cover more than 70 to 80 miles in the "longer" training weeks of the winter.

Actually, from the 3-mile run to the marathon, the training is very similar. A three-miler can train for a marathon by working over some longer distance intervals (but not run any more miles of intervals), but about the only real change in his training would be the addition of a long run of 20 to 30 miles once a month for his Sunday run. Three- and six-milers have discovered that super-high mileage is not as necessary to successful marathoning as theorists would suggest. Also, running the marathon does not mean that the athlete cannot compete in the track races successfully. Experience has proven that it can be done with success.

The tactics of the longer distance runs are essentially the same regardless of the racing distance: find out what the opponent can do, then determine how he can be beaten.

The schedules can be adapted by the athlete for training for almost any racing distance between the 1-mile run and the marathon, for the principles and patterns are the same. Only the paces and quantities differ.

The Steeplechase

The steeplechase is the real test of an athlete. The training for the steeplechase is basically the same as that a two- or three-miler would do. The only real difference involves the hurdling activities. Ideally, the athlete would run a steeplchase about once a month, or hopefully no more often than every two weeks until he got into a situation where he would have to race twice as part of a single competition. Otherwise, running the steeplechase too often can cause the steeplechaser to be "flattened out" from giving too much in his practice and early competitive seasons.

The difference between training for the flat races and the steeplechase is, as mentioned above, the hurdle training. At Oregon, hurdles and small logs (up to three feet in diameter, and lying on their sides) are around the track and athletics areas of the campus for the runners to use in informal practice. One principle of training is that *every* distance runner does some steeplechase training, whether or not he ever runs a steeplechase in competition. This practice helps the teacher discover his potential steeplechasers, some of whom might not be inclined to volunteer for such a tough event. The runners will practice jumping over the obstacles or stepping on and then over them while running on their own.

Some pace work will be done over a distance of 220 yards on the track over the hurdles. This is done with two settings of hurdles. In one case, only two hurdles are used, one set at the end of the first straight and the other at the end of the turn as the second straight begins. In the other case, about five hurdles are run, set 15 to 20 yards apart and included in a 220-yard run. In both cases, the runner will run about four of these intervals while working on his hurdling. He will be trying to hurdle as a hurdler would. During the early part of the year, the hurdles will be set at 30 inches in height; as the preseason training progresses,

Photographs 3.3*a* & *b*   Steeplechase runners at the 1971 AAU championship meet.

the hurdles will be raised to the 3-foot level of the steeplechase barriers.

The steeplechasers will practice over the water jump and barrier once a week. Except during regular competitions, the water jump does not have any water in the pit. The athletes will run in a loop, going over the barrier or water jump perhaps four times. Except for this practice situation, they will practice with the regular hurdles. The reason for this is simple: the regular hurdles can be hit, and they will give. The water jump barrier will not move at all. The other barriers are over 12 feet long and weigh well over 200 pounds. They do not move too freely, either. Finally, if the athlete prefers to step on the barriers, rather than hurdle over them, he must work on this regularly. The athletes will sometimes place a barrier at the edge of the long jump pit and practice running down the runway and stepping onto and going over the barrier.

As suggested above, the steeplechaser should not compete too much in his event, for it causes a lot of wear and tear on him. Also, he should not hurdle too much, for it can be hard on the legs.

American steeplechasing would be helped greatly if the race were added to the high school competitive schedule. As it is, few athletes are exposed to steeplechasing before college. It would be good if high school athletes could run a shortened race of perhaps 2 kilometers (1¼ miles). When the race is longer than a mile, it begins to highlight the experts. This would provide pre-college experience to many runners, and it would be one more event for competitors, allowing more participants. This is the real objective of the entire sport: the joy of competition.

Figure 3.5a Steeplechase Training Schedule

Steeplechase NAME DATE December

1. A. Light jogging B.
2. Fartlek A. Varied (1) 30 min. (2) 40 min.
   B. Steady (1) 2-4 mi. (2) 4-6 mi. (3) 7-10 mi.
   (4) 8-15 mi.
3. Weight program
4. High knee and power run
5. Intervals
   A. 110 (1) 18-16-14 (2) 17-15-13
   B. 165 (1) 25 (2)
   C. 220 (1) 35 (2) 27-29
   D. 330 (1) 52 (2) 48 (3) 45 (4)
   E. 440 (1) 70-73 (2)
   F. 660 (1) 75 (2) 72 (3) 68 (4)
   G. 880 (1) 72-75 (2) 68-70 (3)
   I. 3/4 (1) 72-75 (2) 69-71 (3)
   J. Mile (1) 72-75 (2) 69-72 (3)
   K.
   L.
5. H. Same interval as above with hurdles
6. Sets A. 660-440-330-220-110
   (1) 1:45-68-49-32-15 (2)
   B. 440-660-440-220 (1) 64 (2)
   C.
7. Squad meeting
8. Special A. Sauna B. Swim C.
9. Drills A. Hurdle; X drill (1) 30 in. (2) 36 in.
   B. 165 sprint-float-sprint
   C. 165 middle 1-step accelerate
   D. Last 165 (WJ & hurdle)
   E. Intermediate hurdles (1) 165 (2) 220
   F. 3 mi.–4 hurdles (1) 90 (2) 85 (3) 80 (4)
   G. 40-30 drill (1) 4 laps (2) 6 (3)
   H. 70-90 drill (1) 1-1 (2) 2-1 (3) 3-1 (4)
   I. Cut-downs (1) 110 (2) 165 (3) 220 (4) 330
   (5) 440 (6) 880 (7)
   J. Simulate race drill (1) 1st 880-last 880
   (2) 10 mi.-3/4 drill (3) 2 mi. at 80 pace
   K.
10. A. Test B. Trial C. Compete
    (1) 3/4 date pace (2) Over (3) Under
11. Hill interval A. 110 B. 220 C.
12. With coach (A) Bill B. (B) Bill D. (C)
14. A. Wind sprint B. Hurdle drill
    C. Spring and bound D.
15. Finish work
16. Acrobatics or apparatus
17. 3/4 effort
18.
19.
20. Secondary event
21. A. Pictures B. Film

M	9A–2A(2)–4X 9I(1)
T	2 5F–6 5D–2B(2)–4 9I(4)
W	2B(3)
T	4X 5BH–9J(3)–5A(1)
F	1A
S	10B(1)(3 mi.)–2B(2)–6X 9I(4)
S	2B(4)

M	2A(2)
T	12–24 5D
W	2B(3)
T	2A(2)
F	1A
S	2B(3)
S	2B(3)

M	2A(2)
T	3x 5I–3x 5G–3 5E–6 5D
W	2B(3)–5A(1)
T	4 5C(2)–2B(2)–5A(1)
F	2B(2)
S	9G(2)–2B(1)–6 5D
S	2B(3)

M	
T	
W	
T	
F	
S	
S	

Figure 3.5b Steeplechase Training Schedule

Steeplechase NAME DATE January

1. A. Light jogging B. 45 min.
2. Fartlek A. Varied (1) 30 min. (2)
   B. Steady (1) 2-4 mi. (2) 4-6 mi. (3) 7-10 mi.
   (4) 12-15 mi.
3. Weight program
4. High knee and power run
5. Intervals
   A. 110 (1) 18-16-14 (2) 17-15-13
   B. 165 (1) 25 (2)
   C. 220 (1) 35 (2)
   D. 330 (1) 52 (2) 48 (3) 45 (4)
   E. 440 (1) 70-73 (2)
   F. 660 (1) 75 (2) 72 (3) 68 (4)
   G. 880 (1) 72-75 (2) 68-70 (3)
   I. 3/4 (1) 72-75 (2) 69-71 (3)
   J. Mile (1) 72-75 (2) 69-72 (3)
   K.
   L.
5. H. Same interval as above with hurdles
6. Sets A. 660-440-330-220-110
   (1) 1:45-68-49-32-15 (2)
   B. 440-660-440-220 (1) 64 (2)
   C.
7. Squad meeting
8. Special A. Sauna B. Swim C.
9. Drills A. Hurdle; X drill (1) 30 in. (2) 36 in. (3) Water barrier drill
   B. 165 sprint-float-sprint
   C. 165 middle 1-step accelerate
   D. Last 165 (WJ & hurdle)
   E. Intermediate hurdles (1) 165 (2) 220
   F. 3 mi.-4 hurdles (1) 90 (2) 85 (3) 80 (4)
   G. 40-30 drill (1) 4 laps (2) 6 (3)
   H. 70-90 drill (1) 1-1 (2) 2-1 (3) 3-1 (4)
   I. Cut-downs (1) 110 (2) 165 (3) 220 (4) 330
   (5) 440 (6) 880 (7)
   J. Simulate race drill (1) 1st 880-last 880
   (2) 10 mi.-3/4 drill (3)
   K.
10. A. Test B. Trial C. Compete
    (1) 3/4 date pace (2) Over (3) Under
11. Hill interval A. 110 B. 220 C.
12. With coach (A) Bill B. (B) Bill D. (C)
14. A. Wind sprint B. Hurdle drill
    C. Spring and bound D.
15. Finish work
16. Acrobatics or apparatus
17. 3/4 effort
18.
19.
20. Secondary event
21. A. Pictures B. Film

Day	Week 1	Week 2	Week 3	Week 4
M	2A(2)-9A(1)	2A(2)-9A(1)	2A(2)-9H(2)	
T	1A-9F(3)-5A(2)	1A-4x 5HG-4x 5E-1A-9I(4)	1A-8x 5D-1A-5A(1)	
W	7-9A(3)-2B(2)-5A(1)	9A(3)-2B(2)-5A(1)	9A(3)-2B(2)-5A(1)	
T	2x 5J-3x 5G-9I(4)-1A	4x 5HC-1A-5A(2)	9F-5A(1)	
F	1A	1A	1A	
S	15x 5D(123)	16x 5B(1)-2A(1)-5A(1)	Oregon indoor meet	
S	2B(3)	2B(3)	2B(3)	

Figure 3.5c Steeplechase Training Schedule

Steeplechase NAME DATE *February*

1. A. Light jogging B.
2. Fartlek A. Varied (1) 30 min. (2) *45 min.*
   B. Steady (1) 2-4 mi. (2) 4-6 mi. (3) 7-10 mi.
   (4) *12-15 mi.*
3. Weight program
4. High knee and power run
5. Intervals
   A. 110 (1) 18-16-14 (2) 17-15-13
   B. 165 (1) 25 (2)
   C. 220 (1) 35 (2)
   D. 330 (1) 52 (2) 48 (3) 45 (4)
   E. 440 (1) 70-73 (2)
   F. 660 (1) 75 (2) 72 (3) 68 (4)
   G. 880 (1) 72-75 (2) 68-70 (3)
   I. 3/4 (1) 72-75 (2) 69-71 (3)
   J. Mile (1) 72-75 (2) 69-72 (3)
   K.
   L.
5. H. Same interval as above with hurdles
6. Sets A. 660-440-330-220-110
   (1) 1:45-68-49-32-15 (2)
   B. 440-660-440-220 (1) 64 (2)
   C.
7. Squad meeting
8. Special A. Sauna B. Swim C.
9. Drills A. Hurdle; X drill (1) 30 in. (2) 36 in. *(3) Water barrier*
   B. 165 sprint-float-sprint
   C. 165 middle 1-step accelerate
   D. Last 165 (WJ & hurdle)
   E. Intermediate hurdles (1) 165 (2) 220
   F. 3 mi.–4 hurdles (1) 90 (2) 85 (3) 80 (4)
   G. 40-30 drill (1) 4 laps (2) 6 (3)
   H. 70-90 drill (1) 1-1 (2) 2-1 (3) 3-1 (4)
   I. Cut-downs (1) 110 (2) 165 (3) 220 (4) 330
   (5) 440 (6) 880 (7)
   J. Simulate race drill (1) 1st 880-last 880
   (2) 10 mi.-3/4 drill (3)
   K.
10. A. Test B. Trial C. Compete
    (1) 3/4 date pace (2) Over (3) Under
11. Hill interval A. 110 B. 220 C.
12. With coach (A) Bill B. (B) Bill D. (C)
14. A. Wind sprint B. Hurdle drill
    C. Spring and bound D.
15. Finish work
16. Acrobatics or apparatus
17. 3/4 effort
18. *Regular steeplechase course* *A. Mile B. 880*
19. *C. 440*
20. Secondary event
21. A. Pictures B. Film

M	*9A – 2A(2)*
T	*5D (6x) – 2B(1) – 9I(1) (6x)*
W	*9A(3) (4x) – 2B(3)*
T	*5HG (4x) – 5E (4x) – 2B(1) – 9I(4) (6x)*
F	*1A*
S	*5C (12x) – 10A(2) – 9I(1) (6x) (6 mile run)*
S	*2B(4)*
M	*9E(2) (3x) – 2A(2)*
T	*5D (4x) – 5C (4x) – 2B(1) – 5A(1)*
W	*9A(3) (4x) – 2B(3)*
T	*5I (2x) – 5HG (2x) – 5E (2x) – 2B(1) – 9I(1) (4x)*
F	*1A*
S	*5C (8x) – 2B(2) – 9I(4) (6x)*
S	*2B(4)*
M	*9E(2) (2x) – 2A(2)*
T	*5D (12x) – 1A – 9I(1) (4x)*
W	*9A(3) (4x) – 2B(2)*
T	*5C (2x) – 9F(3) – 9I(1) (4x)*
F	*1A –*
S	*18A(72-75) – 18B(70-72) – 18C(64-66) – 2B(1) – 5A*
S	*2B(4)*
M	*9A – 2A(2) – 9I(1) (4x)*
T	*5D (6x) – 2B(3) – 5D (6x)*
W	*2B(2)*
T	*9E(1) (6x) – 2B(1) – 9I(1) (6x)*
F	*1A – 9A*
S	*5I (2x) – 5G (3x) – 9I(5) (4x) – 1A – 9I(3) (4x)*
S	*2B(4)*

Figure 3.5d Steeplechase Training Schedule

Steeplechase NAME DATE March

1. A. Light jogging B. 45 min.
2. Fartlek A. Varied (1) 30 min. (2)
   B. Steady (1) 2-4 mi. (2) 4-6 mi. (3) 7-10 mi.
   (4) 12-15 mi.
3. Weight program
4. High knee and power run
5. Intervals
   A. 110 (1) 18-16-14 (2) 17-15-13
   B. 165 (1) 25 (2)
   C. 220 (1) 35 (2)
   D. 330 (1) 52 (2) 48 (3) 45 (4)
   E. 440 (1) 70-73 (2)
   F. 660 (1) 75 (2) 72 (3) 68 (4)
   G. 880 (1) 72-75 (2) 68-70 (3)
   I. 3/4 (1) 72-75 (2) 69-71 (3)
   J. Mile (1) 72-75 (2) 69-72 (3)
   K.
   L.
5. H. Same interval as above with hurdles
6. Sets A. 660-440-330-220-110
   (1) 1:45-68-49-32-15 (2)
   B. 440-660-440-220 (1) 64 (2)
   C. 300-220-110
7. Squad meeting
8. Special A. Sauna B. Swim C.
9. Drills A. Hurdle; X drill (1) 30 in. (2) 36 in. (3) Water barrier
   B. 165 sprint-float-sprint
   C. 165 middle 1-step accelerate
   D. Last 165 (WJ & hurdle)
   E. Intermediate hurdles (1) 165 (2) 220
   F. 3 mi.-4 hurdles (1) 90 (2) 85 (3) 80 (4)
   G. 40-30 drill (1) 4 laps (2) 6 (3)
   H. 70-90 drill (1) 1-1 (2) 2-1 (3) 3-1 (4)
   I. Cut-downs (1) 110 (2) 165 (3) 220 (4) 330
   (5) 440 (6) 880 (7)
   J. Simulate race drill (1) 1st 880-last 880
   (2) 10 mi.-3/4 drill (3)
   K.
10. A. Test B. Trial C. Compete
    (1) 3/4 date pace (2) Over (3) Under
11. Hill interval A. 110 B. 220 C.
12. With coach (A) Bill B. (B) Bill D. (C)
14. A. Wind sprint B. Hurdle drill
    C. Spring and bound D.
15. Finish work
16. Acrobatics or apparatus
17. 3/4 effort
18. Regular steeplechase course D. 3/4 mi.
19.
20. Secondary event
21. A. Pictures B. Film

M	2A(2)
T	4x 4x 4x 5E-5HD-2B(1)-9I(3)
W	2B(2)
T	6C-2B(1)-6C
F	1A
S	4x 10B(Mile)-1A-9I(4)
S	2B(3)
M	2A(2)
T	6x 6x 5D-2B(1)-9I(3)
W	2B(2)
T	2x 4x 4x 18D(72)-5G-5E-1A-9I(1)
F	1A
S	6x 5G-2B(2)-9I(4)
S	2B(3)
M	9A-2A(2)
T	4x 4x 6x 5D-5HD-1A-9I(3)
W	2A(4)
T	4x 4x 5C-2B(1)-9I(1)
F	1A
S	10C-Fresno
S	2B(4)
M	3x 3x 2x 2x 2x 5HD-5D-2B(1)-5D-5C-9D
T	2B(2)
W	2A(1)
T	5F-5D-5A-1A-5A(2)
F	1A
S	10C
S	2B(4)

Figure 3.5e Steeplechase Training Schedule

Steeplechase NAME DATE April

1. A. Light jogging B.
2. Fartlek A. Varied (1) 30 min. (2) 45 min.
   B. Steady (1) 2-4 mi. (2) 4-6 mi. (3) 7-10 mi.
   (4) 12-15 mi.
3. Weight program
4. High knee and power run
5. Intervals
   A. 110 (1) 18-16-14 (2) 17-15-13
   B. 165 (1) 25 (2)
   C. 220 (1) 35 (2)
   D. 330 (1) 52 (2) 48 (3) 45 (4)
   E. 440 (1) 70-73 (2)
   F. 660 (1) 75 (2) 72 (3) 68 (4)
   G. 880 (1) 72-75 (2) 68-70 (3)
   I. 3/4 (1) 72-75 (2) 69-71 (3)
   J. Mile (1) 72-75 (2) 69-72 (3)
   K.
   L.
5. H. Same interval as above with hurdles
6. Sets A. 660-440-330-220-110
   (1) 1:45-68-49-32-15 (2)
   B. 440-660-440-220 (1) 64 (2) 62
   C. 660-330-110 D. 330-220-110
7. Squad meeting
8. Special A. Sauna B. Swim C.
9. Drills A. Hurdle; X drill (1) 30 in. (2) 36 in. (3) Water barrier
   B. 165 sprint-float-sprint
   C. 165 middle 1-step accelerate
   D. Last 165 (WJ & hurdle) (1) 220
   E. Intermediate hurdles (1) 165 (2) 220 (3) 440
   F. 3 mi.-4 hurdles (1) 90 (2) 85 (3) 80 (4)
   G. 40-30 drill (1) 4 laps (2) 6 (3)
   H. 70-90 drill (1) 1-1 (2) 2-1 (3) 3-1 (4)
   I. Cut-downs (1) 110 (2) 165 (3) 220 (4) 330
   (5) 440 (6) 880 (7)
   J. Simulate race drill (1) 1st 880-last 880
   (2) 10 mi.-3/4 drill (3) 4 mi. at 80 pace
   K.
10. A. Test B. Trial C. Compete
    (1) 3/4 date pace (2) Over (3) Under
11. Hill interval A. 110 B. 220 C.
12. With coach (A) Bill B. (B) Bill D. (C)
14. A. Wind sprint B. Hurdle drill
    C. Spring and bound D.
15. Finish work
16. Acrobatics or apparatus
17. 3/4 effort
18. Regular steeplechase course A. 3/4 mi.
19.
20. Secondary event
21. A. Pictures B. Film

M	2A(2)
T	6B(2)
W	2B(2)
T	2x 2x 2x 2x 5I-5HG-5E-9D(1)
F	1A
S	6x 9E(3)-2B(3)-9I(3)
S	2B(3)

M	2A(2)
T	2x 3x 3x 18A-5G-9I(5)-1A-9E(2)
W	7-2B(2)
T	6C-1A-6D
F	1A
S	10C
S	2B(4)

M	9A-2A(2)
T	3x 3x 3x 5HD-9I(6)-2B(1)-5HD
W	4x 2B(2)-9I(1)
T	9J(3)-9D(1)-9D-5A
F	2B(1)-5A(2)
S	1A
S	10C-Twilight meet

M	2B(3)
T	2x 4x 2x 2x 5HG-9I(5)-2B(1)-9D(1)-9C
W	2B(2)
T	2x 2x 2x 2x 5D-5C-5A-2B(1)-5A
F	1A
S	10C-Washington
S	2B(3)

Figure 3.5f Steeplechase Training Schedule

Steeplechase NAME DATE *May*

1. A. Light jogging B. *1–3 miles*
2. Fartlek A. Varied (1) 30 min. (2) *45 min.*
   B. Steady (1) 2-4 mi. (2) 4-6 mi. (3) 7-10 mi.
   (4) *12–15 mi.* *(5) 8–12 mi easy*
3. Weight program
4. High knee and power run
5. Intervals
   A. 110 (1) 18-16-14 (2) 17-15-13
   B. 165 (1) 25 (2)
   C. 220 (1) 35 (2) *32*
   D. 330 (1) 52 (2) 48 (3) 45 (4) *46*
   E. 440 (1) 70-73 (2) *62 (3) hurdles in 68*
   F. 660 (1) 75 (2) 72 (3) 68 (4)
   G. 880 (1) 72-75 (2) 68-70 (3) *64 (4) hurdles in 70*
   I. 3/4 (1) 72-75 (2) 69-71 (3)
   J. Mile (1) 72-75 (2) 69-72 (3)
   K.
   L.
5. H. Same interval as above with hurdles
6. Sets A. 660-440-330-220-110
   (1) 1:45-68-49-32-15 (2)
   B. 440-660-440-220 (1) 64 (2)
   C.
7. Squad meeting
8. Special A. Sauna B. Swim C.
9. Drills A. Hurdle; X drill (1) 30 in. (2) 36 in. *(3) Water barrier*
   B. 165 sprint-float-sprint
   C. 165 middle 1-step accelerate
   D. Last 165 (WJ & hurdle) *(1) 220*
   E. Intermediate hurdles (1) 165 (2) 220
   F. 3 mi.–4 hurdles (1) 90 (2) 85 (3) 80 (4)
   G. 40-30 drill (1) 4 laps (2) 6 (3)
   H. 70-90 drill (1) 1-1 (2) 2-1 (3) 3-1 (4)
   I. Cut-downs (1) 110 (2) 165 (3) 220 (4) 330
   (5) 440 (6) 880 (7)
   J. Simulate race drill (1) 1st 880-last 880
   (2) 10 mi.-3/4 drill (3)
   K. *Pace over 4 hurdles per 440*
10. A. Test B. Trial C. Compete
    (1) 3/4 date pace (2) Over (3) Under
11. Hill interval A. 110 B. 220 C.
12. With coach (A) Bill B. (B) Bill D. (C)
14. A. Wind sprint B. Hurdle drill
    C. Spring and bound D.
15. Finish work
16. Acrobatics or apparatus
17. 3/4 effort
18. *Regular steeplechase course*
19.
20. Secondary event
21. A. Pictures B. Film

M	*2A(2)*
T	*3X 9I(6)–3X 9I(5)–3X 9I(3)–2B(1)–3X 9I(3)*
W	*2B(2)*
T	*2X 9E(2)–2B(1)–2X 9D(1)*
F	*1A*
S	*Mile trial*
S	*2B(3)*

M	*2A(2)*
T	*5G(3)–9K(880 in 2:20) 5G(3)–5D(4)– 9K(330 in 51)–5D(4)–2A*
W	*2B(2)*
T	*6X 5C(2)–2B(1) 2X 5C (water barrier + 1 hurdle)*
F	*Light*
S	*10C – Northern Division meet*
S	*2B(5)*

	A.M.	P.M.
M	*2B(1)*	*2A(2)*
T	*Light*	*9K(880 in 2:20)–3X 9I(5)(66-64-62)–1A–3X 9I(4)(49-47-45)*
W	*Light*	*2X 9(3)–1A*
T	*Travel*	*Light grass*
F		*10C – Pac 8 Meet*
S		*Light grass – 8X 5A*
S		*2B(5)*

Day	A.M.	P.M.
M	*2B(1)*	*2A (2)*
T	*2B(1)*	*6X 5E(2)–2A(1)–6X 9I(4)*
W	*2B(1)*	*2B(2)*
T	*Light*	*4X 5G(3-4)–4X 5E(2-3)–4X 9I(3)(33-31-29-27)*
F	*Light*	*Light*
S		*3X 9I(4)(hurdles in 52-50-48)–2B(3)–3X 9I(4)(48-45-42)*
S		

Figure 3.5g Steeplechase Training Schedule

Steeplechase NAME DATE June

1. A. Light jogging B.
2. Fartlek A. Varied (1) 30 min. (2)
   B. Steady (1) 2-4 mi. (2) 4-6 mi. (3) 7-10 mi. (4)
3. Weight program
4. High knee and power run
5. Intervals
   A. 110 (1) 18-16-14 (2) 17-15-13
   B. 165 (1) 25 (2)
   C. 220 (1) 35 (2) 27
   D. 330 (1) 52 (2) 48 (3) 45 (4) 51 over hurdles
   E. 440 (1) 70-73 (2)
   F. 660 (1) 75 (2) 72 (3) 68 (4)
   G. 880 (1) 72-75 (2) 68-70 (3)
   I. 3/4 (1) 72-75 (2) 69-71 (3)
   J. Mile (1) 72-75 (2) 69-72 (3)
   K.
   L.
5. H. Same interval as above with hurdles
6. Sets A. 660-440-330-220-110
   (1) 1:45-68-49-32-15 (2)
   B. 440-660-440-220 (1) 64 (2)
   C.
7. Squad meeting
8. Special A. Sauna B. Swim C.
9. Drills A. Hurdle; X drill (1) 30 in. (2) 36 in.
   B. 165 sprint-float-sprint
   C. 165 middle 1-step accelerate
   D. Last 165 (WJ & hurdle)
   E. Intermediate hurdles (1) 165 (2) 220
   F. 3 mi.–4 hurdles (1) 90 (2) 85 (3) 80 (4)
   G. 40-30 drill (1) 4 laps (2) 6 (3)
   H. 70-90 drill (1) 1-1 (2) 2-1 (3) 3-1 (4)
   I. Cut-downs (1) 110 (2) 165 (3) 220 (4) 330 (5) 440 (6) 880 (7)
   J. Simulate race drill (1) 1st 880-last 880 (2) 10 mi.-3/4 drill (3) 6 laps – 80 sec. pace
   K.
10. A. Test B. Trial C. Compete
    (1) 3/4 date pace (2) Over (3) Under
11. Hill interval A. 110 B. 220 C.
12. With coach (A) Bill B. (B) Bill D. (C)
14. A. Wind sprint B. Hurdle drill
    C. Spring and bound D.
15. Finish work
16. Acrobatics or apparatus
17. 3/4 effort
18.
19.
20. Secondary event
21. A. Pictures B. Film

M	Light	Light grass – 5A(2)
T	Light	5D(4) – 2x 5C(2) – 9J(3)
W	Light	1A
T		10C – Trials – NCAA meet
F		1A
S		10C – Finals – NCAA meet
S		
M		
T		
W		
T		
F		
S		
S		

M	
T	
W	
T	
F	
S	
S	
M	
T	
W	
T	
F	
S	
S	

Racing Tactics

Bolotnikov, Pyotr. "Code of tactical commands," *Track Technique,* No. 28 (June 1967), pp. 875–77.

Kelly, Duane B. "Running indoor curves," *Track Technique,* No. 18 (December 1964), pp. 568–69.

Krüger, Arnd. "Periodization, or peaking at the right time," *Track Technique,* No. 54 (December 1973), pp. 1720–24.

McNab, Tom. "The question of 'peaking,'" *Track Technique,* No. 53 (September 1973), pp. 1691–94.

Rompotti, Kalevi. "Racing tactics," in *International Track and Field Coaching Encyclopedia,* pp. 51–80. West Nyack, N.Y.: Parker Publishing Company, 1970.

Tulloh, Bruce. "Racing strategy," *Track Technique,* No. 49 (September 1972), pp. 1559–60.

Cross Country

Anderson, Bob, and Henderson, Joe. "Cross country's future," *Track and Field Quarterly Review* 72: 162–63.

Ayres, Edward. "Peaking your cross country team for key races," *Scholastic Coach* 38 (October 1968): 28, 30, 48.

Canfield, Harold W. "Speeding up cross country results recording," *Track Technique,* No. 53 (September 1973), pp. 1674–75.

Clark, Marshall. "High school cross country," *Track and Field Quarterly Review*, February 1964, pp. 46–49.

Delavan, Philip. "Cross-country scoring by computer," *Track and Field Quarterly Review* 72: 165–67.

Estes, Gene. "Fartlek variations for cross country training," *Track Technique*, No. 43 (March 1971), pp. 1356–57.

———. "A pre-season cross-country training camp," *Athletic Journal* 48 (May 1968): 14, 82–83.

Francis, Alex. "Cross country training," *Track Technique,* No. 25 (September 1966), pp. 798–99.

Freeman, William H. "Training for cross country," *Scholastic Coach* 37 (April 1968): 34, 36, 93.

Greer, Harvey. "A cross-country recruiting film," *Scholastic Coach* 38 (January 1969): 54, 84–85.

Jones, Ralph E. "Promoting interest in cross country," *Scholastic Coach* 39 (April 1970): 72, 74.

Lumian, Norman C. "Promoting cross country," *Scholastic Coach* 30 (September 1960): 42, 44, 60–63.

Matthews, Reginald S., and Torrance, Dale H. "The need for cross country in physical education," *Athletic Journal* 41 (September 1960): 26, 82.

Newton, Joe, and Schindl, Karl. *The Long Green Line: Championship High School Cross Country*. Oak Brook, Ill.: All American Publishing Company, 1969. 210 pp.

Osborne, Robert, and Jones, Alan, "Computerized cross country scoring and timing," *Track Technique*, No. 45 (September 1971), pp. 1430–31.

Rosandich, Thomas. "Easing cross country race administration," *Track Technique*, No. 50 (December 1972), pp. 1590–91.

Schmidt, Verlyn J. "Conducting a cross country clinic," *Track and Field Quarterly Review* 72: 168–75.

Van Deventer, Don. "Common characteristics of cross country training programs," *Track and Field Quarterly Review* 71: 158–65.

Steeplechase

Elliott, Charles. "Steeplechase: technical analysis," *Track and Field Quarterly Review* 72: 1306–07.

Huntsman, Stan. "The distance training of Doug Brown," *Track and Field Quarterly Review* 73 (September 1973): 178–79.

Kressler, Raymond. "Rider College steeplechase clinic," *Track and Field Quarterly Review* 71: 35–38.

Saunders, Tony. "Steeplechase technique and training," *Track Technique*, No. 35 (March 1969), pp. 1102–3.

Watts, Denis. "Hints on steeplechasing," *Track Technique*, No. 41 (September 1970), pp. 1306–7.

Werner, Chick. "The steeplechase," in *Track in Theory and Technique,* pp. 201–11. Richmond, Calif.: Worldwide Publishing Co., 1962.

two

The Sprints and the Hurdles

The short sprints and relays

Perhaps the first thing which the prospective sprinter should keep in mind is that training is not a "sometime" thing. Sprint training requires the same training consistency that any other event requires. Several general principles of training should be kept in mind. First, the training should be full time, in the sense that it should continue throughout the year, as opposed to training only for four to six months of the year. Second, the athlete's fitness should be raised to a high level and maintained at that level throughout the year. Third, the "hard-easy" principle is perhaps the most conducive to long-term progress (the hard-easy principle is the use of a recovery day of "light" training following each day of "hard" training). Fourth, the athlete should train *to* the competition, trying to improve *gradually* in three-quarter-effort trials. He should *not* be trying to sprint full out in trials, because a sprinter can get into top shape very quickly, compared to other competitors, and the athlete does not want to reach this level of performance until the competitive season has begun. Finally, outside influences upon the athlete must be considered. The coach must help his athletes to set up and understand their priorities while they are competing for a school team. The first priority is, and must always be, to graduate. The athlete's academic work must *always* take precedence. Hopefully, the next order of business will be preparation for athletic competition. Much of an athlete's eventual achievement will depend upon how good he wants to be and how much he *is willing to work* to succeed. Hopefully the coach will exert a good influence on the athlete in helping him to determine his priorities.

Sprinters are recruited by testing candidates over a 40-yard course, with anyone running 5.2 seconds or less being a prospect. Sprinters are not picked by size or body build. They come in all sizes, including very short, and all shapes, occasionally including round. While sprinters may be "born" to the event, they do not fit an easily defined mold.

Training Methods for the Sprint

Training is begun in the fall with group workouts, changing over to individual schedules after the start of the new year. The fall program consists of conditioning and technique workouts two or three days a week. There is also a program of hill running one day a week, beginning with six 40-yard runs up a moderately steep hill. The sprinter concentrates his thoughts on his arm drive and knee lift. He does *not* go full effort. The hill run is lengthened by 10 yards per week, until the athletes are running 6 × 90 yards up the hill. They can then go to 6 × 40–60 yards at seven-eighths effort. The whole workout will consist of a mile jog to the golf course, the hill training session, a mile jog back to the track, then four medium-effort sprints of 55 or 110 yards.

There is also some sort of test effort every two weeks. This is partly to give the runner experience at his race, though they are rarely run too fast. Usually there will be several races at one-half to three-quarters effort. There may also be underdistance or overdistance runs, such as 60, 100, 220, 300, and 440 yards for 100- and 220-runners. Athletes running the 440 will occasionally run 300 or 500 yards, and a 385-yard run is a good test for a potential quarter-miler. The fastest effort ever done in practice is three-quarters to nine-tenths effort; the sprinter *never* runs full effort in practice. The risk of injuries, such as pulls, in training is not worth taking.

A helpful practice for the coach is Sunday training sessions. The biggest reason for this practice is to speed the recovery of any Saturday night "party people." If not for this practice, they would do nothing on Sunday, then take Monday and Tuesday to recover, and thus effectively miss most of the practice week, particularly if the competitive season is in full swing.

The sprinters should have a "routine" for beginning their practice sessions. At Oregon, a routine is used which is begun by jogging one or two laps with several other sprinters while practicing the relay pass. The sprinter might work with two or three or even five people. The sprinters jog Indian file (in a straight line), and the runner in the rear starts passing the baton forward. The next runner in the line drops his left hand back, receives the baton, brings it forward, and switches it to his right hand (this will be discussed later in the chapter), then passes it ahead to the next runner in line. When he has passed the baton, he moves out and trots to the head of the line to wait for the baton to reach him again.

The runner will receive the baton with his left hand, so that when the runner behind him has the baton, he will swing his arms back in the regular cadence five times, with the left arm being counts one, three, and five. On the fifth count, the left hand *stays* extended downward and to the rear, awaiting the baton.

After the jogging and relay drill, the athlete will work on the "high knee–fast leg" drill. This is a two-part drill, done preferably on a grass or sawdust surface. The high knee drill is done slowly and is used to exercise the small groin muscles. The runner will jog either in place or slowly across the grass, moving on the toes and lifting the knee until the thigh is parallel to the ground, then dropping his foot back to the grass. The knees are not lifted beyond this thigh-parallel-to-the-ground position because that is as high as the knees ever go in normal sprinting. Any more stretching simply risks injury. The fast leg drill is done next, and it *is* done fast. The arms are moved very quickly, as in a sprint race, and the feet are sprinting in place, but they are just barely lifted off the ground. The faster the arms move in sprinting, the faster the legs move. There is a similar drill in football.

The warm-up routine is concluded by having the sprinters go through two to four easy starts. These are done very easily and are primarily designed to give the sprinters more starts without imposing any additional strain.

For training sessions, the track is marked with pegs at 55-yard intervals. The 110s are run from the middle of the turn to the middle of the straight. When told to run 13 to 15 seconds, the athlete should run progressively from the slower to the faster time, as in 4 × 110 in 13 to 15 seconds (run 15, 14, 13.5, 13). After a long run, the sprinter should run several 55s. These are not hard or fast runs. The long runs for the sprinters are usually 2 to 3 miles. To gain real benefits from an overdistance run, the athlete must raise his pulse rate to at least 150 beats per minute and hold it at that level for at least 7 minutes. Because of the variability of fall and winter weather, a whole pattern may be changed to take advantage of a good day. If the weather conditions permit nothing else, the runners can jog in the hallways.

Weight training is also beneficial to the sprinter. At this point we will simply mention that most runners who have been very successful have done some sort of weight training. At Oregon it is not assigned, but it is recommended that athletes develop their own programs. An example might be the training done by Oregon's Harry Jerome, whose weight workouts were as follows:

Exercise	*Repetitions*	*Sets*	*Times per week*
Military press	6	2	3
Half or quarter squats	6	2	2
Bench press	6	2	3
Sit-ups	15	2	3
Pullovers (bent or straight)	6	2	3
Dead lift (bent leg)	6	2	2

The sprinters today will also do a step-up lunge onto a 24-inch bench while carrying weights.

The athlete's equipment is perhaps as important as his training. The lighter the uniform is, the better the runner will perform. Fat is useful only for keeping him warm and aiding in his recovery period. A shoe is needed which is sturdy, comfortable, and light. A sweat shirt with a hood is the only practical kind for practice sessions. Cotton long johns, dyed in a school color, are better than regular sweat pants. They are not bulky, and can be worn either over or under the running shorts. They will last about a year. Competition gear should be light and comfortable. Some runners do not wear socks, or wear them only in cold weather or practice sessions. This is largely a matter of personal preference.

The athlete should *not* train if he has a cold or other sickness or infection. An athlete with a cold can return to hard training, fully recovered, in about six days, *if* the cold is cared for. If the cold is not cared for, and the athlete continues to train, it may linger for weeks. If the ailment is physical, such as an injury of some sort, the athlete should be cared for in the training room, then get out on the track.

There are many outside influences which the athlete should try to avoid, although not all outside activities are bad ones. The best influence, from the team's standpoint, is to have a strong team esprit de corps. Many students go "down the drain" every year, unfortunately. This number decreased when the draft boards were most active. Some students do not want to be the only ones to flunk out of school, so they will "recruit" others to flunk out, to go partying, or to enter the army with them. Many cases can be found of such a person handicapping other students who are easily led. Some athletes will meet "hangers-on" who want to be seen with them, consequently taking the athlete to places or situations which are detrimental to him. Parties are always great to have, but they should not be too big, nor should they be planned before there is anything to celebrate. Above all, the athlete must have *dedication* and *perseverance.* An athlete must be a champion *every* day if he expects to be one *one* day.

The activities on the days of meets need to be considered also. For a dual meet held on a Saturday, the sprinters will train on Monday and Wednesday, going light on Thursday and Friday. If the meet begins at 1:30 P.M., the squad meets to eat together between 8:30 and 9 A.M. It does not really matter what the meal is, since it is too early to affect the meet. The athlete might have a small steak, a cup of tea, some Jell-O, and a cup of bouillon. A cup of tea and some toast might be the best meal, but many athletes are too "psyched" to limit themselves to this. The primary function of this meal, however, is to get the athletes up and functioning. The athletes will dress about an hour and a half before they run. They will be out for the warm-up an hour before the race; the warm-up will conclude about fifteen minutes before the meet begins. They might do striding on the grass or sawdust, running perhaps a 110, 165, 220 at an easy pace. When time for the race comes, they will jog a bit, set the blocks, and go.

For a conference meet, the procedure depends upon the schedule of the

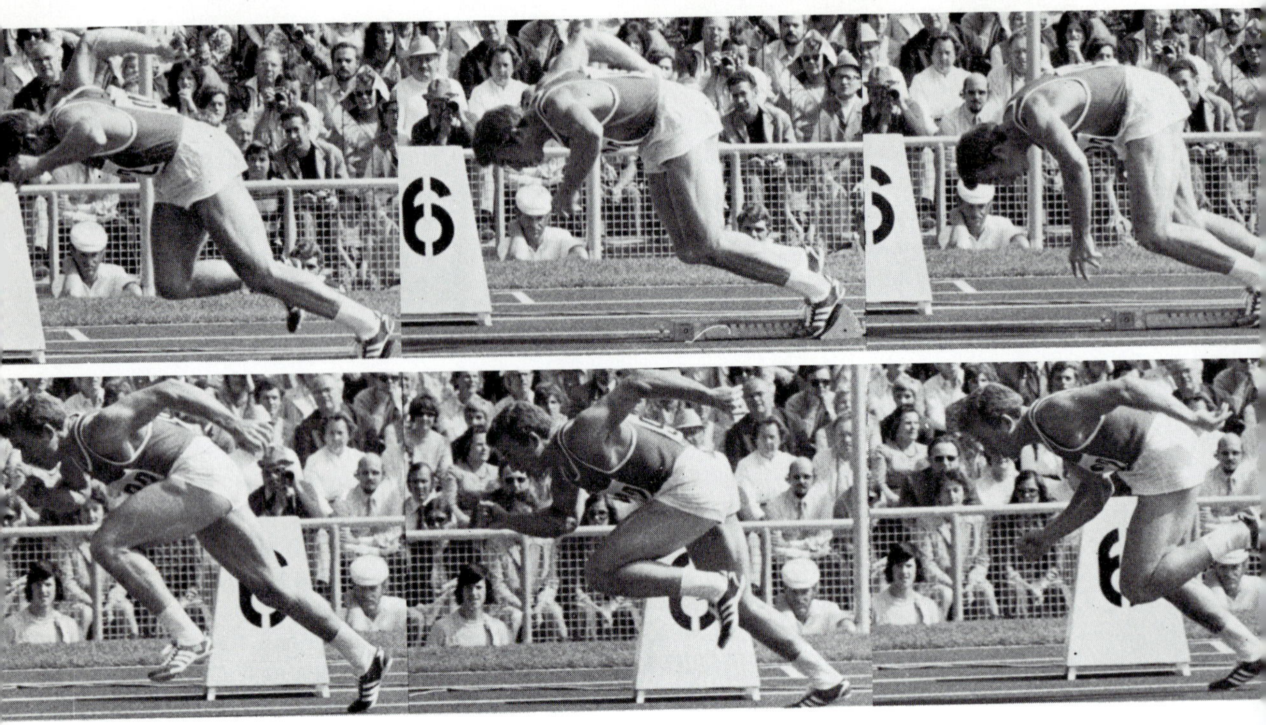

Photographs 4.1*a-l* Valeriy Borzov, U.S.S.R., champion in the 100 and 200 meters.

meet. The athlete may run on two consecutive afternoons. There may be morning trials, however, in which case the team may get up at 6 A.M., if the race is at 10 A.M. For a national meet, where the sprinter might have to run three days in a row, he will try to have his meals no later than four hours before the race. If there is ample time between races, he should have liquids or toast, but nothing which is slow to digest. Almost no training should be done during the week before the conference or NCAA meets, beyond taking a few starts and some passing of the baton.

Starting Techniques for the Sprint

A good start is essential to successful sprinting. There are three types of starts, each named for the position of the sprinter's feet relative to each other. The "bunch" start has the feet close together, bunched up, and the athlete tends to be close to the starting line. With the "medium" start, the feet are a bit farther apart, and the man is not quite so close to the line. With the "elongated" start, the feet are not close together, and the sprinter is not at all crowding the starting line.

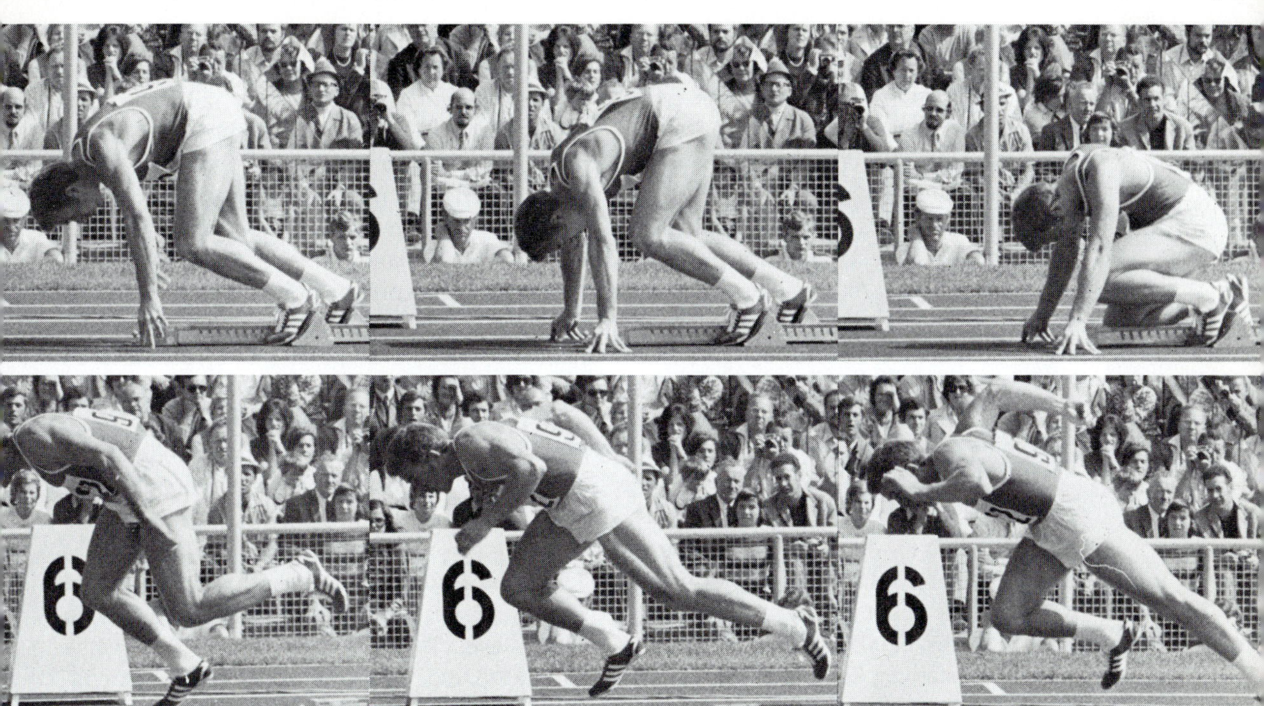

Some athletes like to use the bunch start because they believe it gives the quickest start. Research has shown that while the bunch start is fastest off the blocks for about 30 yards, it is *not* the fastest for the whole race. Most often the medium start results in the fastest time for the entire race. All the same, the block settings are very much a personal matter with sprinters. Jesse Owens used a bunch start, with the front block set a scant 8 inches from the line and the rear block another foot to the rear, or 20 inches from the line. This was in the days when the bunch start was believed to be the best, which might have been the reason for this setting. Bobby Morrow, triple gold medal winner at the 1956 Olympics, set his front block 21 inches from the line and his rear block another 14 inches back, or 35 inches from the line. This is more between the medium and elongated starting positions. Armin Hary, first man to run 10.0 for the metric short sprint, set his front block at 23 inches and his rear block 10 inches farther back, or 33 inches from the line.

For figuring out each athlete's settings, experimentation in practice is necessary. The blocks might first be set at a 15-inch and 15-inch spacing, or 15 inches from the line to the first block and 30 inches to the rear block. The position of the hands should be marked, so they will become as standard as the block settings. They need to be wide enough for the legs to come through without hindrance, but not so wide that the sprinter's first move will be to fall on his chin. The athlete should take starts at many different settings. When a few seem to be the most advantageous, he should run some timed starts for 30 or 40 yards from each of those settings to learn which actually is fastest for him. The athlete should *not* be told the times until the tests are completed, otherwise he might subconsciously "prove" a setting to be better in relation to the others than it really is, simply because he believes the setting is faster.

The commands of the starter are "on your marks," "set," and then the gun is fired. At the command of "on your marks," the sprinter gets into his down position on the blocks, setting himself to the starting position. His hips should be about 4 inches higher than the shoulders, and the angle at the knee should be about 110 degrees. The athlete should not try to anticipate the gun (which leads to false starts), but he should have practiced reacting to *any* sharp sound.

When the gun is fired, the athlete should concentrate on getting the back leg out and down. This was the practice of Harry Jerome, who ran 9.2 and 10.0 for world records at Oregon. Though he did not concentrate on driving off the rear block with his back leg, he did drive with the leg in actual practice. The chest is driven upward and out. If the left foot is forward in the blocks, then the left hand is thrust forward as the right leg is brought out of the rear block. While leaving the blocks, the hips are kept relatively level. They should not rise or fall while starting. Each athlete will have his own little idiosyncrasies, so he must work constantly to master his own style.

Running the Sprint

When the sprinter is in full stride and clear of the blocks, his upper body will be relatively erect, rather than leaning forward. Though this statement might seem questionable, photographic studies of Olympic runners have proven its validity. In this erect position, the athlete can more easily raise his knees and reach out with his feet. This will enable him to lengthen his stride. The arms swing roughly from hip level to shoulder level. If they are swung higher than this, there is a tendency for the runner's strides to be shorter. Usually the faster the arms move, the faster the legs will move. The sprinter should keep on his toes and run with a high knee action, as practiced in the high knee drill. If he tends to toe out (putting the feet down pointing at an angle toward the side of the track, which is a weaker driving position than when the toes point straight ahead in the running direction), practicing running along a straight line can help to correct this. The head should be kept up at all times facing the birds, rather than forward parallel to the ground or rolled back.

Relaxation is extremely important in sprinting. All great sprinters have it, and it can be taught. The shoulders and hands need to be relaxed, for they can cause the runner to tense his upper body. If the shoulders and hands are tense, the arms will move more slowly, consequently slowing down the leg speed. Many runners have been taught to judge their relaxation by whether or not the jaw is relaxed, since it will seem to be flopping or bouncing along when relaxed. One good exercise for learning to relax while sprinting can be done by running 165s. The first 55 yards will be worked hard, then the next 55 yards will be "floated," then the last 55 yards will again be worked hard. The runner should try to run the floated 55 within a tenth of a second as fast as the worked 55s. The object is to develop the ability to relax and float for a while in a race with little or no real slowing down of the running speed.

Finally, the sprinter should finish well. He should learn to reach out for the tape with a properly timed lean or lunge. Some runners will use a quick "dip" toward the tape, others will lunge toward it, while still others will lunge and at the same time turn the shoulder for additional reach toward the tape. The timing is crucial at this point, requiring considerable practice. In all cases, the sprinter should sprint *through* the tape, continuing on for about 10 yards. The primary reason for this is that many runners are subconsciously slowing down as they approach the tape, when they should be moving strongly through it.

Relay Techniques and Training

The relays are very tactical races, even though they are run at top speed. The placement of personnel in a 440-yard relay may be done on the basis of several considerations. They might be placed by their best sprinting times. The best starter might be the first runner. The poorest receiver in the group might be the first runner. A runner with more endurance than the others might take the first leg, which tends to be the longest, just as the runner with the least endurance might be made anchor man, having the shortest run. Some runners perform better around a turn than do others. There are many situations of personal strengths and weaknesses of runners which must be considered. The fastest runner might be put in the third leg, to upset the opponents by what appears to be a sudden breakthrough. Some teams run better from in front than behind, which might be a reason to start the fastest runner first. The sprinters should be timed around a turn to find which ones are fastest. They should be timed twice at this, once starting from a down position and once from a stand. Some athletes are faster with a running start than they are from a crouch.

With a sprint relay the underhand or "blind" hand-off is used. There has been considerable discussion over the idea of switching the baton from one hand to the other while running, as opposed to keeping it in the same hand throughout the run. At Oregon, the baton is still switched over, and for a very good reason. A relay team must practice together often. The athletes have other races to run, though, and occasionally one of the regulars will not be able to run on the relay. So a different person goes into his spot, and if the man is not as practiced at the technique, or if he is not used to his position in the sequence of passes, a pass is missed.

Instead, we use the inside pass. The athlete receives the baton with his left hand and switches it to his right hand as he runs. He passes from his right hand

Photograph 4.2*a-d* The French relay team demonstrates the underhand hand-off.

into the next runner's left hand. The receiver is in the outside of the lane, which allows him to move at more of a straight angle into the turn. Successful relay racing is the result of repeated practice and precision. One Oregon team which used this technique set a world record for the 440-yard relay around two turns of 40.0, though three of the men were hurdlers.

The warm-up routine, which includes relay practice, has already been described. For further practice on the relay, the regular team members will work on the passes using two check marks, one called "lean" and the other called "go." Practice will begin with the first check 5 yards before the relay zone and the other check 5 yards before that, or 10 yards out. The passer and receiver will run through the hand-off at half speed on this round. When the runner with the baton hits the first mark, 10 yards from the passing zone, the receiver will lean forward, preparatory to running. When he hits the second mark, 5 yards away, the receiver will begin his own sprint. The same five-count arm swing will be

Figure 4.1a Short Sprint Training Schedule

Short Sprint NAME DATE September/October

1. A. Jog 1 or 2 laps with relay pass B. High knee (slow) and fast leg
2. Fartlek: A. Holmer (varied-pace)—stride, sprint, recover—stride, meet a challenge or challenge, recover. Finish feeling exhilarated, not exhausted.
   B. Lydiard (steady pace)—slow, 10-30 min. (1) Hendricks (2) Golf course (3)
3. A. Weights and jogging—get chart B. Jogging and stretching
4. High knee and fast leg
5. Starts A. 3 at 1/2 speed, 3 at 7/8—30 yds.
   (1) On your own (2) Gun
   B. 50 yds. C. Grass D.
6. Intervals Y. Fast 20-55 in middle A. 110
   (1) 18-16-14 (2)
   B. 165 (1) 22 (2)
   C. 220 (1) 30 (2)
   D. 110-220-110 (1)
   E.
7. Squad meeting
8. Special A. Sauna B. Swim C.
9. Relay work A. Routine B. 55 C. Trial
10. A. Trial B. Compete
11. Bunches A. 330 B. 165 C. 80
12. Hill with: A. Coach B. Leader
14. A. Wind sprints B. Hurdle drill C. Spring and bound
    D. Alternate run and jog, at least 880
15. Finish work—50-70 at 3/4—last 30-50 at 9/10
    A. 100 B. 220
16. Back to back A. 55 B.
17. 3/4 effort A. 100 B. 300 C. 500
18.
19.
20.
21. A. Pictures B. Film
22. A. 100 yds. at 8/10—float at 70 (3 steps), then go
    B. 220 C. Parts
23. A. 550-330-110 (80-48-14) B. 300-200-100 (1)
    C. 165-110-55
24. Turn work (40 at 9/10) (30 at 1/2) (40 at 9/10)

Date	Dist.	3/4	Date P.	Goal P.

M	7-Organization-equipment-lockers
T	Meet on use of weights
W	7 Discussion of facilities-14A
T	3A
F	1A-1B-2A(1)
S	Registration completed
S	recreation
M	1B-23A-6A(1) 2x-880 jog
T	
W	12B-6A(1) 2x
T	
F	10A-200 meters at 7/8 effort to 9/10 effort
S	
S	
M	1A-23A-6A(1) 2x-jog 880
T	3A
W	12B
T	3A
F	1A-11ABC 2x-6B(1)
S	
S	
M	1A-1B-23A-6B 3x-6A-2B(1)
T	3A
W	12B
T	
F	10A—100 and 300
S	
S	

Figure 4.1b Short Sprint Training Schedule

Short Sprint NAME DATE *October/November*

1. A. Jog 1 or 2 laps with relay pass B. High knee (slow) and fast leg
2. Fartlek: A. Holmer (varied-pace)—stride, sprint, recover—stride, meet a challenge or challenge, recover. Finish feeling exhilarated, not exhausted.
   B. Lydiard (steady pace)—slow, 10-30 min. (1) Hendricks (2) Golf course (3)
3. A. Weights and jogging—get chart B. Jogging and stretching
4. High knee and fast leg
5. Starts A. 3 at 1/2 speed, 3 at 7/8—30 yds.
   (1) On your own (2) Gun
   B. 50 yds. C. Grass D.
6. Intervals Y. Fast 20-55 in middle A. 110
   (1) 18-16-14 (2)
   B. 165 (1) 22 (2)
   C. 220 (1) 30 (2)
   D. 110-220-110 (1)
   E.
7. Squad meeting
8. Special A. Sauna B. Swim C.
9. Relay work A. Routine B. 55 C. Trial
10. A. Trial B. Compete
11. Bunches A. 330 B. 165 C. 80
12. Hill with: A. Coach B. Leader
14. A. Wind sprints B. Hurdle drill C. Spring and bound
    D. Alternate run and jog, at least 880
15. Finish work—50-70 at 3/4—last 30-50 at 9/10
    A. 100 B. 220
16. Back to back A. 55 B.
17. 3/4 effort A. 100 B. 300 C. 500
18.
19.
20.
21. A. Pictures B. Film
22. A. 100 yds. at 8/10—float at 70 (3 steps), then go
    B. 220 C. Parts
23. A. 550-330-110 (80-48-14) B. 300-200-100 (1)
    C. 165-110-55
24. Turn work (40 at 9/10) (30 at 1/2) (40 at 9/10)

Date	Dist.	3/4	Date P.	Goal P.

M	*1B–5A–21A–23A–6C (2x)–2B(1)*
T	*3A–21B*
W	*12B–6A (2x)(1)*
T	*3A*
F	*300y (2x)–100y (4x)–2A(1)*
S	*1A–1B*
S	

M	*1A–5A–23A–6A (4x)–2A(1)*
T	*3A–21B*
W	*12B–6A(1)*
T	
F	*100y (10x)*
S	*10A–300 yards*
S	

M	*1A–5A–500y (1x)–300y (2x)–200y (3x)–100y (4x)–2A(1)*
T	*3B–21B*
W	*12*
T	*3A*
F	*100y (10x) (sets of 4-4-2)–2A(1)*
S	
S	

M	*1A–5A–23A–6B (3x)–10A(1)*
T	*3A*
W	*12–6B (3x)*
T	
F	*10A–100y and relay*
S	*10A–Relay and 300y*
S	*recreation*

Figure 4.1c Short Sprint Training Schedule

Short Sprint NAME DATE November/December

1. A. Jog 1 or 2 laps with relay pass B. High knee (slow) and fast leg
2. Fartlek: A. Holmer (varied-pace)—stride, sprint, recover—stride, meet a challenge or challenge, recover. Finish feeling exhilarated, not exhausted.
   B. Lydiard (steady pace)—slow, 10-30 min. (1) Hendricks (2) Golf course (3)
3. A. Weights and jogging—get chart B. Jogging and stretching
4. High knee and fast leg
5. Starts A. 3 at 1/2 speed, 3 at 7/8—30 yds.
   (1) On your own (2) Gun
   B. 50 yds. C. Grass D.
6. Intervals Y. Fast 20-55 in middle A. 110
   (1) 18-16-14 (2)
   B. 165 (1) 22 (2)
   C. 220 (1) 30 (2)
   D. 110-220-110 (1)
   E.
7. Squad meeting
8. Special A. Sauna B. Swim C.
9. Relay work A. Routine B. 55 C. Trial
10. A. Trial B. Compete
11. Bunches A. 330 B. 165 C. 80
12. Hill with: A. Coach B. Leader
14. A. Wind sprints B. Hurdle drill C. Spring and bound
    D. Alternate run and jog, at least 880
15. Finish work—50-70 at 3/4—last 30-50 at 9/10
    A. 100 B. 220
16. Back to back A. 55 B.
17. 3/4 effort A. 100 B. 300 C. 500
18.
19.
20.
21. A. Pictures B. Film
22. A. 100 yds. at 8/10—float at 70 (3 steps), then go
    B. 220 C. Parts
23. A. 550-330-110 (80-48-14) B. 300-200-100 (1)
    C. 165-110-55
24. Turn work (40 at 9/10) (30 at 1/2) (40 at 9/10)

Date	Dist.	3/4	Date P.	Goal P.

M	1A-1B-6D-23B (2-3X)
T	5A-3A
W	12
T	
F	10A-100 (2X)-300 (1X)-14A
S	
S	2A
M	1A-1B-5A-23B-23C (2-3X)
T	7-3A-21B
W	1-5A-9A-6D-23A
T	
F	10A-Relay (1X)-100 (1X)
S	10A-100 (1X)-300 (1X)
S	
M	
T	
W	
T	
F	
S	
S	
M	
T	
W	
T	
F	
S	
S	

Figure 4.1d Short Sprint Training Schedule

Short Sprint NAME DATE January

1. A. Jog 1 or 2 laps with relay pass B. High knee (slow) and fast leg
2. Fartlek: A. Holmer (varied-pace)—stride, sprint, recover—stride, meet a challenge or challenge, recover. Finish feeling exhilarated, not exhausted.
   B. Lydiard (steady pace)—slow, 10-30 min. (1) Hendricks (2) Golf course (3)
3. A. Weights and jogging—get chart B. Jogging and stretching
4. High knee and fast leg
5. Starts A. 3 at 1/2 speed, 3 at 7/8—30 yds.
   (1) On your own (2) Gun
   B. 50 yds. C. Grass D.
6. Intervals Y. Fast 20-55 in middle A. 110
   (1) 18-16-14 (2)
   B. 165 (1) 22 (2)
   C. 220 (1) 30 (2)
   D. 110-220-110 (1)
   E.
7. Squad meeting
8. Special A. Sauna B. Swim C.
9. Relay work A. Routine B. 55 C. Trial
10. A. Trial B. Compete
11. Bunches A. 330 B. 165 C. 80
12. Hill with: A. Coach B. Leader
14. A. Wind sprints B. Hurdle drill C. Spring and bound
    D. Alternate run and jog, at least 880
15. Finish work—50-70 at 3/4—last 30-50 at 9/10
    A. 100 B. 220
16. Back to back A. 55 B.
17. 3/4 effort A. 100 B. 300 C. 500
18.
19.
20.
21. A. Pictures B. Film
22. A. 100 yds. at 8/10—float at 70 (3 steps), then go
    B. 220 C. Parts
23. A. 550-330-110 (80-48-14) B. 300-200-100 (1)
    C. 165-110-55
24. Turn work (40 at 9/10) (30 at 1/2) (40 at 9/10)

Date	Dist.	3/4	Date P.	Goal P.

M	New Year activities
T	Travel-settle in
W	Register-check equipment-organization
T	3A-14A or jog the halls
F	
S	Relay work or stairs
S	recreation

M	1A-1B-5A-23C-14A (2x over 23C)
T	7-3A-14A
W	12, if no rain. If rain, 1B-5A-9A
T	3A
F	1A-1B-9A
S	
S	

M	1A-23B-23C-2A(1) (2x over 23B)
T	3A-21B
W	1A-12-6A(1) (2x over 12)
T	1A-3A
F	1A-5A-23B-2B(1) (2x over 5A)
S	10A-100-300-2B(1) (1x over 10A, 1x over 300)
S	

M	1A-5A-10A (40 or 60 at 9/10)-1B-14A
T	1A-5A (easy)
W	1A-5A-10A (40 to 60 at 9/10)-2A(1)
T	7 at 4:30 pm
F	Gear ready-jog
S	10A here or 10B-Portland
S	recreation

Figure 4.1e Short Sprint Training Schedule

Short Sprint NAME DATE February

1. A. Jog 1 or 2 laps with relay pass B. High knee (slow) and fast leg
2. Fartlek: A. Holmer (varied-pace)—stride, sprint, recover—stride, meet a challenge or challenge, recover. Finish feeling exhilarated, not exhausted.
   B. Lydiard (steady pace)—slow, 10-30 min. (1) Hendricks (2) Golf course (3)
3. A. Weights and jogging—get chart B. Jogging and stretching
4. High knee and fast leg
5. Starts A. 3 at 1/2 speed, 3 at 7/8—30 yds.
   (1) On your own (2) Gun
   B. 50 yds. C. Grass D.
6. Intervals Y. Fast 20-55 in middle A. 110
   (1) 18-16-14 (2)
   B. 165 (1) 22 (2)
   C. 220 (1) 30 (2)
   D. 110-220-110 (1)
   E.
7. Squad meeting
8. Special A. Sauna B. Swim C.
9. Relay work A. Routine B. 55 C. Trial
10. A. Trial B. Compete
11. Bunches A. 330 B. 165 C. 80
12. Hill with: A. Coach B. Leader
14. A. Wind sprints B. Hurdle drill C. Spring and bound
    D. Alternate run and jog, at least 880
15. Finish work—50-70 at 3/4—last 30-50 at 9/10
    A. 100 B. 220
16. Back to back A. 55 B.
17. 3/4 effort A. 100 B. 300 C. 500
18.
19.
20.
21. A. Pictures B. Film
22. A. 100 yds. at 8/10—float at 70 (3 steps), then go
    B. 220 C. Parts
23. A. 550-330-110 (80-48-14) B. 300-200-100 (1)
    C. 165-110-55
24. Turn work (40 at 9/10) (30 at 1/2) (40 at 9/10)

Date	Dist.	3/4	Date P.	Goal P.

M	2x 4x 1A-1B-14A-5A-6C(2)-6A(2)-14A
T	12
W	1x 2x 6x 1A-1B-300-200-100-14A
T	12 or 1A
F	1x 2x 4x 1A-5A-300-200-100-14A
S	22A or 12
S	grass run or recreation

M	4x 4x 1A-5A-6A(3)-9A-6C(2)-2A(1)
T	3A-14A-7 (5 pm)
W	1A-2B(1)
T	4x 4x 1A-5A-6C(2)-6A(4)-14A
F	3A
S	2A(1)
S	

M	1x 2x 4x 1A-14A-5A-300-200-100-2B(1)
T	3A
W	1A-1B-2B(1)
T	3B
F	1A-9A-9B
S	1x 1x 10A-75y-300y-9A
S	recreation

M	2x 4x 1x 1A-5A-9A-200-100-300
T	3A-2B(1)
W	12
T	9A
F	1A-5A-14A-easy 500y.
S	
S	2B(1)

Figure 4.1f Short Sprint Training Schedule

Short Sprint NAME DATE *March*

1. A. Jog 1 or 2 laps with relay pass B. High knee (slow) and fast leg
2. Fartlek: A. Holmer (varied-pace)—stride, sprint, recover—stride, meet a challenge or challenge, recover. Finish feeling exhilarated, not exhausted.
   B. Lydiard (steady pace)—slow, 10-30 min. (1) Hendricks (2) Golf course (3)
3. A. Weights and jogging—get chart B. Jogging and stretching
4. High knee and fast leg
5. Starts A. 3 at 1/2 speed, 3 at 7/8—30 yds.
   (1) On your own (2) Gun
   B. 50 yds. C. Grass D.
6. Intervals Y. Fast 20-55 in middle A. 110
   (1) 18-16-14 (2)
   B. 165 (1) 22 (2)
   C. 220 (1) 30 (2)
   D. 110-220-110 (1)
   E.
7. Squad meeting
8. Special A. Sauna B. Swim C.
9. Relay work A. Routine B. 55 C. Trial
10. A. Trial B. Compete
11. Bunches A. 330 B. 165 C. 80
12. Hill with: A. Coach B. Leader
14. A. Wind sprints B. Hurdle drill C. Spring and bound
    D. Alternate run and jog, at least 880
15. Finish work—50-70 at 3/4—last 30-50 at 9/10
    A. 100 B. 220
16. Back to back A. 55 B.
17. 3/4 effort A. 100 B. 300 C. 500
18.
19.
20.
21. A. Pictures B. Film
22. A. 100 yds. at 8/10—float at 70 (3 steps), then go
    B. 220 C. Parts
23. A. 550-330-110 (80-48-14) B. 300-200-100 (1)
    C. 165-110-55
24. Turn work (40 at 9/10) (30 at 1/2) (40 at 9/10)

Date	Dist.	3/4	Date P.	Goal P.

M	*3A-4-5A-23B-6D-500 (1x)-2B(1)*
T	*9A-7 (5pm)*
W	*1B-12-6A (4x)*
T	*1A-9A-2A(1)-8C*
F	*Grass run*
S	*10A-Relay-300y (1x)*
S	*recreation*

M	*1B-5A-23B-6D-2A(1)*
T	*9A-2-7 (5pm)*
W	*1A-4-2B(1)-6A(1) (2x)*
T	*21-9A*
F	*1A-5A-6C-6A (4x)-9A-2 (grass)*
S	*Exams start-9A-grass*
S	

M	*Exams-easy workout-2B*
T	*Relay in pairs-14A*
W	*1A-5A (if no exams)-2B(1)*
T	
F	*Gear ready*
S	*Travel-10B-100 and/or 220*
S	*Jog and settle in-spring trip*

Day	A.M.	P.M.
M	*Jog*	*1A-5A-11ABC (2x)-grass*
T	*14A*	*9A-23A-2B*
W	*Jog*	*1A-5A-6A (4x)-500 (1x)-2*
T	*14A*	*9A-2*
F		*Light and swim*
S	*10B-Meet and bus home*	
S		

Figure 4.1g Short Sprint Training Schedule

Short Sprint NAME DATE April

1. A. Jog 1 or 2 laps with relay pass B. High knee (slow) and fast leg
2. Fartlek: A. Holmer (varied-pace)—stride, sprint, recover—stride, meet a challenge or challenge, recover. Finish feeling exhilarated, not exhausted.
   B. Lydiard (steady pace)—slow, 10-30 min. (1) Hendricks (2) Golf course (3)
3. A. Weights and jogging—get chart B. Jogging and stretching
4. High knee and fast leg
5. Starts A. 3 at 1/2 speed, 3 at 7/8—30 yds.
   (1) On your own (2) Gun
   B. 50 yds. C. Grass D.
6. Intervals Y. Fast 20-55 in middle A. 110
   (1) 18-16-14 (2)
   B. 165 (1) 22 (2)
   C. 220 (1) 30 (2)
   D. 110-220-110 (1)
   E.
7. Squad meeting
8. Special A. Sauna B. Swim C.
9. Relay work A. Routine B. 55 C. Trial
10. A. Trial B. Compete
11. Bunches A. 330 B. 165 C. 80
12. Hill with: A. Coach B. Leader
14. A. Wind sprints B. Hurdle drill C. Spring and bound
    D. Alternate run and jog, at least 880
15. Finish work—50-70 at 3/4—last 30-50 at 9/10
    A. 100 B. 220
16. Back to back A. 55 B.
17. 3/4 effort A. 100 B. 300 C. 500
18.
19.
20.
21. A. Pictures B. Film
22. A. 100 yds. at 8/10—float at 70 (3 steps), then go
    B. 220 C. Parts
23. A. 550-330-110 (80-48-14) B. 300-200-100 (1)
    C. 165-110-55
24. Turn work (40 at 9/10) (30 at 1/2) (40 at 9/10)

Date	Dist.	3/4	Date P.	Goal P.

M	New term – Register 1A – 1B – 5A – 9A – 4x 6B – 4x 6A – 1x 300
T	9A
W	1A – 1B – 12
T	9A
F	9A – gear ready
S	10B – relay carnival
S	2B – 4x 6A
M	1A – 6D – 4x 6B – 1x 500 – 7 (5 pm)
T	5A (easy) – light grass
W	1A – 2B (1)
T	1 – 5A – 9A – 6D
F	gear ready – 7 (5 pm)
S	10B – Home meet
S	Easy grass
M	1A – 1B – 14A – 1x 300 (easy)
T	1-5A-100 (7/8 effort)-200 (7/8 effort) 2-(grass)
W	1 – 14A – 14 or 2B
T	Light
F	Light
S	10B – Conference / Dual meet
S	Easy grass
M	1A – 1B – 14A – 1x 300 (easy)
T	1 – 5B – 2x 100 (7/8 effort) – 14B – grass
W	1 – 4 – 14A
T	Light
F	Travel
S	10B – Competition
S	Home – loosen up

Figure 4.1h Short Sprint Training Schedule

Short Sprint NAME DATE May

1. A. Jog 1 or 2 laps with relay pass B. High knee (slow) and fast leg
2. Fartlek: A. Holmer (varied-pace)—stride, sprint, recover—stride, meet a challenge or challenge, recover. Finish feeling exhilarated, not exhausted.
   B. Lydiard (steady pace)—slow, 10-30 min. (1) Hendricks (2) Golf course (3)
3. A. Weights and jogging—get chart B. Jogging and stretching
4. High knee and fast leg
5. Starts A. 3 at 1/2 speed, 3 at 7/8—30 yds.
   (1) On your own (2) Gun
   B. 50 yds. C. Grass D.
6. Intervals Y. Fast 20-55 in middle A. 110
   (1) 18-16-14 (2)
   B. 165 (1) 22 (2)
   C. 220 (1) 30 (2)
   D. 110-220-110 (1)
   E.
7. Squad meeting
8. Special A. Sauna B. Swim C.
9. Relay work A. Routine B. 55 C. Trial
10. A. Trial B. Compete
11. Bunches A. 330 B. 165 C. 80
12. Hill with: A. Coach B. Leader
14. A. Wind sprints B. Hurdle drill C. Spring and bound
    D. Alternate run and jog, at least 880
15. Finish work—50-70 at 3/4—last 30-50 at 9/10
    A. 100 B. 220
16. Back to back A. 55 B.
17. 3/4 effort A. 100 B. 300 C. 500
18.
19.
20.
21. A. Pictures B. Film
22. A. 100 yds. at 8/10—float at 70 (3 steps), then go
    B. 220 C. Parts
23. A. 550-330-110 (80-48-14) B. 300-200-100 (1)
    C. 165-110-55
24. Turn work (40 at 9/10) (30 at 1/2) (40 at 9/10)

Date	Dist.	3/4	Date P.	Goal P.

M	4x 1A-1B-2B(1)-6A-7(4:15 pm)
T	9B
W	1A-1B-5A-grass run
T	7 (3:15 pm)-9A-5A
F	Light
S	10B-Home meet
S	14A (easy)

M	7 (3:15 pm)-9B-4-14A
T	1x 1x 4x 1x 1A-5A-300-165-110-500 (easy)
W	9A-9B-14A
T	7 (3:30 pm)-5A
F	Gear ready
S	10B-Dual meet
S	2B(1) (easy)

M	1x 7 (3:30)-4-9A-300 (easy)
T	4x 1-5A-6D-6A-grass run
W	9A-light grass
T	4x 7 (3:30)-1-5A-6D (grass)
F	Gear ready
S	10B-Invitational or relay meet
S	Home and jog

M	1A-9A-9B-easy 300-14A
T	1A-1B-light
W	1-5A-6D-14A
T	7 (3:30 pm)-Light, gear ready
F	Preliminaries, Pac 8 Meet
S	Finals, Pac 8 Meet
S	Loosen up

Figure 4.1i Short Sprint Training Schedule

Short Sprint NAME DATE *June*

1. A. Jog 1 or 2 laps with relay pass B. High knee (slow) and fast leg
2. Fartlek: A. Holmer (varied-pace)—stride, sprint, recover—stride, meet a challenge or challenge, recover. Finish feeling exhilarated, not exhausted.
   B. Lydiard (steady pace)—slow, 10-30 min. (1) Hendricks (2) Golf course (3)
3. A. Weights and jogging—get chart B. Jogging and stretching
4. High knee and fast leg
5. Starts A. 3 at 1/2 speed, 3 at 7/8—30 yds.
   (1) On your own (2) Gun
   B. 50 yds. C. Grass D.
6. Intervals Y. Fast 20-55 in middle A. 110
   (1) 18-16-14 (2)
   B. 165 (1) 22 (2)
   C, 220 (1) 30 (2)
   D. 110-220-110 (1)
   E.
7. Squad meeting
8. Special A. Sauna B. Swim C.
9. Relay work A. Routine B. 55 C. Trial
10. A. Trial B. Compete
11. Bunches A. 330 B. 165 C. 80
12. Hill with: A. Coach B. Leader
14. A. Wind sprints B. Hurdle drill C. Spring and bound
    D. Alternate run and jog, at least 880
15. Finish work—50-70 at 3/4—last 30-50 at 9/10
    A. 100 B. 220
16. Back to back A. 55 B.
17. 3/4 effort A. 100 B. 300 C. 500
18.
19.
20.
21. A. Pictures B. Film
22. A. 100 yds. at 8/10—float at 70 (3 steps), then go
    B. 220 C. Parts
23. A. 550-330-110 (80-48-14) B. 300-200-100 (1)
    C. 165-110-55
24. Turn work (40 at 9/10) (30 at 1/2) (40 at 9/10)

Date	Dist.	3/4	Date P.	Goal P.

M	1A - 1B - 15A (2X) - 300 (1X)
T	1 - 9A - 14A
W	1 - 5A - 24 - 4 - grass run
T	1 - 9A - jog
F	1 - 5A - 14A
S	10B - Relay
S	Squad picnic
M	1A - 1B - grass run
T	1A - 14A
W	1-5A-grass 14A-100 (1X) (7/8 effort)-220 (1X) (7/8 effort)-Jog
T	1-grass run-100 (7/8 effort)-220 (7/8 effort)-grass run
F	1A-(light) 14A
S	7 - 1A - 14A (light)
S	1-5A-100 (1X) (7/8 effort)-200 (2X) (7/8 effort)-4-14A
M	1 - easy grass
T	1-5 (easy) - 14A (easy)
W	Light
T	10B Championship, or light run
F	10B Championship
S	10B Championship
S	
M	
T	
W	
T	
F	
S	
S	

used, as described earlier, and on the fifth count, the left hand will stay back ready to receive the baton. The sprinter will *not* look back at any time after he has started his own run. Gradually the practice speed is increased and the check marks are moved out, until they are determined correctly for a full-speed run. Each pair of relay runners will practice two or three passes at each of the three exchange zones. The alternate team member will practice as the first and the last man in the relay. By doing this, there is no damage to the interior of the relay team, so mistakes by the alternate cannot hurt the relay team too much. The coach should keep in mind that a team of not-too-good sprinters can form a very respectable relay team, if they are trained well enough to be very precise and consistent in their relay techniques.

Short Sprint Bibliography

Sprinting

Badar, Norbert. "Training for the sprints," *Track and Field Quarterly Review*, December 1966, pp. 27–31.

Balsevitch, V., and Siris, P. "Selection of sprint gifted children," trans. by Glenn B. Hoidale, *Track Technique,* No. 42 (December 1970), pp. 1342–43.

Bowerman, William J., and Brown, Gwilym S. "The secrets of speed," *Sports Illustrated* 35 (2 August 1971): 22–29.

Brown, Oliver. "Sprint training at Worthing High School (Houston, Texas)," *Track and Field Quarterly Review* 71: 89–105.

de Vries, Herbert A. "The 'looseness' factor in speed and O_2 consumption of an anaerobic 100-yard dash," *Research Quarterly* 34 (October 1963): 305ff.

Dintiman, George B. "Effects of various training programs on running speed," *Research Quarterly* 35 (December 1964): 456ff.

Ecker, Tom. "The sprinter's acceleration and forward lean," *Athletic Journal* 50 (April 1970): 28, 31.

Farmer, Dixon. "Sprinters *can* be made," *Scholastic Coach* 42 (March 1973): 26, 28, 109.

Grodjinovsky, Amos, and Magel, John R. "Effect of warm-up on running performance," *Research Quarterly* 41 (March 1970): 116–19.

Hoffman, Karol. "Stride length and frequency of female sprinters," trans. by S. J. Szymanski, *Track Technique,* No. 48 (June 1972), pp. 1522–24.

Jackson, Andrew S., and Baumgartner, Ted A. "Measurement schedule of sprint running," *Research Quarterly* 40 (December 1969): 708–11.

———, and Cooper, John M. "A multiple timing system for measuring the components of the sprint-velocity curve," *Research Quarterly* 40 (December 1970): 857–59.

Jesse, John P. "Explosive strength for sprinters," *Track and Field Quarterly Review*, February 1965, pp. 21–25.

Jordan, Payton. "Sprinting and training for runners," *Track and Field Quarterly Review,* October 1964, pp. 51–55.

Kruczalak, Eugeniusz. "Strength training for sprinters," *Track Technique*, No. 35 (March 1969), pp. 1106–8.

McNab, Tom. "Some observations on strength-training for sprinters," *Athletics Coach* 5 (March 1971): 6–7.

Marlow, Bill. *Sprinting and Relay Racing*. London: AAA, 1972. 48 pp.

Milakov, Milan, and Cox, Vernon. "Improving speed by training on sloping surfaces," *Track Technique*, No. 8 (June 1962), pp. 654–55.

Nett, Toni. "Armin Hary's training," *Track Technique*, No. 4 (June 1961), pp. 122–23.

O'Connor, W. Harold. "Progress in sprinting," *Scholastic Coach* 40 (March 1971): 14, 104–5.

Schmolinski, Gerhardt. "Hurdle training integral part of total training," trans. by Walter Morris, *Track Technique,* No. 45 (September 1971), pp. 1427–29.

Sevigne, Frank. "Sprinting," *Track and Field Quarterly Review*, March 1969, pp. 19–23.

Sylvia, Alfred J. "The body mechanics of sprinting," *Athletic Journal* 36 (March 1966): 14–15, 95–97.

Werschoshanskiu, Semjonow. "Strength training for sprinters," *Track Technique,* No. 54 (December 1973), pp. 1717–20.

Whelan, Press, and Etchberry, Pat. "Sprint training of Jim Green," *Track and Field Quarterly Review* 71: 216–23.

Winter, Bud. "Sprint form training," *Track and Field Quarterly Review* 72: 18–24.

Sprint Start

Clark, Bob. "The standing start!" *Scholastic Coach* 40 (March 1971): 15–16, 109.

Desipres, M. "Comparison of the kneeling and standing sprint starts," *Athletics Coach* 6 (September 1972): 23–24.

Ecker, Tom, and Hay, Jim. "The standing start?" *Athletic Journal* 53 (February 1973): 14.

Ernst, Richard D. "Starting mechanics and technique," *Track and Field Quarterly Review* 70 (August 1970): 21–23.

Fecher, Ron. "Teaching the start to the junior high school sprinter," *Athletic Journal* 49 (December 1968): 28–30, 54–55, 57.

Jackson, Andrew S., and Cooper, John M. "Effects of hand spacing and rear knee angle on the sprinter's start," *Research Quarterly* 41 (October 1970): 378–82.

Justin, Brother. "The sprint start," *Track Technique*, No. 41 (September 1970), pp. 1293–95.

Kahler, Robert W. "A contrast of gestalt and association theories as applied to track starting," *Track and Field Quarterly Review*, March 1967, pp. 70–73.

Meneley, Ronald C., and Rosemier, Robert A. "Effectiveness of four track starting positions on acceleration," *Research Quarterly* 39 (March 1968): 161–65.

Plotnicki, Ben. "Tips for the beginning official starter (officiating)," *Track Technique*, No. 35 (March 1969), p. 1108.

Short, John. "Standing start modernized," *Track Technique*, No. 39 (March 1970), pp. 1227–28.

Sigerseth, Peter O., and Grinaker, Vernon F. "Effect of foot spacing on velocity in sprints," *Research Quarterly* 33 (December 1962): 599ff.

Spence, Dale W. "The art of track starting," *Track and Field Quarterly Review*, October 1965, pp. 19–22.

Stock, Malcolm. "The influence of various track starting positions upon speed," *Athletic Journal* 44 (April 1964): 18, 68–69.

Suryanarayana, V. "The Surya standing start," *Track Technique*, No. 50 (December 1972), pp. 1595–96.

Toomsalu, Ruddi. "Sprint start speed factors," *Track Technique*, No. 11 (March 1963), pp. 325–27.

Winter, Bud. *The Rocket Sprint Start*. Privately published, 1961. 24 pp.

The 440-yard run and mile relay

At one time the one-lap race was considered a distance race and similar to the half-mile, but that day is long gone. Today the athlete who runs 440 yards with the world leader is a sprinter with top speed to which has been added much endurance. Who knows what the best prescription for training this runner is? Curtis Mills reached a world-best level on relatively hard work every day, and his coach's basic pattern was intervals up to 600 meters. Jim Bush's world record holders had a pattern that carried through the competitive season and was varied only to meet the competitive situation. Hoover Wright had a pattern that was flexible enough to accommodate the backgrounds of seven world-class athletes. However, their temperaments were such that his day was divided into from four to seven sections to accommodate the "secret" parts of their formulas.

Curtis Mills's training workouts looked like this:

Early fall (September to December)

Monday:	2 × 220, 660, 2 × 220, 440, 2 × 220 or 2 × 110, 2 × 220, 660, 2 × 220, 2 × 110
Tuesday:	2 × 110, 2 × 330, 550, 330, 2 × 110 or 2 × 220, 660, 2 × 220, 330, 2 × 110
Wednesday:	2 × 220, 660, 440, 220
Thursday:	Seven-man continuous 880 relay
Friday:	330, 220, 110, 220, 330

January and February

Monday:	2 × 110, 2 × 220, either 660 or 440, 2 × 220, 2 × 110
Tuesday:	2 × 220, 550, 2 × 220 or 2 × 660
Wednesday:	5 × 300 or 7 × 220 or 10 × 150
Thursday:	5 × 220 or 6 × 150
Friday:	10 × 150 (six medium–four fast)
Saturday:	3 × 150, 3 × 110

March and April

Monday:	2 × 500 (400 in 50 seconds), 2 × 150 fast
Tuesday:	4 × 300 (31.5-second average)
Wednesday:	4 × 220 (22.0 average)
Thursday:	5 × 150 or 6 × 100, flying start
Friday:	Rest
Saturday:	Track meet

For Jim Bush's men at UCLA, the competitive pattern was as follows:

Monday:	1 to 2 slow 500s, 2 to 3 medium 300s, 3 to 5 comfortable 150s
Tuesday:	Run a 200, slow on the turn and quickening on the straight, with emphasis on either "arms" or "legs," given audibly
Wednesday:	Hill work, if one is available (his 440 men were urged to use their hill as often as possible any day)
Thursday:	150s, using "arms" and "legs"
Friday:	300s, 200s, and 100s, and follow with the hill

Hoover Wright's pattern was similar to the following:

Photographs 5.1*a-e* Oregon runner Otis Davis, 1960 Olympic champion in the 440-meter low hurdles.

Monday:	1 × 500 or 600, 3 × 300, 6 × 100
Tuesday:	1 × 300, 3 × 200, 6 × 100
Wednesday:	1 × 400, 3 × 200, 6 × 100
Thursday:	3 × 200, 6 × 100
Friday:	6 × 100

From the above three sets of training patterns, all of which have produced world-class runners, three things are apparent:

1. A plan is there, and it is flexible, but it must be followed.
2. The success of the program is in direct proportion to the talent that is present.
3. If the training pattern is not enjoyable, no lasting success is possible.

The program presented in the workouts which follow this discussion has been flexible, geared to the needs of the individual, and has produced one Olympic champion and world record holder, as well as numerous other national contenders and international relay runners. In many respects the training is similar to that of the short sprints, so the material in the previous chapter should also be studied.

The top 440 runner will have the speed of a top quality 220 runner, but he must add the strength to continue his pace, combined with the ability to relax while running at nearly top speed. A look at photographs of world-class sprinters at top speed will reveal this relaxation (See Photographs 5.1 and 5.2). The runner will train with a combination of short, fast intervals and longer intervals run at a gradually quickening race pace. The total training distance for an interval workout would be from 2½ to 3 times the racing distance, or about three laps of the track.

Strength is developed through fartlek running at a comfortable pace, hill work, and overdistance runs (such as 550 to 660 yards) at paces a bit below the usual race pace. Too much long work will temporarily cut down on quickness, though it can be regained quickly. Quarter-milers tend not to like longer runs. An 880-yard run will help the endurance, but if the runner lacks confidence and courage, he will look out the window when the 880 is mentioned. The desire to run this distance is most important.

The runner must develop a floating sprint stride. In running 110s, sprint the first 55 yards, then float the next 55 yards, trying to relax as much as possible with a minimum of decrease in pace. The hips will loosen up. The athlete will not stride longer; his stride length will be the same or shorter. It is an attempt to relax while running. When it is learned well, the sprinter may find that he will actually increase his speed.

Tactics in the 440 relate more to the runner's own pace than to his opponent's. Most races are run entirely in lanes, so relative positions are difficult to determine before entering the final straight, 100 yards or so from the finish. The athlete should sprint as far as he can go comfortably from the start, anywhere from 55 to 150 yards. He should carry a sprinter's stride until the cadence slows, then drop to a sprint for 20 to 30 yards and go into his "float." Again, the float is a relaxation, not a period of slowing down the pace. The pace should be maintained as much as possible, so long as relaxation can be achieved. The athlete should accelerate at a time when he can carry his acceleration to the finish. If the athlete is ahead, he should float until he is challenged, for if he "ties up," he has had it.

Photographs 5.2*a-f* Ludmila Bragina, in the 1500 meters.

Sprinting Mechanics

One of the earlier American studies of posture for sprinters was done by Dr. Donald B. Slocumb, an orthopedic physician and surgeon, and he graciously included the author in his research. The first step of the study was to study the posture of champions in full sprint. The posture of 400-meter men, from William Carr and Ben Eastman through Otis Davis, the 1960 Olympic champion, was studied in both still and motion pictures. In the short sprint, the top runners from Jesse Owens to Armin Hary and Dave Sime (1960 Olympics) were carefully analyzed. Without exception their posture was almost 90 degrees in relation to the surface being covered.

The purpose of the study was to determine from a medical standpoint what mechanical devices might be designed to simulate near-perfect mechanics of motion. From an athletic consideration, it was to determine how the champions did it. Analytically it was determined that freedom of motion was best accomplished if the posture was upright, as detailed in Chapter 2. Among the less talented and up through the fairly good sprinters, there were deviations from the perpendicular. The question was how to correct this for an athlete so that he might more nearly do as the champions do.

Muscle tone is more important than the command to "stand straight." The most important muscles are the abdominals, pectorals, and latissimi dorsi (the stomach, chest, and back). The weakest set of muscles of a number of athletes tested was the abdominal muscles. To correct that weakness and also to prescribe exercises for general body activity, a set of ten self-testing and self-exercising weight activities was devised.

Posture is the second fault in mechanics of action. If the head is forward, something will have to balance that 5 kilograms of ugly fat. It is usually the buttocks, which will move into an awkward position. Several simple exercises were used, following the theory that better muscle tone would result in better posture. Two simple exercises for the athletes were the following:

1. Standing with the heels about 4 inches from a door, post, or other flat surface, slightly bend the knees. Rotate the hips forward and under with a "nasty" motion and at the same time tighten the abdominal muscles. Walk for about 4 to 8 seconds, then relax the abdominal muscles, return to the door and repeat the exercise four or five times.

2. Lie on the back, then bring the knees up, keeping the heels on the floor. Contract the abdominal muscles and rotate the hips until the back is flat. Lift one foot and gradually straighten that leg during a slow five-count. Bring the leg back in a five-count, and relax, then follow the exercise with the other foot and leg.

Lateral movement should be eliminated through practice. Swaying the head from side to side, swinging the arms too far across the chest, and making similar lateral motions will result in a compensating action by the legs. The coach and the athlete—through work, observation, pictures, and videotape—can make the training interesting as well as productive. The training schedules themselves should be studied next. They are preceded by a discussion of the concluding event in the typical meet, therefore a crucial event in close contests—the mile relay.

The Mile Relay

Though relay racing was discussed in the previous chapter, we have an expanded discussion here; and the relay bibliography is included as a part of this chapter, for whether an athlete runs the 100, 220, or 440, and runs in the 440 relay or mile relay, he must be concerned with the methods and training of all the sprinting races.

The mile relay is worth five points in a dual meet, so it is important. If possible, the team should try to win before the relay, so no athlete will be overworked by *having* to run the relay. The object of the race is *not* to please the spectators, a point often lost on network television when it covers contests. If the meet depends upon the mile relay, put a runner who will give a good position in the first leg. The weakest man will run second, the Number 2 runner will run third, and the top runner will anchor. As a variation, if a weak runner is in the third position on the other team, the coach might put his best man up against him to build a lead to carry through the last runner.

The training for the mile or 1600-meter relay should be a regular, meaningful routine. On the schedule it appears as number 9, as well as appearing as part of the warming-up activities. For the warm-up, two or three athletes jog around the track or across the training area. The receiver watches the incoming

Figure 5.1a 440-Yard Run Training Schedule

440-Yard Run NAME DATE September/October

1. A. Warm-up routine: Jog 1 or 2 laps with relay pass.
2. Fartlek A. Holmer (varied-pace)—stride, sprint, recover—stride, meet a challenge or challenge, recover. Finish feeling exhilarated, not exhausted.
   B. Lydiard—slow, steady, 10-30 min. (1) Hendricks (2) Golf course (a) 10 min. (b) 30 min. (c)
3. A. Weights and jogging—get chart B. Jogging and stretching
4. High knee and fast leg
5. Starts A. 2 at 1/2, 2 at 7/8 on curve, 50 yds.
   B. Curve 110 (1) On your own (2) Gun C. Grass
   D.
6. Intervals Y. Fast 20-55 in middle
   A. 110-220-110 (1) 14-30-14 (2)
   B. 165 (1) 22-20-18 (2)
   C. 220 (1) 30 (2)
   D. 330 (1)
   E. 110 (1) 13 (2)
7. Squad meeting
8. Special A. Sauna B. Swim C. Hill
9. Relay work A. Routine B. 55 C.
10. A. Trial B. Compete
11. Bunches A. 550 (1) 70-75 (2)
    B. 330 (1) 42-45 (2)
    C. 165 (1) 20-22 (2)
12. With A. Coach B. Leader
14. Wind sprints A. Straight B. Curve
15. Finish work A. 1st 110, jog 330, last 110
    B.
16. Back to back A. B.
17. 3/4 effort A. 220 B. 300 C.
18. Alternate run and jog at least 880
19.
20.
21. A. Pictures B. Film
22. Simulated 440 A. 110-110-110 B. 165-165-165
23. Simulated 220 A. 110-110 B. 165-165

Date	Dist.	3/4	Date P.	Goal P.

M	Organization-lockers-equipment
T	Leaders meet on use of weights
W	7-Discuss nonschool facilities-14A
T	3A
F	1A-4
S	Registration complete
S	recreation
M	1-4-11A-14A
T	3A (light)
W	8C-4X 100y (easy on grass)
T	
F	10A-200 meters of 7/8 effort to 9/10-18
S	
S	
M	1-11A-11B-6E-6A(1)-18
T	
W	12A-8C
T	3A
F	1A-11A-11B-6E-4
S	
S	
M	1-4-11ABC (1-2X) - 6C (3X) - 2B(1)
T	3A
W	8C (12B)
T	10A-100y and 300y
F	
S	
S	

Figure 5.1b 440-Yard Run Training Schedule

440-Yard Run NAME DATE October/November

1. A. Warm-up routine: Jog 1 or 2 laps with relay pass.
2. Fartlek A. Holmer (varied-pace)—stride, sprint, recover—stride, meet a challenge or challenge, recover. Finish feeling exhilarated, not exhausted.
   B. Lydiard—slow, steady, 10-30 min. (1) Hendricks (2) Golf course (a) 10 min. (b) 30 min. (c)
3. A. Weights and jogging—get chart B. Jogging and stretching
4. High knee and fast leg
5. Starts A. 2 at 1/2, 2 at 7/8 on curve, 50 yds.
   B. Curve 110 (1) On your own (2) Gun C. Grass
   D.
6. Intervals Y. Fast 20-55 in middle
   A. 110-220-110 (1) 14-30-14 (2)
   B. 165 (1) 22-20-18 (2)
   C. 220 (1) 30 (2)
   D. 330 (1)
   E. 110 (1) 13 (2)
7. Squad meeting
8. Special A. Sauna B. Swim C. Hill
9. Relay work A. Routine B. 55 C.
10. A. Trial B. Compete
11. Bunches A. 550 (1) 70-75 (2)
    B. 330 (1) 42-45 (2)
    C. 165 (1) 20-22 (2)
12. With A. Coach B.
14. Wind sprints A. Straight B. Curve
15. Finish work A. 1st 110, jog 330, last 110
    B.
16. Back to back A. B.
17. 3/4 effort A. 220 B. 300 C.
18.
19.
20.
21. A. Pictures B. Film
22. Simulated 440 A. 110-110-110 B. 165-165-165
23. Simulated 220 A. 110-110 B. 165-165

Date	Dist.	3/4	Date P.	Goal P.

M	1-4-5A (easy) - 11ABC
T	3A
W	4-5 (easy) - 8C
T	21A - 3A
F	1-6A - 14A
S	1-4-5A - 10A (500y) - 2B (1)
S	recreation

M	1-11ABC - 2A (1 or 2)
T	3-14A
W	1-6E 4x (2) - 8C - 6E 4x
T	3A
F	10A - Relay - 300y or 100y
S	Choice
S	

M	1-4-5A - 11ABC
T	3A
W	4-6A - 8C - 6E 4x
T	3A
F	Light
S	10A - Relay 1x - 385y 1x - 2B (1)
S	recreation

M	1-4-5A - 11ABC 1-2x - 2B (1)
T	4-8B
W	1-6A - 2B (1)
T	3A
F	1-9A - 2B (1)
S	Choice
S	recreation

Figure 5.1c 440-Yard Run Training Schedule

440-Yard Run NAME DATE November/December

1. A. Warm-up routine: Jog 1 or 2 laps with relay pass.
2. Fartlek A. Holmer (varied-pace)—stride, sprint, recover—stride, meet a challenge or challenge, recover. Finish feeling exhilarated, not exhausted.
   B. Lydiard—slow, steady, 10-30 min. (1) Hendricks (2) Golf course (a) 10 min. (b) 30 min. (c)
3. A. Weights and jogging—get chart B. Jogging and stretching
4. High knee and fast leg
5. Starts A. 2 at 1/2, 2 at 7/8 on curve, 50 yds.
   B. Curve 110 (1) On your own (2) Gun C. Grass
   D.
6. Intervals Y. Fast 20-55 in middle
   A. 110-220-110 (1) 14-30-14 (2)
   B. 165 (1) 22-20-18 (2) 9/10 effort
   C. 220 (1) 30 (2) 28
   D. 330 (1)
   E. 110 (1) 13 (2)
7. Squad meeting
8. Special A. Sauna B. Swim C. Hill
9. Relay work A. Routine B. 55 C.
10. A. Trial B. Compete
11. Bunches A. 550 (1) 70-75 (2)
    B. 330 (1) 42-45 (2)
    C. 165 (1) 20-22 (2)
12. With A. Coach B.
14. Wind sprints A. Straight B. Curve
15. Finish work A. 1st 110, jog 330, last 110
    B.
16. Back to back A. B.
17. 3/4 effort A. 220 B. 300 C.
18.
19.
20.
21. A. Pictures B. Film
22. Simulated 440 A. 110-110-110 B. 165-165-165
23. Simulated 220 A. 110-110 B. 165-165

Date	Dist.	3/4	Date P.	Goal P.

M	1-11ABC-2B(1)
T	3A
W	1-6C(2)-6E(1)-8C (4x over 6C(2), 4x over 6E(1))
T	3A
F	4-6B(2)-2B(1)-6E (3x over 6B(2), 4x over 6E)
S	
S	recreation
M	1-4-11ABC-2B(1) (1-3x over 11ABC)
T	3A
W	1-5A-8C-6E(1) (4x over 6E(1))
T	3A
F	10A (Relay-880 or 440)
S	
S	
M	
T	
W	
T	
F	
S	
S	
M	
T	
W	
T	
F	
S	
S	

Figure 5.1d 440-Yard Run Training Schedule

440-Yard Run NAME DATE January

1. A. Warm-up routine: Jog 1 or 2 laps with relay pass.
2. Fartlek A. Holmer (varied-pace)—stride, sprint, recover—stride, meet a challenge or challenge, recover. Finish feeling exhilarated, not exhausted.
   B. Lydiard—slow, steady, 10-30 min. (1) Hendricks (2) Golf course (a) 10 min. (b) 30 min. (c)
3. A. Weights and jogging—get chart B. Jogging and stretching
4. High knee and fast leg
5. Starts A. 2 at 1/2, 2 at 7/8 on curve, 50 yds.
   B. Curve 110 (1) On your own (2) Gun C. Grass
   D.
6. Intervals Y. Fast 20-55 in middle
   A. 110-220-110 (1) 14-30-14 (2)
   B. 165 (1) 22-20-18 (2)
   C. 220 (1) 30 (2)
   D. 330 (1)
   E. 110 (1) 13 (2)
7. Squad meeting
8. Special A. Sauna B. Swim C. Hill
9. Relay work A. Routine B. 55 C.
10. A. Trial B. Compete
11. Bunches A. 550 (1) 70-75 (2)
    B. 330 (1) 42-45 (2)
    C. 165 (1) 20-22 (2)
12. With A. Coach B.
14. Wind sprints A. Straight B. Curve
15. Finish work A. 1st 110, jog 330, last 110
    B.
16. Back to back A. B.
17. 3/4 effort A. 220 B. 300 C.
18. 330-220-110
19. 110s-1st, 2d, 3d, 4th
20.
21. A. Pictures B. Film
22. Simulated 440 A. 110-110-110 B. 165-165-165
23. Simulated 220 A. 110-110 B. 165-165

Date	Dist.	3/4	Date P.	Goal P.

M	Register-orientation-equiment
T	2-4x 1-4-2B-6B
W	8C or 8A
T	3A
F	3x Easy 10A-Relay-300y or 100y-18
S	
S	
M	2x 4x 1-4-6B-19-2
T	3A
W	2-3x 2-3x 1-14-6B - 6A-jog
T	Light
F	7
S	10B-Indoor meet
S	
M	2-3x 3-5x 1-11A-11B-11C-2B(1)
T	3A
W	6x 1-6E-14 or 8C
T	3A
F	10-Relay-385y-jog
S	
S	
M	1-14A-2
T	3A
W	4x 14A-8C-6E
T	1-14A
F	1-4-6A-18
S	2B(1)
S	

Figure 5.1e 440-Yard Run Training Schedule

440-Yard Run NAME DATE February

1. A. Warm-up routine: Jog 1 or 2 laps with relay pass.
2. Fartlek A. Holmer (varied-pace)—stride, sprint, recover—stride, meet a challenge or challenge, recover. Finish feeling exhilarated, not exhausted.
   B. Lydiard—slow, steady, 10-30 min. (1) Hendricks (2) Golf course (a) 10 min. (b) 30 min. (c)
3. A. Weights and jogging—get chart B. Jogging and stretching
4. High knee and fast leg
5. Starts A. 2 at 1/2, 2 at 7/8 on curve, 50 yds.
   B. Curve 110 (1) On your own (2) Gun C. Grass
   D.
6. Intervals Y. Fast 20-55 in middle
   A. 110-220-110 (1) 14-30-14 (2)
   B. 165 (1) 22-20-18 (2)
   C. 220 (1) 30 (2)
   D. 330 (1)
   E. 110 (1) 13 (2)
7. Squad meeting
8. Special A. Sauna B. Swim C.
9. Relay work A. Routine B. 55 C. Hill
10. A. Trial B. Compete
11. Bunches A. 550 (1) 70-75 (2)
    B. 330 (1) 42-45 (2)
    C. 165 (1) 20-22 (2)
12. With A. Coach B.
14. Wind sprints A. Straight B. Curve
15. Finish work A. 1st 110, jog 330, last 110
    B.
16. Back to back A. B.
17. 3/4 effort A. 220 B. 300 C.
18. 300-200-100
19.
20. Alternate sprint and float
21. A. Pictures B. Film
22. Simulated 440 A. 110-110-110 B. 165-165-165
23. Simulated 220 A. 110-110 B. 165-165

Date	Dist.	3/4	Date P.	Goal P.

M	2-3x 3-5x 1x 1-2B(1)(a)-6D-11C - 6E - 11A
T	4x 6E-3A
W	4x 1x 4x 1-6E-11A-20-55y
T	3A
F	2
S	10B or 10A (Relay-385y)
S	recreation

M	1-5A-11A-6B(1)-2B(1)
T	3A
W	4x 8C-6E
T	3A
F	2x 4-9A-500y
S	Light
S	Light

M	2x 4x 1-4-18-6A-6E-2B(b)
T	9A-3A-8A
W	8C
T	9A-3A
F	Light
S	10A-Relay-330y or 385 y
S	easy run

M	4x 1x 1-4-18-6A-6E-500y (1/2 effort)
T	3A
W	1x 2x 1-4-6C-100y-2B(1)
T	9 (easy)
F	9 (easy)
S	10A or 10B (indoor)
S	

Figure 5.1f 440-Yard Run Training Schedule

440-Yard Run NAME DATE *March*

1. A. Warm-up routine: Jog 1 or 2 laps with relay pass.
2. Fartlek A. Holmer (varied-pace)—stride, sprint, recover—stride, meet a challenge or challenge, recover. Finish feeling exhilarated, not exhausted.
   B. Lydiard—slow, steady, 10-30 min. (1) Hendricks (2) Golf course (a) 10 min. (b) 30 min. (c)
3. A. Weights and jogging—get chart B. Jogging and stretching
4. High knee and fast leg
5. Starts A. 2 at 1/2, 2 at 7/8 on curve, 50 yds.
   B. Curve 110 (1) On your own (2) Gun C. Grass
   D. *165 yds.* *E. 265 yds.*
6. Intervals Y. Fast 20-55 in middle
   A. 110-220-110 (1) 14-30-14 (2)
   B. 165 (1) 22-20-18 (2)
   C. 220 (1) 30 (2)
   D. 330 (1)
   E. 110 (1) 13 (2)
7. Squad meeting
8. Special A. Sauna B. Swim C. *Hill*
9. Relay work A. Routine B. 55 C.
10. A. Trial B. Compete
11. Bunches A. 550 (1) 70-75 (2)
    B. 330 (1) 42-45 (2)
    C. 165 (1) 20-22 (2)
12. With A. Coach B.
14. Wind sprints A. Straight B. Curve
15. Finish work A. 1st 110, jog 330, last 110
    B. *Jog 220, 440 moves in last 220*
16. Back to back A. B.
17. 3/4 effort A. 220 B. 300 C.
18. *330 – 220 – 110*
19. *165s - 1st, 2nd, last – race moves*
20.
21. A. Pictures B. Film
22. Simulated 440 A. 110-110-110 B. 165-165-165
23. Simulated 220 A. 110-110 B. 165-165

Date	Dist.	3/4	Date P.	Goal P.

M	*1-4-5B-(1x) 600y-(4x) 6E-(1x) 440(65-70)-2B (1 or 2)*
T	*9A – 3A*
W	*4-5B(2)-18-8C-(4x) 5C*
T	*9A-21A*
F	*1-10A (Relay-385y)*
S	*2*
S	*2*
M	*4-19-11ABC-2A(1)-(4x) 6E*
T	*9A-3A*
W	*1-5D(2)-8C*
T	*3A*
F	*3B*
S	*10A-Relay-15B-2B(1)*
S	*2 (easy)*
M	*Exam week-5E-5D-6B(1)-2B*
T	*9A*
W	*1-(2x) 5B-(2x) 6C(2)-8C*
T	*9A-3A*
F	*Gear ready*
S	*10B-Meet-1 event*
S	*Travel for spring vacation*
M	*10A (165-220-165)-18-2B*
T	*9A (easy)-2B-(4x) 6E*
W	*18-2B*
T	*(4x) 6E-9A (easy)*
F	*Gear ready - jog*
S	*10B-Relay and 1 event*
S	*Home-reregister and settle in*

Figure 5.1g 440-Yard Run Training Schedule

440-Yard Run NAME DATE *April*

1. A. Warm-up routine: Jog 1 or 2 laps with relay pass.
2. Fartlek A. Holmer (varied-pace)—stride, sprint, recover—stride, meet a challenge or challenge, recover. Finish feeling exhilarated, not exhausted.
   B. Lydiard—slow, steady, 10-30 min. (1) Hendricks (2) Golf course (a) 10 min. (b) 30 min. (c)
3. A. Weights and jogging—get chart B. Jogging and stretching
4. High knee and fast leg
5. Starts A. 2 at 1/2, 2 at 7/8 on curve, 50 yds.
   B. Curve 110 (1) On your own (2) Gun C. Grass
   D.
6. Intervals Y. Fast 20-55 in middle
   A. 110-220-110 (1) 14-30-14 (2)
   B. 165 (1) 22-20-18 (2)
   C. 220 (1) 30 (2)
   D. 330 (1)
   E. 110 (1) 13 (2)
7. Squad meeting
8. Special A. Sauna B. Swim C. *Hill*
9. Relay work A. Routine B. 55 C.
10. A. Trial B. Compete
11. Bunches A. 550 (1) 70-75 (2)
    B. 330 (1) 42-45 (2)
    C. 165 (1) 20-22 (2)
12. With A. Coach B.
14. Wind sprints A. Straight B. Curve
15. Finish work A. 1st 110, jog 330, last 110
    B.
16. Back to back A. B.
17. 3/4 effort A. 220 B. 300 C.
18. *110s – 1st, 2nd, 3rd, last –*
19. *330 – 220 – 110*
20.
21. A. Pictures B. Film
22. Simulated 440 A. 110-110-110 B. 165-165-165
23. Simulated 220 A. 110-110 B. 165-165

Date	Dist.	3/4	Date P.	Goal P.

M	*7-4-[2x] 6C-18-[4x] 6E-11A-2B*
T	*4-9A*
W	*1-4-10A (165-275)-[4x] 6E-8C*
T	*9A*
F	*Gear ready*
S	*10B*
S	*Loosen up*

Day	A.M.	P.M.
M	*1*	*1-19-grass run*
T	*4*	*1-10A (275-165)-[2x] 6A-11A*
W	*1*	*8C-8B*
T	*4*	*9A-[2x] 6C-grass run*
F	*9A-grass*	
S	*10B*	
S	*grass run*	

Day	A.M.	P.M.
M	*1*	*6A-10A(165-275)-[4x] 6E-[1x] 500y*
T	*Jog*	*1-9A-grass-3A*
W	*4*	*1-10A(165-330)-[4x] 5C-1*
T	*Jog*	*1A*
F	*Gear ready*	
S	*10B*	
S	*loosen up*	

Day	A.M.	P.M.
M	*3A*	*1-5-9A-grass*
T	*4*	*1-6A-6B(1)-[1x] 500y-2(grass)*
W	*3A*	*4-9A-grass-8C*
T	*4*	*9A*
F	*Gear ready*	
S	*10B*	
S	*8B*	

Figure 5.1h 440-Yard Run Training Schedule

440-Yard Run NAME DATE *May*

1. A. Warm-up routine: Jog 1 or 2 laps with relay pass.
2. Fartlek A. Holmer (varied-pace)—stride, sprint, recover—stride, meet a challenge or challenge, recover. Finish feeling exhilarated, not exhausted.
   B. Lydiard—slow, steady, 10-30 min. (1) Hendricks (2) Golf course (a) 10 min. (b) 30 min. (c)
3. A. Weights and jogging—get chart B. Jogging and stretching
4. High knee and fast leg
5. Starts A. 2 at 1/2, 2 at 7/8 on curve, 50 yds.
   B. Curve 110 (1) On your own (2) Gun C. Grass
   D.
6. Intervals Y. Fast 20-55 in middle
   A. 110-220-110 (1) 14-30-14 (2)
   B. 165 (1) 22-20-18 (2)
   C. 220 (1) 30 (2) *22.5*
   D. 330 (1)
   E. 110 (1) 13 (2) *7/8 effort*
7. Squad meeting
8. Special A. Sauna B. Swim C. *Hill*
9. Relay work A. Routine B. 55 C.
10. A. Trial B. Compete
11. Bunches A. 550 (1) 70-75 (2)
    B. 330 (1) 42-45 (2)
    C. 165 (1) 20-22 (2)
12. With A. Coach B.
14. Wind sprints A. Straight B. Curve
15. Finish work A. 1st 110, jog 330, last 110
    B. *1st 165, jog, last 165*
16. Back to back A. B.
17. 3/4 effort A. 220 B. 300 C.
18.
19.
20.
21. A. Pictures B. Film
22. Simulated 440 A. 110-110-110 B. 165-165-165
23. Simulated 220 A. 110-110 B. 165-165

Date	Dist.	3/4	Date P.	Goal P.

	A.M.	P.M.
M	*Jog*	*1x 100y – 2x 6C – 4x Short hill – 4x Medium hill – 2B*
T	*9A*	*9A*
W	*Jog*	*5A – 1x 300 – 1x 200 – 5x 100 – 1x 500*
T	*9A*	*9A*
F	*1-10A (400y at 3/4 to 7/8 effort)*	
S	*10B*	
S	*Loosen up*	

M	*Jog*	*6B(1) – 2B(1)*
T	*9A*	*1-10A (385-165) – 1x 500 – Jog*
W	*Jog*	*5B – 15B – 8C*
T	*9A*	*9A*
F	*Gear ready for trials*	
S	*10B – Northern Division meet*	
S	*Loosen up*	

M	*7 – Jog*
T	*2x 6C(2) – 6E(2) – 1x 250 (3/4 effort)*
W	*9A – 5 (easy) – 4x 6E – 1x 500*
T	*Travel and loosen up*
F	*10B – Conference – trials*
S	*10B – Conference – finals*
S	*Loosen up at home*

M	
T	
W	
T	
F	
S	
S	

Figure 5.1i 440-Yard Run Training Schedule

440-Yard Run NAME DATE June

1. A. Warm-up routine: Jog 1 or 2 laps with relay pass.
2. Fartlek A. Holmer (varied-pace)—stride, sprint, recover—stride, meet a challenge or challenge, recover. Finish feeling exhilarated, not exhausted.
   B. Lydiard—slow, steady, 10-30 min. (1) Hendricks (2) Golf course (a) 10 min. (b) 30 min. (c)
3. A. Weights and jogging—get chart B. Jogging and stretching
4. High knee and fast leg
5. Starts A. 2 at 1/2, 2 at 7/8 on curve, 50 yds.
   B. Curve 110 (1) On your own (2) Gun C. Grass
   D.
6. Intervals Y. Fast 20-55 in middle
   A. 110-220-110 (1) 14-30-14 (2)
   B. 165 (1) 22-20-18 (2)
   C. 220 (1) 30 (2)
   D. 330 (1)
   E. 110 (1) 13 (2)
7. Squad meeting
8. Special A. Sauna B. Swim C. Hill
9. Relay work A. Routine B. 55 C.
10. A. Trial B. Compete
11. Bunches A. 550 (1) 70-75 (2)
    B. 330 (1) 42-45 (2)
    C. 165 (1) 20-22 (2)
12. With A. Coach B.
14. Wind sprints A. Straight B. Curve
15. Finish work A. 1st 110, jog 330, last 110
    B.
16. Back to back A. B.
17. 3/4 effort A. 220 B. 300 C.
18. 165s – 1st, 2nd, last – race moves
19. 110s – 1st, 2nd, 3rd, 4th
20. 220 – 1st, last – race moves
21. A. Pictures B. Film
22. Simulated 440 A. 110-110-110 B. 165-165-165
23. Simulated 220 A. 110-110 B. 165-165

Date	Dist.	3/4	Date P.	Goal P.

M	1-2A(1) – 18-19 – 1X 500y – 2(grass)
T	9A – 14A (grass)
W	1-2A(1) – 20 – Relay 110s
T	10B – 440 of 50y dashes
F	9B
S	10A – 330y – Relay
S	Grass Jog -- 9A
M	100 (7/8 effort) – 2X 220 – 9 (passing)
T	2-3X 90 (grass) – 9
W	Travel – check facility
T	10B – Trials
F	10B – Semifinal – mile relay trial
S	10B – Final – mile relay final
S	
M	
T	
W	
T	
F	
S	
S	
M	
T	
W	
T	
F	
S	
S	

runner, takes two to five steps, presents the left hand (inside hand on the track), continues running while receiving the baton, immediately transfers it to his right (outside) hand, and if there are three athletes in the warm-up drill, he prepares to pass it to the third runner when he presents his hand. When the front runner has the baton, he "peels off" and drops to the rear of the line, preparing to repeat the procedure. This is continued during the one or two laps of warm-up activities.

As in the short relay blind pass, the inside pass is used, since dropping the inside arm tends to pull the receiver to the inside. That is the place in the running lane where we want the runner as he goes into and around the turn. The receiver is to look back over his left shoulder. His left arm is "pumped" in coordination with the stride two, three, or possibly as many as five times as the incoming athlete approaches. When the passer appears to be in position (the receiver is watching his approach), the receiver swings his left arm out from the elbow and to the rear, keeping the palm up and the thumb slightly elevated. The passer is swinging his arms as he approaches, and as the receiver presents his upturned hand, the passer places the baton on it on his downward and outward swing.

Practice for the competitive mile relay is best done in the actual zone The zone for the long relay is 20 meters and does not have the extra 10 meters allowed in the 4 × 100 relay.

One of the first drills is to have the first runner approach at jog pace, while the second runner waits in the zone. He has put a mark about 5 meters back, and as the Number 1 runner crosses the mark, the Number 2 runner leaves the rear of the passing zone, swinging both arms as in sprinting. However, his eyes are on the incoming teammate. The receiver presents his left hand on the second or third count, depending upon the speed of the approach, receives the baton, and continues accelerating into the bend at 440 pace, then tapers off. The next part of the drill is for the Number 2 runner to pass to Number 3, then Number 3 to Number 4, then Number 4 to Number 1.

A second drill, which is used after the mechanics of passing have become set, is to have Number 1 pass to Number 2 and at the same time have Number 3 pass to Number 4 in a lane just inside or outside the lane used by Number 1 and Number 2. After each pass, the two-runner groups change lanes and partners, such as Number 2 passing to Number 3 and Number 4 to Number 1.

In dual meets it is usually the practice to put the best runner at the anchor position, second best runner on the third leg, third best runner as the lead-off, and the weakest runner in the second slot. The only logical reason for such placement is the prestige connected with the anchor position. In a very competitive dual meet situation, a coach sometimes calls for the best runner to run first to build up a lead that may cause the opposing team to make an error and "tie up" in either the first or second leg of the relay. If the outcome of the meet has already been decided, the reasons for running the relay are:

1. It is a regularly scheduled event, and it is an obligation to the spectator as well as to the opponent.

2. It is an opportunity for the team members to work together in positions to practice for upcoming competition and also to determine if they are capable of coming back from one of the flat races. If a runner cannot come back, he had better not enter one of the *big* relays on hope.
3. It is a help for the runners in the regular approach to top condition.

Sprint and Relay Bibliography

The 440

Bell, Sam. "The 440 yard dash," *Track and Field Quarterly Review* 72: 92–93.

Bush, Jim. "The classic 440-yard dash," *Athletic Journal* 52 (March 1972): 18–19, 82.

———. "The 440 yard dash and mile relay at U.C.L.A.," *Track and Field Quarterly Review* 72: 227–33.

O'Shea, John P. "Effects of varied, short-term weight training programs on improving performances in the 400-meter run," *Research Quarterly* 40 (March 1969): 248–50.

Thomas, Charles, and Mills, Curtis. "Training schedule of Curtis Mills," *Track and Field Quarterly Review* 71: 27–34.

Relay Racing

Bell, Sam. "Fundamentals for sprint relays," *Track and Field Quarterly Review* 72: 94–95.

Colfer, George. "Passing the baton," *Athletic Journal* 53 (March 1973): 14–15, 116–18.

———. "Techniques of relay racing," *Athletic Journal* 53 (February 1973): 32, 87–88.

Gibson, Ken. "Baton passing drills," *Scholastic Coach* 38 (March 1969): 44.

Giles, Kelvin B. "Teaching the sprint relay in schools," *Track Technique,* No. 45 (September 1971), p. 1431.

Justin, Brother. "Speed in relay passes," *Track Technique,* No. 51 (March 1973), pp. 1620–21.

Larkin, Richard A. "Improved techniques in speed relay baton exchanges," *Athletic Journal* 47 (January 1967): 8–9.

Morriss, John. "Relay racing," *Track and Field Quarterly Review*, June 1967, pp. 40–47.

Olsen, Paul V. "Baton passing the 'natural' way," *Scholastic Coach* 39 (March 1970): 34, 36, 96.

Pardivala, Jal D. "Art of baton passing," *Track Technique,* No. 24 (June 1966), pp. 739–41.

Santos, Jim. "Speed exchange pass for all relay races," *Scholastic Coach* 39 (April 1970): 66, 106.

Tozer, M. D. W., ed. "A comparison of relay take-over methods," *Athletics Coach* 4 (September 1970): 7–10.

Walker, Leroy T. "Elementary fundamentals in sprint relay racing," *Scholastic Coach* 33 (February 1964): 38, 70–71.

———. "Relay racing techniques," *Track and Field Quarterly Review*, February 1964, pp. 67–69.

West, John. "Coaching the speed pass," *Track and Field Quarterly Review* 71: 166–68.

Wolfe, Vern. "Relay exchanges," *Track and Field Quarterly Review*, March 1969, pp. 24–26.

Wright, Stan. "Sprint relay passes," *Track and Field Quarterly Review,* October 1969, pp. 19–26.

The high hurdles

In the beginning God did not create hurdlers. They either develop themselves or are developed by the teacher-coach. If the coach has to develop his hurdlers, he needs an organized training plan. Training methods and procedures are extremely important, so they will be discussed first.

Training Procedures for the High Hurdles

The warm-up routine of the hurdler should ensure that the circulation is moving well, the body temperature is adjusted, and the runner feels warm, but not tired. Extreme stretching should be avoided. If extreme or violent stretching exercises are performed in practice, the extra adrenalin flowing on the day of competition makes the hurdler more liable to pull or strain a muscle before the competition ever starts. No muscles need to be stretched any more in warming up than they will be stretched in performing the competitive activities.

From the dressing room the hurdler jogs a quarter-mile to the track, then covers about a half-mile alternating jogging and easy stretching. He finishes with another quarter-mile and is then ready for the day's activities. It may be noted that the X drill is a graduated warm-up routine, as well as a training routine.

Practice has indicated that if an athlete works hard on one day, he will probably need a recovery period the next day. This is generally true for all athletic events. By alternating hard and easy days of training, the athlete can prepare well for his competitive events and at the same time use his easy days to benefit from activities such as easy jogging, weight training, and swimming. Often the hurdlers may work with the sprinters on activities such as relay work on these easier days.

For a hard day, the hurdler begins with warming-up jogging and stretching, then goes through the X drill, working perhaps on his trail leg. He will progress from five-stepping to the sides and over the top to three-stepping to the sides and over the top. He might begin by doing the X drill with the hurdles set at 30 inches, then repeat it with the hurdles at 36, 39, and 42 inches. He might then run several intervals, followed by easy fartlek, with the workout concluded by four progressively quickening (but *never* all-out) 110s.

As the athlete gets into condition, the coach will realize that there will be competitive situations where the hurdler may race on two or even three days consecutively. If this is so, preparation for such a situation should begin about a month ahead of time. On one day the athlete might warm up with his usual routine, do the X drill, then simulate a racing situation, which might be done by running through a full set of hurdles, or running five hurdles back-to-back, or perhaps running the first three hurdles and last three hurdles, with jogging between. This would be followed by a warm-down or cool-out at the end of practice. It will have been neither a hard nor an easy day, but the runner is conditioning himself mentally and physically for the big races that are coming.

The next day, rather than taking it easy, he would again warm up, perhaps take three or four starts, work on the hurdles as on the previous day (going through a full flight either in part, in segments, or in the first and last parts), then cool down again.

The third day, if he is preparing for three hard days of competition in a row, would begin with a warm-up, then simulate the racing situation. Following this he would take the hardest workout of the week. After all, when a runner gets into shape by planned work, if he is preparing for the competition ahead, he does not want to do so much resting that he gets out of condition. The continuation of this procedure might see him running a series of 110s or 165s, or he might do enough relay work to have done the equivalent of a half-mile of running, then finish with a jog through the hills, if he wishes, or a series of moderate wind sprints.

As a final note on training, a good practice is regular test efforts every two weeks until the competitive season begins. These usually are not over the full distance. For the high hurdles these would most commonly be at 60 yards (four or five hurdles), 70 yards (five or six hurdles), or 90 yards (seven hurdles—three-fourths of the racing distance). These might be all-out trials, but more commonly they would be aimed at running at a set pace or at a rate of gradual improvement from one trial to the next. Also, they would generally be over hurdles set below the regular competitive height during the winter (36 or 39 inches, rather than 42 inches for the college highs).

Who Are the Hurdlers?

Hurdlers are usually agile men with quick reactions. They should be strong and fiercely competitive, and usually they will not be easily agitated or distracted. The coach should not try to place hurdlers in a single physical group. While most hurdlers are tall and tend toward ranginess, there have been world-class hurdlers as short as 5 feet 8 inches and successful high school hurdlers even shorter. One thing should always be remembered where hurdlers are concerned: they are sprinters first and hurdlers second. A slow man on the flat will be slow over the hurdles. Though your hurdlers may not be as fast as your best sprinters, they will not likely be far behind. In 1962 the University of Oregon set a world record of 40.0 seconds for the 440-yard relay with a team of three hurdlers and one sprinter.

The test used for discovering hurdling potential is described in Chapter 18. When the prospects are located, the next step is teaching them to hurdle. This procedure can be discouraging to the draftees, because it is human nature to avoid anything which might hurt, and the prospect of hitting a hurdle and perhaps falling on the track may cause runners to shy away from trying to hurdle really well. The athletes must have no fear of the hurdles. Two things can be done to minimize the prospects' fears: (1) most hurdle practice, at least in the learning and early practice stages, should be done on the grass; and (2) soft-top hurdles should be used. These simple precautions will do much to limit the fears of the athletes.

At this point, as we prepare to teach hurdling, the distinction should be made between the terms "lead leg" and "trail leg." The leg which goes over the hurdle first is called the "lead leg," while the leg which follows the body over the hurdle is the "trail leg." It makes no difference which leg the high hurdler uses as his lead leg. He will find that he naturally prefers one leg to the other. For a race which goes around a turn on the track, there are some advantages to leading with the left leg. However, not all the best runners of such races lead with the left leg. The arm opposite the lead leg is called the "lead arm," since it leads over the hurdle in conjunction with the lead leg. If a man leads with his right leg, his left arm will be his lead arm, and his right arm will be his "trail arm."

The athletes should first try walking over the hurdles. Pull three hurdles over backward and place them 5 yards apart. Boxes or other objects about 12 to 15 inches in height might be used as well. Have the hurdlers walk over the obstacles, concentrating on lifting the lead *knee*. After several repetitions of this exercise, they should walk through concentrating on the trail leg and turning the toe out, until they have the feel of the basic hurdling action. They will then be ready to learn the "X drill," used at Oregon to teach hurdling and review the basic techniques regularly. The term "X" has no meaning, other than as a name for the routine. We begin with three hurdles set at the low height (30 inches). The high hurdles are ordinarily set 10 yards apart, with 15 yards from the start to the first hurdle. For our teaching drill we begin with 14 yards to the first

Figure 6.1a High Hurdle Training Schedule

High Hurdle NAME DATE September/October

1. A. Warm-up: jog 1 or 2 laps with relay pass. Hurdle X drill at 36 and/or 39 in. B. High knee and fast leg drill C. 2 starts to 1 hurdle
2. Fartlek: A. Holmer (varied-pace)—stride, sprint, recover—stride, meet a challenge or challenge, recover. Finish feeling exhilarated, not exhausted. B. Lydiard—slow, steady (1) Park run (2) Golf course (a) 10 min. (b) 20 min. (c)
3. A. Weights and jogging B. Jogging and stretching
4. High knee and fast leg
5. Starts A. 2 at 1/2 speed, 2 at 7/8 speed, 30 yds. B. Same as A, 50 yds. (1) On your own (2) Gun C. Highs D. IH E. Back to back highs, 5 hurdles F. First 3, jog, last 3
6. Intervals Y. Fast 20-55 in middle Z. Over intermediates A. 110 (1) 18-15-14-12 (2) 17-15-13 (a) Curve (b) Straight (c) B. 165 (1) 22 (2) 20 (3) C. 165-110-55 (1) 22-13-6 (2) D. 220 (1) 30 (2) 28 (3) E. 330 (1) (2) F. 550 G.
7. Squad meeting
8. Special A. Sauna B. Swim C. Hill
9. Relay work A. Routine B. 55 C. Trial
10. Test effort A. Trial B. Compete (1) 40 (2) 60 (3) 90 (4) Full
11. Bunches A. 550 (1) 75-80 (2) B. 330 (1) 45-48 (2) C. 110 (1) 12 (2) D. 300-200-100 (1)
12. With A. Coach B.
14. A. Wind sprints (1) Curve (2) Straight B. Hurdle X drill C. Spring and bound D. Alternate run and jog at least 880 E.
15. Finish work A. First 3, jog, last 3 B. Full 10—float at 5, then go last 5 C. Last 5 hurdles
16. X drill—for fundamentals (a) 36 (b) 39 (c) 42 A. 5 step to side B. 5 step to top C. 3 step to side D. 3 step to top (1) Lean (buck) (2) Trail leg (3) Lead leg (4) Off arm (5) Lead arm (6) Quickness (7) On toes
17. 3/4 speed A. 330 B. 500 C.
18. 5 hurdles A. First 5 B. Last 5
19. Simulated hurdling on the grass
20.
21. A. Pictures B. Film
22. Simulated race A. 220 B. 440 C. (1) Over hurdles

M	Organization-lockers-equipment
T	Meet on use of weights
W	Discuss off-school courses-14A
T	3A
F	1A-1B-2A(1)-
S	
S	recreation
M	4x 1B-19-2A-6A(1)-14D
T	3A
W	8C
T	3A
F	10A-200 meters at 7/8 to 9/10 effort
S	
S	
M	2x 1A-19-6A(1)-Jog 880
T	3A
W	12-Jog
T	3A
F	2x 1A-11ABC-1B(1)
S	
S	
M	1A-1B-16ABCD(a)(b)
T	3A
W	8C
T	3A
F	
S	
S	

Figure 6.1b High Hurdle Training Schedule

High Hurdle NAME DATE October/November

1. A. Warm-up: jog 1 or 2 laps with relay pass. Hurdle X drill at 36 and/or 39 in. B. High knee and fast leg drill C. 2 starts to 1 hurdle
2. Fartlek: A. Holmer (varied-pace)—stride, sprint, recover—stride, meet a challenge or challenge, recover. Finish feeling exhilarated, not exhausted. B. Lydiard—slow, steady (1) Park run (2) Golf course (a) 10 min. (b) 20 min. (c)
3. A. Weights and jogging B. Jogging and stretching
4. High knee and fast leg
5. Starts A. 2 at 1/2 speed, 2 at 7/8 speed, 30 yds. B. Same as A, 50 yds. (1) On your own (2) Gun C. Highs D. IH E. Back to back highs, 5 hurdles F. First 3, jog, last 3
6. Intervals Y. Fast 20-55 in middle Z. Over intermediates A. 110 (1) 18-15-14-12 (2) 17-15-13 (a) Curve (b) Straight (c) Hill B. 165 (1) 22 (2) 20 (3) C. 165-110-55 (1) 22-13-6 (2) D. 220 (1) 30 (2) 28 (3) E. 330 (1) (2) F. 550 G.
7. Squad meeting
8. Special A. Sauna B. Swim C.
9. Relay work A. Routine B. 55 C. Trial
10. Test effort A. Trial B. Compete (1) 40 (2) 60 (3) 90 (4) Full
11. Bunches A. 550 (1) 75-80 (2) B. 330 (1) 45-48 (2) C. 110 (1) 12 (2) D. 300-200-100 (1)
12. With A. Coach B.
14. A. Wind sprints (1) Curve (2) Straight B. Hurdle X drill C. Spring and bound D. Alternate run and jog at least 880 E.
15. Finish work A. First 3, jog, last 3 B. Full 10—float at 5, then go last 5 C. Last 5 hurdles
16. X drill—for fundamentals (a) 36 (b) 39 (c) 42 A. 5 step to side B. 5 step to top C. 3 step to side D. 3 step to top (1) Lean (buck) (2) Trail leg (3) Lead leg (4) Off arm (5) Lead arm (6) Quickness (7) On toes
17. 3/4 speed A. 330 B. 500 C.
18. 5 hurdles A. First 5 B. Last 5
19. Simulated hurdling on the grass
20.
21. A. Pictures B. Film
22. Simulated race A. 220 B. 440 C. (1) Over hurdles

M	1B-5A-21A-11A-6A(1)-2B(1) (2-4x)
T	3A
W	12 or 8-6A(1)
T	3A
F	300y (2x)-100y (4x)-2A(1)
S	3B
S	

M	1A-5A-19-6A (4x)-2A(1)
T	3A-21B
W	12 or 8-6A(1)
T	
F	10A (100y or 5 hurdles)
S	10A (300y)
S	

M	1A-5A-100y (1x)-300y (2x)-200y (3x)-100y (4x)
T	3B-21B
W	12 or 8
T	3A
F	10A (100y or Hurdles)-2A(1)
S	
S	

M	1A-5A-19-6B (3x)-10A(1)
T	3A
W	8 or 12-6B (3x)
T	
F	10A (100y and Relay)
S	10A (Relay and 300y flat)
S	

Figure 6.1c High Hurdle Training Schedule

High Hurdle NAME DATE November/December

1. A. Warm-up: jog 1 or 2 laps with relay pass. Hurdle X drill at 36 and/or 39 in. B. High knee and fast leg drill
   C. 2 starts to 1 hurdle
2. Fartlek: A. Holmer (varied-pace)—stride, sprint, recover—stride, meet a challenge or challenge, recover. Finish feeling exhilarated, not exhausted.
   B. Lydiard—slow, steady (1) Park run
   (2) Golf course (a) 10 min. (b) 20 min. (c)
3. A. Weights and jogging B. Jogging and stretching
4. High knee and fast leg
5. Starts A. 2 at 1/2 speed, 2 at 7/8 speed, 30 yds.
   B. Same as A, 50 yds. (1) On your own (2) Gun
   C. Highs D. IH E. Back to back highs, 5 hurdles
   F. First 3, jog, last 3
6. Intervals Y. Fast 20-55 in middle
   Z. Over intermediates A. 110 (1) 18-15-14-12
   (2) 17-15-13 (a) Curve (b) Straight (c)
   B. 165 (1) 22 (2) 20 (3)
   C. 165-110-55 (1) 22-13-6 (2)
   D. 220 (1) 30 (2) 28 (3)
   E. 330 (1) (2)
   F. 550 G.
7. Squad meeting
8. Special A. Sauna B. Swim C. Hill
9. Relay work A. Routine B. 55 C. Trial
10. Test effort A. Trial B. Compete (1) 40
    (2) 60 (3) 90 (4) Full
11. Bunches A. 550 (1) 75-80 (2)
    B. 330 (1) 45-48 (2)
    C. 110 (1) 12 (2)
    D. 300-200-100 (1)
12. With A. Coach B.
14. A. Wind sprints (1) Curve (2) Straight
    B. Hurdle X drill C. Spring and bound
    D. Alternate run and jog at least 880
    E.
15. Finish work A. First 3, jog, last 3
    B. Full 10—float at 5, then go last 5
    C. Last 5 hurdles
16. X drill—for fundamentals (a) 36 (b) 39
    (c) 42 A. 5 step to side B. 5 step to top
    C. 3 step to side D. 3 step to top (1) Lean (buck)
    (2) Trail leg (3) Lead leg (4) Off arm
    (5) Lead arm (6) Quickness (7) On toes
17. 3/4 speed A. 330 B. 500 C.
18. 5 hurdles A. First 5 B. Last 5
19. Simulated hurdling on the grass
20.
21. A. Pictures B. Film
22. Simulated race A. 220 B. 440 C.
    (1) Over hurdles

M	1A-16ABCD-2X 6ZB-2X 11A
T	3A
W	8 or 12
T	
F	10A (2X 100-1X 300)-14A
S	
S	2A
M	1A-1B-5C-11A-2X 6ZB
T	7-3A-21B
W	1-5A-9A-6D-11A
T	
F	10A (Relay)-10A(3)-2B(1)
S	10A (100-300)
S	
M	
T	
W	
T	
F	
S	
S	
M	
T	
W	
T	
F	
S	
S	

Figure 6.1d High Hurdle Training Schedule

High Hurdle NAME DATE January

1. A. Warm-up: jog 1 or 2 laps with relay pass. Hurdle X drill at 36 and/or 39 in. B. High knee and fast leg drill C. 2 starts to 1 hurdle
2. Fartlek: A. Holmer (varied-pace)—stride, sprint, recover—stride, meet a challenge or challenge, recover. Finish feeling exhilarated, not exhausted. B. Lydiard—slow, steady (1) Park run (2) Golf course (a) 10 min. (b) 20 min. (c)
3. A. Weights and jogging B. Jogging and stretching
4. High knee and fast leg
5. Starts A. 2 at 1/2 speed, 2 at 7/8 speed, 30 yds. B. Same as A, 50 yds. (1) On your own (2) Gun C. Highs D. IH E. Back to back highs, 5 hurdles F. First 3, jog, last 3
6. Intervals Y. Fast 20-55 in middle Z. Over intermediates A. 110 (1) 18-15-14-12 (2) 17-15-13 (a) Curve (b) Straight (c) B. 165 (1) 22 (2) 20 (3) C. 165-110-55 (1) 22-13-6 (2) D. 220 (1) 30 (2) 28 (3) E. 330 (1) (2) F. 550 G.
7. Squad meeting
8. Special A. Sauna B. Swim C. Hill
9. Relay work A. Routine B. 55 C. Trial
10. Test effort A. Trial B. Compete (1) 40 (2) 60 (3) 90 (4) Full
11. Bunches A. 550 (1) 75-80 (2) B. 330 (1) 45-48 (2) C. 110 (1) 12 (2) D. 300-200-100 (1)
12. With A. Coach B.
14. A. Wind sprints (1) Curve (2) Straight B. Hurdle X drill C. Spring and bound D. Alternate run and jog at least 880 E.
15. Finish work A. First 3, jog, last 3 B. Full 10—float at 5, then go last 5 C. Last 5 hurdles
16. X drill—for fundamentals (a) 36 (b) 39 (c) 42 A. 5 step to side B. 5 step to top C. 3 step to side D. 3 step to top (1) Lean (buck) (2) Trail leg (3) Lead leg (4) Off arm (5) Lead arm (6) Quickness (7) On toes
17. 3/4 speed A. 330 B. 500 C.
18. 5 hurdles A. First 5 B. Last 5
19. Simulated hurdling on the grass
20.
21. A. Pictures B. Film
22. Simulated race A. 220 B. 440 C. (1) Over hurdles

M	Register-lockers-2B
T	4B
W	1A-4A-16ABCD-4x 6A(13-15)-8C or 12
T	9A-3A-4B-6C
F	1-5A-16ABCD-3x 6B-2B(1)
S	11 or 2
S	

M	1A-4A-16-2x 6A2(a)-2x 6A2(b)-4x 6A(13)
T	3A-4B-7
W	1A-5A-2x 4 hurdles-8 or 12
T	3A (grass)
F	1A-4A-2x 5B(2)-Jog-2x 6A2(a)-2x 6A2(b)-2A(1)
S	
S	

M	1-5A-6A(1)-6B-2B(1)
T	1-3 (grass)
W	1-5B(2)-16(2,3)(b,c)
T	1-3-Jog
F	10A (Relay-hurdles)
S	
S	

M	1-5A(2)-16(2,3)-11A
T	3A
W	1-5A(2)-10A(2)-6B
T	3A
F	Gear ready-jog
S	10B-indoors, or 3B
S	

Figure 6.1e High Hurdle Training Schedule

High Hurdle NAME DATE February

1. A. Warm-up: jog 1 or 2 laps with relay pass. Hurdle X drill at 36 and/or 39 in. B. High knee and fast leg drill
   C. 2 starts to 1 hurdle
2. Fartlek: A. Holmer (varied-pace)—stride, sprint, recover—stride, meet a challenge or challenge, recover. Finish feeling exhilarated, not exhausted.
   B. Lydiard—slow, steady (1) Park run
   (2) Golf course (a) 10 min. (b) 20 min. (c)
3. A. Weights and jogging B. Jogging and stretching
4. High knee and fast leg
5. Starts A. 2 at 1/2 speed, 2 at 7/8 speed, 30 yds.
   B. Same as A, 50 yds. (1) On your own (2) Gun
   C. Highs D. IH E. Back to back highs, 5 hurdles
   F. First 3, jog, last 3
6. Intervals Y. Fast 20-55 in middle
   Z. Over intermediates A. 110 (1) 18-15-14-12
   (2) 17-15-13 (a) Curve (b) Straight (c)
   B. 165 (1) 22 (2) 20 (3)
   C. 165-110-55 (1) 22-13-6 (2)
   D. 220 (1) 30 (2) 28 (3)
   E. 330 (1) (2)
   F. 550 G.
7. Squad meeting
8. Special A. Sauna B. Swim C. Hill
9. Relay work A. Routine B. 55 C. Trial
10. Test effort A. Trial B. Compete (1) 40
    (2) 60 (3) 90 (4) Full
11. Bunches A. 550 (1) 75-80 (2)
    B. 330 (1) 45-48 (2)
    C. 110 (1) 12 (2)
    D. 300-200-100 (1)
12. With A. Coach B.
14. A. Wind sprints (1) Curve (2) Straight
    B. Hurdle X drill C. Spring and bound
    D. Alternate run and jog at least 880
    E.
15. Finish work A. First 3, jog, last 3
    B. Full 10--float at 5, then go last 5
    C. Last 5 hurdles
16. X drill—for fundamentals (a) 36 (b) 39
    (c) 42 A. 5 step to side B. 5 step to top
    C. 3 step to side D. 3 step to top (1) Lean (buck)
    (2) Trail leg (3) Lead leg (4) Off arm
    (5) Lead arm (6) Quickness (7) On toes
17. 3/4 speed A. 330 B. 500 C.
18. 5 hurdles A. First 5 B. Last 5
19. Simulated hurdling on the grass
20.
21. A. Pictures B. Film
22. Simulated race A. 220 B. 440 C.
    (1) Over hurdles

M	2x 4x 1A-4AB-5A(2)-16(bc)-6B-6A-Jog
T	3-8A or 8B
W	1A-4A-11A(1)-12 to 8C
T	3A-4B
F	2x 4x 1A-5A(2)-16(bc)-5A-6D(2)-6A(14)-2B(1)
S	8C-3
S	recreation

M	2x 1-4A-16(bc)(5)-11A-11B-2B(1)
T	3A-8A or 8B
W	4x 1-6A(2)-8C
T	3A-8A or 8B
F	1-Jog-
S	10A(4)-36" and 39"-Relay-Jog
S	Jog

M	3x 2x 1A-16(1)(bc)-6B(3)-6D(2-1)-2B(1)
T	2x 4x 1A-6D(2-1)-6A(13)-11ABC
W	8C
T	2x 1A-4A-5B-6A(13)-2B(1)
F	10A (Relay-75y Highs)-11ABC
S	3-2B(1)
S	recreation

M	2x 1-4A-16(4)(bc)-11A-11B-2B(1)
T	3A-8A or 8B
W	4x 6AZ-8C
T	3A-8A or 8B
F	2A(1)
S	10A(3)-10A(300y IH)
S	Recreation

Figure 6.1f High Hurdle Training Schedule

High Hurdle NAME DATE *March*

1. A. Warm-up: jog 1 or 2 laps with relay pass. Hurdle X drill at 36 and/or 39 in. B. High knee and fast leg drill C. 2 starts to 1 hurdle
2. Fartlek: A. Holmer (varied-pace)—stride, sprint, recover—stride, meet a challenge or challenge, recover. Finish feeling exhilarated, not exhausted.
   B. Lydiard—slow, steady (1) Park run (2) Golf course (a) 10 min. (b) 20 min. (c)
3. A. Weights and jogging B. Jogging and stretching
4. High knee and fast leg
5. Starts A. 2 at 1/2 speed, 2 at 7/8 speed, 30 yds.
   B. Same as A, 50 yds. (1) On your own (2) Gun
   C. Highs D. IH E. Back to back highs, 5 hurdles
   F. First 3, jog, last 3
6. Intervals Y. Fast 20-55 in middle
   Z. Over intermediates A. 110 (1) 18-15-14-12
   (2) 17-15-13 (a) Curve (b) Straight (c)
   B. 165 (1) 22 (2) 20 (3)
   C. 165-110-55 (1) 22-13-6 (2)
   D. 220 (1) 30 (2) 28 (3)
   E. 330 (1) (2)
   F. 550 G.
7. Squad meeting
8. Special A. Sauna B. Swim C. *Hill*
9. Relay work A. Routine B. 55 C. Trial
10. Test effort A. Trial B. Compete (1) 40 (2) 60 (3) 90 (4) Full
11. Bunches A. 550 (1) 75-80 (2)
    B. 330 (1) 45-48 (2)
    C. 110 (1) 12 (2)
    D. 300-200-100 (1)
12. With A. Coach B.
14. A. Wind sprints (1) Curve (2) Straight
    B. Hurdle X drill C. Spring and bound
    D. Alternate run and jog at least 880
    E.
15. Finish work A. First 3, jog, last 3
    B. Full 10—float at 5, then go last 5
    C. Last 5 hurdles
16. X drill—for fundamentals (a) 36 (b) 39
    (c) 42 A. 5 step to side B. 5 step to top
    C. 3 step to side D. 3 step to top (1) Lean (buck)
    (2) Trail leg (3) Lead leg (4) Off arm
    (5) Lead arm (6) Quickness (7) On toes
17. 3/4 speed A. 330 B. 500 C.
18. 5 hurdles A. First 5 B. Last 5
19. Simulated hurdling on the grass
20.
21. A. Pictures B. Film
22. Simulated race A. 220 B. 440 C.
    (1) Over hurdles

M	*1A – 4A – 6A [4x] (12–13) – 11A (2) – 2B (a)*
T	*9A – 3A*
W	*1A – 16AB – 6A [4x] (12–13) – 8C*
T	*9A – 2B (a)*
F	*10A (Relay) – 300 yds. [1x] – 2B (a)*
S	*10A (4) – 300 yds. – 2B (b)*
S	*Study – jog*

M	*Exam week – jog, study, rest*
T	
W	*1-4-5A – 16ABCD – 6A2 [1–2x] – JOG*
T	
F	*1-4-5A – 1st. 3 – 6A(1)2 [2x] – 6A(2)2 [2x] – 200 yds. [1x] (grass)*
S	*Meet – 1 race*
S	*Jog – settle in spring trip*

	A.M.	P.M.
M	*Jog*	*Hill jog*
T	*Jog*	*4A – 5A(2) [2x] – 6B – 6A [4x] (12–13)*
W	*JOG*	*9A*
T	*Jog*	*1A – 1st. 3 [2x] – 5B – 200 yds. [1x] (grass)*
F		*Light – gear ready*
S		*Meet*
S		*Home*

M	*Register – 1A – 9A – 6C – 6B – 6A [4x]*
T	*9A*
W	*1A – 5A – 5A(1) – 5B – 6A(1) – 300 yds or 500 yds. [1x]*
T	*Light – 9A*
F	*Gear ready*
S	*Relay meet*
S	*jog*

Figure 6.1g High Hurdle Training Schedule

High Hurdle NAME DATE April

1. A. Warm-up: jog 1 or 2 laps with relay pass. Hurdle X drill at 36 and/or 39 in. B. High knee and fast leg drill C. 2 starts to 1 hurdle
2. Fartlek: A. Holmer (varied-pace)—stride, sprint, recover—stride, meet a challenge or challenge, recover. Finish feeling exhilarated, not exhausted. B. Lydiard—slow, steady (1) Park run (2) Golf course (a) 10 min. (b) 20 min. (c)
3. A. Weights and jogging B. Jogging and stretching
4. High knee and fast leg
5. Starts A. 2 at 1/2 speed, 2 at 7/8 speed, 30 yds. B. Same as A, 50 yds. (1) On your own (2) Gun C. Highs D. IH E. Back to back highs, 5 hurdles F. First 3, jog, last 3
6. Intervals Y. Fast 20-55 in middle Z. Over intermediates A. 110 (1) 18-15-14-12 (2) 17-15-13 (a) Curve (b) Straight (c) B. 165 (1) 22 (2) 20 (3) C. 165-110-55 (1) 22-13-6 (2) D. 220 (1) 30 (2) 28 (3) E. 330 (1) (2) F. 550 G.
7. Squad meeting
8. Special A. Sauna B. Swim C. Hill
9. Relay work A. Routine B. 55 C. Trial
10. Test effort A. Trial B. Compete (1) 40 (2) 60 (3) 90 (4) Full
11. Bunches A. 550 (1) 75-80 (2) B. 330 (1) 45-48 (2) C. 110 (1) 12 (2) D. 300-200-100 (1)
12. With A. Coach B.
14. A. Wind sprints (1) Curve (2) Straight B. Hurdle X drill C. Spring and bound D. Alternate run and jog at least 880 E.
15. Finish work A. First 3, jog, last 3 B. Full 10—float at 5, then go last 5 C. Last 5 hurdles
16. X drill—for fundamentals (a) 36 (b) 39 (c) 42 A. 5 step to side B. 5 step to top C. 3 step to side D. 3 step to top (1) Lean (buck) (2) Trail leg (3) Lead leg (4) Off arm (5) Lead arm (6) Quickness (7) On toes
17. 3/4 speed A. 330 B. 500 C.
18. 5 hurdles A. First 5 B. Last 5
19. Simulated hurdling on the grass
20.
21. A. Pictures B. Film
22. Simulated race A. 220 B. 440 C. (1) Over hurdles

M	1A-4-5A-16-6A-7
T	9-3A
W	9A-1A-1B-8C-110 (4x)
T	16ABCD(c)
F	5A-9A
S	Meet-Relay-120 Highs
S	Home-loosen up
M	9A-16-250y (1x)
T	1A-5A(2)-6A-11B-7 (4x)
W	9A-500 (easy grass) (1x)
T	1A-5A(1)-5B-5C-6B
F	Travel-loosen up
S	Dual meet
S	Home-loosen up
M	9A-1A-6B-6A-300y-Jog (4x 1x)
T	9A-Jog
W	9A-1A-3A-15B-15C-2B(1)
T	9A
F	Light
S	Meet-home
S	Jog
M	1-5A-16-5B-6B-Light jog (2x)
T	9A-3A
W	1-5A-5B-12-8
T	Relay and jog
F	5 (2 starts)-9A-Gear ready
S	Dual meet
S	Loosen up

Figure 6.1h High Hurdle Training Schedule

High Hurdle NAME DATE May

1. A. Warm-up: jog 1 or 2 laps with relay pass. Hurdle X drill at 36 and/or 39 in. B. High knee and fast leg drill C. 2 starts to 1 hurdle
2. Fartlek: A. Holmer (varied-pace)—stride, sprint, recover—stride, meet a challenge or challenge, recover. Finish feeling exhilarated, not exhausted. B. Lydiard—slow, steady (1) Park run (2) Golf course (a) 10 min. (b) 20 min. (c)
3. A. Weights and jogging B. Jogging and stretching
4. High knee and fast leg
5. Starts A. 2 at 1/2 speed, 2 at 7/8 speed, 30 yds. B. Same as A, 50 yds. (1) On your own (2) Gun C. Highs D. IH E. Back to back highs, 5 hurdles F. First 3, jog, last 3
6. Intervals Y. Fast 20-55 in middle Z. Over intermediates A. 110 (1) 18-15-14-12 (2) 17-15-13 (a) Curve (b) Straight (c) B. 165 (1) 22 (2) 20 (3) C. 165-110-55 (1) 22-13-6 (2) D. 220 (1) 30 (2) 28 (3) E. 330 (1) (2) F. 550 G.
7. Squad meeting
8. Special A. Sauna B. Swim C. Hill
9. Relay work A. Routine B. 55 C. Trial
10. Test effort A. Trial B. Compete (1) 40 (2) 60 (3) 90 (4) Full
11. Bunches A. 550 (1) 75-80 (2) B. 330 (1) 45-48 (2) C. 110 (1) 12 (2) D. 300-200-100 (1)
12. With A. Coach B.
14. A. Wind sprints (1) Curve (2) Straight B. Hurdle X drill C. Spring and bound D. Alternate run and jog at least 880 E.
15. Finish work A. First 3, jog, last 3 B. Full 10—float at 5, then go last 5 C. Last 5 hurdles
16. X drill—for fundamentals (a) 36 (b) 39 (c) 42 A. 5 step to side B. 5 step to top C. 3 step to side D. 3 step to top (1) Lean (buck) (2) Trail leg (3) Lead leg (4) Off arm (5) Lead arm (6) Quickness (7) On toes
17. 3/4 speed A. 330 B. 500 C.
18. 5 hurdles A. First 5 B. Last 5
19. Simulated hurdling on the grass
20.
21. A. Pictures B. Film
22. Simulated race A. 220 B. 440 C. (1) Over hurdles

M	1A-5A-16-5B (2x)-6AZ
T	9A-14A
W	7-5ABC-Jog
T	Gear ready
F	Light
S	Dual meet
S	Light
M	A.M. 9A | P.M. 1-16-5B-5C (grass)-200yds. (1x)
T	3A
W	1-5ABC-6BZ-jog
T	Light
F	Travel
S	Invitational meet
S	Home-loosen up
M	9A-19-14A
T	1A-5A-16-5B-5C-6B
W	1-9A-6A
T	1-5A-16-14A
F	Gear ready
S	Northern Division meet
S	
M	
T	
W	
T	
F	
S	
S	

Figure 6.1i High Hurdle Training Schedule

High Hurdle NAME DATE June

1. A. Warm-up: jog 1 or 2 laps with relay pass. Hurdle X drill at 36 and/or 39 in. B. High knee and fast leg drill
   C. 2 starts to 1 hurdle
2. Fartlek: A. Holmer (varied-pace)—stride, sprint, recover—stride, meet a challenge or challenge, recover. Finish feeling exhilarated, not exhausted.
   B. Lydiard—slow, steady (1) Park run
   (2) Golf course (a) 10 min. (b) 20 min. (c)
3. A. Weights and jogging B. Jogging and stretching
4. High knee and fast leg
5. Starts A. 2 at 1/2 speed, 2 at 7/8 speed, 30 yds.
   B. Same as A, 50 yds. (1) On your own (2) Gun
   C. Highs D. IH E. Back to back highs, 5 hurdles
   F. First 3, jog, last 3
6. Intervals Y. Fast 20-55 in middle
   Z. Over intermediates A. 110 (1) 18-15-14-12
   (2) 17-15-13 (a) Curve (b) Straight (c)
   B. 165 (1) 22 (2) 20 (3)
   C. 165-110-55 (1) 22-13-6 (2)
   D. 220 (1) 30 (2) 28 (3)
   E. 330 (1) (2)
   F. 550 G.
7. Squad meeting
8. Special A. Sauna B. Swim C. Hill
9. Relay work A. Routine B. 55 C. Trial
10. Test effort A. Trial B. Compete (1) 40
    (2) 60 (3) 90 (4) Full
11. Bunches A. 550 (1) 75-80 (2)
    B. 330 (1) 45-48 (2)
    C. 110 (1) 12 (2)
    D. 300-200-100 (1)
12. With A. Coach B.
14. A. Wind sprints (1) Curve (2) Straight
    B. Hurdle X drill C. Spring and bound
    D. Alternate run and jog at least 880
    E.
15. Finish work A. First 3, jog, last 3
    B. Full 10—float at 5, then go last 5
    C. Last 5 hurdles
16. X drill—for fundamentals (a) 36 (b) 39
    (c) 42 A. 5 step to side B. 5 step to top
    C. 3 step to side D. 3 step to top (1) Lean (buck)
    (2) Trail leg (3) Lead leg (4) Off arm
    (5) Lead arm (6) Quickness (7) On toes
17. 3/4 speed A. 330 B. 500 C.
18. 5 hurdles A. First 5 B. Last 5
19. Simulated hurdling on the grass
20.
21. A. Pictures B. Film
22. Simulated race A. 220 B. 440 C.
    (1) Over hurdles

M	1A-4-14A
T	5 (easy)-9A (easy)
W	9A
T	Easy jog
F	Prelims.
S	Conference finals
S	Picnic
M	Exams-light-study
T	light-study
W	1A-5A-5B-14A
T	1A-5A-5C-14A
F	1A-5ABC-14A
S	Light
S	9A
M	Light
T	9A
W	Light
T	Championship
F	Championship
S	Championship
S	
M	
T	
W	
T	
F	
S	
S	

hurdle and 8 yards between hurdles, then move to 14 and 9, then finally to 15 and 10.

The first step in the X drill is walking to the side of the hurdles. The athletes walk past the hurdles, keeping them on their lead leg side. As they approach each hurdle, they lift the lead knee and step over the hurdle with that leg only, keeping the trail leg out to the side of the hurdle. This exercise is repeated, then the men switch sides to practice with the trail leg. Again they walk past the hurdles, taking care to place the lead foot past the hurdle, then bring the trail leg over the hurdle with the toe turned out, so the foot will cross the hurdle parallel to its top. This exercise is also repeated.

The hurdlers next progress to trotting past the hurdles, using the same exercises as above, but taking only five steps between each hurdle. After the habit of leading with the knee has been acquired, the lead leg exercises are no longer used as part of the X drill. First they trot through two repetitions to the side exercising the trail leg, then they complete this stage of the drill by five-stepping over the top of the hurdles, using all aspects of correct form. This is also repeated twice.

The final stages in the drill are a switch to three steps between the hurdles. First two repetitions are run to the side using the trail leg, then two are run straight across the tops of the hurdles. While the previous exercises must be rather slow, the three-stepping exercises must be rather fast.

Several points of form are emphasized during the X drill:

1. The lead leg is directed by lifting the knee. If the knee is lifted in the approach to each hurdle, the foot will almost automatically clear the hurdle, and it will be less likely to be directed off to the side. The leg can also be elevated more quickly than if the hurdler led with the foot, since a short pendulum (the thigh) can move more swiftly than a longer one (the whole leg).
2. Pull the trail knee through and into sprinting position. The trail foot does not have to be thrust forward to reach into the next step if the knee is handled properly and the hurdler keeps on his toes and tries for a quick-stepping rhythm.
3. The toe of the trail foot must be rotated upward until the foot clears the hurdle in a position parallel to the top, rather than hitting the hurdle.
4. The shoulders must be kept level. To do this the trail hand (on the side of the lead foot) reaches about as far forward as the lead knee (but straight ahead, not across the knee), while the lead arm extends fully straight ahead and downward across the hurdle (this combination is sometimes referred to as "a hand and a half"). If either hand comes across the body, the hurdler will tend to land off balance and moving toward the side of the track.
5. The hurdler should strive to stay on his toes, trying not to run flat-footed or land on the heels before or after clearing the hurdle.
6. The "buck" or "dive," the lean over the hurdle by the upper torso, should

be held until the toe is almost on the ground. The trailing foot can then be pulled straight forward, clearing the hurdle with less effort.

The X drill is practiced as the conclusion of the warm-up exercises on each day when the hurdlers will be practicing their hurdling, which is usually two or three times a week. When working on technique with the X drill, only one fundamental is practiced at a time, such as running through the drill concentrating on keeping on the toes or getting the rhythm of the buck or dive. Working on everything at once may prove too confusing to the athlete.

Analysis of Hurdling Technique

The hurdler begins his race from a sprint starting position in the starting blocks, usually with a medium to elongated block setting, permitting better balance in preparation for the take-off over the hurdles. From a sprint start the runner may not be entirely upright when he reaches the first hurdle, eight steps later. As he approaches the hurdle, he concentrates on lifting the knee, rather than the lead foot. Notice the form of the hurdler, Willie Davenport, in Photograph 6.1*a*, page 138; in this picture he is preparing to attack the hurdle. His lead arm is coming forward in an elevated position, raising his center of gravity and facilitating hurdle clearance. He is raising his knee in preparation for attacking the hurdle.

Photograph 6.1*c* shows him just as he loses contact with the ground in clearing the hurdle. Notice that he is leaning into the hurdle well, but with no awkward exaggeration. He has led with the knee until his thigh is at its peak angle in the hurdle clearance; his foot has not been extended toward the hurdle yet.

Photograph 6.1*d* shows little basic change from the previous illustration, except that the foot has now reached out for the hurdle. The body lean is more pronounced, but still is not exaggerated. The trail leg has lost contact with the ground, but it has not yet begun to come forward to clear the hurdle.

The hurdler has begun his actual clearance in Photograph 6.1*e*. He shows good forward lean without being excessively stretched over the hurdle. His lead foot has crossed the top of the hurdle, and he is just beginning to bring his lead arm down to assist the final stages of his clearance. The hurdler reaches over the hurdle, then downward. As the arm descends, the hurdler's body will begin to straighten, and his lead leg will be forced down into contact with the track. The trail knee is beginning to come forward at this time.

The hurdler is halfway through his clearance in Photograph 6.1*f*. His trunk is gradually becoming upright, and his lead leg is reaching downward as his lead arm is brought down and to the rear. The body has not yet lost its forward lean. The trail leg is almost into the clearing position and has begun to come forward.

Photograph 6.1*g* shows the hurdler completing the hurdle clearance portion of his flight. His body has cleared the hurdle, and his lead leg is coming down to make contact with the ground, while the lead arm is now down and beginning

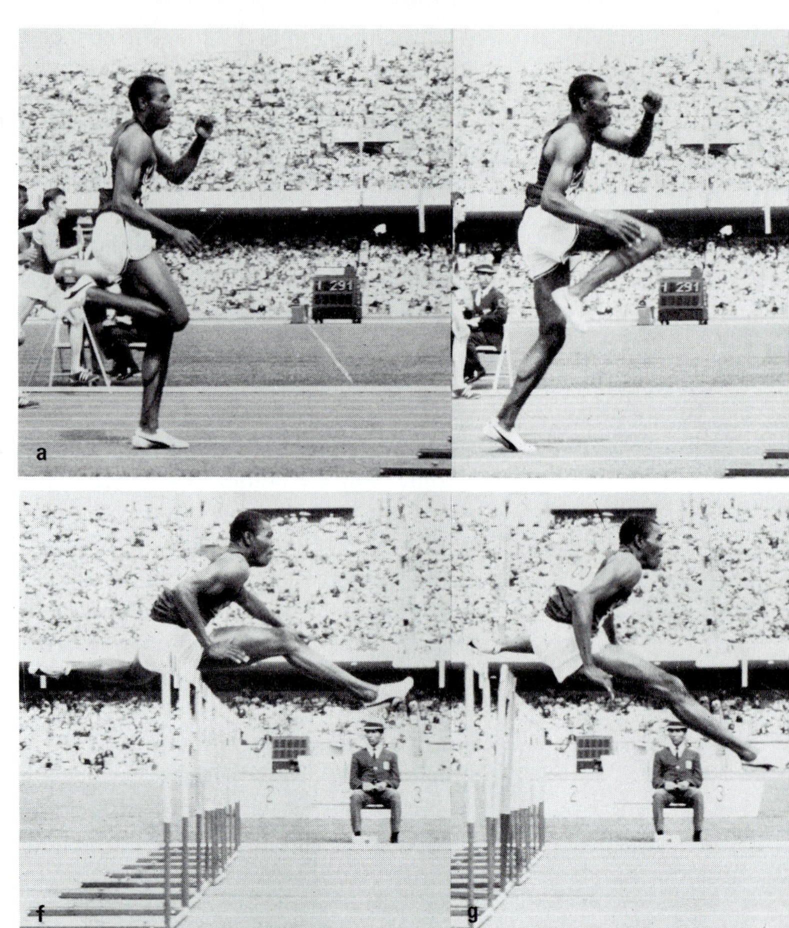

to move backward. He is beginning to bring his trail leg, led by the knee, through (under) his lead arm. Notice that the position of the trail foot is very good. It is parallel to the hurdle top as he completes his clearance. The apparent high clearance of the hurdler at this point is a result of the camera angle. The clearance is actually quite close. At this point the hurdler's center of gravity, which reached its apex before it reached the hurdle, is descending.

The hurdler is about to land in Photograph 6.1*h*. Notice his excellent balance and body position at this point. He is reaching down to land on his toe, rather than on his whole foot, and at the same time his line of sight is directed to the tops of the upcoming hurdles. His trail leg is being brought through the arm in a high position and not permitted to drop quickly toward the track. The trail arm is beginning to show as it moves forward into the preparation for the first step after landing.

He has landed in Photograph 6.1*i*, with the force almost causing his heel to

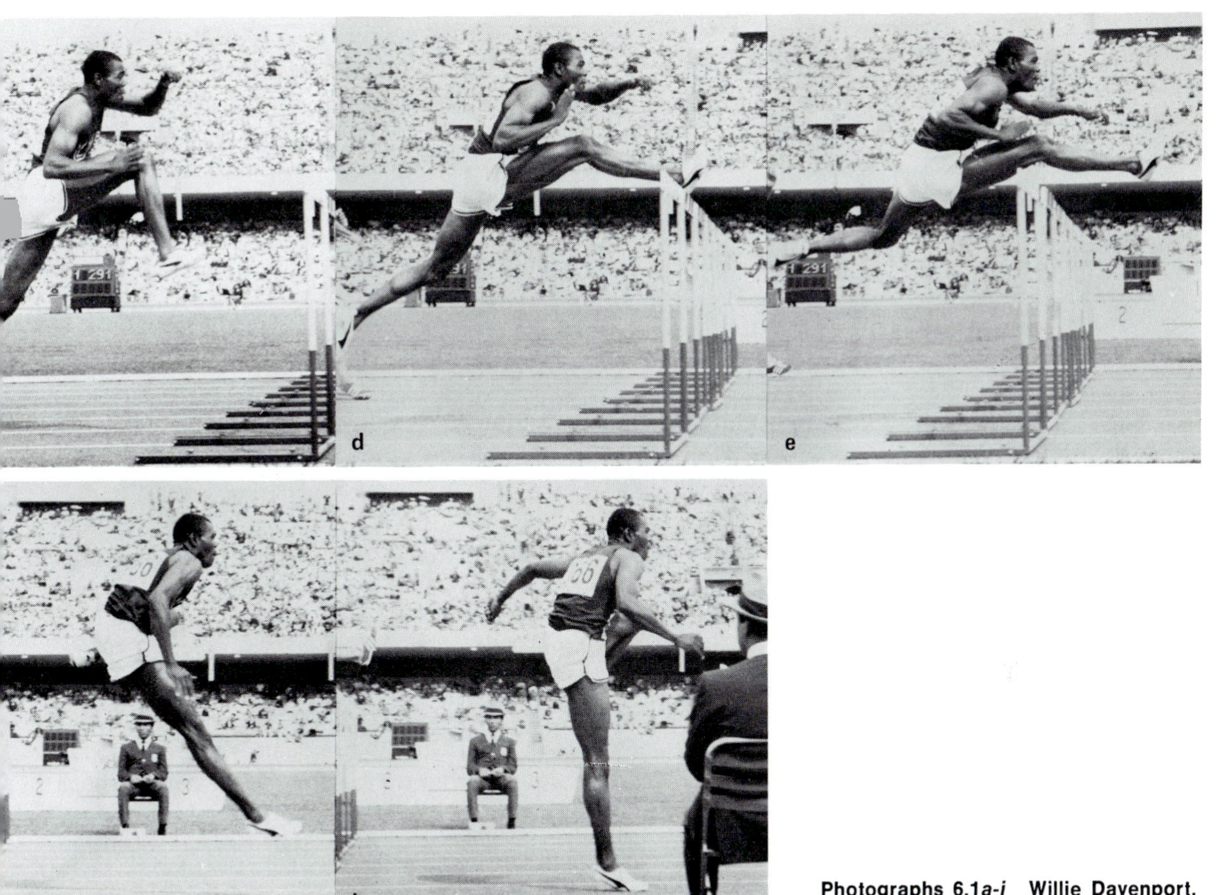

Photographs 6.1*a-i* Willie Davenport, U.S.A., in the high hurdles.

drop to the track. He actually has landed on the toes. The trail leg has been brought through well, and is now ready for the next sprinting stride. Notice that he has brought his knee forward, but he has not reached out into the next stride with his foot. The leg is in good sprinting position, which is all that is necessary to ensure a satisfactory stride length. He is keeping his body (and center of gravity) high, so his clearance of the next hurdle will not be too difficult.

Hurdling Faults and Their Correction

The hurdler should be observed regularly from three different vantage points. The common one is from the side. Many problems can be detected from this angle, but for better balance of observation, the coach should also watch from in front of and behind the hurdler. Many balance and mechanical problems will

Photographs 6.2*a-g* Annelie Erhardt of East Germany in the 400 meters.

appear from the front or rear which may be too subtle to detect from the side. If the hurdler is landing off balance, observation from the front or rear may reveal that he is trying to lead with his foot, rather than with his knee, resulting in his lead foot moving across to the side of the hurdle, leaving him off balance when he touches down.

Several hurdling faults need to be discussed at this point. Hitting the hurdle is likely the most common fault. It can result from a number of errors, such as taking off either too close to or too far from the hurdle, not having the steps down properly, insufficient altitude, or poor clearance form (bringing the lead leg down too fast, loafing over the hurdle, dragging the trail knee, or failing to turn the trail foot upward to clear the hurdle).

Another problem is running either off of or onto the heel. If the hurdler is back on his heel (flat-footed) when he prepares to clear the hurdle, he cannot generate as much speed, and he is giving away 3 to 5 inches of additional height which could be used to make the hurdle clearance easier. If he lands on his heel, rather than staying on his toe, he cannot maintain his momentum or speed as well as when on the toe, nor can he accelerate as quickly.

Improper use of the hands is another weakness. If the lead hand is thrown sharply upward, rather than straight ahead, it causes the body to remain in a too-erect position and the legs stay too low to clear the hurdle well. If the trail hand is not kept in a good position, it can result in the hurdler's balance being upset. A very common fault, especially with shorter or less-experienced hurdlers, is to throw the trail arm and hand straight out to the rear when clearing the hurdle. While balance may be maintained by this maneuver, the hurdler is delayed in picking up his sprint when he lands, because the trail hand leads the way into the first sprinting stride after the hurdle, and it is difficult to pull it back into position.

Crossing over the direction of travel with the lead foot is another troublesome error. If the lead foot deviates to the left or right of the direction of the

body's flight, the hurdler will land off balance and will have to use valuable energy in correcting his line of travel and his balance. If the runner is leading with his knee, he should not develop this problem. If he leads with his foot, the problem could become quite common.

Another balance problem is dropping the shoulder or turning the shoulder out of line. Ideally, the shoulders should always be squared facing the line of travel. If they turn out of line or one of them drops, the hurdler is getting off balance and further problems may develop. To combat this problem, the "hand and a half" is recommended. Since both arms are moved forward to some degree at the same time, there is less tendency to move the shoulders out of line than if one arm went forward and the other swung to the rear.

Some hurdlers will lock the knee or otherwise use too straight a lead leg in clearing the hurdle. While it may look picturesque, it adds to the clearance time, since the leg cannot be brought down into sprinting position as quickly as when it is slightly flexed. The runner will be sailing gracefully through the air while his opponents are down and sprinting for the next barrier.

Clearing the hurdle with the body in a too-erect position and straightening up too soon are closely related hurdling faults. If the hurdler clears the obstacle as though he were sitting on it, he is wasting energy, because he has to raise his center of gravity an additional 6 inches or more. Straightening up too soon handicaps the runner because of the law of physics concerning equal and opposite reactions: the leg will be forced down too quickly. The hurdler will hit the ground too soon and be off balance, and he may come down on the hurdle in the process. This may result from bringing the trail leg through too fast.

Galloping is a common problem with inexperienced hurdlers. By listening to the hurdler's foot (strike), a blind man could detect galloping. The steps should be quick and *regularly spaced.* If the runner is overstriding or trying to stretch too much to reach a hurdle, his steps will be all too obviously irregular, in both sight and sound.

The hurdler should at all times remember that the primary objective is to get to the finish line as quickly as possible. It is a sprint race with obstacles in the way. The hurdling form should not be developed in a way which gains beauty only to lose speed.

High Hurdle Bibliography

Carnes, Jimmy. "Teaching the hurdles," *Athletic Journal* 53 (February 1973): 56–57, 62.

Covey, Bob. "The high hurdles — training and technique," *Track and Field Quarterly Review,* March 1969, pp. 27–34.

Freeman, William H. "Training for hurdling," *Scholastic Coach* 37 (February 1968): 46, 48.

Jacoby, Edward G. "Speed in high hurdling," *Scholastic Coach* 38 (March 1969): 7, 54, 56.

Jesse, John. "Explosive power and muscular stamina for the hurdler," *Track and Field Quarterly Review,* February 1965, pp. 31–37.

Jett, Kirby, and Hodges, Gordon. "The 120 yard high hurdles and the 440 intermediate hurdles," *Track and Field Quarterly Review* 71: 106–8.

Jones, Hayes. "High hurdling," in *Track in Theory and Technique*, pp. 138–42. Richmond, Calif.: Worldwide Publishing Company, 1962.

Le Masurier, John. *Hurdling*, 3d ed. London: AAA, 1972. 39 pp.

Maughan, Ralph B. "The 120 yard high hurdles," *Track and Field Quarterly Review,* October 1966, pp. 60–65.

Ottoson, Ron. "From beginner to finished hurdler," *Scholastic Coach* 38 (April 1969): 10–11, 80–81.

Powell, John T. "How to introduce hurdling," *Track and Field Quarterly Review*, October 1965, pp. 60–64.

Rohe, Chuck. "High hurdling technique exemplified by Richmond Flowers," *Athletic Journal* 48 (March 1968): 44, 46–47.

Ross, Wilbur L. *The Hurdler's Bible,* 2d ed. Arlington, Va.: Yates Printing Company, 1969. 177 pp.

Ruckert, Jim. "The short hurdler," *Scholastic Coach* 37 (February 1968): 23, 29.

Santos, Jim. "Endurance training for hurdlers," *Track and Field Quarterly Review* 71: 169–72.

Sharpley, Frank. "Teaching beginners to hurdle," *Track Technique*, No. 4 (June 1961), pp. 119–22.

Simonyi, Gabor. "High hurdling the Guy Drut way," *Scholastic Coach* 42 (April 1973): 12–13, 110, 112.

Singh, Jagmohan. "Points sometimes overemphasized in high hurdles," *Track Technique,* No. 21 (September 1965), pp. 668–69.

Sorsby, Bill. "Hurdling," in *Track in Theory and Technique*, pp. 135–37. Richmond, Calif.: Worldwide Publishing Company, 1962.

Talley, Thad. "Hurdling at Arkansas State University," *Track and Field Quarterly Review* 70 (August 1970): 15–17.

Walker, Leroy T. "The high hurdler — 'what you see is what you get,' " *Track and Field Quarterly Review* 72: 210–12.

The intermediate and low hurdles

7

The 180-yard low hurdles might be described as an American anachronism, for it is a competitive event only in high schools in the United States. We will give little discussion of it here, for it can be adequately prepared for in training for other events. Some of Jerry Tarr's workouts called for periodic running of three low hurdles on the turn and on the straight, yet most of his time was spent on the high hurdles, plus sprint work. He still ran 22.8 for the 220-yard lows around a full turn, which would be the pace for about 18.6 or 18.7 for the high school race around a turn. The high school race primarily requires a good sprinter who can lift his feet. The race calls for a minimum of hurdling skill, for with a modicum of training a good sprinter will beat a good hurdler over the race nine times out of ten. Many excellent college sprinters have turned in world-class times in the lows with almost no hurdle training. It requires a bit more knee lift at intervals, but little else, beyond running like blazes throughout the race. Beyond these considerations, the training can be similar to that given for the intermediate hurdles. Fortunately, some states have begun the transition to the 330 intermediate hurdles, a fortunate step in light of the total lack of carry-over of the race beyond the high school level.

Training Techniques for the Intermediate Hurdles

The intermediate hurdler should think of himself as having the speed of a sprinter, the skill of a high hurdler, and the endurance of a half-miler. If he has the courage to believe this, he has the potential to become a great intermediate hurdler. The intermediates, while related to the highs, is an entirely different event. In tough competition, it is a tremendously unusual individual who can do both events and do them with the utmost skill. The danger is that he might have to put so much into the preliminary events that he would end up totally exhausted after three days of competition in each event, particularly after meeting other outstanding athletes who were competing only in one event. When Rex Cawley was competing in both races, he found it very difficult to accomplish the double in national competition. When Jerry Tarr won both events in the national meet, he would not have appeared in both events except that the competition in the highs was not very strong. Most important for him, only eight intermediate hurdlers showed up, allowing him to go all the way through his high-hurdle qualifying rounds without having to run an "all-out" race before his finals in either race. Besides, some high hurdlers are unable to cover the entire distance of the 440-yard intermediate hurdles, possibly because physiologically they cannot accommodate the carbon dioxide build-up, or perhaps because they are mentally lazy and do not want to prepare themselves to run this tough event.

What does the intermediate hurdler do? He should run off the blocks, attempting to reach the first hurdle in 6 seconds (49 yards). This is, of course, after he has developed his stride to the point that he reaches it quickly, but comfortably. From the first to the second hurdle takes about 4 seconds for most world-class athletes. We do not believe it is realistic for a beginning hurdler to try to reach the first hurdle in 6 seconds, the second in 10 seconds, the third in 14, the fourth in 18, and the fifth hurdle in 22, as a world-class performer might try to do. Rather, the beginning hurdler should start from a standing start, or down in the traditional sprint start, and run the first hurdle comfortably but quickly in about 7 seconds. He should then trot back and cover the same distance again, but this time going over the first three hurdles. He should take a recovery, jogging completely around the track; then when he reaches the head of the last straight, he should run the last three hurdles down the straight, trying to hit between 4 and 5 seconds between each hurdle. He should then take another full-lap recovery jog, then run the three hurdles on the bend, again trying to get between 4 and 5 seconds between each hurdle. He should complete another lap recovery jog, then run the last two hurdles, for about 110 yards, and try to finish up as he would in the 440-yard hurdle race.

A variation of this exercise is to run the first 110, recover with a quarter, run the middle 220 of the race, jog another lap, then finish with the last 110 yards of the hurdles. Some of the athletes at the Olympic Training Camp at Tahoe in 1968 used an exercise consisting of running 110 yards of hurdles, jogging back to the start, running 220 yards of hurdles, jogging back to the start, then running 330 yards of hurdles.

Too much hurdling is liable to produce banged-up knees and sore ankles from hitting the hurdles, so the intermediate hurdler should run through the X drill over the high hurdles, then run through intervals of hurdles totaling once or twice his racing distance, and then think of himself as a half-miler. He should

Figure 7.1a Intermediate Hurdle Training Schedule

Intermediate Hurdle NAME DATE September/October

1. Warm-up: jog 1 or 2 laps with relay pass, easy stretch, X drill
   B. High knee (slow) and fast leg
2. Fartlek A. Holmer (varied-pace)
   B. Lydiard—slow, steady (1) Park run (2) Golf course
   (a) 10 min. (2) 30 min. (3)
3. A. Weights and jogging B. Jogging and stretching
4. High knee and fast leg B. Arms emphasis
5. Starts A. 2 at 1/2 effort, 2 at 7/8
   B. Over 2 hurdles (1) 30 in. (2) 36 in.
   C. Back to back (1) 3 hurdles (2)
   D. First 3, slow jog, go last 3
6. Y. Over hurdles Z. Flat A. 110 (1) 18-16-14
   (2) B. 165-110-55
   C. 220 (1) 30 (2)
   D. 330 E. 165 F. 440 G.
7. Squad meeting
8. Special A. Sauna B. Swim C. Hill
9. Relay A. Routine B. 55 C. 110
10. A. Trial B. Compete (1) Full distance
    (2) 3/4 distance (3) First 3, last 3
11. A. 550-330-110 (1) 70-75, 42-45, 12-13
    B. 330-220-110 (1) 39-42, 25-27, 12-13
12. With A. Coach B.
14. A. Wind sprints B. Hurdle X drill
    C. Spring and bound
    D. Alternate run and jog at least 880
15. Finish work A. Jog 1st 330, go last 110
    B. Jog 1st 220, go last 220 C. Go last 330
    D. Finish work lane 2-5-8
16. Parts of race Y. Hurdles Z. Flat
    A. 110s—1st, 2d, 3d B. 165s—1st, 2d, last
    C.
17. 3/4 effort A. 220 B. 330 C. 550 D.
18. X drill A. 36 in. B. 39 in. C. 42 in.
    (1) 5 step to side (2) 5 step the top
    (3) 3 step to side (4) 3 step the top
19. A. Lead arm B. Off arm C. Hand and a half
20. A. On toes B. Shoulders level
21. A. Pictures B. Film
22. Simulated race A. 220 B. 440 C.
    D. Parts of race Y. Over hurdles

Date	Dist.	3/4	Date P.	Goal P.

M	Organization-equipment-lockers
T	7-use of weights-information
W	7-running courses, procedures-14A
T	1C
F	1A-1B
S	1A-1B
S	recreation
M	1A-11A-14A
T	3A (light)
W	4x 8C-6A (easy on grass)
T	
F	10A (220 at 7/8-9/10ths)-14D
S	
S	
M	4x 1A-11A-11B-6A(1)-14D
T	
W	12-8C
T	3
F	1A-11AB-1B
S	
S	
M	1-2x 3x 1A-1B-11AB-6B-2B(1)
T	3A
W	8C
T	
F	10A (100y and 300y)
S	
S	

Figure 7.1b Intermediate Hurdle Training Schedule

Intermediate Hurdle NAME DATE October/ November

1. Warm-up: jog 1 or 2 laps with relay pass, easy stretch, X drill
   B. High knee (slow) and fast leg
2. Fartlek A. Holmer (varied-pace)
   B. Lydiard—slow, steady (1) Park run (2) Golf course
   (a) 10 min. (2) 30 min. (3)
3. A. Weights and jogging B. Jogging and stretching
4. High knee and fast leg B. Arms emphasis
5. Starts A. 2 at 1/2 effort, 2 at 7/8
   B. Over 2 hurdles (1) 30 in. (2) 36 in.
   C. Back to back (1) 3 hurdles (2)
   D. First 3, slow jog, go last 3
6. Y. Over hurdles Z. Flat A. 110 (1) 18-16-14
   (2) B. 165-110-55
   C. 220 (1) 30 (2)
   D. 330 E. 165 F. 440 G.
7. Squad meeting
8. Special A. Sauna B. Swim C. Hill
9. Relay A. Routine B. 55 C. 110
10. A. Trial B. Compete (1) Full distance
    (2) 3/4 distance (3) First 3, last 3
11. A. 550-330-110 (1) 70-75, 42-45, 12-13
    B. 330-220-110 (1) 39-42, 25-27, 12-13
12. With A. Coach B.
14. A. Wind sprints B. Hurdle X drill
    C. Spring and bound
    D. Alternate run and jog at least 880
15. Finish work A. Jog 1st 330, go last 110
    B. Jog 1st 220, go last 220 C. Go last 330
    D. Finish work lane 2-5-8
16. Parts of race Y. Hurdles Z. Flat
    A. 110s—1st, 2d, 3d B. 165s—1st, 2d, last
    C.
17. 3/4 effort A. 220 B. 330 C. 550 D.
18. X drill A. 36 in. B. 39 in. C. 42 in.
    (1) 5 step to side (2) 5 step the top
    (3) 3 step to side (4) 3 step the top
19. A. Lead arm B. Off arm C. Hand and a half
20. A. On toes B. Shoulders level
21. A. Pictures B. Film
22. Simulated race A. 220 B. 440 C.
    D. Parts of race Y. Over hurdles

Date	Dist.	3/4	Date P.	Goal P.

M	4x 1A-4B-5B (easy)-11AB-14D
T	3A
W	1B-5B (easy)-18A-8C
T	21A-3A
F	3x 1A-18A(1)(3)-6D-14A
S	1A-1B-5A-10A (500y)-2B(1)
S	recreation

M	1A-1B-11AB-2A (park)
T	3-14A
W	4x 4x 1A-6A-8C-6A
T	3
F	10A (Relay-300y or 500y)
S	Your choice
S	

M	1A-4B-5B-11A-2A
T	3
W	4x 1B-4A-8C-6A
T	1B
F	2x 1A-6B-Jog
S	10 (Relay-385y)-2B(1)
S	

M	1-2x 1A-1B-5A-11A-2B
T	1B-8B
W	8C
T	3A
F	1A-9A-2B(1)
S	With or observe runners
S	recreation

Figure 7.1c Intermediate Hurdle Training Schedule

Intermediate Hurdle NAME DATE November/December

1. Warm-up: jog 1 or 2 laps with relay pass, easy stretch, X drill
   B. High knee (slow) and fast leg
2. Fartlek A. Holmer (varied-pace)
   B. Lydiard—slow, steady (1) Park run (2) Golf course
   (a) 10 min. (2) 30 min. (3)
3. A. Weights and jogging B. Jogging and stretching
4. High knee and fast leg B. Arms emphasis
5. Starts A. 2 at 1/2 effort, 2 at 7/8
   B. Over 2 hurdles (1) 30 in. (2) 36 in.
   C. Back to back (1) 3 hurdles (2)
   D. First 3, slow jog, go last 3
6. Y. Over hurdles Z. Flat A. 110 (1) 18-16-14
   (2) 13 B. 165-110-55
   C. 220 (1) 30 (2) 28
   D. 330 E. 165 F. 440 G.
7. Squad meeting
8. Special A. Sauna B. Swim C. Hill
9. Relay A. Routine B. 55 C. 110
10. A. Trial B. Compete (1) Full distance
    (2) 3/4 distance (3) First 3, last 3
11. A. 550-330-110 (1) 70-75, 42-45, 12-13
    B. 330-220-110 (1) 39-42, 25-27, 12-13
12. With A. Coach B.
14. A. Wind sprints B. Hurdle X drill
    C. Spring and bound
    D. Alternate run and jog at least 880
15. Finish work A. Jog 1st 330, go last 110
    B. Jog 1st 220, go last 220 C. Go last 330
    D. Finish work lane 2-5-8
16. Parts of race Y. Hurdles Z. Flat
    A. 110s—1st, 2d, 3d B. 165s—1st, 2d, last
    C.
17. 3/4 effort A. 220 B. 330 C. 550 D.
18. X drill A. 36 in. B. 39 in. C. 42 in.
    (1) 5 step to side (2) 5 step the top
    (3) 3 step to side (4) 3 step the top
19. A. Lead arm B. Off arm C. Hand and a half
20. A. On toes B. Shoulders level
21. A. Pictures B. Film
22. Simulated race A. 220 B. 440 C.
    D. Parts of race Y. Over hurdles

Date	Dist.	3/4	Date P.	Goal P.

M	1A - 18AB(1,3) - 11A - 11B - 2B
T	3A
W	1A - 4x 6C(2) - 4x 6A(2) - 8C
T	3A
F	1B - 3x 6E (9/10 effort) - 2B - 4x 6A (7/8 effort)
S	
S	recreation
M	1A - 1B - 18AB(1,2,3,4) - 11AB - 2B(1)
T	3A
W	1A - 5B - 8C - 4x 6A(2)
T	3A
F	10A (Relay - 880 or 440)
S	
S	
M	
T	
W	
T	
F	
S	
S	
M	
T	
W	
T	
F	
S	
S	

Figure 7.1d Intermediate Hurdle Training Schedule

Intermediate Hurdle NAME DATE January

1. Warm-up: jog 1 or 2 laps with relay pass, easy stretch, X drill
   B. High knee (slow) and fast leg
2. Fartlek A. Holmer (varied-pace)
   B. Lydiard—slow, steady (1) Park run (2) Golf course
   (a) 10 min. (2) 30 min. (3)
3. A. Weights and jogging B. Jogging and stretching
4. High knee and fast leg B. Arms emphasis
5. Starts A. 2 at 1/2 effort, 2 at 7/8
   B. Over 2 hurdles (1) 30 in. (2) 36 in.
   C. Back to back (1) 3 hurdles (2)
   D. First 3, slow jog, go last 3
6. Y. Over hurdles Z. Flat A. 110 (1) 18-16-14
   (2) 13 B. 165-110-55
   C. 220 (1) 30 (2)
   D. 330 E. 165 F. 440 G.
7. Squad meeting
8. Special A. Sauna B. Swim C. Hill
9. Relay A. Routine B. 55 C. 110
10. A. Trial B. Compete (1) Full distance
    (2) 3/4 distance (3) First 3, last 3
11. A. 550-330-110 (1) 70-75, 42-45, 12-13
    B. 330-220-110 (1) 39-42, 25-27, 12-13
12. With A. Coach B.
14. A. Wind sprints B. Hurdle X drill
    C. Spring and bound
    D. Alternate run and jog at least 880
15. Finish work A. Jog 1st 330, go last 110
    B. Jog 1st 220, go last 220 C. Go last 330
    D. Finish work lane 2-5-8
16. Parts of race Y. Hurdles Z. Flat
    A. 110s—1st, 2d, 3d B. 165s—1st, 2d, last
    C.
17. 3/4 effort A. 220 B. 330 C. 550 D.
18. X drill A. 36 in. B. 39 in. C. 42 in.
    (1) 5 step to side (2) 5 step the top
    (3) 3 step to side (4) 3 step the top
19. A. Lead arm B. Off arm C. Hand and a half
20. A. On toes B. Shoulders level
21. A. Pictures B. Film
22. Simulated race A. 220 B. 440 C.
    D. Parts of race Y. Over hurdles

Date	Dist.	3/4	Date P.	Goal P.

M	Class or squad organization-4A-3
T	Complete registration-7(procedures)-2B
W	1A-4A-1B-5C(1)-8D
T	7-3A-4B-6ZB
F	1-5A-4A-11A-2A
S	Workout
S	

M	1A-4A-4B-5B-16A-6C2(1)-2B (2x over 5B, 4x over 6C2)
T	1-4A-3A
W	1A-5A-4A-16B-11A-Jog
T	3A-8C
F	1-4A-5A-16B-11B-Jog
S	
S	

M	1-5A-16A-16B-11B-2A
T	3A
W	1-5A-6A(2)-6YB-Jog (4x over 6A(2), 2x over 6YB)
T	3A-grass run or 8C
F	1-4A-5B-6YA-6YB-2B (2x over 5B, 2x over 6YA, 2x over 6YB)
S	10 hurdles
S	

M	1-5A-16A-16B-11B-Jog
T	7-3A
W	1-5A-16B-11B-8A
T	3A
F	Gear ready
S	10A or B-Indoor meet
S	

Figure 7.1e Intermediate Hurdle Training Schedule

Intermediate Hurdle NAME DATE February

1. Warm-up: jog 1 or 2 laps with relay pass, easy stretch, X drill
   B. High knee (slow) and fast leg
2. Fartlek A. Holmer (varied-pace)
   B. Lydiard—slow, steady (1) Park run (2) Golf course
   (a) 10 min. (2) 30 min. (3)
3. A. Weights and jogging B. Jogging and stretching
4. High knee and fast leg B. Arms emphasis
5. Starts A. 2 at 1/2 effort, 2 at 7/8
   B. Over 2 hurdles (1) 30 in. (2) 36 in.
   C. Back to back (1) 3 hurdles (2)
   D. First 3, slow jog, go last 3
6. Y. Over hurdles Z. Flat A. 110 (1) 18-16-14
   (2) 13 (3) 12 B. 165-110-55
   C. 220 (1) 30 (2) 26-28
   D. 330 E. 165 F. 440 G.
7. Squad meeting
8. Special A. Sauna B. Swim C. Hill
9. Relay A. Routine B. 55 C. 110
10. A. Trial B. Compete (1) Full distance
    (2) 3/4 distance (3) First 3, last 3
11. A. 550-330-110 (1) 70-75, 42-45, 12-13
    B. 330-220-110 (1) 39-42, 25-27, 12-13
12. With A. Coach B.
14. A. Wind sprints B. Hurdle X drill
    C. Spring and bound
    D. Alternate run and jog at least 880
15. Finish work A. Jog 1st 330, go last 110
    B. Jog 1st 220, go last 220 C. Go last 330
    D. Finish work lane 2-5-8
16. Parts of race Y. Hurdles Z. Flat
    A. 110s—1st, 2d, 3d B. 165s—1st, 2d, last
    C.
17. 3/4 effort A. 220 B. 330 C. 550 D.
18. X drill A. 36 in. B. 39 in. C. 42 in.
    (1) 5 step to side (2) 5 step the top
    (3) 3 step to side (4) 3 step the top
19. A. Lead arm B. Off arm C. Hand and a half
20. A. On toes B. Shoulders level
21. A. Pictures B. Film
22. Simulated race A. 220 B. 440 C.
    D. Parts of race Y. Over hurdles

Date	Dist.	3/4	Date P.	Goal P.

M	1A - 18 - 4A - 5A - 6A (2) 4X
T	1A - 4A - 6E (18-19) 3X - 6A (3) 4X - 4A
W	7 - A - 18AB - 4A - 6A 4X - 8C
T	1A - 3
F	Jog and gear ready
S	10
S	Easy jog

Day	A.M.	P.M.
M	1B	3A - 6YC 4X
T		1A - 16YB - 300yds. 2X - 2A - 300yds (34) 2X
W	1B	1A - 6A 4X - 8C - 4 - 6A
T		1A - 18 - 16C - 2B - 6A 2-4X
F		Jog
S		Jog
S		10A (660yds.)
M	1B - 6A 3X	2B - 6A 4X
T		1A - 18 - 11B 2X - 2B - 14A
W	1B	1A - 6F 3-4X - (54-56) - 2A
T		1A - 6C (2) 6-8X
F	1B	
S		1B - (660 - 440 - 220) 1X - 2A
S		
M	1B	18AB - 16A - (600-300-100) 1X - 2A - 6A 4X
T		1A - 4A - 16B - 6C 2-4X - 2A - 6A 4X
W		3 - 8C
T	1B	6C (2) 6-8X - 2A - 6A 4X
F		18AB
S		10 (440yds. and IH or HH and IH)
S		2A

Figure 7.1f Intermediate Hurdle Training Schedule

Intermediate Hurdle NAME DATE March

1. Warm-up: jog 1 or 2 laps with relay pass, easy stretch, X drill
   B. High knee (slow) and fast leg
2. Fartlek A. Holmer (varied-pace)
   B. Lydiard—slow, steady (1) Park run (2) Golf course
   (a) 10 min. (2) 30 min. (3)
3. A. Weights and jogging B. Jogging and stretching
4. High knee and fast leg B. Arms emphasis
5. Starts A. 2 at 1/2 effort, 2 at 7/8
   B. Over 2 hurdles (1) 30 in. (2) 36 in.
   C. Back to back (1) 3 hurdles (2)
   D. First 3, slow jog, go last 3
6. Y. Over hurdles Z. Flat A. 110 (1) 18-16-14
   (2) B. 165-110-55
   C. 220 (1) 30 (2)
   D. 330 E. 165 F. 440 G. 550 F. 660
7. Squad meeting
8. Special A. Sauna B. Swim C. Hill
9. Relay A. Routine B. 55 C. 110
10. A. Trial B. Compete (1) Full distance
    (2) 3/4 distance (3) First 3, last 3
11. A. 550-330-110 (1) 70-75, 42-45, 12-13
    B. 330-220-110 (1) 39-42, 25-27, 12-13
12. With A. Coach B.
14. A. Wind sprints B. Hurdle X drill
    C. Spring and bound
    D. Alternate run and jog at least 880
15. Finish work A. Jog 1st 330, go last 110
    B. Jog 1st 220, go last 220 C. Go last 330
    D. Finish work lane 2-5-8
16. Parts of race Y. Hurdles Z. Flat
    A. 110s—1st, 2d, 3d B. 165s—1st, 2d, last
    C. Last 220 (1) 22
17. 3/4 effort A. 220 B. 330 C. 550 D.
18. X drill A. 36 in. B. 39 in. C. 42 in.
    (1) 5 step to side (2) 5 step the top
    (3) 3 step to side (4) 3 step the top
19. A. Lead arm B. Off arm C. Hand and a half
20. A. On toes B. Shoulders level
21. A. Pictures B. Film
22. Simulated race A. 220 B. 440 C.
    D. Parts of race Y. Over hurdles

Date	Dist.	3/4	Date P.	Goal P.

	A.M.	P.M.
M	1A	18BC–1X 10HH–16C(1)–16A–Jog
T		2X 16B
W	1B	18AB–1X 10HH–1X Last 265 at 220 pace–2A–4X 6A
T		9B
F	1B	3X 5B(2)
S		10A (full 120HH–full 440IH)
S		
M	1B	18BC–16B–11B–2A
T	1A	1B–3
W	1B	18AB–5D–15B–2A–4X 6A
T		1A–3
F	1B	5B–Jog
S		10B (IH and mile relay)
S		Travel–spring vacation
M	1B	18AB–16B–1X (660–440–220)–2A–Jog
T	1B	18AB–15C–15A–2–4X 6C
W	1B	18BC–2A–4X 6A
T	1B	18BC·5–16B–15B–4X 6A
F	1B	3A
S		10B—Dual meet
S		Travel home–re-register
M	1B	18AB–5C–Last 265 yds.–6G–6F–Jog
T		9–3A
W	1B	18AB–5D(HH)–Last 265 yds.–2A–4X 6A
T	7	Light
F		Gear ready
S		10B–HH and IH
S		Jog

Figure 7.1g Intermediate Hurdle Training Schedule

Intermediate Hurdle NAME DATE April

1. Warm-up: jog 1 or 2 laps with relay pass, easy stretch, X drill
   B. High knee (slow) and fast leg
2. Fartlek A. Holmer (varied-pace)
   B. Lydiard—slow, steady (1) Park run (2) Golf course
   (a) 10 min. (2) 30 min. (3)
3. A. Weights and jogging B. Jogging and stretching
4. High knee and fast leg B. Arms emphasis
5. Starts A. 2 at 1/2 effort, 2 at 7/8
   B. Over 2 hurdles (1) 30 in. (2) 36 in.
   C. Back to back (1) 3 hurdles (2)
   D. First 3, slow jog, go last 3
6. Y. Over hurdles Z. Flat A. 110 (1) 18-16-14
   (2) B. 165-110-55
   C. 220 (1) 30 (2)
   D. 330 E. 165 F. 440 G.
7. Squad meeting
8. Special A. Sauna B. Swim C. Hill
9. Relay A. Routine B. 55 C. 110
10. A. Trial B. Compete (1) Full distance
    (2) 3/4 distance (3) First 3, last 3
11. A. 550-330-110 (1) 70-75, 42-45, 12-13
    B. 330-220-110 (1) 39-42, 25-27, 12-13
12. With A. Coach B.
14. A. Wind sprints B. Hurdle X drill
    C. Spring and bound
    D. Alternate run and jog at least 880
15. Finish work A. Jog 1st 330, go last 110
    B. Jog 1st 220, go last 220 C. Go last 330
    D. Finish work lane 2-5-8
16. Parts of race Y. Hurdles Z. Flat
    A. 110s—1st, 2d, 3d B. 165s—1st, 2d, last
    C.
17. 3/4 effort A. 220 B. 330 C. 550 D.
18. X drill A. 36 in. B. 39 in. C. 42 in.
    (1) 5 step to side (2) 5 step the top
    (3) 3 step to side (4) 3 step the top
19. A. Lead arm B. Off arm C. Hand and a half
20. A. On toes B. Shoulders level
21. A. Pictures B. Film
22. Simulated race A. 220 B. 440 C.
    D. Parts of race Y. Over hurdles

Date	Dist.	3/4	Date P.	Goal P.

M	1A-4A-5A-16C-11A-Jog
T	9B-2A
W	3x 1A-18BC-16B-6D(39-42)-8C
T	9B-1A
F	Gear ready-14A (grass)
S	10B-Dual meet
S	Loosen up

M	1x 1A-18AB-16C-(660-440-220)-2B
T	3-9A-20 min. jog
W	2x 4x 1A-5A-16C-300yds.-8C-grass 55yds.
T	9A-16A
F	Gear ready-jog
S	10B-Dual meet
S	Loosen up

M	1x 1A-4A-18AB-5C-16B-Jog-500yds.
T	3A
W	1x 4x 1A-5A-5B-18BC-15B-300yds.-6A(grass)
T	3A
F	Gear ready
S	10B-Dual meet
S	1A-10A-2A

M	1A-18A-Jog
T	1A-4A-18AB-16A-15B-16ZA-Jog
W	4x 3-grass hurdle-6ZB
T	1A-5A-18BC-10A (120 yds.-36")- 16YA-16YB-2A
F	Easy
S	10B-Quadrangular meet
S	Jog

Figure 7.1h Intermediate Hurdle Training Schedule

Intermediate Hurdle NAME DATE *May*

1. Warm-up: jog 1 or 2 laps with relay pass, easy stretch, X drill
   B. High knee (slow) and fast leg
2. Fartlek A. Holmer (varied-pace)
   B. Lydiard—slow, steady (1) Park run (2) Golf course
   (a) 10 min. (2) 30 min. (3)
3. A. Weights and jogging B. Jogging and stretching
4. High knee and fast leg B. Arms emphasis
5. Starts A. 2 at 1/2 effort, 2 at 7/8
   B. Over 2 hurdles (1) 30 in. (2) 36 in.
   C. Back to back (1) 3 hurdles (2)
   D. First 3, slow jog, go last 3
6. Y. Over hurdles Z. Flat A. 110 (1) 18-16-14
   (2) B. 165-110-55
   C. 220 (1) 30 (2)
   D. 330 E. 165 F. 440 G.
7. Squad meeting
8. Special A. Sauna B. Swim C. *Hill*
9. Relay A. Routine B. 55 C. 110
10. A. Trial B. Compete (1) Full distance
    (2) 3/4 distance (3) First 3, last 3
11. A. 550-330-110 (1) 70-75, 42-45, 12-13
    B. 330-220-110 (1) 39-42, 25-27, 12-13
12. With A. Coach B.
14. A. Wind sprints B. Hurdle X drill
    C. Spring and bound
    D. Alternate run and jog at least 880
15. Finish work A. Jog 1st 330, go last 110
    B. Jog 1st 220, go last 220 C. Go last 330
    D. Finish work lane 2-5-8
16. Parts of race Y. Hurdles Z. Flat
    A. 110s—1st, 2d, 3d B. 165s—1st, 2d, last
    C.
17. 3/4 effort A. 220 B. 330 C. 550 D.
18. X drill A. 36 in. B. 39 in. C. 42 in.
    (1) 5 step to side (2) 5 step the top
    (3) 3 step to side (4) 3 step the top
19. A. Lead arm B. Off arm C. Hand and a half
20. A. On toes B. Shoulders level
21. A. Pictures B. Film
22. Simulated race A. 220 B. 440 C.
    D. Parts of race Y. Over hurdles

Date	Dist.	3/4	Date P.	Goal P.

M	*1A-5A-18AB-5C-16B-Jog-4X 6A*
T	*Grass hurdle - 4A*
W	*5A-5D-4A (grass)*
T	*5A-16A-Jog (grass)*
F	*Gear ready*
S	*10B - Dual meet*
S	*Loosen up*
M	*1B-4X 6A-4A-grass hurdle*
T	*1A-18AB-2x 6YE (first)-2x 6YA (last)-2A*
W	*3*
T	*1-18-grass hurdle-Jog*
F	*Gear ready, grass hurdle*
S	*10B-Northern Division meet*
S	*1X 500yds - 2B*
M	*1B-3A-2A*
T	*1A-18AB-5C-16B-jog-14A*
W	*7 - light grass*
T	*Grass hurdle - 14A (grass)*
F	*Prelims - Pac 8 meet*
S	*Finals - Pac 8 meet*
S	*Loosen up*
M	
T	
W	
T	
F	
S	
S	

Figure 7.1i Intermediate Hurdle Training Schedule

Intermediate Hurdle NAME DATE June

1. Warm-up: jog 1 or 2 laps with relay pass, easy stretch, X drill
   B. High knee (slow) and fast leg
2. Fartlek A. Holmer (varied-pace)
   B. Lydiard—slow, steady (1) Park run (2) Golf course
   (a) 10 min. (2) 30 min. (3)
3. A. Weights and jogging B. Jogging and stretching
4. High knee and fast leg B. Arms emphasis
5. Starts A. 2 at 1/2 effort, 2 at 7/8
   B. Over 2 hurdles (1) 30 in. (2) 36 in.
   C. Back to back (1) 3 hurdles (2)
   D. First 3, slow jog, go last 3
6. Y. Over hurdles Z. Flat A. 110 (1) 18-16-14
   (2) B. 165-110-55
   C. 220 (1) 30 (2)
   D. 330 E. 165 F. 440 G.
7. Squad meeting
8. Special A. Sauna B. Swim C. Hill
9. Relay A. Routine B. 55 C. 110
10. A. Trial B. Compete (1) Full distance
    (2) 3/4 distance (3) First 3, last 3
11. A. 550-330-110 (1) 70-75, 42-45, 12-13
    B. 330-220-110 (1) 39-42, 25-27, 12-13
12. With A. Coach B.
14. A. Wind sprints B. Hurdle X drill
    C. Spring and bound
    D. Alternate run and jog at least 880
15. Finish work A. Jog 1st 330, go last 110
    B. Jog 1st 220, go last 220 C. Go last 330
    D. Finish work lane 2-5-8
16. Parts of race Y. Hurdles Z. Flat
    A. 110s—1st, 2d, 3d B. 165s—1st, 2d, last
    C.
17. 3/4 effort A. 220 B. 330 C. 550 D.
18. X drill A. 36 in. B. 39 in. C. 42 in.
    (1) 5 step to side (2) 5 step the top
    (3) 3 step to side (4) 3 step the top
19. A. Lead arm B. Off arm C. Hand and a half
20. A. On toes B. Shoulders level
21. A. Pictures B. Film
22. Simulated race A. 220 B. 440 C.
    D. Parts of race Y. Over hurdles

Date	Dist.	3/4	Date P.	Goal P.

M	Light and 9A
T	1x 1A-5A-16C-500yds.-2A
W	2x 1A-5A-16B-300yds.-2A
T	Light-14A
F	Jog
S	1x 1A-5A-16C-500yds.-2A
S	1A-5A-16AY-2A
M	1A-5A-10A (10 highs at 39")-16B-2A
T	Light-gear ready
W	Travel-loosen up
T	Semifinals (N.C.A.A)-14D-14A
F	Trials-14D-14A NCAA
S	Finals NCAA
S	
M	
T	
W	
T	
F	
S	
S	
M	
T	
W	
T	
F	
S	
S	

Photographs 7.1*a-j* John Akii-Bua, Uganda, in the intermediate hurdles.

then use what we call step-down sets, running one or two sets of 660-440-220. This consists of a 660 at a 30-to 35-seconds-per-220 pace, for 1:30 to 1:45, then a recovery of 660 yards (or however much is needed). This is followed by a 440 at a slightly faster pace, also in the 30- to 35-seconds-per-220 pace. After a 440 jog, the set is concluded with a 220 in 28 to 32 seconds, and a 220 recovery jog. The runner might then run a second set, or he might take a run for a few miles through the local countryside, if it is countryside. Two courses through rolling hills are used at Oregon. Hill running is exhilarating, and it is also an excellent resistance exercise, just as is weight training.

The hurdlers also follow a regular schedule of weight training. It is identical to the one used by the sprinters and longer-distance runners. Ten exercises are used which will exercise the entire body. If the runner wishes, he can develop his own routines beyond these basic exercises as he becomes familiar with the training. It is the prerogative of the individual athletes. The basic routine can be done in 10 minutes, so the athlete can benefit without feeling that excessive time is required of him.

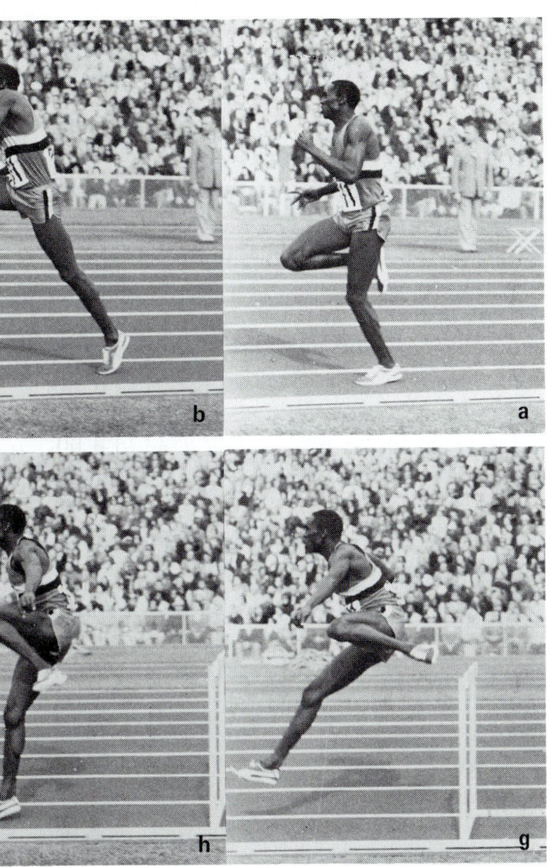

The most important thing for the hurdler is that he establish a routine which will look after the various parts of his race, giving enough attention to the mechanical fundamentals of his event and to the pleasures of the preparation, so he will go into the competition with the belief that he is fully prepared to turn in his very best effort.

For more details on basic hurdling skills and training, with more extensive bibliographical coverage, see Chapter 6, "The high hurdles."

Analysis of Intermediate Hurdle Form

The example of running style for the intermediate hurdles shown here is that of John Akii-Bua, who set a world record of 47.8 seconds for the 440-yard hurdles in 1972. The form is not very different than that used for the high hurdles, since the intermediate hurdles are 3 feet tall.

In the first frame (Photograph 7.1*a*) he is gathering himself to go over the hurdle. He leads with the right leg, and he is bringing the lead knee through high as he begins to move it toward the hurdle. He is also bringing his lead (left) hand forward. Because of the strenuousness of the intermediate hurdle race, the hurdling form exhibited often may appear technically inferior. This results primarily from fatigue and may also be seen in the steeplechase.

The next frame (Photograph 7.1*b*) shows good drive in leading with the knee as he attacks the hurdle. He is fully up on the trail toe as he pushes off. The lead hand can now be seen coming across the body. While a straight-ahead thrust of the lead hand might in most instances be preferred, there may be individual matters of technique which make this cross-swing the most technically advantageous method for this hurdler. The chest and head are also beginning to lean forward into the hurdle, though he appears to be ducking his head a bit.

As he attains full flight before reaching the hurdle (Photograph 7.1*c*), the lead thigh has been raised slightly, and the lead foot is now reaching out to clear the hurdle. The lead arm is still coming across the body, but it is high, helping to raise the center of gravity for the hurdle clearance.

The hurdler has reached the barrier in the fourth frame (Photograph 7.1*d*), and his lead leg is fully extended, though it is not locked. The body and lead arm are in excellent position for the hurdle clearance. The trail leg and foot are beginning to turn to the side and move forward for their clearance of the hurdle.

The hurdler is next seen (Photograph 7.1*f*) descending over the hurdle. He is beginning to drop his lead foot and lead hand, and his trail hand has just begun to move forward. His trail knee and foot are raised into position for clearing the hurdle, and they have moved well forward.

The hurdler is preparing to land in the next picture (Photograph 7.1*g*). His toe is extended for the landing, and he is bringing his trail knee through (under) his right arm. In the eighth picture (Photograph 7.1*h*), he has touched down, landing well on the toes. He can be seen bringing the trail knee through for the next stride, but the trail knee is not being brought through in as high a position as in the high hurdles. Note that both arms seem to be moving in arcs about the body, rather than forward or to the rear, as one would hope for in a good hurdle clearance.

Finally, the hurdler is moving into his first stride after landing (Photograph 7.1*j*). His body position is good, pushing off with his toes and bringing his trail knee into the sprinting position. His arms are high, keeping his center of gravity high, but the trail arm appears to be almost out of control, being extended far to the rear, which requires the expenditure of additional effort to return to control.

The primary differences between the hurdling form for the high and intermediate hurdles are few. They result in large part from the lower hurdle height, which requires less lift and effort to clear, therefore less technical excellence is necessary. Because the intermediate race is longer, the pace is slower, and the hurdler may be a bit more upright in his clearance. Also, the additional length adds a considerable fatigue factor, which further modifies the form exhibited by the hurdlers.

Intermediate and Low Hurdle Bibliography

Bartusek, Borivoj. "400-meter hurdles training and technique," trans. by Charles L. Sullivan, *Track Technique*, No. 38 (December 1969), pp. 1212–14.

Farmer, Dixon. "Getting the most from the intermediates," *Athletic Journal* 50 (February 1970): 34, 64–65.

_______. "Intermediate hurdles," *Track and Field Quarterly Review* 70 (May 1970): 55–63.

Hirschi, Willard. "440 intermediate hurdles: continuous change," *Track and Field Quarterly Review* 73 (March 1973): 26–33.

Hirth, Hans. "Training the 400-meter hurdler," trans. by Walter Morris, *Track Technique*, No. 47 (March 1972), pp. 1488–90.

Le Masurier, John. "David Hemery, golden hurdler," *Athletic Coach* 2 (December 1968): 10–13.

May, Joe. "Intermediate hurdles," *Track and Field Quarterly Review,* March 1967, pp. 36–43.

Mitchell, Les. "Bend running in the quarter hurdles," *Track Technique*, No. 33 (September 1968), pp. 1045–46.

O'Connor, W. Harold. "Intermediate hurdling," *Scholastic Coach* 38 (February 1969): 10–11, 42–43.

Singh, Jagmohan. "Pace judgement and stride plan in 400 meter hurdles," *Track Technique*, No. 20 (June 1965), pp. 615–17.

Smith, Bill. "Hemery's rush for gold," *Athletic Journal* 49 (January 1969): 8–9, 140–43.

Snyder, Larry. "Intermediate hurdles," *Track and Field Quarterly Review,* April 1964, pp. 40–47.

three

The Jumps

The high jump

The Watusi warriors of Africa were, and probably still are, the world record holders in free-style high jumping. Many termite hills are found in their part of Africa. As a sport these men compete regularly in high jumping, using the termite hills as take-off platforms. Using a rock-hard, rounded hill seven inches tall to give a "lift" at the take-off, these warriors consistently cleared 7 feet above the take-off point. In 1956 the Watusi record for the high jump stood at 8 feet ½ inch, compared to the "official" world record of 7 feet ¼ inch. The record holder was a thirty-seven-year-old man. The Swedish or Russian ½-inch sole is the limit for "built-up" jumping shoes for "official" jumping, but it had its beginnings in the Watusi ingenuity.

The high jumper is usually average or above average in height and possessing good spring. He will likely be a tenacious worker, but not necessarily well coordinated. The general test for high jumpers is the jump-and-reach, or Sargent jump, but do not consider it an infallible guide. There have been world-class high jumpers no taller than 5 feet 8 inches tall. On the jumping test, Dick Fosbury, who went over 7 feet 4 inches, was outjumped by some weight men on his college team.

The technique as a whole is simple. Most jumpers use an approach of six to eight steps, taking off from the foot nearest the crossbar. A kick is coordinated by an upward swing of the arms, and the jumper goes into a layout designed to get him across the bar, then down to the landing pit. Some variations upon this have occurred since the advent of the "Fosbury flop," so the flop will be discussed separately to avoid confusion.

Discussion of the Major High Jump Styles

There are several major techniques or "styles" of jumping, some of which are rarely used today. The oldest style is the "scissors," with the jumper running up to the bar and kicking up first one leg and then the other, clearing the bar in a sitting-up position. It is the least efficient way to jump. Another form seldom seen is the "Eastern cut-off," a slightly more efficient, but confusing, variation of the scissors.

The Western roll is still used, though only a few athletes compete using this style. It is made with a traditional approach from the side, taking off from the inside foot. The athlete goes into a layout on top of the bar, clearing it on his *side,* bringing his take-off leg through between the bar and his kicking leg. If the jump is high enough, he will land on his two hands and his take-off foot. This is still an excellent style to learn for its assistance in developing proper take-off habits.

The most common style today is the "straddle," which has several variations. Also called the "belly roll," this is as efficient a technique as can be found, although there are questions concerning possible mechanical advantages of the Fosbury flop. The belly roll is the best name, perhaps, simply because it perfectly describes the clearance of the bar. The approach and take-off are the same as for the Western roll, but the athlete clears the bar while facing down toward it, rolling around and over it. There are variations of this style, such as the true belly roll, with the jumper in a beautiful layout which perfectly parallels the bar. There is a variation sometimes referred to as the dive straddle, since the head clears the bar ahead of the leg, similar to Brumel's style.

There is an occasional version of a "dive" style of jumping. Perhaps the most prominent recent dive was by AAU champion Bobby Avant, who bettered 7 feet with an uncomfortable dive form very similar to a high jumper trying a forward roll over the bar. Unfortunately, sawdust pits were still common, which had a hard effect upon his cervical vertebrae.

The most recent variation is the Fosbury flop, which won the 1968 Olympic title. It is a variation of the occasionally seen back layout, which in turn came from the scissors (which was Fosbury's procedure as he developed the style). From a scissors jump with an approach to the side, the jumper lifts first the inside leg, then the outside leg to clear the bar, as one might go over a low fence one leg at a time while sitting down. A more efficient style evolved from this, using the same basic take-off, but with the back in a layout position, so that the jumper cleared the bar while lying on his back. From this start, Fosbury gradually arrived at a curved run and a clearance which took the body over

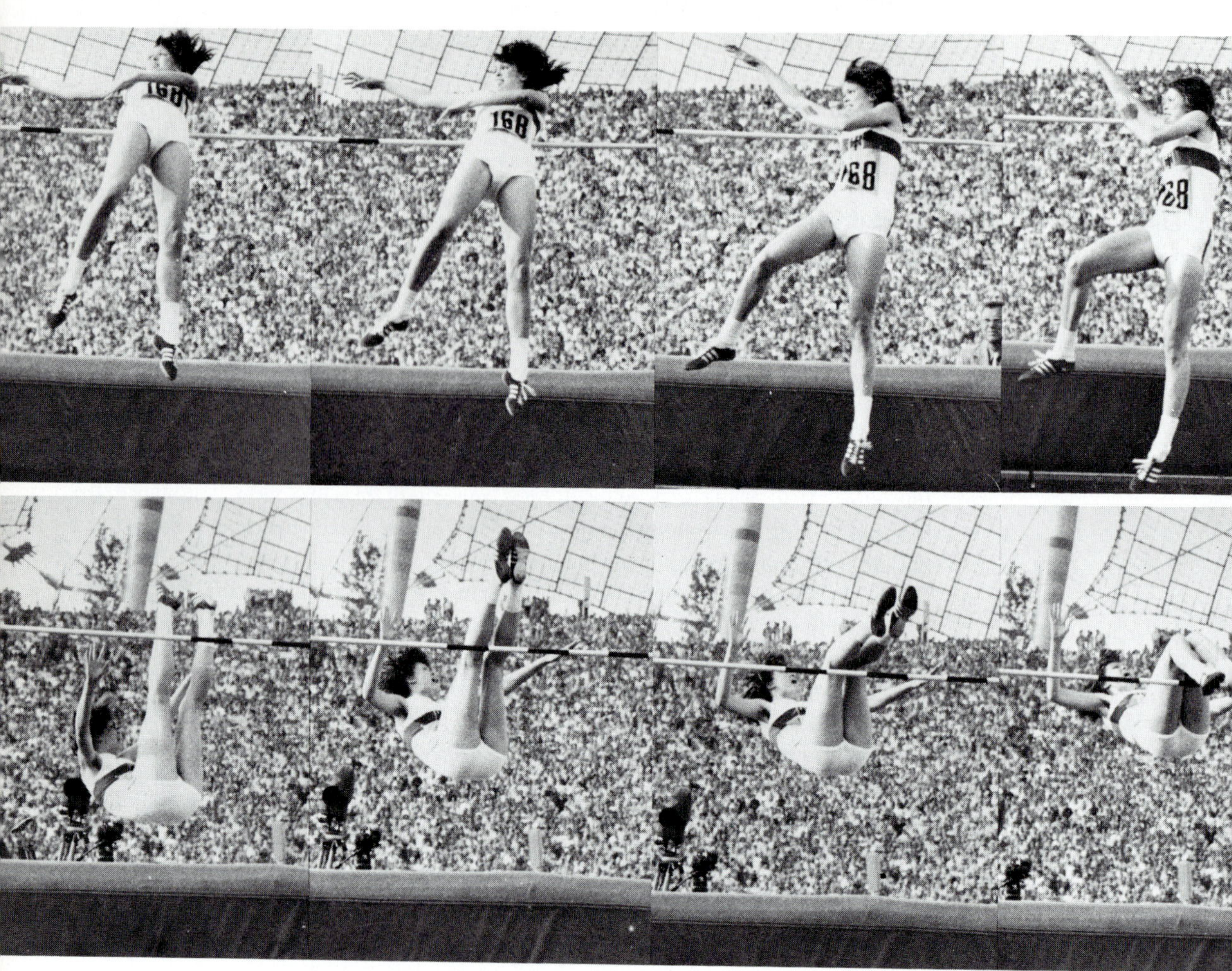

Photographs 8.1*a-p* Ulrika Meyfarth, West Germany, in the high jump.

the bar at a 90-degree angle to the bar. It has been conjectured that from the standpoint of the raising of the center of gravity, the flop *may* be more efficient than the straddle.

Actually, three styles should be discussed in detail: (1) the Western roll, (2) the straddle, and (3) the flop, or back layout. The approach and take-off for the Western roll and the straddle are virtually identical. The jumper will start from a check mark about eight strides from his take-off point. Most often he will be running toward the bar in a line which forms an angle of between 30 and 45 degrees in relation to the crossbar. The speed of the approach varies with the individual jumper. Some jumpers make a slow approach, relying heavily upon spring for their height, while other jumpers make a fast approach, relying on leg strength to enable them to convert their forward momentum to upward

momentum. Generally the last three strides will be longer and faster, as the athlete lowers his center of gravity and "gathers" for the take-off. The jumper plants the heel of his take-off foot solidly, coordinating the "brake" on his forward momentum with a swift upward kick of the lead leg and upward thrust of the arms, designed to convert his momentum as mentioned. On the take-off, the plant foot will be put down out ahead of the jumper's center of gravity. The jump is then coordinated as cited previously.

The clearance method of the Western roll and the straddle forms has been recited already. The Western roll jumper will kick up with his outside leg, then bring his trail leg up and through between the bar and the lead leg. The straddle jumper will kick up, but the lead leg will continue over the bar, *after* which the trail leg will clear the bar, so that the athlete goes over the bar on his stomach.

If the height of the jump is great enough, he will continue to rotate as he falls, landing on his back.

Analysis of Common Jumping Faults

A common fault when jumping with the straddle style is leaning into the crossbar. The result is a poor jump, usually hitting the crossbar as the jumper rises into the air. This is where work on the Western roll can be helpful, since the athlete can hardly perform the Western roll if he has leaned into the bar at the take-off. Some earlier jumpers would use the Western roll at the lower heights

Photographs 8.2*a-n*   Valeriy Brumel, world record holder, executing the "dive-straddle."

during meets, then switch over to the straddle as they reached the higher, more difficult heights.

Delaying the arm and leg lift is a fault which can destroy a jump because it allows most of the momentum of the jumper's approach run to go to waste. The forward momentum must be converted to upward momentum at just the right time, or the jumper will have to rely entirely upon his spring. If he does this, he is unlikely to make a successful jump.

Placing the take-off foot out of position also affects the conversion of forward to upward momentum, because the take-off foot acts as the "brake" for the forward run. When it applies the brakes, the arms and kicking leg are supposed to simultaneously provide lift, converting the direction of the momentum.

If the foot is planted improperly, the runner may continue forward into the bar, or he may convert his momentum to the wrong direction.

If the height is reached too soon or too late, the jumper will generally miss. This fault is corrected by moving the starting and take-off points either in or out from the landing area by several inches. If the height is reached too soon, the jumper is taking off too far from the bar and should move his marks in a bit closer. In this case the jumper will generally hit the bar while coming down on the other side of it. If he reaches his height too late, he has taken off too close to the bar, usually hitting it as he rises into the air. He should then move his marks outward a bit.

Finally, the jumper may show poor mechanics while clearing the crossbar. In this case, he might have sufficient height for the jump, yet still knock off the bar. There are contrasting styles of clearance readily visible to the observer. The Russians usually show the mechanically correct method of clearance by rotating the left shoulder downward to raise the left leg over the crossbar. The traditional clearance is a roll of the entire body over the bar. The Russian method would not *seem* to be correct, but when studied closely it shows itself quite effective. It requires better conditioning, strength, and technique than the older style, and is more suited to the Russian approach, which is faster and more vigorous than is commonly seen with straddle jumpers. The fast approach is a characteristic which Russian straddle jumpers share with the Fosbury flop–style jumpers.

Analysis of a Straddle Sequence

Valeriy Brumel held the world record in the high jump for better than ten years. The sequence used here was taken in a jump of over 7 feet 5 inches. Brumel's speedy approach is clearly visible (Photograph 8.2*a*, page 164) as he drops his center of gravity and takes a long last stride leading to his take-off point. He drives upward with his kicking leg and both arms (Photographs 8.2*b* to *e*). His kick begins as a straight-leg kick, but the knee gradually bends, perhaps to permit greater acceleration in the later stages of the take-off. He reaches over the bar and down with his right arm (Photographs 8.2*f* and *g*) and also brings his head over the bar and down soon (Photographs 8.2*h* to *j*). This technique is used in a variation of the straddle sometimes called the "dive-straddle." As he clears the bar and falls toward the pit (Photographs 8.2*k* to *n*), he keeps his feet widely apart, facilitating his final clearance and preventing sloppiness over the bar.

The Fosbury "Flop"

Four advantages of the Fosbury flop, or reverse layout, make it worth the coach's consideration. First, the style is very easy to learn. Second, there are fewer technical points to give problems, compared to other jumping forms.

Third, the form permits greater utilization of the athlete's natural speed than other forms. Fourth, the sensation of flight created by the form is more fun to many jumpers than other ways of jumping.

These advantages do not necessarily mean that there are no risks to the form. One risk should not be overlooked: only a good foam rubber landing pit should *ever* be used for jumping with this form. Sawdust or shavings are *not* safe as a landing area. The risks of back or neck injury are considerable if any landing area other than a large, deep foam rubber pit is used.

The "flop" style of jumping is much simpler in practice than it appears. Most athletes take an eight-step approach, the first step being with the right foot if the jumper plants with his left foot on the take-off. Some jumpers will rock into the first step, as Fosbury did, though it is mostly a personal thing which is the result of nervousness or a way of helping the jumper build his concentration.

If the athlete takes off on his left foot, he will approach the bar from the right side of the pit (Figure 8.1). He should measure his starting point when his

Figure 8.1 Fosbury-Style Approach.

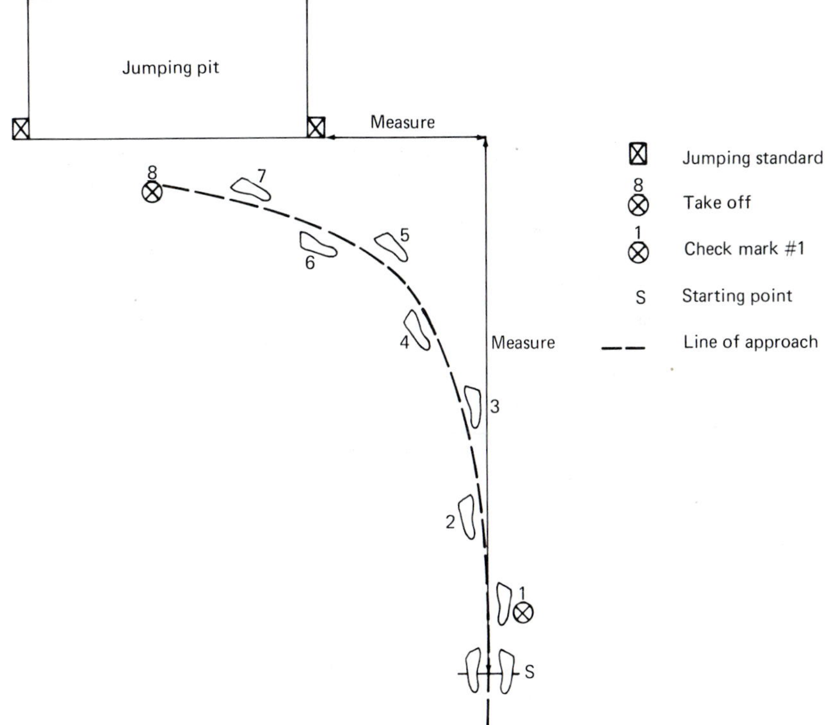

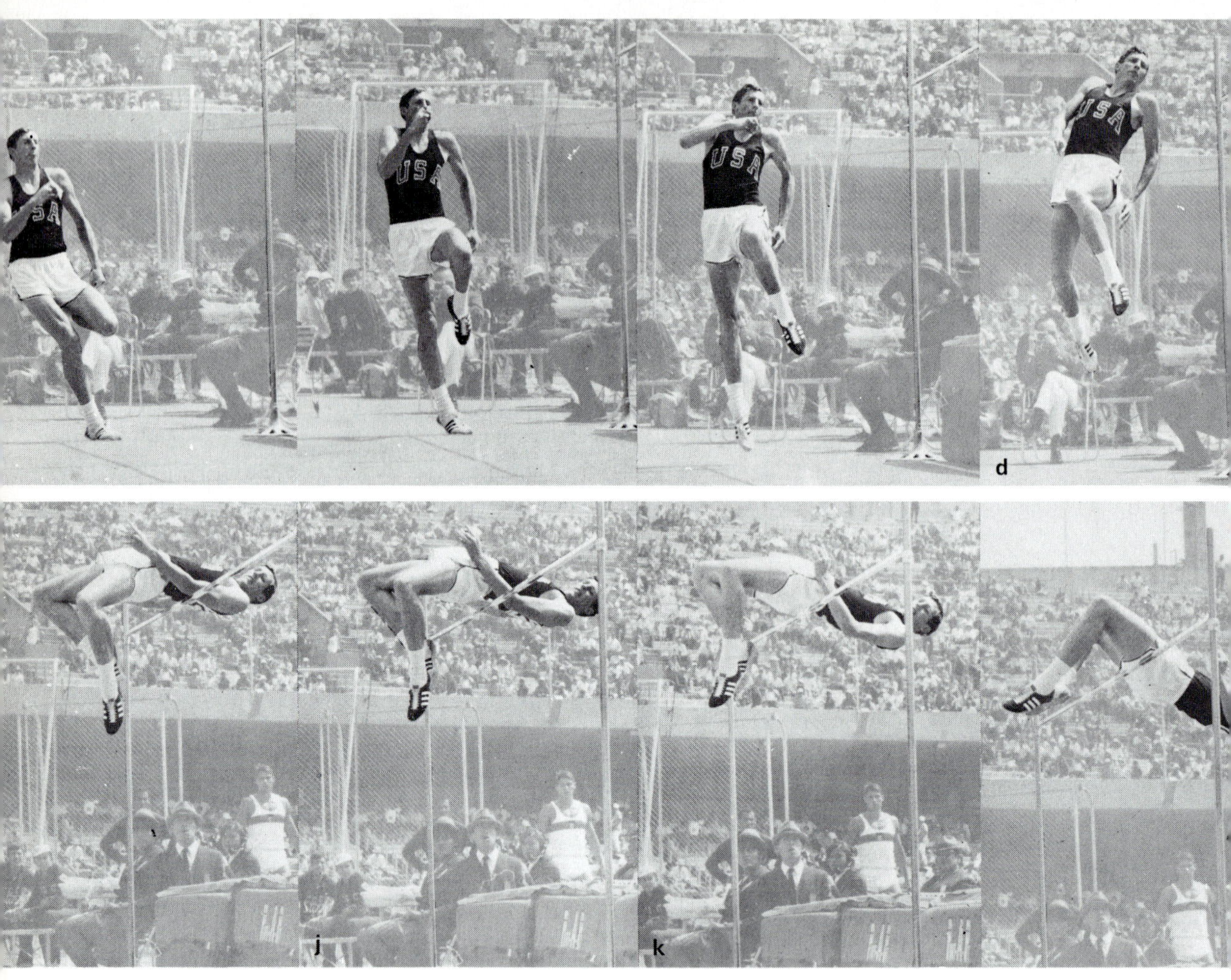

approach run has become consistent. He would measure the distance to the right of the right standard to a point even with the start of his run, then measure out from that point to his actual starting position. Though the measurements will be straight lines, the run will be a curving approach, similar to an inverted "J." Some beginners with the style will use almost a half-circle approach, but as they master the style, the approach will gradually straighten until it is only a small curve.

With the curving approach, the jumper will begin his approach by running almost straight in toward the corner of the pit, rather than toward his take-off point. Around the fourth or fifth step he will curve his run to his left until he is running in at a very shallow angle to the bar. He gradually accelerates during his run, then lowers his center of gravity by stretching his stride around the

Photograph 8.3*a-n* Dick Fosbury in a 7-foot high jump using the "flop."

sixth or seventh step. His take-off stride will then find his body already starting to move upward in the air.

When taking off, the kick is coordinated with an upward swing of one or both arms. The kick is with the upper part of the leg only, a bent leg kick that gives the sensation of kicking with the knee, rather than the entire leg. This kick, combined with the curving run, will cause the athlete to turn his back to the bar as he rises off the ground. By arching his back, he clears that part of his body over the bar. As the athlete clears the bar, he may appear to be lying flat on his back from his head to his knees, with his lower legs still hanging down. He will then lift the knees and feet to clear the bar. An upward swing of both arms may facilitate this movement. If the feet are kicked up to clear the bar, the landing in the pit will be high on the back or in the upper neck region, and the jumper may do a backward roll when he lands. Otherwise, the landing will be flat on the back.

There are four primary faults, three of them technical. The most common fault is dragging the hips through the crossbar. This can be avoided to some degree by keeping the hips tucked forward while clearing the bar. Arching the back or dropping the shoulders can also aid in clearing the hips.

A second fault is dragging the feet through the crossbar. It may be corrected by swinging the feet upward, naturally, but it can be assisted by throwing the arms upward as the hips clear the crossbar.

The third fault is getting one's height at the wrong place, which may result in the shoulders hitting the crossbar either as the athlete is taking off or as he is clearing the bar in landing. It can usually be corrected by moving the athlete's starting mark either out or in by several inches. Some athletes will find that their mark for starting the approach will have to gradually be moved farther from the landing pit as they attempt greater heights.

The fourth fault, though not exactly a technical one, is still important: too slow an approach run. Unlike the straddle form of jumping, a very slow run will not necessarily permit the jumper to clear the bar. He will more likely land on it, since he crosses perpendicular, rather than parallel, to the bar. Too slow a run will usually result in the failure to attain sufficient height for the jump.

Analysis of a Flop Sequence

The Dick Fosbury sequence, page 168, is a 7-foot jump in competition. In the first picture (Photograph 8.3*a*), Fosbury has lowered his center of gravity and is in the last step of his approach. Notice that as he takes off (Photograph 8.3*d*), he is much more upright, perhaps the result of the greater height needed for bar clearance. As he rises and turns in the air (Photograph 8.3*f*), his hands drop to his sides and his legs attain roughly the same position relative to each other. Atop the bar (Photograph 8.3*j*) he has a flat back, then begins to raise his knees (Photograph 8.3*k*) as his hips clear the bar. He raises his arms to assist in the clearance of the feet (Photographs 8.3*m* and *n*), though the full result of this move is not visible until well after the bar is cleared (Photograph 8.3*n*). He lands on his upper back, which is quite safe in a proper foam rubber pit.

Training for the High Jump

The first thing for the coach to remember in training high jumpers is that the best style for one athlete is *not* necessarily the same for another. Also, the amount of work which a jumper can tolerate varies greatly from one jumper to the next. Les Steers, Oregon's world record holder in the 1940s, jumped twice a day, sometimes taking 20 to 30 jumps on the morning of a meet as a warm-up.

The first thing to do with a group of jumping prospects is to learn their dominant or kicking leg. Have them run over a low hurdle several times, then hand-vault over a sawhorse. This should bring out the kicking leg clearly, since the athletes are going to prefer one leg to the other. They might then be taught the Western roll style of jumping, since it is helpful to learn and at the same time has great carry-over value to the take-off for the straddle jump. At one time this progression of learning to jump was considered the proper learning sequence, though it is not emphasized too much today. It is still very helpful, though.

After the lead foot has been determined, the athlete should work on his check marks. It helps to have two check marks in the approach, as a safety factor. The first mark is four steps from the take-off point, and the second check mark is another four steps out, giving an eight-step approach (Figure 8.2). The last four steps from the check to take-off are measured, as is the distance from the check to a line extended from the crossbar and the distance from this juncture to the nearest jumping standard. It is very important to know the jumper's check marks. It is helpful to have a short check mark, in case the jumper has to compete in bad wind conditions. It is easier to vary a short run to hit the take-off properly than to vary a full run.

The jumper will warm up, then work on a routine. He will first work on the check marks, then work on the take-off, concentrating on the two-count rise. The last two steps of the approach are longer and faster than the preceding steps, lowering the center of gravity. The jumper gets down, then rises over

Figure 8.2 Approach Check Marks (Straddle).

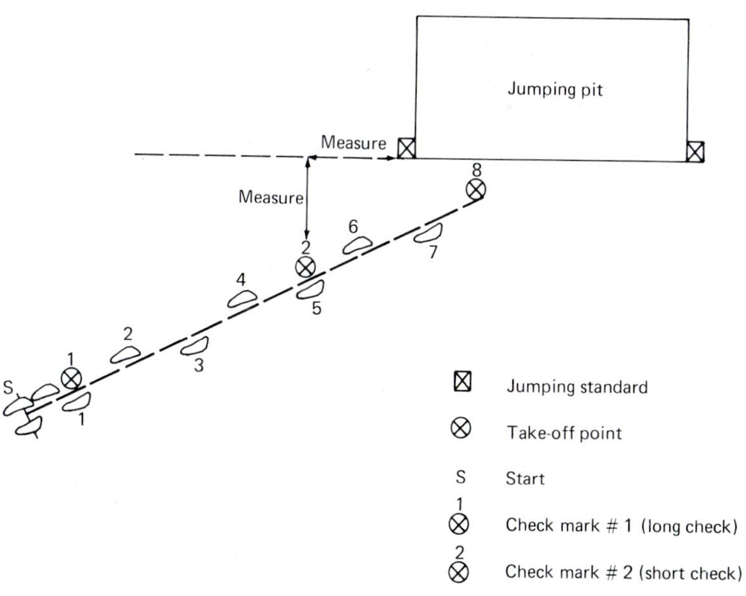

his last two steps, so he will go into the air with increased momentum. The jumper should try to get both arms and the lead leg rising to aid the momentum and raise the center of gravity.

Form work comes next, with the athlete working from 6 to 8 inches under his best mark at that time of year. If he has jumped a best of 6 feet 6 inches at that time of year, he would do form work at 5 feet 10 inches to 6 feet. He might take his last three jumps at increasing heights, but not permitting as many as three misses at one height. The jumper should be able to finish while feeling that he might have made it. He also needs to get used to seeing the crossbar at higher heights.

Weight lifting is useful in improving the jumper's spring. Some jumpers will do much leg work, emphasizing leg presses. The Russians particularly emphasize weight training. The athlete should be sure he is exercising the muscle within the usual limits of its movement in performing the event. As an example, full squats are risky, and they are *never* done while high jumping.

Training Program for "Floppers"

The training program for a back layout jumper can be a problem to plan, but not because of the work involved. After the jumper has mastered the form, he may prefer to do little jumping. For some as yet undiscovered reason, the flop jumper seems to thrive on little or no jumping during the season. If his form is good during the meets, there is rarely any reason for him to jump during the week. If a form problem did appear in a meet, he might work on that aspect of his form by jumping on Monday or Tuesday before a Friday or Saturday meet. If his performances begin to get worse, he may actually be jumping and practicing *too* much. A flopper is more likely to flourish under the old-fashioned light training methods than under the modern hard training methods, strange as it may seem. The time for perfecting the form with much jumping is during the fall and winter when there is plenty of time and no pressure.

Dick Fosbury's training is a good example of the way an athlete might train for this type of jumping, after he has learned the style well. This schedule is for a typical week during the competitive season, with a meet each Saturday:

Monday:	Sprints Runs up 80 rows of stadium seats, *or* Hopping halfway up stadium seats
Tuesday:	Weight training
Wednesday:	Same as Monday
Thursday:	Weight training
Friday:	Usually light (*might* repeat Monday's workout)

His weight training program, which he had followed for only two years before the Olympic Games, was as follows (on a Universal Gym):

Leg presses: 1 set × 10 at 390 lbs.
1 × 8 at 450 lbs.
1 × 6 at 510 lbs.
1 × 4 at 540 lbs.
1 × 2–3 at 600 lbs.

Toe presses: 2 sets × 25 at 150 lbs.

During the competitive season, he did no shoulder work, did only some of the leg work, and added partial jumping squats with the feet close together and alternating feet on the landing, usually doing two sets of 15 with 135 pounds.

How much should a high jumper practice? One year we found ourselves with no "class" returnees, so the physical education classes were screened for material, giving us two candidates capable of 5 feet 10 inches. In the interest of "science" one was put on a typical Les Steers overload, or heavy training schedule. The other jumper was given a minimal program of jumping and other activities. At season's end, both jumpers had achieved 6 feet 6 inches. Obviously either the ideal program had been followed by each jumper by random chance, or there is no ideal program.

This chapter will first present typical training schedules for the fall. These can be used either for the athlete in training or, scaled down, for a physical education unit. Winter and spring schedules follow. The progression of training and preparation for competition in the spring is produced in the graphic training schedules following. The fundamentals of approach, take-off, clearance, and related body mechanics will be explained after the schedules are presented.

Interpretation of One Week of Training Schedules

Monday: Class organization is intended for a physical education unit. Squad organization is in the event that fall track is conducted. The objectives and goals of the program are covered. Equipment and responsibility for attendance and separate workouts are discussed.

Tuesday: (16) Easy acrobatics might be done in the gymnastics room where more equipment is available. Such rudimentary activities as the forward roll and cartwheels can be done at the track.

(4A) The short check mark is a fundamental drill covered in the section following the schedules.

(14F) In the general schedule, run 55 yards, then jog 55 yards, and repeat the exercise for a distance of 440 to 880 yards or more.

Wednesday: (7) Squad meeting, time and place to be written on the board in the squad dressing room.

(1B) Weight activities of the athlete's choice or according to the suggestions given in the section on weight training. This is followed by jogging and comfortable running.

(8A or B) A sauna or swim, depending upon preference and availability of the pool.

Thursday: (1) In pairs or threes, take a warm-up jog of 440 or 880 yards. Each runner handles the baton, passing it forward. When the front runner receives the baton, he drops to the rear, and the exercise is continued.

(4A) Short check work, already mentioned.

(19) The superscript ^{6} means the exercise is done six times. Set the bar at an easily cleared height, such as 5 feet. One or more jumpers go through and jump as fast as they can make their clearance and get back to repeat the jump from one to six times. If the jumper misses, he is through jumping. This exercise is for conditioning and fun.

(14F) Repeated 55s, already mentioned.

Friday: (1B) Weight activities, already mentioned.

(15A) A run through the park (2 to 3 miles), comfortable pace, but with some stress for conditioning.

Saturday: (3) A full workout according to the section on weights or the athlete's already established weight workout activities.

Sunday: Recreational activities should be included on this day. Sunday can also be a very productive practice day and is very useful in bringing to life the athlete who overdoes Saturday night and would otherwise not revive until Tuesday or Wednesday.

The Training Schedules Explained

4A. Short check mark. This is used for learning a method of arriving at a take-off point that achieves maximum height directly over the crossbar. Usually four steps are taken from the one check mark to the take-off. Standing one or two steps from the check, the jumper thinks through the fundamental, if he is working on one fundamental, then shuts out the thinking process. He advances the one or two steps to the check, then takes four steps to the take-off and executes the jump. This distance will vary from 18 to 25 feet, depending upon the athlete's needs and stride length. The jumper should take three practice approaches while being observed, then average the length of the three runs to determine his short check mark. This mark should be measured daily, since better physical condition and weather differences (heat, cold, etc.) will cause variations in the approach.

4B. Long check mark. The long check mark uses two checks. The jumper will begin one or two steps from the first check, then will take four strides to the

Figure 8.3a High Jump Training Schedule

High Jump NAME DATE September/October

1. A. Jog 1 or 2 laps, relay pass—2s or 3s B. Weights and jog
   C.
2. Fartlek A. Varied pace B. Slow, steady
3. Weights
4. Check mark A. Short B. Long
5. A. Rhythm (2-4-6-8) B. Settle and 2-count rise
   C. Lead leg and lead arm
   D.
6. A. Head B. Layout and bar clearance
   C. Up and down—not up and out
7. Squad meeting
8. Special A. Sauna B. Swim C. Hill
   D.
9. A. Take off B. Arm lift C. CG over take-off foot
   D.
10. A. Trial B. Compete (1) Up 2 in. to 3 in. on a make, down 4 in. on a miss (2) 2 jumps 2 in. above average best
11. Alternate from Straddle to Western roll to Fosbury
12. With coach A. B.
14. A. Wind sprints B. Starts or 1. 110s 2.
    C. High knee and fast leg
    D. Hurdle drill, 3 lows 8 to 10 yds. E. Spring and bound
    F. Alternate run-jog at least 880
15. A. Hendricks B. Laurel C. Steps
16. Easy acrobatics or apparatus
17. High kicking A. Basket B. Target
18. Form jumping A. Short B. Long
    6 in.—12 in. under best
19. Speed jumping—4 to 8 fast, or a miss
20. Secondary event
21. A. Pictures B. Film C.
22. Experimental work

Date	Result	3/4	Date	Goal

M	Class or squad organization
T	16-4A-14F
W	7-1B-8A or 8B
T	6x 1A-4A-19-14F
F	1B-15A
S	3
S	recreation

M	2-4x 1A-14F-4A-5C-18A
T	1B-16-14E
W	1A-14F-5A-5B-14D
T	1B-16-17B
F	1-10A-18A-14F
S	2B
S	recreation

M	1A-14F-4A-5A-18A
T	1B-16-17-14E
W	1-14F-4B-9A-5B-14D
T	1-16-17
F	1-10A1-18A
S	3-14F
S	recreation

M	2-4x2-4x 1-14F-4A-4B-9A-18A
T	1B-14E-14F
W	1-4B-9A-5B-14D
T	1B-16-17
F	6-10x6-10x 1-18A-18B-14F
S	1B-14F
S	recreation

Figure 8.3b High Jump Training Schedule

High Jump NAME DATE January

1. A. Jog 1 or 2 laps, relay pass—2s or 3s B. Weights and jog
   C.
2. Fartlek A. Varied pace B. Slow, steady
3. Weights
4. Check mark A. Short B. Long
5. A. Rhythm (2-4-6-8) B. Settle and 2-count rise
   C. Lead leg and lead arm
   D.
6. A. Head B. Layout and bar clearance
   C. Up and down—not up and out
7. Squad meeting
8. Special A. Sauna B. Swim C. Hill
   D.
9. A. Take off B. Arm lift C. CG over take-off foot
   D.
10. A. Trial B. Compete (1) Up 2 in. to 3 in. on a make, down 4 in. on a miss (2) 2 jumps 2 in. above average best
11. Alternate from Straddle to Western roll to Fosbury
12. With coach A. B.
14. A. Wind sprints B. Starts or 1. 110s 2.
    C. High knee and fast leg
    D. Hurdle drill, 3 lows 8 to 10 yds. E. Spring and bound
    F. Alternate run-jog at least 880
15. A. Hendricks B. Laurel C. Steps
16. Easy acrobatics or apparatus
17. High kicking A. Basket B. Target
18. Form jumping A. Short B. Long
    6 in.–12 in. under best
19. Speed jumping—4 to 8 fast, or a miss
20. Secondary event
21. A. Pictures B. Film C.
22. Experimental work

Date	Result	3/4	Date	Goal

M	New term or start new year
T	Class or squad organization
W	Register–11–3–or classes
T	7–Register–lockers–11–3
F	1–14A–3–15A
S	3–11
S	Recreation
M	1–4A–5B–9A–14F
T	1A–3
W	1–5A–5C–6C
T	1A–3–15A
F	1–14F–5B–5C–9A–14F
S	1A–3–14A
S	recreation
M	1–3–14D
T	1A–5B–4A (2–4x)–4B (2–4x)–5A
W	1–3–14F–15A
T	1–4B–6B–9A
F	1–3–14E–15B
S	1–10–6A–14E
S	recreation
M	1–3–14F
T	1A–4A–4B–5B–5C–6B
W	1–3–14A
T	1A–5A–5B–5C–14B
F	1–3–14A
S	3–14A
S	recreation–3

Figure 8.3c High Jump Training Schedule

High Jump NAME DATE February

1. A. Jog 1 or 2 laps, relay pass—2s or 3s B. Weights and jog
   C.
2. Fartlek A. Varied pace B. Slow, steady
3. Weights
4. Check mark A. Short B. Long
5. A. Rhythm (2-4-6-8) B. Settle and 2-count rise
   C. Lead leg and lead arm
   D.
6. A. Head B. Layout and bar clearance
   C. Up and down—not up and out
7. Squad meeting
8. Special A. Sauna B. Swim C. Hill
   D.
9. A. Take off B. Arm lift C. CG over take-off foot
   D.
10. A. Trial B. Compete (1) Up 2 in. to 3 in. on a make, down 4 in. on a miss (2) 2 jumps 2 in. above average best
11. Alternate from Straddle to Western roll to Fosbury
12. With coach A. B.
14. A. Wind sprints B. Starts or 1. 110s 2.
    C. High knee and fast leg
    D. Hurdle drill, 3 lows 8 to 10 yds. E. Spring and bound
    F. Alternate run-jog at least 880
15. A. Hendricks B. Laurel C. Steps
16. Easy acrobatics or apparatus
17. High kicking A. Basket B. Target
18. Form jumping A. Short B. Long
    6 in.–12 in. under best
19. Speed jumping—4 to 8 fast, or a miss
20. Secondary event
21. A. Pictures B. Film C.
22. Experimental work

Date	Result	3/4	Date	Goal

M	1-4A-4B-5A-5B-14D-14E
T	3-14A
W	1-4A-4B-15A or 15C
T	14E-3
F	2-3x 1-4A-5B2-9
S	Swim or weights
S	recreation
M	1A-14D-5C-14C
T	3-8A or B
W	3x 3x 1-5A-5B-5C
T	Light
F	1-10
S	Sprint & hurdle trials 10:30 am
S	
M	1A-4B-5C-5B-18-Jog
T	1B
W	6x 1A-18-8C or 15A
T	1B
F	1A-4A-4B-5B-5C-14E-14F
S	Jog & 3
S	recreation
M	2x 2x 3x 3-6x 1A-4A-4B-5A-5B-14E-14F
T	1B-8A or 8B
W	1B-16
T	1B-16
F	1A-10A1-10A2
S	3 or 14E
S	recreation

Figure 8.3d High Jump Training Schedule

High Jump NAME DATE *March*

1. A. Jog 1 or 2 laps, relay pass—2s or 3s B. Weights and jog
   C.
2. Fartlek A. Varied pace B. Slow, steady
3. Weights
4. Check mark A. Short B. Long
5. A. Rhythm (2-4-6-8) B. Settle and 2-count rise
   C. Lead leg and lead arm
   D.
6. A. Head B. Layout and bar clearance
   C. Up and down—not up and out
7. Squad meeting
8. Special A. Sauna B. Swim C. Hill
   D.
9. A. Take off B. Arm lift C. CG over take-off foot
   D.
10. A. Trial B. Compete (1) Up 2 in. to 3 in. on a make, down 4 in. on a miss (2) 2 jumps 2 in. above average best
11. Alternate from Straddle to Western roll to Fosbury
12. With coach A. B.
14. A. Wind sprints B. Starts or 1. 110s 2.
    C. High knee and fast leg
    D. Hurdle drill, 3 lows 8 to 10 yds. E. Spring and bound
    F. Alternate run-jog at least 880
15. A. Hendricks B. Laurel C. Steps
16. Easy acrobatics or apparatus
17. High kicking A. Basket B. Target
18. Form jumping A. Short B. Long
    6 in.—12 in. under best
19. Speed jumping—4 to 8 fast, or a miss
20. Secondary event
21. A. Pictures B. Film C.
22. Experimental work

Date	Result	3/4	Date	Goal

M	1A-8B
T	1B-8A or B
W	7-1A-4B (2x)-9B-9A-19-14D-14F
T	Light
F	1A-10A1-18-15A
S	Light
S	Light
M	1-14E-4B-9B (4x)-9C (10x)-14E-14D
T	1B-8B
W	1-4-9A-18-14F
T	Jog
F	4-10A1-17
S	3-16-14E
S	recreation
M	1A-4-6B-9B-14E-14F
T	Easy grass running
W	7-4-18
T	Light
F	Gear ready and/or travel
S	First meet (10B-20)
S	Light workout

	A.M.	P.M. Spring trip
M	1A-Jog	1A-4-5B-6C-14F
T	1A-3	Grass running
W	1A-Jog	1A-18
T	1A-3	Light
F	Travel home—loosen up	
S	Division early season relay meet	
S	Loosen up	

Figure 8.3e High Jump Training Schedule

High Jump NAME DATE April

1. A. Jog 1 or 2 laps, relay pass—2s or 3s B. Weights and jog
   C.
2. Fartlek A. Varied pace B. Slow, steady
3. Weights
4. Check mark A. Short B. Long
5. A. Rhythm (2-4-6-8) B. Settle and 2-count rise
   C. Lead leg and lead arm
   D.
6. A. Head B. Layout and bar clearance
   C. Up and down—not up and out
7. Squad meeting
8. Special A. Sauna B. Swim C. Hill
   D.
9. A. Take off B. Arm lift C. CG over take-off foot
   D.
10. A. Trial B. Compete (1) Up 2 in. to 3 in. on a make, down 4 in. on a miss (2) 2 jumps 2 in. above average best
11. Alternate from Straddle to Western roll to Fosbury
12. With coach A. B.
14. A. Wind sprints B. Starts or 1. 110s 2.
    C. High knee and fast leg
    D. Hurdle drill, 3 lows 8 to 10 yds. E. Spring and bound
    F. Alternate run-jog at least 880
15. A. Hendricks B. Laurel C. Steps
16. Easy acrobatics or apparatus
17. High kicking A. Basket B. Target
18. Form jumping A. Short B. Long
    6 in.—12 in. under best
19. Speed jumping—4 to 8 fast, or a miss
20. Secondary event
21. A. Pictures B. Film C.
22. Experimental work

Date	Result	3/4	Date	Goal

M	1A-5B-4B-18-19-14D
T	1B-17-14E-14F
W	7-1A-5B-9A-18-14E
T	3
F	Light and gear ready
S	Relay meet
S	Field open 11 to 3
M	1-4B-4A-5B-9A-19-14D
T	1B-17-14E-14F
W	7-1A-4B-10A1 and 2-18 jog
T	3
F	1-4B-18 (4-6x)-gear ready
S	Dual meet
S	Church-field open 11-3
M	1-4A-4B-5B-18-19-14D
T	17-3-14E-14F
W	7-1-5B-9A-6B-18-14D
T	3
F	Gear ready
S	Dual meet
S	Light workout
M	7-1-4A-4B-5B-18-19-14D
T	17B-1B-14E-14F
W	7-1-4-10A1 (4-6x)-10A2 (2x)-14F
T	Light
F	Travel
S	Dual meet
S	Home and loosen up

Figure 8.3f High Jump Training Schedule

High Jump NAME DATE May

1. A. Jog 1 or 2 laps, relay pass—2s or 3s B. Weights and jog
   C.
2. Fartlek A. Varied pace B. Slow, steady
3. Weights
4. Check mark A. Short B. Long
5. A. Rhythm (2-4-6-8) B. Settle and 2-count rise
   C. Lead leg and lead arm
   D.
6. A. Head B. Layout and bar clearance
   C. Up and down—not up and out
7. Squad meeting
8. Special A. Sauna B. Swim C. Hill
   D.
9. A. Take off B. Arm lift C. CG over take-off foot
   D.
10. A. Trial B. Compete (1) Up 2 in. to 3 in. on a make, down 4 in. on a miss (2) 2 jumps 2 in. above average best
11. Alternate from Straddle to Western roll to Fosbury
12. With coach A. B.
14. A. Wind sprints B. Starts or 1. 110s 2.
    C. High knee and fast leg
    D. Hurdle drill, 3 lows 8 to 10 yds. E. Spring and bound
    F. Alternate run-jog at least 880
15. A. Hendricks B. Laurel C. Steps
16. Easy acrobatics or apparatus
17. High kicking A. Basket B. Target
18. Form jumping A. Short B. Long
    6 in.—12 in. under best
19. Speed jumping—4 to 8 fast, or a miss
20. Secondary event
21. A. Pictures B. Film C.
22. Experimental work

Date	Result	3/4	Date	Goal

M	7-Jog
T	Light
W	Memorial Day Traditional Dual meet
T	1A-4B-10A1-14E
F	1B-17-14F
S	Jog
S	Field open 11-3--Squad picnic 5 pm
M	1-14E-14D-14F
T	1-4-5C-6B-18-14E
W	Light & Jog
T	Light & Jog
F	1-4
S	Light
S	1-5-18-Jog
M	7-1-5-18-Jog
T	Light
W	7-Light
T	Championship starts
F	Championship-High jump qualifying
S	Championship-High jump finals
S	
M	
T	
W	
T	
F	
S	
S	

second check (his short check), then take another four strides to the take-off point. This approach is described in more detail a bit later in the chapter.

5A. Rhythm jumping (2-4-6-8). This activity was introduced at the Olympic Development Jumping Camp at Duke University. The athlete pays attention only to developing a rhythm. For learning purposes the athlete stands at a long check mark and comes in to the jump either counting or having the coach count the even-numbered strides "2-4-6-8," with "8" being the take-off. It is for rhythm, speed, and to get rid of a jerky or uneven approach. The other fundamentals work more smoothly if a good rhythmical approach is achieved.

5B. Settle and 2-count rise. This technique is used either consciously or because of the superior coordination of every great high jumper. To acquire this technique, the athlete starts learning with a short check mark. Usually he will find that on the second step before the take-off he will settle and then start to rise on the step before take-off, so that the body weight as well as the momentum will be going up at the instant of the take-off. Some great jumpers have made the settle on the last step before the take-off, then started to rise on the same step, taking off on the next step.

5C. Lead leg and lead arm. The lead leg and lead arm, which are approaching the bar for clearance, should be hurried upward well before the take-off foot leaves the ground. The lifting of the leg and arm raises the center of gravity, bringing the total mass of the body nearer the crossbar. The fact that the body mass is going up makes the relative weight of the body mass less. This leg-arm movement must be executed before the take-off, or the physical principle of the "equal and opposite reaction" will tend to destroy the effect of the lift, because it will be taking effect against the strong base of the take-off and will be negated by the action of the extremities being in motion at this time.

5D. A vacant space for use when some unlisted specific is needed in an individual's schedule.

6A. Head. The head is ten pounds of dead weight which can either help or hinder the jumper. If the chin is raised, the head can help the jumper direct himself upward off the ground. If the chin is dropped, it can hamper the take-off. If the chin is tipped toward the crossbar, it will lead the body into a premature lean into the bar, a common fault leading to poor jumping.

6B. *Layout and bar clearance.* The center of gravity is what rises, and the body and extremities rotate around it. The first motion is up, then by the last actions at the point of take-off, the body coordination is affected by the arms and legs, turning the body and helping it to "lay out" atop the crossbar. The rotation around the bar is accomplished by lowering the head, which is beyond the bar, and lifting the take-off leg.

6C. Up and down — not up and out. The jumper who uses more speed than he can control tends to cover space in the wrong direction. The rule is "use as much speed as can be controlled." If the jumper takes off too close with speed uncontrolled, he will go into the crossbar. The speed jumper should be farther out than the "stroller." The fast jumper who is going into the bar should experiment with a more acute angle, going down more toward the crossbar as do the "floppers," another speed jump.

9A. Take-off. An exact take-off spot is a necessity, and check marks must be determined which will assist the jumper in hitting that spot on every approach run. When the spot is reached, the most important part of the technique is maintaining body position and lift. A leanout not only makes for a premature turn and striking the crossbar, but it can make the jumper 2 to 4 inches shorter by lowering his center of gravity by that distance.

9B. Arm lift. The left arm will almost automatically rise with the right leg. The coordination of the double-arm lift (both arms together) is an acquired one. As the right foot is planted on the last step before the final plant and take-off, both arms are dropped back only as far as the plane of the body, then both lift vigorously as the lead (right) leg is driven up toward the crossbar. The arms are at about bar height as the take-off foot leaves the ground. As the body rises, the right arm reaches across the bar, and the most natural thing is for the left elbow to smoothly come to the side and proceed to the rear until the hand is at about the hip area. It is also believed helpful for take-off leg clearance if the right arm will rise, lifting to the outside and triggering a compensating action by the take-off leg.

9C. Center of gravity over take-off foot. The center of gravity should be maintained at as high a position as possible as the take-off is executed. As the jumper makes his final step, he should pass directly over the take-off foot. If there is to be a fault out of line, it should be in the direction of the bar, not away from the bar. Crossing the left foot across the line of approach (and away from the bar) will lower the center of gravity and lean the jumper into the crossbar.

10A. Trial. A warm-up procedure should be acquired for trials and experimented with to determine what is best for competition. The trials themselves are a learning situation. A competitive trial is only to eliminate someone if there are more entries available than can be used in the competition. If there is one outstanding jumper, he should be an automatic entry, but he should compete in the trials for the learning experience. The other jumpers are also learning, but they will also be competing for the other two spots in the dual meet entries.

Let the athletes set the crossbar at a good starting height for each individual, within reason. In item *10A1,* the athlete raises the bar 2 to 3 inches if he clears the height, and he lowers the bar 4 inches if he misses. One jumper may start at 5 feet 6 inches, while a good jumper might start at 6 feet 4 inches. If the weak jumper misses his height, he will jump next at 5 feet 2 inches. The good jumper might have his next jump at 6 feet 6 inches to 6 feet 7 inches, depending upon how good he is and how early in the season it is.

10A2. Two jumps 2 inches above average best. If the jumpers have reached their approximate best and have had two misses at a height, they may have two more jumps at 2 or 3 inches above their best seasonal mark. They should not be allowed three misses, for psychological reasons, since it would put them out of the competition. In practice, the jumpers should never take more than two misses at a submaximal height.

11. Alternate from Straddle to Western to Fosbury. This is an experimental exercise for variety of activity, teaching body control, and perhaps discovering an additional jumping "weapon." The jumper works with several different jumping styles, going from the straddle or "belly roll" to the Western roll to the Fosbury flop style of jumping, learning better body control and perhaps discovering if he can do better with a different form.

16. Easy acrobatics or apparatus. If possible, have some apparatus in the practice area. Also take advantage of the usually superior equipment and instruction of a good gymnastics teacher. It is great exercise for body control, as well as pleasurable and a good change of pace.

17. High kicking. High kicking is used for work on the take-off and for timing in the leg lift in relation to the take-off. It consists of short approaches followed by high kicks with the lead leg toward a high target of some sort.

18. Form jumping. Form jumping should be done at a minimal height. It is possible to concentrate on the techniques and mechanics without being concerned about the height of the jump. Acquire the tools, then do the job in the meet.

19. Speed jumping. The crossbar is set at an easy height, perhaps a foot under the jumper's best. In rotation the jumpers take their jumps as fast as they can get into the pit and back out again. A miss puts the jumper out. Winner is the last man out, or a single jumper takes four to eight or so "speed" jumps.

20. Secondary event. Every athlete should have a second event, if only for a change of scenery. He should also consider himself a part of the team. He may get the extra point which will win his letter or the team's meet. The greatest high jumper in Oregon history, Les Steers, could also throw the javelin, hurdle, and pole vault. He also held the world record for the high jump for well over a decade.

Bezeg, Adam. "Improving spring in the high jump," *Track Technique*, No. 28 (June 1967), pp. 895–96.

Chityakov, T. "The high jump approach," trans. by Peter Tschiene, *Track Technique*, No. 40 (June 1970), pp. 1282–84.

Cooper, John M. "Kinesiology of high jumping," *Track and Field Quarterly Review* 72: 104–8.

Dobroth, John. "Teaching beginners to high jump," *Track Technique*, No. 47 (March 1972), pp. 1509–10.

Dyatchkov, Vladimir M. "The high jump," trans. by James Hay, *Track Technique*, No. 34 (March 1969), pp. 1059–74.

_______. "High jump exercises," *Track Technique*, No. 25 (September 1966), pp. 779–81.

_______. "High jumping," *Track Technique*, No. 36 (June 1969), pp. 1123–57.

_______. "How Russian high jumpers succeeded at Rome," trans. by Gar Williams, *Track Technique*, No. 4 (June 1961), pp. 100–2.

_______. "Problems involved in the training of Soviet high jumpers," *Track Technique*, No. 5 (September 1961), pp. 138–40.

_______. "Specialized exercises for high jumpers," *Track Technique*, No. 34 (March 1969), p. 1075.

Freeman, William H. "Coaching the Fosbury flop," *Atheltic Journal* 51 (January 1971): 16, 71–72.

Hay, James G. "A kinematic look at the high jump," *Track Technique*, No. 53 (September 1973), pp. 1697–1703.

_______. "Pat Matzdorf: how he trains," *Track Technique*, No. 48 (June 1972), pp. 1519–20.

Hooper, Bernard J. "Rotation, part 4," *Track Technique*, No. 12 (June 1963), pp. 356–61.

_______. "Rotation, part 6," *Track Technique*, No. 15 (March 1964), pp. 468–71.

Kerssenbrock, Klement. "Analyzing the Fosbury flop," trans. by Karel Spilar, *Track Technique*, No. 41 (September 1970), pp. 1291–93.

_______, and Spilar, Karel. "Matzdorf vs. Brumel: techniques of the highest high jumpers," *Track Technique*, No. 48 (June 1972), pp. 1514–19.

Oglesby, Burch E. "Russian power high jumping," in *The Best in Track and Field from Scholastic Coach*, pp. 17–22. New York: Scholastic Coach Athletic Services, 1970.

Ozolin, Nikolay. "The high jump takeoff mechanism," trans. by Gar Williams, *Track Technique*, No. 52 (June 1973), pp. 1668–71.

Page, Peter. "Mechanical analysis of the high jump," *Track Technique*, No. 32 (September 1968), pp. 1022–24.

Paish, Wilf. "Fosbury is not a flop," *Athletics Coach* 6 (May 1972): 5–7.

Sharpley, Frank. "Teaching beginners to high jump," *Track Technique*, No. 5 (September 1961), pp. 134–37.

Wagner, Berny. "The amazing Fosbury flop," *Scholastics Coach* 39 (April 1970): 14–15, 92.

_______. "The high jump," *Track and Field Quarterly Review*, March 1969, pp. 35–39.

Watts, D. C. V. *High Jump.* London: AAA, 1969. 40 pp.

The long jump

"One giant leap for mankind" was taken on the surface of the moon by an astronaut during the summer of 1969. In the Mexican Summer Olympics of 1968 a great leap for posterity was made by Bob Beamon as he broke the world and Olympic long jump records. Twenty-eight feet was anticipated, but the breaking of the 29-foot barrier was astounding. How? A superb athlete, perfect conditions, and competition of the highest order combined to produce this phenomenal leap of 29 feet 2½ inches (8.90 meters). How long will his record stand? Until equal or better conditions prevail, and until equally superb or better athletes meet for a great competition.

Since long jumpers have the same interest in physiology, philosophy, and mechanics as do the sprinters, the first presentation is of the training schedules. Doers want to *do.* Thinkers, having patience, will find supplemental material and references later.

Analysis of Long Jump Sequences

For comparative purposes, two athletes are shown performing the long jump. Both Olympic gold medalists, they use the hitch-kick or "walking-in-air" style. The first athlete is Bob Beamon, shown in Photographs 9.1*a to m*, page 186. The second jumper is Ralph Boston, pictured in Photographs 9.2*a to l*, page 188.

Photographs 9.1*a-m* Bob Beamon, U.S.A., Olympic gold medalist.

Unfortunately neither of the photographs show the last several strides of the approach, which would show whether the athletes are rising as they reach the take-off board. Movies would suggest that they are rising, similar to the two-count rise recommended earlier. Both jumpers seem to run off the board in the same way that a hurdler does in the early stages of attacking a hurdle (Photographs 9.1*a*, 9.2*a*), though Beamon may be observed fouling on his take-off. Only after they are rising into the air do the individual styles appear. While Boston kicks his lead leg until it extends in front of him (Photograph 9.2*b*), Beamon (Photographs 9.1*b* to *c*) does not extend the kicking leg very far forward, holding to a form more similar to actually running through the air.

As the jumper nears the end of his one-and-one-half-stride hitch-kick, he brings his lead leg forward to a position almost parallel to the ground, then brings the trail leg forward to a similar position, trying to keep his legs up as long as possible. Boston (Photographs 9.2*h* to *l*) does an excellent job of this phase of the jump, while Beamon's late position in the air (Photographs 9.1*i* to *j*) seems almost phenomenal. Notice with both of the jumpers that as the hands are swept down-

ward, the legs come up. If the arms move back upward, the legs will automatically begin to drop, as seen in the Beamon jump (Photographs 9.1*l* to *m*).

The hang is another long jump style, which has been used successfully by a third Olympic gold medalist, Wolfgang Klein, in a jump of 25 feet 11 inches (7.9 meters). Klein takes off similarly to the hitch-kickers, but does not extend his lead leg forward very far before he brings the trail leg forward to join it. He moves through the air as if suspended from a trapeze, then raises his feet into the landing position by swinging his arms over and downward. His final landing position is a strong one, with the feet extended and held relatively high.

From the mechanical angle, when a body is moving through the air, a movement or action of one part of the body will cause an equal and opposite reaction in the opposite part of the body (opposite in relation to the center of gravity). Consequently, when the arms are swung downward, the reaction is for the legs to swing upward. This action is utilized to elevate the feet before landing, adding distance to the jump.

The reason for the athlete's movements in the air is a matter of debate. Very

Photographs 9.2*a-l* Ralph Boston, U.S.A., demonstrating the "hitch-kick" style.

likely movements such as the hitch-kick are used primarily to enable the athlete to maintain his balance while in flight. There is no proven advantage of the hitch-kick over the hang style. All other factors being equal, the distances attained would be identical. Once the body leaves the ground, only its take-off velocity and angle, coupled with the pull of gravity and wind resistance, will determine where the center of gravity will land. *Nothing* which the athlete does in the air will change the flight path of his center of gravity.

This does not mean the athlete cannot alter his jumping distance after take-off. He can vary the distance by the degree to which he holds up his legs, since they can touch down anywhere within 2 to 3 feet *on either side* of his center of gravity's landing point. This means that a jump in which the center of gravity traveled 20 feet could yield a *measured* jump of anywhere between 17 and 23 feet! Thus the proper use of the arms and legs is of paramount importance.

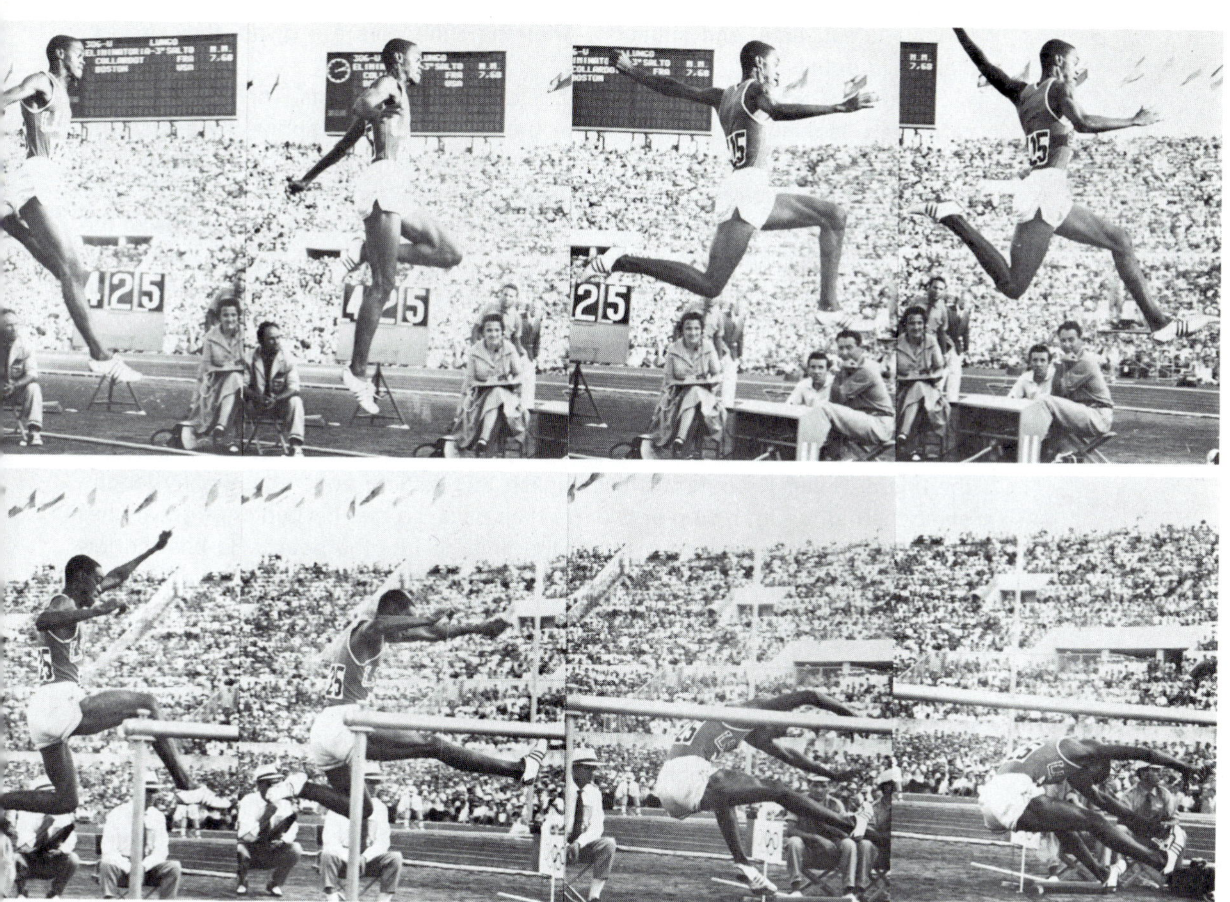

Comments on the Long Jump and Training

The long jump is "the lazy man's event." It is an event in which training injury is a very real risk. The long jumper should not take too many jumps in any one session, nor should he jump too often. He is an athlete blessed with both agility and speed. Speed alone will not make a really good jumper, though most world-class long jumpers are capable of 9.6 to 10.0 seconds in the 100-yard dash. There have been exceptionally speedy runners in the event, such as Jesse Owens; they were also very agile, as well as fleet of foot. Long jumpers should be well coordinated, with explosive reactions. This is also an event which may attract the most strongly competitive athletes.

The training schedules are made for and from the ordinary athletes' practices and projected activities. Fit them to your own athletes' needs. Alter them to your talent, time, and situation. After the schedules are given, they are explained in detail.

Two tests are useful in determining long jump prospects. The first is the 40-yard dash, looking for 5.2 seconds or better, just as with sprint prospects. The standing long jump should also be used, giving some indication of native long jumping spring. Look for a standing leap of 7 feet 6 inches or more here.

The basic jump involves a run of 120 feet or more, with relaxation during the last 20 to 30 feet, an attempt to go high into the air after the take-off, then landing with as much outward reaching of the feet as possible. The jumper should try to go into the air in a gradual rise to the board over his last two steps. This technique is sometimes referred to as the "two-count rise." As an example, consider a jumper who hits the take-off board with his left foot. On the third and fourth strides before hitting the board, he settles down, lowering his center of gravity to hit a low point when he puts down his left foot two strides before he hits the board. Some jumpers will accomplish this settling action by slightly lengthening their stride for a step or two. He then rises, so that his center of gravity has already begun its upward ascent by the time he hits the board. He hits the low point on the left foot, then rises onto the right foot, then rises to the left foot, which hits the board, where he drives on upward into the air.

An excellent training technique is the use of short run "pop-ups." These are done with a run of 50 feet or less, usually taking an eight-step approach. The jumpers work on the two-count rise, doing pop-ups from the area in front of the take-off board, trying to fly off the runway and get good height in their jumps.

The two biggest problems long jumpers encounter in action are bad check marks and bad take-offs. Consider the check marks first. Finding the starting point for a jumper's approach run is like locating a target with mortar fire. Have the jumper start from the take-off board and run eight strides up the runway two or three times, marking the location of the eighth stride each time. Then mark the average of the three marks as a starting check mark and have the jumper begin practicing with it. This approach is long enough for practicing most technique work, except for perfecting the full approach run.

How long should a jumper's approach run be? Probably 120 feet or so will be enough. Most world-class jumpers take 120 to 140 feet. Some jumpers who take as much as a 150-foot approach run (there is no legal limit) are probably wasting energy, rather than gaining benefits. Often a jumper using an overly long approach will not improve after his second jump, probably because he becomes fatigued. Most people can reach their top sprinting speed in 40 yards, so a longer run is rarely of any benefit.

There are about as many ideas on the number and location of check marks as there are long jumpers plus coaches. Some jumpers use only one check, located at the start of the full approach, while others use two or three marks. We suggest three marks as the most useful number. The first is at the start of the long approach. The jumper leaves this mark running at half effort for four strides. He then hits the second mark, at which point he accelerates to three-fourths or seven-eighths speed, running for the next six steps, at which point he hits the final check. This mark is ten steps from the take-off board. This part of the approach is run at full speed, or as close to it as the jumper can keep under control and convert to upward momentum when the actual jump takes place.

There are, as mentioned above, many versions of what is desirable in the use of check marks. The jumper can use a 2-4-6 set of checks or any other combination which he finds most useful for his own particular jumping style. One highly recommended practice is to have two check marks two steps apart (hit both marks with the same foot) somewhere in the middle of the approach run. If the first mark is missed, any stride adjustment can be checked quickly. If both marks are missed, the jumper can terminate his run at that point, rather than risk wasting a jump.

Some jumpers may have trouble with their check marks in the switch from high school to college jumping; being accustomed to the allowable 2-foot-wide take-off board used in some secondary schools, the switch to hitting the collegiate or international board, which is only 8 inches wide, is a major adjustment.

A jumper should keep in mind the benefits of the short run (8 to 12 strides) in the competitive situation. If there is a strong head wind, the jumper may find it especially tiring or difficult to jump well after a full approach battling the wind. In this case, the jumper should use the short approach instead. He will save energy on his approach run, energy which can be applied to additional speed to give a jumping edge over those who are sticking with the more exhausting long run. Also, if the jumper has opened with two fouls, leaving him with only one jump to make the finals, he should use the surer short run.

On the take-off, the jumper should pass over his plant foot. He should hit the board and go off over the foot, *not* reach out for the board. Actually, the last stride (onto the board) will be slightly shorter than the other approach strides, so essentially he "runs off the board," since he is rising through his last two strides. However, some coaches advocate "stamping" the foot on the board. Also, he should take care not to bring his "kicking foot" across the body, misdirecting his line of flight to the side. At the take-off board the jumper should shift his line of sight from the board to the horizon. The chest should be kept up, and he should concentrate on getting his knee lift off the board. The movements in the air are done only to keep the body balanced in flight and to prepare for the landing. The "hang" style of jumping is the easiest way to keep one's "in-flight" coordination. While in the air the primary considerations are getting the feet extended forward (not letting them drop toward the pit) and holding the hands up and out.

Putting a mark in the pit is actually of little real benefit (and is also illegal), for after the jumper has left the ground, the laws of physics determine how far he will go. *Nothing* done in the air will cause his body to travel any farther, nor can he do anything to shorten his flight. The only effect the jumper has on the distance of his jump after he is in the air is the extension of his legs and feet. If he drops them too quickly, he will land *before* his center of gravity would have landed, thus getting a poorer jump. If he keeps them up and extended perfectly, they can land as much as 2 feet or more *ahead* of the center of gravity. This, then, is the importance of extending the feet, for it can make a difference of 3 or more *feet* between the distance achieved by two jumps which were equal in all other respects.

The Long Jump Schedules Interpreted

Monday: Organization: The physical education class or squad meets to discuss objectives and goals and explain responsibilities for regular attendance or for separate individual workouts. Use and care of facilities are also explained.

Tuesday: (1A) In groups of two or three, jog one or two laps of the track. A relay fundamental is used, with the joggers carrying a baton and passing it forward as they jog single file. When the baton reaches the jogger at the head of the line, he drops to the rear and begins passing the baton again.

(14F) Run 55 yards, then jog slowly or walk for 55 yards, until 440 or 880 yards or more have been covered.

(3) Weight training activities according to the schedules or the routine of the athlete.

Wednesday: (1A) Warm-up activities already described.

(4A) Short check mark, described in detail after the presentation of the schedules.

(14C) High knee drill, followed by the fast leg, both described in detail after the schedules.

Thursday: (3) Weight training activities.

(16) Acrobatics or apparatus work of a gymnastic nature.

Friday: (1A) Warm-up routine.

(15A) A run to Hendricks Park and two times up the short hill, which is about 50 yards long.

Saturday: (1B) A weight training session, followed by a jogging session.

(14F) Alternating runs and jogs or walks of 55 yards for 440 to 880 yards, as described earlier.

Sunday: Recreational activities are recommended. Workout procedures are gradually worked into the program as the year progresses. For those who need training and exercise, this is a day to restore physical well-being.

Figure 9.1a Long Jump Training Schedule

Long Jump NAME DATE September/October

1. A. Jog 1 or 2 laps, relay pass 2s or 3s B. Weights and jog C.
2. Fartlek A. Varied pace B. Slow, steady
3. Weights
4. Check marks A. Short B. Long 1. Height 2. Landing C. Take off
5. Height work A. Emphasize body control B. Apparatus C Take off D.
6. Flight A. Hitch-kick 1½ B. Hang C.
7. Squad meeting
8. Special A. Sauna B. Swim C. Hill D.
9. Landing A. Over the feet B. Around the feet C.
10. Test or trial—compete, record below A. 3/4 to 7/8 effort B. Full effort C.
11. Short run and jump—last 4 steps relax A. Feather the board B. Pound the board C. Over the foot D. 2-count rise—height E. Off platform F. Landing
12. With Coach A. B.
14. A. Wind sprints B. Starts—go 30-50 yds. C. High knee and fast leg D. Hurdle drill 3 lows 8-10 yds. apart E. Spring and bound F. Alternate walk-run 55 yds., go 880 H.
15. A. Hendricks B. Laurelwood 1. Short hill 2. Long hill C. Stadium steps D.
16. Acrobatics or apparatus
17.
18. A. 330-165-110 B. 110-220-110 C.
19.
20. Secondary event
21. A. Pictures B. Film C. Videotape

Date	Result	3/4	Date	Goal

M	Class or squad organization
T	1A-14F-3
W	1A-4A-14C
T	3-16
F	1A-15A-15A1 (2x)
S	1B-14F
S	weights and long walk
M	1A-9A (4-8x)-14F
T	1B-3-Jog
W	7-1A-14C-14D-14E-14A
T	1B-3-Jog
F	1A-14F-11F-14F
S	3 or 15A
S	weights and run
M	1A-14E-15A1 (3x)-15A2 (3x)-14F
T	1A-3-8A
W	1A-14E-14A-14E-14D
T	1A-3-14F
F	1A-14E-15A1 (2x)-15A2 (2x)-Jog
S	jog Hendricks Park
S	jog Hendricks Park
M	1A-14C-9A-8A or B
T	3-Jog
W	1A-4A (2x)-4B (2x)-14D-14B-Jog
T	1B-14F-Jog
F	1A-4A-10A (3x)-Jog
S	Help on track trials or run SPRINT or hurdle
S	run

Figure 9.1b Long Jump Training Schedule

Long Jump NAME DATE October/November

1. A. Jog 1 or 2 laps, relay pass 2s or 3s B. Weights and jog C.
2. Fartlek A. Varied pace B. Slow, steady
3. Weights
4. Check marks A. Short B. Long 1. Height 2. Landing C. Take off
5. Height work A. Emphasize body control B. Apparatus C Take off D.
6. Flight A. Hitch-kick 1½ B. Hang C.
7. Squad meeting
8. Special A. Sauna B. Swim C. Hill D.
9. Landing A. Over the feet B. Around the feet C.
10. Test or trial—compete, record below A. 3/4 to 7/8 effort B. Full effort C.
11. Short run and jump—last 4 steps relax A. Feather the board B. Pound the board C. Over the foot D. 2-count rise—height E. Off platform F. Landing
12. With Coach A. B.
14. A. Wind sprints B. Starts—go 30-50 yds. C. High knee and fast leg D. Hurdle drill 3 lows 8-10 yds. apart E. Spring and bound F. Alternate walk-run 55 yds., go 880 H.
15. A. Hendricks B. Laurelwood 1. Short hill 2. Long hill C. Stadium steps D.
16. Acrobatics or apparatus
17.
18. A. 330-165-110 B. 110-220-110 C.
19.
20. Secondary event
21. A. Pictures B. Film C. Videotape

Date	Result	3/4	Date	Goal

M	1-14C-18B-110 in 15-16
T	1-3-14E
W	7-1-4B-4A-5C-14D-4x 11D-20
T	3-14C
F	1-4A-4B
S	15A or B
S	3
M	1-5-4A-4B-20-11D-Jog
T	3-16-8A
W	1-14E-4B-10A-2x 18B-Jog
T	3- 8A or B
F	1-14E-4A-4B-14D-2x 18B-Jog
S	15A or 3
S	18A or 3
M	1A-1C-14D-2-4x 4B-2-4x 5D
T	3
W	7-1C-14B-11A-11D-18A
T	3
F	1-4B-9-15A
S	10 and sprint or hurdle trial
S	3
M	1-14A-14D-4B-2-4x 11C-2-4x 11D-14A
T	3
W	1-14C-4A-4B-11F-2x 11B1-2x 11B2-Jog
T	3
F	1-14B-4B-11D-18A
S	3
S	15A or B

Figure 9.1c Long Jump Training Schedule

Long Jump NAME DATE January

1. A. Jog 1 or 2 laps, relay pass 2s or 3s B. Weights and jog
   C.
2. Fartlek A. Varied pace B. Slow, steady
3. Weights
4. Check marks A. Short B. Long 1. Height
   2. Landing C. Take off
5. Height work A. Emphasize body control B. Apparatus
   C Take off D.
6. Flight A. Hitch-kick 1½ B. Hang C.
7. Squad meeting
8. Special A. Sauna B. Swim C. Hill D.
9. Landing A. Over the feet B. Around the feet
   C.
10. Test or trial—compete, record below
    A. 3/4 to 7/8 effort B. Full effort C.
11. Short run and jump—last 4 steps relax A. Feather the board
    B. Pound the board C. Over the foot
    D. 2-count rise—height E. Off platform F. Landing
12. With Coach A. B.
14. A. Wind sprints B. Starts—go 30-50 yds.
    C. High knee and fast leg
    D. Hurdle drill 3 lows 8-10 yds. apart
    E. Spring and bound
    F. Alternate walk-run 55 yds., go 880
    H.
15. A. Hendricks B. Laurelwood 1. Short hill 2. Long hill
    C. Stadium steps D.
16. Acrobatics or apparatus
17.
18. A. 330-165-110 B. 110-220-110 C.
19.
20. Secondary event
21. A. Pictures B. Film C. Videotape

Date	Result	3/4	Date	Goal

M	Recheck all gear-squad or class organize
T	1-9A-15A-locker arrangements
W	1A-11D-14D-14F
T	7-1B-8A
F	1A-14C-11D-14F
S	1A-14A or C
S	jog the halls
M	1A-14C-4A-11A-14A
T	7-3-14F
W	1A-14C-4A-11D-14F
T	3-8A or B or Jog
F	1A-14C-4B-11A-14A
S	3-14D
S	or 8A
M	1-14F-4B-11C-18A
T	14F-8A
W	2-4x 1-14C-4B-10A short run-14A
T	14F-14C
F	1A-4B-11A-11D-18A
S	3-15A-15C
S	
M	1-4B-4A-9A-11A-14F
T	3
W	2x 2x 1A-4B-4A-9D-18B-18C-14F
T	Light
F	Gear ready
S	Compete indoors
S	Light

Figure 9.1d Long Jump Training Schedule

Long Jump NAME DATE February

1. A. Jog 1 or 2 laps, relay pass 2s or 3s B. Weights and jog
   C.
2. Fartlek A. Varied pace B. Slow, steady
3. Weights
4. Check marks A. Short B. Long 1. Height
   2. Landing C. Take off
5. Height work A. Emphasize body control B. Apparatus
   C Take off D.
6. Flight A. Hitch-kick 1½ B. Hang C.
7. Squad meeting
8. Special A. Sauna B. Swim C. Hill D.
9. Landing A. Over the feet B. Around the feet
   C.
10. Test or trial—compete, record below
    A. 3/4 to 7/8 effort B. Full effort C.
11. Short run and jump—last 4 steps relax A. Feather the board
    B. Pound the board C. Over the foot
    D. 2-count rise—height E. Off platform F. Landing
12. With Coach A. B.
14. A. Wind sprints B. Starts—go 30-50 yds.
    C. High knee and fast leg
    D. Hurdle drill 3 lows 8-10 yds. apart
    E. Spring and bound
    F. Alternate walk-run 55 yds., go 880
    H.
15. A. Hendricks B. Laurelwood 1. Short hill 2. Long hill
    C. Stadium steps D.
16. Acrobatics or apparatus
17.
18. A. 330-165-110 B. 110-220-110 C.
19.
20. Secondary event
21. A. Pictures B. Film C. Videotape

Date	Result	3/4	Date	Goal

M	2x 2x 6-10x 3-6x 1-4A-4B-5A - 5B-14D-14E
T	3-14A
W	3x 3x 7-1-4A1-4A2-15A or 15C or 8C
T	14E-3
F	2-3x 1-4A-15A or B, 1 and 2-14E
S	8B or 3
S	long walk
M	1A-14D-5C-14C-Jog
T	3-8A or B
W	3x 3x 1-5A-5B-5C
T	Light
F	1-10-8C
S	Sprint and hurdle trials
S	
M	1-14A-14C-11D-14E-14C
T	3-16
W	7-14B-4B-4A-14F
T	3-8A or B
F	2x 1-4A-18A-18B-15A
S	8-15A
S	3
M	1A-14D-5C-14C
T	3-8A or C
W	3x 3x 7-5A-5B-5C-15
T	3-8A
F	1-10-run a 275-15
S	
S	

Figure 9.1e Long Jump Training Schedule

Long Jump NAME DATE March

1. A. Jog 1 or 2 laps, relay pass 2s or 3s B. Weights and jog C.
2. Fartlek A. Varied pace B. Slow, steady
3. Weights
4. Check marks A. Short B. Long 1. Height 2. Landing C. Take off
5. Height work A. Emphasize body control B. Apparatus C Take off D.
6. Flight A. Hitch-kick 1½ B. Hang C.
7. Squad meeting
8. Special A. Sauna B. Swim C. Hill D.
9. Landing A. Over the feet B. Around the feet C.
10. Test or trial—compete, record below A. 3/4 to 7/8 effort B. Full effort C.
11. Short run and jump—last 4 steps relax A. Feather the board B. Pound the board C. Over the foot D. 2-count rise—height E. Off platform F. Landing
12. With Coach A. B.
14. A. Wind sprints B. Starts—go 30-50 yds. C. High knee and fast leg D. Hurdle drill 3 lows 8-10 yds. apart E. Spring and bound F. Alternate walk-run 55 yds., go 880 H.
15. A. Hendricks B. Laurelwood 1. Short hill 2. Long hill C. Stadium steps D.
16. Acrobatics or apparatus
17.
18. A. 330-165-110 B. 110-220-110 C.
19.
20. Secondary event
21. A. Pictures B. Film C. Videotape

M	1A-14B-14E-11D [3-5X]-11A [3-5X]-14F
T	3-14F [3X]
W	7-1C-14E-14A [2-4X]-9C [2-4X]-9A [2X]-9B [2X]-14D-14F
T	3-14F or set of 300-200-1-
F	1C-4A [3X]-4B [3X]-5A [3-4X]-9A-Jog
S	3-Jog
S	park run

M	1A-14C-14E-14B [3X]-4A [3X]-4B [3X]-run 110 [4X]
T	14A-3
W	7-1C-4B [3X]-4A2 [3X]-14D
T	3-14A
F	Gear ready and jog
S	Meet routine-compete-after meet routine
S	run

	A.M.	P.M.
M	1A-3	1-4A [2X]-4B [2X]-5C [2X]-14F
T	Jog	1-14E-20-4A [2X]
W	Light	Light
T	1-14E	1-14C-4B [2X]-4B1 [2X]-4B2 [2X]-14F
F	Jog	Gear ready-light exercise
S	Meet routine-compete-after meet routine	
S		

M	
T	
W	
T	
F	
S	
S	

Date	Result	3/4	Date	Goal

Figure 9.1f Long Jump Training Schedule

Long Jump NAME DATE April

1. A. Jog 1 or 2 laps, relay pass 2s or 3s B. Weights and jog C.
2. Fartlek A. Varied pace B. Slow, steady
3. Weights
4. Check marks A. Short B. Long 1. Height 2. Landing C. Take off
5. Height work A. Emphasize body control B. Apparatus C Take off D.
6. Flight A. Hitch-kick 1½ B. Hang C.
7. Squad meeting
8. Special A. Sauna B. Swim C. Hill D.
9. Landing A. Over the feet B. Around the feet C.
10. Test or trial—compete, record below A. 3/4 to 7/8 effort B. Full effort C.
11. Short run and jump—last 4 steps relax A. Feather the board B. Pound the board C. Over the foot D. 2-count rise—height E. Off platform F. Landing
12. With Coach A. B.
14. A. Wind sprints B. Starts—go 30-50 yds. C. High knee and fast leg D. Hurdle drill 3 lows 8-10 yds. apart E. Spring and bound F. Alternate walk-run 55 yds., go 880 H.
15. A. Hendricks B. Laurelwood 1. Short hill 2. Long hill C. Stadium steps D.
16. Acrobatics or apparatus
17.
18. A. 330-165-110 B. 110-220-110 C.
19.
20. Secondary event
21. A. Pictures B. Film C. Videotape

Date	Result	3/4	Date	Goal

M	7-1-14C-4A-4B-11D-1C
T	1-14C-3
W	1-4A-4B-14E-14A
T	1-4B-Jog-3
F	Light
S	Meet
S	Jog and 8A or 8B
M	7-1-14C-5B-14A 7 at 4:45 p.m.
T	1-4B-11-14F
W	1-14E-14D
T	1-4B-11A-11D-14E
F	Light
S	Big meet-relay and long jump
S	Jog
M	7-14C-4B-14A
T	1-4B-11D-11F-Jog
W	1-14E-11-14F
T	1-4B-4A-11D
F	Travel and loosen up
S	Compete
S	1-8A-Jog
M	7-1-14A-4B-14E-14F
T	1-4B-11A-4B1-14F
W	3
T	1-4B-11D
F	Light
S	Dual meet-away
S	Home-8A-Jog

Figure 9.1g Long Jump Training Schedule

Long Jump NAME DATE May

1. A. Jog 1 or 2 laps, relay pass 2s or 3s B. Weights and jog
   C.
2. Fartlek A. Varied pace B. Slow, steady
3. Weights
4. Check marks A. Short B. Long 1. Height
   2. Landing C. Take off
5. Height work A. Emphasize body control B. Apparatus
   C Take off D.
6. Flight A. Hitch-kick 1½ B. Hang C.
7. Squad meeting
8. Special A. Sauna B. Swim C. Hill D.
9. Landing A. Over the feet B. Around the feet
   C.
10. Test or trial—compete, record below
    A. 3/4 to 7/8 effort B. Full effort C.
11. Short run and jump—last 4 steps relax A. Feather the board
    B. Pound the board C. Over the foot
    D. 2-count rise—height E. Off platform F. Landing
12. With Coach A. B.
14. A. Wind sprints B. Starts—go 30-50 yds.
    C. High knee and fast leg
    D. Hurdle drill 3 lows 8-10 yds. apart
    E. Spring and bound
    F. Alternate walk-run 55 yds., go 880
    H.
15. A. Hendricks B. Laurelwood 1. Short hill 2. Long hill
    C. Stadium steps D.
16. Acrobatics or apparatus
17.
18. A. 330-165-110 B. 110-220-110 C.
19.
20. Secondary event
21. A. Pictures B. Film C. Videotape

Date	Result	3/4	Date	Goal

M	1-4-5A-11D-9A-20-15F
T	3-Jog
W	1-4-11D-9A-14E-14F
T	3-Jog
F	Travel and loosen up
S	Major meet
S	Home-1-14C-8B-8A
M	Jog
T	Jog
W	Twilight meet or trials
T	11C-11D-11F
F	4A-4B-15A
S	Squad picnic
S	walk or jog
M	1-4A-4B1-11C-14E-jog
T	1-4B-14A
W	Jog-3
T	Jog-4
F	1-4A-4B-Jog
S	3x 1-14E-4B-10A
S	Jog and weights
M	4x 1-14E-14A-14B-pop-ups--75 yards-jog
T	2-3x 1-14E-4A-4B-Easy 14D
W	Easy grass running
T	Easy grass running
F	Qualify
S	Championship
S	

A long jump training chart is used for communication and for the convenience of coach and athlete. Several of the numbers have common interpretations for all events, simplifying scheduling and recording for the coach. Those used particularly for long jump training are explained as follows:

4. Check mark. The long jump check mark is a very important fundamental. We recommend that the jumper first establish a short check mark to be used when jumping against the wind, or when there have been two fouls in the preliminaries and a "must" jump is necessary to qualify for the finals. The "short check" is important in training for other fundamentals, also.

4A. Short check. The short check is a one-mark approach, the distance being 50 to 70 feet, depending upon the length of the athlete's strides. The approach will be 10 strides in most cases, though one variation uses a short check of 8 strides. Figure 9.2 illustrates the stride pattern for a 10-stride shot approach for a jumper who leaves the board from his left foot.

4B. Long check mark. This mark has several variations. The most commonly used one is the 4-8-10 step. Using "S" for the start (Figure 9.3), checks 1, 2, and 3, and "T" for take-off, a procedure for establishing the marks would be: start the athlete at S and the coach or observer on the runway or track about 20 feet away. Two walking steps lead to check 1 with the left foot, and running at half-speed and gradually increasing, on the fourth step the jumper is at check 2. The observer marks the location of this step, and the procedure is repeated for a total of three efforts. The average distance, usually 20 to 25 feet, establishes the first two check marks.

The procedure is repeated for check 3. The jumper begins at S and reconfirms checks 1 and 2 as he goes through three efforts, running at three-fourths effort, gradually increasing his speed. The observer again marks each of the three efforts and takes the average, eight steps being taken from check 2 to check 3.

Figure 9.2 Short Check Approach: Long Jump.

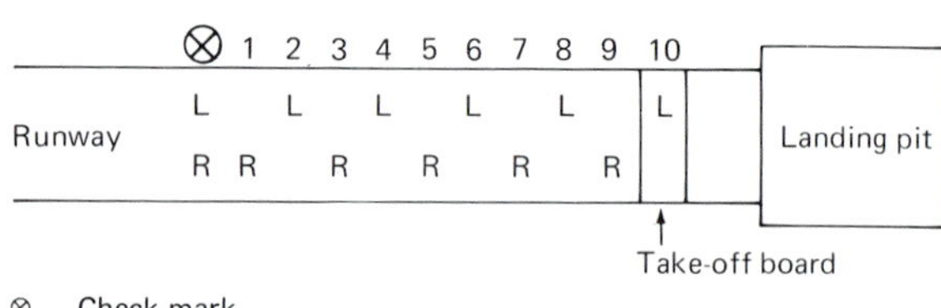

Figure 9.3 Long Check Approach: Long Jump.

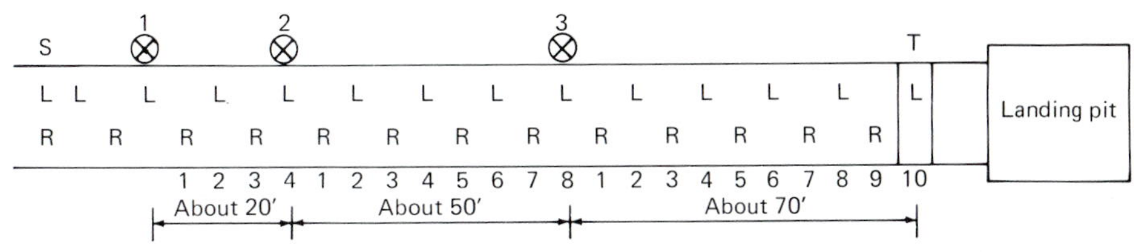

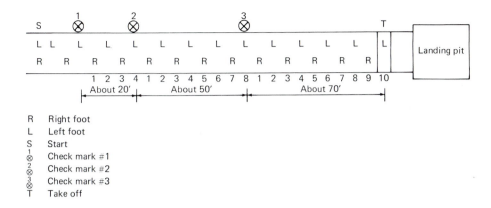

R Right foot
L Left foot
S Start
⊗1 Check mark #1
⊗2 Check mark #2
⊗3 Check mark #3
T Take off

The "T" is established in the same manner, with the speed gradually increasing from seven-eighths to nine-tenths effort. It may be necessary for the jumper to establish the "T" mark on another day, particularly if his fitness level is low.

4A1. Short run, height. This is a drill to emphasize the slight settle on the second-to-last step, a slight rise on the next-to-last step, and final lift at the take-off. The perfect jump would find the jumper's center of gravity rising at an angle of about 45 degrees, with the maximum height achieved at the approximate midpoint of the jump.

4A2. Short run, landing. This is a reflex action. The between-the-feet or over-the-feet action is the most common landing. The feet must be dropped soon enough for the forward momentum to carry the jumper over the feet, or a slight spread of the feet should be used to let the jumper go between the feet, forcing the hips forward. This action (the same as in item *9A*) also depends on the jumper reaching forward and through between the knees.

A second excellent method is landing with one knee slightly stiffened (also used in item *9B*). At the instant of foot contact with the landing surface, the opposite arm and hand reach across the body, while the arm on the same side as the locked knee is moved outward. This action causes a rotation around the feet. This is difficult to coordinate and is only for the very agile athlete.

4C. Check mark, take-off. The take-off here is for the emphasis of having the take-off foot under the hip, not across the center of gravity. A cross step by the take-off foot (planting the foot across the line of the run to the board) will cause a compensating motion across the body by the arm opposite the take-off leg. This also causes the lead leg to cross over the line of the approach to the pit. Not only will the take-off be spoiled, but the flight will be a fight for balance, resulting in a poor landing.

Figure 9.4 Height Work: Long Jump.

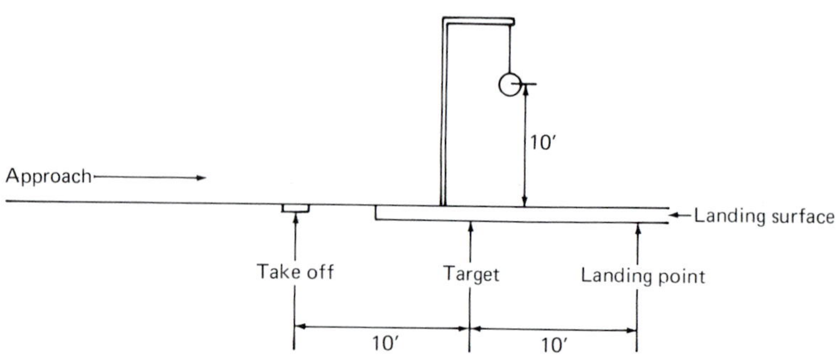

5. Height work. Height work is of such importance that not only is it treated within check mark fundamentals, but it is also a separate fundamental requiring special attention. In a 20-foot jump, the center of gravity should reach its peak height at a point 10 feet from the take-off. The body should be perpendicular to the ground at the midpoint of the jump. A pole vault standard with an arm extension (Figure 9.4) and a hanging target made of a towel or sponge may be used for practicing this fundamental. The target is suspended about 10 feet above the pit and 10 feet from the take-off. The jumper works to get his head up about 9 to 10 feet above ground level at this point.

6. Flight. There are two major methods of body control in the air in preparation for landing. Neither propels the center of gravity any farther. The importance of the flight is to gain balance so the feet can be thrust as far forward as possible and so the center of gravity can pass forward past the feet at impact without the hands or buttocks making sand marks.

6A. Hitch-kick. As the take-off foot pushes off the board, the lead knee is brought to hip height, followed by the take-off leg coming into a running position, then extending, and the lead leg coming up into the extended position for a 1½-step "walk in the air." Ralph Boston developed a 2½-step walk. This great, gifted athlete could handle the technique. Only those who can benefit from the technique should use it. It is strongly recommended that the 1½-step be mastered before the athlete even plays with the 2½-step style.

6B. Hang. At the take-off the lead knee is lifted, the arms lift, and as the lead knee is lowered, the take-off leg is brought alongside, but the legs are spread and the knees are slightly bent. The jumper, with his arms over his head and his legs hanging down, appears to hang until past the midpoint of the jump, when the legs and arms are brought forward and the jumper awaits the pull of gravity for the landing.

9. Landing. This work was described with the check mark work. It may be practiced with either the long or short approaches (items *8A* and *8B* with *4A* and *4B*).

10. Test effort. The coach or athlete should record the results of this effort on the lower left area of the training sheet. The three-fourths to seven-eighths effort is a usual procedure for practice. There is no benefit in an athlete being exhausted on Tuesday or Wednesday. The trials are a learning and technique procedure. Assuming a jumper has an average of 22 feet in competition, we believe a reasonable trial or test jump would be 20 feet. A "hot" practice effort might well equal or better the competitive average, but technique combined with controlled process will make for the big jumps in the big meets.

11A. Feather the board. The technique strived for here is to try to achieve a running up into the air, rather than a pounding of the take-off board. It is believed that an emphasis *up* rather than down gives maximum lift.

11B. Pound the board. This means exactly what it says, and it is a technique used by many fine jumpers and advocated by many coaches. The jumper should use what suits him and gets results. Heel bruises and muscle pulls are the great dangers in the "pound" technique. In practicing either of these techniques, the jumper should take off either in front of the board or on the grass, rather than from the board.

11C. Over the foot. The coach or a teammate should watch the jumper from the rear to determine that the take-off foot is directly under the hip, and not across a line dropped perpendicular to the center of gravity. Such a crossover will cause many compensating equilibrium problems which will detract from the jumping distance.

11D. Two-count rise, height. The two-count rise (Figure 9.5) is a very important technique. The jumper settles on his third-to-last (left foot for a left-footed take-

Figure 9.5 Two-Count Rise: Long Jump.

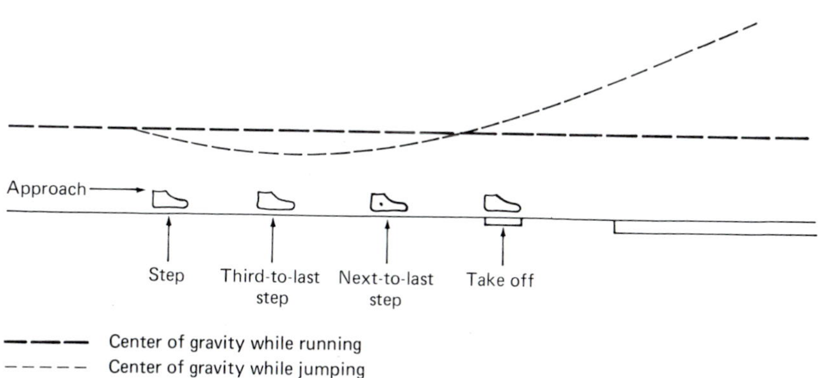

off) step, is just barely rising on his next-to-last step, and on the last step gives the final propulsion and lift. Theoretically, if the body is already rising, it not only weighs proportionately less, but also utilizes the body's momentum to detract from the body's weight. The jumping leg has a tremendous advantage in lifting a mass which is already moving upward.

11E. Off platform. A platform of plywood with one edge on a 2 by 4 makes an inclined plane with a slight elevation, which enables the jumper to artificially attain additional height, giving more time to work on body control in the air.

14E. Spring and bound. A secondary event might be the relay, the 100, or sometimes the triple jump. The dangers of the triple jump are the same as the long jump: stone bruise, muscle pull, back problems, and such. If an athlete would limit himself to a total of four to six jumps total in both events, perhaps it would then be a good double. However, he may turn out to be only fair in both events, when he could be great in one event if he concentrated.

Long Jump Bibliography

Campbell, Donald E. "Velocity curve of the horizontal approach of the competitive long jumper," *Research Quarterly* 42 (December 1971): 444–49.

Ecker, Tom. "The long jump landing position," *Athletic Journal* 50 (May 1970): 26, 78.

Flynn, James E. "Cinématographic study of the kinematic and temporal analysis of the takeoff in the running long jump," *Track and Field Quarterly Review* 73 (December 1973): 222–29.

Giovinazzo, Nick. "Teach them to land," *Athletic Journal* 50 (January 1970): 16, 23, 88–89.

Greer, Harvey. "Basic long jumping technique," *Track Technique,* No. 44 (June 1971), pp. 1398–99.

Jesse, John P. "Weight training for long and triple jumpers," *Track and Field Quarterly Review*, October 1965, pp. 44–50.

McNab, Tom. "The long jump approach: problems of accuracy," *Athletics Coach* 6 (June 1972): 12–13.

Miler, Rajko. "Landing in the long jump," *Track Technique*, No. 19 (March 1969), pp. 600–1.

Nulton, John E. "Long jump or triple jump," *Athletics Journal* 51 (February 1971): 44–47, 73–74.

______. "Specialized conditioning for long and triple jumpers," *Scholastic Coach* 40 (February 1971): 14–16, 84, 86, 88–89.

Plagenhoef, Stan. "A biomechanical analysis of Beamon, Williams, and an average college long jumper," *Track and Field Quarterly Review* 73 (December 1973): 214–21.

Ramey, Melvin R. "Effective use of force plates for long jump studies," *Research Quarterly* 43 (May 1972): 247–52.

Ryan, Frank. "Beamon's style: the 'height' of fashion," *Scholastic Coach* 39 (September 1969): 18–20.

Sharpley, Frank. "Teaching beginners to broad jump," *Track Technique*, No. 10 (December 1962), pp. 315–18.

Ter-Ovanesyan, Igor. "Ter-Ovanesyan on the long jump," *Track Technique*, No. 27 (March 1967), pp. 858–60.

Vaupas, Antanas. "Training of the long jump," *Track Technique*, No. 30 (December 1967), pp. 938–39.

Verhoshanskiy, Yuriy. "Depth jumping in the training of jumpers," *Track Technique*, No. 51 (March 1973), pp. 1618–19.

Watts, Denis C. V. *The Long Jump*. 5th ed. London: AAA, 1972, 56 pp.

The triple jump

10

The triple jump is a relatively recent addition to American high school and college dual meets. The lack of previous competition in the United States was reflected quite clearly in Olympic competitions. There might be an occasional international-class athlete, but the Americans were no real threat in the major competitions. However, the quality of triple jumping has risen phenomenally in the United States over the last decade. Hopefully the broadened scope of competition will eventually produce a gold medalist in this event, last won by an American in 1904.

A prospective triple jumper needs several natural qualities if he hopes to be successful. Speed and leg strength are essential. The speed will be there or it will not. The leg strength can be developed. Perhaps the most important factor in successful triple jumping is balance. Finally, rhythm is necessary, since the triple jump is, as its title implies, a series of jumps, rather than a single effort.

Analysis of the Triple Jump

The triple jump has been called the "hop, step, and jump," and on occasion, incorrectly, the "hop, skip, and jump." The approach is made similar to the long jump approach, with the jumper beginning the jumping sequence when he steps upon a take-off board. The first part of the action is the "hop," so called because the jumper will land on the same foot which he placed on the take-off board. This action of taking off and then landing on the same foot requires considerable leg strength if the jumper is to continue through the other two phases of the jump.

From the landing at the end of the hopping phase, the jumper moves into a "step," in which he takes off on the foot upon which he landed when completing his hop, then lands on the opposite foot, completing the step and preparatory to the last phase of the action, which is the "jump." The jump is simply a normal long jumping action, with the athlete taking off from the foot upon which he landed when completing the stepping phase of the jump. The jumping portion of the sequence is most commonly done with the form of the "hang" style of long jumping, described in Chapter 9. If the triple jumper takes off on his left foot (placing that foot on the board when beginning the jumping sequence), his stepping pattern will be take off (left foot) to land (left foot) at completion of hop, to land (right foot) at completion of step, to land (both feet) in pit at completion of jumping phase. (See Photographs 10.1*a-p,* of Victor Saneyev, for an example of the triple jump.)

The approach run for the triple jump is similar to the run for the long jump, with the primary exceptions that (1) it is not generally as long as the long jump run and (2) the two-count rise, employed in assisting the long jump take-off, is not used. The triple jumper is primarily seeking controlled speed to the point of the take-off.

At the take-off, the jumper does *not* want to get much height off the board. The action off the board is very similar to the normal sprinting action. The jumper wishes to conserve as much of his horizontal momentum as possible. This momentum at the time of his take-off must last through not one but *three* take-offs. The jumper wants to hit the board both balanced and relaxed. His balance at this point is very important, as any imbalance at the take-off will likely result in a very weak later portion of the jump. The jumper should try to hit the board with his hips a bit more forward than they would be in the normal sprinting position.

On each of the landings the landing foot should be pulled back quickly just before it strikes the ground. This maneuver is designed to allow the jumper to preserve as much of his momentum as possible through the landing and subsequent take-off actions. If the foot is not pulled backward, but remains very far ahead of the jumper, it will act as a brake when he lands, removing most of his potential momentum which could have been applied to the next jumping phase.

The coach and jumper should *listen* to the rhythm of the jump as it is performed. It should be regular for all three portions of the jump. If the middle portion sounds too quick, the stepping phase is probably not being done properly. The step is generally the hardest portion of the jump to learn and develop properly. The jumper should work at developing his strength in each leg equally. He will generally use the same leg for taking off in both the long jump and the triple jump.

Comments on the Triple Jump and Training

One competitive suggestion for teachers and coaches: do not use an athlete in both the long jump and triple jump. There are several reasons for this suggestion.

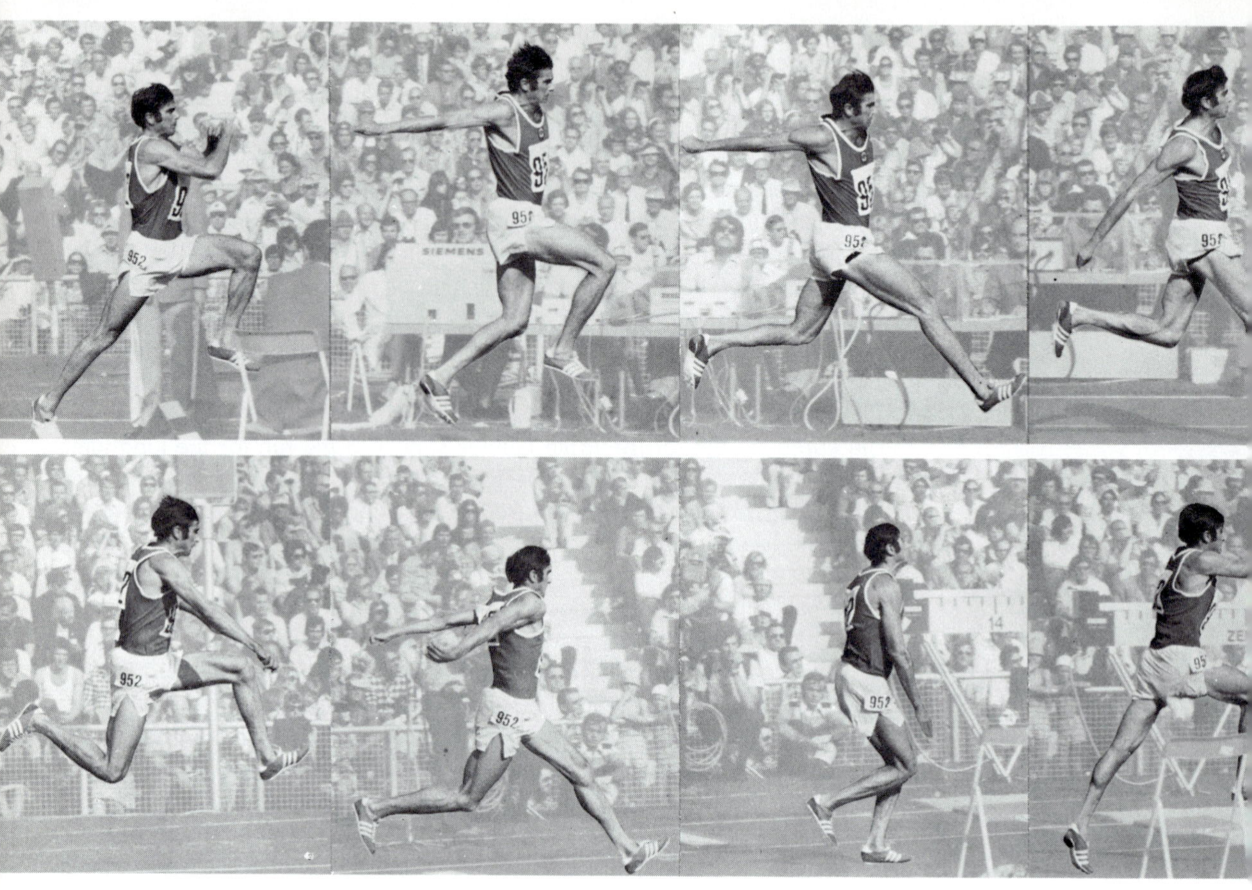

Photographs 10.1*a-p* Victor Saneyev, U.S.S.R., in the triple jump.

The primary reason is that both events are very hard on the athlete's legs. The risk of injury with much jumping is great with either event. If the jumper competes in both events, his risk of injury is doubled — as are the coach's chances of losing the athlete. Also, an athlete will tend to be better in one or the other of the two events. Only at the low level of accomplishment will he be likely to show an equal level of achievement in the events. Practically no international-class jumper in either event has been better than national class (and there is quite a bit of difference) in the other. Generally the long jumpers have the best speed, while the triple jumpers are longer on leg strength, which they can utilize despite their lesser natural speed.

Prospective triple jumpers are generally found by testing with a standing triple jump, which is also a good training drill. The high school student who goes past 24 feet or the collegian who exceeds 28 feet is probably a good prospect. The teacher should watch the prospects, looking for rhythm and balance. Hurdlers are often good prospects. Rhythm can be developed by jumping first from

standing jumps, then going to jumps taken from a short run of three steps or so. While jumping, the athletes should always wear heel cups for their protection.

Several types of drills can be used as a vital part of triple jump training. Three types of drills are rhythm drills, power bounding, and box drills. The rhythm drills are done by using a five-to-seven-step approach, followed by 10 consecutive jumps, with any combination of landings (i.e., any combination of hops and steps). The primary object of this drill is to work on the rhythm of the hopping and stepping, and it is judged by the tone and distance covered by the jumper in the 10-step sequence. As the athlete improves, the distance which he covers will increase, while the time required for the series will decrease. One experienced triple jump coach suggests that 120 feet in 5.5 seconds indicates that an athlete will be a good triple jumper.

The power bounding drills are performed working on either height or distance. There are several possible variations of the drill. The athlete will go intervals of 50 to 100 yards *on soft surfaces* hopping on either one leg or the other, working on either height or distance of hops. This exercise will be done six to eight times as fast as the athlete can go. The jumpers might also work on a hop-step drill. In this drill the jumper also covers 50 to 100 yards, except that he alternates his hopping (H) and stepping (S) (i.e., HSHSHSHS, etc.), working on his double-arm action and trying to develop a more powerful lead leg.

The box drills are done with boxes of various heights, with 18 inches the most common height. At Oregon, boxes 16 inches high × 20 inches across in the jumping direction × 30 inches wide are used. Usually three to five boxes are used, or sections of logs might even be used, since a log is only a box that hasn't been made into a box. These are spaced at intervals along the runway or on the grass. To begin the drill, the boxes are only a few yards apart. According to the drill, or as the jumpers become more adept, they can be moved farther apart. One drill is to go over the boxes, stepping on the ground with the take-off leg and stepping on the boxes with the leg which leads into the stepping phase of the triple jump. The purpose of the drill is to get the jumper in the habit of getting his stepping leg up, which is necessary to get onto the box and also to get a long step in the actual jump. Another drill, done with the boxes farther apart, is to work on both hopping and stepping. The athlete hops *between* the boxes, then steps *over* a box, hops to the next box, steps over again, and so forth. If the athlete takes off on his left leg (LL), the pattern would be LL, box, RL, box, LL, box, RL, and so forth, always with a hop over and a step between. Because of the boxes, the jumper learns to get the trail leg up fast. In performing the step, the jumper needs to learn to get both legs up, one forward and one to the rear.

Rope jumping is also a good leg-strengthening exercise, jumping on one leg for half a minute, then resting for 15 seconds or so, then jumping for an equal period of time on the other leg. During the fall period of training, the jumpers will generally work on drills three days a week, working over the boxes on Mondays and Fridays and on the rhythm drills on Wednesdays. Fall is a good time for building the athlete's strength and sense of the movements, leaving the period immediately before the season for more specific technique work.

A warm-up routine is used for the triple jump, as for the other events, but since the triple jump is a relatively recent addition to the dual meet schedule, the routine used at Oregon is still in a state of flux. At the moment, the routine is begun with work on power bounding. This is followed by several series of three triple jumps taken following approaches of varying lengths. The first three jumps are taken from a stand. The next three jumps are taken with a 30-foot approach run. Three jumps are taken from a 60-foot approach, then three jumps are taken with a 90-foot approach. Actually, this is quite enough actual jumping for a triple jumper, and it may even be more than he should do, except on occasion. The rest of his workouts would consist of drills and selected sprinters' exercises. The coach should be careful not to overwork a triple jumper and expose him to needless injury. Examples of the fundamentals of triple jumping may be seen on the training sheets in Figure 10.1.

Several principles of triple jumping have been cited by Oglesby, a number of which might be mentioned here. One which is often overlooked by beginning

Figure 10.1a Triple Jump Training Schedule

Triple Jump NAME DATE September/October

1. Warm-up routine to include A. Jogging-flexibility
   B. Easy high knee, fast leg
2. Fartlek A. Holmer B. Lydiard
3. Weight routine
4. Bounding drills A. Height, B. Distance } L.R (50-100 yds.)
   6-8 repeats fast as you can control
   C. Hop-step drill—double arm action—powerful lead leg (50-100 yds.) 6-8 repeats
5. Rhythm drills: 5-7-9-step approach
   A. S - S - S - J
   B. H - H - H - S - J
   C. LL RR LLL R LL—10 successive—for time and distance—124 ft.—excellent! D.
6. Box drills
   A. L □ L □ L □ L □ L □—step leg up to get on box (R over each box)
   B. L □ R □ L □ R □ L □ R
   C. L □ R □ L □ R □ L (L R L R over boxes)
   D. R □ L □ R □ Pit (R R L over boxes) | 4m |
   Reverse RRLRRL to LLRLLR
   E. R □ R—L □ R—R □ L—R □ R Pit | 10 ft. |
   Reverse RRLRRLRR to LLRLLRLL
   F. R—R □ R—L □ R—R □ Pit (L, L over boxes) | 16 ft. | | 10 ft. |
   G. R □ R □ R □ Pit (L L L over boxes) 8 ft. work for 20 ft.
   H. R □ R □ L □ Pit (R L L over boxes)
7. Squad meeting
8. Special A. Sauna B. Swim C. Film D.
9. Short approach triple jump A. Standing B. 3-step C. 5-step D. 7-step E. 9-step F. 11-step
10. Full approach A. Check marks B. Jumping C. Competition or trial
11. Rope jumping: 30 sec., 15 sec. rest
12. Hurdle X drill
14. Intervals A. 110 B. 165 C. 220 D. 300 E. 330 F. 440 G. 660-440-330-220-110
15. Hill work A. Laurelwood B. Emerald St. C. Stadium steps

Day	Week 1
M	6-8x 1AB-14C
T	1AB-3-2A
W	15A-7
T	1AB-3-2B
F	4x 1AB-14G-14A
S	1AB-3-2A
S	

Day	Week 2
M	3x 3x 3x 1AB-14E-14C-14A
T	1AB-3-2A
W	15A
T	1AB-3-2A
F	4x 4x 1AB-14D-14A-2B
S	1AB-3-2A
S	

Day	Week 3
M	6x 1AB-4AB-14G-14A
T	1AB-3-2B
W	1AB-12-15A
T	1AB-3-2A
F	3x 4x 4x 1AB-4ABC-5ABC-14D-14A
S	1AB-3-2B
S	

Day	Week 4
M	5x 4x 3x 3x 1AB-4ABC-5A-5B-5C-14G-14A
T	1AB-3-2B
W	1AB-12-15A-8C
T	1AB-3-2A
F	4x 3x 3x 2x 3x 4x 1AB-4ABC-5A-5B-5C-14F-14E-14C-14B
S	1AB-3-2A
S	

Figure 10.1b Triple Jump Training Schedule

Triple Jump NAME DATE November

1. Warm-up routine to include A. Jogging-flexibility
   B. Easy high knee, fast leg
2. Fartlek A. Holmer B. Lydiard
3. Weight routine
4. Bounding drills A. Height } L.R (50-100 yds.)
   B. Distance }
   6-8 repeats fast as you can control
   C. Hop-step drill—double arm action—powerful lead leg (50-100 yds.) 6-8 repeats
5. Rhythm drills: 5-7-9-step approach
   A. S - S - S - J
   B. H - H - H - S - J
   C. LL RR LLL R LL—10 successive—for time and distance—124 ft.—excellent! D.
6. Box drills
   A. L □ L □ L □ L □ L □—step leg up to get on box (R above each box)
   B. L □ R □ L □ R □ L □ R
   C. L □ R □ L □ R □ L (L, R, L, R above boxes)
   D. R □ L □ R □ Pit (R, R, L above boxes) | 4m |
   Reverse RRLRRL to LLRLLR
   E. R □ R—L □ R—R □ L—R □ R Pit | 10 ft. |
   Reverse RRLRRLRR to LLRLLRLL
   F. R—R □ R—L □ R—R □ Pit (L above boxes) | 16 ft. | | 10 ft. |
   G. R □ R □ R □ Pit (L above boxes) 8 ft. work for 20 ft.
   H. R □ R □ L □ Pit (R, L, L above boxes)
7. Squad meeting
8. Special A. Sauna B. Swim C. Film D.
9. Short approach triple jump A. Standing B. 3-step
   C. 5-step D. 7-step E. 9-step F. 11-step
10. Full approach A. Check marks B. Jumping
    C. Competition or Trial
11. Rope jumping: 30 sec., 15 sec. rest
12. Hurdle X drill
14. Intervals A. 110 B. 165 C. 220 D. 300
    E. 330 F. 440 G. 660-440-330-220-110
15. Hill work A. Laurelwood B. Emerald St.
    C. Stadium steps

M	3x 4x 1AB-4AB-5ABC-14C-14G
T	1A-3
W	1A-12-15A
T	1A-3
F	3x 2x 2x 4x 1AB-4ABC-6ABCD-14E-14C-14A
S	1A-3-2A
S	

M	3x 6x 1AB-4ABC-5ABC-14C
T	1AB-3-2A
W	15A-8C
T	1AB-3-2A
F	3x 3x 1AB-4ABC-6BCDE-14D-14G
S	1A-3-2A
S	

M	5x 3x 2x 3x 4x 1AB-4ABC-5AB-5C-14F-14E-14C-14A
T	1A-3-2B
W	1AB-15A-7
T	1A-3-2B
F	3x 1AB-4ABC-9ABC-14G
S	1A-3-2B
S	

M	5x 3x 3x 3x 3x 1AB-4ABC-5AB-5C-14D-14B-14A
T	1A-3-2B-8C
W	1AB-12-15A
T	1A-3-2B
F	3x 3x 3x 3x 1AB-4ABC-6CDEF-14E-14C-14A
S	1AB-3-2B
S	

Figure 10.1c Triple Jump Training Schedule

Triple Jump NAME DATE December

1. Warm-up routine to include A. Jogging-flexibility
   B. Easy high knee, fast leg
2. Fartlek A. Holmer B. Lydiard
3. Weight routine
4. Bounding drills A. Height, B. Distance } L.R (50-100 yds.)
   6-8 repeats fast as you can control
   C. Hop-step drill—double arm action—powerful lead leg (50-100 yds.) 6-8 repeats
5. Rhythm drills: 5-7-9-step approach
   A. S - S - S - J
   B. H - H - H - S - J
   C. LL RR LLL R LL—10 successive—for time and distance—124 ft.—excellent! D.
6. Box drills
   A. L □ L □ L □ L □ L □—step leg up to get on box (R on each box)
   B. L □ R □ L □ R □ L □ R
   C. L □ R □ L □ R □ L (L R L R on the boxes)
   D. R □ L □ R □ Pit (R R L on the boxes) |4m|
   Reverse RRLRRL to LLRLLR
   E. R □ R—L □ R—R □ L—R □ R Pit |10 ft.|
   Reverse RRLRRLRR to LLRLLRLL
   F. R—R □ R—L □ R—R □ Pit |16 ft.| |10 ft.|
   G. R □ R □ R □ Pit (L over each box) 8 ft. work for 20 ft.
   H. R □ R □ L □ Pit (R L L over the boxes)
7. Squad meeting
8. Special A. Sauna B. Swim C. Film D.
9. Short approach triple jump A. Standing B. 3-step
   C. 5-step D. 7-step E. 9-step F. 11-step
10. Full approach A. Check marks B. Jumping
    C. Competition or Trial
11. Rope jumping: 30 sec., 15 sec. rest
12. Hurdle X drill
14. Intervals A. 110 B. 165 C. 220 D. 300
    E. 330 F. 440 G. 660-440-330-220-110
15. Hill work A. Laurelwood B. Emerald St.
    C. Stadium steps

M	1AB-4ABC-5AB (5x)-5C (3x)-14G-14A (4x)
T	1AB-3-2A
W	1AB-12-15B
T	1AB-3-2A
F	1AB-4ABC-6DEFG (4x)-14D (5x)
S	1AB-3-2A
S	
M	1AB-4ABC-5A (6x)-5B (5x)-5C (4x)-14G-14A (4x)
T	1AB-3-2A
W	1AB-12-15B (3-5x)
T	1AB-3-2A
F	1AB-2B
S	1AB-4AC-9BCD (2x)-14E (2x)-14C (2x)-14A (2x)
S	
M	
T	
W	
T	
F	
S	
S	
M	
T	
W	
T	
F	
S	
S	

Figure 10.1d Triple Jump Training Schedule

Triple Jump NAME DATE *January*

1. Warm-up routine to include A. Jogging-flexibility B. Easy high knee, fast leg
2. Fartlek A. Holmer B. Lydiard
3. Weight routine
4. Bounding drills A. Height / B. Distance } L.R (50-100 yds.)
   6-8 repeats fast as you can control
   C. Hop-step drill—double arm action—powerful lead leg (50-100 yds.) 6-8 repeats
5. Rhythm drills: 5-7-9-step approach
   A. S - S - S - J
   B. H - H - H - S - J
   C. LL RR LLL R LL—10 successive—for time and distance—124 ft.—excellent! D.
6. Box drills
   A. L □ L □ L □ L □ L □—step leg up to get on box (R over each box)
   B. L □ R □ L □ R □ L □ R
   C. L □ R □ L □ R □ L (L R L R over boxes)
   D. R □ L □ R □ Pit (R R L over boxes; | 4m |)
   Reverse RRLRRL to LLRLLR
   E. R □ R–L □ R–R □ L–R □ R Pit (| 10 ft. |)
   Reverse RRLRRLRR to LLRLLRLL
   F. R–R □ R–L □ R–R □ Pit (L, L over boxes; | 16 ft. | | 10 ft. |)
   G. R □ R □ R □ Pit (L L L over boxes; 8 ft. work for 20 ft.)
   H. R □ R □ L □ Pit (R L L over boxes)
7. Squad meeting
8. Special A. Sauna B. Swim C. Film D.
9. Short approach triple jump A. Standing B. 3-step C. 5-step D. 7-step E. 9-step F. 11-step
10. Full approach A. Check marks B. Jumping C. Competition or Trial
11. Rope jumping: 30 sec., 15 sec. rest
12. Hurdle X drill
14. Intervals A. 110 B. 165 C. 220 D. 300 E. 330 F. 440 G. 660-440-330-220-110
15. Hill work A. Laurelwood B. Emerald St. C. Stadium steps

Day	Week 1
M	*1AB – 4AB – 6X 14C*
T	*1AB – 3 – 2B*
W	*1AB – 12 – 15B – 7*
T	*1AB – 3 – 2A*
F	*1AB – 4BC – 3X 6EFGH – 4X 14D – 4X 14A*
S	*1AB – 3 – 2B*
S	

Day	Week 2
M	*1AB – 4ABC – 4X 5A – 3X 5B – 3X 5C – 14G – 4X 14A*
T	*1AB – 3 – 2B*
W	*1AB – 10A – 15B*
T	*1AB – 3 – 2A*
F	*1AB – 4ABC – 3X 5AB – 3X 9ABC – 14E – 2X 14C – 3X 14A*
S	*1AB – 3 – 2B*
S	

Day	Week 3
M	*1AB – 4ABC – 10A – 4X 5ABC – 14G – 3X 14A*
T	*1AB – 3 – 2B*
W	*1AB – 12 – 10A – 15B*
T	*1AB – 3 – 2A*
F	*1AB – 4ABC – 10A – 4X 6FGH – 14F – 2X 14E – 3X 14C – 3X 14A*
S	*1AB – 3 – 2B*
S	

Day	Week 4
M	*1AB – 4AB – 10A – 3X 5AB – 3X 9CDE – 14G – 4X 14A*
T	*1AB – 3 – 2B*
W	*1AB – 10A – 15B – 7*
T	*1AB – 3 – 2A*
F	*1AB –*
S	*1AB – 10C*
S	

Figure 10.1e Triple Jump Training Schedule

Triple Jump NAME DATE *February*

1. Warm-up routine to include A. Jogging-flexibility
   B. Easy high knee, fast leg
2. Fartlek A. Holmer B. Lydiard
3. Weight routine
4. Bounding drills A. Height / B. Distance } L.R (50-100 yds.)
   6-8 repeats fast as you can control
   C. Hop-step drill—double arm action—powerful lead leg (50-100 yds.) 6-8 repeats
5. Rhythm drills: 5-7-9-step approach
   A. S - S - S - J
   B. H - H - H - S - J
   C. LL RR LLL R LL—10 successive—for time and distance—124 ft.—excellent! D.
6. Box drills
   A. L □ L □ L □ L □ L □—step leg up to get on box (R over each box)
   B. L □ R □ L □ R □ L □ R
   C. L □ R □ L □ R □ L (L R L R over boxes)
   D. R □ L □ R □ Pit (R R L over boxes) | 4m |
   Reverse RRLRRL to LLRLLR
   E. R □ R—L □ R—R □ L—R □ R Pit | 10 ft. |
   Reverse RRLRRLRR to LLRLLRLL
   F. R—R □ R—L □ R—R □ Pit (L, L over boxes) | 16 ft. | | 10 ft. |
   G. R □ R □ R □ Pit (L L L over boxes) 8 ft. work for 20 ft.
   H. R □ R □ L □ Pit (R L L over boxes)
7. Squad meeting
8. Special A. Sauna B. Swim C. Film D.
9. Short approach triple jump A. Standing B. 3-step C. 5-step D. 7-step E. 9-step F. 11-step
10. Full approach A. Check marks B. Jumping C. Competition or Trial
11. Rope jumping: 30 sec., 15 sec. rest
12. Hurdle X drill
14. Intervals A. 110 B. 165 C. 220 D. 300 E. 330 F. 440 G. 660-440-330-220-110
15. Hill work A. Laurelwood B. Emerald St. C. Stadium steps

M	1AB-4ABC-5ABC-14G-14A (4x)
T	1AB-3-2B
W	1AB-12-15B
T	1AB-3-2A
F	1AB-4ABC-6DEFG (4x)-14D (3x)-14A (3x)
S	1AB-3-2B
S	

M	1AB-4ABC-5ABC-14G-14A (4x)
T	1AB-3-2B
W	1AB-10A-15B-7
T	1AB-3-2A
F	1AB-10A-14C (6-8x)
S	1AB-4AC-9DEF (3x)-2B
S	

M	1AB-4ABC-5ABC-14D (3-5x)
T	1AB-3-2B
W	1AB-10A-15B
T	1AB-3-2A
F	1AB-4AC-6EFGH (4x)-14G-14A (4x)
S	1AB-3-2B
S	

M	1AB-4AC-10A-5ABC-9CDE (3x)-14C (4x)-14A (4x)
T	1AB-3-2B
W	1AB-10A-15B
T	1AB-3-2A
F	1AB-10A-14B (2x)-14A (3x)
S	1AB-4AC-10A-9EF (2x)-10B (2x)-14G
S	

Figure 10.1f Triple Jump Training Schedule

Triple Jump NAME DATE March

1. Warm-up routine to include A. Jogging-flexibility
   B. Easy high knee, fast leg
2. Fartlek A. Holmer B. Lydiard
3. Weight routine
4. Bounding drills A. Height, B. Distance } L.R (50-100 yds.)
   6-8 repeats fast as you can control
   C. Hop-step drill—double arm action—powerful lead leg (50-100 yds.) 6-8 repeats
5. Rhythm drills: 5-7-9-step approach
   A. S - S - S - J
   B. H - H - H - S - J
   C. LL RR LLL R LL—10 successive—for time and distance—124 ft.—excellent! D.
6. Box drills
   A. L ☐ L ☐ L ☐ L ☐ L ☐—step leg up to get on box (R R R R R)
   B. L ☐ R ☐ L ☐ R ☐ L ☐ R
   C. L ☐ R ☐ L ☐ R ☐ L (L R L R)
   D. R ☐ L ☐ R ☐ Pit (R R L) | 4m |
   Reverse RRLRRL to LLRLLR
   E. R ☐ R—L ☐ R—R ☐ L—R ☐ R Pit | 10 ft. |
   Reverse RRLRRLRR to LLRLLRLL
   F. R—R ☐ R—L ☐ R—R ☐ Pit (L L) | 16 ft. | | 10 ft. |
   G. R ☐ R ☐ R ☐ Pit (L L L) 8 ft. work for 20 ft.
   H. R ☐ R ☐ L ☐ Pit (R L L)
7. Squad meeting
8. Special A. Sauna B. Swim C. Film D.
9. Short approach triple jump A. Standing B. 3-step
   C. 5-step D. 7-step E. 9-step F. 11-step
10. Full approach A. Check marks B. Jumping
    C. Competition or Trial
11. Rope jumping: 30 sec., 15 sec. rest
12. Hurdle X drill
14. Intervals A. 110 B. 165 C. 220 D. 300
    E. 330 F. 440 G. 660-440-330-220-110
15. Hill work A. Laurelwood B. Emerald St.
    C. Stadium steps

M	3x 1AB-4AC-10A-5ABC-14G-14A
T	1AB-3-2B
W	1AB-10A-15B-7
T	1AB-3-2A
F	4x 3x 3x 1AB-4AC-6EFGH-14D-14A
S	1AB-3-2B
S	
M	3x 1AB-4AC-10A-5ABC-14G-14A
T	1AB-3-2B-8C
W	1AB-10A-15B
T	1AB-3-2A
F	3x 3x 3x 1AB-4AC-9DEF-14D-14A
S	3x 3x 1AB-3-14C-14A
S	
M	4x 1AB-4AC-10A-5ABC-14G-14A
T	1AB-3-2B
W	2x 3x 3x 3x 1AB-4AC-10A-9CDE-14C-14B-14A-7
T	1AB-3-2A-8C
F	1AB-
S	1AB-10C
S	
M	3x 1AB-4AC-10A-5AB-14G-14A
T	1AB-10A-3-2B
W	2x 2x 2x 3x 1AB-10A-9CDE-14D-14C-14A-7
T	1AB-10A-3(light)-2A-8C
F	1AB-
S	1AB-10C
S	

Figure 10.1g Triple Jump Training Schedule

Triple Jump NAME DATE April

1. Warm-up routine to include A. Jogging-flexibility
   B. Easy high knee, fast leg
2. Fartlek A. Holmer B. Lydiard
3. Weight routine
4. Bounding drills A. Height, B. Distance } L.R (50-100 yds.)
   6-8 repeats fast as you can control
   C. Hop-step drill—double arm action—powerful lead leg (50-100 yds.) 6-8 repeats
5. Rhythm drills: 5-7-9-step approach
   A. S - S - S - J
   B. H - H - H - S - J
   C. LL RR LLL R LL—10 successive—for time and distance—124 ft.—excellent! D.
6. Box drills
   A. L □ L □ L □ L □ L □—step leg up to get on box (R R R R R above boxes)
   B. L □ R □ L □ R □ L □ R
   C. L □ R □ L □ R □ L (L R L R above boxes)
   D. R □ L □ R □ Pit (R R L above boxes) | 4m |
   Reverse RRLRRL to LLRLLR
   E. R □ R—L □ R—R □ L—R □ R Pit | 10 ft. |
   Reverse RRLRRLRR to LLRLLRLL
   F. R—R □ R—L □ R—R □ Pit (L L above boxes) | 16 ft. | | 10 ft. |
   G. R □ R □ R □ Pit (L L L above boxes) 8 ft. work for 20 ft.
   H. R □ R □ L □ Pit (R L L above boxes)
7. Squad meeting
8. Special A. Sauna B. Swim C. Film D.
9. Short approach triple jump A. Standing B. 3-step
   C. 5-step D. 7-step E. 9-step F. 11-step
10. Full approach A. Check marks B. Jumping
    C. Competition or Trial
11. Rope jumping: 30 sec., 15 sec. rest
12. Hurdle X drill
14. Intervals A. 110 B. 165 C. 220 D. 300
    E. 330 F. 440 G. 660-440-330-220-110
15. Hill work A. Laurelwood B. Emerald St.
    C. Stadium steps

M	3x 2x 1AB-4AC-10A-6EFG-14G-14B-7
T	1AB-10A-3-2B-8C
W	2x 2x 3x 1AB-10A-9CDE-14D-14C-14B
T	1AB-10A-3 (light)-2A-8C
F	1AB
S	1AB-10C-7
S	

M	1AB-4AC-10A-5ABC-14G-7
T	1AB-10A-3-2B-8C
W	2x 3x 4x 1AB-4AC-10A-5ABC-14D-14C-14A
T	1AB-10A-3 (light)-2A
F	1AB
S	1AB-10C-7
S	6x 1AB-14A

M	3x 1AB-4AC-10A-6DEF-14G-7
T	1AB-10A-3-2B-8C
W	3x 3x 1AB-10A-5ABC-14C-14A
T	1AB-3 (light)-2B
F	1AB
S	1AB-10C-7
S	1AB-4AC-3

M	3x 1AB-4AC-10A-5ABC-14G-14B-7
T	1AB-10A-3-2B
W	2x 3x 3x 1AB-10A-9CDE-14D-14A
T	1AB-10A-3 (light)-2B
F	1AB
S	1AB-10C-7
S	4x 4x 1AB-14C-14A

Figure 10.1h Triple Jump Training Schedule

Triple Jump NAME DATE *May*

1. Warm-up routine to include A. Jogging-flexibility B. Easy high knee, fast leg
2. Fartlek A. Holmer B. Lydiard
3. Weight routine
4. Bounding drills A. Height, B. Distance } L.R (50-100 yds.)
   6-8 repeats fast as you can control
   C. Hop-step drill—double arm action—powerful lead leg (50-100 yds.) 6-8 repeats
5. Rhythm drills: 5-7-9-step approach
   A. S - S - S - J
   B. H - H - H - S - J
   C. LL RR LLL R LL—10 successive—for time and distance—124 ft.—excellent! D.
6. Box drills
   A. L □ L □ L □ L □ L □—step leg up to get on box (R over each box)
   B. L □ R □ L □ R □ L □ R
   C. L □ R □ L □ R □ L (L R L R over boxes)
   D. R □ L □ R □ Pit (R R L over boxes) | 4m |
   Reverse RRLRRL to LLRLLR
   E. R □ R—L □ R—R □ L—R □ R Pit | 10 ft. |
   Reverse RRLRRLRR to LLRLLRLL
   F. R—R □ R—L □ R—R □ Pit (L, L over boxes) | 16 ft. | | 10 ft. |
   G. R □ R □ R □ Pit (L L L over boxes) 8 ft. work for 20 ft.
   H. R □ R □ L □ Pit (R L L over boxes)
7. Squad meeting
8. Special A. Sauna B. Swim C. Film D.
9. Short approach triple jump A. Standing B. 3-step C. 5-step D. 7-step E. 9-step F. 11-step
10. Full approach A. Check marks B. Jumping C. Competition or Trial
11. Rope jumping: 30 sec., 15 sec. rest
12. Hurdle X drill
14. Intervals A. 110 B. 165 C. 220 D. 300 E. 330 F. 440 G. 660-440-330-220-110
15. Hill work A. Laurelwood B. Emerald St. C. Stadium steps

M	1AB-4AC-10A-(2X) 6DEFG-14G-7
T	1AB-3-2B
W	1AB-10A-(2X) 9BCD-(3X) 14D-(3X) 14A
T	1AB-3(light)-2B
F	1AB-10A
S	1AB-10C-7
S	1AB-10A-(2X) 9DEF-2B
M	1AB-10A-14G-(3X) 14A-7
T	1AB-3-2B-8C
W	1AB-4AC-10A-5ABC-(2X) 14D-(4X) 14A
T	1AB-3(light)-2A
F	1AB-
S	1AB-10C-7
S	1AB-10A-(5X) 14C
M	1AB-4AC-10A-(2X) 6DEFG-14G-7
T	1AB-3-2B-8C
W	1AB-4AC-10A-5AB-(3X) 14D-(3X) 14A
T	1AB-10A-3(light)-2A
F	1AB
S	1AB-10C-7
S	1AB-10A-(2X) 9BCD-(4X) 14A
M	1AB-4AC-10A-14G-(4X) 14A-7
T	1AB-3-2B
W	1AB-4AC-10A-5ABC-(6X) 14C
T	1AB-3(light)-2A
F	1AB
S	1AB-10C-7
S	1AB-10A-4ABC-2A

Figure 10.1i Triple Jump Training Schedule

Triple Jump NAME DATE June

1. Warm-up routine to include A. Jogging-flexibility
   B. Easy high knee, fast leg
2. Fartlek A. Holmer B. Lydiard
3. Weight routine
4. Bounding drills A. Height, B. Distance } L.R (50-100 yds.)
   6-8 repeats fast as you can control
   C. Hop-step drill—double arm action—powerful lead leg (50-100 yds.) 6-8 repeats
5. Rhythm drills: 5-7-9–step approach
   A. S - S - S - J
   B. H - H - H - S - J
   C. LL RR LLL R LL—10 successive—for time and distance—124 ft.—excellent! D.
6. Box drills
   A. L □ L □ L □ L □ L □—step leg up to get on box (R over each box)
   B. L □ R □ L □ R □ L □ R
   C. L □ R □ L □ R □ L (L R L R over boxes)
   D. R □ L □ R □ [Pit] (R R L over boxes; | 4m |)
   Reverse RRLRRL to LLRLLR
   E. R □ R—L □ R—R □ L—R □ R [Pit] (| 10 ft. |)
   Reverse RRLRRLRR to LLRLLRLL
   F. R—R □ R—L □ R—R □ [Pit] (L, L over boxes; | 16 ft. | | 10 ft. |)
   G. R □ R □ R □ [Pit] (L L L over boxes; 8 ft. work for 20 ft.)
   H. R □ R □ L □ [Pit] (R L L over boxes)
7. Squad meeting
8. Special A. Sauna B. Swim C. Film D.
9. Short approach triple jump A. Standing B. 3-step C. 5-step D. 7-step E. 9-step F. 11-step
10. Full approach A. Check marks B. Jumping C. Competition or Trial
11. Rope jumping: 30 sec., 15 sec. rest
12. Hurdle X drill
14. Intervals A. 110 B. 165 C. 220 D. 300 E. 330 F. 440 G. 660-440-330-220-110
15. Hill work A. Laurelwood B. Emerald St. C. Stadium steps

M	1A-1B-4A-4C-10A-5ABC-14D (3X)-14C (3X)-14A (3X)-7
T	1A-1B-3-2B
W	1A-1B-4A-4C-10A-9CDE (2X)-14F-14E (2X)-14C (3X)-14A (4X)
T	1A-1B-3-2B
F	1A-1B-4A-4C-10A-5AB-14A (6X)
S	1A-B-4A-4C-10A-6DEF (2X)-14G-14A (4X)
S	1A-1B-10A
M	1A-1B-4A-4C-5ABC (2X)-9BCD (2X)-14D (3X)-14A (3X)
T	1A-1B-3-2B-8C
W	1A-1B-10A-5AB-14C (4X)
T	1A-1B-10A-14A (3X)-8C
F	10C
S	10C
S	
M	
T	
W	
T	
F	
S	
S	
M	
T	
W	
T	
F	
S	
S	

jumpers is that each of the three parts of the jump should be roughly the same length. This is the reason for the work on rhythm. If the rhythm of the jump does not sound regular, the jump probably is not a balanced one. Too many jumpers lose distance because they have a poor step on the middle of their jump, but how many of them realize that they may be sacrificing distance because they go too far on the hop, trying to make up for the step before they ever reach it?

Also, the teacher should emphasize that the hop and step are relatively flat jumps. If much height is gained, the athlete may be unable to make the transition to the later phases of the jump because of a lack of leg strength or other reasons. Too much of the momentum developed by the approach run may be lost by too much height early in the jump. There are several differing schools of jumping technique in the world, with differing ideas on this problem, but for most jumpers the flat technique is the safest and most productive.

The jumper must make sure he is not reaching out to land at the end of the hop-and-step phases of the jump, which would act as a brake on his forward momentum. He should bring the landing foot back just before he lands. This action may take away inches from the distance attained on the phase of the jump just being finished, but it can add feet to the final distance achieved in the total jump.

The most important principle suggested is one which no prospective triple jumper should forget: "Triple jumpers are made."

One other note relates to the "double-arm swing," referred to elsewhere in this chapter. This refers to a coordinated swinging action of *both* arms in the same direction and at the same time at certain portions of the jump. This consists of a forward and upward swing of both arms at the time of the take-off of each phase of the jump. It is used by expert jumpers to give additional impetus to each phase of the jump. It is a relatively recent technique and will require considerable practice, but if mastered it can be of considerable benefit to the jumper.

Triple Jump Bibliography

Davis, Ira. "The hop-step and jump," *Track and Field Quarterly Review*, April 1964, pp. 26–31.

Ganslen, Richard V. "The dynamics of efficient triple jumping," *Athletic Journal* 44 (March 1964): 12–13, 94–101.

Horn, Darryll. "Fine points of the triple jump," *Track and Field Quarterly Review*, December 1968, pp. 25–28.

Jesse, John P. "Weight training for long and triple jumpers," *Track and Field Quarterly Review*, October 1965, pp. 44–50.

Kleinen, Heinz. "Winter conditioning and training for triple jumpers," trans. by Jess Jarver, *Track Technique*, No. 20 (June 1965), pp. 620–24.

Korenberg, V. "Striding movements during the pushoff," trans. by Gar Williams, *Track Technique*, No. 23 (March 1966), pp. 710–14.

McNab, Tom. "Polish triple jumping," *Track Technique*, No. 29 (September 1967), pp. 899–902.

_______. *Triple Jump.* London: AAA, 1968. 56 pp.

Oglesby, Burch E. "Nine basic principles of triple jumping," *Scholastic Coach* 39 (April 1970): 48, 50.

Prihoda, L. "The Olympic triple jump in Tokyo: shallow or steep jump technique," ed. by Toni Nett, *Athletics Coach* 2 (March 1966): 14–18.

Rose, Jack. "The triple jump," *Track and Field Quarterly Review* 20 (August 1970): 18–20.

Sharpley, Frank. "Teaching beginners to triple jump," *Track Technique*, No. 18 (December 1964), pp. 562–64.

Simmons, Steve. "The triple jump," *Track and Field Quarterly Review* 72: 110–19.

Simonyi, Gabor. "Double arm action in triple jumping," *Track Technique*, No. 43 (March 1971), pp. 1377–81.

_______. "Teaching the triple jump," *Track Technique*, No. 48 (June 1972), pp. 1525–28.

_______. "Triple jumping with a double-arm swing," *Scholastic Coach* 39 (March 1970): 9–11, 91–95.

Starzynski, Tadeusz. "Analysis of jumping axes," *Track and Field Quarterly Review* 72: 120–21.

_______. "Exercises to prevent injuries to jumpers," *Track Technique*, No. 51 (March 1973), pp. 1610–13.

_______. "Triple jump training," trans. by Robert Z. Opiola, *Track Technique*, No. 45 (September 1971), pp. 1436–40.

Toomsalu, Ruddi. "Training and technique of Soviet hop-step-jumpers," *Track Technique*, No. 1 (September 1960), pp. 26–30.

Verhoshanskiy, Yuriy. "Depth jumping in the training of jumpers," trans. by Dr. Michael Yessis, *Track Technique*, No. 51 (March 1973), pp. 1618–19.

Yoon, Pat Tan Eng. "Research into the hop step and jump," in *Track in Theory and Technique,* pp. 252–273. Richmond, Calif.: Worldwide Publishing Company, 1962.

_______. "The triple jump," in *International Track and Field Coaching Encyclopedia*, pp. 204–27. West Nyack, N.Y.: Parker Publishing Company, 1970.

The pole vault

The legend of the little boy of Dutch ancestry who used a pole to vault the irrigation ditches which watered his father's grapes in the San Joaquin Valley of California is surpassed only by the actual feats of "Dutch" Warmerdam, who became the first man to vault an official 15 feet. His world record, set with a bamboo pole, stood for nearly two decades. His technique is still studied and copied for its excellence.

Other pole vaulting lore has it that the Dutch and the Irish both used the pole as a means of transport — over either canals, in the case of the Dutch, or swollen streams by the Irish. The pole was left at "the crossing" for the next user. We must assume either that traffic was equal in both directions or that poles were abundant.

An Overview of Vaulting

Pole vaulters vary in size probably as much as any other athletes in track. The vaulter will be an athlete with good speed and superior coordination. He will also have another natural endowment: determination. The pole vault requires years of hard work if its technical components are to be mastered. Because of the time requirement, the best vaulters often have been athletes who grew up with the pole, so to speak. The youngster who started vaulting at age ten has considerable advantage over the vaulter who started only after entering high school or college. No test is suggested for discovering pole vaulters. If other sports are to be checked for candidates, gymnasts will usually make the best prospects. They are apt to have the required natural abilities and have developed some measures of speed, agility, and strength.

Most pole vaulters need an approach of over 100 feet, good relaxation prior to the plant, and a smooth, well-placed planting of the pole so that the take-off will be a swift flow off the ground and into position for the swing and rise which precede the turn, and finally a smooth flow from the turn into the "off the pole" phase. Gravity will bring the vaulter down to the ground, but a good landing is almost as important as any other part of the vault, though the newer developments in landing pits are rapidly diminishing the landing risks. A bad landing in a poor pit will take more out of a vaulter than a night on the town.

The multiplicity of techniques in pole vaulting makes it one of the most difficult of sports events. It consists of at least six separate "events" which must be combined into a smooth-flowing motion from the beginning of the run, through the planting of the pole, the take-off, the hang, the turn-rise, the crossing of the bar, and the dismounting or landing. Good vaulting technique requires a well-balanced combination of abilities, including speed, coordination, strength, and determination.

For these reasons, experience is important in pole vaulting. It has been shown repeatedly that pole vaulters who started practicing this event when they were about ten years old always have an advantage over those who did not begin until they are in high school or college. The early beginners have already learned to handle the pole easily, to feel it as an extension of themselves — or to feel that they are an extension of the pole. It may also be true that youngsters who have the necessary combinations of natural ability will find other ways to exercise and express their abilities in other sports unless they are introduced to pole vaulting at an early age.

Analysis of Vaulting Technique

The phases of pole vaulting technique which need to be discussed are: holding the pole; the run, including check marks and how they are set up; the plant; the take-off; the rise and hang; the turn and rise; the crossing of the bar; and the dismount. In this discussion, a right-handed vaulter will be used as an example, thus, the pole is held with the right hand up, but not too far out, and the left hand down the pole.

Holding the Pole

Some vaulters have the mistaken notion that the height of the crossbar — the height which the vaulter is attempting to make at any one time — influences the position of their hands on the pole. This is not true. A vaulter holds the pole where it is most advantageous to him, where he feels he has the best possible control of the pole and is himself in a position in relation to the pole to make maximum use of that control.

The exact position of the hands on the pole, like the exact number of steps in an approach, are matters for the individual athlete to decide for himself on the basis of ample experimentation and adjustment. Once he has chosen and practiced these details thoroughly, he should not change them impulsively, especially in competition. Any further changes should be made only as the vaulter's progress indicates that he is ready, and such adjustments should then be made when there is plenty of time to master the changes before further competition.

As a rule, a good vaulter can always jump 2 feet higher than the height of his hands on the pole. A 14-foot vaulter will, therefore, probably hold his pole at approximately 12 feet. The height of the hold may vary in certain competitive conditions, however. If a strong headwind or crosswind is present, the vaulter may use a shorter run and a lower hold. If the wind is at his back, he might use a longer run and a higher than usual hold.

Approach

The purpose of the approach is to gather maximum momentum and at the same time put the vaulter in his optimum position for the take-off. He places his check mark at the spot where he believes he will be at the moment of take-off. He then practices his run of 100 feet or more, finding the exact number of strides that will put him on that spot without necessitating any stretching or hesitation. After having made these measurements and any adjustments that are necessary, the vaulter has established his check marks and will proceed to practice them.

It has generally been assumed, and has been a matter of practice, that the approach should be planned so that the vaulter reaches his maximum speed and momentum as closely as possible to the moment his pole is planted in the box, giving explosive power to his take-off. One coach of many successful vaulters has suggested that the vaulter should reach maximum speed as soon as possible during his approach run, so that at the time of the plant he is "free wheeling." This approach could perhaps contribute to the smoothness of the entire vaulting technique and be a noticeable advantage to some vaulters. The theory advocates getting the most *controlled* momentum possible at point T, since longer maintained speed contributes to *fluidity.*

Two types of approaches are taught at Oregon: the long run and the short run. The long run, 100 to 130 feet, is generally favored by vaulters and taught as "normal" technique. It is important, however, that vaulters be taught the advantages of a short run and practice it as thoroughly as the long one, so they will be able to use it whenever special conditions warrant using an approach of about 70 feet.

When a strong wind is blowing into the face of the vaulters, it is both exhausting and almost impossible to get off the ground with a full run and hold. A short run (about 70 feet) with a low hold is important for such vaulting into the wind. For practice sessions, it is possible to get in many more vaults with the short run-low hold than with the full run. In big competitive meets, also, when the pole vaulting promises to be a long, drawn-out affair requiring many attempts, the vaulter who can take a short approach and vault from a low hold, at least in the early attempts, will find that he has a great advantage in conserving his energy for his later, higher attempts.

It is sometimes difficult to persuade even experienced vaulters to master the technique of both the long and the short approaches, but for the competitive success of the team, as well as for the individual, it should be considered essential to learn and practice both. Conditions are met frequently which give the advantage to vaulters who can competently vault with a short approach and a low hold.

It is also equally difficult sometimes to persuade an athlete that he should not alter any part of his technique in a competitive situation. To do so not only invites failure, but probably ensures it. This point should be stressed with pole vaulters and particularly stressed with regard to this approach problem. Although the separate technical steps involved in vaulting are quite distinct, they must be synthesized, through continuous practice, into a continuous, smooth-flowing action. To alter any detail will affect, possibly badly, the rest of the routine. The virtuoso of vaulting who has a wealth of experience will know when and if a change is indicated.

Though it has been rumored that some great vaulters use three or more separate approaches, the two approaches suggested here will enable a vaulter to cope quite adequately with most conditions he is likely to meet in competition. Furthermore, two variations of technique are probably all that most young athletes have time to learn and practice adequately. A mature, international-class athlete is quite competent to decide for himself how many variations of technique he can master and use to advantage.

The hand grip is measured from the bottom of the pole to the top of the top hand. The athlete should be vaulting 2 feet or more above his hand grip before raising the grip. Many athletes try to use a higher grip than they can effectively handle, mistakenly believing that it will enable them to vault higher. A good vaulter should be able to clear 14 feet with a grip of no more than 12 feet to 12 feet 6 inches. The pole usually will be taped, generally being made sticky with "firm grip" or a similar substance, giving a more secure handhold. While carrying the pole, the hands are usually gripping the pole about 3 feet apart. This wide grip is retained with the fiber glass pole during the vault; metal vaulting poles will require a lower handhold and a closer grip, not to mention a somewhat different general technique. The pole is carried during the run in a position requiring the least movement for a successful plant at the end of the approach.

For a short-run approach (50 to 70 feet), a vaulter will also use a low hold on the pole, probably about 12 feet. Since any good vaulter can go 2 feet higher than his handhold, a 12-foot hold should be comfortable and quite sufficient for vaulting under conditions that warrant a short approach: into a stiff wind or for early vaults in a long competition. In either of these or similar situations where exhaustion, rather than another competitor, may contribute to defeat, the vaulter who can conserve necessary energy with a short run and a low hold will turn disadvantage into advantage.

Establishing Check Marks

When measuring and establishing check marks, it is not necessary to work on the pole vault runway. In fact, it is probably preferable to work on the track, especially if this facility is dirt- or cinder-surfaced, as the footprints will show and can be carefully noted for more accurate measurements. It is almost impossible for an athlete to establish his check marks alone. It would be ideal if the coach could help each vaulter with this procedure at the beginning of the season. Remember to have the athlete carry the pole while establishing the marks. If the coach cannot assist the vaulter in establishing his marks, then the vaulters should work in groups or pairs, with the experienced vaulters particularly helping the inexperienced ones.

The only reason for establishing check marks is to arrive at the take-off point with optimum controllable speed for the plant. In making the check marks for a full-length approach, one occasionally discovers a vaulter whose stride is so erratic that it is impossible for him to reach the take-off point in the customary 4-6-10 stride pattern. Such an athlete might drop down to a shorter approach, trying perhaps a 4-4-8 combination of strides.

Suppose, however, the candidate's stride is so erratic that he simply cannot establish or meet his check marks. What does the coach do? He has two choices: shoot the candidate, or cut his own throat. If neither seems satisfactory, he can try to help the man improve the evenness of his stride. A good drill for this is to set three low (30-inch) hurdles about 9 yards apart and have the vaulter practice hurdling over the side and over the top, not trying for hurdle style, but for evenness of stride. It might be very helpful if all vaulters would try competing in the hurdles, but it is difficult to persuade many of them to do this. Bob Seagren frequently ran the 400-meter hurdles during his competitive season, and what is good enough for the world champion vaulter should be good enough for those who aspire to reach the same goal. It is hard to tell whether hurdling serves as a particularly good conditioning exercise or whether the benefit comes from improved evenness of stride, but there seems to be a good correlation between excellence in hurdling and vaulting.

For check marks for the short approach, a single mark will suffice. Begin by assuming that the approach will be between 50 and 70 feet and should be accomplished in eight strides. We will measure back 10 feet from the planting box for the take-off point. From there we will measure back 50 feet (or however far the vaulter travels in his eight strides), and locate at that point check mark 1. The vaulter will go through the short approach three times, then average the distance for his measured short run check mark.

As an athlete becomes more fit through the preseason conditioning, and even during the competitive season, the distances between check marks will tend to change. His stride may well be half a foot longer at the end of the season,

Figure 11.1 Earlier Speed Approach: Pole Vault.

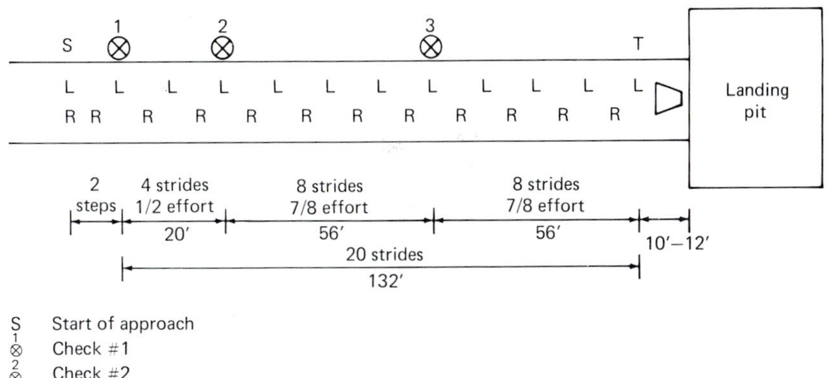

S Start of approach
$\overset{1}{\otimes}$ Check #1
$\overset{2}{\otimes}$ Check #2
$\overset{3}{\otimes}$ Check #3
T Take off

short approach about 4 feet longer, as a rough example. For this reason, check marks should be measured *every day* before practice and before competition, and changed as necessary. Other factors which influence the stride length, such as the condition of the track and wind, will also vary and need to be considered.

The early speed approach, for want of a better name, applies the same principles in setting the marks and measuring the stride (Figure 11.1): from the starting point, two steps to check mark 1, then four strides at half-speed to check mark 2. From check mark 2 to mark 3, the vaulter is going at seven-eighths speed. From check 3 to the take-off, he goes another eight steps, at the same speed, then plants the pole. The big advantage of the early speed approach for the last 100 feet of the approach run is that the vaulter may have better control of his speed for the pole plant, and therefore have better control for the things that follow through the rest of the vault.

Vaulting Faults

Four of the greater faults, which have been described elsewhere, will be mentioned here as a reminder. The first is inaccurate check marks, which can result in the vaulter never getting off the ground. The second is a premature pull and turn, which can hurry up the vault too much, putting the athlete into the crossbar. The third is letting the feet go out, instead of up, which is disastrous, since the hips follow the feet. The fourth fault is working for height in practice, instead of getting the vaulting technique down "pat."

Analysis of a Vaulting Sequence

The first photographic sequence is of Kjell Isaksson of Sweden, who has vaulted almost 18 feet on several occasions. In his approach run (Photograph 11.1a,

Photographs 11.1*a-q* Kjell Isaksson of Sweden, in the pole vault.

◀

i

j

q

Photographs 11.2*a-t* Bob Seagren, U.S.A., 1968 Olympic pole vaulting champion.

page 228), he can be seen carrying the pole low to his right side (he is right-handed). As he raises the pole overhead to prepare for the plant (Photographs 11.1*b* to *c*), a close study will reveal that he has dropped his body's center of gravity a bit, so that as he plants the pole, his body will already be rising from the ground, assisting his take-off. As he plants the pole (Photographs 11.1*c* to *d*), it is held directly over his head along the line of the body's axis. As he lifts off of the runway (Photographs 11.1*d* to *e*), he is leading with his right knee, providing further lift at the take-off. As he hangs from the pole and rises into the air (Photographs 11.1*e* to *f*), he works at preventing his lower hand and arm (left elbow area) from collapsing into the pole. He lays back and begins raising the legs at this time, then when the pole has straightened up, he begins his turn and rise toward the crossbar (Photograph 11.1*k*). When he is ready to clear the bar, he first pushes off with his lower (left) hand (Photograph 11.1*m*), then his upper (right) hand (Photograph 11.2*o*), and finally gets his arms across the bar safely (Photograph 11.1*q*).

The second sequence is of Bob Seagren, the 1968 Olympic champion. He approaches the take-off and gets the pole aligned directly over his head as he plants it in the box (Photographs 11.2*a* to *c*, page 230). He leads with his right knee in assisting his lift off the ground, then hangs in a position on his back as the pole begins to straighten out (Photographs 11.2*d* to *i*). When the pole is almost straight, he begins his pull and turn, pulling on the pole and turning with the legs as he reaches for height (Photographs 11.2*j* to *m*). As he reaches the peak of his vault, he can be seen pushing off first with the left hand and then with the right hand (Photographs 11.2*n* to *q*).

Training for the Pole Vault

What does the teacher-coach want the student-athlete to do, and how does he tell him? The schedule is a continuing line of communication between the teacher and the student, the coach and the athlete. The schedule used at Oregon is a listing of the "fundamentals" of pole vaulting and a day-by-day plan for practicing these fundamentals. It also becomes a record of what the student-athlete did in practice and competition, his rate of progress and his accomplishments.

The practices and patterns which make up the schedules may not always be right, or even the best possible for any individual. They do provide, however, a plan to work from, a place to start. Development may indicate that other things (different exercises, techniques, rates of progress) might be helpful or worth experimenting with, but to begin with, both teacher and student need a lesson plan. The schedules or lesson plans suggested in this chapter are actual schedules which have been used successfully. The virtuoso, the truly gifted, may find adaptations which are particularly helpful to him.

Youngsters should first learn to vault at the age of ten years or so. The procedure suggested here, however, is the same for high school or college freshmen. The teacher should hold a pole upright in the vaulting box. The student will grasp the pole and be swung into the landing pit. He will next trot up to the pole, grasp it, and be swung into the pit by the teacher. The other students might take turns swinging the pole in the teacher's place. If the student will not let go of the pole, he probably will not overcome his fear of vaulting. He should be given something else to do. The final step for the beginner is to run with the pole and vault.

Once the student has the idea of swinging with the pole, he goes over a crossbar set at 2 feet above the ground. He next works with a bar set at 5 or 6 feet above the ground, and out a bit from the vaulting box. He will then proceed to work on the plant. Students should work frequently without a crossbar, so they will worry less about it.

The vaulter then needs to learn to establish a "routine" of practice. The first step in the routine is work on the short run. Using a run of 50 to 70 feet, the vaulter works at perfecting his vaulting technique. He should work on the fundamentals of the pole plant, the take-off, and the lay back and wait. A general training routine might look something like this:

1. Three times a long run (for the steps)
2. Three times a short run (also for the steps)
3. Work with the short run:
   One to three times working on the plant
   One to three vaults working on laying back and waiting
   One to three vaults working on coming off the pole

When working with a short run and low hold, the vaulter should use a pole which will react like the one he uses for the long run and high hold. A long pole (such as 16 feet) will not react the same if a low hold (such as 11 or 12 feet) is used. Also, the vaulters may at times begin to get tired when they are vaulting. If the vaulter is tired and shows it, he should *stop vaulting* for that day. He runs the risk of emphasizing and setting bad habits of vaulting, if he continues.

The Training Schedules Interpreted

This is a translation of a sample week of training from the vaulting schedules in this chapter. The numbers on the schedule sheets represent the fundamentals of pole vaulting. These fundamentals will be described in detail after the schedules are presented. The week of training given here is the first week of training given in the schedules:

Monday: The class or squad meets for the first time. Equipment is discussed, procedures are explained, goals are recommended for individuals, and such things as "hard" and "easy" days with test efforts every seven, ten, or fourteen days are explained.

Tuesday: (1) Warm-up.

(14C) *High knee,* slow running, almost in place, bringing the knees about hip high. Go about 10 yards, then walk 10 yards. This is followed by *fast leg* by barely lifting the feet off the ground, gradually increasing the cadence and bouncing the ball of each foot off the surface in cadence with a short, very rapid arm action. Go about 10 yards, then rest and repeat the high knee, then the fast leg for 50 to 100 yards.

(14F) Run 55 yards, walk 55 yards to recover, then repeat until a distance of 440 to 880 yards or more has been covered. This is a conditioning activity.

(16) Apparatus work, such as ropes, rings, parallel bars, doing other apparatus activities.

Wednesday: (1A) Warm up with jogging, relay routine, stretching, and flexibility exercises.

(17) Run, carrying the pole. This is for conditioning, plus learning that, next to his dog, a vaulting pole is the vaulter's best friend.

(14D) Set up three low hurdles about 8 to 10 yards apart. This exercise is for evenness of stride and perhaps to develop a hurdler, if the skills are acquired.

Thursday: (3) Weight lifting. Most athletes will work out weight training routines of their own. There will be suggested exercises in the weight training section.

Friday: (1) Warm-up.

(14A) Wind sprints, starting slowly, gradually increasing the speed for about 55 yards, then gradually decreasing to a jog and recovering for 55 yards. Cover 440 to 880 yards.

(17) See Wednesday explanation.

(4A) Short check mark drill of 50 to 70 feet. This will be explained in the section on pole vaulting fundamentals.

(6A) Another pole vaulting fundamental, explained after the schedules are presented.

(14F) See Tuesday explanation.

Saturday: (3) Weight training.

(17) Running with the pole.

Sunday: For relaxation, recreation, and workouts, there is no better day than Sunday.

Figure 11.2a Pole Vault Training Schedule

Pole Vault NAME DATE *September/October*

1. Warm-up A. Jog 1 or 2 laps relay pass
   B. Weights and jog C.
2. Fartlek A. Varied B. Slow, steady
3. Weights
4. Check mark A. Short B. Long
5. A. Pole plant B. Take off up C. Lay back and wait (hang)
6. A. Pull when back parallel and pole "up"
   B. Turn and rise, lead foot up C. Off the pole
7. Squad meeting
8. Special A. Sauna B. Swim C. Hill D.
9. A. Short run-low hold form work
   B. Long run form work
10. A. Trials B. Compete (1) Up or down 6 in. on a make or miss
    (2) 2 jumps at 3 in. above average best
    (3) Establish starting height good or bad day
11. Higher grip and check mark adjustment
12. With Coach A. B.
14. A. Wind sprints B. Starts or (1) 100 (2)
    C. High knee and fast leg
    D. Hurdle drill—3 lows at 8-10 yds.
    E. Spring and bound
    F. Alternate run-jog at least 880
15. A. Hendricks B. Laurel C. Stadium steps
16. Easy apparatus or acrobatics
17. Run with the pole 55 yds., walk 110, go 440
18. Warm-up routine
19.
20. Secondary event
21. A. Pictures B. Film
22. Experimental work

Date	Result	3/4	Date	Goal

M	*Class or squad organization*
T	*1-14C-16-14F*
W	*1A-17-14D*
T	*3*
F	*1-14A-17-4A-6A-14F*
S	*1-3-17*
S	*16*
M	*1-^{3}4A-^{3}5A-^{3}6A-9A-14A*
T	*1-3-17*
W	*7-1-^{2}4B-^{2}4A-9A-14A*
T	*1-3-14F*
F	*1-^{2}4B-^{2}4A-^{2}5A-9A-14A*
S	*3*
S	*3-16*
M	*1-^{3}4B-^{2}4A-6B·14D-14A*
T	*1-3-17*
W	*1-^{2}4A-^{2}4B-^{2}5A-^{2}5B-9A-14D*
T	*1-3-15B*
F	*1-^{2}4A-^{2}4B-9A-17*
S	*3*
S	*3-14D*
M	*1-17-^{2}4A-^{2}4B-^{2}5A-^{2}6B-9A-14D*
T	*3-14F*
W	*1-17-^{2}4A-^{2}4B-9A-7*
T	*1-3-15B*
F	*1-4A-4B-10A1-14A*
S	*3*
S	*3*

Figure 11.2b Pole Vault Training Schedule

Pole Vault NAME DATE October/November

1. Warm-up A. Jog 1 or 2 laps relay pass
   B. Weights and jog C.
2. Fartlek A. Varied B. Slow, steady
3. Weights
4. Check mark A. Short B. Long
5. A. Pole plant B. Take off up C. Lay back and wait (hang)
6. A. Pull when back parallel and pole "up"
   B. Turn and rise, lead foot up C. Off the pole
7. Squad meeting
8. Special A. Sauna B. Swim C. Hill D.
9. A. Short run–low hold form work
   B. Long run form work
10. A. Trials B. Compete (1) Up or down 6 in. on a make or miss
    (2) 2 jumps at 3 in. above average best
    (3) Establish starting height good or bad day
11. Higher grip and check mark adjustment
12. With Coach A. B.
14. A. Wind sprints B. Starts or (1) 100 (2)
    C. High knee and fast leg
    D. Hurdle drill—3 lows at 8-10 yds.
    E. Spring and bound
    F. Alternate run-jog at least 880
15. A. Hendricks B. Laurel C. Stadium steps
16. Easy apparatus or acrobatics
17. Run with the pole 55 yds., walk 110, go 440
18. Warm-up routine
19.
20. Secondary event
21. A. Pictures B. Film
22. Experimental work

Date	Result	3/4	Date	Goal

M	1A-14C-17-16
T	3-14D-15B
W	1A-$4B^{3}$-14E-16
T	1-$4A^{2}$-$4B^{2}$-$5B^{2}$-14A-8B
F	1-3-17
S	1A-$4B^{2}$-$5A^{2}$-$6B^{2}$-14D
S	15A

M	1A-17-$4A^{3}$-$5A^{2}$-$6C^{2}$-14A
T	1A-3 or 15B
W	1A-4A-5B-5C-9A-14F
T	1A-14D
F	1B-4B-5C-9A-14F
S	3
S	jog

M	1-14D-4A-4B-5C-9B-15A
T	1A-15B
W	1B-5B-5C-9A-15A or B
T	1B-3-8A
F	1A-10A1-10A2-14D
S	1B
S	

M	1A-14C-4B-6A-6C-9B-2B
T	3-8A
W	7-1A-4A-4B-5A-9A-2B
T	3-8A or B
F	1A-5A-10A1-10A2-14D
S	3
S	

Figure 11.2c Pole Vault Training Schedule

Pole Vault NAME DATE January

1. Warm-up A. Jog 1 or 2 laps relay pass
   B. Weights and jog C.
2. Fartlek A. Varied B. Slow, steady
3. Weights
4. Check mark A. Short B. Long
5. A. Pole plant B. Take off up C. Lay back and wait (hang)
6. A. Pull when back parallel and pole "up"
   B. Turn and rise, lead foot up C. Off the pole
7. Squad meeting
8. Special A. Sauna B. Swim C. Hill D.
9. A. Short run-low hold form work
   B. Long run form work
10. A. Trials B. Compete (1) Up or down 6 in. on a make or miss
    (2) 2 jumps at 3 in. above average best
    (3) Establish starting height good or bad day
11. Higher grip and check mark adjustment
12. With Coach A. B.
14. A. Wind sprints B. Starts or (1) 100 (2)
    C. High knee and fast leg
    D. Hurdle drill—3 lows at 8-10 yds.
    E. Spring and bound
    F. Alternate run-jog at least 880
15. A. Hendricks B. Laurel C. Stadium steps
16. Easy apparatus or acrobatics
17. Run with the pole 55 yds., walk 110, go 440
18. Warm-up routine
19.
20. Secondary event
21. A. Pictures B. Film
22. Experimental work

M	Register–squad meet–4A (3)–4B (3)–14F
T	3
W	1A–14C–16 or 4A–9A–14A
T	7–3
F	1A–18–4B (3)–20–14A
S	16
S	jog
M	1B–4A (2-3)–4B (2-3)–5A (2-3)–9A–14F
T	3–16
W	1A–4A (2-3)–4B (2-3)–15B(8C) or 15C
T	3
F	1B–14C–4B–18–14F
S	16 or 3
S	jog
M	1A–14C–16–4B (2-3)–4A (2-3)–5B (2-3)–9–14A
T	3–8A or B
W	1A–4B (2-3)–15B (8C)
T	3–15A
F	1–4B–10A1–10A2
S	3 or form work
S	jog
M	1B–14C–6–4B (2-3)–4A (2-3)
T	3–8A or B or sun
W	7–1B–5A–6C–15B (8C)
T	3
F	1B–Gear ready
S	10B Indoors
S	jog

Date	Result	3/4	Date	Goal

Figure 11.2d Pole Vault Training Schedule

Pole Vault NAME DATE February

1. Warm-up A. Jog 1 or 2 laps relay pass B. Weights and jog C.
2. Fartlek A. Varied B. Slow, steady
3. Weights
4. Check mark A. Short B. Long
5. A. Pole plant B. Take off up C. Lay back and wait (hang)
6. A. Pull when back parallel and pole "up" B. Turn and rise, lead foot up C. Off the pole
7. Squad meeting
8. Special A. Sauna B. Swim C. Hill D.
9. A. Short run–low hold form work B. Long run form work
10. A. Trials B. Compete (1) Up or down 6 in. on a make or miss (2) 2 jumps at 3 in. above average best (3) Establish starting height good or bad day
11. Higher grip and check mark adjustment
12. With Coach A. B.
14. A. Wind sprints B. Starts or (1) 100 (2)
    C. High knee and fast leg
    D. Hurdle drill—3 lows at 8-10 yds.
    E. Spring and bound
    F. Alternate run-jog at least 880
15. A. Hendricks B. Laurel C. Stadium steps
16. Easy apparatus or acrobatics
17. Run with the pole 55 yds., walk 110, go 440
18. Warm-up routine
19.
20. Secondary event
21. A. Pictures B. Film
22. Experimental work

Date	Result	3/4	Date	Goal

M	1A-17-9A-4D-Jog
T	3-8A
W	7-1-10A-9A-14A
T	3-8B
F	1-4A-4B-5C-6A-14F
S	3-8A or B
S	jog
M	1A-14C-9B-9A-14A
T	1A-16-8A or B
W	1A-18-4B-6C-9A-14A
T	1A-16
F	1A-10A-10B-14D-14A-Jog
S	3-15A
S	jog
M	1-4B-6A-14D-17
T	16-8A or B
W	1-17-12-4A-5C-6C-17
T	3-16
F	1-4B-6B-9A-14D
S	3-14A
S	jog
M	1-4B-5B-6A-9A-14E
T	3 or 16
W	1-10A-10B-14A
T	1-16-8A or B
F	1-4A-4B-5B-9B-14D
S	15A or B
S	jog

Figure 11.2e Pole Vault Training Schedule

Pole Vault NAME DATE March

1. Warm-up A. Jog 1 or 2 laps relay pass
   B. Weights and jog C.
2. Fartlek A. Varied B. Slow, steady
3. Weights
4. Check mark A. Short B. Long
5. A. Pole plant B. Take off up C. Lay back and wait (hang)
6. A. Pull when back parallel and pole "up"
   B. Turn and rise, lead foot up C. Off the pole
7. Squad meeting
8. Special A. Sauna B. Swim C. Hill D.
9. A. Short run-low hold form work
   B. Long run form work
10. A. Trials B. Compete (1) Up or down 6 in. on a make or miss
    (2) 2 jumps at 3 in. above average best
    (3) Establish starting height good or bad day
11. Higher grip and check mark adjustment
12. With Coach A. B.
14. A. Wind sprints B. Starts or (1) 100 (2)
    C. High knee and fast leg
    D. Hurdle drill—3 lows at 8-10 yds.
    E. Spring and bound
    F. Alternate run-jog at least 880
15. A. Hendricks B. Laurel C. Stadium steps
16. Easy apparatus or acrobatics
17. Run with the pole 55 yds., walk 110, go 440
18. Warm-up routine
19.
20. Secondary event
21. A. Pictures B. Film
22. Experimental work

Date	Result	3/4	Date	Goal

M	1A-17-18-5A-9B-14D
T	1B-16
W	1-18-10A1-10A2-9A-5B-Jog
T	1-16-14A
F	1-18-6B-10-14A
S	3-15A or B-8A or B
S	
M	1-18-17
T	1A-4B-5A-5B-10A2
W	1-gear ready or 3-14A
T	Travel-1A-14C-4A-4B
F	Meet routine
S	Travel home
S	Loosen up at 1pm-14
M	7-1A-14A
T	1A-4A-4B-9B-14A
W	16
T	1-4B-9B-14F
F	Gear ready
S	Relay meet
S	Loosen up at 1 p.m.
M	1A-17-4B-5A-9B-14D
T	3-14A
W	1A-18-9B-10A2
T	16
F	Gear ready
S	Travel to meet-10B
S	Loosen up

Figure 11.2f Pole Vault Training Schedule

Pole Vault NAME DATE April

1. Warm-up A. Jog 1 or 2 laps relay pass
   B. Weights and jog C.
2. Fartlek A. Varied B. Slow, steady
3. Weights
4. Check mark A. Short B. Long
5. A. Pole plant B. Take off up C. Lay back and wait (hang)
6. A. Pull when back parallel and pole "up"
   B. Turn and rise, lead foot up C. Off the pole
7. Squad meeting
8. Special A. Sauna B. Swim C. Hill D.
9. A. Short run–low hold form work
   B. Long run form work
10. A. Trials B. Compete (1) Up or down 6 in. on a make or miss
    (2) 2 jumps at 3 in. above average best
    (3) Establish starting height good or bad day
11. Higher grip and check mark adjustment
12. With Coach A. B.
14. A. Wind sprints B. Starts or (1) 100 (2)
    C. High knee and fast leg
    D. Hurdle drill—3 lows at 8-10 yds.
    E. Spring and bound
    F. Alternate run-jog at least 880
15. A. Hendricks B. Laurel C. Stadium steps
16. Easy apparatus or acrobatics
17. Run with the pole 55 yds., walk 110, go 440
18. Warm-up routine
19.
20. Secondary event
21. A. Pictures B. Film
22. Experimental work

Date	Result	3/4	Date	Goal

M	1A - 4A (2X) - 6B (2-4X) - 5A - 9A - 14A
T	1B - 3
W	7 - 1A - 4 - 6A - 10A2 - 9A - 14D
T	1B - 16
F	Meet preparation
S	Premeet - compete - after meet
S	3 or 15B
M	1B - 4 (3X) - 5A (3X) - 5C - 9A - 14A
T	3 - 8A or B
W	7 - 1A - 4B (3X) - 10A1 - 9A - 14D
T	Jog - 8A or B
F	Light
S	Meet routine
S	16
M	1A or 17 - 4B - 5A - 5C - 9A - 14E
T	1B - 14C - 14D
W	1A - 4B - 10A - 9A - 14F
T	3 - 8B - 14A grass
F	Light
S	Dual meet
S	1A - 11 - 9B
M	17 - 16 - 8A or B
T	1A - 11 - 10A - 9A - 9B
W	3 - 16 - 8A or B
T	1A - 18 - 11 - 9B - 9A
F	Light
S	Compete
S	1A - recheck grip - 11

Figure 11.2g Pole Vault Training Schedule

Pole Vault NAME DATE May

1. Warm-up A. Jog 1 or 2 laps relay pass
   B. Weights and jog C.
2. Fartlek A. Varied B. Slow, steady
3. Weights
4. Check mark A. Short B. Long
5. A. Pole plant B. Take off up C. Lay back and wait (hang)
6. A. Pull when back parallel and pole "up"
   B. Turn and rise, lead foot up C. Off the pole
7. Squad meeting
8. Special A. Sauna B. Swim C. Hill D.
9. A. Short run–low hold form work
   B. Long run form work
10. A. Trials B. Compete (1) Up or down 6 in. on a make or miss
    (2) 2 jumps at 3 in. above average best
    (3) Establish starting height good or bad day
11. Higher grip and check mark adjustment
12. With Coach A. B.
14. A. Wind sprints B. Starts or (1) 100 (2)
    C. High knee and fast leg
    D. Hurdle drill—3 lows at 8-10 yds.
    E. Spring and bound
    F. Alternate run-jog at least 880
15. A. Hendricks B. Laurel C. Stadium steps
16. Easy apparatus or acrobatics
17. Run with the pole 55 yds., walk 110, go 440
18. Warm-up routine
19.
20. Secondary event
21. A. Pictures B. Film
22. Experimental work

Date	Result	3/4	Date	Goal

	A.M.	P.M.
M	Jog	1A-4B-5A-5C-9A-14D (3 over 4B, 3 over 5A, 3-6 over 5C)
T	Jog	3
W	Jog	7-1A-18-10B2-14A1
T	Jog	Light
F		Light
S		Be good, be tough, be relaxed Traditional meet
S		Pole plant and swing

M	14F - easy 14D
T	1A-18-10A-9A-14C
W	7-15B or grass run
T	1A-4A-4B-5A-14D (2 over 4A, 4B, 5A)
F	Light
S	Dual meet
S	Grass run

M	1B-4B-5A-5C-9A or B-14E (3 over 4B, 3 over 5A, 3-6 over 5C)
T	3 and light
W	1A-4B-5B-10B2
T	Light
F	Light
S	Championship
S	Grass run

M	
T	
W	
T	
F	
S	
S	

4A. Short check mark. A short approach is recommended for early season work, since the vaulter can do more vaulting with a shorter run. It is also helpful in competitions which have bad weather conditions, such as a strong headwind, a vicious crosswind, or rain. The short approach was recommended for training and inclement weather competition by Dean Cromwell, the greatest of track coaches and coach of many Olympians and world record holders.

An approach of 50 to 70 feet is used to reach the take-off point, which will be 9 to 11 feet from the vaulting box. The approach is 6 to 10 steps, with a two-step approach to the one check mark (Figure 11.3). With the short approach, a low hold on the pole is used. It should be low enough for positive control in any conditions and high enough for respectable clearance. A handhold of eleven and one-half feet will permit a clearance of 13 to 14 feet. A lower, calibrated pole should be used for this short check–low hold vaulting. When the vaulter can consistently clear 14 to 15 feet, he should acquire a pole with a lower calibration for the short run practice and for bad weather competition.

The vaulter stands in a forward-leaning position, pole on the ground or at the ready. He concentrates on his total vault, then with a walking two-step approach hits the check mark and gradually accelerates in 10 steps to the "T," or take-off point. When starting fall or winter training, the vaulter can work on the check mark on the runway or on the track. He carries the pole, hits the check with his left foot, then accelerates through 10 steps to the take-off. His coach or observer marks the T spot. This run is repeated two more times, and the T marks are averaged to give the length of the short check. This mark is then transferred to the runway. Ten feet from the box a T mark is placed. The vaulter can now practice his approaches on the runway.

Figure 11.3 Short Check Mark: Pole Vault.

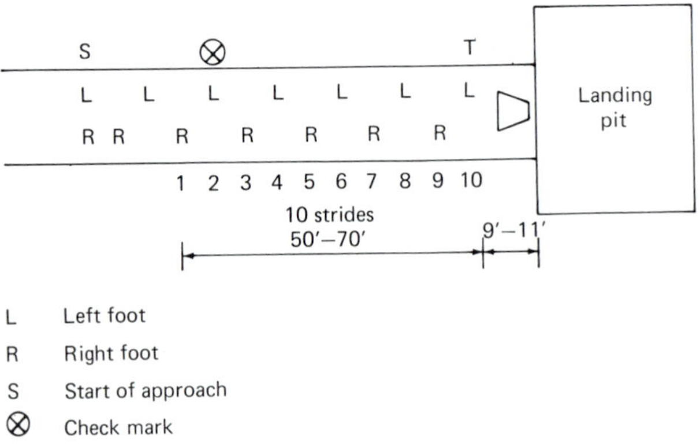

Figure 11.4 Long Check Mark: Pole Vault.

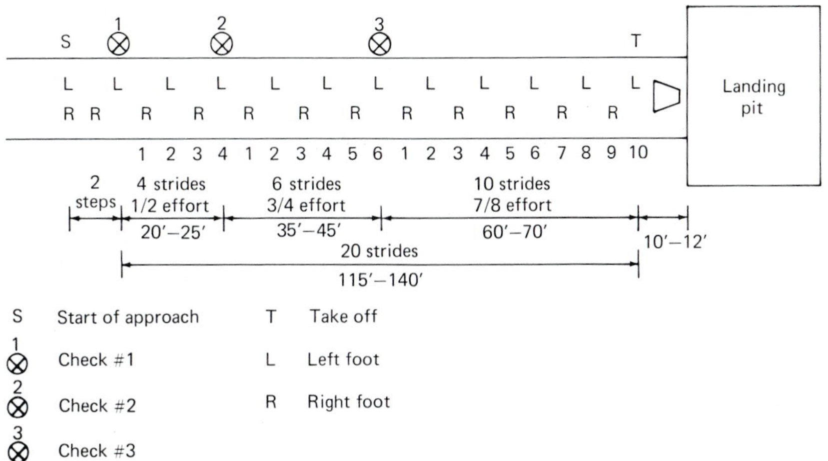

The distance of the short check should increase as the season progresses and the vaulter reaches peak condition, assuming the conditions are ideal. Wind in the face, cold weather, and physical disability will cause the distance to be shorter.

4B. Long check mark. The long run and regular high hold are for the time when the parts of the technique, fundamentals, and physical condition are approaching their peak. As with other events needing check marks, the method varies with athletes and coaches. Having check marks is as important to the vaulter as navigation points are to the astronaut going to the moon.

The vaulter stands two steps behind check mark 1 (Figure 11.4). He stands with both feet together or right foot forward, whichever is more comfortable for him. He should think through the entire technique of his vault before starting his approach. His first step will be with his left foot hitting the first check mark.

Assuming that the stride of the vaulter, going at half effort at this point, is 5 feet, he would then take 20 feet to reach check mark 2 with his left foot. (This is not to suggest that the vaulter try for a set length of stride; it is simply an illustration.) It is not intended that the vaulter either try for any particular stride length or run through a full approach when he is establishing his check marks. He should run through this part of the procedure from his starting point before check 1 through check 2 so he can establish what the length of his stride is and exactly what this distance should be. The vaulter will take three tries, then use the average of the three results.

After he has established the distance between point 1 and point 2, the vaulter will work at measuring his stride at three-quarters effort, so he can put in check mark 3, which will be six strides after point 2. If his stride is 6 feet, for example, he will cover about 36 feet between checks 2 and 3. The vaulter will now return to his starting point and run through marks 1 and 2, then see how close he comes to check 3 in six additional strides. Again, this run will be done three times and an average distance taken.

The next distance is to the T, or take-off, 10 to 12 feet from the box. If the vaulter is tired or erratic, the procedure is stopped until the next day for working on the check marks. To zero in on the take-off, have the vaulter run the complete approach, marking the track or runway each of the three times. After checking through the first three check marks, the vaulter's intention is to reach a speed which might be called seven-eighths effort while taking 10 strides to point T. If a vaulter's stride at this speed is 7 feet, as an example, this part of the approach will consume 70 feet. He will measure this as before, taking three trials and averaging their lengths.

The technique of setting the check marks must be practiced and re-checked every vaulting day. Measuring is a must. The champion vaulter is not only an artist, he is a careful technician.

5A. The pole plant. The second phase of the vault consists of planting the pole in the vaulting box. It should be accomplished in two or three counts. It is important that the vaulter look at the box rather than the crossbar as he plants the pole. There are two planting techniques, the overhand and the straight underhand. It is simply a matter of personal preference which is used. The plant should not be too fast. The count or steps should be carefully practiced and a rhythm established. It is not to be hurried in competition, either.

The pole should be aligned straight into the box and along the vaulter's nose. If it is off to the side, it throws him out of line. The delivery of the pole into the box should be smooth and well timed. The vaulter should try to be rising in the last two steps leading into the plant, so he will seem to float off the ground, rather than seeming to be pushing off hard. The vaulter should not pull the pole toward himself during the plant or take-off, but neither should he hold it out to the side, since that would throw him off to the side during his rise.

5B. The take-off. The pole should be straight overhead during the take-off, and the vaulter should be right between his hands. Vaulters used to take off under the right hand, but the "glass" pole has changed that. Now as the vaulter leaves the ground, his head is about halfway between his hands as they grasp the pole. The lead knee should be quick in leaving the ground. The higher the hold on the pole, the straighter the angle between the pole and the ground, and the higher the vaulter will go. The vaulter at this critical stage needs to be on guard against several faults: being off to the side; settling down during the last several strides; and having the arms too bent, which may result in their collapsing as he rises into the air.

5C. The lay back and wait (hang). The vaulter should not pull the pole toward him, but should hold the pole away as he rises in order to get into the "hang." As the pole bends, he should not sit down, as this puts more pressure on the pole, a frequent cause of broken poles. One Oregon vaulter habitually rose in this sitting position; he also broke eight poles in one year. Even if the sitting position does not break the pole, it requires greater exertion to get the man off the ground, which means that he could have gone higher and risen more easily, had he not dropped into the sitting position.

6A. Pull when back parallel and pole "up." A vaulter does hang as the pole continues to move upward. Then he concerns himself with getting his center of gravity up in the air. Too often a vaulter watches his feet. When he sees that they are high enough, he believes he is high enough. But it is not the feet, but the center of gravity which determines the height of the vault. Think of the hips or waist as rising to crossbar height before the turn is started. Get the center of gravity up, and good things will happen in the pole vault.

6B. The turn and rise. If the turn is too soon, the vaulter may stall the pole. He has to stay behind the pole throughout the bend. The action is like performing a curl with the right hand and a press with the left hand, simultaneously. When the hips and center of gravity are at the height of the crossbar, and the bottom of the pole is perpendicular to the ground, *then* the vaulter should pull and turn. This will cause the pole to straighten and the vaulter to rotate around his center of gravity. The lead foot continues up as the turn is completed.

6C. Off the pole. This is the final stage of the vault, as the hands are rising and the vaulter's body is clearing the crossbar. The vaulter needs to learn to use his feet and legs to clear the upper body, leaving only the problem of a safe landing, which is no problem if a good, modern landing pad is used.

9. Technical work.

9A. Short run–low hold form work. Using the short approach already described, the vaulter works on the aspects of form referred to with the letters in item 6 on the training sheet. Many more productive vaults can be made with a short approach than with the long run.

9B. Long run form work. This work is done as in item *9A,* practicing on technique, fundamentals, or individuals. The full approach with all checks is used, however.

10. Trials. Trials are meant for a "progress report," as well as a learning situation. The starting level of the competition should be within the capability of the weakest or youngest vaulter. The vaulters should rotate their turns, with the crossbar going up or down according to the talents of each vaulter.

10A1. Up or down 6 inches on a make or miss. The practice at Oregon is to move the bar up if the height is cleared and lower the bar if the height is missed. Assume that vaulter A starts at 12 feet and misses. His next jump is at 11 feet 6 inches. Vaulter B starts at 13 feet (in squad rotation, not according to the height being attempted) and clears it, so his next height will be 13 feet 6 inches. A clears 11 feet 6 inches on his next attempt, so he goes back up to 12 feet.

10A2. Two jumps at 3 inches above average best. When the vaulters acquire some consistency, which usually takes about 6 weeks, they will then occasionally practice beyond the season's best mark (average). Assume that vaulter B reaches 15 feet 3 inches and he is given two attempts to make the height. He does not get a third attempt, for psychological reasons. Three misses would put him out of the competition, and it is preferred that he quit while feeling that he might have made it on that third jump.

10A3. Starting height (establish) good or bad day. The starting height which the vaulter can use with assurance should be established according to the runway, the weather, and the vaulter's ability. The vaulters should jump in rotation and move the standards to their capability.

11. Higher grip and check mark adjustment. Some vaulters are almost promiscuous in their changes of handholds (height at which the hand grips the pole). The height of the vaulter's hold should not change until he has mastered the technique to a near-maximum height. Particularly, the vaulter should not vary his hold out of hope or panic in competition. When the vaulter is "ready," then he should start with a 3-to-6-inch or possibly as much as a foot increase in the handhold. His routine should be reestablished, including the variation in check marks, the change in timing to a longer "hang," and possibly the delayed release of the pole's stored energy at the turn and "off the pole" phases of the vault. These changes may take several vaulting sessions and should start with no crossbar and work through to a successful trial situation.

16. Easy apparatus or acrobatics. The apparatus room and gymnastic equipment offer great opportunity for variation and pleasant exercise. Vaulting skills can be related, but most important the athlete acquires mastery of his bodily movements.

20. Secondary event. The secondary event for the pole vaulter may be for competitive pleasure, conditioning, or team points. The great Bob Richards was such a master of all events that he was a world-class decathlon competitor. Bob Seagren frequently ran the 400-meter hurdles. Temperament is an ingredient necessary to athletic or any other success. The real champion makes it work for him! An athlete should have a secondary event for pleasure as well as self-mastery. The champions do, the losers do not!

Pole Vault Bibliography

Ariel, Gideon. "The contribution of the pole to the vault," *Track and Field Quarterly Review* 72 (December 1972): 217–22.

Cramer, John L. "Analytic profile of the world's first 18′ vaulter," *Scholastic Coach* 40 (February 1971): 8–9, 80–82.

_______. "Fiberglass controversy in retrospect," *Track and Field Quarterly Review*, November 1970, pp. 51–57.

_______. "Fiberglass pole vaulting by the champions, part 1: individual differences," *Scholastic Coach* 38 (January 1969): 14–16, 74–75.

_______. "Part 2: techniques," No. 6 (February 1969), pp. 14–16, 63–67.

_______. "Part 3: training methods," No. 7 (March 1969), pp. 34, 36, 38, 52.

_______. "Part 4: recommendations," No. 8 (April 1969), pp. 14–15, 79–80.

_______. "Wolfgang Nordwig — style personified," *Scholastic Coach* 40 (April 1971): 8–9, 96–99.

Ecker, Tom. "Poles and pits," *Track Technique*, No. 39 (March 1970), pp. 1228–30.

Falk, Bill. *Taking the Mystery out of Fiberglass Pole Vaulting*. Providence, R.I.: M-F Athletic Company, 1972. 32 pp.

Ganslen, Richard V. *Mechanics of the Pole Vault*, 7th ed. Denton, Tex.: privately published by Richard Ganslen, 1970. 160 pp.

Hay, James G. "Pole vaulting: a mechanical analysis of factors influencing pole-bend," *Research Quarterly* 38 (March 1967): 34–40.

Jarver, Jess. "Fiberglass vaulting mechanics," *Track Technique*, No. 47 (March 1972), pp. 1483–86.

Jesse, John P. "Weight training for pole vaulters," *Track and Field Quarterly Review*, April 1964, pp. 19–25.

Kaufmann, David A. "A biomechanical block diagram of the pole vault," *Track Technique*, No. 54 (December 1973), pp. 1732–34.

Mitchell, John T. "The world's first 16′ high school vaulter," *Track and Field Quarterly Review*, December 1965, pp. 29–31.

Olsen, Tom. "ABC's of fiberglass vaulting," *Track Technique*, No. 17 (September 1964), pp. 516–17.

_______. "Teaching beginners to vault in ten easy steps," *Track Technique*, No. 21 (September 1965), pp. 660–61.

Pappa, John, and LaQuard, Bill. "Conditioning a vaulter," *Athletic Journal* 50 (February 1970): 17–18.

Rohrbough, Jon. "Approach velocity in pole vaulting," *Track Technique*, No. 52 (June 1973), pp. 1663–65.

Sharpley, Frank. "Teaching beginners to pole vault," *Track Technique*, No. 3 (March 1961), pp. 75–79.

Simonyi, Gabor. "Vertical carry in pole vaulting," *Track Technique*, No. 39 (March 1970), pp. 1235–37.

Wood, Ian. *Pole Vaulting*. London: AAA, 1966. 44 pp.

four

The Throws

The shot-put

12

Some of the best shot-put prospects never enjoy the fierce, lonely effort that is the reward for stepping into the circle and culminating the months and years of preparation for the explosion that leads to an Olympic gold medal. It is the nature of football to be demanding of time and organization that consumes the best of the physical giants who might otherwise be a Matson, a Woods, a Steinhauer, or a Feuerbach. It is also the nature of the individual sport that many of the team sport giants are not psychologically equipped to face the possibility of having their abilities measured with absolute objectivity.

The shot-put is traditionally considered the strong athlete's event in track and field. The collegiate shot-putter is typically big and strong. The bigger and stronger he is, the more likely he is to be successful. This is not as strictly the case with high school shot-putters. Since the high school shot is only 12 pounds, compared to 16 pounds for the collegian, a smaller athlete who is "nifty," that is, fast and explosive, can compete with the larger athlete on this level of competition.

Progress in the shot-put has been tremendous over the last several decades. In the late 1930s, Oregon's best putter, Bill Foskett, was skirting the edges of the 50-foot barrier, but thirty years later his son Bob broke his record by more than 10 feet with an effort of better than 60 feet. The 70-foot mark has been passed, and now many other athletes are on the verge of making it a "typical" distance for world-class competitors.

The test for shot-putters, described in detail in Chapter 18, is simply to have every candidate try taking several tosses from a standing position. Anyone who can better 20 feet is considered a potential shot-putter.

Technique of the Shot-Put

The action of shot-putting, as it is currently practiced, begins with the putter standing in the rear of the 7-foot throwing circle and facing *away* from the direction of the put. From this position the thrower carries the shot to the front of the ring, to add speed to its movement, and in the process of crossing the ring he lifts, turns, pushes the shot upward, and finally gives a final "flip" of the wrist to impart final momentum to the shot as it leaves his hand.

The shot is held on the hard part of the hand, the section at the base of the fingers, where the pads are at the top of the palm. It is held by four fingers (three fingers and the thumb, with the "little" finger often curled under). At one time putters tried to hold the shot out on the fingers. However, few men are strong enough to keep it out there, and throwing the shot while holding it that way can hurt the arm all the way to the elbow. The putter should squeeze the shot a bit, helping to keep better control. The elbow should be kept behind the shot at all times. The hand might be turned out to keep the elbow in a good position.

The four stages of the shot-putting action are: (1) the athlete moves to the center of the circle; (2) he lifts himself, imparting a change in the direction of the shot; (3) when he reaches the center of the circle, the putter begins to turn toward the direction of the final put, and (4) he pushes the shot outward until it leaves the hand. These stages are not as separate as the description would suggest. The movement is a continuous, uninterrupted action. According to the laws of motion, the shot weighs less when it is moving, so long as it is pushed along the *same* line of travel along which it is already traveling.

The method of shot-putting now considered "traditional" is also sometimes referred to as the "O'Brien style" for its developer, Parry O'Brien. Before O'Brien, putters made a turn of only about 90 degrees while crossing the ring to make a toss. In the early 1950s O'Brien developed the style of beginning the movement facing completely away from the direction of the throw, using a full 180-degree turn before throwing. The primary advantage of his style was that the shot was in contact with the athlete's hand for an additional foot or so of movement, permitting greater momentum to be developed and applied to the final action in releasing the shot.

As an example, we will use an athlete who throws with his right hand. He begins standing at the rear of the circle, facing away from the direction of his throw. The shot is cradled in the hand and held alongside the neck at the chin. The forearm at this time extends downward toward the ground. The athlete's weight is on his right foot, with his left foot reaching back a bit, in preparation for the movement across the ring. The athlete will begin by raising his left hand

Photographs 12.1*a-p*   Randy Matson in the shot-put.

or extending it to the rear of the circle. This is primarily a matter of attaining balance. The athlete must be in a good state of balance before he begins the movement across the circle.

Analysis of a Shot-Put Sequence

This set of photographs is of Randy Matson, the first man to break the 70-foot barrier in the shot-put. The first picture (Photograph 12.1*a*, above) shows him at the rear of the circle, with the shot under his chin and his body well balanced. He then prepares for his move across the ring by reaching down and to the rear

with his arm, while his left leg reaches back in the direction of the throw (Photograph 12.1*b*). The leg will, in a sense, "pull" him across the ring, since he will quickly extend it, after first pulling it in (Photograph 12.1*c*), with this quick push of the leg across the circle (Photograph 12.1*f*) used to help start the body moving across the circle. At the end of this first phase (Photograph 12.1*h*), he will be in a position which is still somewhat crouched, and his right leg will have been drawn back under his body, so that it is still the primary support of the thrower's weight. The right foot will be at the center of the circle or slightly across it on the throwing side, depending mostly upon the size of the thrower, and it will be turned slightly to the athlete's right, forming an angle of about 120 to 140 degrees to the direction of the throw. The left foot will have come into contact with the toeboard, leaving the athlete in a strong throwing position, since he can use his legs as well as his arms in supplying force to the throw. The arm holding the shot is still hanging down at this point, though the picture shows that the athlete has begun to bring his left arm around into the movement of the turn.

The athlete begins the "lift," in which the upper body is being raised, and in the late stages of the lift, he moves into the turn toward the direction of the throw, putting him in the position seen in Photograph 12.1*i*. Both legs are still somewhat bent, so the thrower can get additional force out of each leg. The upper torso is coming up and around, with the left arm leading the way to provide additional force to the turn. The putting arm is just beginning to come out from the body, though it is still hanging downward.

As the thrower makes the turn, the throwing arm goes out to the side. This results in a strong throwing position in the front of the circle (Photograph 12.1*j*). While turning, the putter has shifted his weight forward from the right foot to the left foot, so he is now working in the front of the ring. Though he is forward in the circle, he is still receiving power from the right leg, which can be seen still pushing from the center of the circle. The left leg is still slightly bent, so it can still apply additional lift. The right arm is out to the side, and the shot has just begun to leave its position next to the thrower's chin. He is also pulling around with his left arm, and his eyes are aimed upward, coordinated with the direction along which he wants to thrust his right arm.

He has turned a bit more and is pushing the shot up and out in Photograph 12.1*k*. The continued leg thrust is still noticeable here, reaching its end in Photograph 12.1*l* as his rear foot loses contact with the ground. At this point, however, he is just short of losing contact with the shot itself, as the arm is almost completely extended. In Photograph 12.1*m*, he has given the final "flip" to the shot; it is on its way; and his feet are off the ground as he begins his "reverse" to the final position (Photograph 12.1*p*) which is used to prevent him from fouling by stepping out of the circle.

The purpose of the ring crossing, as mentioned before, is to add momentum to the shot. The amount of speed will vary with the individual. It should be only as much as the athlete can *control,* since otherwise he will likely throw himself off balance, gaining little from the additional speed. The direction of the shot should not be changed from the time the athlete begins moving in the rear of the circle until the shot is released. The final angle of the release of the shot should be at an angle of about 45 degrees, or slightly under that angle, for the optimum distance.

Faults in Shot-Put Technique

One fault already mentioned refers to the speed of the thrower's movement across the ring. If the athlete has more speed than control, the throw will not be very successful. Control is perhaps the most important factor in successful putting, control and balance at all times. Without these, most additional speed will be wasted.

If the thrower changes the direction of the shot's movement at any time before the release, this will handicap the throw considerably. The laws of physics will work for the athlete as long as that line of movement is followed. If the direction is changed, the laws will work against the thrower, making the shot become (from the standpoint of ease or power) much heavier for the thrower.

Bad placement of the back foot (the left foot for a right-handed thrower) is another fault. The result can be any number of other problems, ranging from a change in the direction of the put to the failure to gain control and balance throughout the put. If the thrower is not balanced and does not have everything well under control in the rear of the circle, he should not begin his throw. If he begins the shift and reaches the center of the circle in the wrong position, he will be better off if he stops at that point and starts over, rather than take what may be a poor throw.

Turning before lifting is a fault which will result in the athlete either trying to put the shot at too steep an angle, resulting in less distance, or making a relatively flat throw, with the same result.

Premature putting is a common fault which results in poorer throws. If the shot is tossed prematurely, the entire force of the interacted movements of the body will not yet have been applied to the put. The result is predictable. This may be related to the position from which the thrower begins his movements, so a change in his placement in the circle may correct the problem.

The Shot-Put Routine

The "routine" is designed to give the shot-putter the "feel" of what he should be doing when he goes through the entire putting action. It consists of two groups of exercises, the first group performed in the front area of the circle, and the other group involving crossing the ring. These exercises should help the putter review the "basics" of his event, progressing in effort from "easy" to "medium" to "hard."

The first part of the routine is done with the putter in the front of the circle. Actually, this means that he begins at the *start* of the final phase of the put, with his body over his flexed right leg and his left leg extended back to the toeboard. This part of the exercise is called the "stand." The shot is held while the athlete goes through the action of the lift and turn, but with one difference: the athlete does *not* push the shot. The arm goes out to the side, just as though the shot were to be pushed, but the hand stays at the neck area. The shot is allowed to fall from the hand, but it travels only as far as the force of the body, with absolutely no arm action, causes it to go. The second drill repeats the first one, except that the hand *follows* (but does not push) the shot as it leaves the hand. The third drill does involve pushing the shot as it leaves, but it is not a hard push. The last standing drill has the athlete lifting, turning, and pushing *hard.*

The second part of the routine is done by crossing the ring, using the full action of throwing. When crossing the ring in the routine, the thrower should start slow and finish fast. The full crossing drill is to give the feel of the event, rather than to work on the speed of the crossing. The first drill is similar to the second drill from a stand. The athlete crosses the circle, lifts, turns, and lets the shot leave his hand, following it with the hand, but *not* pushing it. The second, third, and fourth drills with the ring crossing involve pushing the shot at the completion of the action. The second drill has the putter make a "medium" effort push, the third drill has him making a "hard" effort push, and on the fourth drill, the athlete will try to "explode," unleashing all his force into the put. At all times the feet should be spread enough for the athlete to get his hips into the throw. Some throwers have worked on the final push of the throwing arm by trying to develop a "punching" action. One exercise used for this action has been to work at hitting a punching bag while on one's knees, which requires the man to push upward at about the angle of the putting action.

Training for the Shot-Put

For the purposes of records, a condensed or coded training sheet for the shot-put is more practical than one page for every day of training or even every week. While preparing a written workout may be a bit easier, it can also be sloppier in thought. At Oregon a workout sheet is prepared in a manner similar to the sheets used for the other events. It lists the exercises considered "fundamental" to training for the shot-put. Because all the exercises are listed on the sheet, the coach or teacher is less likely to forget to assign vital portions of the training regime.

The shot-put training schedules are organized so that either an individual or a group, such as the members of a physical education class, can devote a unit of ten weeks to one or more events. The schedule is a guide, not a dictum. The routines are introduced and repeated regularly. Technique is introduced early in the schedule and those points which are most basic to the event are repeated with the greatest frequency. Also included are agility drills, speed work, and possibly a secondary event. The program is from the simple to the more difficult with a gradual increase in "planned" distance, so that the best technique can be acquired as physical condition and strength improve.

The schedules are arranged so that a month's record is available. There are three particular values to this system: (1) a complete "book" may be kept on the individual athlete, (2) comparisons to previous athletes may be made, and probably the most important, (3) particular fundamentals will not be overlooked.

The athlete and coach should try to follow patterns which have been successful. This is one reason for recording and saving the schedule sheets. In training for technique of the put, it is best to work on only *one* thing or phase of the put at a time. Gradually these can be put together into the complete put. On the schedule sheet, these facets of the put are listed by letters under item 6. This is primarily to avoid confusion and frustration.

On the fartlek running, we would like the putters to be able to run steadily

Figure 12.1a Shot-Put Training Schedule

Shot-Put NAME DATE *September/October*

1. A. Jog 1 or 2 laps, easy stretching B. Weights and jog C.
2. Fartlek run A. Varied pace B. Slow, steady
3. Weights and resistance activities.
4. Routine A. Stand B. Crossing (1) Lift (2) Turn (3) Push
5. Effort A. Stand B. Crossing (1) Easy (2) Medium (3) Hard
6. Technique A. Stand-shot almost in palm B. Crossing—have speed under control (1) Comfortable knee bend (2) Hip push from cock position (3) Left arm in position, pull for torque (4) Eye on ground or target (5) Every 3d or 4th explode (6) Lift well before turn (7) Squeeze the shot (8) Right foot in center of ring (9) Target for 3/4 to 7/8 effort (a) Stand (b) Crossing (10) Left foot timing and position (11) Reach on put and lean into it (12)
7. Squad meeting
8. Special A. Sauna B. Swim C. Steps or hill
9. Alternate stand-step-crossing routine; same letters as item 6
10. Test or compete—record below
11. Cross ring easy. Feeling of exploding. Start slow, finish fast.
12. With coach
14. A. Wind sprints B. Starts, go 25 yds. C. High knee and fast leg D. Hurdles E. Spring and bound F. Alternate walk-run go 880 or more
15. A. Hendricks Park B. Laurelwood Golf Course
16. Tumbling activities
17. Have feeling of low and relaxed. No strain at back or in crossing.
18. A. On staying in the ring B. Lift-turn
19. Ring crossing, feet not too far spread only as fast as you can control. Same as item 6.
20. Secondary event
21. A. Pictures B. Film C. Video

Date	Result	3/4	Now	Goal

M	Organization-equipment-lockers
T	Use of equipment-Safety-training times
W	1A-6A(1)-6A(2)-7-14F
T	(10 am) 21A-3
F	1A-6A(1)-6A(3)-8C-14F
S	3
S	3-14A-14F or recreation
M	1A-6A(1)-6B(1)-6A(2)-6B(2)-14A
T	7-5A(1)(2)(3)-3-14A
W	1A-6A(3)-6B(3)-17
T	3-8B or 8C
F	1A-6B(6)-11-14C
S	3-14D-14F
S	recreation
M	1A-6A(4)-6B(4)-6A(11)-6B(11)-14A
T	3-14F
W	1A-6A(4)-6B(4)-6A(11)-6B(11)-6B(8)-1A
T	3-14F
F	1A-6A(1)-6B(1)-6A(11)-6B(11)-6B(8)
S	3-14F
S	recreation
M	1A-6A(11)-6B(11)-6A(1)-6B(1)-17-20
T	3-14A
W	1A-6A(2)-6B(2)-6A(4)-6B(4)-14B
T	3-14F
F	1A-10A-9A(8)
S	3-14F
S	recreation

Figure 12.1b Shot-Put Training Schedule

Shot-Put NAME DATE October/November

1. A. Jog 1 or 2 laps, easy stretching B. Weights and jog C.
2. Fartlek run A. Varied pace B. Slow, steady
3. Weights and resistance activities.
4. Routine A. Stand B. Crossing (1) Lift (2) Turn (3) Push
5. Effort A. Stand B. Crossing (1) Easy (2) Medium (3) Hard
6. Technique A. Stand-shot almost in palm B. Crossing—have speed under control (1) Comfortable knee bend (2) Hip push from cock position (3) Left arm in position, pull for torque (4) Eye on ground or target (5) Every 3d or 4th explode (6) Lift well before turn (7) Squeeze the shot (8) Right foot in center of ring (9) Target for 3/4 to 7/8 effort (a) Stand (b) Crossing (10) Left foot timing and position (11) Reach on put and lean into it (12)
7. Squad meeting
8. Special A. Sauna B. Swim C. Steps or hill
9. Alternate stand-step-crossing routine; same letters as item 6
10. Test or compete—record below
11. Cross ring easy. Feeling of exploding. Start slow, finish fast.
12. With coach
14. A. Wind sprints B. Starts, go 25 yds. C. High knee and fast leg D. Hurdles E. Spring and bound F. Alternate walk-run go 880 or more
15. A. Hendricks Park B. Laurelwood Golf Course
16. Tumbling activities
17. Have feeling of low and relaxed. No strain at back or in crossing.
18. A. On staying in the ring B. Lift-turn
19. Ring crossing, feet not too far spread only as fast as you can control. Same as item 6.
20. Secondary event
21. A. Pictures B. Film C. Video

Date	Result	3/4	Now	Goal

M	1A-3
T	1A-6A(1)-6B(1)-6B(2)-9AB(1)-20
W	3-14F
T	1A-6A(1)-6B(1)-9AB(8)-14F
F	3
S	
S	

M	1A-3
T	1A-6A(3)-6B(3)-9-14A
W	3-20
T	1A-4 (for distance)-6A(5)-6B(5)-9AB(5)-14F
F	1A-3
S	
S	

M	1A-3-14F or 20
T	1A-5A(4)-9AB(4)-14A
W	1A-3
T	1A-5A(4)-9AB(4)-17-14F
F	1A-3
S	
S	

M	1A-3
T	1A-14F-6A(6)-6B(6)-9AB(6)-17-14A
W	1A-3-14F
T	1A-14A-6A(6)-6B(6)-9AB(6)-11-1A
F	1A-3-14F
S	1A-6A(8)-6B(8)-9AB(8)-11-14A
S	

Figure 12.1c Shot-Put Training Schedule

Shot-Put NAME DATE November/December

1. A. Jog 1 or 2 laps, easy stretching B. Weights and jog C.
2. Fartlek run A. Varied pace B. Slow, steady
3. Weights and resistance activities.
4. Routine A. Stand B. Crossing (1) Lift (2) Turn (3) Push
5. Effort A. Stand B. Crossing (1) Easy (2) Medium (3) Hard
6. Technique A. Stand-shot almost in palm B. Crossing—have speed under control (1) Comfortable knee bend (2) Hip push from cock position (3) Left arm in position, pull for torque (4) Eye on ground or target (5) Every 3d or 4th explode (6) Lift well before turn (7) Squeeze the shot (8) Right foot in center of ring (9) Target for 3/4 to 7/8 effort (a) Stand (b) Crossing (10) Left foot timing and position (11) Reach on put and lean into it (12)
7. Squad meeting
8. Special A. Sauna B. Swim C. Steps or hill
9. Alternate stand-step-crossing routine; same letters as item 6
10. Test or compete—record below
11. Cross ring easy. Feeling of exploding. Start slow, finish fast.
12. With coach
14. A. Wind sprints B. Starts, go 25 yds. C. High knee and fast leg D. Hurdles E. Spring and bound F. Alternate walk-run go 880 or more
15. A. Hendricks Park B. Laurelwood Golf Course
16. Tumbling activities
17. Have feeling of low and relaxed. No strain at back or in crossing.
18. A. On staying in the ring B. Lift-turn
19. Ring crossing, feet not too far spread only as fast as you can control. Same as item 6.
20. Secondary event
21. A. Pictures B. Film C. Video

Date	Result	3/4	Now	Goal

Day	
M	1A-14F-6A(6)-6B(6)-9AB(6)-17
T	1A-3-14F
W	1A-14A-6A(6)-6B(6)-9AB(6)-11
T	1A-3-14A
F	1A-3-6A(8)-6B(8)-9AB(8)-11
S	
S	

Day	
M	3 (easy and very light)
T	6 (form)
W	1A-14A
T	Light
F	10-Test for distance
S	
S	

Day	
M	
T	
W	
T	
F	
S	
S	

Day	
M	
T	
W	
T	
F	
S	
S	

Figure 12.1d Shot-Put Training Schedule

Shot-Put NAME DATE January

1. A. Jog 1 or 2 laps, easy stretching B. Weights and jog C.
2. Fartlek run A. Varied pace B. Slow, steady
3. Weights and resistance activities.
4. Routine A. Stand B. Crossing (1) Lift (2) Turn (3) Push
5. Effort A. Stand B. Crossing (1) Easy (2) Medium (3) Hard
6. Technique A. Stand-shot almost in palm
   B. Crossing—have speed under control
   (1) Comfortable knee bend (2) Hip push from cock position
   (3) Left arm in position, pull for torque
   (4) Eye on ground or target (5) Every 3d or 4th explode
   (6) Lift well before turn (7) Squeeze the shot
   (8) Right foot in center of ring (9) Target for 3/4 to 7/8 effort
   (a) Stand (b) Crossing (10) Left foot timing and position
   (11) Reach on put and lean into it (12)
7. Squad meeting
8. Special A. Sauna B. Swim C. Steps or hill
9. Alternate stand-step-crossing routine; same letters as item 6
10. Test or compete—record below
11. Cross ring easy. Feeling of exploding. Start slow, finish fast.
12. With coach
14. A. Wind sprints B. Starts, go 25 yds.
    C. High knee and fast leg D. Hurdles
    E. Spring and bound F. Alternate walk-run go 880 or more
15. A. Hendricks Park B. Laurelwood Golf Course
16. Tumbling activities
17. Have feeling of low and relaxed. No strain at back or in crossing.
18. A. On staying in the ring B. Lift-turn
19. Ring crossing, feet not too far spread only as fast as you can control. Same as item 6.
20. Secondary event
21. A. Pictures B. Film C. Video

Date	Result	3/4	Now	Goal

M	Class or squad organization—3-5A
T	1A-5A(1,2,3)-9AB(1) (3-6x)-14A
W	3
T	7-6B(2) (6-10x)-9AB(2) (3-6x)-14A
F	3
S	1A-6B(5) (6-10x)-9AB(5) (2-4x)
S	recreation
M	3-14B
T	1A-5A(1,2,3)-5B(1,2,3)-6B(6) (6-10x)-9AB(5) (3-6x)-14F
W	3
T	1A-5B(1,2,3)-6B(6) (6-10x)-9AB(6) (3-6x)-14A
F	3
S	10 (record)-9B(7)-14F
S	recreation
M	3-14B-14F
T	1A-5A(1,2,3)-6AB(8) (6-10x)-9AB(8) (3-6x)-14F
W	3
T	1A-5B(1,2,3)-6AB(4) (6-10x)-9AB(4) (3-6x)-14F
F	3
S	1A-5B(1,2,3)-6A(6) (6-10x)-9AB(6) (3-6x)-19
S	
M	3
T	1A-8A (6-10x)-6A(1) (6-10x)-6A(4)-9AB(4) (3-6x)-14B
W	3
T	1A-19AB(9) (4-6x)-17-14F
F	3
S	10 (form work)
S	

Figure 12.1e Shot-Put Training Schedule

Shot-Put NAME DATE February

1. A. Jog 1 or 2 laps, easy stretching B. Weights and jog
   C.
2. Fartlek run A. Varied pace B. Slow, steady
3. Weights and resistance activities.
4. Routine A. Stand B. Crossing (1) Lift
   (2) Turn (3) Push
5. Effort A. Stand B. Crossing
   (1) Easy (2) Medium (3) Hard
6. Technique A. Stand-shot almost in palm
   B. Crossing—have speed under control
   (1) Comfortable knee bend (2) Hip push from cock position
   (3) Left arm in position, pull for torque
   (4) Eye on ground or target (5) Every 3d or 4th explode
   (6) Lift well before turn (7) Squeeze the shot
   (8) Right foot in center of ring (9) Target for 3/4 to 7/8 effort
   (a) Stand (b) Crossing (10) Left foot timing and position
   (11) Reach on put and lean into it (12)
7. Squad meeting
8. Special A. Sauna B. Swim C. Steps or hill
9. Alternate stand-step-crossing routine; same letters as item 6
10. Test or compete—record below
11. Cross ring easy. Feeling of exploding. Start slow, finish fast.
12. With coach
14. A. Wind sprints B. Starts, go 25 yds.
    C. High knee and fast leg D. Hurdles
    E. Spring and bound F. Alternate walk-run go 880 or more
15. A. Hendricks Park B. Laurelwood Golf Course
16. Tumbling activities
17. Have feeling of low and relaxed. No strain at back or in crossing.
18. A. On staying in the ring B. Lift-turn
19. Ring crossing, feet not too far spread only as fast as you can control. Same as item 6.
20. Secondary event
21. A. Pictures B. Film C. Video

Date	Result	3/4	Now	Goal

M	3-14A
T	1A-4-6A(1)-9AB(1)-17-14F
W	3
T	2x 1A-4AB(1, 2, 3)-9-14A
F	Gear ready-weigh shot-7
S	Indoor meet or 10
S	3
M	3-14B or 14F
T	1A-6B(1)-19B(3)-14F-8A-14F
W	1A-3
T	1A-6A(2)-19B(2)-17-19B(8)-11-14A
F	3
S	1A-6A(4)-19B(4)-9-17-14F
S	3
M	1A-3
T	20x 20x 1A-6A(1)-6B(1)-14F
W	1A-3
T	20x 20x 20x 1A-9B(11)-18-6A(3)-11-14F
F	1A-3
S	7-20
S	3
M	20-40x 10-20x 1A-9B(5)-9B(11)-11-14A
T	3-14B
W	20x 20x 20x 20x 1A-9B(11)-18-5B-19B(2)-14F
T	3-14B
F	10
S	3
S	3

Figure 12.1f Shot-Put Training Schedule

Shot-Put NAME DATE *March*

1. A. Jog 1 or 2 laps, easy stretching B. Weights and jog
   C.
2. Fartlek run A. Varied pace B. Slow, steady
3. Weights and resistance activities.
4. Routine A. Stand B. Crossing (1) Lift
   (2) Turn (3) Push
5. Effort A. Stand B. Crossing
   (1) Easy (2) Medium (3) Hard
6. Technique A. Stand-shot almost in palm
   B. Crossing—have speed under control
   (1) Comfortable knee bend (2) Hip push from cock position
   (3) Left arm in position, pull for torque
   (4) Eye on ground or target (5) Every 3d or 4th explode
   (6) Lift well before turn (7) Squeeze the shot
   (8) Right foot in center of ring (9) Target for 3/4 to 7/8 effort
   (a) Stand (b) Crossing (10) Left foot timing and position
   (11) Reach on put and lean into it (12)
7. Squad meeting
8. Special A. Sauna B. Swim C. Steps or hill
9. Alternate stand-step-crossing routine; same letters as item 6
10. Test or compete—record below
11. Cross ring easy. Feeling of exploding. Start slow, finish fast.
12. With coach
14. A. Wind sprints B. Starts, go 25 yds.
    C. High knee and fast leg D. Hurdles
    E. Spring and bound F. Alternate walk-run go 880 or more
15. A. Hendricks Park B. Laurelwood Golf Course
16. Tumbling activities
17. Have feeling of low and relaxed. No strain at back or in crossing.
18. A. On staying in the ring B. Lift-turn
19. Ring crossing, feet not too far spread only as fast as you can
    control. Same as item 6.
20. Secondary event
21. A. Pictures B. Film C. Video

Date	Result	3/4	Now	Goal

Day	Week 1
M	1A-6A(1)-6B(1)-17-14A-14F-6A(4)-6B(4)
T	3-14F-20
W	1A-11-17-10 (4x)-10 (4x)-10 (4x)-14A
T	3-20-14A
F	1A-11-17-10 (4x)-10 (4x)-10 (4x)-10 (4x)-14A
S	19-20
S	19-20

Day	Week 2
M	1A-6A(3)-6B(3)-6B(8)-19-14F
T	3-20-14F
W	7-1A-11-6B(8)-17-14A
T	3-20-14F
F	1A-8B(8)-11-17-14A
S	Exams and jog
S	

Day	Week 3
M	3-14F-20
T	1A-4A-4B-5A-5B-17-14A-14F
W	3-20-14F
T	1A-11-17-10 (4x)-14A
F	Travel
S	10-Meet
S	Settle in-spring trip

Day	A.M.	P.M.
M	1A-3	1A-6B(8)-4A(1,2,3)-4B(1,2,3)-14A
T	1-14F	1-20-3-14F
W	1-3	1A-17-6A(8)-6B(8)-14A-14F
T		1A-6B(8)-4A-4B-11-14F
F	Light	Light
S	10-Triangular meet	
S	Travel home	

Figure 12.1g Shot-Put Training Schedule

Shot-Put NAME DATE April

1. A. Jog 1 or 2 laps, easy stretching B. Weights and jog C.
2. Fartlek run A. Varied pace B. Slow, steady
3. Weights and resistance activities.
4. Routine A. Stand B. Crossing (1) Lift (2) Turn (3) Push
5. Effort A. Stand B. Crossing (1) Easy (2) Medium (3) Hard
6. Technique A. Stand-shot almost in palm
   B. Crossing—have speed under control
   (1) Comfortable knee bend (2) Hip push from cock position
   (3) Left arm in position, pull for torque
   (4) Eye on ground or target (5) Every 3d or 4th explode
   (6) Lift well before turn (7) Squeeze the shot
   (8) Right foot in center of ring (9) Target for 3/4 to 7/8 effort
   (a) Stand (b) Crossing (10) Left foot timing and position
   (11) Reach on put and lean into it (12)
7. Squad meeting
8. Special A. Sauna B. Swim C. Steps or hill
9. Alternate stand-step-crossing routine; same letters as item 6
10. Test or compete—record below
11. Cross ring easy. Feeling of exploding. Start slow, finish fast.
12. With coach
14. A. Wind sprints B. Starts, go 25 yds. C. High knee and fast leg D. Hurdles E. Spring and bound F. Alternate walk-run go 880 or more
15. A. Hendricks Park B. Laurelwood Golf Course
16. Tumbling activities
17. Have feeling of low and relaxed. No strain at back or in crossing.
18. A. On staying in the ring B. Lift-turn
19. Ring crossing, feet not too far spread only as fast as you can control. Same as item 6.
20. Secondary event
21. A. Pictures B. Film C. Video

Date	Result	3/4	Now	Goal

M	1A - 3 - 14A
T	1A - 6A(6) 3x - 6B(6) 3x - 9A(4) 4-6x - 9A(2) 4-6x - 14F
W	3-14B
T	1-5A - 6A(7) - 11 - 20
F	Easy
S	10- Dual meet
S	Your choice
M	3-14B
T	7-1A - 6A(6) 3-4x - 6A(4) 3-4x - 9
W	3-20
T	7-1A - 6A(1) 3-4x - 6B(1) 3-4x - 11 - 14A
F	Easy jog
S	10- Dual meet
S	Your choice
M	3-14B (easy)
T	1A - 6A(2) 3x - 6A(6) 3x - 6A(2) 3x - 9 - 14F
W	3-20
T	7-1A - 6A(2) 2-3x - 6A(3) 3-4x - 6B(9) 4x - Easy 20
F	Travel
S	10- Dual meet
S	Home and loosen up
M	2-14F
T	12-21B - 5A - 6A - 6B - 9 - 14F
W	2-20
T	12-16(8) - 6B(8) - 17 - 19 - 14A
F	Gear ready
S	10- Dual meet
S	Your Choice

Figure 12.1h Shot-Put Training Schedule

Shot-Put NAME DATE May

1. A. Jog 1 or 2 laps, easy stretching B. Weights and jog C.
2. Fartlek run A. Varied pace B. Slow, steady
3. Weights and resistance activities.
4. Routine A. Stand B. Crossing (1) Lift (2) Turn (3) Push
5. Effort A. Stand B. Crossing (1) Easy (2) Medium (3) Hard
6. Technique A. Stand-shot almost in palm
   B. Crossing—have speed under control
   (1) Comfortable knee bend (2) Hip push from cock position
   (3) Left arm in position, pull for torque
   (4) Eye on ground or target (5) Every 3d or 4th explode
   (6) Lift well before turn (7) Squeeze the shot
   (8) Right foot in center of ring (9) Target for 3/4 to 7/8 effort
   (a) Stand (b) Crossing (10) Left foot timing and position
   (11) Reach on put and lean into it (12)
7. Squad meeting
8. Special A. Sauna B. Swim C. Steps or hill
9. Alternate stand-step-crossing routine; same letters as item 6
10. Test or compete—record below
11. Cross ring easy. Feeling of exploding. Start slow, finish fast.
12. With coach
14. A. Wind sprints B. Starts, go 25 yds.
    C. High knee and fast leg D. Hurdles
    E. Spring and bound F. Alternate walk-run go 880 or more
15. A. Hendricks Park B. Laurelwood Golf Course
16. Tumbling activities
17. Have feeling of low and relaxed. No strain at back or in crossing.
18. A. On staying in the ring B. Lift-turn
19. Ring crossing, feet not too far spread only as fast as you can control. Same as item 6.
20. Secondary event
21. A. Pictures B. Film C. Video

Date	Result	3/4	Now	Goal

M	1-3-14A-14F
T	7-12-6A(2)-9A(2)-10-17-14B
W	Form work and 20
T	3x 3x 1A-Distance-11-17-12-Distance-11-8
F	Travel
S	10-Dual meet
S	Home and loosen up

M	1-3-14F
T	12 with Coach-Technique and target (Aug.-10%)
W	12A-as on Tuesday, 10% less than average.
T	Light-3
F	Light-3
S	10-Twilight meet
S	Your choice

M	Target 10% less than average-3-14A
T	1-4-9AB(5)-18A-11-14A
W	3-14A
T	1-9(11)
F	Light-gear ready
S	10-Northern Division
S	4 puts-3

M	Light-3
T	1-4-9AB(5)-17-14F
W	1-4-11-form work-14A
T	Light
F	Travel
S	10-Pac 8 Meet
S	

Figure 12.1i Shot-Put Training Schedule

Shot-Put NAME DATE Late May or June

1. A. Jog 1 or 2 laps, easy stretching B. Weights and jog
   C.
2. Fartlek run A. Varied pace B. Slow, steady
3. Weights and resistance activities.
4. Routine A. Stand B. Crossing (1) Lift
   (2) Turn (3) Push
5. Effort A. Stand B. Crossing
   (1) Easy (2) Medium (3) Hard
6. Technique A. Stand-shot almost in palm
   B. Crossing—have speed under control
   (1) Comfortable knee bend (2) Hip push from cock position
   (3) Left arm in position, pull for torque
   (4) Eye on ground or target (5) Every 3d or 4th explode
   (6) Lift well before turn (7) Squeeze the shot
   (8) Right foot in center of ring (9) Target for 3/4 to 7/8 effort
   (a) Stand (b) Crossing (10) Left foot timing and position
   (11) Reach on put and lean into it (12)
7. Squad meeting
8. Special A. Sauna B. Swim C. Steps or hill
9. Alternate stand-step-crossing routine; same letters as item 6
10. Test or compete—record below
11. Cross ring easy. Feeling of exploding. Start slow, finish fast.
12. With coach
14. A. Wind sprints B. Starts, go 25 yds.
    C. High knee and fast leg D. Hurdles
    E. Spring and bound F. Alternate walk-run go 880 or more
15. A. Hendricks Park B. Laurelwood Golf Course
16. Tumbling activities
17. Have feeling of low and relaxed. No strain at back or in crossing.
18. A. On staying in the ring B. Lift-turn
19. Ring crossing, feet not too far spread only as fast as you can control. Same as item 6.
20. Secondary event
21. A. Pictures B. Film C. Video

Date	Result	3/4	Now	Goal

M	1-2-11-17-14F
T	Light
W	3x 10-14A-14F
T	Semi-competition
F	Light
S	3x 1A-3-6B(8)-17-10-14F
S	3x 1A-10-17-14A-14F
M	Jog
T	Jog
W	1-3-6B(1)(2)-17-14A
T	2x 1-3-6B(8)-17-10-14A
F	Jog
S	Jog
S	3x 1-6A(1)-6B(1)(3)-10-9A(8)-17-14A
M	1-3-9A(8)-17-14F
T	Medium-3 puts-14B
W	Light
T	Light
F	Qualify-NCAA meet
S	Finals
S	Home
M	
T	
W	
T	
F	
S	
S	

for at least 7 minutes. This running is good for the cardiovascular system, and a steady run of at least 7 minutes is necessary to gain much cardiovascular benefit from such a run.

The athletes need to use weight training activities which will develop enough body mass for successful putting. While suggested training exercises are outlined for the athletes, they do not follow a rigidly set weight training schedule. Each athlete basically develops his own program of weight training activities. This is in keeping with the belief that the athlete should not be overcoached. By the time an athlete is a collegian, he should have enough background to know fairly well what activities of this nature are most beneficial for him, if he has been a very successful putter. As the weight lifters try to arrange their schedules so they can do their lifting activities together, they also pick up ideas from each other. Weight training definitely helps, though it can also be overdone. The ultimate object is feet thrown, not pounds lifted. Weight training is done three times a week in the fall, going to two to three sessions per week in the winter, and one or two in the spring (Tuesday, for a Saturday meet).

The hard-easy schedule is followed to some degree, though not so closely as with running activities. The pattern will also vary, according to the time of year. For example, in January the putter might go hard on alternating days, such as Monday, Wednesday, and Friday. In February or early March, preparation for future two-day meets will begin. Since the athlete will have to qualify on one day, then throw again the next day in finals, this sequence is simulated in practice. The thrower would go hard on both Monday and Tuesday, with other hard days on Thursday and Saturday. In preparing for a big meet, the thrower might go hard on Monday and Tuesday, then go light until the meet, either on Friday for trials or on Saturday, if it is a one-day meet.

A brief word concerning the equipment is necessary, since it can affect the distance of the put, though not to the extent possible with different discoi or javelins. The athlete has the choice of iron, steel, or brass instruments. Brass is the smallest shot, but is no longer popular with the better putters. Shot-putters want the largest legal implement they can get. This gives them greater leverage to exert while throwing. Some high school throwers have gone so far as to use the larger indoor shot outdoors, when it has been allowed. However, the birdshot filled instruments are not as good as the solid metal or rubber-covered, solid metal ones, since they give the effect of trying to throw a bean bag.

Shot-Put Bibliography

Ariel, Gideon. "Computerized biomechanical analysis of the world's best shot putters," *Track and Field Quarterly Review* 73 (December 1973): 199–206.

Bosen, K. O. "Hammer and shot flight angles and velocities," *Track Technique*, No. 24 (June 1966), pp. 767–68.

Dalrymple, Alex. "Putting the shot for beginners," *Track Technique*, No. 7 (March 1962), pp. 204–6.

Davis, Dave. "General weight training for throwers," *Track Technique*, No. 51 (March 1973), pp. 1632–35.

Ecker, Tom. "Angle of release in shot putting," *Athletic Journal* 50 (February 1970), 52–53.

"Foot contact at the instant of release in throwing," trans. by Charles L. Sullivan, *Track Technique*, No. 9 (September 1962), pp. 271–74.

Garfoot, Brian. "Analysis of the trajectory of the shot," *Track Technique*, No. 32 (June 1968), pp. 1003–6.

Grigalka, Otto. "Fundamental shot put technique," trans. by Fritz Kuhn and Glenn B. Hoidale, *Track Technique*, No. 49 (September 1972), pp. 1573–75.

Hartzog, Lew. "The shot put with George Woods," *Track and Field Quarterly Review*, October 1966, pp. 68–70.

Harvey, Jack. "Shot putting at the University of Michigan," *Track and Field Quarterly Review*, December 1969, pp. 13–18.

Healey, Joe. "Weight training and shot putting," *Track and Field Quarterly Review*, April 1964, pp. 52–61.

Hood, Don W. "A more scientific approach to shot putting," *Athletic Journal* 51 (April 1971): 59–60, 88.

Jesse, John P. "Explosive power for the shot put," *Track Technique*, No. 14 (December 1963), pp. 424–27.

———. "New approach to shot put strength training," *Track and Field Quarterly Review*, October 1965, pp. 49–56.

Long, Dallas. "The shot put," *Track and Field Quarterly Review*, February 1964, pp. 28–36.

Maggard, Dave. "Technique and training for the shot put," *Track and Field Quarterly Review* 70 (May 1970): 29–33.

Pendrak, Mike. "Developmental program for shot putters," *Scholastic Coach* 40 (March 1971): 8–9, 109.

Pickering, Ron. *Shot Putting*. London: AAA, 1972. 44 pp.

Scoles, Gordon. "Rear leg action in the shot put," *Scholastic Coach* 41 (April 1972): 44, 46.

Simonyi, Gabor. "Form of Wladyslaw Komer," *Scholastic Coach* 42 (March 1973): 7–9, 94, 96, 98–102.

Thomas, Charles. "Training for the shot put and discus double," *Athletic Journal* 46 (January 1966): 51–52, 71–72.

———. "The training techniques of Randy Matson," *Track and Field Quarterly Review*, December 1965, pp. 21–28.

Tschiene, Peter. "Perfection of shot put technique," *Track Technique*, No. 37 (September 1969), pp. 1187–89.

The discus throw

13

Back in the late 1920s the world record for the discus throw was just edging into the lower 160s in feet, but today the mark is edging into the lower 230s. How have athletes progressed this far? Three reasons might be suggested as contributing factors:

1. There are more athletes throwing in the schools today, and they continue to throw for longer periods of time. Besides being a four-time Olympic champion, Al Oerter was probably the best technician the world has ever seen, and certainly the best Olympic competitor.

2. The facilities are better to throw from, and the discoi are now delicate instruments, well balanced and physically prepared to achieve aerodynamic wonders. Concrete or similar surfaces have taken most of the chance out of footing. Nonskid shoes or surfaces take care of some of the disadvantages of rain, and the throwing circles are often placed so as to take advantage of the prevailing winds.

3. Technique has evolved from the slow turn through speed and agility which was introduced by Fortune Gordien to the careful analysis of body mechanics and the principles of physics and aerodynamics.

The discus often seems like a difficult event to learn, because the plate-like shape of the discus does not lend itself to being held or handled easily by the beginning athlete. The beginner should first take the discus and hold it with the fingers spread comfortably along the edge and practice tossing it upward into the air, letting it roll off the fingers. Beginners can work in groups of three, forming a triangle and rolling the discus on its side along the ground to one another. Then the candidates can practice "sailing" it through the air to each other.

The routine for the discus progresses from the stand to stepping into the throw to using the turn. The first part of this stand-step-turn cycle is throwing from a standing position in the circle. If the thrower is right-handed, his right foot (trail leg) will be in the center of the circle and pointing at an angle of 120 degrees or so from the direction of the throw. The left foot will be in the front of the circle and a bit to the left of center, so the thrower will have room to get his hips into the throw. The body is back over the trail leg before throwing. The athlete will rotate his body into the throw, keeping a long throwing arm (not bending it) and pulling the discus through the throwing position. The body shifts during the throwing action from the right leg to the left leg, throwing over a relatively straight leg.

The second part of the routine consists of stepping into the final position and throwing. The turn is not used at this time. As the thrower steps into the final portion, he will drop down slightly, so that as he goes into the actual throw, he will lift and "unwind," as though he were a coiled spring being released.

The final part of the routine uses the full turn and throw. From the starting position in the circle, located in the rear of the circle, with the feet planted comfortably facing away from the throwing direction, the athlete turns, moving into the throwing position, and throws. The progression is turn, step (trail leg plant), step (lead leg plant, both feet now in throwing position), throw. The athlete should try to stay close to the center of the ring, allowing himself room for his follow-through after the throw. When throwing, he should use only as much speed as he can control; otherwise, he will handicap his throw much more than he can help it. Also, he should drop down only as low as he can control, then lift and unwind as he throws.

Analysis of the Discus Throw Technique

The photographic sequence of the discus throw which is included here depicts an athlete who has been outstanding for a number of years, Ludwik Danek. When studying the sequence, athletes and coaches should remember two particular points: (1) a sequence covers only a single throw and may vary in some respects from the athlete's usual throwing form in his most successful throws, and (2) each athlete will have facets of form which are peculiar to himself, differences which work for him but would not work for many other athletes. Thus, this sequence is an example, rather than a law.

The sequence, on page 270, begins as Danek is turning. In Photograph 13.1*d* the 1972 Olympic champion is turning on his left foot, keeping his body low and his throwing arm extended and behind him (behind the line of his

217
217
217
217

d e

k l m

Photographs 13.1*a-r* Ludwik Danek, Czechoslovakia, in the discus throw.

shoulders). As he turns about his foot (Photographs 13.1*e* to *g*), he drops the discus down, so it will then rise to the point of its release. From these pictures it is evident that he is turning very rapidly. Photograph 13.1*h* shows him driving off the foot on which he was turning, preparing to go into the "power position" in the center of the ring. The drive off the left foot is very evident from this angle. At this stage of the action he has bent the lead arm considerably, which speeds up his turn. This may or may not be a virtue at this point, since the thrower does not wish to get too much "ahead of himself."

The right foot has landed in Photographs 13.1*k* and *l* and is turning into the throwing power position. In Photographs 13.1*m* and *n*, his left foot is coming down in the front of the ring as he brings himself into a strong position for the last phases of the throw. When both feet have touched down, his weight is over the rear (right) foot in the center of the circle, and he is still down a bit in a semi-crouch. As he brings the discus around to the release position, he shifts his weight forward toward the front foot, also straightening his legs, so his body (Photograph 13.1*o*) is rising, causing the discus to move in a pattern like the edge of a screw, circling in an upward direction. After the release (Photograph 13.1*q*), the thrower reverses his foot position in the front of the circle, preventing a foul.

Discus Throwing Tips

When throwing the discus, the use of the entire body and legs is important. The "arm" thrower will succeed only against poor competition. As the thrower moves into the throw, he is rising upward, gradually lifting with his legs and adding to the force applied to the discus. When the throw is being made, the hips are cocked. The hip is thrown forward like a punch, adding to the power of the throw. If the lead foot is placed directly in front of the body, though, the hips cannot be thrown forward, since they have nowhere to go. The thrower should lead into the release of the discus with his nose and chin, which should be pointed straight ahead when he releases the discus.

All the unwinding (hips, chest, etc.) must *precede* the arm. This leading gets a sling or whip action into the arm. The farther the discus can be pulled in this manner, the greater the velocity which can be imparted to it. Connected with these actions are the left arm coordination and the footwork of the throw, which are very important.

The direction the discus will go depends upon where the left foot points when the hips are cocked. The best throws have a low trajectory, which comes through the thrower's shoulder. The athlete wants a "low screamer" into the wind at an angle of about 22 degrees in relation to the ground. Exercises using wooden pegs set at different angles in relation to the throwing circle as targets are helpful in developing the ability to throw the discus where it should be going for the greatest benefit to the thrower.

Discus Throwing Faults

One fault of discus throwers is getting ahead of the feet. When this happens, the throw becomes an "arm" throw, since the rest of the body contributes nothing to it. The body will often be thrown off balance. This sometimes is a result of trying to cross the ring too fast, when the thrower cannot keep himself under control and handle the extra speed.

Another fault is throwing too soon. This problem also results in the same problems as the first fault. The thrower is getting little benefit from any portion of the body other than his arm.

Some throwers tend to carry the discus too low at the end of the turn, resulting in a steeply angled release and a flight which is too high. This is another problem of control of the arms. Its correction is extremely important, since a high trajectory results in a very poor discus flight.

Finally, lack of control over the direction in which the discus will travel can be a handicap for the thrower. Keeping within the legal throwing zone is not too great a problem for most throwers. However, wind conditions can be very disadvantageous at times, or they can be used to the athlete's considerable benefit. The athlete should learn to aim his throws, using exercises such as the suggested peg exercise.

A Typical Training Week for the Discus Thrower

Schedules are given for the entire year for the discus thrower, but the basic training principle is the hard-easy training cycle. An example of one week of training along the suggested hard-easy cycle is given here and can be considered a "typical" week of training:

Monday: Warm-up routine:
Four standing throws, working on leading with the chest and nose
Four throws after a turn, working as above
Four throws standing, work on a long pull
Four throws turning, working on a long pull
Four to six throws alternately standing and crossing the ring
25-yard wind-sprints

Tuesday: Weight training work
Jogging and flexibility exercises

Wednesday: Same throwing cycles of standing, then turning, as Monday, except working on (1) keeping the hips ahead of the arm, (2) throwing through the shoulder, and (3) left arm coordination.

Thursday: Weight training work
Jogging and flexibility exercises

Figure 13.1a Discus Throw Training Schedule

Discus Throw NAME DATE *September/October*

1. A. Jog 1 or 2 laps, easy stretching B. Weights and jog
   C.
2. Fartlek run A. Varied pace B. Slow, steady
3. Weights and resistance activities
4. A. Stand, foot in center of ring
   B. Cross the ring C. Stand, step, turn
5. A. Stand (1) Easy (2) Medium (3) Hard
   B. Cross (1) Easy (2) Medium (3) Hard
6. A. Standing throws B. Crossing the ring
   (1) Knee bend and lift (2) Maximum reach back or torque
   (3) Lead with chest and nose (4) Long pull
   (5) Hips cocked to uncocked (6) Through the shoulder
   (7) Other arm coordination (8) Back knee bend-lift
   (9) Discus flight
7. Squad meeting
8. Special A. Sauna B. Swim C. Steps or hill
9. Alternate standing and crossing the ring, same numbers as in item 6.
10. Trial or competition—record results below
    A. 3/4 to 7/8 effort B. 9/10 to full effort
11. Cross ring easy, feeling of exploding at finish. Start slow, finish fast.
12. With A. Coach B.
14. A. Wind sprints B. Starts, go 25 yds.
    C. High knee and fast leg D. Hurdles E. Spring and bound
    F. Alternate run-walk, go 880 or more
15. A. Park run B. Golf course run
16. Tumbling activities for agility
17. Get over rear leg—lift with legs
18. Position A. Staying in the ring B. Good position at end of turn—lift and unwind
19. A. Throw into net B. Throw at target C. Ring crossing, feet not too far spread, speed you can control. Same as item 6.
20. Secondary event work
21. A. Pictures B. Film C. Video
22. A. Slow down and be back over rear leg for long lift and unwind
    B. Pull the discus—lift and push with toes

Date	3/4	7/8	Goal	Date

M	*Class or squad organization*
T	*3-14F*
W	*1A-14B-6A(4)-6B(4)-19B-14F*
T	*21A-3*
F	*1-14A-6A(5)-6A(8)-19A-14F*
S	*3-14F*
S	*1B*
M	*1-14A-4X 6A(4)-4X 9A(4)-4X 6B(4)-4X 6A(5)-14C*
T	*3-14C*
W	*7-14A-9A(5)-19B-11*
T	*3-14A*
F	*1-14A-6A(1)-19C(5)*
S	*Choice*
S	*3*
M	*1-14A-4C-4X 6A(7)-4X 6B(7)-19-14A*
T	*3-2A*
W	*1-14F-6A(3)-6B(3)-6A(8)-6B(8)-14A*
T	*3-8A or 8B*
F	*1-14A-6A(9)-19B-19C-14F*
S	*7*
S	
M	*1-14A-5-10X 19C(5)-5-10X 19C(2)-17-14F*
T	*2B-14A*
W	*7-1-14A-10A-12-9A(9)-14A*
T	*3-8*
F	*1-19C-10A-19B-14A*
S	*3*
S	*1-19B*

Figure 13.1b Discus Throw Training Schedule

Discus Throw NAME DATE October/November

1. A. Jog 1 or 2 laps, easy stretching B. Weights and jog
   C.
2. Fartlek run A. Varied pace B. Slow, steady
3. Weights and resistance activities
4. A. Stand, foot in center of ring
   B. Cross the ring C. Stand, step, turn
5. A. Stand (1) Easy (2) Medium (3) Hard
   B. Cross (1) Easy (2) Medium (3) Hard
6. A. Standing throws B. Crossing the ring
   (1) Knee bend and lift (2) Maximum reach back or torque
   (3) Lead with chest and nose (4) Long pull
   (5) Hips cocked to uncocked (6) Through the shoulder
   (7) Other arm coordination (8) Back knee bend-lift
   (9) Discus flight
7. Squad meeting
8. Special A. Sauna B. Swim C. Steps or hill
9. Alternate standing and crossing the ring, same numbers as in item 6.
10. Trial or competition—record results below
    A. 3/4 to 7/8 effort B. 9/10 to full effort
11. Cross ring easy, feeling of exploding at finish. Start slow, finish fast.
12. With A. Coach B.
14. A. Wind sprints B. Starts, go 25 yds.
    C. High knee and fast leg D. Hurdles E. Spring and bound
    F. Alternate run-walk, go 880 or more
15. A. Park run B. Golf course run
16. Tumbling activities for agility
17. Get over rear leg—lift with legs
18. Position A. Staying in the ring B. Good position at end of turn—lift and unwind
19. A. Throw into net B. Throw at target C. Ring crossing, feet not too far spread, speed you can control. Same as item 6.
20. Secondary event work
21. A. Pictures B. Film C. Video
22. A. Slow down and be back over rear leg for long lift and unwind
    B. Pull the discus—lift and push with toes

Date	3/4	7/8	Goal	Date

M	1A-4-6A(7)-9A(7)-19B-2B
T	7-1A-20
W	1A-5A-5B-9A(4)-9A(5)-14A
T	1A-3
F	10-20-14F
S	3
S	3

M	1A-14A-6A(4)-6B(4)-9A(4)-2A (4x, 4x, 4-8x)
T	3
W	1A-9A(3)-11-14F
T	3
F	1A-20
S	3
S	3

M	1A-14A-9A(2)-14A (3x)
T	10-20
W	7-3
T	1A-14F-4A
F	1A-4-5-11-18A-14F
S	3
S	3

M	1-14A-19C(5)-19C(2)-22A-14A (5-10x, 5-10x)
T	3
W	1-4A-4B-5AB-9A(5)
T	Light-3
F	1-14A-10A-14A-10A-19C-Jog (3x, 3x)
S	3
S	3

Figure 13.1c Discus Throw Training Schedule

Discus Throw NAME DATE *November/December*

1. A. Jog 1 or 2 laps, easy stretching B. Weights and jog
   C.
2. Fartlek run A. Varied pace B. Slow, steady
3. Weights and resistance activities
4. A. Stand, foot in center of ring
   B. Cross the ring C. Stand, step, turn
5. A. Stand (1) Easy (2) Medium (3) Hard
   B. Cross (1) Easy (2) Medium (3) Hard
6. A. Standing throws B. Crossing the ring
   (1) Knee bend and lift (2) Maximum reach back or torque
   (3) Lead with chest and nose (4) Long pull
   (5) Hips cocked to uncocked (6) Through the shoulder
   (7) Other arm coordination (8) Back knee bend-lift
   (9) Discus flight
7. Squad meeting
8. Special A. Sauna B. Swim C. Steps or hill
9. Alternate standing and crossing the ring, same numbers as in item 6.
10. Trial or competition—record results below
    A. 3/4 to 7/8 effort B. 9/10 to full effort
11. Cross ring easy, feeling of exploding at finish. Start slow, finish fast.
12. With A. Coach B.
14. A. Wind sprints B. Starts, go 25 yds.
    C. High knee and fast leg D. Hurdles E. Spring and bound
    F. Alternate run-walk, go 880 or more
15. A. Park run B. Golf course run
16. Tumbling activities for agility
17. Get over rear leg—lift with legs
18. Position A. Staying in the ring B. Good position at end of turn—lift and unwind
19. A. Throw into net B. Throw at target C. Ring crossing, feet not too far spread, speed you can control. Same as item 6.
20. Secondary event work
21. A. Pictures B. Film C. Video
22. A. Slow down and be back over rear leg for long lift and unwind
    B. Pull the discus—lift and push with toes

Date	3/4	7/8	Goal	Date

M	*1A-6A(4)-6A(5)-6B(3)-9-14F*
T	*3*
W	*1A-21A-17-11*
T	*3*
F	*1-14A*
S	*3*
S	*recreation*
M	*1-14F-6A(2)-6B(2)-11-14A*
T	*3-8A or 8B*
W	*1-14F-6B(4)-11*
T	
F	*10A-10B*
S	*Assist with cross country*
S	*recreation*
M	
T	
W	
T	
F	
S	
S	
M	
T	
W	
T	
F	
S	
S	

Figure 13.1d Discus Throw Training Schedule

Discus Throw NAME DATE January

1. A. Jog 1 or 2 laps, easy stretching B. Weights and jog C.
2. Fartlek run A. Varied pace B. Slow, steady
3. Weights and resistance activities
4. A. Stand, foot in center of ring B. Cross the ring C. Stand, step, turn
5. A. Stand (1) Easy (2) Medium (3) Hard
   B. Cross (1) Easy (2) Medium (3) Hard
6. A. Standing throws B. Crossing the ring
   (1) Knee bend and lift (2) Maximum reach back or torque
   (3) Lead with chest and nose (4) Long pull
   (5) Hips cocked to uncocked (6) Through the shoulder
   (7) Other arm coordination (8) Back knee bend-lift
   (9) Discus flight
7. Squad meeting
8. Special A. Sauna B. Swim C. Steps or hill
9. Alternate standing and crossing the ring, same numbers as in item 6.
10. Trial or competition—record results below
    A. 3/4 to 7/8 effort B. 9/10 to full effort
11. Cross ring easy, feeling of exploding at finish. Start slow, finish fast.
12. With A. Coach B.
14. A. Wind sprints B. Starts, go 25 yds.
    C. High knee and fast leg D. Hurdles E. Spring and bound
    F. Alternate run-walk, go 880 or more
15. A. Park run B. Golf course run
16. Tumbling activities for agility
17. Get over rear leg—lift with legs
18. Position A. Staying in the ring B. Good position at end of turn—lift and unwind
19. A. Throw into net B. Throw at target C. Ring crossing, feet not too far spread, speed you can control. Same as item 6.
20. Secondary event work
21. A. Pictures B. Film C. Video
22. A. Slow down and be back over rear leg for long lift and unwind
    B. Pull the discus—lift and push with toes

Date	3/4	7/8	Goal	Date

M	Week of class organization – 3
T	Squad organization – 1 – 3
W	Registration – 1 – 3 – 16
T	7 – 1A – 4AB – 6A(7) – 6B(7) – 4AB
F	3 – 5
S	1A – 4AB – 6A(6) – 11 – 14A
S	
M	1A – 3 – 14A – 6A(5) – 6B(5) – 11 – 14A
T	1A – 3
W	1A – 6A(4) – 6B(4) – 11 – 4AB – 14F
T	1A – 3
F	1A – 4AB – 5 – 10 – 4AB – 14F
S	3
S	3
M	1A – 4AB – 9A(8) – 17 – 14A
T	3
W	1A – 14A – 4AB – 6A(1) – 6B(1) – 11 – 18A – 14F
T	3
F	10(4 to 6 throws) – 4AB – 14A
S	3
S	3
M	1A – 3 – 14A
T	1A – 4AB – 9A(1) – 14A – 14F
W	7 – 1A – 3 – 14F
T	1A – 6A – 11 – 22 – 14A
F	3 – 14A
S	1A – 4AB – 9A(8) – 18B – 22 – 14F
S	3 – 14F

Figure 13.1e Discus Throw Training Schedule

Discus Throw NAME DATE February

1. A. Jog 1 or 2 laps, easy stretching B. Weights and jog
   C.
2. Fartlek run A. Varied pace B. Slow, steady
3. Weights and resistance activities
4. A. Stand, foot in center of ring
   B. Cross the ring C. Stand, step, turn
5. A. Stand (1) Easy (2) Medium (3) Hard
   B. Cross (1) Easy (2) Medium (3) Hard
6. A. Standing throws B. Crossing the ring
   (1) Knee bend and lift (2) Maximum reach back or torque
   (3) Lead with chest and nose (4) Long pull
   (5) Hips cocked to uncocked (6) Through the shoulder
   (7) Other arm coordination (8) Back knee bend-lift
   (9) Discus flight
7. Squad meeting
8. Special A. Sauna B. Swim C. Steps or hill
9. Alternate standing and crossing the ring, same numbers as in item 6.
10. Trial or competition—record results below
    A. 3/4 to 7/8 effort B. 9/10 to full effort
11. Cross ring easy, feeling of exploding at finish. Start slow, finish fast.
12. With A. Coach B.
14. A. Wind sprints B. Starts, go 25 yds.
    C. High knee and fast leg D. Hurdles E. Spring and bound
    F. Alternate run-walk, go 880 or more
15. A. Park run B. Golf course run
16. Tumbling activities for agility
17. Get over rear leg—lift with legs
18. Position A. Staying in the ring B. Good position at end of turn—lift and unwind
19. A. Throw into net B. Throw at target C. Ring crossing, feet not too far spread, speed you can control. Same as item 6.
20. Secondary event work
21. A. Pictures B. Film C. Video
22. A. Slow down and be back over rear leg for long lift and unwind
    B. Pull the discus—lift and push with toes

Date	3/4	7/8	Goal	Date

M	6-10x 1-6A(9)-17-9A(1)-6A(6)-14A
T	3-1A
W	6-10x 6-10x 1-14A-6A(6)-6B(6)-19B-14F
T	3-1A
F	1-21-10-9A(6)
S	3
S	
M	1-14A-3
T	6-10x 6-10x 6-10x 1-14A-19B-6A(5)-6B(5)-9A(5)-14A
W	3
T	4-6x 6-10x 1-14A-19A-6A(3)-10(today or Sat.)-14F
F	3
S	10-20
S	
M	1-3-14A
T	6-10x 6-10x 6-10x 1-14A-6A(3)-9A(8)-9A(6)-14A
W	1-3-8A or 8B
T	4-8x 1-14A-9B-6A(6)-14A
F	Jog-3
S	1-14A-19B-10B-14E
S	
M	1A-3-14B
T	6-10x 6-10x 1A-14A-6A(6)-6B(6)-11-19A
W	3
T	1A-10-20-16
F	3
S	3
S	

Figure 13.1f Discus Throw Training Schedule

Discus Throw NAME DATE March

1. A. Jog 1 or 2 laps, easy stretching B. Weights and jog
   C.
2. Fartlek run A. Varied pace B. Slow, steady
3. Weights and resistance activities
4. A. Stand, foot in center of ring
   B. Cross the ring C. Stand, step, turn
5. A. Stand (1) Easy (2) Medium (3) Hard
   B. Cross (1) Easy (2) Medium (3) Hard
6. A. Standing throws B. Crossing the ring
   (1) Knee bend and lift (2) Maximum reach back or torque
   (3) Lead with chest and nose (4) Long pull
   (5) Hips cocked to uncocked (6) Through the shoulder
   (7) Other arm coordination (8) Back knee bend-lift
   (9) Discus flight
7. Squad meeting
8. Special A. Sauna B. Swim C. Steps or hill
9. Alternate standing and crossing the ring, same numbers as in item 6.
10. Trial or competition—record results below
    A. 3/4 to 7/8 effort B. 9/10 to full effort
11. Cross ring easy, feeling of exploding at finish. Start slow, finish fast.
12. With A. Coach B.
14. A. Wind sprints B. Starts, go 25 yds.
    C. High knee and fast leg D. Hurdles E. Spring and bound
    F. Alternate run-walk, go 880 or more
15. A. Park run B. Golf course run
16. Tumbling activities for agility
17. Get over rear leg—lift with legs
18. Position A. Staying in the ring B. Good position at end of turn—lift and unwind
19. A. Throw into net B. Throw at target C. Ring crossing, feet not too far spread, speed you can control. Same as item 6.
20. Secondary event work
21. A. Pictures B. Film C. Video
22. A. Slow down and be back over rear leg for long lift and unwind
    B. Pull the discus—lift and push with toes

M	3-14F
T	10-20x 1A-6A(9)-11A(1)-11A(5)-14F
W	1B-3-14A
T	1A-22A-20-14A-Gear ready
F	Gear ready
S	10-Meet or trials
S	

	AM	PM
M	Jog	1A-3
T	Jog	1A-6A(2)-9A(2)-22
W	Jog	3
T	Jog	4x 1A-10-11-14A
F	Light-gear ready	
S	10-Meet	
S	Home	

M	1-14A-6A(6)-6B(6)-11-19B-14F
T	1A-3
W	1-10 or 20-19B-18B
T	1-16-14F
F	1-18B-9A(2)-11-14F-9A(3)-18B
S	1A-1B-14F
S	1A-14F

M	1A-14F-18B-19B-9A(4)-18B-19A
T	1A-3
W	1A-6A(3)-19B
T	1-3
F	Gear ready
S	10-Meet
S	Jog or recreation

Date	3/4	7/8	Goal	Date

Figure 13.1g Discus Throw Training Schedule

Discus Throw NAME DATE April

1. A. Jog 1 or 2 laps, easy stretching B. Weights and jog
   C.
2. Fartlek run A. Varied pace B. Slow, steady
3. Weights and resistance activities
4. A. Stand, foot in center of ring
   B. Cross the ring C. Stand, step, turn
5. A. Stand (1) Easy (2) Medium (3) Hard
   B. Cross (1) Easy (2) Medium (3) Hard
6. A. Standing throws B. Crossing the ring
   (1) Knee bend and lift (2) Maximum reach back or torque
   (3) Lead with chest and nose (4) Long pull
   (5) Hips cocked to uncocked (6) Through the shoulder
   (7) Other arm coordination (8) Back knee bend-lift
   (9) Discus flight
7. Squad meeting
8. Special A. Sauna B. Swim C. Steps or hill
9. Alternate standing and crossing the ring, same numbers as in item 6.
10. Trial or competition—record results below
    A. 3/4 to 7/8 effort B. 9/10 to full effort
11. Cross ring easy, feeling of exploding at finish. Start slow, finish fast.
12. With A. Coach B.
14. A. Wind sprints B. Starts, go 25 yds.
    C. High knee and fast leg D. Hurdles E. Spring and bound
    F. Alternate run-walk, go 880 or more
15. A. Park run B. Golf course run
16. Tumbling activities for agility
17. Get over rear leg—lift with legs
18. Position A. Staying in the ring B. Good position at end of turn—lift and unwind
19. A. Throw into net B. Throw at target C. Ring crossing, feet not too far spread, speed you can control. Same as item 6.
20. Secondary event work
21. A. Pictures B. Film C. Video
22. A. Slow down and be back over rear leg for long lift and unwind
    B. Pull the discus—lift and push with toes

M	1A-9A(4)-11-19B-14A-14F
T	1-9A(5)-11-19A-14F-14A
W	7-1A-3-grass
T	1-22A-18B
F	Light and gear ready
S	10-Meet
S	3-10-14F
M	Light
T	1A-6A(8)-6B(8)-22B-19B-14F
W	7-Light
T	1-6A(6)-6B(6)-18B-11-14F
F	Gear ready
S	10-Meet
S	3A-1A
M	1A-18B-9A(5)-11-14A-14B
T	1A (light)
W	1-6A(3)-18B-11-14A-14B
T	Light
F	Gear ready
S	10-Meet
S	1A-18B-9A(3)-11-10-14F
M	Light
T	1-6A(4)-6B(4)-19B-11-3
W	7-Light
T	Gear ready
F	Jog
S	10-Meet
S	3

Date	3/4	7/8	Goal	Date

Figure 13.1h Discus Throw Training Schedule

Discus Throw NAME DATE May

1. A. Jog 1 or 2 laps, easy stretching B. Weights and jog
   C.
2. Fartlek run A. Varied pace B. Slow, steady
3. Weights and resistance activities
4. A. Stand, foot in center of ring
   B. Cross the ring C. Stand, step, turn
5. A. Stand (1) Easy (2) Medium (3) Hard
   B. Cross (1) Easy (2) Medium (3) Hard
6. A. Standing throws B. Crossing the ring
   (1) Knee bend and lift (2) Maximum reach back or torque
   (3) Lead with chest and nose (4) Long pull
   (5) Hips cocked to uncocked (6) Through the shoulder
   (7) Other arm coordination (8) Back knee bend-lift
   (9) Discus flight
7. Squad meeting
8. Special A. Sauna B. Swim C. Steps or hill
9. Alternate standing and crossing the ring, same numbers as in item 6.
10. Trial or competition—record results below
    A. 3/4 to 7/8 effort B. 9/10 to full effort
11. Cross ring easy, feeling of exploding at finish. Start slow, finish fast.
12. With A. Coach B.
14. A. Wind sprints B. Starts, go 25 yds.
    C. High knee and fast leg D. Hurdles E. Spring and bound
    F. Alternate run-walk, go 880 or more
15. A. Park run B. Golf course run
16. Tumbling activities for agility
17. Get over rear leg—lift with legs
18. Position A. Staying in the ring B. Good position at end of turn—lift and unwind
19. A. Throw into net B. Throw at target C. Ring crossing, feet not too far spread, speed you can control. Same as item 6.
20. Secondary event work
21. A. Pictures B. Film C. Video
22. A. Slow down and be back over rear leg for long lift and unwind
    B. Pull the discus—lift and push with toes

Date	3/4	7/8	Goal	Date

M	Light
T	Light
W	7-10 (Meet-night)
T	1A-9A(7)-18B-22B-14B-14A
F	Light
S	Light
S	Squad picnic
M	1A-10
T	3x 1-19B-3
W	Light
T	Light
F	1-9A(6)-18B-19B-14A-14F
S	1-9A(8)-18B-17-14F-14A
S	3x 1-19B-3 or form work
M	1-3 (light)-14B
T	3-6x 11-Jog
W	Light
T	Light
F	Qualifying-Pac 8 Meet
S	Finals-Pac 8 Meet
S	
M	
T	
W	
T	
F	
S	
S	

Figure 13.1i Discus Throw Training Schedule

Discus Throw NAME DATE June

1. A. Jog 1 or 2 laps, easy stretching B. Weights and jog C.
2. Fartlek run A. Varied pace B. Slow, steady
3. Weights and resistance activities
4. A. Stand, foot in center of ring B. Cross the ring C. Stand, step, turn
5. A. Stand (1) Easy (2) Medium (3) Hard
   B. Cross (1) Easy (2) Medium (3) Hard
6. A. Standing throws B. Crossing the ring
   (1) Knee bend and lift (2) Maximum reach back or torque
   (3) Lead with chest and nose (4) Long pull
   (5) Hips cocked to uncocked (6) Through the shoulder
   (7) Other arm coordination (8) Back knee bend-lift
   (9) Discus flight
7. Squad meeting
8. Special A. Sauna B. Swim C. Steps or hill
9. Alternate standing and crossing the ring, same numbers as in item 6.
10. Trial or competition—record results below A. 3/4 to 7/8 effort B. 9/10 to full effort
11. Cross ring easy, feeling of exploding at finish. Start slow, finish fast.
12. With A. Coach B.
14. A. Wind sprints B. Starts, go 25 yds. C. High knee and fast leg D. Hurdles E. Spring and bound F. Alternate run-walk, go 880 or more
15. A. Park run B. Golf course run
16. Tumbling activities for agility
17. Get over rear leg—lift with legs
    Position A. Staying in the ring B. Good position at end of turn—lift and unwind
    A. Throw into net B. Throw at target C. Ring crossing, feet not too far spread, speed you can control. Same as item 6.
20. Secondary event work
21. A. Pictures B. Film C. Video
22. A. Slow down and be back over rear leg for long lift and unwind
    B. Pull the discus—lift and push with toes

Date	3/4	7/8	Goal	Date

M	Exams start - 3
T	1A - 6A(6) - 11A - 17 - 18B - 14F
W	Light
T	1A - 10 (3X) as in Trials
F	1A - 10 (3X) as in Finals
S	Final exams completed
S	1A - Form work or loosen up
M	17 - 18B
T	Easy form work
W	Travel and loosen up
T	1st day Prelims - NCAA Meet
F	2nd day Prelims - NCAA
S	Finals - NCAA
S	
M	
T	
W	
T	
F	
S	
S	
M	
T	
W	
T	
F	
S	
S	

Friday or Saturday: Semitrials: find out how many throws it takes for the man to reach his best mark. Throw in sets of three throws, with 5-minute breaks, as in competition. Where do the throws begin to taper off? Where are the longer ones? Might throw three and three, sprint for a bit, throw four and four, sprint again, and so forth.

Discus Throw Bibliography

Cooper, Carl W. "The discus throw," *Track and Field Quarterly Review,* February 1964, pp. 64–66.

Davis, Dave. "General weight training for throwers," *Track Technique,* No. 51 (March 1973), pp. 1632–35.

Dunn, George, Jr. "Common errors in the discus," *Athletic Journal* 49 (March 1969): 52.

"Foot contact at the instant of release in throwing," trans. by Charles L. Sullivan, *Track Technique,* No. 9 (September 1962), pp. 271–74.

Ganslen, Richard V. "Aerodynamic and mechanical forces in discus flight," *Athletic Journal* 44 (April 1964): 50, 52, 68, 88–89.

Gemer, George V. "The Munich discus throw: observations and comments," *Track Technique,* No. 53 (September 1973), pp. 1695–96.

Gordien, Fortune. "Stress 'technique' in the discus," *Scholastic Coach* 42 (February 1973): 26, 28.

Ivanova, L. "A new strength training approach for discus throwers," *Track Technique,* No. 50 (December 1972), pp. 1602–3.

Jesse, John P. "A new look at strength development for discus throwers," *Track and Field Quarterly Review,* June 1966, pp. 23–31.

Le Masurier, John. *Discus Throwing.* 2d ed. London: BAAB, 1972. 40 pp.

Lockwood, Bert. "The double-turn throw," *Track Technique,* No. 35 (March 1969), pp. 1111–14.

Long, Leo. "Discus throwing technique," *Athletic Journal* 53 (February 1973): 8–9, 91–94.

Maughan, Ralph B. "Discus throwing technique," *Track and Field Quarterly Review,* October 1967, pp. 40–43.

Morris, Frank. "Common errors in the discus," *Scholastic Coach* 42 (March 1973): 24, 103.

———. "Form study of Ricky Bruch," *Scholastic Coach* 42 (April 1973): 14–15, 117.

———. "Mechanics of the discus," *Scholastic Coach* 42 (February 1973): 59–60, 99.

———. "Simplifying discus technique," *Track Technique,* No. 50 (December 1972), pp. 1603–5.

O'Connor, W. Harold. "The legs in discus throwing," *Scholastic Coach* 37 (February 1968): 7, 58–59.

Paisch, Wilf. "Teaching the discus throw," *Track Technique,* No. 42 (December 1970), pp. 1331–33.

Powell, John T. "Danek's discus delivery," *Track and Field Quarterly Review,* December 1966, pp. 32–35.

Robison, Clarence. "Discus throwing," *Track and Field Quarterly Review,* October 1964, pp. 61–65.

Simonyi, Gabor, and Felton, Sam. "Discus throwing from A to Silvester," *Scholastic Coach* 39 (April 1970): 9–11, 108–14.

Thomas, Charlie. "Training for the shot and discus double," *Athletic Journal* 46 (January 1966): 51–52, 71–72.

_______. "The training technique of Randy Matson," *Track and Field Quarterly Review,* December 1965, pp. 21–28.

Thomas, Robert. "Variables in the discus throw," *Track and Field Quarterly Review*, May 1968, pp. 37–57.

Vrabel, Jan. "Discus and the wind," *Track Technique,* No. 21 (September 1965), pp. 644–45.

Wachowsky, E., and Tan Eng Yoon, Pat. "Significant deviations from correct discus technique," *Track Technique,* No. 19 (March 1965), pp. 586–88.

Ward, Paul. "Analysis of the discus throw," *Track Technique,* No. 37 (September 1969), pp. 1176–83.

The javelin throw

14

The javelin throw is perhaps the most military of track and field events. It was contested by the Greeks as an event important to military prowess, for the javelin was an important weapon of that period. The ability to throw the javelin well was a mark of military skill in that day. Today the military has no need for javelins, but the event survives. Children still play at throwing spears, then graduate to the intricacies of the javelin. Technique becomes all-important, for the throwing form used with the javelin is not a natural motion. While the military value of the javelin throw has passed, the beauty of a good throw survives.

Analysis of a Javelin Throw Sequence

The sequence used here shows a world record holder. Photograph 14.1, page 286, is of Janis Lusis, the Russian Olympic champion. Photograph 14.1*k* picks him up on his cross step as he pushes off step two of his final five steps. The speed of his approach is evident (Photograph 14.1*l*) as the cross step continues, then he plants his right foot (Photograph 14.1*m*) to begin the actual throw. His throwing arm is extended back, and his lead arm is across his body. As he continues into the throw (Photograph 14.1*n*), he is already bringing his lead arm around to provide more pull for the throw. His left leg is extended to plant and provide a break on his forward momentum, which will be transferred to the javelin. As he plants the heel of the left foot (Photograph 14.1*o*), he is in a strong throwing

Photographs 14.1*a-t*   Janis Lusis of Russia, in the javelin throw.

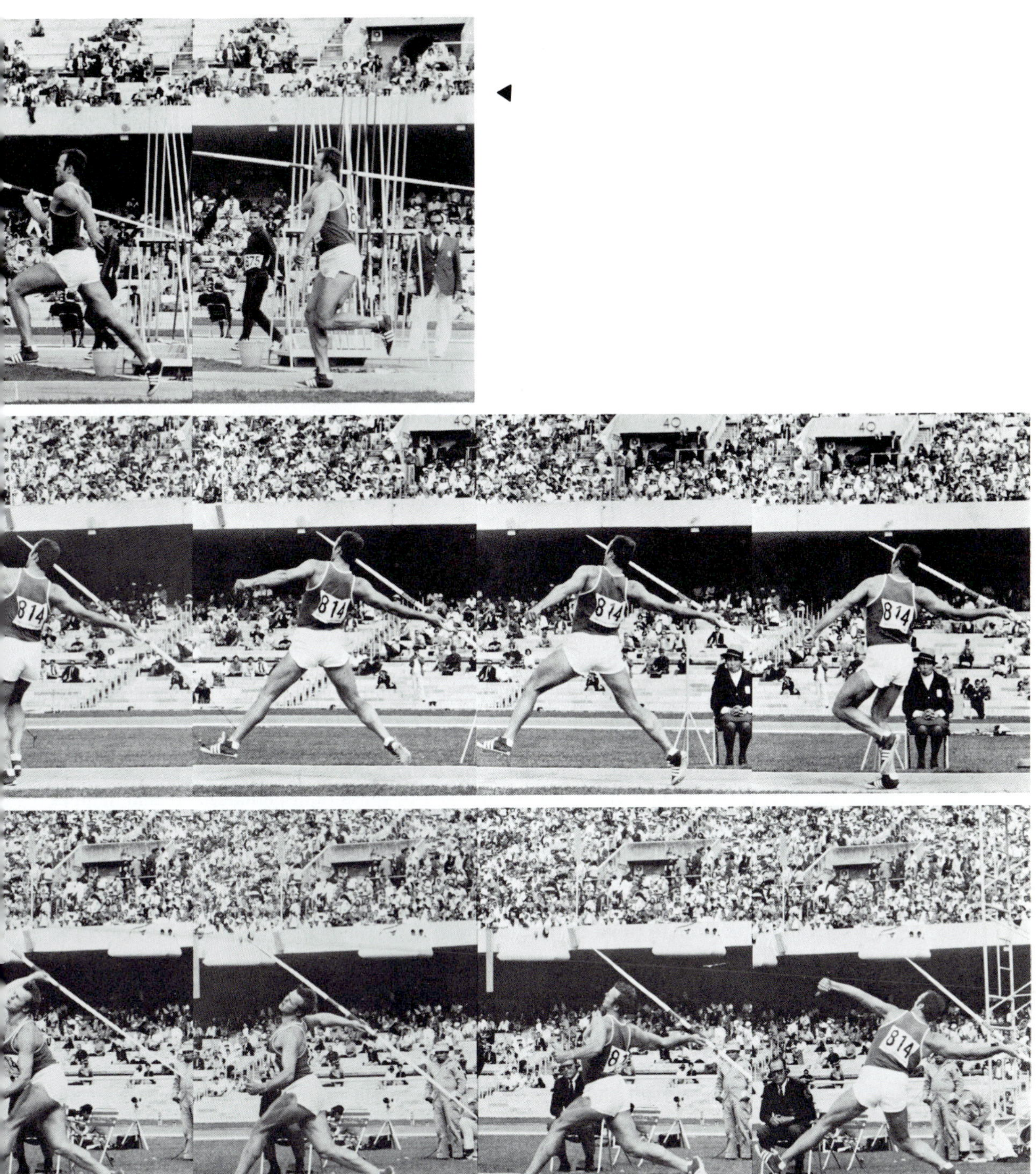

814
p
o

position. He is already pulling the javelin forward and bringing his left arm around to provide additional pull. He is providing additional push with his right leg and beginning to rotate his torso into the throw. As he continues the throw (Photograph 14.1*p*), he has rotated his body into the throw, and he is keeping his lead leg rigid, forcing the body to go over it. As he releases the javelin, he still has his pushing right foot in contact with the ground (Photograph 14.1*s*). In Photograph 14.1*t* he is continuing forward, still going *over* the left foot. He will land on his right foot, the fifth step of the final five, stopping his forward movement short of the foul line.

Common Faults of Javelin Throwers

One of the greatest faults, especially with American throwers, is the tendency to throw the javelin to the side, rather than bring it across the shoulder. This probably results from the common throwing technique used with a baseball, which may be delivered over the elbow, held out to the side of the shoulder, or even thrown side-armed. This throwing form not only will result in a poorer throw, but will also put a much greater strain on the arm and elbow than the correct over-the-shoulder delivery.

Another fault is throwing the javelin, rather than *pulling* it. Most of the work in a good javelin throw is done before the hand comes over the shoulder, rather than after the hand has passed the shoulder and is in the process of throwing. Much better results will be gained by concentrating on *pulling* the javelin through the throw.

A great weakness in many throwers is the lack of body pull. The arm is not everything in throwing the javelin. The thrower must coordinate the entire body into the throw. When the athlete learns to throw with the arms and legs and body, he is beginning to develop from a learner to a *thrower.*

Premature lift of the left foot (if the thrower is right-handed) can also hamper good throwing considerably, as previously mentioned. This problem may also develop from American ball games, using a "reverse" of the feet after throwing, much as one does in the shot. The thrower should stay on the left leg until he goes *over* it. It should not be pulled out at any stage of the throw, since it is helping to contribute to the shifting of the athlete's momentum from straight ahead to the launching of the javelin itself.

A final fault is not technical: throwing the javelin hard too often in practice. Notice that all the training described here consists of throwing at levels varying from easy throwing to seven-eighths effort, but *never* at full effort. Frequent full effort throwing usually has one result: injuries, most frequently to the elbow region. Holding back the effort of the throws will not hamper the success of the thrower. In 1964 Oregon had a thrower with a very bad elbow, Gary Reddaway. In the first meet of the season, in late March, he threw well enough to qualify for the NCAA meet. He was then held out of all other meets until the NCAA in mid-June. He went through his practice routines doing *only* easy throwing, and that with a tennis ball. He was able to get into the NCAA finals on a single throw of 219 feet 10 inches. He made a vast improvement on his second throw in the finals to 246 feet 1½ inches and finished in the middle as Oregon took the first three places.

One point which might help in holding back athletes who want to throw hard consistently: do not let them use new javelins in practice. They will want to see how far they will go. With an old javelin, the athletes know it will not go as far, so they will settle down and work on technique instead. All the throwing in routines can be done just as well, and probably more safely, with weighted balls, such as a tennis ball filled with shotgun bird shot.

Comments on Javelin Training

There is no ideal size to look for in the prospective javelin thrower. Top throwers have been as large as 6 feet 6 inches or so tall, yet the world record has been held by men as small as 5 feet 7 inches tall and 165 pounds in weight. The coach is looking for the well-coordinated individual with a good throwing arm. Tests such as the softball or football throw have been used for locating prospects, but perhaps the most accurate indicator is throwing an 800-gram weighted ball, the same weight as the javelin.

There are two major grips to be considered in holding the javelin, the fork and Finnish grips. The fork grip is a simple style, consisting of holding the javelin between the index and middle fingers, with the fingers against the rear of the cord grip of the javelin. This style has been used partly because of its simplicity and partly for other reasons (Oregon's Boyd Brown, who set an American record at 234 feet 1½ inches in 1940, used the fork grip because he had lost his thumb in an accident).

The Finnish grip consists of laying the cord grip of the javelin through the palm at the middle of the hand, the middle finger encircling the spear at the rear of the cord grip, with the thumb around the opposite side of the grip, and the index finger extended back and to the same side of the javelin as the middle finger. Keep in mind that the object is to see how far you can throw the javelin, not how prettily it can be held.

Where the approach run to the throw is concerned, there have been two major styles of throwing the javelin. The simplest, but not necessarily the best, is the old-fashioned "American hop" in which the thrower runs up to the throwing position, then turns sideways with a hop to get into a good throwing position. Unfortunately, while the approach is simple to learn, much of the benefit of a speedy run is lost with this style of throwing.

The Finnish style, or variations of it, is the most commonly used style in the world today. As the thrower reaches the final steps of his approach, he gradually turns his feet slightly to the side of his throwing arm and goes into a fast cross step or series of cross-steps to get into a powerful throwing position. While this style is more difficult to learn than the American style, it has greater advantages in the utilization of the thrower's speed. The basic throwing motion, regardless of the grip or approach style, is close to the ear and over the shoulder.

The Finns have a long and illustrious history as javelin throwers and will continue to produce champions with their youth program. Consequently, much of the current knowledge and theory of javelin technique has come from their experience. While the gradual refinement of technique has played an important role in the improvement of records in the javelin, technological advances in javelin design and construction have also contributed greatly to longer throws. At one time the javelin was little more than a long, unwieldy stick. Now it is an aerodynamically designed precision tool continually undergoing further advances in its design. The athletes, too, have "gimmicks," some of which make their implements illegal, such as tampering with the grip, shaft construction, and weight of the javelin. The first approved world record (1912) was 204 feet 5½ inches; the current record is 100 feet beyond that point.

In training the thrower should progress from standing throws to throws with a short run, then to throws with a full run. This is done in a regular routine which is repeated before every workout in which any throwing is done. The standing technique can be done beneficially with a weighted ball instead of the javelin. The ball is about the same weight as the javelin.

The first step of the routine is throwing three times from a stand at a target about 30 feet away. The thrower begins with his weight back over his rear leg and the knee bent (the right leg, if he throws right-handed). The front (left) leg is extended well to the front, pointing in the direction of the throw. The hips are turned at an angle of about 30 degrees away from the line of direction of the throw. The torso is back, with the hips over the rear leg. The right arm (throwing arm) is extended to the rear comfortably, but not stretched. The left arm is usually across the chest, leading the torso in rotating into the throw. The hips and legs are used to give additional thrusting power and rotation to the body to impart to the javelin. The javelin is thrown when maximum pull, rotation, and whip of the body have been applied to the throw. The throwers will work at this last phase of the throw from the standing position for five to ten hours, then progress to the trotting throws.

The next step in the routine is the 3-4-5 exercise, which consists of going through the last three steps of the approach and throwing the weight or javelin three times at a target about 60 feet away. This gives the feel of moving the body into the final stages of the throw.

The last step in the routine is taking three throws going through the approach from the last check mark through the last five steps of the approach. These throws will be at a target about 90 feet away. After the routine is completed, the thrower may move on to more warm-up throws with an approach run.

The throwers may work with the trotting throws next. The purpose of the trotting throw is to add momentum to the other mechanics of the throw. With an easy trot of 10 to 20 steps, the javelin or weighted ball is brought back into throwing position, then thrown easily for 50 to 100 feet. This exercise is repeated about five times.

The final stage of the warm-up might be taking several throws, usually about five, with the full-approach run. This is especially important for getting the approach pattern and check marks down pat. Three check marks are recommended, though some throwers may use two marks or only one. The first mark will be 90 to 110 feet from the rear of the throwing arc, keeping in mind that international rules do not allow a run exceeding 120 feet. From the starting check mark to the second check should be four strides, then another ten strides to the final check, at the point where the last five strides, including the cross-stepping, are begun. The thrower wants to reach the throwing point with as much speed as he can control, though excessive speed hinders successful throwing more than it assists it. We want to reach the throwing point with good position and control. The last check mark, five strides from the completion of the throw, will be about 30 feet or so behind the throwing arc.

After the check marks have been practiced, nine throws with the javelin are taken, but *none* of them will be hard throws at full effort. Three throws will be made at half effort, followed by three throws at three-quarters effort, and finally three throws at seven-eighths effort.

For the progression of throwing in a competitive situation, the check marks should be set up first, then the warm-up cycle taken and followed by one or two throws. Do not throw away the "good ones." The thrower may find it helpful to follow a cycle or pattern with his competitive throws. The first throw would be a medium effort only, since the primary object of this throw is to get a safe throw, qualifying for the finals at the start of the competition. The second throw is a relatively hard throw, about seven-eights to nine-tenths effort, a bit of gamble. The thrower should attempt to explode with a full effort "big" throw on his third attempt. The same cycle is recommended for the final three throws, medium to hard to explosion.

For a general pattern of training, a good practice for the preseason is to throw on Monday, Wednesday, and Friday. When the season arrives, if the athlete's competitions are on Saturdays, he would throw on Saturday, be off (from throwing) on Sunday and Monday, then throw again on both Tuesday and Wednesday (to help him prepare for the experience of two-day competitions later in the season). He would do no throwing on Thursday and Friday leading into the next Saturday's competition. For a very big meet, there should be no throwing after Monday.

Several technical points of the approach and throw should be noted at this point. The lead foot comes into the throwing position pointed straight ahead or slightly to the right of the direction of the throw, while the trail foot is pointed slightly to the side. This allows the thrower to rotate his hips into the throw. The lead foot is not moved until the body has passed *over* it. The lead foot should come down either flat or on its ball. If the landing is made on the heel, the knee will be more likely to collapse and absorb much of the momentum of the approach run, rather than forcing the body to pass up and over the leg, passing the body's momentum on to the throw as a summation of forces. The lead arm should not be brought through too fast, or it will get too far ahead of the throw, limiting its effectiveness. The head should continue looking straight ahead throughout the throwing action, though there is a tendency to pull it down to the left as the throw is being made. The thrower should try either to look ahead or to watch the tip of the javelin. If the head is turned aside, the shoulders may not be squared to the throw or the legs may not be properly utilized. A very common throwing fault is pulling the front leg from under the body and executing a reverse, rather than going over the leg. Finally, the faster the javelin is thrown, the lower the trajectory can be. About 30 degrees is considered the ideal with the newer aerodynamic javelins. Always throw through the shaft and to the point of the javelin, trying to send it off at the optimum 30-degree angle, if possible.

Weight training is advantageous for the javelin thrower, as it is for the participants in most athletic events. The use of balls of various weights can be very beneficial. Some throwers recommend throwing javelins or balls weighing more than the regulation javelin. Whether the benefits of such training are physical or psychological is difficult to say at the moment, though most studies done along this line have not indicated any significant benefits. A similar idea calls for the use of underweight javelins and balls, such as the 600-gram javelin used in training for the 800-gram javelin. Theory suggests that the lighter implement will permit faster arm movement, gradually increasing the speed of arm movement, which will then be applied to the regulation javelin. This method has been successfully used by some individuals, but there have been no scientific studies of the technique published yet.

Interpretation of a Week's Training

The first week of the javelin throw training schedules will be translated from the numbers to show how the charts are interpreted. The training week begins on Monday and ends on the following Sunday.

Monday: The first week of training in the javelin, as with the other events, leads off with the organization of the class, if it is for physical education, or of the squad concerning equipment, practice periods, principles, squad meetings, and so forth.

Tuesday: (1A) This number represents the usual warm-up jog and flexibility exercises.

(5A) Starting in a standing position, the athlete throws into the grass nearby (15 to 30 feet away), or into a sand pit or other soft surface, gradually increasing the effort of his throws.

(16) Simple acrobatic activities not only are excellent conditioners, but also teach body control.

(14F) When time permits, every workout should be concluded with easy running.

Wednesday: (3) Weight training activities. In the section on weight training there are suggested resistance exercises. Most athletes develop their own weight training routines.

(14F) Running activities, alternating 55-yard intervals of running and walking or jogging for a half-mile or more.

(7) Squad meeting. The meeting time will be posted on the blackboard in the team dressing room.

Thursday: (1A) Warming-up activities already described.

(4A) Short check mark establishment is a critical and technical exercise. It is explained in some detail in the section which follows the schedules.

(19A) A softball or weighted ball of 1 to 3 pounds is an excellent substitute for throwing the javelin. It does not put the pressure on the arm which a javelin held in a bad position will. The same techniques as for the javelin are emphasized. If no net is available, throw up and down a field.

(14A) Wind sprints are short dashes of 25 to 50 yards with a recovery of 50 to 100 yards, whatever is needed. The thrower starts slowly, gradually increases to almost full effort, then slows down to recovery pace.

Friday: All Friday's activities have been described above.

Saturday: Weight training or some special activity. A sauna, if available, is recommended, as are many other healthful activities.

Sunday: What better way to finish a week or start a new one than in light recreation? We also use workout activities on occasion for the athlete who needs special attention on technique. It is also a great way to bring back to life those who spend "all hours" on the weekend in extracurricular expression of their personalities.

Explanation of the Fundamentals of Javelin Training

4A. Short check mark. The check marks for the javelin thrower are as important as those used in the jumping events. The "class" thrower knows almost to the inch how close he will come to the "scratch" line. This technique should be practiced on each throwing day.

To establish a short check mark, which is used for technique throwing, for inclement weather, or for when the thrower is having a bad competitive day, the thrower begins two steps before the first check mark (Figure 14.2). The first check mark is hit with the left foot, then the thrower continues for six steps to hit the T with his left foot. The T point is the start of the five-count final approach which includes the cross-step.

Figure 14.1a Javelin Throw Training Schedule

Javelin Throw NAME DATE September/October

1. A. Jog 1 or 2 laps, easy stretching B.
2. Fartlek A. Varied pace B. Steady pace
3. Weights and jogging
4. Check mark A. Short B. Long
5. A. Stand, throw 10 to 30 times
   B. Routine: throw 3 of each—easy, medium, hard.
   (1) 3 step, 45 ft.-90 ft. (2) 5 step, 90 ft.-150 ft.
   (3) Run and throw, 150 ft.-180 ft.
6. A. Short approach B. Long approach
   (1) Position of feet—keep lead foot down
   (2) Rear foot under—be over it
   (3) Body to right, body proceeds arm (4) Good pull
   (5) Cock the hand—rotate palm up
   (6) Over the shoulder, close to the ear
   (7) Through the shaft—keep tip low
   (8) Lead foot down quickly—pass over it
   (9)
7. Squad meeting
8. Special A. Sauna B. Swim C. Steps or hill
   D.
9. Full run and form throws—numbers as in item 6.
10. Test or compete—record below A. 1/2 to 3/4
    B. 3/4 to 7/8 C. 9/10
11. A. Start slow—finish fast B. Explosion
    C. Easy-medium-hard D.
12. With Coach A. B.
14. A. Wind sprints B. Starts, 25-40 yds.
    C. High knee and fast leg D. Hurdle drill
    E. Spring and bound F. Alternate walk-run, go 880 or more
15. A. Hendricks Park B. Laurel Golf Course C.
16. Tumbling activities
17. Have feeling of back and relaxed, no strain over rear leg
18. Work on staying behind scratch line
19. A. Throw ball into net B. Throw at target
20. Secondary event
21. A. Pictures B. Film C. Video

Date	3/4	7/8	Now	Goal

M	Class or squad organization
T	1A-5A-16-14D
W	3-14D-7
T	1A-4A-19A-14A
F	1A-5A-16-14D
S	3 or 8A
S	recreation
M	3-8A or B
T	1A-5A-6A(7)-4-7 at Student Union
W	3-4 or 8A
T	4-3-16
F	1A-5A-5B-14A
S	3-14D-8A or B
S	recreation-study
M	3-14A-Tuesday 12:30 S.U.
T	1A-5A-5B-14A-12:30 S.U.
W	3-8B
T	1A-4A-3-16
F	1A-Check gear-easy jog
S	1A-4A-4B-10A-14D
S	Usual
M	3-14A
T	1A-6A(2)-6B(2)-5B-4B-14D
W	3-14D
T	14A-3-16
F	1A-6A(2)-6B(2)-19A-14D
S	3
S	Usual

Figure 14.1b Javelin Throw Training Schedule

Javelin Throw NAME DATE October/November

1. A. Jog 1 or 2 laps, easy stretching B.
2. Fartlek A. Varied pace B. Steady pace
3. Weights and jogging
4. Check mark A. Short B. Long
5. A. Stand, throw 10 to 30 times
   B. Routine: throw 3 of each—easy, medium, hard.
   (1) 3 step, 45 ft.-90 ft. (2) 5 step, 90 ft.-150 ft.
   (3) Run and throw, 150 ft.-180 ft.
6. A. Short approach B. Long approach
   (1) Position of feet—keep lead foot down
   (2) Rear foot under—be over it
   (3) Body to right, body proceeds arm (4) Good pull
   (5) Cock the hand—rotate palm up
   (6) Over the shoulder, close to the ear
   (7) Through the shaft—keep tip low
   (8) Lead foot down quickly—pass over it
   (9)
7. Squad meeting
8. Special A. Sauna B. Swim C. Steps or hill
   D.
9. Full run and form throws—numbers as in item 6.
10. Test or compete—record below A. 1/2 to 3/4
    B. 3/4 to 7/8 C. 9/10
11. A. Start slow—finish fast B. Explosion
    C. Easy-medium-hard D.
12. With Coach A. B.
14. A. Wind sprints B. Starts, 25-40 yds.
    C. High knee and fast leg D. Hurdle drill
    E. Spring and bound F. Alternate walk-run, go 880 or more
15. A. Hendricks Park B. Laurel Golf Course C.
16. Tumbling activities
17. Have feeling of back and relaxed, no strain over rear leg
18. Work on staying behind scratch line
19. A. Throw ball into net B. Throw at target
20. Secondary event
21. A. Pictures B. Film C. Video

Date	3/4	7/8	Now	Goal

Day	Week 1
M	1A-3
T	Choice
W	1A-4A-5A(1)-5A(2)-5A(3)-19B-14D
T	3
F	1A-4A-4B-10B-14A-10A
S	3
S	Choice

Day	Week 2
M	1A-3
T	Choice
W	1A-4A-4B-5A-6A(8)-6A(7)-14D
T	3
F	1A-4A-4B-5A-6A(3)-17-14D
S	3-16
S	Usual

Day	Week 3
M	1A-3
T	3 or choice
W	1A-4A-4B-21-10A-19A-14A or 14D
T	Choice
F	1A-19A-19B-2A or 2B
S	3
S	Choice

Day	Week 4
M	1A-3-14A-8
T	3
W	1A-4A-4B-6A(8)-6B(8)-18-14C-2B
T	3-8A
F	1A-4A-4B-10(3 short run - 3 long run)
S	3
S	Choice

Figure 14.1e Javelin Throw Training Schedule

Javelin Throw NAME DATE *March*

1. A. Jog 1 or 2 laps, easy stretching B.
2. Fartlek A. Varied pace B. Steady pace
3. Weights and jogging
4. Check mark A. Short B. Long
5. A. Stand, throw 10 to 30 times
   B. Routine: throw 3 of each—easy, medium, hard.
   (1) 3 step, 45 ft.-90 ft. (2) 5 step, 90 ft.-150 ft.
   (3) Run and throw, 150 ft.-180 ft.
6. A. Short approach B. Long approach
   (1) Position of feet—keep lead foot down
   (2) Rear foot under—be over it
   (3) Body to right, body proceeds arm (4) Good pull
   (5) Cock the hand—rotate palm up
   (6) Over the shoulder, close to the ear
   (7) Through the shaft—keep tip low
   (8) Lead foot down quickly—pass over it
   (9)
7. Squad meeting
8. Special A. Sauna B. Swim C. Steps or hill
   D.
9. Full run and form throws—numbers as in item 6.
10. Test or compete—record below A. 1/2 to 3/4
    B. 3/4 to 7/8 C. 9/10
11. A. Start slow—finish fast B. Explosion
    C. Easy-medium-hard D.
12. With Coach A. B.
14. A. Wind sprints B. Starts, 25-40 yds.
    C. High knee and fast leg D. Hurdle drill
    E. Spring and bound F. Alternate walk-run, go 880 or more
15. A. Hendricks Park B. Laurel Golf Course C.
16. Tumbling activities
17. Have feeling of back and relaxed, no strain over rear leg
18. Work on staying behind scratch line
19. A. Throw ball into net B. Throw at target
20. Secondary event
21. A. Pictures B. Film C. Video

Date	3/4	7/8	Now	Goal

M	2-14A
T	1A-5A-6A(9)-6A(6)-4B-19B(150-180')-14D
W	1A-3
T	1A-12-10B(190-210')-Target at 200'-14D
F	1A-3-14C
S	Secondary event test
S	Usual

M	3-14A
T	1A-4A-4B-5A-6B(2)-6B(1)-5B-14D
W	3-8A or B
T	1-12-6A(8)-6B(8)-19B-20-8A or B
F	3
S	1-10-14D
S	study

M	3-8A or B
T	1A-4A-4B-5A-5B-6B(2)-6B(1)-17-14A
W	3-8A or B
T	1A-5A-5B-6B(3)-6B(5)-19A
F	3
S	3 or 14A
S	study

M	1A-3-2
T	1A-4A-4B-5A-5B-17-14A
W	1A-4A-4B-3 medium throws-8A
T	3-14D
F	Light and gear ready
S	Travel and compete
S	recreation

Figure 14.1f Javelin Throw Training Schedule

Javelin Throw NAME DATE April

1. A. Jog 1 or 2 laps, easy stretching B.
2. Fartlek A. Varied pace B. Steady pace
3. Weights and jogging
4. Check mark A. Short B. Long
5. A. Stand, throw 10 to 30 times
   B. Routine: throw 3 of each—easy, medium, hard.
   (1) 3 step, 45 ft.-90 ft. (2) 5 step, 90 ft.-150 ft.
   (3) Run and throw, 150 ft.-180 ft.
6. A. Short approach B. Long approach
   (1) Position of feet—keep lead foot down
   (2) Rear foot under—be over it
   (3) Body to right, body proceeds arm (4) Good pull
   (5) Cock the hand—rotate palm up
   (6) Over the shoulder, close to the ear
   (7) Through the shaft—keep tip low
   (8) Lead foot down quickly—pass over it
   (9)
7. Squad meeting
8. Special A. Sauna B. Swim C. Steps or hill
   D.
9. Full run and form throws—numbers as in item 6.
10. Test or compete—record below A. 1/2 to 3/4
    B. 3/4 to 7/8 C. 9/10
11. A. Start slow—finish fast B. Explosion
    C. Easy-medium-hard D.
12. With Coach A. B.
14. A. Wind sprints B. Starts, 25-40 yds.
    C. High knee and fast leg D. Hurdle drill
    E. Spring and bound F. Alternate walk-run, go 880 or more
15. A. Hendricks Park B. Laurel Golf Course C.
16. Tumbling activities
17. Have feeling of back and relaxed, no strain over rear leg
18. Work on staying behind scratch line
19. A. Throw ball into net B. Throw at target
20. Secondary event
21. A. Pictures B. Film C. Video

Date	3/4	7/8	Now	Goal

M	3-14A or 14D
T	3x 3x 1A-4A-4B-5A-6A2-6A6-6B2-6B6-19B-14D
W	2-8B
T	3x 3x 3x 1-12-5A-6A2-6B2-6B2-4A-4B-19B
F	Gear ready-jog & stretch-no javelin
S	Compete
S	Form work
M	2-4
T	3x 3x 7-1A-5A-6A6-6B6-6A3-4A-4B-14B
W	1A-4A-4B-3 medium throws-3
T	2-8
F	Jog and stretch
S	Compete
S	Travel home and loosen up
M	1A-3
T	1A-3-14A
W	3x 3x 1A-4-5-6A1-6A3-9B2-9B6-14D
T	1A-3
F	Light-all gear ready
S	Compete
S	Home and loosen up
M	3-14A
T	3x 3x 3x 3x 7-1A-4A-4B-6A8-6A6-9A2-9A6-19A-14D
W	2-8
T	3x 1A-12-5A-4A-4B-9A2-jog
F	Gear ready and travel
S	Compete
S	Loosen up-4-5A

Figure 14.1c Javelin Throw Training Schedule

Javelin Throw NAME DATE January

1. A. Jog 1 or 2 laps, easy stretching B.
2. Fartlek A. Varied pace B. Steady pace
3. Weights and jogging
4. Check mark A. Short B. Long
5. A. Stand, throw 10 to 30 times
   B. Routine: throw 3 of each—easy, medium, hard.
   (1) 3 step, 45 ft.-90 ft. (2) 5 step, 90 ft.-150 ft.
   (3) Run and throw, 150 ft.-180 ft.
6. A. Short approach B. Long approach
   (1) Position of feet—keep lead foot down
   (2) Rear foot under—be over it
   (3) Body to right, body proceeds arm (4) Good pull
   (5) Cock the hand—rotate palm up
   (6) Over the shoulder, close to the ear
   (7) Through the shaft—keep tip low
   (8) Lead foot down quickly—pass over it
   (9)
7. Squad meeting
8. Special A. Sauna B. Swim C. Steps or hill
   D.
9. Full run and form throws—numbers as in item 6.
10. Test or compete—record below A. 1/2 to 3/4
    B. 3/4 to 7/8 C. 9/10
11. A. Start slow—finish fast B. Explosion
    C. Easy-medium-hard D.
12. With Coach A. B.
14. A. Wind sprints B. Starts, 25-40 yds.
    C. High knee and fast leg D. Hurdle drill
    E. Spring and bound F. Alternate walk-run, go 880 or more
15. A. Hendricks Park B. Laurel Golf Course C.
16. Tumbling activities
17. Have feeling of back and relaxed, no strain over rear leg
18. Work on staying behind scratch line
19. A. Throw ball into net B. Throw at target
20. Secondary event
21. A. Pictures B. Film C. Video

Date	3/4	7/8	Now	Goal

M Reorganize class or squad
T 3-8B
W 1A-5A-6B-6A-2
T 3-8A or B
F 1A-5A-6B(1)-6A(8)-14A
S 3
S walk, or recreation
M 3-8A
T 3-16-8B
W 1A-5A-12-6A(5)-6A(3)-19A-14D
T 3-8A
F 1A-5A-6A(5)-6A(7)-14A
S 3
S 2 or good walk
M 3
T 16
W 1A-12(4 pm)-5A-6B(6)-6B(8)-5A
T 3-8A or B
F 1A-14A-6A(1)-6B(1)-6B(7)-14D
S 3
S 3
M 1A-3-14A
T 3-16
W 1A-5A-6A(6)-6A(3)-19A-14D
T 1A-3-14A
F 1A-5A-5B-Easy 11A and B-14C
S 3-2
S Choice

Figure 14.1d Javelin Throw Training Schedule

Javelin Throw NAME DATE February

1. A. Jog 1 or 2 laps, easy stretching B.
2. Fartlek A. Varied pace B. Steady pace
3. Weights and jogging
4. Check mark A. Short B. Long
5. A. Stand, throw 10 to 30 times
   B. Routine: throw 3 of each—easy, medium, hard.
   (1) 3 step, 45 ft.-90 ft. (2) 5 step, 90 ft.-150 ft.
   (3) Run and throw, 150 ft.-180 ft.
6. A. Short approach B. Long approach
   (1) Position of feet—keep lead foot down
   (2) Rear foot under—be over it
   (3) Body to right, body proceeds arm (4) Good pull
   (5) Cock the hand—rotate palm up
   (6) Over the shoulder, close to the ear
   (7) Through the shaft—keep tip low
   (8) Lead foot down quickly—pass over it
   (9)
7. Squad meeting
8. Special A. Sauna B. Swim C. Steps or hill
   D.
9. Full run and form throws—numbers as in item 6.
10. Test or compete—record below A. 1/2 to 3/4
    B. 3/4 to 7/8 C. 9/10
11. A. Start slow—finish fast B. Explosion
    C. Easy-medium-hard D.
12. With Coach A. B.
14. A. Wind sprints B. Starts, 25-40 yds.
    C. High knee and fast leg D. Hurdle drill
    E. Spring and bound F. Alternate walk-run, go 880 or more
15. A. Hendricks Park B. Laurel Golf Course C.
16. Tumbling activities
17. Have feeling of back and relaxed, no strain over rear leg
18. Work on staying behind scratch line
19. A. Throw ball into net B. Throw at target
20. Secondary event
21. A. Pictures B. Film C. Video

Date	3/4	7/8	Now	Goal

M 1A-3-14A or 14D
T 1A-6B(5)-6B(2)-6B(6)-14A
W 3
T 1A-5A-5B-4A-4B-14D
F 3-8A or B
S 3
S study and recreation
M 1A-3-14A
T 1A-4A-4B-6B(2) 3X-6B(6) 3X-5B-14A
W 3
T 1A-4A-4B-5A-5B-6A(2)-19A-14A
F 3
S 1A-5A-6B(2)-11B-14D
S study or recreation
M 1A-3
T 1A-4A-4B-5A-5B-19B-14D
W 7-1A-3
T 1A-5A-6B(2)-6A(1)-5B-14D
F 3-8A or 8B or 16
S 1A-12-10A-5B-14A or D
S Usual
M 1A-3-16
T 1A-5A-6B(6)-6B(7)-19B-14A
W 2-8A or B
T 1A-10-12-4B-10-5B
F 3-8A or B
S 3
S Usual

Figure 14.1g Javelin Throw Training Schedule

Javelin Throw NAME DATE May / June

1. A. Jog 1 or 2 laps, easy stretching B.
2. Fartlek A. Varied pace B. Steady pace
3. Weights and jogging
4. Check mark A. Short B. Long
5. A. Stand, throw 10 to 30 times
   B. Routine: throw 3 of each—easy, medium, hard.
   (1) 3 step, 45 ft.-90 ft. (2) 5 step, 90 ft.-150 ft.
   (3) Run and throw, 150 ft.-180 ft.
6. A. Short approach B. Long approach
   (1) Position of feet—keep lead foot down
   (2) Rear foot under—be over it
   (3) Body to right, body proceeds arm (4) Good pull
   (5) Cock the hand—rotate palm up
   (6) Over the shoulder, close to the ear
   (7) Through the shaft—keep tip low
   (8) Lead foot down quickly—pass over it
   (9)
7. Squad meeting
8. Special A. Sauna B. Swim C. Steps or hill
   D.
9. Full run and form throws—numbers as in item 6.
10. Test or compete—record below A. 1/2 to 3/4
    B. 3/4 to 7/8 C. 9/10
11. A. Start slow—finish fast B. Explosion
    C. Easy-medium-hard D.
12. With Coach A. B.
14. A. Wind sprints B. Starts, 25-40 yds.
    C. High knee and fast leg D. Hurdle drill
    E. Spring and bound F. Alternate walk-run, go 880 or more
15. A. Hendricks Park B. Laurel Golf Course C.
16. Tumbling activities
17. Have feeling of back and relaxed, no strain over rear leg
18. Work on staying behind scratch line
19. A. Throw ball into net B. Throw at target
20. Secondary event
21. A. Pictures B. Film C. Video

Date	3/4	7/8	Now	Goal

M	Light 2 and 14A
T	1A-6A(8)-6A(3)-4A-4B-3x 6A(2)-3x 6A(6)-5B-Jog
W	2-21B
T	Gear ready
F	Preliminaries-Regional or Conference
S	Finals
S	Home and loosen up
M	Easy
T	1A-2x 5B-4A-4B-3x 10B-14A or 14D
W	Help with frosh or JV meet-Jog
T	1A-5B-14A
F	Invitational meet, travel and loosen up
S	Invitational meet, or simulate
S	Usual Sunday routine
M	Runway and form work at Championship area
T	Light
W	Light
T	Qualify for Championship
F	Light
S	Championship finals
S	Usual
M	
T	
W	
T	
F	
S	
S	

Figure 14.2 Short Check Mark: Javelin Throw.

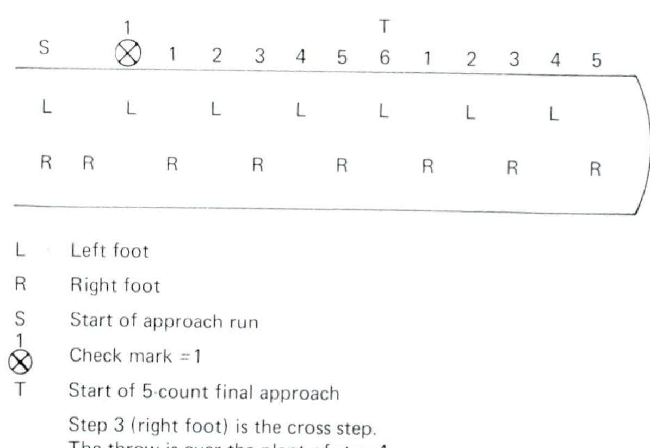

4B. Long check mark. The long check marks are for competitive throwing. The more speed the javelin thrower can *use* (control) and still get an effective throwing position, the farther his throws should travel. This technique is not easily acquired, so it should be started early in the year and practiced with consistent regularity. The rules do not permit an approach longer than 120 feet. Most fine javelin men will use from 90 feet to the 120-foot maximum.

The athlete stands at the rear of his approach (Figure 14.3), then takes a four-step trotting start from S, the start of the run, to the first check mark. The coach or an observer marks his last step while he repeats the four steps twice. The average for this first part of the approach is about 20 feet. The average of the thrower's three trials is his first check mark.

The same procedure is followed to establish the distance from the first check mark to T, with three trials made and the distances averaged. However, the athlete runs through the approach from the start, S, through check 1 and on through the 10 steps to T, rather than running only the 10 steps for a measurement. This part of the approach will usually average around 55 to 65 feet.

The final measurement adds in the approach run through the last five steps, including the follow-through. From the starting point, the thrower takes his four steps to check 1; 10 steps to T, the start of the final approach; and the final five steps, which will include the throw and the follow-through. This long run is also done three times for an average. The "five-count," or last five steps of the approach, will vary from 25 to 35 feet in most cases.

The type of approach, as well as wind and weather conditions, can make considerable difference in the length of the "short" approach, and even more dramatic variations in the "long" approach. Competitive areas vary from soft grass, cinders, and mud to urethane, which is the all-weather surface of the world's finest tracks. It is imperative that the athlete who aspires to his best

Figure 14.3 Long Check Mark: Javelin Throw.

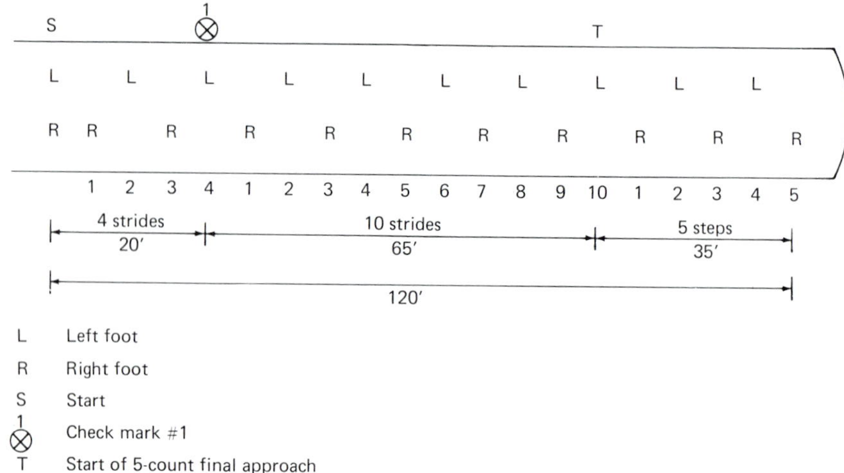

should have among his "tools" a short as well as a long approach and a full knowledge of his distances on different kinds of approach surfaces.

5A. Stand, throw 10 to 30 times. This is a routine warm-up drill. From a standing position the athlete throws the javelin from 10 to 30 feet into a soft surface, gradually increasing the effort of his throws. This is also an opportunity to work on technical procedures.

5B. Routine. This is a continuation of the warm-up, but it is also a technique drill. In the "3-step, throw 45–90 ft." (*5B1*), the javelin is already held back in the throwing position. The athlete takes two approach steps (Figure 14.4), then executes steps 3, 4, and 5 of the final approach, throwing over the left foot on step 4. Three easy throws are taken with this approach, with the athlete trying to throw only in the range between 45 and 90 feet. The emphasis is upon perfecting the technique of the approach and throw, not on distance achieved.

Figure 14.4 Three-Step Routine: Javelin Throw.

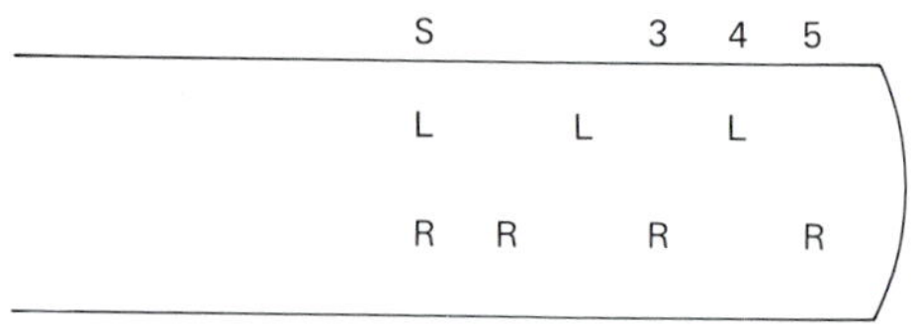

S Start of 2-step approach
R Right foot
L Left foot
3-4-5 Throwing approach

Figure 14.5 Five-Step Routine: Javelin Throw.

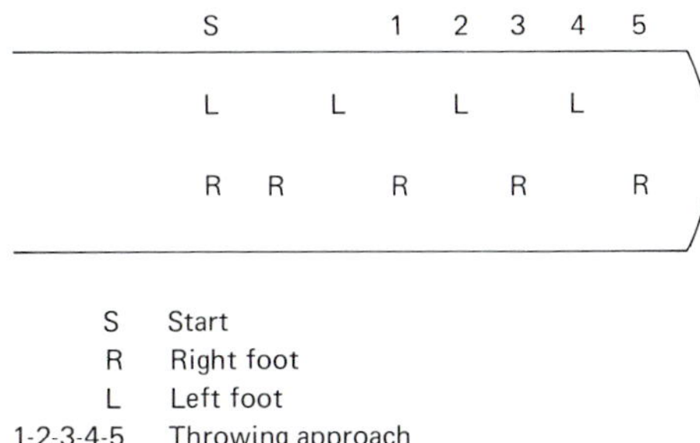

S Start
R Right foot
L Left foot
1-2-3-4-5 Throwing approach

In the "5-step, 90–150 ft." (*5B2*), the athlete takes two approach steps to the final check point, then executes the five-step final approach and delivery, taking three easy throws. The approach should be rhythmical, hitting the "check" with the left foot (for a right-handed thrower) and going through the five final steps, with step 3 the cross-step, step 4 (the left foot) being the plant leg over which the throw is made, and step 5 the follow-through step (Figure 14.5).

The "run and throw, 150–180 ft." (*5B3*) is the final approach. It is used to gain additional momentum, but the emphasis is on the rhythm of the approach and whatever point of technique the athlete feels needs attention. Again, these throws are for approach and technique work. No throws are made for distance. The distances listed are general suggestions for collegiate throwers who can throw from 220 feet to 260 feet or better.

6A. Short approach and *6B. Long approach* are for technique emphasis. As with all other events, we believe that concentration on one part of the technique at a time will produce the best results. Eventually the athlete, as with a well-timed machine, fits all cogs of the meshing gears together. He then produces gradually increasing efforts as the season progresses. The numbers listed below, such as (1), are the numbers of the individual techniques listed under *6A* and *6B.*

1. *Position of feet — keep lead foot down.* This drill's purpose is to provide a throwing foundation while maintaining motion. Starting from the T mark in Figure 14.6, the first step of the five-count approach is a rhythmical, slightly longer, straight-ahead step. At the same time, the javelin starts back toward the throwing position. On the second step, the left foot turns slightly to the right, the javelin is now almost in the throwing position, and the torso is turned partially to the right. On the third step, the right foot is turned slightly to the right (this is the cross-step), the javelin reaches its final throwing position, and the torso is turned as far to the right as is practical for the individual. The final left foot position (step 4) is almost straight ahead, but is still slightly to the right in its aim. The right leg momentum is increased by a slight push, the left foot remains planted, and the final step or reverse (step 5) is made to the final position on the right foot.

Figure 14.6 Foot Position in the Final Approach: Javelin Throw.

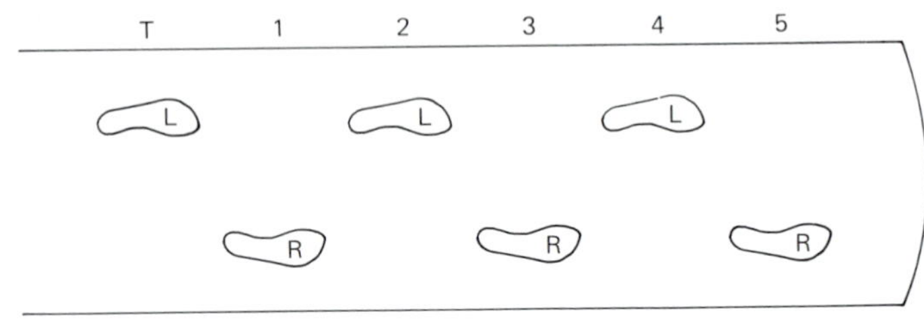

T Start of final approach
L Left foot
R Right foot

2. *Rear foot under — be over it.* On the third step of the final approach the torso should be turned as far toward a right angle to the throwing direction as the javelin thrower can get it back into the delivery. This position varies with some individuals. Some excellent throwers keep the torso almost directly ahead, getting a "bow" effect, rather than a "lay back" over the back (right) leg, which is the method most commonly used. The action starts from a slightly bent right knee, and the hip has also been "cocked." The torso is turned to the right, and the javelin is back, with the thrower's left arm across the chest or pointed in the direction of the throw. The head and nose are aimed in the direction of the throw. The right knee straightens; the hip thrusts the torso back to a position "across" the direction of the throw (this is a turn of 45 degrees, not 90 degrees).

3. *Body to right, body precedes arm.* This position is taken on the third step in Figure 14.6 and continues into the fourth step. The torso is turned to the right to make it easier to place the javelin in the back throwing position. The left arm should be across the chest or, as some athletes carry it, pointed toward the throwing direction. As the left foot comes down (step 4), the left arm swings in an arc below shoulder height and comes to the direction of the throw. The torso is turned quickly to the direction of the throw, and the throwing arm flows into the throw.

4. *Good pull.* The javelin is pulled, as one would pull on a rope. The pull of the body's turn and momentum, which is transferred from the feet to the hips to the torso and finally to the pulling arm, adds momentum to the javelin before the actual throw is made.

5. *Cock and hand — rotate palm up.* The throwing hand should be rotated "up" (palm up). The emphasis on the throwing hand should be "palm up at the start of the throw, palm down at the finish."

6. *Over the shoulder, close to the ear.* The javelin on delivery should pass over the shoulder and close enough to the head that it (the head) tilts slightly to the left during the delivery. The side-arm delivery is the most certain way to have certain elbow injuries.

7. *Through the shaft — keep tip low.* The shaft should be delivered at about 30 degrees. In delivering it, the thrower should watch the point to see that it does

not wander to the right or tip up on delivery. As the javelin leaves, all the thrower should be able to see is the "tail-tip," which should appear no larger than a silver dollar. A tipped-up shaft will show the whole javelin and result in a high, bad flight.

8. *Lead foot down quickly — pass over it.* The lead foot (step 4) should come down quickly. The thrower should use as much power and momentum flowing. The left leg is planted quickly, the foot pointed slightly to the right, and the knee almost straight and straightening up into the throw as the body passes over it.

10. Test or compete — record below. The number indicates a trial or an actual throwing "all out." 10A is a throw of one-half to three-fourths effort. 10B is a throw at three-fourths to seven-eighths effort, and 10C is a throw at nine-tenths effort. The best throw is recorded, along with the date, at the bottom of the training sheet.

11A. Start slow — finish fast. The emphasis on the approach run should be to gain momentum with relaxed speed at the end of the throw. The beginner tends to slow down at the end, not only stopping the feet, but also stopping the torso. He gains very little from such an approach. It is true that the feet stop in a good approach. The feet stopping at the end of a fast approach make the body a catapult or whip, which increases the momentum of the javelin before the final throwing motion.

11B. Explosion. The athlete is trying to "explode" with a burst of energy at the end of the throw. If done well and timed perfectly, it can help the thrower put more into his throwing.

11C. Easy — medium — hard. This is work on a throwing cycle for competition. The first throw is relatively "easy," in other words a "safe" throw, a sure mark. The second throw in the qualifying round would be a bit harder, a "medium" throw. The last throw is "hard," an attempt to "explode" and get a big improvement in the mark. The same throwing cycle is used in the final round of three throws.

17. Have feeling of back and relaxed over rear leg, no strain. The final throwing position (steps 3 and 4 in Figure 14.6) is one of a slight lean back over the right or rear leg, which is bent. As the body is turned into the throw, it makes a bow or sling for shooting the "arrow."

18. Work on staying behind scratch line. All javelin throwers need some practice in staying behind the scratch line, some because after a good throw they wander over the line, causing a foul. A thrower also needs to know how much momentum he can use and still have room for his follow-through.

19A. Throw ball into net. If a net is available, a softball or weighted ball up to

3 pounds can be used to work on technique as well as arm strength and flexibility.

19B. Throw at target. Target throwing is used to keep the athlete from competing every practice day. It is also used so that a good wind can better be used by varying the direction of approach in the throwing area.

19C. Approach speed. The thrower should constantly be working for more approach speed. How much speed? Armas Valste of Finland said, "As much speed as you can control." Work regularly to attain greater *controlled* speed.

20. Secondary event. A secondary event should be a pleasurable diversion. It may also be a team point winner. Les Tipton, Oregon and Olympic athlete, helped win a dual track meet with a third in the high hurdles.

Javelin Throw Bibliography

Bankhead, William H., and Thorsen, Margaret A. "A comparison of four grips used in throwing the javelin," *Research Quarterly* 35 (October 1964): 438ff.

Cantello, Al. "The javelin throw," *Track and Field Quarterly Review* 70 (May 1970): 41–46.

Davis, Dave. "General weight training for throwers," *Track Technique,* No. 51 (March 1973), pp. 1632–35.

Doolittle, John H. "A new look at European javelin technique," *Athletic Journal* 45 (February 1965): 22, 24, 51–52.

FitzSimmons, John. "Javelin lessons from Budapest," *Track Technique,* No. 32 (June 1968), p. 1007.

Fromm, John R. "Javelin training programs," *Athletic Journal* 51 (February 1971): 64–65, 77–78.

Ganslen, Richard V. "Javelin aerodynamics," *Track Technique,* No. 30 (December 1967), pp. 940–43.

Haines, Joe. "Developing a European-styled javelin thrower," *Scholastic Coach* 39 (April 1970): 52, 54.

_______. "Javelin interval training," *Track Technique,* No. 51 (March 1973), p. 1638.

_______. "A study of America's top javelin throwers," *Scholastic Coach* 41 (April 1972): 84.

Haldeman, Neil. "Pitching velocity: can you increase it?" *Scholastic Coach* 39 (April 1970): 30, 32–33.

Held, Dick. "Russian vs. American javelin styles," *Scholastic Coach* 39 (March 1970): 16–18.

Jaworski, Edmund. "Daniela Jaworska — how she trains," *Track Technique,* No. 51 (March 1973), pp. 1635–37.

Kovalakides, Nick. "Four A's of javelin throwing," *Track and Field Quarterly Review* 70 (May 1970): 14–15.

_______. "Throwing the javelin" (3 parts), *Scholastic Coach*, No. 6 (February 1968), pp. 12–13, 64; No. 7 (March 1968), pp. 46, 48–49; No. 8 (April 1968), pp. 28, 30, 54.

Kuznetsov, Vladimir L. "Mastery of javelin throwing techniques," trans. by Robert Buckeye and Wally Swerchowsky, *Track Technique,* No. 2 (December 1960), pp. 46–52.

Markov, D. "Javelin technique," trans. by Robert Buckeye and Wally Swerchowsky, *Track Technique,* No. 19 (March 1965), pp. 603–7.

May, Joe. "The javelin throw," *Track and Field Quarterly Review,* March 1966, pp. 42–46.

Mazzalitis, V. "Javelin throwing, Russian style," ed. by V. V. Sadvski, trans. by Frank Covelli and Dick Bank, *Track Technique,* No. 33 (September 1968), pp. 1027–45.

Noah, Pop. "Javelin training of Bill Schmidt," *Track and Field Quarterly Review* 71: 84–88.

Paish, Wilf. "Analysis of European javelin throwers," *Track Technique,* No. 27 (March 1967), pp. 848–49.

———. "Javelin techniques of world class performers," *Track Technique,* No. 24 (June 1966), pp. 747–49.

———. *Javelin Throwing.* London: AAA, 1972. 48 pp.

Ranson, Roland. "A technique analysis of Scandinavian and Russian world class javelin throwers," *Track and Field Quarterly Review* 72: 30–42.

Ryan, Frank. "Teaching the javelin throw," in *Track in Theory and Technique,* pp. 366–71. Richmond, Calif.: Worldwide Publishing Co., 1962.

Shannon, Ken. "Javelin analysis," *Track and Field Quarterly Review* 73 (March 1973): 34–40.

Tucker, Ed. "The evolution of the stubby," *Track and Field Quarterly Review* 73 (December 1973): 246–50.

———. "The javelin — Finnish style," *Athletic Journal* 49 (February 1969): 54, 91–92.

Wade, Michael G. "Finnish javelin throwing — a comparative viewpoint," *Track Technique,* No. 28 (June 1967), pp. 881–84.

———. "A javelin refutation," *Track Technique,* No. 23 (March 1966), pp. 728–31.

Wilkinson, Charles D., III. "Predicting potential in the javelin," *Athletic Journal* 50 (January 1970): 46, 83.

Witchey, Ronald. "Factors influencing javelin performance," *Track Technique,* No. 52 (June 1973), pp. 1666–67.

The hammer throw

by Arne Nytro, Norway

The Historical Development of the Hammer Throw

Mankind has used the hammer as both tool and weapon for thousands of years, and probably men were also throwing the hammer for distance in the earliest times. The first competitions in which we know hammer throwers took part were the Fenach Taill Lenn Games on the Black Water in Ireland, held from about 500 B.C. to 500 A.D. Little is known about the implement and the rules of that period, but the event is thought to be of Celtic origin.

The hammer has been thrown in Scotland since about 300 A.D. From Scotland the event was introduced into England, where it was a popular sport during the sixteenth century. It is known that Kings Edward II (1307–1327) and Henry VII (1485–1509) encouraged and took part in the hammer throw. The implement of that period was either a blacksmith's hammer or a round stone with a wooden handle.

In the 1860s the hammer throw was introduced into university sports, and the implement was a 16-pound shot with an oak handle. The athletes threw from behind a line drawn anywhere in the stadium. After 1880 the seven-foot circle was used, and the hammer's handle was four feet long and constructed of iron or wood.

The hammer throw became popular on the east coast of the United States in the middle 1800s. The implements and rules were those used in the United Kingdom. Today's rules are based on the 1908 rules, but they are more specific.

The modern style of throwing the hammer was developed by the Irish and Irish-American throwers, who dominated the event from the 1900 Olympic Games in Paris through the 1932 Games in Los Angeles. Their styles were more personal and varied than today's style. They used one, two, or three turns, and they always turned on the ball of the foot, as do today's discus throwers.

From 1936 the Germans took the lead with throwers such as Ervin Black and Karl Hein. Their coach, Stepp Christman, invented the "heel-toe, toe" rotation, which made it possible to take four turns. This pattern is the basis for the hammer style of today, but the turns are faster today than they were then. After finishing each turn, they "waited" until the hammerhead was in front of the thrower, and this caused the "hang" in the implement at the beginning of the turn.

The Hungarian Imre Nemeth, the 1948 Olympic champion, and the Norwegian Sverre Strandli, the first man to throw the hammer over 200 feet, started the hammer renaissance around 1950 by developing the style which is used by all of the top men today. In this style the thrower's body is always ahead of the implement in all of the turns. They never "wait" for it. With this technique the hammer acquires greater acceleration and develops greater release speed.

The International Hammer Throw Rules

Rule 181: General Rules

3. A competitor must commence the throw from a stationary position.
4. A competitor may touch the inside of the iron band around the circle, but it will be a foul throw if he touches the top of the band or the area outside the band with any part of his body. [This rule is implemented by Rule 185 (4).] If no rule has been violated, a competitor may interrupt a trial which has been started, lay his implement down, return to the stationary position again, and begin a fresh trial, provided there is not more than one such interruption in each trial.
5. The competitor cannot leave the circle until the implement has landed, and then he shall from a standing position leave the rear half of the circle.
6. The implement must land within the inner edges of lines marking a 45° sector.

Rule 185: Throwing the Hammer

1. All throws must be from a circle 2.135 meters (7 feet) in diameter.
2. When throwing the hammer, gloves for the protection of the hands are permitted. The gloves must be smooth on the back and the front and the fingertips must be exposed, i.e., the tips of the fingers on the gloves must not be closed.
3. The competitor in his starting position prior to the preliminary swings or turns is allowed to put the head of the hammer on the ground outside the circle.
4. It shall not be considered a foul throw if the head of the hammer touches the ground when the competitor makes the preliminary swings or turns; but if,

after having so touched the ground, he stops throwing so as to begin the throw again, this shall count as a trial throw. (For implement, refer to Rule 207. For cage and circle, refer to Rules 208 and 209.)

5. If the hammer breaks during a throw or while in the air, it shall not count as a throw provided it was made in accordance with the rules. If the competitor thereby loses his equilibrium and commits a foul, it shall not count against him.

Rule 207: Hammer Construction

1. Head: The head shall be of solid iron or other metal not softer than brass, or a shell of such metal, filled with lead or other solid material. It must be completely spherical in shape. If a filling is used this must be inserted in such a manner that it is immovable and that the center of gravity shall not be more than 6 millimeters (0.25 inch) from the center of the sphere.
2. Handle: The handle shall be of single unbroken and straight length of spring steel wire not less than 3 millimeters (0.118 inch) or No. 11 Standard Wire Gauge (0.116 inch) in diameter, and such that it cannot stretch appreciably while the hammer is being thrown. The handle may be looped at one or both ends as a means of attachment. For an example of an approved hammer handle, see Figure 15.1.
3. Grip: The grip may be either of single or double loop construction, but must be rigid and without hinging joints of any kind and so made that it cannot stretch appreciably while being thrown. It must be attached to the handle in

Figure 15.1 Internationally Approved Hammer Handle.

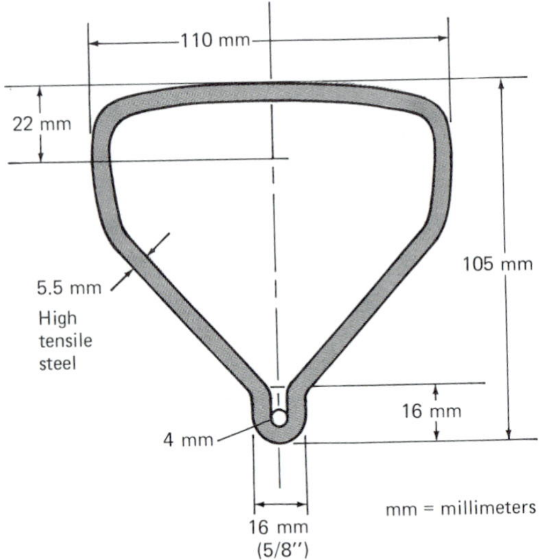

such a manner that it cannot be turned within the loop of the handle to increase the overall length of the hammer.

4. Connection: The handle shall be connected to the head by means of a swivel which may be either plain or ball bearing. The grip shall be connected to the handle by means of a loop. A swivel may not be used.
5. The hammer shall conform to the following specifications:
   Weight of hammer complete as thrown (minimum): 7.26 kilograms (16 lbs.)
   Length of hammer complete as thrown measured from the inside of the grip:
      Minimum: 117.5 centimeters (3 feet 10¼ inches)
      Maximum: 121.5 centimeters (3 feet 11¾ inches)
   Diameter of head:
      Minimum: 102 millimeters (4 inches)
      Maximum: 120 millimeters (4¾ inches)

Comments on the Rules

1. The edge of the throwing circle is indicated by a band of iron or steel three-quarters of an inch high placed with the top edge of the circle level with the surrounding ground.
2. Use a leather glove on the hand closest to the handle. Some throwers have taped the fingers before they put on the glove.
3. All types of training shoes without spikes can be used in practice, but in competition, shoes made especially for the hammer throw are used.

Technique of the Hammer Throw

The following description of throwing the hammer is based on a "normal" style for a right-handed thrower. The essential points in the technique, those which are common to all good throwers, will be described. All throwers have their personal "trademarks" or stylistic differences, but if they are good throwers, their style is based on common mechanical principles and their biological background. These things will be discussed later in the chapter.

A throw can be broken down into four parts: (1) the starting position and the grip; (2) the preliminary swings (the winds); (3) the turns (usually three, sometimes four), and (4) the release. But, remember that the hammer throw is one flowing motion from the start of the winds to the release, with no pauses between the different phases of the throw.

Starting Position and the Grip

The athlete stands in the rear of the circle, with his back facing the direction of the throw. His feet are about two feet apart, and his toes are one inch forward from the edge of the circle. The knees are bent at an angle of approximately 150°. The thrower lays the hammerhead in front of him, with the grip in his right hand.

Photographs 15.1*a-l* Gyula Zsivotsky, Hungary, in the hammer throw.

He swings the implement to the rear and lands the ball behind him and in front of the right half of the circle. He turns the upper body to the right, so that the shoulder axis is parallel to the throwing direction. He straightens the left arm *fully* and takes the hammer grip in the left hand (glove hand) — second finger point. He places the right hand over the left and crosses the thumbs with the left thumb on top (Figure 15.2), and looks forward (toward the rear of the circle).

Preliminary Swings (the Winds)

Next, the athlete straightens his back and draws the left arm forward and upward with a smooth lifting movement. At the same time, the upper body is twisted to the left, beginning the winds. (The hammer thrower pictured in Photographs 15.1*a-l*, above, is Gyula Zsivotsky.)

The arms sweep the hammer in a wide path. When the ball is left-front, the thrower bends the elbows, lowers the left shoulder, moves the hips to the right

and passes the hands over the right part of the head. The face and the left shoulder are pointing ahead (to the rear of the circle). The left arm is straight.

The second wind is executed the same way, but faster. The thrower uses the pelvis to counter the pull of the hammerhead. He bends the knees more, and when the hammerhead is right-front for the second time, the turns begin.

The Turns

1. The first turn. The implement is moving fast at this point. The athlete starts turning the left leg when the ball is right-front. A split-second later, the right leg starts, and he turns on the left heel and the right toe-ball. The body weight is over the right foot, and the left leg is working against the centrifugal force of the hammer. The lower back is straight, and the shoulders are relaxed.

The athlete turns the left foot approximately 160° in the first phase of the turn,

Figure 15.2 Proper Hammer Grip.

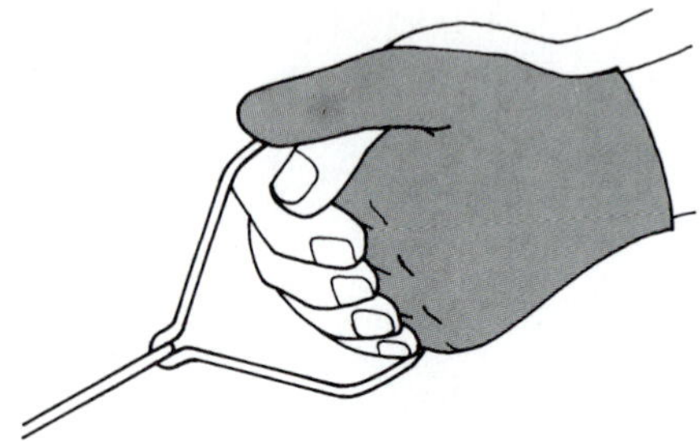

continues on the outer side of the foot, and completes the rest of the full 360° turn on the ball of the foot (Figure 15.3).

After the right leg has left the ground, the thrower tries to keep the right knee as close as possible to the left leg, and to move the right hip and leg so fast that they are ahead of the shoulders, arms and hammer when the right foot hits the ground. This is a good position from which to give greater velocity to the hammer. Only when both feet are on the ground can the thrower gain speed. When the right leg is in the air, speed is lost (look at Figure 15.4).

2. *The second and third turns.* The next two turns should follow the same path as the first, but to increase the speed of the hammer, the lower body (hips and legs) must move faster and faster. One must bend the knees more, and when the hammerhead is up, the hips are lower.

When the hammerhead is on the right, the hips are higher and turned to the left. In other words, the upper body is over the right foot when the hammerhead

Figure 15.3 Footwork Accompanying the Hammer Throw.

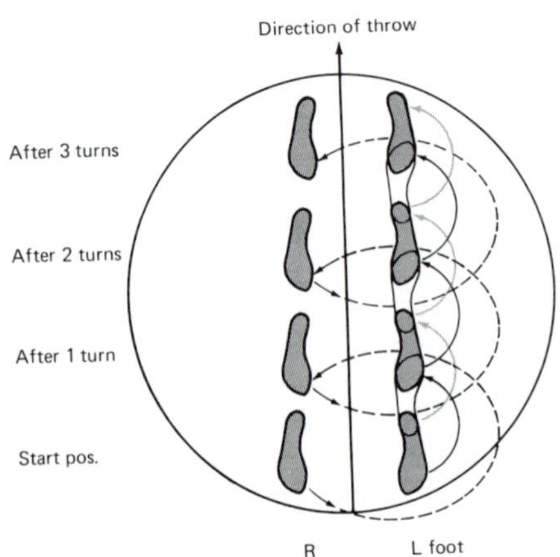

Figure 15.4 Graph Illustrating the Speed of the Hammerhead.

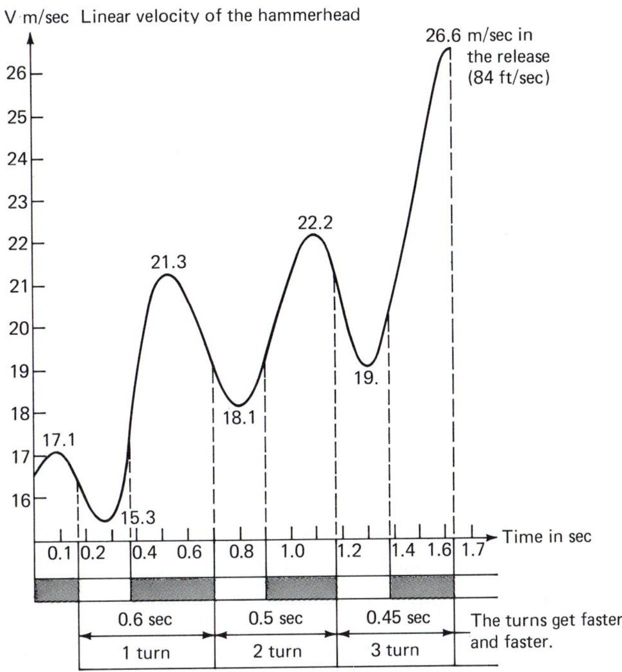

Graphical picture showing the speed of the hammerhead in a 66.7 m throw of Y. Bakarinov, U.S.S.R.

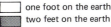

one foot on the earth
two feet on the earth

is to the left, and it is over the left foot when the hammerhead is to the right. All of this is done to control the centrifugal force and to maintain balance. The thrower should keep his head raised and look ahead over the straight left upper arm.

At the end of the third turn, the twist (torque) between the upper body and lower body begins to tighten despite the fast footwork, and the thrower must concentrate on the release of the hammer. During the turns, the lowest and the highest points of the body are moving closer and closer to the center line of the circle, but must *never move across it* (Figures 15.5 and 15.6).

The Release

If the three turns have been executed correctly, the speed of the implement has increased from turn to turn (Figure 15.4). The final acceleration comes from the

Figure 15.5 Highest and Lowest Points of the Hammer Throw.

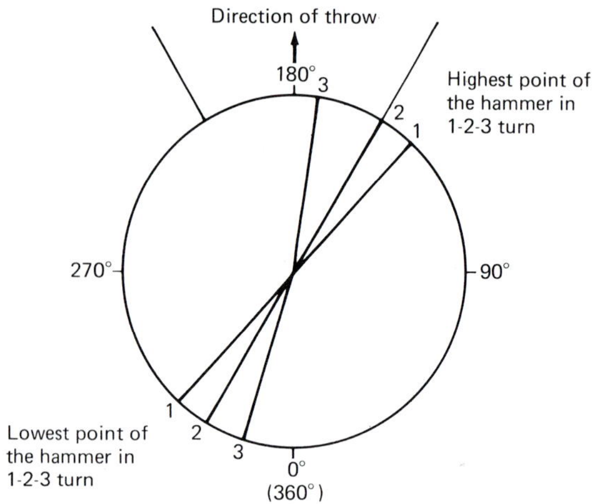

extension of the knees, hips and back. Therefore, in the beginning of the third turn, the thrower must concentrate on this last effort: just as the right foot hits the ground, he starts a final explosive pull. He extends the whole body, and throws the head backward.

The Organic-Mechanical Basics of the Throw

The length of a throw depends upon two things: (1) the speed of the implement at the moment of the release, and (2) the angle of release. (In the hammer, no aerodynamic problems arise as in the javelin and discus.) The speed of the implement is related to the athlete's anatomical and physiological make-up, including such characteristics as his muscular power, his neuromuscular reactions, his coordination, and his stature. The athlete's ability to use his biological background to increase the speed from the winds through the turns until the release constitutes his technique. The angle of release also depends upon the thrower's technique.

From a theoretical point of view, a tall man with a heavy build will have the advantage in the hammer, but a small thrower who is powerful can also succeed. The hammer thrower must build up an optimum of muscular power to provide a base for advanced technique; the beginner has to train for hours daily to this end. Years of training are required before he can achieve champion status, and then he must continue to train to maintain his strengths and to try to overcome his weaknesses.

Figure 15.6 Path of the Hammerhead.

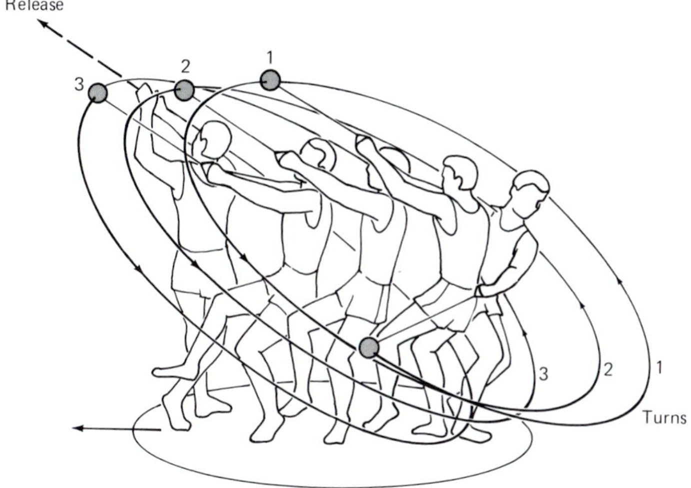

The Organic Background

The hammer thrower has to be strong in all the muscles of his body, but the following muscle groups must be stronger than the others:

1. In the legs:
   a. the extensors of the hip (the gluteals and others),
   b. the extensors of the knee (the femoris group), and
   c. the plantar flexors (gastrocnemius and soleus).
2. In the lower body:
   a. the twisters of the trunk (obliquus abdominis externis and internis),
   b. the muscles controlling the shoulders and arms (trapezius, rhomboids, deltoids, latissimus),
   c. the extensors of the trunk (erector spinae, quadratus lumborum), and
   d. the finger flexors.

These muscle groups must be given special consideration in the power-building training.

The Mechanical Background

If we take a closer look at technique as measured in terms of physical principles, we can state that the key word is *speed* or *velocity*. The thrower tries to build up a high central speed, or angular velocity, during the turns by means of fast footwork. At the same time, he tries to maximize the hammerhead's peripheral, or

Figure 15.7 Body's Axis of Rotation during the Hammer Throw.

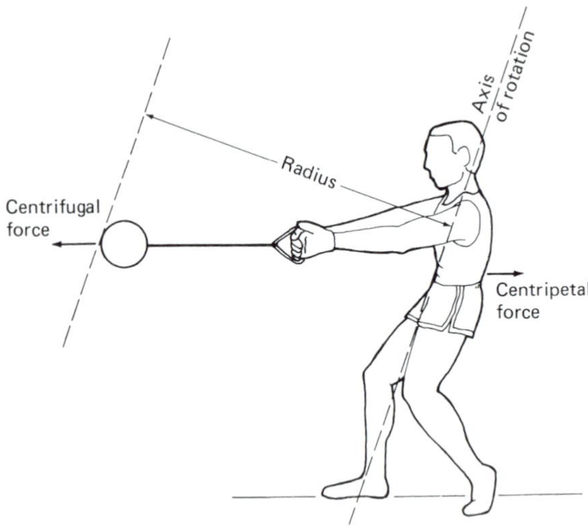

linear, velocity by combining the central speed with a long radius. That necessitates the long arms and relaxed upper body. The body's *axis of rotation* is always moving forward in the circle and describing the outline of a cone (circumduction) (Figure 15.7).

The fastest central speed and the longest arms give not only the highest speed of the hammerhead, but also the greatest pull outward (*centrifugal force*): up to 700 pounds for a throw of 200 feet. To control this force, the thrower must produce an equal force pulling in the opposite direction, called *centripetal force* (Figure 15.8). That requires that he keep the knees bent and the lower back straight to control the centrifugal force exerted by the pull of the hammer.

To understand the relationship between the speed and the angle of delivery refer to the nomograph, page 320, that the Russian hammer thrower and engineer Anatoliy Samotsvetov constructed (Figure 15.9). Nomographs can help the coach discover his throwers' potential and correct their faults.

In Samotsvetov's case, he had measured the length of the throw as 200 feet. With a stopwatch he had timed the flight of the hammer, from the release to the landing, as 2.9 seconds. From the nomograph he can determine that the angle of release was 33° and the velocity was 82 feet/second. But, using the nomograph, he can also see that if his thrower had increased his angle of release to 43° and maintained the same speed of release, he might have reached 215 feet!

Training for the Hammer Throw

The main goal of training for the hammer throw is to build up general and specific strength and to develop good technique. Roughly, one can say that one-quarter of the training will be allotted to developing technique and the other three-quarters

Figure 15.8 **Body's Centripetal Force Resists the Hammer's Outward Pull.**

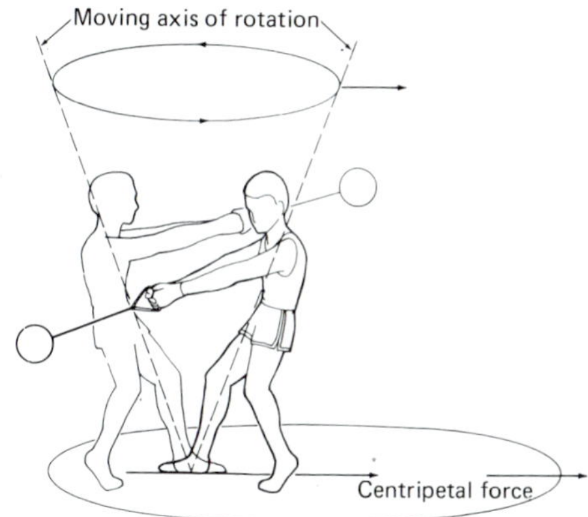

will be allotted to general and special conditioning, using a variety of methods, such as running, games, jumping, flexibility, and technical training and barbell work. The training can be done both indoors and outdoors, depending on local conditions.

Types of Training

Running. There are several types of running and each has its purpose: jogging is done to warm up; fartlek and long, slow runs are done to develop stamina or to cool off after a hard practice; and sprinting, 20 to 40 yards, is done to build up speed.

Games. Games are a combination of running and jumping, but they are more fun. Basketball, volleyball and soccer are fine for warming up and for recreation.

Flexibility. This training will consist of all kinds of arm swings and hip circling to improve these movements and to develop flexibility in the shoulders and the hip region.

Jumping. Jumping is an important training activity because it develops explosive power and speed in the lower extremities. Specifically, broad and high jumps, continuous hops and steps, step-jumping, and rope-skipping develop these skills.

Technical training. This training is important both to the novice and to the champion, the former to learn good technique and the latter to try to improve his pattern and speed.

Technical training can be done best outdoors, but it is also possible to do it indoors. If the athlete cannot train at the main stadium, it would be worth the effort for him to construct a concrete circle in a quiet place out of the way of activity. Indoors, the athlete can train for technique with sandbags on a rope or with a hammer thrown into a nylon net or a canvas "wall."

Technical training for the hammer throw consists of countless swings and turns and releases, practiced in various combinations with hammers of ordinary weights and heavier and lighter implements.

Weight training. Strength is a must for a hammer thrower, and the only way to develop strength is to work against resistance. Of the two types of resistance training, isotonic and isometric, we advocate the isotonic (dynamic), and the exercises included here (Figures 15.10 and 15.11) are only for that type of training.

Figure 15.9 Relationship between Speed and Angle of Delivery of the Hammer.

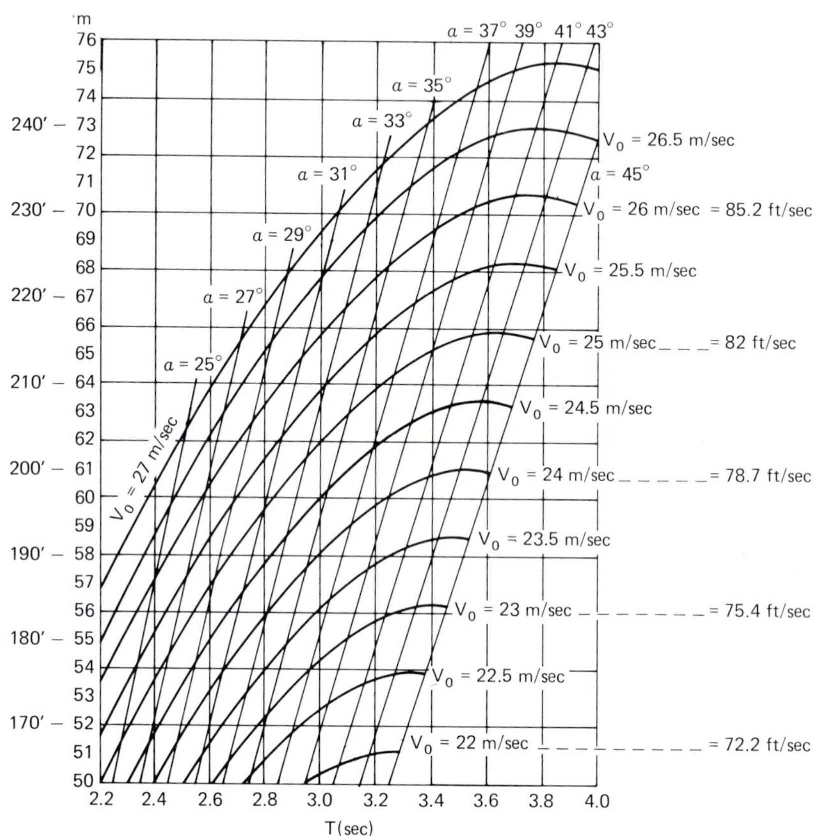

m = Distance thrown in meters
V_0 = Velocity of hammer at release
a = Release angle
T = Flight time of hammer

Figure 15.10 Exercises for the Lower Body.

A. Without Weights

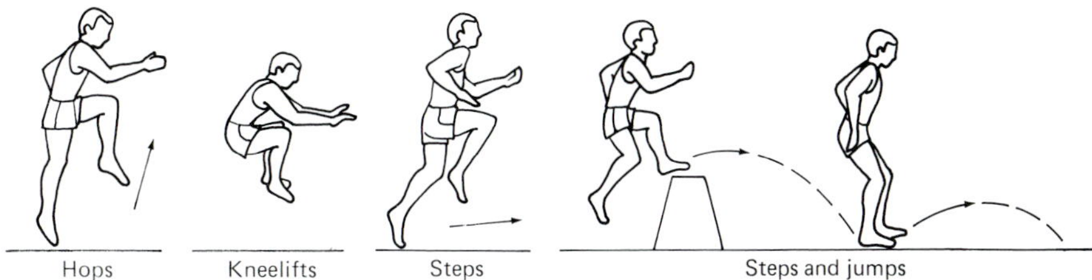

B. With Heavy Weights

Strength training can be divided into "basic" training, with heavy weights, and "specific" training, with smaller weights. The basic training concentrates on the muscles in the legs, back and arms. The weights used are 70 to 90 percent of the maximum that can be lifted. One to six repetitions are done in three sets. The pauses between the sets are two to three minutes.

In the specific training, smaller implements and lighter weights are used: for examples, sandbags, medicine balls, shots, barbell discs, light and heavy hammers (Figure 15.12). They are all used in exercises which follow the same pattern as the swings, turns and delivery. They are executed *as fast as possible* and with adequate rests between each try.

Planning

In all training programs, the athlete must have one plan which encompasses goals over the long term, such as a year; and one or more plans geared toward short-range goals, such as plans for the preseason months, for competition-season, and for days and weeks (look at the year plan, Table 15.1). All these plans must be flexible enough to accommodate the unpredictable: sickness, injuries, stress from studies, social events or personal problems.

In planning a long-term training program, the athlete should keep certain points in mind:

1. In the *off-season* the aim is to build up and maintain overall physical fitness and strength. At least three days a week should be devoted to this kind of training and at least one day to technical and more specific training.
2. In the *competitive season* the athlete still requires two days of all-around training, mixed with auxiliary exercises more specific to the hammer. Technical training should be done two to three days a week.
3. The ratio of general conditioning to specific training in the training schedule depends largely on the athlete's stage of development. A beginner must spend more time on the basic training than the thrower who has years of practice and several competitions behind him. The experienced thrower must reduce the basic weight training to a level sufficient only to maintain basic strength and should spend most of his training time on technique and special weight training.
4. The thrower chooses his weights and the number of repetitions and sets according to his level of development (but within the bounds of accepted training methods).
5. Besides weight training and throwing, the athlete should always try to fit in sprints, jumps and flexibility training. It is best to do this training on the same day as the technical training.
6. The number of throws during one "practice day" must never be over forty, and 30 to 40 percent of the throws should be for distance.
7. One of the days of technical training should concentrate on special problems of technique such as (a) winds and turns without throwing, (b) continuous turns (5-10) with the hammer or a shot in the hands, and (c) easy turns with stress on the release.

Table 15.1 Training for the Hammer Throw: Suggested Sample Schedule for One Year

	PRESEASON		COMPETITIVE SEASON
	Sept. Oct. Nov. Dec. (*4–5 days a week*)	*Jan. Feb. March* (*5–6 days a week*)	*Apr. May June July Aug.* (*4–5 days a week*)
Mon.	Basic strength training	Fartlek	Basic strength training—Long, slow run
Tues.			Throwing and specific strength training
Wed.	Basic strength training	Games	Specific strength—Light throwing and basic strength Jumps—sprints
Thurs.	Technical training	Throwing	Throwing Throwing—sprints
Fri.	Basic strength training	Specific strength	
Sat.			Competition or throwing; sprints and jumps
Sun.	Throwing—sprints—jumps		
Aim Type of work	All-around strength Increasing the weights	Specific strength Same weights Increasing the speed	Preparation for competition—Technique Reducing the weights Increasing the speed

8. Warm-up exercises are essential for physical and mental preparedness. The warm-up should always move from slow movements to more vigorous movements; for example, jogging and wind sprints should be followed by calisthenics.

Figure 15.11 Exercises for the Upper Body.

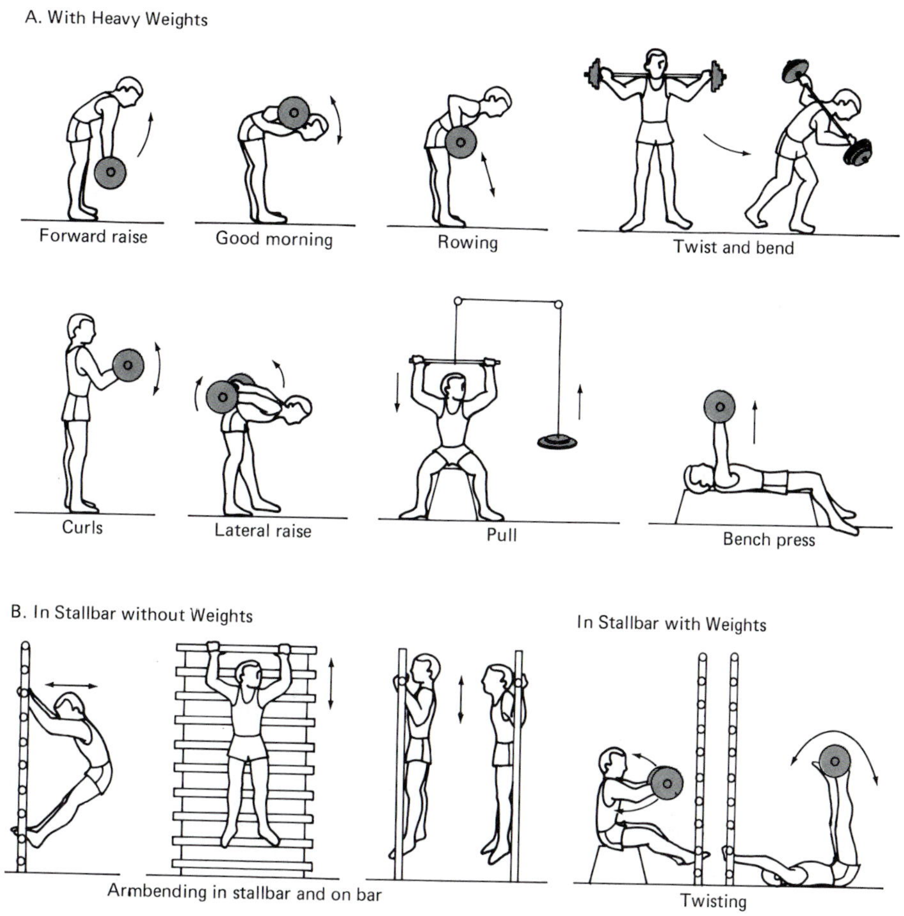

A. With Heavy Weights

Forward raise
Good morning
Rowing
Twist and bend

Curls
Lateral raise
Pull
Bench press

B. In Stallbar without Weights

In Stallbar with Weights

Armbending in stallbar and on bar

Twisting

Figure 15.12 Training Exercises with Small Weights.

Sample Week Programs

Preseason

Monday:
1. Warm-up
2. Barbell work:
   a. Squats, 3 sets of 6
   b. Two-handed curls, 2 sets of 10
   c. Dead lift, 3 sets of 4
   d. Sit-up, with twist, 3 sets of 10
   e. Clean, 3 sets of 6
   f. Rowing, flat back, 2 sets of 6
   g. Leg press (in machine), 2 sets of 6
   h. Pull (in machine), 2 sets of 6
3. Exercise for flexibility
4. 1-to-2-mile slow run

Tuesday: No training

Wednesday:
1. Warm-up
2. Barbell work:
   a. Squats, 3 sets of 6
   b. Clean, 3 sets of 6
   c. Dead lift, 3 sets of 4
   d. Good morning, flat back, 3 sets of 4
   e. Forward, upward raise, 2 sets of 4
   f. Standing, trunk twist and bend, 2 sets of 8
   g. Rowing, flat back, 3 sets of 6
3. Exercise for flexibility
4. 1-to-2-mile slow run

Thursday:
1. Warm-up: one-handed winds
2. Technical training:
   a. 5 to 10 winds and throws with two hammers or a 25- or 50-pound weight
   b. Winds, three turns and throw, with ordinary hammer; fifteen throws with 70 percent intensity; ten throws of maximum effort.
3. Jumps:
   a. Five to ten 20-to-40-yard sprints with standing starts
   b. Five series of hops, 15 yards on each leg
   c. Five series of steps, 25 yards long
4. Auxiliary exercises:
   a. Arm bending on stallbar, bar or beam, 3 sets of ten
   b. Twisting exercises with small weights
5. Exercise for flexibility
6. Slow run

Friday:

1. Warm-up
2. Barbell work:
   a. Squats, 3 sets of 6
   b. Bench press, 3 sets of 6
   c. Good morning exercise, 2 sets of 6
   d. Clean, 3 sets of 6
   e. Shoulder shrug, 2 sets of 10
   f. Swing bell circling
   g. Sitting on bench, extended arms twisting
   h. Lying: leg raise and twist
   i. Pull (in machine), 2 sets of 6
3. Exercise for flexibility
4. 1-to-2-mile slow run

Saturday: No training

Sunday: Same as Thursday

Competition Season

Monday:

1. Warm-up
2. Barbell work:
   a. One-half squat, 3 sets of 6
   b. Clean and jerk, 3 sets of 6
   c. Sit-up with twist incline board
   d. Up and down on a box, 20 times
   e. Rowing, flat back, 3 sets of 6
   f. Leg press (in machine), 2 sets of 6
   g. Pull (in machine), 3 sets of 6
3. Exercise for flexibility
4. Jog

Tuesday:

1. Warm-up
2. Barbell work:
   a. Throwing with weights (25-to-50-pound)
   b. Throwing a shot backwards, forwards and sideways
   c. Pull-up on bar
   d. Twisting exercises with the shot in sitting and laying position
3. 2-to-3-mile slow run

Wednesday:

1. Warm-up
2. Throwing:
   a. Continuous turns
   b. 20 easy throws
   c. 10 throws at maximum effort
3. Exercises for flexibility
4. Jog

Thursday:
1. Warm-up
2. Throwing:
   a. Winds and throw without turns
   b. 20 throws with 3 turns for style
3. Jumps:
   a. Five series of hops, 15 yards on each leg
   b. Five series of steps, 25 yards long
4. Run:
   a. Standing start, 5 x 30-yard sprint
   b. 1-mile slow run

Friday: No training

Saturday: Competition, or:
1. Warm-up
2. Six throws, maximum effort, with 3 to 5 min. between each. Then 15-minute jog, and six more throws at maximum effort as before.
3. Wind sprints
4. Exercise for flexibility
5. Jog

Sunday: No training

The training load before an important meet is very important, especially during the last two weeks. It determines not only the readiness of the athlete for competition, but also his rate of recovery after competition. We recommend that the training load for the last eight to twelve days before competition be lessened 50 to 60 percent. During the last week, the number of throws should be reduced to half that of the previous weeks and the intensity of these throws should be 80 to 90 percent of maximum; in short, a reduction in both load and intensity of training is recommended before a meet.

Just before the meet, the following warm-up is suggested:

1. Slow run for 10 to 20 minutes
2. Short windsprints, 20 to 40 yards
3. General calisthenics
4. Winding the hammer and slow turns
5. 2 to 3 easy throws
6. 1 to 2 harder throws (not maximum)

How to Teach a Beginner to Throw the Hammer

Introduce the hammer throw event to prospective athletes through films, film loops, sequence photos, pictures and first-hand observation of a good hammer-thrower. Explain the mechanical principles, especially the relationship between centrifugal force and centripetal force. Explain the danger involved in the hammer throw and how to avoid accidents, stressing the need for strict discipline and organization on the practice field, with no "horseplay."

A beginner must first be familiarized with the pull of the hammer; therefore he must start with the turns, or winds. The turns are to be learned first without the hammer, then with the hammer, and these steps should not be hurried. It takes years to become a champion: Sverre Strandli (Norway), European champion and two-time world record holder, competed for seven years before he doubled the results of his first competition.

Phase 1: Winds and Release

These can be done on cinders, grass, or an artificial surface. Give the athlete the hammer and teach him how to *hold* it, with the left hand first, then the right. (It is not necessary for the beginner to use gloves.)

Have him take a broad stance (over hipwidth between the feet) with bent knees, an upright body, and a raised head. Then have him turn the hammer around his head. Stress long arms on the right side and in front of the body and a very fast movement over the head. The left elbow should be in front of the left eye and the right shoulder turning right.

Slow winds come next. The lowest point of the ball is on the right (Figure 15.5). The athlete should move the pelvis in the direction opposite to the ball. Note that initially the hammer will pull the athlete out of balance, but after a while he will become familiar with the implement and be able to control the winds.

When he is able to control the winds, have him release the hammer in the throwing direction. Practice two winds and release until he is familiar with the motion, especially with releasing his grip at the right moment.

Phase 2: The Footwork

The athlete should first practice the footwork without an implement. Two parallel lines should be drawn two feet apart and eight to ten feet long on the ground. The athlete will place his feet on the end of the lines and heel-toe parallel with them, facing away from the direction of travel. He will start turning in the following sequence: (1) Left heel — right toe; (2) Left toe. The right foot should be kept down as long as possible, but once in the air, the athlete should move fast, with the right knee close to the left leg.

After a full 360° turn, the athlete will land on the same line, two feet from the starting point (Figure 15.3). He will continue to turn the whole length of the lines. In the beginning it is wise for a novice to make the turns in two phases: (1) heel-toe, and (2) toe. But it should be stressed that the eventual object is to turn as smoothly as possible, in one flowing movement.

In order to develop control of the footwork, give the athlete a *baseball bat* (Figure 15.13). He will rest the right elbow on the right hip, and place the bat in the right hand with his palm up. He will then grip the bat with his left hand, palm

Figure 15.13 Footwork Training with a Baseball Bat.

down, and elbow straight. The thick end of the bat should then point out to the right.

He should then practice the turns with the bat, keeping in mind that the hammer always has to be behind the thrower, just as the bat is. He should pay special attention to keeping the left arm long and straight.

Next, the athlete should take the hammer and try to make slow turns with the hammer head one to two feet above the ground, all the way around.

Phase 3: Winds, One Turn and Throw

When the athlete has some control over the basic movements described in phases 1 and 2, he can start throwing with one turn. He should do two winds, one turn, and throw. These should be easy winds. When the ball is approaching from the right side to the front, the thrower transmits his body weight over to the right leg and starts turning the left leg on the heel, maintaining a straight back and long arms. The hammer ball is always to the right.

Phase 4: Winds, Two Turns and Throw

The difficulties increase with two turns, but they are not insurmountable for the beginning thrower. If he feels the hammer's increasing pull with the increasing speed, he should let this tension be transmitted through the relaxed, long arms to the body and legs, leaning backwards and bending the legs a little more. He should move the right leg and hip forcefully and quickly in the turns so that they are always ahead of the hammer ball. The arms should be passive.

Phase 5: Winds, Three Turns and Release

Making a throw with two controlled turns prepares the athlete for the final and most difficult stage of the throw: three turns, *with increasing speed from turn to turn.* Until now we have more or less broken the hammer throw into stages. The aim has been to master the simple movements first, and then the more complicated ones. But the throwing distance in competition cannot be seen in parts. The throw is an *entire action* from the start of the winds, through the three or four turns, to the release: a smooth, powerful action without pauses or stops. It requires constantly increasing speed from turn to turn until the final powerful sweep in the release.

Common Faults

A. In the starting position:

1. Placing the wrong hand on the grip.
2. Not starting with the hammerhead far enough behind.

B. In the preliminary swings:

1. Bending the elbows and lifting the shoulders.
2. Bending the trunk forward.
3. Not bending the knees.
4. The lowest point of the hammers are too far in front of the athlete.
5. Not emphasizing the forward and upward part of the swing.
6. Going too far left with the hands when passing over the head.
7. Not countering the hips in relation with the shoulders.
8. Not raising the left heel when turning the trunk right to "meet" the hammer.

C. In the turns:

1. Starting the turning of the feet too late and too slow, so the hammer takes the lead.
2. Not placing the body weight over the bent right leg.
3. Moving the right leg too slowly and too far from the left in the turn.
4. Bending the head and upper body forward.
5. Bending the elbows.
6. Not turning the left foot 180°, so the thrower ends in the left side of the circle.
7. Stretching the left knee so the thrower gets too long a turn and ends on the right side of the circle.
8. The trail of the hammer is too steep.

D. In the delivery:

1. The body is too far to the right.
2. The legs are too extended, so the thrower does not get any power from them, and the delivery is too flat.
3. The thrower uses only his upper body in the delivery.
4. The thrower bends his upper body and the hammerhead touches the ground.

E. After the delivery:

1. Stopping the rotation, instead of following through.
2. Stepping out of the front half of the circle.

Hammer Throw Bibliography

Black, Irving S. "Teaching beginning hammer throwers," *Track Technique,* No. 46 (December 1971), pp. 1460–61.

Bosen, K. O. "Hammer and shot flight angles and velocities," *Track Technique,* No. 24 (June 1966), pp. 767–68.

______. "Some problems in hammer throwing," *Track and Field Quarterly Review* 73 (December 1973): 239–42.

Davis, Dave. "General weight training for throwers," *Track Technique,* No. 51 (March 1973), pp. 1632–35.

Doherty, J. Kenneth. *Track and Field Omnibook.* Swarthmore, Pa.: privately published by Kenneth J. Doherty, 1972.

Ecker, Tom. *Track and Field Dynamics.* Los Altos, Calif.: 1971.

Felton, Samuel M., Jr. "Instant hammer throwers!" *Scholastic Coach* 40 (April 1971): 60, 62, 66–68.

______. "The hammer throw," in *International Track and Field Coaching Encyclopedia,* pp. 307–50. West Nyack, N. Y.: Parker Publishing Company, 1970.

______. *Modern Hammer Throwing.* Rosemont, Pa.: 1967.

______, and Simonyi, Gabor. "Modern European hammer technique," *Scholastic Coach* 38 (March 1969): 10–11, 70, 72, 74, 76, 78–80.

______. "Part 2," *Scholastic Coach* 38 (April 1969): 16–18, 82–84, 86.

Frenn, George. "The hammer throw," *Athletic Journal* 47 (February 1967): 52, 54–57, 84.

Gilligan, William. "Hammer throwing and the 35 lb. weight," *Track and Field Quarterly Review,* March 1966, pp. 47–55.

Harmati, Sandor. "Gyula Zsivotzky's training profile," *Track Technique,* No. 26 (December 1966), pp. 826–29.

Hopper, Bernard J. "Some mechanical features of the hammer release," *Track Technique,* No. 31 (March 1968), pp. 972–75.

Jabs, Rolf-Gunther. "Analyzing the 1972 Olympic hammer," *Track Technique,* No. 52 (June 1973), pp. 1656–59.

______. "Psychological considerations in hammer throwing," *Track Technique,* No. 19 (March 1965), pp. 596–97.

______. "Hammer throwing principles, part 1," *Track Technique,* No. 21 (September 1965), p. 670.

______. "Part 2," *Track Technique,* 22 (December 1965), pp. 695–96.

______. "Part 3," *Track Technique,* 23 (March 1966), pp. 722–24.

Johnson, Carlton. "Teaching hammer in schools," *Athletics Coach* (June 1971): 2–8.

Johnson, Sam. "Fundamental skills of throwing the hammer," *Track Technique,* No. 4 (June 1961), pp. 104–8.

Kintisch, Irv. "Teaching the hammer throw," *Track and Field Quarterly Review* 70 (August 1970): 11–14.

Lutkowski, J. "Development of young hammer throwers," *Track Technique,* No. 39 (March 1970), pp. 1237–39.

Nett, Toni. *Die Tecknik bei Stoss und Wurf.* West Berlin: 1961.

———. "Fundamentals of the technique of hammer throwing," in *Track in Theory and Technique*, pp. 373–76. Richmond, Calif.: Worldwide Publishing Co., 1962.

Payne, Howard. *Hammer Throwing.* London: AAA, 1969. 147 pp. ($2.00 postpaid).

Raymond, Doug. "The hammer throw," *Track and Field Quarterly Review* 73 (March 1973): 41–44.

Samosvetov, Anatoliy. "Die Wirksamkeit der Abwurfphase beim Hammerwurf," *Leichtathletik* (West Berlin), No. 20, 1969.

Schmolinsky, G. *Leichtathletik.* East Berlin: 1971.

Scoles, Gordon. "Pulling strength for hammer throwers," *Track and Field Quarterly Review* 73 (December 1973): 243–45.

Simonyi, Gabor. "Non-turning hammer throwing," *Track Technique,* No. 54 (December 1973), pp. 1728–31.

———. "Hammer throwing, part 1," *Track Technique,* No. 14 (December 1963), pp. 434–38.

———. "Part 2," *Track Technique,* No. 15 (March 1964), pp. 464–66.

———. "Part 3," *Track Technique,* No. 16 (June 1964), pp. 491–93.

Sjutsch, E. "Four or five hammer turns?" *Track Technique,* No. 6 (December 1961), p. 165.

Wilt, Fred. "Hammer teaching progressions," *Track and Field Quarterly Review* 70 (November 1970): 24–26.

five

The All-around Athlete

The decathlon

The decathlon might be called the "acid test" of athletics, for its demands upon the participants are great. The name "decathlon" comes from the Greek *deca*, meaning "ten," since it includes ten separate events. The competition lasts for two days, with five different events contested each day, following a set sequence. The first day begins with the 100-meter sprint, followed in order by the long jump, shot-put, high jump, and 400 meters. The second day opens with the 110-meter hurdles, proceeds through the discus throw, pole vault, and javelin throw, then concludes with the 1500-meter run.

The decathlon is scored by a table devised by the IAAF on a range of 1 to 1,200 points per event, with the 1,000-point level roughly equivalent to the "decathlon world record" for that event (best mark made solely in decathlon competition). A score of 5,000 points for an inexperienced person shows decathlon potential, provided weaknesses in any individual event are not too glaring. A score of 7,000 points is beginning to reach national class, while the world-class level begins around 7,800 points.

Training for the Decathlon

Though occasional references to the decathlon may be found, they are few and give little detail of decathlon training in actual practice. Three systems or methods of decathlon training will be described here. The first is that of "Ducky" Drake, former UCLA coach and developer of two world record holders and Olympic medalists. The discussion is based upon written accounts[1,2] and personal contacts with Mr. Drake. The second system is that of Friedel Schirmer, the West German decathlon coach, considered by many[3] to be the leading decathlon coach in the world today. The discussion of his training methods is based primarily upon two published versions of an address[7,8] delivered to an international gathering of coaches in Athens in 1969. The third system is the one practiced at Oregon, which has produced one world-class decathlete.

Little attention has been paid to the potential all-around training which can be gained from decathlon training. Bill Toomey, 1968 Olympic champion, has stated[3] that he improved in his previous specialty events while training for the whole decathlon, rather than training for one or two events. Schirmer points out[7] that the first thing the decathlete needs to do is attain a high level of physical conditioning. Some writers have suggested useful variations of the decathlon for physical education classes, but few schools follow up these possibilities. Parks[6] suggested that variations of the decathlon might be used indoors with students of elementary and junior high school age, while Sylvia[10] devised a simplified scoring table for use in high school and college physical education classes. Bowerman[4] has used a variation called the "three-quarter decathlon" in classes for almost twenty years, with a recently revised scoring table more closely related to the international tables, thus more indicative of genuine decathlon potential.

The decathlon is a strenuous event, or one might even refer to it as a "sport," as ten events are included. The short time in which the athletes must produce major efforts creates a need for stamina. One writer[11] suggests that the three major physical needs of the decathlete are skill, strength, and stamina. He points out that the psychological considerations are many, since the athlete needs long-term powers of concentration to endure the mental strain of up-and-down competition spread over two days.

A study of the 1968 Olympic decathlon competition was made, with the observer comparing in particular the first six finishers to the last six finishers. His conclusion was that points were more easily lost than gained, so the key to success was a balance of skill over *all* the events. This touches upon the old argument of whether the decathlete should concentrate on his "specialty" event or events to make up for his weak events, or concentrate on his weaker events so they will not detract so much from his final score. Until ten or fifteen years ago, perhaps the leading idea was to work on one or several "big" events which would pile up a mass of points. This idea is no longer accepted, perhaps because the competition is not so easily beaten as before. Sykes shows another weakness of the old idea with his study: what happens if the athlete does not "come through" on his big event?

He will likely lose. Shirmer,[3] feeling that American athletes spend too much time training for their best events, says, "I concentrate on weaknesses. Only after a man has brought himself up to the required level do we permit him to work mainly on his best events."

The Drake System of Decathlon Training

"Ducky" Drake, who produced two great athletes, Rafer Johnson and C. K. Yang, likes to work on a three-day cycle, six days a week, concentrating on the athlete's weaker events. He divides the decathlon into three groups of three events each: the runs, the jumps, the throws, plus the 1500 meters. On each of the three days of the cycle the athlete works on one event from each of the groups, so he covers all ten events in three days (no special 1500-meter training is done, except for a 5-mile cross country run once a week). The three days a week also include weight training, so the training pattern for a week looks like this:[2]

Monday	*Tuesday*	*Wednesday*
Pole vault Javelin Intervals: 10 × 165 30 min. weights	High jump Shot-put Hurdles Intervals: 6 × 330	Long jump Discus Intervals: 10 × 220 30 min. weights
Thursday	*Friday*	*Saturday*
Pole vault Discus Hurdles Intervals: 10 × 110	High jump Javelin Intervals: 4 × 110 2 × 220 2 × 330 30 min. weights	Long jump Shot-put Hurdles Cross country with intervals (fartlek)

Most of the running is fartlek and short intervals, ranging from 110 to 330 yards, with equal rests. Drake feels that the pole vault needs much work, since it is difficult, but it is also good for general development, since it helps develop the arms and shoulder girdle, strengthening the athlete for the weight events. He tries to rotate his decathletes into different events during the dual meet season, so they will have competitive experience in *all* the events.

Drake states that the decathlete needs speed, strength, and endurance. Because stamina is very necessary, much repetition work with running is needed. He points out that both of his great decathletes had exceptional coordination, so they were able to make adjustments in form quickly. Most of the best American decathletes until recent times have been hurdlers, perhaps because the hurdles (and pole vault also) require the most all-around skill. A final important quality of great decathletes pointed out by Drake is the ability to relax between events, conserving the athlete's physical and mental energy.

The Schirmer System of Decathlon Training

Schirmer is one of the few coaches who specialize in the decathlon, and the athletes of this former Olympic decathlon competitor have made an outstanding showing, setting a number of records and winning several medals in Olympic competition. He emphasizes the need to first develop a good base of conditioning of the body, which can then benefit more from the specific training in the techniques of the events. He mentions in particular three points of value to decathlon training:

1. Training to increase muscular strength ensures basic conditioning, making the learning of techniques easier and faster. However, *too much* training to increase muscular strength may impair the specific sense of movement.
2. Training to increase organic strength has little effect upon the mastering of techniques. Also, it *might not* give increases in the muscular strength.
3. Training aimed at improving the sense of movement has a favorable influence upon technique.

He also stresses the importance of planning decathlon training before it begins, considering the aims of training and the different means of training needed for the different muscle groups. The sequence of training exercises should be clearly thought out as to their training aim. Schirmer notes that some carry-over is gained from the training for one event to certain other events, if practiced in a certain order, such as training for the hurdles after working on the hitch-kick in the long jump.

A proponent of "weak event training," Schirmer feels that the decathlete should train first in his weak events, until he has reached the 7,400-point level, which is the lower realms of world-class competition. When this level is reached, the athlete should then try to become *especially* good in two or three "specialty events" in which he might earn the large point scores which make the difference between the 7,400- and 8,000-point decathletes.

He also notes several "principles of decathlon training":

1. Technique and speed training should be practiced only after long pauses, when the muscles are well rested.
2. If a single day's training covers several kinds of exercises, the athlete should go in the following order of practice:
   a. Technique
   b. Force
   c. Conditioning
3. The decathlete should use the event technique best suited to *himself,* rather than the best technique in an absolute sense, as he might use if he were a specialist in that event.
4. Speed and power training can benefit greatly by intense concentration before and during the exercises, thus yielding better results in less time with less effort. Weight training in particular requires full concentration and great technical precision.

Schirmer recommends a four-day training cycle, if the various types of training are done on different days:

First day:	Technique and speed work
Second day:	Power training
Third day:	Speed and endurance training
Fourth day:	Rest, or easy day

For the period immediately following a decathlon competition, he suggests two days of rest, easy warming up on the third day, easy coordinated running on the fourth day, and easy technical work on the fifth day, with no endurance or strength training during this period. The athlete should be ready to compete in a single event one week after the decathlon and another high-level (such as national-class) decathlon within two weeks.

The Oregon System of Decathlon Competition

A decathlon class was added to the Oregon physical education activity program around 1953. At first only the freshmen track team participated, though this is no longer the case. Offered during the fall term, the class yields three results with freshmen track athletes:

1. It gives them basic conditioning.
2. It teaches them sympathy or gives them more understanding of the problems of the athletes in events which have been alien to them.
3. It shows the coach if any athlete has undetected talent in an unsuspected event. One such discovery was Les Tipton, a high school hurdler who threw the javelin 160 feet in the decathlon class. Switched to the javelin, he threw over 260 feet as a senior, winning the NCAA title.

Scoring the Decathlon

A special point table is used for the Oregon decathlon, since it is a "three-quarter" decathlon: all the running events are only three-fourths of the usual distance. The 100 meters was converted to 75 yards, though 60 yards (with a starting-time-loss conversion factor) is now used, since it is a more commonly run distance. The 400 meters became a 330-yard run, the 110-meter (or 120-yard) high hurdles became the 90-yard highs (set at the high school height of 39 inches), and the 1500-meter run became a 1320-yard (three-fourth mile) run. All other events use standard conditions and implements of the standard size and weight. The athlete may skip one of the ten events, taking an automatic 100 points for that event.

The old scoring tables were revised in 1971 to be very close to the values of the IAAF tables, giving them more accurate predictive value to potential achievement in a regulation decathlon. The tests (three in the ten-week term: pretest, midterm, and final exam) are spread over three days, instead of two, and cover a five-day period, testing on Monday, Wednesday, and Friday. A simpler, quicker scale, but one which cannot be used for comparative purposes to the IAAF tables, is the one compiled by Sylvia.[10] It has here been amended to cover fourteen events, since his testing suggestion was that the student could substitute one of the additional events for one of the ten regulation events (or his variations of them), usually replacing the javelin, which is not allowed in many states in high school competition, or the pole vault. The softball, football, or 800-gram weighted ball throw might be substituted for the javelin, using the same scoring tables. Thus three versions of the decathlon might be used in physical education classes (or as an "interest-getter" for the track team in the fall, preseason, or just after the competitive season has been concluded). The events are as follows:

IAAF "Official"	*Bowerman "Three-quarter College"*	*Sylvia "School"*
100 meters	60 yards	100 yards
Long jump	Long jump	Long jump
Shot-put (16 pounds)	Shot-put (16 pounds)	Shot-put (12 pounds)
High jump	High jump	High jump
400 meters	330 yards	440 yards
110-meter hurdles (42 inches)	90-yard highs (39 inches)	120-yard lows (30 inches)
Discus throw (2 kilograms)	Discus throw (2 kilograms)	Discus throw (high school)
Pole vault	Pole vault	Pole vault
Javelin throw	Javelin throw	Javelin or ball throw
1500-meter run	Three-quarter-mile run	1-mile run

The IAAF version takes the first five events on the first day and the second five events on the second day. A short version of the scoring table is shown at the end of this chapter as an example of the scoring methods (see Appendix A, page 384). All implements are official and all international rules apply, *except* that:

1. There are only *three* attempts in the throwing events, not six.
2. There are only *three* attempts in the long jump, not six.
3. The runner is not disqualified until the *third* false start.
4. The athlete must attempt every event, or he is disqualified.
5. Records cannot be set if the wind exceeds four meters per second in those events where the wind velocity must be fixed.

The Bowerman version takes three days, four of the events being contested on the first day. There might be some rearrangement of the event order on the second day, if wished, such as opening with the hurdles, then the discus, then concluding with the 330-yard run. Starts are without blocks and running from a three- or four-point start (see Chapter 18 on testing), with the clock started when the hand is lifted from the track. The long jump is measured from the take-off point, so that there are no "scratch" jumps. The Bowerman tables are also reproduced at the end of this chapter (see Appendix B, pages 385–86).

The Sylvia version can also use the informal aspects of the Bowerman version. No stated length of time is offered for completing this decathlon. For the hurdles, the low hurdles are used, set at the low hurdle spacings (20 yards apart), though the hurdles might be set at the low height with the high hurdle spacings. One event may be substituted for an additional event, the choices being the 220 and 880 (scored by Sylvia) and the 2-mile and triple jump (based upon Sylvia's tables). His scoring tables are also reprinted at the end of this chapter (see Appendix C, pages 387–89).

Each of the versions has its advantages, with the primary advantage of the Sylvia version being its scoring simplicity, while the primary advantage of the Bowerman version is its close scoring similarity to the IAAF tables, permitting great predictive value without running the more exhausting full distances or making metric conversions. In all cases, the IAAF competition rules are followed basically, with the modifications mentioned above.

Training for the Decathlon

The decathlon training at Oregon has produced one outstanding decathlete, Dave Edstrom, who scored 8,176 points on the 1952 tables then in force (7,870 on the 1962 tables) and was a member of the 1960 U.S. Olympic Team. The training follows the Oregon hard-easy principle. Since there are always two consecutive days of competition, the training follows a pattern of two hard days, followed by two easy days. The events are practiced in the order in which they are encountered in competition.

On the first hard day, the athlete warms up, then takes four to six sprint starts. He then does a few short sprints, going 30, then 50 yards, possibly adding a 70-yard sprint. He then proceeds to the long jump, where he first works on his check marks, then works on "pop-ups." He next follows the shot-put outine, first putting from a stand, then crossing the ring and putting, all while working on *one* aspect of the technique. He then moves to the high jump area, working first on his check marks, then taking about six jumps working on one of the techniques. He then concludes the workout with four 110s and a fartlek run.

On the second hard day, he warms up, goes through several sprint starts, then goes to the hurdles. He goes through the X drill, then runs either a set of "back-to-back 5s" or "first 3 — last 3." He then moves to the discus, where he works on one aspect of his technique, first throwing from a stand (with his back foot in the center of the ring, rather than hanging over the front of the ring), then working with the turn. He then works on the pole vault, first setting his check marks, then working on his pole plant, then the take-off, and finishing with perhaps half a dozen vaults. He then runs through the javelin routine, first throwing the weighted balls from a stand, then going to the 3-4-5 throwing sequence, then the full count check, then moving several times through the full run. The full run work

Figure 16.1a Decathlon Training Schedule

Decathlon NAME DATE September/October

1. Warm-up A. Jogging and stretching
   B. Relay work
2. Fartlek A. Varied pace B. Slow, steady C. Light
3. A. Jogging and stretching B. Weights and jogging
   C. Easy jogging
4. 100 m A. High knee—fast leg B. Starts C. Finish work
5. Long jump A. Check marks (1) Short (2) Long
   B. Pop-ups, 2-count rise
6. Shot-put A. Routine B. Standing
   C. Across the ring
7. Squad meeting
8. Special A. Sauna B. Swim C. Hill or steps
9. High jump A. Check marks B. Take off
   C. Clearance B. Jumping E. Rhythm
10. Test effort A. 100 meters B. Long jump C. Shot
    D. High jump E. 400 meters F. 110 m G. Discus
    H. Pole vault J. Javelin K. 1,500 m L.
    (1) 3/4 racing distance
11. Intervals X. Easy Y. Hurdles
    Z. Fast in middle 20–50 yds. A. 55 B. 110 C. 165
    D. 220 E. 330 F. 440 G. 550 H. 660 J.
    (1) Goal pace (2) Date pace
12. With coach: A. B.
14. 110 m hurdles A. X drill B. Starts C.
15. Discus throw A. Routine B. Standing
    C. Across the ring D. Alternate stand and across
    E.
16. Pole vault A. Check marks B. Approach
    C. Pole plant D. Take off E. Vaulting F.
17. Javelin A. Standing throws B. Trot and throw
    C. Full run X. Check marks D. Technique throws
    E.
18. Sets Y. Over hurdles A. 110-220-110 (1) Goal pace
    B. 165-110-55 (2) Date pace C. 330-220-110
    (3) D. 660-440-220 E.
19. Weak event work A. Throw B. Jump C. Run
    (1) Weakest (2) 2d weakest
20.
21. A. Pictures B. Film C. Video

M	Class organization-1A-2B1
T	
W	1A-10A1-10C-10B
T	
F	1A-10D-10E1
S	
S	

M	1A-10F1-10J-2A1 or 8X 11D (35-40)
T	
W	1A-2B2
T	
F	1A-10G-10H-2A or 8X 11D (35-40)
S	
S	

M	1A-14A1-9A-9D1-5A1-5B-2C
T	
W	1A-14A1-14B3-5B-6A-2B1
T	
F	1A-14A1-14B2-9A-9C-6B-2A1
S	
S	

M	1A-14A1-15A1-15E1-17B1-2C
T	
W	1A-14A1-17A-9A-9D-3X 11C-2C
T	
F	1A-10F1 (30")-9D-15B-2B1
S	
S	

Figure 16.1b Decathlon Training Schedule

Decathlon NAME DATE *October/November*

1. Warm-up A. Jogging and stretching
   B. Relay work
2. Fartlek A. Varied pace B. Slow, steady C. Light
3. A. Jogging and stretching B. Weights and jogging
   C. Easy jogging
4. 100 m A. High knee—fast leg B. Starts C. Finish work
5. Long jump A. Check marks (1) Short (2) Long
   B. Pop-ups, 2-count rise
6. Shot-put A. Routine B. Standing
   C. Across the ring
7. Squad meeting
8. Special A. Sauna B. Swim C. Hill or steps
9. High jump A. Check marks B. Take off
   C. Clearance B. Jumping E. Rhythm
10. Test effort A. 100 meters B. Long jump C. Shot
    D. High jump E. 400 meters F. 110 m G. Discus
    H. Pole vault J. Javelin K. 1,500 m L.
    (1) 3/4 racing distance
11. Intervals X. Easy Y. Hurdles
    Z. Fast in middle 20-50 yds. A. 55 B. 110 C. 165
    D. 220 E. 330 F. 440 G. 550 H. 660 J.
    (1) Goal pace (2) Date pace
12. With coach: A. B.
14. 110 m hurdles A. X drill B. Starts C.
15. Discus throw A. Routine B. Standing
    C. Across the ring D. Alternate stand and across
    E.
16. Pole vault A. Check marks B. Approach
    C. Pole plant D. Take off E. Vaulting F.
17. Javelin A. Standing throws B. Trot and throw
    C. Full run X. Check marks D. Technique throws
    E.
18. Sets Y. Over hurdles A. 110-220-110 (1) Goal pace
    B. 165-110-55 (2) Date pace C. 330-220-110
    (3) D. 660-440-220 E.
19. Weak event work A. Throw B. Jump C. Run
    (1) Weakest (2) 2d weakest
20.
21. A. Pictures B. Film C. Video

M	*1A–14A2–4B–15D–9D–2C*
T	
W	*1A–14A2–9D–6A–2A1*
T	
F	*1A–14A2–5A–5B–6B–6C–2B2*
S	
S	

M	*1A–10A1–10C–10D–2C*
T	
W	*1A–10B–10E1–2B2*
T	
F	*1A–10F1 (36")–10G–10H*
S	
S	

M	*1A–14A23–5B1–10J–10K–3C*
T	
W	*1A–14A23–5B–16A–16E–6A–2C*
T	
F	*1A–14A23–16E–9D or 6B–6A or 17D*
S	
S	

M	
T	
W	
T	
F	
S	
S	

Figure 16.1c Decathlon Training Schedule

Decathlon NAME DATE November/December

1. Warm-up A. Jogging and stretching
   B. Relay work
2. Fartlek A. Varied pace B. Slow, steady C. Light
3. A. Jogging and stretching B. Weights and jogging
   C. Easy jogging
4. 100 m A. High knee—fast leg B. Starts C. Finish work
5. Long jump A. Check marks (1) Short (2) Long
   B. Pop-ups, 2-count rise
6. Shot-put A. Routine B. Standing
   C. Across the ring
7. Squad meeting
8. Special A. Sauna B. Swim C. Hill or steps
9. High jump A. Check marks B. Take off
   C. Clearance B. Jumping E. Rhythm
10. Test effort A. 100 meters B. Long jump C. Shot
    D. High jump E. 400 meters F. 110 m G. Discus
    H. Pole vault J. Javelin K. 1,500 m L.
    (1) 3/4 racing distance
11. Intervals X. Easy Y. Hurdles
    Z. Fast in middle 20-50 yds. A. 55 B. 110 C. 165
    D. 220 E. 330 F. 440 G. 550 H. 660 J.
    (1) Goal pace (2) Date pace
12. With coach: A. B.
14. 110 m hurdles A. X drill B. Starts C.
15. Discus throw A. Routine B. Standing
    C. Across the ring D. Alternate stand and across
    E.
16. Pole vault A. Check marks B. Approach
    C. Pole plant D. Take off E. Vaulting F.
17. Javelin A. Standing throws B. Trot and throw
    C. Full run X. Check marks D. Technique throws
    E.
18. Sets Y. Over hurdles A. 110-220-110 (1) Goal pace
    B. 165-110-55 (2) Date pace C. 330-220-110
    (3) D. 660-440-220 E.
19. Weak event work A. Throw B. Jump C. Run
    (1) Weakest (2) 2d weakest
20.
21. A. Pictures B. Film C. Video

M	1A-14A23-5A-5B-9D-15D-2A1
T	
W	4x 1A-14A23-9D-17D2-17D4-16E-11D (35-40)
T	
F	1A-14A23-6B-6C-5A-15D-2B2
S	
S	
M	1A-14A23-5 or 9 or 16-6 or 15 or 17-2C
T	
W	Choice
T	
F	Choice
S	
S	
M	1A-10A1-10B-10C-10J-3C
T	
W	1A-10C-10D-10E1-3C
T	
F	1A-10F1 (39")-10H-10K1-3C
S	
S	
M	
T	
W	
T	
F	
S	
S	

Figure 16.1d Decathlon Training Schedule

Decathlon NAME DATE January

1. Warm-up A. Jogging and stretching B. Relay work
2. Fartlek A. Varied pace B. Slow, steady C. Light
3. A. Jogging and stretching B. Weights and jogging C. Easy jogging
4. 100 m A. High knee—fast leg B. Starts C. Finish work
5. Long jump A. Check marks (1) Short (2) Long B. Pop-ups, 2-count rise
6. Shot-put A. Routine B. Standing C. Across the ring
7. Squad meeting
8. Special A. Sauna B. Swim C. Hill or steps
9. High jump A. Check marks B. Take off C. Clearance B. Jumping E. Rhythm
10. Test effort A. 100 meters B. Long jump C. Shot D. High jump E. 400 meters F. 110 m G. Discus H. Pole vault J. Javelin K. 1,500 m L. (1) 3/4 racing distance
11. Intervals X. Easy Y. Hurdles Z. Fast in middle 20-50 yds. A. 55 B. 110 C. 165 D. 220 E. 330 F. 440 G. 550 H. 660 J. (1) Goal pace (2) Date pace
12. With coach: A. B.
14. 110 m hurdles A. X drill B. Starts C.
15. Discus throw A. Routine B. Standing C. Across the ring D. Alternate stand and across E.
16. Pole vault A. Check marks B. Approach C. Pole plant D. Take off E. Vaulting F.
17. Javelin A. Standing throws B. Trot and throw C. Full run X. Check marks D. Technique throws E.
18. Sets Y. Over hurdles A. 110-220-110 (1) Goal pace B. 165-110-55 (2) Date pace C. 330-220-110 (3) D. 660-440-220 E.
19. Weak event work A. Throw B. Jump C. Run (1) Weakest (2) 2d weakest
20.
21. A. Pictures B. Film C. Video

M	3-6x 3x Squad organization- 4A-4B - 5B - 11C-2A1
T	3x 4x 1A-14A1-9E-11C-11F (75-80)-2B1
W	7-3B
T	3-6x 3x 1A-4A-4B-5B - 6B1-11C-2A1
F	3x 4x 1A-14A1-9E-11C-11F(75-80)-2B1
S	3B
S	3A

M	6x 1A-14A2-14B2-15D-16A1-11E(50-52)-2B-3B
T	10-15x 10-15x 3x 1A-14A2-14B2-17A - 17B - 18B-18C
W	7-3B
T	6x 1A-14A2-14B2-15D-16A1-11E(50-52)-2B
F	10-15x 10-15x 3x 1A-14A2-14B2-17A - 17B - 18B-18C
S	3B
S	3A

M	3-6x 3x 1A-4A-4B-5B-6B1-11C-2A1
T	4x 1A-10A1 or 10F(60y)-14A1-9E-11F-2B1
W	7-3B
T	3-6x 3x 1A-10A1 or 10F(60y)-4A-4B-5B -11C-2A1
F	4x 1A-14A1-9E-11F(75-80)-2B1
S	3B
S	3A

M	1A-14A2-16A1-16B1-16E1- 6x/11E(50-52)-2A13B
T	10-15x 4x 1A-14A2-15B-16A1-17B1-18C-11B-2B1
W	3B
T	10-15x 10-15x 4x 1A-14A2-16A1-16B1-17A - 17B - 18C - 11B
F	3-6x 3-6x 6x 1A-14A2-15B-15D-16A1-16E1-11E-2A1
S	3B
S	3A

Figure 16.1e Decathlon Training Schedule

Decathlon NAME DATE February

1. Warm-up A. Jogging and stretching
   B. Relay work
2. Fartlek A. Varied pace B. Slow, steady C. Light
3. A. Jogging and stretching B. Weights and jogging
   C. Easy jogging
4. 100 m A. High knee—fast leg B. Starts C. Finish work
5. Long jump A. Check marks (1) Short (2) Long
   B. Pop-ups, 2-count rise
6. Shot-put A. Routine B. Standing
   C. Across the ring
7. Squad meeting
8. Special A. Sauna B. Swim C. Hill or steps
9. High jump A. Check marks B. Take off
   C. Clearance B. Jumping E. Rhythm
10. Test effort A. 100 meters B. Long jump C. Shot
    D. High jump E. 400 meters F. 110 m G. Discus
    H. Pole vault J. Javelin K. 1,500 m L.
    (1) 3/4 racing distance
11. Intervals X. Easy Y. Hurdles
    Z. Fast in middle 20–50 yds. A. 55 B. 110 C. 165
    D. 220 E. 330 F. 440 G. 550 H. 660 J.
    (1) Goal pace (2) Date pace
12. With coach: A. B.
14. 110 m hurdles A. X drill B. Starts C.
15. Discus throw A. Routine B. Standing
    C. Across the ring D. Alternate stand and across
    E.
16. Pole vault A. Check marks B. Approach
    C. Pole plant D. Take off E. Vaulting F.
17. Javelin A. Standing throws B. Trot and throw
    C. Full run X. Check marks D. Technique throws
    E.
18. Sets Y. Over hurdles A. 110-220-110 (1) Goal pace
    B. 165-110-55 (2) Date pace C. 330-220-110
    (3) D. 660-440-220 E.
19. Weak event work A. Throw B. Jump C. Run
    (1) Weakest (2) 2d weakest
20.
21. A. Pictures B. Film C. Video

M	1A-4A-5B-6A-6B-11C (3X) -2A1-3B
T	1A-14A2-15B-16A1-17B1 (10-15X) -18C-11B (4X) -2B1
W	7-3B
T	1A-14A2-16A1-16B1-16E1-1B1
F	1A-6A-6C-9A-9D-18C-3C-11B (4X)
S	2A1-3B
S	19-2B2 or 3A
M	1A-14A23-15A-15B (4-6X) -16A1-10K1-3C-3B
T	1A-14A2-14B2-16A1-16B-17A (10-15X) -17B (10-15X) -11F (4X)
W	1A-10D-2A2-3B
T	1A-14A23-14B1-15D (6X) -15C (6X) -16A-16E-11F (4X) -2B
F	1A-14A2-14B3-10G-16A-16C-17B-17C (2X) -11C (3X) -3C
S	1A-10F1-2A1-3B
S	19-2B2 or 3A
M	1A-4A-10A-5A-5B-6A-11C2 (4X) -2B1-3B
T	1A-14A2-6A-6B-9A-9E-18B2 (2X) -11B (4X) -2B
W	7-1A-10B-2A2-3B
T	1A-4A-4B-5A-5B-6A-11G-2B1-11B (4X)
F	1A-14A2-5A-10C-9A-9E-11E2 (6X) -3C
S	2A1-3B
S	19-2B2 or 3A
M	1A-14A23-15A-15B (4X) -16A-10E-2B-3B
T	1A-14A23-14B2-16A1-16B-17A-17B-11F1 (4X)
W	1A-10H-2A2-3B
T	1A-14A23-14B1-15D (6X) -15C (6X) -16A-16E-11E2 (6X) -2B
F	1A-4A-16A-17B (10-15X) -10J-2B
S	10F-3B
S	19-2B2 or 3A

Figure 16.1f Decathlon Training Schedule

Decathlon NAME DATE March

1. Warm-up A. Jogging and stretching
   B. Relay work
2. Fartlek A. Varied pace B. Slow, steady C. Light
3. A. Jogging and stretching B. Weights and jogging
   C. Easy jogging
4. 100 m A. High knee—fast leg B. Starts C. Finish work
5. Long jump A. Check marks (1) Short (2) Long
   B. Pop-ups, 2-count rise
6. Shot-put A. Routine B. Standing
   C. Across the ring
7. Squad meeting
8. Special A. Sauna B. Swim C. Hill or steps
9. High jump A. Check marks B. Take off
   C. Clearance B. Jumping E. Rhythm
10. Test effort A. 100 meters B. Long jump C. Shot
    D. High jump E. 400 meters F. 110 m G. Discus
    H. Pole vault J. Javelin K. 1,500 m L.
    (1) 3/4 racing distance
11. Intervals X. Easy Y. Hurdles
    Z. Fast in middle 20–50 yds. A. 55 B. 110 C. 165
    D. 220 E. 330 F. 440 G. 550 H. 660 J.
    (1) Goal pace (2) Date pace
12. With coach: A. B.
14. 110 m hurdles A. X drill B. Starts C.
15. Discus throw A. Routine B. Standing
    C. Across the ring D. Alternate stand and across
    E.
16. Pole vault A. Check marks B. Approach
    C. Pole plant D. Take off E. Vaulting F.
17. Javelin A. Standing throws B. Trot and throw
    C. Full run X. Check marks D. Technique throws
    E.
18. Sets Y. Over hurdles A. 110-220-110 (1) Goal pace
    B. 165-110-55 (2) Date pace C. 330-220-110
    (3) D. 660-440-220 E.
19. Weak event work A. Throw B. Jump C. Run
    (1) Weakest (2) 2d weakest
20.
21. A. Pictures B. Film C. Video

M	1A-14A23-4A-5A2-5B1-6A-11G-3C-11CY [3X]-3B
T	1A-4C-6B [3X]-6C [3X]-9A2-9D-11B1 [3X]-18B2-2B
W	7-1A-14A2-19A1-3B
T	1A-4B-19A2-2A1
F	1A-14A2-15A-16A1-16A2-17CX [3X]-3C-11B [4X]
S	10:00-10:30-11:00-11:30-12:00-12:30 1A-10A- 10B- 10C- 10D- 10E-3C
S	3C
M	1A-14A23-14B2-15A-18C2-2B-11B [4X]-3B
T	1A-10A23-14B3-16A-16E-17A [10-15X]-17B-11E2 [6X]-2B
W	7-1A-19A1-3B
T	1A-14A2-14B1-2A1
F	1A-5A-5B1-6A-9A2-3C-11B [4X]
S	10:00-10:30-11:00-11:30-12:15-12:45 1A - 10F - 10G - 10H - 10J - 10K-3C
S	3C
M	14A-19-16-2A1-3B
T	1A-4B-5A [3-6X]-5B [3-6X]-6A-9A-9D2-11C [3X]-3C
W	14A23-14B1-15A [4-6X]-15D-16A-16E-17D-11E [6X]-3B
T	1A-19-3A
F	3C - Gear ready
S	10 - Early season meet
S	3A
M	14A-19-16-2A1-3B
T	1A-4A-5A-5B-6A [3-6X]-9A-9B-11D2 [4X]-2B
W	14A-15D [3-6X]-16A-16C-17X-17D [10-15X]-18C [2-3X]
T	1A-19-4B or 14B1-11C [2X]-3B (light)
F	3C-Gear ready
S	Dual meet
S	3C

Figure 16.1g Decathlon Training Schedule

Decathlon NAME DATE *April*

1. Warm-up A. Jogging and stretching
   B. Relay work
2. Fartlek A. Varied pace B. Slow, steady C. Light
3. A. Jogging and stretching B. Weights and jogging
   C. Easy jogging
4. 100 m A. High knee—fast leg B. Starts C. Finish work
5. Long jump A. Check marks (1) Short (2) Long
   B. Pop-ups, 2-count rise
6. Shot-put A. Routine B. Standing
   C. Across the ring
7. Squad meeting
8. Special A. Sauna B. Swim C. Hill or steps
9. High jump A. Check marks B. Take off
   C. Clearance B. Jumping E. Rhythm
10. Test effort A. 100 meters B. Long jump C. Shot
    D. High jump E. 400 meters F. 110 m G. Discus
    H. Pole vault J. Javelin K. 1,500 m L.
    (1) 3/4 racing distance
11. Intervals X. Easy Y. Hurdles
    Z. Fast in middle 20–50 yds. A. 55 B. 110 C. 165
    D. 220 E. 330 F. 440 G. 550 H. 660 J.
    (1) Goal pace (2) Date pace
12. With coach: A. B.
14. 110 m hurdles A. X drill B. Starts C.
15. Discus throw A. Routine B. Standing
    C. Across the ring D. Alternate stand and across
    E.
16. Pole vault A. Check marks B. Approach
    C. Pole plant D. Take off E. Vaulting F.
17. Javelin A. Standing throws B. Trot and throw
    C. Full run X. Check marks D. Technique throws
    E.
18. Sets Y. Over hurdles A. 110-220-110 (1) Goal pace
    B. 165-110-55 (2) Date pace C. 330-220-110
    (3) D. 660-440-220 E.
19. Weak event work A. Throw B. Jump C. Run
    (1) Weakest (2) 2d weakest
20.
21. A. Pictures B. Film C. Video

M	7-14A234-4B-5A-5B-6B-6C-9A-9D-11C (3-4X) -3C
T	14A-14B2-15D (3-6X) -16A-16E-17X-17D-18D1-11B (4X)
W	1A-14B1-19-3C
T	3C-Gear ready
F	10-Decathlon-first day
S	10-Decathlon-second day
S	3C

M	14A-4A-5A-5B-6B-6C-9A-9D-11E (3-4X) -3B
T	3A-19A-19B-19C-3C
W	14A-15B2-15D-16A-16E-17X-17D-11E2 (6X) -3B
T	14A-14B1-19-3C
F	3C-Gear ready
S	Dual meet
S	3A

M	14A-4A-5A-5B-6B-6C-9A-9E-18B (2-3X) -3C-3B
T	3A-19A-19B-19C-3C
W	14A-14B3-15D-16A-16D-17X-17C-11F1 (4X) -3B
T	14A-14B1 or 4B-19-3C
F	3C-Gear ready
S	Dual meet
S	3A

M	1A-4A-4B-6A-6C-9A-9B-11C1 (2-3X) -3C-3B
T	14A-14B1-15A-15C-16A-16C-17X-17D-11E1 (6X)
W	1A-19B-19A-19C-3B-3C
T	3C-Gear ready
F	10-Decathlon-first day
S	10-Decathlon-second day
S	3A

Figure 16.1h Decathlon Training Schedule

Decathlon NAME DATE May / June

1. Warm-up A. Jogging and stretching B. Relay work
2. Fartlek A. Varied pace B. Slow, steady C. Light
3. A. Jogging and stretching B. Weights and jogging C. Easy jogging
4. 100 m A. High knee—fast leg B. Starts C. Finish work
5. Long jump A. Check marks (1) Short (2) Long B. Pop-ups, 2-count rise
6. Shot-put A. Routine B. Standing C. Across the ring
7. Squad meeting
8. Special A. Sauna B. Swim C. Hill or steps
9. High jump A. Check marks B. Take off C. Clearance B. Jumping E. Rhythm
10. Test effort A. 100 meters B. Long jump C. Shot D. High jump E. 400 meters F. 110 m G. Discus H. Pole vault J. Javelin K. 1,500 m L. (1) 3/4 racing distance
11. Intervals X. Easy Y. Hurdles Z. Fast in middle 20–50 yds. A. 55 B. 110 C. 165 D. 220 E. 330 F. 440 G. 550 H. 660 J. (1) Goal pace (2) Date pace
12. With coach: A. B.
14. 110 m hurdles A. X drill B. Starts C.
15. Discus throw A. Routine B. Standing C. Across the ring D. Alternate stand and across E.
16. Pole vault A. Check marks B. Approach C. Pole plant D. Take off E. Vaulting F.
17. Javelin A. Standing throws B. Trot and throw C. Full run X. Check marks D. Technique throws E.
18. Sets Y. Over hurdles A. 110-220-110 (1) Goal pace B. 165-110-55 (2) Date pace C. 330-220-110 (3) D. 660-440-220 E.
19. Weak event work A. Throw B. Jump C. Run (1) Weakest (2) 2d weakest
20.
21. A. Pictures B. Film C. Video

M	1A-4A-4B-5A-5B-6A-9A-9E-(2-3x) 18B-3B-3C
T	14A-14B1-15A-16A-16B-17X-17D-(4-6x) 11E-2B-
W	1A-4B or 14B1-19A1-19B1-3C
T	3C-Gear ready
F	Qualify-division or conference
S	Finals-division or conference
S	3A

M	1A-19B-19A-19C-3B-2B1
T	14A-19B1-19C1-19A1-3C
W	1A-4A-4B-5A-5B-6A-9A-9D-18C1-3C
T	14A-14B1-15A-16A-16E-17X-(3x) 17B-18D1-(4x) 11B-3C
F	3A-3B-2B1
S	3A
S	1A-4A-4B-4C-5A-5B-6A-(3x) 6C-9A-9B-18C1-3B-3C

M	14A-14B1-15A-(3x) 15C-16A-16C-17X-(3x) 17B-(4-6x) 11E1-3C
T	3C
W	3C-Gear ready
T	NCAA-Decathlon-first day
F	NCAA-Decathlon-second day
S	3A
S	3A

M	
T	
W	
T	
F	
S	
S	

is done last during the early season training, but it is done first during the late season training. Finally, the decathlete does what he can handle from a distance workout, usually about a mile of intervals (such as 8 x 220, or 6 x 330, or 4 x 440), then concludes the second hard day with a fartlek run. The third and fourth days are "easy" days, with activities such as jogging and stretching, with perhaps some swimming or weight training. The fifth day is a return to the first day of hard training, beginning the cycle again.

Notice that Schirmer's four-day sequence can also be fairly called a hard-easy pattern, since the second day is primarily weight-type training, while the fourth day is rest. For more specialized training suggestions, or for clarification of the workout sequence cited above, the chapters on the individual events should be studied. The decathlon is indeed a champion's event, the supreme test of the true athlete.

Explanation of a Week of Decathlon Training

The preceding training sheets listing the decathlon workouts are abbreviated forms of the regular decathlon training sheet, which is presented and explained on pages 350–53. The fall training schedules show workouts for only three days per week. During that part of the year, the decathlon is offered as a physical education class for the freshmen track team and any other interested students. On the days which list no workouts, the track team follows the workouts for each athlete's specialty events.

Monday: The class is introduced to the course and given an explanation of training, testing, and grading procedures.

(1A) Warm-up routine, with jogging and stretching activities, followed by the high knee–fast leg drill.

(2B1) Run 15 minutes of Lydiard fartlek (slow, steady running).

Tuesday: No workout is listed, so track men will follow the workout scheduled for their regular competitive event. Nontrack members of the physical education class may do as they choose.

Wednesday: (1A) Warm-up activities, as above.

(10A1) Test effort for the 100-meter event. This will be run at three-fourths the full distance, which in this case has been cut to a 60-yard dash.

(10C) First test in the shot-put, with each man getting three attempts. The throws are measured only to the nearest foot in the first test.

(10B) Test in the long jump. Again, each man gets three attempts.

The jump is measured from the take-off point, so there are no scratch jumps.

Thursday: Same description as for Tuesday.

Friday: (1A) Warm-up activities.

(10D) Test on the high jump.

(10E1) Test for the 400 meters. This test will be run at three-fourths distance, which is 330 yards.

Saturday: Same description as Tuesday.

Explanation of the Decathlon Training Sheets

The training sheets used to present the schedules are not the same as those used for the actual assignment of workouts. The sheet which is commonly used is shown in Figure 16.2. That sheet will be discussed only briefly.

Almost no new material appears on the decathlon training sheet which has not already been described in the chapters devoted to the individual events. The events comprising the decathlon are listed in the order in which they appear in the competition. For an explanation of the fundamentals of each event, the chapter on that event should be consulted. The few new descriptions which appear here are explained below.

10. Test effort. These are the trials used in the other events. They will be encountered every two to three weeks during training. They are never full effort, but are an attempt at controlled improvement.

10A1. 100 meters, three-fourths racing distance. The running events will rarely be contested over the full racing distance. The early trials will be at 60 yards. The later trials may be longer, moving up to 70 and then 80 yards.

10E1. 400 meters, three-fourths racing distance. This racing distance will also generally be run at less than the full distance in trials. The most common distance is 330 yards, though later trials may be at other fractional distances, such as 275 yards or 385 yards.

10F1. 110-meter hurdles, three-fourths racing distance. For the decathlon classes, the usual trial (and the final exam) is 90 yards. For other nonclass trials, other distances may be used, such as 60, 70, and 75 yards. For the class, the first trial is over the 30-inch (low) hurdles, the midterm is over the 36-inch (intermediate) hurdles, and the final exam is over the 39-inch (high school) hurdles. The hurdle spacings are not changed, 15 yards to the first barrier and 10 yards between each hurdle. Few trials will ever be at the full 42-inch international height.

Figure 16.2 Decathlon Training Sheet

Decathlon NAME

M	M
T	T
W	W
T	T
F	F
S	S
S	S

—/—/ to —/—/ —

1. Warm-up: A. Jogging and stretching—1 or 2 laps, high knee (slow)-fast leg B. Relay
2. Fartlek: A. Holmer (varied pace) B. Lydiard (slow, steady) C. Light fartlek
3. A. Jogging and stretching B. Weights and jogging C. Easy jogging
4. 100 meters A. High knee and fast leg exercise B. Starts: 3 at 1/2 speed, 3 at 7/8—30 yds. C. Finish work: 50-70 at 3/4, last 50-30 at 9/10 D. (1) 20-40-60
5. Long jump A. Check marks (1) Short—about 50 ft. (2) Long B. Pop-ups, 2-count rise C.
6. Shot-put A. Routine B. Standing put (1) Easy (2) Medium (3) Hard (4) Explode (a) Lift (b) Turn (c) Push C. Across the ring D.
7. Squad meeting
8. Special A. Sauna B. Swim C. Steps or hill
9. High jump A. Check marks (1) Short (2) Long (2 marks) B. Take off C. Clearance D. Jumping (1) Low, easy height (2) 4-6 in. under best (3) E. Rhythm 2-4-6-8 F.
10. Test effort A. 100 m B. Long jump C. Shot D. High jump E. 400 m F. 110 m G. Discus H. Pole vault J. Javelin K. 1,500 m L. (1) 3/4 racing distance
11. Intervals X. Easy Y. Hurdles Z. Fast 20-50 yds. in middle of interval A. 55 B. 110 C. 165 D. 220 E. 330 F. 440 G. 550 H. 660 J. (1) Goal pace (2) Date pace (3)
12. With coach: A. B.
14. 110 m hurdles A. X drill (1) 30 in. (2) 36 in. (3) 39 in. (4) 42 in. (a) Buck (b) Trail leg (c) Lead leg (d) Off arm (e) Lead arm (f) B. Starts over hurdles (1) 2 at 1/2 speed, 2 at 7/8 speed (2) Back-to-back 5s (3) First 3—last 3 C.
15. Discus throw A. Routine B. Standing throws (center of ring) (1) Lead with chest and nose (2) Long pull (3) Hips (cocked to uncocked) ahead of arm (4) Through the shoulder (5) Left arm coordination (6) Left arm, reach back (7) (a) Easy (b) Medium (c) Hard (d) Explode C. Across the ring, numbers as B D. Alternate stand and across E.
16. Pole vault A. Check marks (1) Short (2) Long B. Approach C. Pole plant D. Take off E. Vaulting (1) Low hold (2) High hold (a) 12 in. below best (b) F.
17. Javelin A. Standing throws B. Trot and throw (1) 345 (2) Full count (a) Over shoulder (b) Close to ear (c) Good pull (d) Cock the hand (e) Left foot on ground (f) Right foot under (g) Body turned to right, then precede arm with body (h) Through shaft—don't tip it up (i) C. Full run X. Check mark (1) 1/2 effort (2) 2/3 effort (3) 7/8–9/10 effort (4) D. Technique throws (1) Standing at 30 ft.-60 ft. target (2) 3-step and throw at 45 ft.-90 ft. target (3) 5-step and throw at 120 ft.-150 ft. target (4) Full run and checks at 150 ft.-180 ft. target E.
18. Sets Y. Hurdles (1) 30 in. (2) 36 in. A. 110-220-110 (1) Goal pace B. 165-110-55 (2) Date pace C. 330-220-110 (3) D. 660-440-220
19. Weak event work A. Throw B. Jump C. Run (1) Weakest (2) 2d weakest event
20.
21. A. Pictures B. Film C. Video

10K1. 1500 meters, three-fourths racing distance. This race will usually be tested either for three-fourths of a mile or for the full distance, which is 119½ yards less than a mile. For the decathlon class, the distance is always three-fourths of a mile.

11X. Intervals, easy. The intervals listed are to be run at a comfortable, relatively easy pace. A listing of three times 11CX means to run three times an easy 165 yards.

11Y. Intervals, over hurdles. This notation may be used if the decathlete is also training for the 400-meter hurdles as a dual meet event. A notation of 11EY means run a 330 over the hurdles (set at the intermediate hurdle spacings).

11Z. Intervals, fast 20 to 50 yards in the middle of the interval. This notation is used for a short interval, such as 110 or 165 yards, and is an exercise to increase the speed or to learn to accelerate quickly in a race.

11A1. Intervals, goal pace. The distance given is merely an example. The "1" notation for either fundamental 11 (intervals) or 18 (sets) means that the distance is to be run at the athlete's "goal pace," a term which is explained in Chapter 2 "The fundamentals of distance training."

11A2. Intervals, date pace. The distance is again an example. The "2" notation means that the given interval or set is to be run at the athlete's current date pace, as explained in Chapter 2.

18AY. Sets, over hurdles. The "A" notation is only an example. The "Y" notation, meaning to run over the hurdles, is used if the athlete is training for the intermediate hurdles.

18AY1. Sets, over 30-inch hurdles. The "Y1" notation means that the set is run over 30-inch (low) hurdles set at the intermediate hurdle spacings.

18AY2. Sets, over 36-inch hurdles. The "Y2" notation means that the set is run over the regular intermediate height hurdles at the intermediate hurdle spacings.

19. Weak event work. On occasion, the athlete will be told to use some of his time in training in one of his weaker events, since each athlete has his own individual weak events.

19A. Weak event work, throw. Work on one of the weaker throwing events, the shot, discus, or javelin.

19B. Weak event work, jump. Work on one of the weaker jumping events, the high jump, long jump, or pole vault.

19C. Weak event work, run. Work on one of the weaker running events, the two sprints, the distance run, or the hurdles.

19A1. Weak event work, (throw), weakest event. The choice of the throws is only an example. The "1" notation means to work in the athlete's weakest event in that group of events.

19A2. Weak event work, (throw), second-weakest event. The "2" notation means to work on the athlete's second-weakest event in that group of events.

Footnotes

1. Elvin C. Drake, "The Decathlon," in *Clinic Notes,* eds. Don Canham and Phil Diamond (Ann Arbor: National Collegiate Track Coaches Association, 1956), pp. 206–8.

2. ———. "Decathlon," in *Track in Theory and Technique,* ed. Thomas P. Rosandich (Richmond, Calif.: Worldwide Publishing Company, 1962), pp. 377–78.

3. "One Throw to Go," *Newsweek,* 12 August 1968, p. 70.

4. Robert H. McCollum and William J. Bowerman, "The Three-Quarter Distance Decathlon for College Men," *Athletic Journal* 42 (April 1962): 14, 74.

5. Tom McNab, *Decathlon* (London: AAA, 1972), 71 pp.

6. Robert C. Parks, "Organizing an Indoor Decathlon in Elementary or Junior High School Physical Education Classes," *Track and Field Quarterly Review,* 71:4, pp. 34–35.

7. Friedel Schirmer, "Technical Evaluation and Observations from the Decathlon at the Games of Mexico," *Track and Field Quarterly Review,* 70:4, pp. 55–63.

8. ———. "Decathlon Training, West German Style," *Track Technique,* No. 42 (December 1970), pp. 1338–41.

9. Robin C. Sykes, "Balance — the Decathlon Keyword," *Track Technique,* No. 45 (September 1971), pp. 1442–43.

10. Alfred J. Sylvia, "A Decathlon for High School and College," *Athletic Journal,* 44 (April 1964): 38, 40.

11. Richard Wotruba, "Training for the Decathlon," *Track and Field Quarterly Review* (October 1965), pp. 70–74.

six

Administration

Organizing and administering the track and field program

17

A good track and field program must be developed around the concept of community interest in track and field. Local interest in track will do much to assure good track teams, for the more able athletes will be drawn to track more than to other sports. For this reason the administrative aspect of track athletics must include the community program as well as the school's program itself. On the high school level a good community program will enhance the school's program immeasurably and provide many future athletes. On the college level, this program will not function so much as a feeder as a community service and as a means of developing community interest in the sport.

Community Track Programs

Good examples of community programs which can be developed either by or through the school are all-comers' summer track programs and jogging programs. Each will be described as it has been practiced in Eugene, Oregon.

The benefits of a community all-comers' summer track program are many. From the standpoint of the coach there is one particular value which outweighs the others: a body of spectators is developed for the sport. If young people are competing in the summer meets, many of their parents will come to see the meets. The many contests involved in a meet are exciting, and they are not difficult to understand. Many persons will discover that they have been missing a good spectator sport. Consequently, when the school has track meets, the body of potential spectators will have grown. Bigger crowds mean more interest, and more interest means more athletes.

A second value lies with the participants themselves. Naturally they will benefit from the health and fitness standpoint; that is understood. However, many young people are never really exposed to the sport, despite the possibility that they might have considerable natural aptitude for it. There are community programs in football, basketball, and baseball — why not track and field? Young people will find it an enjoyable experience, even if they do not develop into future track athletes. Some of them, however, will develop into track athletes. Several competitors in the Olympic Games were first exposed to track at the all-comers' meets in Eugene.

The program should reach up as well as down across the age groups. For the young children the competition is fun, but does not necessarily require any fine skills which might prove embarrassing to the low-skilled growing child. To the junior high school student, it is similar to high school athletics, and may be interesting from that point of view. To the high school student, it is a chance to compete without the pressure of success or failure involved in team-scored meets, plus a chance to experiment with new events, which is also an aspect of its allure to college athletes. To the graduate of high school or college, it is a chance to continue to compete, even if no longer allied with a team. For older adults, it is a return to the pleasures of competition, or a discovery of those pleasures for the first time. For every competitor, it is an enjoyable social event, for the all-comers' meet is decidedly informal. Of course, events are held for both females and males.

The All-Comers' Program in Eugene, Oregon

The all-comers' program was begun in Eugene, Oregon, in 1957 as an attempt to promote summer track and field competition. The original intention was to provide competition for the college athletes. The first meets averaged thirty or thirty-five competitors, spread over a dozen or more events — not overly impressive for a metropolitan area with over 150,000 people. To expand participation, the high school age groups were added. The number of participants grew. As the bottom age limit continued to drop, the number of entries in the meets snowballed. A typical meet today has hundreds of participants. To make organizing and officiating easier, the meets were split into two meets per weekend. On Friday evening, beginning around 5 P.M., the adult meet (ages fifteen and up) is staged, lasting usually until 7:30 or 8 P.M. On Saturday morning the younger version of the meet is staged from 10 A.M. until about noon, and it is a sight to behold.

All events are subdivided into several age groups, beginning at the bottom with the 6-and-under group, then moving up by two-year groups (7 to 8, 9 to 10, etc.) through the eighteen-year-olds (17 to 18), followed by an "open" division. In some events, adult categories covering ten-year blocks have been used where adults aged forty or older wished to compete (40 to 49, 50 to 59, etc.). This is most common in the jogger's mile. There are, of course, races for the boys and for the girls. To simplify matters and limit the demand for officials, all field events are completed before the running events begin. Through age twelve the short sprint is 60 yards and is contested on the grass infield in heats, with awards to each heat — no finals. A heat of seven- and eight-year-olds might have thirty or forty runners. Competitors are limited in the number of events which they can enter, to prevent monopolizing of the ribbons. All awards, either three or five places, are stamped with the "All-Comers' Meet" stamp, the year, and the place of finish. No date, other than the year, and no event designation are used. For children, the entry fee is 25 cents for up to four events. For adults, it is 25 cents for each event.

For the six-and-under groups (to enter, they must be able to pronounce their name), there are three events: the 60-yard dash, on the grass; the 220-yard run, around a turn; and the standing long jump. To save time on the long jump, a board with the distances is placed alongside the pit, so the length of the jump can be given without using a measuring tape. Since five places are awarded, five pegs are used to mark the leading five jumpers. Anyone not in those five takes the board measurement. After the event is completed, the five leaders have their jumps measured by tape. A similar technique is used in all throwing events, plus the running long jump. Arcs at 5-foot intervals are used for the shot, and similar marks assist the discus and javelin.

The hurdle races are shorter races and are also run on the grass, regardless of the age group. For running events, if the number of entries is small for an age group, several groups will run together to save time, though the results will still be tabulated separately. Finally, the winners of each event for each age group are typed out and reported to the local newspapers for publication. Seeing his name in the paper increases the athlete's interest in the sport, and seeing their child's name in the paper increases the parents' interest in the sport.

For the adult section, all standard track events which are more common are run, up through the 2-mile. Those interested in a 3-mile run the first 2 miles with the 2-mile racers. If there is sufficient interest, other races, such as the 3,000-meter steeplechase, are run. There is also a jogger's mile, the first running event every Friday evening, beginning around 5:45 or 6 P.M. The men and women run together in this event, since neither sex has a natural advantage over the other. Each entry writes down his or her predicted time for the mile and turns it in before the race. The person running closest to the estimated time wins. No watches or timing aids are allowed. Speed is no advantage. If one runner runs 5:05 after predicting 5:08, while another predicted 7:00 and ran 6:58, the 6:58 runner would win, being only 2 seconds off. This race is run in two groups. The first race is the "over 7:30," or slow group, those predicting a run no faster than that time. The second race is the "fast group," those running no slower than 7:30

(predicted) and no faster than 5:00. Anyone breaking 5:00 is declared a racer and disqualified. These two races attract entries from ten years and under to seventy years and older.

The summer meets are held for four or five weekends each summer, beginning on the weekend after the Fourth of July and running through mid-August. They are usually preceded by several clinics for young people in the different events, given at schools throughout the community by local teachers and coaches and announced ahead of time in the newspapers and over radio and television. The summer track program is sponsored by the Oregon Track Club, the successor to the Emerald Empire Athletic Association, a group of local citizens interested in the advancement of track and field in the Eugene–Springfield, Oregon, metropolitan area and the state of Oregon. Incidentally, the experience at putting on large meets regularly had much to do with Eugene winning bids to have the NCAA Track and Field Championships several times, as well as the AAU Meet and the 1972 U.S. Olympic Trials, in a metropolitan area which ranked only 139th in the United States in population in 1970. Further information about all-comers' meets is in the *Oregon Manual,* printed by the United States Track and Field Federation.

Community Jogging Program

The second valuable community program is the jogging program. It performs several vital services, for not only does it acquaint the adults of the community with the track program to some degree, but also it is an excellent public service to the local citizens' state of physical fitness. The jogging boom in the United States began in Eugene, Oregon. Late in 1962, a small group of Oregon distance runners traveled to New Zealand with Bill Bowerman as American representatives for a series of races organized by the sports bodies of the two nations. Bowerman was introduced to a popular activity called "jogging" by the outstanding New Zealand coach Arthur Lydiard. Deeply impressed by his own miserably unfit showing when jogging with the New Zealanders, some of them in their seventies, Bowerman publicized Lydiard's jogging program upon his return to Oregon in January of 1963. He immediately extended an invitation to interested adults to join him in jogging sessions at the Oregon track. A small number of outings brought a mass of hundreds of people swarming over the track at one time.

Bowerman stopped at that point and set out to develop a definite, safe jogging program. Working with a local cardiologist, Dr. W. E. Harris, he experimented with a group of adults, aged twenty-five to sixty-six, to discover how much work the typical adult male and female could take while benefiting, but not undergoing undue stress. The result of the studies was publicized nationwide, bringing correspondence from around the world asking for jogging programs. A small booklet of programs was prepared, then a book of over 120 pages was written, giving the principles and techniques of jogging, plus a number of graduated schedules for getting started and then continuing in jogging.

Jogging is simply a program designed to promote physical fitness by improving the condition of the body's cardiovascular system through a program of regular exercise consisting of slow, easy running. It is *not* a strenuous exercise program. The key is a quote from Arthur Lydiard: "Train, don't strain." It is the jogger's motto. The ideal is easy, comfortable running. For this reason, anyone running the jogger's mile under 5 minutes is disqualified: if he is moving that fast, he is no longer jogging; he is running or racing.

The school's track coach is the natural person to introduce jogging to the community, if it is not already known. This can be done under the auspices of the school itself or through community groups, such as the Department of Parks and Recreation, if there is one, or the YMCA, or any similar interested group. The coach can volunteer to speak to groups on jogging, explaining the principles and demonstrating the techniques, or even better, having his athletes demonstrate the techniques.

Groups could be welcomed if they wish to use the school track for jogging when it is not being used for school activities. Jogging classes or groups might be led at the track by members of the track team. This is excellent community relations, for it benefits the local people in terms of health, and at the same time it makes them a bit more aware of the track team through the influence of the coach and the contact with his athletes. Detailed programs are outlined in the book *Jogging,* by William J. Bowerman and W. E. Harris, which has been published in paperback and hardback in many nations around the world.

These two particular programs, the all-comers' meets and the jogging program, can be extremely helpful in building a place in the community for the school's track program. They build interest and provide experience while offering activities which will be genuine public services. They should not be expected to be overnight successes; they may take years to develop to the point that major benefits to the community and to the school's programs can be seen. The time invested will be worthwhile.

Nonvarsity School Track Programs

This suggested concern for a strong community program does not mean that the school program should be neglected or played down in any way. However, it should be projected beyond the traditional narrow bounds in which it has been used. The school program of track and field activities should not be limited to the varsity program, for it has much wider applicability to student needs. Two particular phases of the nonvarsity program should be considered: the physical education classes and the intramural program. In both cases, these should not be all-male programs; they are as enjoyable and beneficial to women as to men.

The school's physical education classes should have as their prime objective the physical fitness of the students, followed closely by providing activities which the students will enjoy and which have carry-over value to their adult life. The track and field activities carry this appeal as do few of the other competitive sports. The first question asked by the physical education teacher is: what activities can we offer? The second question might concern their value to the students' lives and the school's physical education program.

Thre basic units might be suggested for the high school curriculum: cross country, track and field, and jogging. Cross country has as perhaps its greatest value the cardiovascular benefits derived from the training. Few sports require as much of the competitor's cardiovascular and respiratory systems. Further, there is the small advantage held by the undersized student in such competition. The best cross country runners are often the smallest of the school's athletes. The smaller student, at a disadvantage in most sports because of his size, will be happy to find a sport in which he does not begin at a disadvantage.

Track and Field Events

The track and field unit has a great advantage in the variety of activities which it offers. Every student should be able to find some event at which he can be a passable success, and training in all the events gives as well-rounded physical training as can be found in any physical fitness activities. There are several possible variations of the track and field unit. The men might have a unit on the decathlon, using the training methods and scoring tables mentioned in Chapter 16. This provides some standardization of grading, plus gives natural competition over the whole unit and within each of the ten subparts of the unit. For the women, the pentathlon (100-meter hurdles, long jump, shot-put, high jump, and 200 meters) or a variation of the decathlon might be used.

Jogging

A class in jogging does not give immediate large gains in physical fitness to most young students, but it is more valuable than many activities for its long-term usability. A class involving running aids the student in building a physical fitness base which might be a good start before going into more strenuous physical activities. Women might find it interesting when presented in terms of weight control. Finally, it can be carried out throughout the ordinary person's lifetime with no more equipment than a pair of shoes and no other people as teammates or competitors. No other lifetime sport can offer this claim. Also, if physical education activities are offered on a five-day-a-week basis, it can be sandwiched into another unit, such as on Tuesdays and Thursdays, as an alternate activity to help prevent boredom with the other activity.

The college physical education program allows a greater variety of course offerings, with more specialized instruction. Activity courses might be offered in track and field, cross country, decathlon, and jogging. In larger schools some interested students might like a class in road running. For the women, a few might be interested in cross country, but a number might be interested in the pentathlon or a variation of the decathlon class. Many might be interested in a jogging class. Classes in track and jogging can easily be used as coeducational activities. Some women might be interested in coeducational classes also in cross country and road running. Class schedules can easily be adapted from the fall training schedules given in the chapters on decathlon and other special activities.

Intramural Sports

Intramural sports is another area of potential interest in track and field activities which should not be overlooked by the physical education teacher or athletics coach. Common intramural offerings are a single cross country meet and a single track and field meet. Considerable student interest might result from the offering of a decathlon for the men and perhaps a pentathlon for the women.

High schools commonly offer a single cross country intramural race, with the cross country lettermen or team members not allowed to compete. This often takes place in November, sometimes being called a "Turkey Race," with the winner receiving a turkey. One variation is to have team competition, either by physical education classes or homeroom units in the high school or by fraternities, dormitory units, or nonaffiliated or day-student groups on the college level. Awards might be ribbons, medals, or small trophies. In some cases, the winners (individual and team) might have an award of a turkey given in their name to a needy family.

Track and field competition should be both team and individual competition, organized around units similar to those suggested for cross country. On the college level, there might be sufficient interest in team competition to permit the organization of a small number of dual meets between teams, with all the meets conducted at the same time.

Decathlon and pentathlon competitions would be individually scored, though variations of team scoring are possible. These are good events to stage to discover the school's best "all-around" athletes. For suggestions on scoring such contests, see the appendixes to Chapter 16 on the decathlon.

Bibliography

Bowerman, William J., and Harris, W. E. *Jogging.* New York: Grosset & Dunlap, 1968. 128 pp.

Doherty, J. Kenneth. *The Track and Field Omni book.* Swarthmore, Pa.: privately published by Kenneth J. Doherty, 1972.

Jackson, J. Oliver. "How to promote the track and field program," *JOHPER* 33 (January 1963), 56–57.

Luke, Brother G. "Stimulating interest in track and field," *Track and Field Quarterly Review,* October 1965, pp. 23–26.

Rosandich, Thomas. "Track and field promotion and administration." In *Track in Theory and Technique*, ed. Thomas Rosandich, pp. 381–406. Richmond, Calif.: Worldwide Publishing Co., 1962.

Locating and testing prospects in the school

Few coaches have the good fortune to inherit a team of good athletes. Most coaches begin each year needing new athletes to fill at least several of the events, if not all of them. No prospect should be overlooked in this search. The physical education classes are one of the best sources of prospects, whether you coach in high school or college.

Testing the Physical Education Classes

The coach will benefit from a practice of testing all physical education classes in several events as a regular procedure. Most of the tests described here have been used for several decades and are proven indicators of talent.

Sprint Test

The first test is for sprinters. Each person should be timed in a 40-yard dash. The class can run on the football field, starting on the goal line and finishing where the coach is standing on the 40-yard line (Figure 18.1). Have each person go down in a three-point stance (both feet and one hand on the ground)

Figure 18.1 Test for Sprinters.

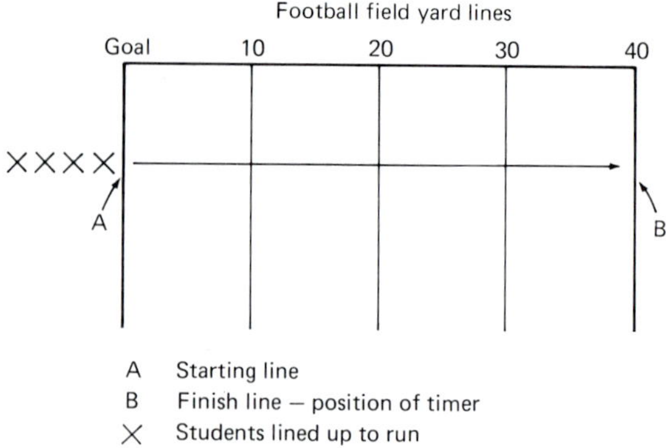

for the start. No one is needed to start the runner, if they run one at a time, since the timer starts the watch when the athlete lifts his hand from the ground. Each person is given only one trial, since untrained runners will rarely improve their sprint times on a second or third attempt. Any person running 5.2 seconds or faster is a prospective sprinter.

Hurdling Test

The next test is for hurdling prospects. The same 40-yard distance is used, but three hurdles are added to the course (Figure 18.2). The first hurdle is 14 yards from the start, and the other two hurdles are at 8-yard intervals past the first one. If you are starting the runners on the goal line, the hurdles will be on the 14-, 22-, and 30-yard lines, with the finish on the 40-yard line. The hurdles are set at low hurdle height (2 feet 6 inches). Anyone running 6.2 seconds or faster is a prospect.

Distance Run Test

Distance runners are found with an 880-yard run. The class can be divided into two groups, one group lined up facing the other and numbered in sequence, with each member of group one having a counterpart with the same number in group two. Each runner will get the finishing time of his counterpart in the other group and report it after he has run, the number one runner in the first group reporting the time of the number one runner in the second group, and so forth. After one group has run and had its times recorded, the second group will run and have its times taken and reported to the recorder by the first group. If only the best times are of interest, everyone can be run at the same time and the top runners pulled to the side as they finish. Any untrained person running 2:30 or faster is a prospective distance man.

Figure 18.2 Test for Hurdlers.

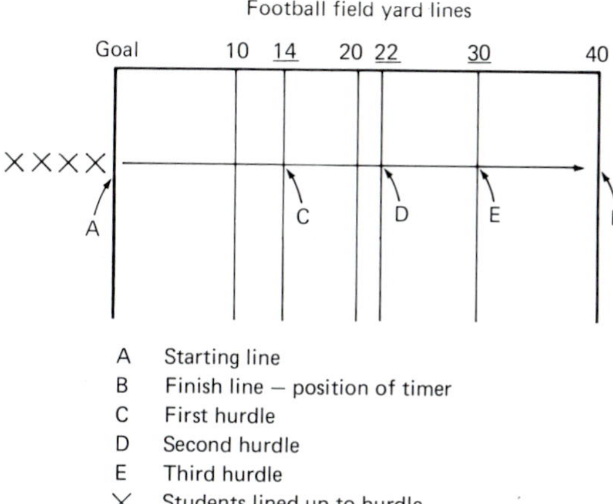

High Jumper Test

For high jumpers, use the jump and reach (Sargent jump) test. A strip of masking tape can be placed on the wall, running upward from about 6 feet to 11 feet above the floor. It should be marked at 1-inch intervals over that distance, with larger marks and numerals for every 6 inches. Each jumper stands next to the wall at the tape and raises his arm to see how high he can touch with his fingers while flat-footed on the floor. He then crouches and jumps, touching as high up the strip of tape as he can reach with his hand, while the coach notes the height he reaches (Figure 18.3). If the man has a standing reach of 7 feet 3 inches and a reach of 9 feet 10 inches on the jump, his mark is 31 inches, the difference between the two marks. Anyone with a difference of 30 inches or more is a high jump prospect.

Figure 18.3 Jump and Reach for High Jumpers.

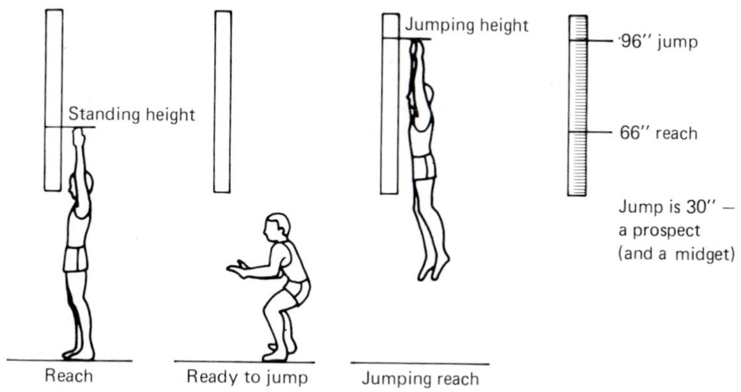

Figure 18.4 Standing Long Jump Positioning.

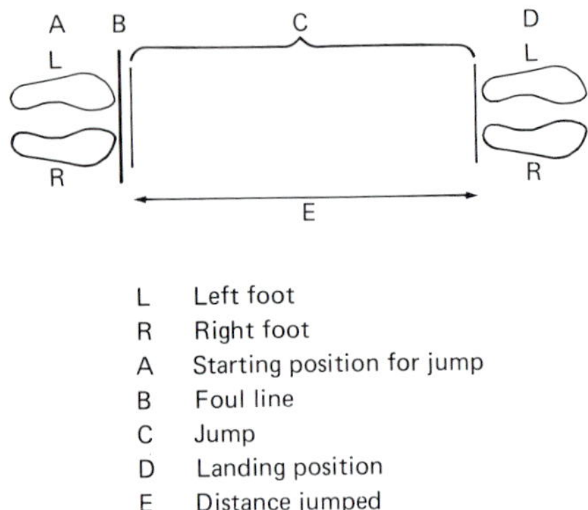

L Left foot
R Right foot
A Starting position for jump
B Foul line
C Jump
D Landing position
E Distance jumped

Long Jump Tests

Two tests are used in conjunction for long jump prospects. The first is the sprint test already described: 40 yards in 5.2 seconds or less. The second test is the standing long jump. This can be done into the long jump pit, or it can be done indoors on any floor providing relatively nonslip footing. A strip of masking tape can be placed upon the floor running outward at a right angle to the take-off point, beginning 4 feet from the take-off point and marked at 1-inch intervals to 11 feet (Figure 18.4). Have each jumper stand directly behind the take-off line with the toe of each foot touching the line, then leap as far forward as he can. Anyone jumping 7 feet 6 inches or farther is a prospect. The leap can be into a pit, onto a tumbling mat (mark where the corners should be on the floor, since the mat will move with each landing), or on the floor (a bit uncomfortable).

Triple Jump Test

The standing triple jump is used as a test for triple jump prospects. The teacher will want to demonstrate the technique first, since it may seem strange to the students. The jumper will take off over one foot, land on the same foot, go into a step, landing on the other foot, then make a jump like a long jump to conclude the sequence (Figure 18.5). The same take-off line can be used as for the standing long jump, but the coach might put marks with chalk or masking tape at 6-inch intervals from 20 to 32 feet away from the take-off point. If this is not done with the landing in a jumping pit or on a mat, it should be done on a grassy area, such as the football field. The jumper can "swing" into the jump, starting with one foot behind the take-off foot to provide some push into the jump. Any high school athlete jumping 24 feet or any college man reaching 28 feet is a prospect for the triple jump. The coach is looking for men with good rhythm and balance, so the hurdlers are often good prospects.

Figure 18.5 Standing Triple Jump Sequence.

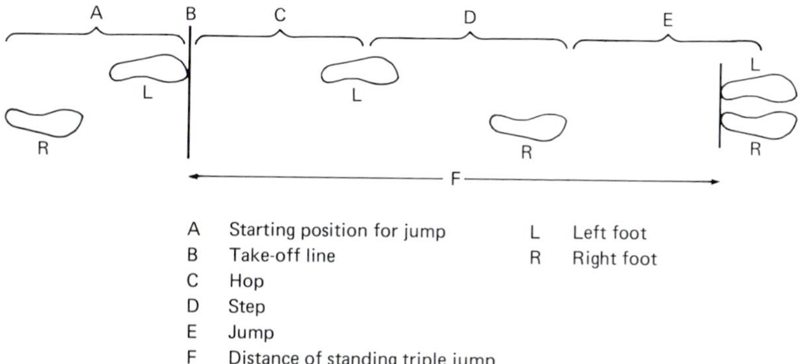

Shot-Put and Javelin Throw Tests

We find shot-putters by using the standing put. A throwing line is marked on the ground with chalk, then lines are made at 10 feet, 15 feet, and 1-foot intervals from 20 to 30 feet from the throwing line. The men take turns throwing from a standing position facing the direction of their throw (no turn is used). Anyone putting over 20 feet is a prospect.

Javelin throwers are found by using a softball, football, or an 800-gram weighted ball (about 1¾ pounds). These are reasonably valid indicators of talent and will add years to the life expectancy of the person marking the distances of the throws. The goal line of the football field can be used as a throwing line (Figure 18.6). Each thrower is allowed to run up to the line as he wishes, so long as he does not cross it. Any person throwing the softball 200 feet or more is a prospect. Some research has indicated that the distance reached throwing the 800-gram weighted ball gives the closest approximation of the actual distance which can be reached with the javelin. If the goal line of the football field is used as the throwing line, the 200-foot mark will be 10 feet before the 30-yard line at the opposite end of the field.

Locating Prospects for Other Events

We have no test which we have used to discover discus throwers or pole vaulters. Your shot-putters generally will throw the discus, eventually showing themselves stronger in one event or the other after they have become more competent in the skills of each event. Pole vaulting requires a unique combination of skills which shows most readily in skilled gymnasts. A pole vaulter may be a man who is a fair sprinter, long jumper, and hurdler. One world record holder in the pole vault competed occasionally as an intermediate hurdler and had run under 2:00 in the half-mile.

Figure 18.6 Test for Javelin Throwers.

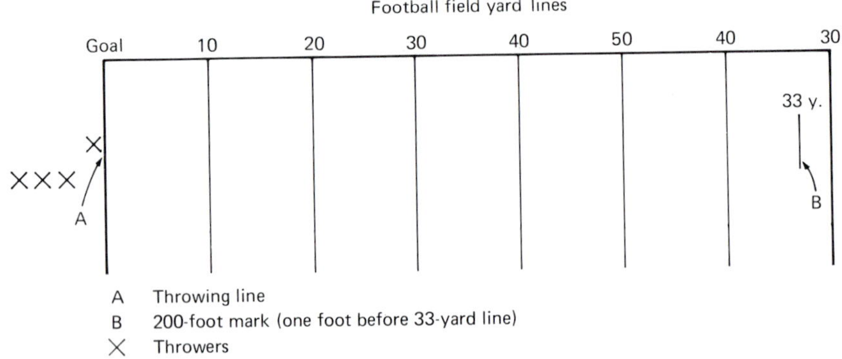

General Comments on Testing and Recruitment

Tests may not be absolute indicators of talent. Some athletes have off days; others are late bloomers. The tests suggested here seek to discover some native ability without requiring the prospect to have prior training in the events. For this reason, the coach can test his prospects who turn out for the team on their first day of practice, or he can test everyone in his classes (if he teaches physical education) during the first week of school. Athletes do not always realize that they have the talent for a given event, so all prospects should be tested for all events, rather than be asked what event they want to try and be trained only in that event.

If the tests are to be given in a short time and several teachers or assistants are available for recording the results at different stations, the tests might be conducted in this manner (see also Figure 18.7):

Test number	*Test*	*Site*	*Prospective event*
1	Jump and reach	Gym	High jump
2	Standing long jump	Gym	Long jump (40 yards)
3	40-yard dash	Field	Sprint–long jump
4	40-yard hurdles	Field	Hurdles
5	Ball throw	Field	Javelin throwers
6	Standing triple jump	Field	Triple jump
7	Shot-put	Shot area	Shot-put
8	880-yard run	Track	Distance runs

The students can proceed from one test to the next as they complete each item, except that the 880 would be run in one or two large groups. Athletes or managers could handle some of the events, to lessen the number of persons needed to administer the tests. The coach could get through all the tests in one afternoon, if all prospects are present, if the procedure is carefully explained to

Figure 18.7 Field Testing with Several Teachers Available.

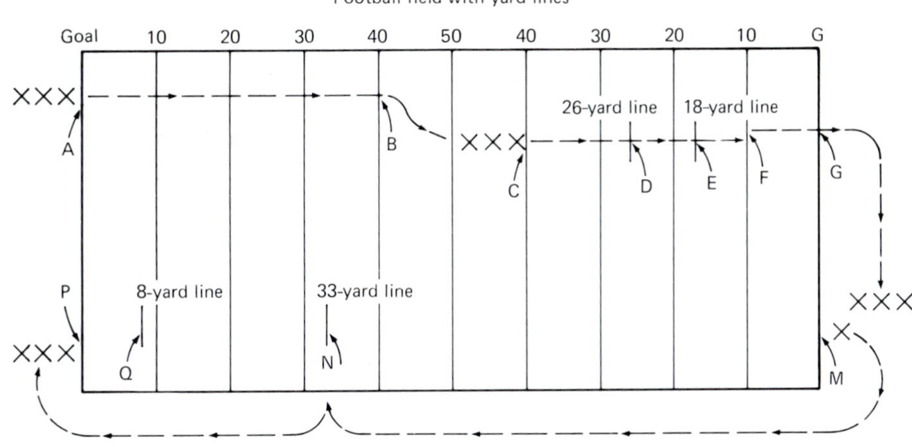

Test 1: 40-yard dash – A to B
Test 2: 40-yard hurdles – C to G (hurdles at D, E, F)
Test 3: Ball throw from M, prospects throwing to N (if softball)
Test 4: Standing triple jump – P to Q (high school prospect)

them, and if the whole process is well organized. (See Table 18.1, page 370, for an example of a prospective athlete's testing summary.)

The coach should endeavor to make his sport popular with the students. He should try to see that it is enjoyed, for this will be an important criterion for a young person in going out for a team. No matter how "in" a sport may be at first, if the coach does not make it an enjoyable experience, he will lose many prospects and eventually lose any vestiges of status which the sport might have carried. If a sport becomes popular, three-quarters of the recruiting problem is solved.

Every coach has wondered at some time to what lengths he should go to (1) get a prospect to come out for his sport and (2) convince him to stay if he shows a desire to quit. There are many benefits of competition for every man, but it is difficult to say whether or not these benefits are realized if an athlete stays on a team when he might prefer not to be there. Is it worth the continuous effort to convince a hesitant athlete to stay on the team? We suspect that it is not. The coach is going to waste much time which could be better used with athletes who would appreciate the assistance. Also, the team risks losing a valuable member late in the season with no trained replacement, when his loss might have been covered by other athletes had it occurred before the season began. Thus the effect upon team morale of a potential dropout could be minimized. Finally, an athlete might threaten to quit simply to get attention from the coach. Most coaches will have enough work to fill their time without adding the pampering of prima donnas to their list of chores.

Table 18.1: Summary of Testing

Event	*Test and prospect's mark*
Sprints	40 yards in 5.2 seconds
Distances	880 in 2:30 (untrained)
Hurdles	40-yard lows in 6.2 seconds
High jump	Jump and reach of 30 inches
Long jump	7 feet 6 inches in standing long jump, plus 40 yards in 5.2 seconds
Triple jump	Standing jump of 24 feet (high school) or 28 feet (college), rhythm and balance
Pole vault	All-around gymnastic ability
Shot-put	Standing put of 20 feet
Discus	Try shot-putters
Javelin	200 feet with softball or football, or good javelin distance with 800-gram weighted ball

Coaching aids

Coaching aids refer to anything which can be used to make the job of the coach a little bit easier. Every coach has his little coaching secrets or his little devices which he feels help the training of his athletes or make his job easier. A few examples of such aids will be given in this section, and the coach or teacher can then use his imagination to develop further aids.

Audiovisual Materials as Coaching Aids

Motion Pictures

Perhaps the most obvious and most useful of today's coaching aids is the motion picture. Movies are of inestimable value to the coach, for the coach can see exactly and repeatedly what the athlete is doing, whether it is right or wrong. The current adjunct to the use of movies, even more useful perhaps, is the videotape apparatus. Videotapes have all the advantages of movies, plus one greater advantage: the recorded action can be played back immediately. The athlete can make an effort, such as throwing the javelin, then he can watch the throw several times, studying his weaknesses and discussing with the coach exactly how they might be corrected. He can then take another throw, study it on videotape, and repeat the process indefinitely. Research has shown that if the results of an effort are given immediately, there is a strong positive effort to try to improve, while withholding or falsifying results creates negative feelings.

While the videotape recording has the advantage of immediacy in providing results, movies have the advantage of relative permanence of use. Tapes are usually used for a while, then erased or used to record new programs. Movies are kept. This has several benefits. First, the athlete can study the films of a practice session or meet in the context of how well he did on that particular occasion. Next, he can compare that first film to an earlier or later film to observe his progress, and determine whether he is correcting his earlier technical faults. Finally, he can run two projectors at a time, showing his throws on one projector and a world-class athlete on another. He can then simultaneously compare his technical form to that of the champion athlete.

Sequence Photographs

Sequence pictures are also very helpful, for they permit the athlete to study phases of the form of his event at any time. These are usually pictures of champion athletes, many of which are shown in the various coaching publications. The athlete can post them in his room or on his locker, giving him something to study at odd moments. They are not as good as movies or videotapes, however, because a sequence photograph may catch the athlete at "in-between positions" which might give an incorrect impression of the important aspects of his performance technique.

Equipment Aids

The coach can work at developing useful pieces of training equipment. One such piece of equipment is the soft hurdle top, described in the hurdling chapters. It permits the athletes to work to improve their hurdling technique without worrying about whether they will hit a hurdle and sustain an injury. This aids in making practice more thorough and therefore more efficient. Many coaches have developed such pieces of improved equipment or have adapted one piece of equipment to use in another event, such as using the trampoline with mats draped over the side as an indoor high jumping pit. The coach needs only his ingenuity, plus an understanding of what would help the athlete in his practice.

The pace clock, described in Chapter 2 on distance training, is another great coaching aid. When combined with a small clock's electric motor and a large face and large second hand, and placed in a prominent area easy to see from most points on the track, the pace clock acts as a team manager or assistant coach, providing timing to the nearest second to a large number of athletes without any use of team personnel or school watches. This makes it possible to train many athletes in a minimum of time, for on assigned interval workouts, once the athletes have learned the basics of training, they can conduct an interval training session without the assistance of a coach, manager, or stopwatch.

Chart Aids

Perhaps the greatest aids are the workout charts, such as those demonstrated in the chapters on training. These have several advantages. First, they serve as a brief, but thorough, record of the training used in each event each year, which also allows a comparison of training from year to year or champion to champion. They can show the progress of athletes by showing where they are compared to where they were at the same time in the previous year. Finally, they can help the coach to cover all aspects of the athlete's training. Because they list all the fundamentals of the athlete's event, they assist the coach in checking whether he has assigned workouts which cover each of those fundamentals, therefore developing a more thorough training program. It is devices such as these which make the job of the coach much simpler and more pleasurable.

Bibliography

Bowerman, William J. "Homemade electronic timer," *Athletic Journal* 43 (February 1963): 62.

Crakes, James G. "What about the air-filled pit," *Scholastic Coach* 37 (January 1968): 74–75.

De Bacy, Diane. "Effect of viewing video tapes of a sport skill performed by self and others on self-assessment," *Research Quarterly* 41 (March 1970): 27–31.

Ehrenheim, Bob. "Do-it-yourself portable indoor track," *Athletic Journal* 53 (February 1973): 30, 95–96.

Ellis, Art, and Moawad, Bob. "Small format films get the job done," *Scholastic Coach* 40 (January 1971): 28, 30, 74.

Houston, Robert J. "Use a workout clock in your track program," *Athletic Journal* 43 (January 1963): 54.

MacDonald, Harold, "Building a portable banked track section," *Track Technique*, No. 40 (June 1970), pp. 1280–81.

McCarthy, Chris. "The art of repairing shoes," *Distance Running News* 2 (April 1967): 6–7.

Nelson, Dale O., and Biancani, Al. "Are starting blocks too narrow?"*Athletic Journal* 51 (February 1971): 16, 75.

Newcomb, Cyrus B., Jr. "Consider the Super 8," *Athletic Journal* 51 (October 1970): 56, 58, 60, 69–70.

"Pennsylvania's practice track bubble," *Scholastic Coach* 37 (January 1968): 11.

Slee, Dennis. "An 8-mm color film as a 'guest speaker,' " *Scholastic Coach* 39 (January 1970): 24, 26, 90–91, 93.

Steitz, Edward. "The synthetic surface revolution," *Scholastic Coach* 39 (January 1970): 22, 100–101.

Theibert, P. R. "The impossible dreams," *Scholastic Coach* 37 (January 1968): 10–11, 71–73.

Tolliver and Curl Paving Contractors. "Building a low-cost rubberized asphalt track," *Track and Field Quarterly Review,* December 1964, pp. 58–61.

"Suggested specifications for an asphalt rubber sand surfacing for track and field event runways," *Track and Field Quarterly Review,* May 1968, pp. 30–32.

Westervelt, Sheldon. "Those existing rubber tracks — how have they been working out?" *Track and Field Quarterly Review,* October 1965, pp. 13–16.

Wright, Edward J. "Effects of light and heavy equipment on acquisition of sports-type skills by young children," *Research Quarterly* 38 (December 1967): 705–14.

Yanosy, Alex, Jr. "High jumping done safely indoors," *Athletic Journal* 46 (January 1966): 19.

Organizing and administering competitions

Few persons realize the difficulties involved in putting on a track and field competition which is well run. The meet must be run well to ensure two things:

1. The better it is run, the more efficiently the athletes can prepare and the more successfully perform.
2. The better it is run, the more appeal it will hold for your spectators.

The net result of this care will be happier, more successful athletes; happier and more numerous spectators; and a happier, more successful coach. This is what every person wants ultimately.

The Meet Director

For most small meets the track coach is considered the meet director, but he should carefully consider other possibilities. The success of any given meet depends heavily upon the work of the meet director. During a meet the coach is concerned with helping his athletes, within the bounds of the rules. He cannot successfully fulfill that function and at the same time direct a meet properly. Because of this conflict in duties, both of which are important, he should pick and train a meet director to direct the meets at his school, if at all possible. (Most coaches will react by saying that it is not possible, and 99 out of every 100 of them will be wrong.)

The meet director is the key to the success of the meet. He must be a leader, he must be an administrator, and he must be willing to take charge and run the meet. He will have to be more knowledgeable of the rules than the coach (not as difficult a task as most coaches think), and he must have the resolve to enforce them strictly and fairly, no matter whom they affect. He must be skillful in handling persons, and he must be as nonpartisan as possible. The only quality given above which is not necessary in a good meet director is that he be a "he."

Responsibilities of the Meet Director

The responsibilities of the meet director are many. To clearly understand the duties of the people in charge of running a meet, any person who plans to run a meet should get the appropriate rulebooks, depending upon his affiliation and the auspices under which the meet is being run (the rulebooks are listed in Chapter 1). As an example, an NAIA school would use the "high school" rulebook. For some clarifications of the rules and a clearer understanding of what should be done, copies of the IAAF rulebook and the officiating manual published by the USTFF are highly recommended. The director must keep in mind that there are variations in rules and specifications from one set of rules to another. If an NCAA school puts on a high school meet, it must be run under the high school rulebook. For its own meets it uses the NCAA rules. If it puts on an AAU meet, it must use the AAU rules; while an Olympics must follow the international rules (IAAF). If you are confused, now you know why it is difficult to be a good track coach and meet director at the same time.

The preliminary details of the meet, the major details, must first be determined: when, where, the schedule, and the finances. For a dual meet there is no real problem. The date and place have been agreed upon, often being set by the conference itself (except for nonconference meets). The time for starting is often set in the same manner. The order of events is either suggested or clearly stated in most rulebooks below the international level, so there is little problem there. The time to allow for each event, methods of seeding, and heat schedules (if required) are also given in the rulebooks, so they should cause little problem.

Expenses

Expenses may be a matter of some concern, especially for the larger meets. For most dual meets these are only minor problems, if expenses are even considered. Most small track meets charge little or no admission, so shares of gate proceeds are not a concern here. The cost of awards may be defrayed by either having them covered in the annual budget, taking them out of the gate receipts (if there are any), having them donated in some manner, or by charging team or individual entry fees. Track is not a "money sport," so finances usually enter the picture only in very large meets.

Finding a Meet Official

The preparation of the meet officials is the next item of concern. If the officiating is poor, or even the least bit suspect, the meet will not be much of a success. A good number of qualified officials are indispensable to the successful track program. A "spur-of-the-moment" official is almost of less value than no official at all, for his lack of knowledge of the rules deters him from doing the athlete justice. As a timer, his work renders times in short races totally worthless. Find some sports-minded or civic-minded people who might be interested in helping with your meets. If possible, interest a civic group, such as the Jaycees or Kiwanis, for they will provide more people and enthusiasm, plus give more of a sense of group cohesion to the task.

Training a Meet Official

When you have found the officials, you are halfway home. Next they must be trained. Many groups, such as the AAU, have set up regular programs for training, testing, and certifying track and field officials. The track coach will be the first instructor, then when a meet director has been trained, he will either take over the duty of training the officials or share it with the coach. The training should begin with several sessions of reviewing the rules which will be used, in both "the letter of the law" and "the intent of the law." Each official should have his own copy of the rulebook, and he should carry it with him to each meet which he officiates.

After the officials have a good working knowledge of the rules, it would be most beneficial if a field test was provided, so each official could have the opportunity to practice at the track and see the types of situations which he might encounter in an actual competition. This can be done during time trials or some similar semiofficial type of competition. Preferably, the new officials would work under the supervision of an experienced official, so they can be assisted where necessary and evaluated more fairly.

Evaluating the Meet Official

The evaluation of the officials should be based on a combination of performance on a written open-book test on the rules and the official's proficiency test at the track. Each official should also have one or two events or areas in which he specializes. He needs to know the rules in all areas, but he should be certified in specialized areas in which his competence will be high. The AAU has a system of certifying officials on the local, state, and national level which is a good example of what the coach is trying to develop. Once the meet is provided with officials training in this manner, 90 percent of the technical snafus encountered in most meets can be eliminated before they begin.

The Track Meet

The meet officials should have a gathering place off the track, so they will not interfere with other events as they collect. They should have some item of identification, preferably an item of clothing such as a cap or shirt or jacket with a suitable emblem and in a suitable color. This identifies them to the marshals, who have the duty of keeping the competition area clear of noncompetitors, coaches, and others who are not supposed to be on the track, and it makes them readily identifiable to the athletes, who may need to find an official in a hurry. All items used by the officials, such as clipboards, tapes, watches, rakes, etc., should be kept in a single, off-the-track location, where they can be checked out when they are needed for use and checked in as soon as the event is concluded, thereby avoiding many shouts by disgruntled tape-seekers and such. The officials should know who is in charge of an event and who is their immediate superior in case there are any questions which they cannot answer or any protests. They must *always* know either (1) the answer or (2) what person will *definitely* know the answer. Finally, there should be a place in the stands, or at least off the track, where any officials not actively working on an assigned duty can gather, for they ought to be (1) out of the way and (2) enjoying the meet.

Scoring Contingencies

What if there is a record? How many people never think of that contingency? How many people have lost records because the equipment did not meet the required specifications or there was no wind gauge, or problems of that nature. At any respectable meet at which the slightest quality of competition occurs, a wind gauge and trained operator should be used. The track and field area must be surveyed and certified by a surveyor, not a groundskeeper with a 50-foot tape. The track and all starts, finishes, lane markings and staggers, relay zones, and hurdle markings must be surveyed and certified (here is where the all-weather track with permanent lines is a gift from heaven). Circles and elevation plus throwing sectors must be checked. Before the meet, and after a record, implements must be weighed and measured for legality. A last word on weights and measures. A track with a curb has its circumference measured 1 foot (12 inches) out from the curb; a track with no curb and only a painted line for the inside of the track has its circumference measured only 8 inches out from the line. If you are preparing to have an all-weather track built, make sure the architect and builder know and understand that fact. The same is true for the surveyor. Many tracks in this nation are 1 or 2 yards long per lap because no one thought of that one small rule.

A trained man should handle the weights and measures for all field implements. There should be an off-the-track station where all implements are weighed and measured, after which they should be marked in a manner known to the event officials (most common is a spot of paint from a spray-can in an agreed-upon color, which should change from meet to meet). If a record is set, the winning implement is checked again for certification.

Finally, the coach should have available a set of records-sheets (applications for records) for any level at which a competitor could conceivably reach. There are sets for high school records, junior colleges, NAIA, NCAA (university and college divisions), American (AAU) and world (IAAF), not including the record-approval system used in women's athletics below the national citizen's record level. The reason is simple: this is the simplest time to get all the necessary signatures on the paper to certify the record.

Crowd Facilities

The next item to consider in the successful meet is crowd comfort. If the meet is run well, many problems are solved, but suppose there are no seats for the spectators, or they tend to discover splinters where they are hard to remove? The facility must be comfortable with good, safe seating, placed as close as possible to where the action is. There should also be convenient, *clean* rest rooms available close to the seats, as few spectators come to hike, particularly under stress. If admission is charged, people should be there to collect tickets and direct traffic, especially if there are any reserved seats. If possible, concession stands, clean and well run, are good to have, but only if there are enough spectators to warrant it. Keep the people interested and happy, and they will come back. If they will come back, track will grow.

The Meet Announcer

One person is as important to the success of the meet as the meet director, and he is not usually a coach: he is the meet announcer. The meet announcer can put the crowd to sleep (or not disturb their slumbers), or he can get them interested and excited. Every school using an announcer at meets has a customary announcer for all sports events. Is he really the one for the track meet, though? He may not be. The track meet announcer has several characteristics (if he is good):

1. He is a good announcer (voice and delivery).
2. He likes track very much.
3. He is very knowledgeable about track (the rules, the records, the people competing at home and elsewhere).
4. He likes to give thorough information, but he is not in love with the sound of his voice.

If any of the above points are not met, he is not the man (or woman) you want. The first point can be corrected to some degree, and the third point can also be corrected, but if he does not pass number two, get a new person.

Many things are desired from an announcer, but this is what you need the most:

1. Accurate information as soon as it is available.
2. Thorough information, as soon as possible. What is the height of the bar, what jump is it, how far was that throw, what was his time or place, what and when is the next event.
3. Information to help the competitor, such as how long until the next event, the calls for events, running scores, and (if he cannot hear them at the track) accurate lap times for the leader.

Notice that the emphasis is placed upon speed, accuracy, and thoroughness. The announcer should work in that order. The crowd wants results *now.* They want them as accurately as possible (if they are unofficial, announce them as unofficial, for the winner — do not give unofficial place times). As soon as available, they want thorough information. This is where the announcer needs assistants to feed him the information as fast as it happens. An announcer can make a good meet great, and he can make a great meet confusing. Choose and train an announcer with care. You may have to do it yourself.

Publicity and Promotion

Publicity and promotion for the meet are necessary only as the larger meets approach. The coach should make information available for the local news media. Pictures should be available of the better athletes. Written (typed) information should also be available for the media. The coach may have to write everything, including color stories on his meets, but if it is necessary, he should do it. Let the local newspapers, radio and television stations know what is going to happen both before and after it happens. "During" is their responsibility. If a meet charges admission, press passes or photographers' passes should be available if arranged ahead of time (and with set, strict ground rules against hampering the competition if allowed on the field). News of meet schedules and coming events should be sent to all potentially interested bodies well ahead of time, and results should be sent out after the competition is completed (as soon as possible). In a large city, telephone. The more cooperative and helpful you are with the press, the better they will treat you and your team. In the long run, more will get done for the sport of track and field.

Many books have chapters on running contests, whether track meets, sports carnivals, or other large sporting events. They will offer further suggestions on running meets and the problems which are encountered. Perhaps the best way to prepare for a large competition is the method used in Eugene, Oregon, to prepare for any kind of competition which has not been put on recently: the dry run. To prepare for the United States Olympic Trials Decathlon, four preliminary decathlons were held, three small ones were used to train the meet director and his officials in the peculiarities of the decathlon competition and to test their ideas, then the NCAA decathlon provided a national-class test of the final plans. By the time the actual Olympic Trials began, every person connected with the running of the competition knew exactly what was expected of him, most problems had been anticipated, and the competition ran very smoothly. Only experience works out all the bugs.

The way to success in running meets is to try to foresee anything, no matter how minor, which could possibly go wrong and try to correct it before it happens. This is done in every aspect of the meet mentally, as the meet is being planned. It is then done physically in the dry run meets or less important competitions where the theories are tested. Finally, it is put into action at the competition itself, hopefully with all the bugs long since gone. The job of the meet director is to be so thorough that the spectators will think "any idiot could run that." If a meet is run well, the officials and meet directors will hardly ever be noticed. How many sports contests can make that claim?

Bibliography

Gallagher, J. A. "A track meet is only as good as its announcer," *Scholastic Coach* 38 (April 1969): 62, 64, 104–5.

Greer, Harvey. "A summer track program," *Track and Field Quarterly Review,* June 1969, pp. 22–24.

Hamilton, Scott. "Orientation running," *Track Technique,* No. 13 (September 1963), p. 415.

How to Organise and Conduct an Athletics Meeting. London: AAA, n.d. 36 pp.

Lieberman, Seymour. "Physical fitness for the track coach," *Track and Field Quarterly Review,* January 1968, pp. 62–64.

Mirkin, Gabe. "How to organize a 'Run for your Life' program," *Distance Running News* 3 (October 1968): 6–7.

Newland, Robert. "Oregon summer all-comers track meet program," *Track and Field Quarterly Review,* June 1967, pp. 48–60.

Phelps, Dale E. "Conducting a track and field meet with inexperienced personnel," *Athletic Journal* 49 (March 1969): 28, 30, 110.

Sealy, Victor C. *How to Judge Field Events.* Revised by C. A. Sinfield. London: AAA, 1969, 40 pp.

Track and Field Officials' Manual. Tucson: USTFF, 1972. 80 pp.

Appendixes

Summary of IAAF International Tables, First Day

Points	*100 meters*	*Long jump*	*Shot-put*	*High jump*	*400 meters*
1000	10.25	25′11″	61′ 6″	7′ 1½″	46.0
950	10.4	25′ 1¼″	58′ 6″	6′11″	46.9
900	10.6	24′ 3¼″	55′ 6″	6′ 9″	48.0
850	10.8	23′ 5½″	52′ 8″	6′ 6¼″	49.0
800	11.0	22′ 8″	49′10″	6′ 4½″	50.1
750	11.2	21′10½″	47′ 1″	6′ 2″	51.3
700	11.45	21′ 1½″	44′ 5″	6′ 0″	52.5
650	11.7	20′ 4½″	41′11″	5′ 9½″	53.7
600	11.9	19′ 7½″	39′ 5″	5′ 7¼″	55.1
550	12.15	18′11″	37′ 0″	5′ 5¼″	56.4
500	12.4	18′ 2″	34′ 7″	5′ 3½″	57.9
400	12.95	16′ 9½″	30′ 2″	4′11½″	61.1
300	13.55	15′ 6″	26′ 0″	4′ 7½″	64.6
200	14.2	14′ 2½″	22′ 2″	4′ 3½″	68.5
100	14.9	13′ 0″	18′ 8″	4′ 0″	73.0
1	15.69	11′10″	15′ 5″	3′ 9″	78.0

Summary of IAAF Tables, Second Day

Points	*110 mH*	*Discus*	*Pole vault*	*Javelin*	*1500 m*	*1 mile*
1000	13.7	188′ 8″	15′ 8″	265′ 9″	3:40.2	3:59.5
950	14.1	178′10″	15′ 0″	250′ 5″	3:45.3	4:04.8
900	14.5	169′ 3″	14′ 4″	235′ 7″	3:50.6	4:10.3
850	15.0	159′11″	13′ 8″	221′ 2″	3:56.1	4:16.1
800	15.5	150′11″	13′ 1″	207′ 3″	4:02.0	4:22.2
750	16.0	142′ 1″	12′ 5″	193′ 9″	4:08.2	4:28.6
700	16.5	133′ 7″	11′10″	180′ 9″	4:14.5	4:35.3
650	17.1	125′ 4″	11′ 2″	168′ 2″	4:21.3	4:42.4
600	17.8	117′ 4″	10′ 8″	156′ 0″	4:28.4	4:49.8
550	18.4	109′ 8″	10′ 0½″	144′ 4″	4:36.0	4:57.6
500	19.2	102′ 2″	9′ 7″	133′ 2″	4:44.0	5:05.8
400	20.8	88′ 0″	8′ 6″	112′ 1″	5:01.5	5:23.8
300	22.8	74′11″	7′ 6″	92′10″	5:21.3	5:43.9
200	25.3	62′11″	6′ 7″	75′ 4″	5:43.8	6:06.8
100	28.2	51′11″	5′ 9″	59′ 9″	6:09.8	6:32.9
1	31.9	42′ 1″	5′ 4″	52′ 7″	6:39.6	7:02.7

Bowerman Three-quarters Decathlon Tables, Part 1, 1971 revision by Freeman

60 yards		*Long jump*			*Shot-put*			*High jump*			*330 yards*		
Time	*Pts.*	*Ft.*	*Pts.*	*A*	*Ft.*	*Pts.*	*B*	*Ht.*	*Pts.*	*C*	*Secs.*	*Pts.*	*D*
5.9	1040	26′	1000	5	60′	977	1½	7′ 2″	1010	22	34	1050	7
6.0	990	25′6″	970	5	55′	887	1½	7′	966	20	35	980	7
6.2	880	25′	940	5	50′	797	1½	6′10″	926	20	36	910	7
6.4	780	24′6″	910	5	45′	707	1½	6′ 8″	882	22	37	850	6
6.6	680	24′	880	5	40′	617	1½	6′ 6″	840	21	38	790	6
6.8	580	23′6″	850	5	35′	512	2	6′ 4″	796	22	39	730	6
7.0	480	23′	820	5	34′	488	2	6′ 2″	752	22	40	680	5
7.2	410	22′6″	790	5	33′	464	2	6′	708	22	41	630	5
7.4	340	22′	760	5	32′	440	2	5′10″	662	23	42	580	5
7.6	260	21′6″	730	5	31′	416	2	5′ 8″	616	23	43	530	5
7.8	200	21′	700	5	30′	392	2	5′ 6″	570	23	44	490	4
8.0	130	20′6″	664	6	29′	368	2	5′ 4″	520	25	45	440	5
8.1	100	20′	628	6	28′	344	2	5′ 2″	474	23	46	400	4
		19′6″	592	6	27′	320	2	5′	414	30	47	360	4
		19′	556	6	26′	296	2	4′10″	364	25	48	330	3
		18′6″	520	6	25′	272	2	4′ 8″	314	25	49	290	4
		18′	484	6	24′	248	2	4′ 6″	264	25	50	260	3
		17′	412	6	23′	224	2	4′ 4″	210	27	52	190	3½
		16′	340	6	22′	200	2	4′ 2″	156	27	54	130	3
		15′	268	6	21′	164	3	4′	100	28	55	100	3
		14′	184	7	20′	140	2						
		13′	100	7									

KEY
A: Points per inch
B: Points per inch
C: Points per inch
D: Points per 1/10

Bowerman Three-quarters Decathlon Tables, Part 2

90-yard Highs		*Discus*		*Pole vault*		*Javelin*		*¾-mile run*	
10.0	1050	180′	955	16′	1024	250′	950	3:00	965
10.5	960	170′	905	15′6″	988	240′	920	3:05	905
11.0	880	160′	850	15′	952	230′	880	3:10	850
11.5	820	150′	795	14′6″	916	220′	850	3:15	800
12.0	750	140′	740	14′	874	210′	810	3:20	745
12.5	690	135′	710	13′6″	832	200′	780	3:25	700
13.0	640	130′	680	13′	796	190′	740	3:30	650
13.5	580	125′	650	12′6″	760	180′	700	3:35	610
14.0	530	120′	620	12′	718	170′	660	3:40	565
14.5	490	115′	585	11′6″	676	160′	620	3:45	525
15.0	450	110′	550	11′	628	150′	570	3:50	490
16.0	380	105′	520	10′6″	586	140′	530	3:55	455
17.0	310	100′	485	10′	544	130′	490	4:00	420
18.0	250	95′	450	9′6″	496	120′	440	4:05	385
19.0	200	90′	415	9′	448	110′	390	4:10	350
20.0	150	85′	380	8′6″	400	100′	340	4:15	320
20.5	130	80′	340	8′	352	90′	280	4:20	290
		70′	260	7′	244	80′	220	4:25	260
		60′	180	6′	136	60′	100	4:30	235
		52′	100					4:48	100

Decathlon Appendix C

Sylvia High School — College Decathlon Tables, Part 1,

100 yards		*Long jump*		*Shot-put*		*High jump*		*440 yards*	
9.8	1200	23′	1200	55′	1200	6′ 4″	1200	49s	1200
10.0	1100	22′	1150	50′	1150	6′ 2″	1150	50	1100
10.2	1000	21′	1100	45′	1100	6′ 0″	1100	51	1000
10.4	950	20′	1000	40′	1000	5′10″	1000	52	950
10.6	900	19′	900	39′	900	5′ 8″	900	53	900
10.8	850	18′	800	38′	800	5′ 6″	800	54	850
11.0	800	17′	700	37′	700	5′ 4″	700	55	800
11.2	700	16′6″	600	36′	600	5′ 2″	600	56	750
11.4	600	16′	550	35′	500	5′ 0″	500	57	700
11.6	500	15′6″	500	34′	450	4′10″	400	58	650
11.8	400	15′	450	33′	400	4′ 8″	300	59	600
12.0	300	14′6″	400	32′	350	4′ 6″	250	60	550
12.2	250	14′	350	31′	300	4′ 4″	200	61	500
12.4	200	13′6″	300	30′	250	4′ 2″	150	62	450
12.6	150	13′	200	29′	200	4′ 0″	100	63	400
12.8	100	12′6″	100	28′	150			64	350
13.0	50	12′	50	27′	100			65	300
				26′	50			66	250
								67	200
								68	150
								69	100

SOURCE: From Alfred J. Sylvia, "A Decathlon for High School and College," *Athletic Journal* 44 (April 1964): 38, 40. Reprinted by permission of *Athletic Journal*.

120 low hurdles		*Discus*		*Pole vault*		*Javelin*		*1 mile*	
13.4	1200	165′	1200	14′0″	1200	200′	1200	4:25	1200
13.8	1100	150′	1100	13′6″	1150	175′	1100	4:35	1150
14.2	1050	135′	1050	13′	1100	160′	1000	4:40	1100
14.6	1000	120′	1000	12′6″	1050	140′	900	4:45	1050
15.0	950	105′	900	12′	1000	120′	800	4:50	1000
15.3	900	95′	800	11′6″	950	105′	750	4:55	900
15.6	800	90′	700	11′	900	95′	700	5:00	800
15.9	700	85′	600	10′6″	800	90′	650	5:05	700
16.2	600	80′	500	10′	700	85′	600	5:10	650
16.5	500	75′	450	9′6″	600	80′	500	5:15	600
16.8	400	70′	400	9′	500	75′	400	5:20	550
17.1	350	65′	350	8′6″	400	70′	300	5:25	500
17.4	300	60′	300	8′	300	65′	200	5:30	450
17.7	250	55′	250	7′6″	200	60′	150	5:45	350
18.0	200	50′	200	7′	100	55′	100	6:00	250
18.3	150	45′	150			50′	50	6:15	150
18.6	100	40′	100					6:30	50

NOTES:
1. One of the four alternate events may be substituted for one of the regular decathlon events.
2. An 800-gram weighted ball, softball, or football might be substituted for the javelin.

220 yards		*880 yards*		*2 miles*		*Triple jump*	
21.0	1200	1:55	1200	9:30	1200	48′	1200
22.0	1150	1:58	1150	9:50	1150	46′	1150
22.5	1100	2:00	1100	10:00	1100	44′	1100
23.0	1000	2:05	1000	10:10	1050	42′	1000
23.5	900	2:10	950	10:20	1000	40′	900
24.0	850	2:15	900	10:30	900	38′	800
24.5	800	2:20	800	10:40	800	36′	700
25.0	700	2:25	700	10:50	700	35′	600
25.5	600	2:30	600	11:00	650	34′	550
26.0	500	2:35	500	11:10	600	33′	500
26.5	450	2:40	450	11:20	550	32′	450
27.0	400	2:45	400	11:30	500	31′	400
27.5	350	2:50	350	11:40	450	30′	350
28.0	300	2:55	300	12:10	350	29′	300
28.5	250	3:00	250	12:40	250	28′	200
29.0	200	3:05	200	13:10	150	27′	100
29.5	150	3:10	150	13:40	50	26′	50
30.0	100	3:15	100				

Decathlon Metric Conversion Tables

Long jump		*Shot-put*		*High jump*		*Discus throw*		*Pole vault*	
26′	7.92 m	60′	18.29 m	7′ 2″	2.18	190′	57.91	17′	5.18
25′6″	7.77	58′	17.68	7′	2.13	185′	56.39	16′6″	5.03
25′	7.62	56′	17.07	6′10″	2.08	180′	54.86	16′	4.88
24′6″	7.47	54′	16.46	6′ 8″	2.03	175′	53.34	15′6″	4.72
24′	7.32	52′	15.85	6′ 6″	1.98	170′	51.82	15′	4.57
23′6″	7.16	50′	15.24	6′ 4″	1.93	165′	50.29	14′6″	4.42
23′	7.01	48′	14.63	6′ 2″	1.88	160′	48.77	14′	4.27
22′6″	6.86	46′	14.02	6′	1.83	155′	47.24	13′6″	4.11
22′	6.71	44′	13.41	5′10″	1.78	150′	45.72	13′	3.96
21′6″	6.55	42′	12.80	5′ 8″	1.73	145′	44.20	12′6″	3.81
21′	6.40	40′	12.19	5′ 6″	1.68	140′	42.67	12′	3.66
20′6″	6.25	38′	11.58	5′ 4″	1.63	135′	41.15	11′6″	3.50
20′	6.10	36′	10.97	5′ 2″	1.58	130′	39.62	11′	3.35
19′6″	5.94	34′	10.36	5′	1.52	125′	38.10	10′6″	3.20
19′	5.79	32′	9.75	4′10″	1.47	120′	36.58	10′	3.05
18′6″	5.64	30′	9.14	4′ 8″	1.42	115′	35.05	9′6″	2.90
18′	5.49	28′	8.53	4′ 6″	1.37	110′	33.53	9′	2.74
17′6″	5.33	26′	7.92			105′	32.00	8′6″	2.59
17′	5.18	24′	7.32			100′	30.48	8′	2.44
16′6″	5.03	22′	6.71			95′	28.96		
16′	4.88	20′	6.10			90′	27.43		
						85′	25.91		
						80′	24.38		

100 YARDS To convert 100 yards to 100 meters, if the 100-yard time is:
(1) Less than 10.2, add 0.9 secs., i.e., 10.1 yds. = 11.0 m
(2) From 10.2 to 11.1, add 1.0 secs., i.e., 11.1 yds. = 12.1 m
(3) From 11.2 to 12.1, add 1.1 secs., i.e., 12.1 yds. = 13.2 m
(4) From 12.2 to 13.3, add 1.2 secs., i.e., 13.3 yds. = 14.5 m
(5) More than 13.3, add 1.3 secs., i.e., 13.4 yds. = 14.7 m

440 YARDS To convert 440 yards to 400 meters, if the 440-yard time is:
(1) 43.0 or less, *subtract* 0.2 secs., i.e., 43.0 yds. = 42.8 m
(2) From 43.1 to 60.2, subtract 0.3 secs., i.e., 60.2 yds. = 59.9 m
(3) From 60.3 to 77.0, subtract 0.4 secs., i.e., 77.9 yds. = 76.6 m
(4) More than 77.0, subtract 0.5 secs., i.e., 77.2 yds. = 76.7 m
110-meter hurdles almost identical to 120-yard hurdles time.

Javelin throw		1,500 meters	1 mile	1,500 meters	1 mile
250′	76.20	3:43.7	4:00	4:58.3	5:20
240′	73.15	3:47.4	4:04	5:02	5:24
230′	70.10	3:50	4:06.8	5:05.7	5:28
220′	67.06	3:51.2	4:08	5:07.6	5:30
210′	64.01	3:54.9	4:12	5:10	5:32.6
200′	60.96	3:58.6	4:16	5:16.9	5:40
190′	57.91	4:00	4:17.5	5:20	5:43.3
180′	54.86	4:02.3	4:20	5:26.2	5:50
170′	51.82	4:05	4:22.9	5:30	5:54.1
160′	48.77	4:06.1	4:24	5:35.5	6:00
150′	45.72	4:09.8	4:28	5:40	6:04.8
140′	42.67	4:13.5	4:32	5:44.9	6:10
130′	39.62	4:15	4:33.6	5:50	6:15.5
120′	36.58	4:17.2	4:36	5:54.2	6:20
110′	33.53	4:20	4:39	6:00	6:26.2
100′	30.48	4:21	4:40	6:03.5	6:30
90′	27.43	4:24.7	4:44	6:10	6:37
80′	24.38	4:28.4	4:48	6:12.8	6:40
		4:32.2	4:52	6:20	6:47.7
		4:35.9	4:56	6:22.1	6:50
		4:39.6	5:00	6:30	6:58.4
		4:43.3	5:04	6:31.5	7:00
		4:47.1	5:08	6:40	7:09.2
		4:50.8	5:12	6:50	7:19.9
		4:54.5	5:16	7:00	7:30.6

Index of names

Numbers in boldface indicate photograph references.

BEE COUNTY COLLEGE LIBRARY
3800 CHARCO ROAD
BEEVILLE, TEXAS 78102
(512) 354 - 2740